PATTERN RECOGNITION
AND
ARTIFICIAL INTELLIGENCE

ACADEMIC PRESS RAPID MANUSCRIPT REPRODUCTION

Proceedings of the
Joint Workshop on Pattern Recognition and Artificial Intelligence
Held at Hyannis, Massachusetts
June 1–3, 1976

PATTERN RECOGNITION AND ARTIFICIAL INTELLIGENCE

Edited by

C.H. CHEN

College of Engineering
Southeastern Massachusetts University
North Dartmouth, Massachusetts

ACADEMIC PRESS, INC

New York   San Francisco   London   1976

A Subsidiary of Harcourt Brace Jovanovich, Publishers

ACADEMIC PRESS, INC.
111 Fifth Avenue, New York, New York 10003

United Kingdom Edition published by
ACADEMIC PRESS, INC. (LONDON) LTD.
24/28 Oval Road, London NW1

Library of Congress Cataloging in Publication Data

Joint Workshop on Pattern Recognition and Artificial
      Intelligence, Hyannis, Mass., 1976.
      Pattern recognition and artificial intelligence.

      Includes index.
      1.   Artificial intelligence—Congresses.
2.   Pattern recognition systems—Congresses.
I.   Chen, Chi-hau,   Date   II.   Title.
Q334.J64   1976   001.53'5   76-48887
ISBN 0–12–170950–7

CONTENTS

v **211175**

LIST OF CONTRIBUTORS

R. B. Banerji, Department of Computer and Information Science, Temple University, Philadelphia, Pennsylvania 19122

H. G. Barrow, Artificial Intelligence Center, Stanford Research Institute, Menlo Park, California 94025

Eberhard L. Bertsch, Institut für Informatik, Universität des Saarlandes, 66 Saarbrücken, West Germany

J. M. Brayer, Department of Electrical Engineering and Computer Science, University of New Mexico, Albuquerque, New Mexico 87131

Bruce L. Bullock, Hughes Research Laboratories, 3011 Malibu Canyon Road, Malibu, California 90265

Arvola Chan, Laboratory for Computer Science, Massachusetts Institute of Technology, 545 Technology Square, Cambridge, Massachusetts 02139

B. Chandrasekaran, Department of Computer and Information Science, The Ohio State University, Columbus, Ohio 43210

C. L. Chang, Computer Science Department, IBM Research Laboratory, San Jose, California 95193

C. H. Chen, Department of Electrical Engineering, Southeastern Massachusetts University, North Dartmouth, Massachusetts 02747

David B. Cooper, Division of Engineering, Brown University, Providence, Rhode Island 02912

Nelson Corby, Electrical and Systems Engineering Department, Rensselaer Polytechnic Institute, Troy, New York 12181

R. Cunningham, Robotics Laboratory, Jet Propulsion Laboratory, 4800 Oak Grove Drive, Pasadena, California 91103

Rui J. P. de Figueiredo, Department of Electrical Engineering, Rice University, Houston, Texas 77001

E. Diday, Institut de Recherche d'Informatique et d'Automatique, Domaine de Voluceau-Rocquencourt, 78150 le Chesnay, France

Sahibsingh A. Dudani, Hughes Research Laboratories, 3011 Malibu Canyon Road, Malibu, California 90265

S. J. Dwyer, III, Department of Electrical Engineering, University of Missouri, Columbia, Missouri 65201

Eugene C. Freuder, Computer Science Department, Indiana University, Bloomington, Indiana 47401

K. S. Fu, School of Electrical Engineering, Purdue University, West Lafayette, Indiana 47906

Lester A. Gerhardt, Electrical and Systems Engineering Department, Rensselaer Polytechnic Institute, Troy, New York 12181

Michael Hammer, Massachusetts Institute of Technology, Laboratory for Computer Science, 545 Technology Square, Cambridge, Massachusetts 02139

C. A. Harlow, Department of Electrical Engineering, University of Missouri, Columbia, Missouri 65201

Frederick Hayes–Roth, Department of Computer Science, Carnegie–Mellon University, Pittsburgh, Pennsylvania 15213

H. K. Huang, Georgetown University Medical Center, 3900 Reservoir Road, Northwest, Washington, D.C. 20007

Laveen N. Kanal, Computer Science Department, University of Maryland, College Park, Maryland 20742

R. S. Ledley, Georgetown University Medical Center, 3900 Reservoir Road, Northwest, Washington, D.C. 20007

R. W. McLaren, Department of Electrical Engineering, University of Missouri, Columbia, Missouri 65201

Paul Mermelstein, Haskins Laboratories, 270 Crown Street, New Haven, Connecticut 06511

Richard E. Parent, Department of Computer and Information Science, The Ohio State University, Columbus, Ohio 43210

T. Pavlidis, Department of Electrical Engineering and Computer Science, Princeton University, Princeton, New Jersey 08540

Jacques Pitrat, C.N.R.S., 5 Rue de la Moselle, 75019 Paris, France

George C. Stockman, Computer Science Department, University of Maryland, College Park, Maryland 20742

Steven L. Tanimoto, Department of Electrical Engineering and Computer Science, University of Connecticut, Storrs, Connecticut 06268

J. M. Tenenbaum, Artificial Intelligence Center, Stanford Research Institute, Menlo Park, California 94025

J. R. Ullmann, Department of Applied Mathematics and Computer Science, University of Sheffield, Sheffield, England

D. A. Waterman, Information Sciences Department, The Rand Corporation, 1700 Main Street, Santa Monica, California 90406

Y. Yakimovsky, Jet Propulsion Laboratory, 4800 Oak Grove Drive, Pasadena, California 91103

Steven W. Zucker, Department of Electrical Engineering, McGill University, Montreal, Canada H3C 3G1

PREFACE

The Joint Workshop on Pattern Recognition and Artificial Intelligence that was held June 1-3, 1976, at Hyannis, Massachusetts and attended by over 120 participants was organized on selected topics of interest to researchers in both the fields of pattern recognition and artificial intelligence. This volume contains most of the papers presented at the meeting. Other workshop papers along with panel discussion reports appear in a conference record published by the IEEE Computer Society (Catalog Number 76 CH1169-2C) in July, 1976. The 28 chapters included in this volume represent the most important up-to-date developments in the topics of scene analysis, data structure, syntactic methods, biomedicine, speech recognition, statistical pattern recognition, game-playing programs, computer graphics, etc. Indeed, the trend as reflected by the talks given at the meeting has been toward increased interaction between the two fields. This volume should be useful as a supplementary text for graduate courses in pattern recognition and artificial intelligence as well as a reference for researchers in both fields.

I would like to express my gratitude to all the individuals who have helped me with the workshop organization and operation, and to all the reviewers whose suggestions have led to the refinement of papers for the volume. In particular, I would like to thank Dr. Merle M. Andrew for the enlightening opening remarks he gave at the workshop; Professor K. S. Fu, as Chairman of the IEEE Machine Intelligence and Pattern Analysis Technical Committee, for his moral support; and Mrs. Gardiner W. White for typing all the manuscripts of this volume.

Finally I would like to thank Lt. Colonel George W. McKemie of AFOSR for his encouragement and partial financial support, and my wife for her understanding and assistance in relieving me of some of the chores connected with the workshop.

A DATA STRUCTURE WHICH
CAN LEARN SIMPLE PROGRAMS
FROM EXAMPLES OF INPUT-OUTPUT

R. B. *Banerji*
Temple University
Philadelphia, Pa.

I. INTRODUCTION

The structure described in this paper is closely related to a
previously described structure [4,5,9] which was designed to facilitate the description of complex patterns and for the learning of
the description of pattern classes from training samples. The
structure of the language was predicated on the belief that purely
algebraic or structural-linguistic constructs are inadequate for
handling descriptions which depend on complex relations in the objects being classified. The power of at least parts of ω-order
Predicate Calculus was needed using n-ary relations with arbitrary-
ly high n. It was further necessary to ensure that predicates
could be introduced by definition and that these definitions, once
learned by examples, be usable for representation just like any
other predicate of the language. To make this possible, it was
felt necessary that the format for representing n-ary relations be
identical for all values of n. It was also necessary to represent
the entities related, not as abstract symbols, as the individual
symbols are in logic but as sets of property-value pairs: i.e.
there had to be functional constants in the language, or some of
the predicates had to be many-valued.
    Since then, a large number of systems [1,2,3] with compara-
ble capabilities have developed. The exact relationships between
all these have not been thoroughly investigated: but most of
these have sufficient formal precision that such a comparison is
possible. No such comparison, however, will be attempted in this
present paper. Instead, I will only describe one of them, illustrate what I mean by learning simple programs, and how this is intimately related to the learning of descriptions (either of objects or of programs and relations: the difference is non-exis-
tent in the language although the efficiency of the learning process can differ widely, depending on the structure of the entity
being learned.

II. AN INTRODUCTION TO THE LANGUAGE

The two basic entities of the language are objects (which
take the place of individual constants), and descriptions (which
are like definitions in an extendable language).
    The objects are not abstract symbols - instead, they are sets

1

of property-value pairs. Any property or any value can have properties and values of their own, i.e. can be objects in themselves.
Ultimately, of course, they are symbols. Because of this structure, any ordered n-tuple of objects can also be an object--each
of the component objects being the value of some property. As a
result the techniques of describing classes of objects can be used
to describe relations. The basic predicates of the language are
all of the form f(x)=g where f and g are either properties and
values or in more complex cases, have to be interpreted as such.
In our examples, we shall exhibit these more complex atomic sentences.

A description is a statement (involving the Boolean binary
connectives and existential quantifiers and having one free variable) attached to a symbol which is the name of a defined predicate. If x is the free variable of the statement then we will
visualize a description to have the form

$$x \; \epsilon \; P \equiv S(x)$$

where P is the predicate name and S(x) is a statement.

Let us exemplify the ideas involved by some examples of objects and descriptions which can be interpreted as coming from the
arithmetic of integers, represented as binary strings - (value, 0)-
stands for the digit '0'. The description -

$$x \; \epsilon \; digit = (value \; (x)=0) \; or \; (value \; (x)=1)$$

is an elementary description of objects representing binary digits.
This elementary description can then be used to describe the somewhat more complex concept of a numeral or a binary string. In
this description, the least significant digit is the value of the
property "tail" and the rest of the string (up to the "empty" symbol lambda) represents the value of the property "head". Since
the value of "head" looks like a numeral, it leads to the following possible recursive definition

$x\epsilon numeral \equiv (tail \; (x)\epsilon digit)$ and (head(x)=lambda) or (head(x)ϵ
numeral)

A typical object fitting this description would be

[(tail, (value,0); head, (tail, (value,1); head, (tail,

(value,1); head, lambda)))]

representing 110.

The successor function for integers is described as a binary
relation. Each object in this relation is an ordered pair of
numerals. It has two properties which we shall call "first" and
"second". Each has a value belonging to the set "numeral", i.e.

2

satisfying the statement in the description of "numeral".

x ε successor ≡first (x) ε numeral & second (x) ε numeral

   & [{value (tail (first (x)))=0 & value (tail (second(x)))=1

     & head (first (x))= head (second (x))}

  or {value (tail (first(x)))=1 & value (tail (second(x)))=0

    & [{head (first(x))= lambda

     & head (second(x))=(head, lambda; tail, (value,1)))}

  or (∃z) (first (z)= head (first(x)) &

  second(z)=head(second(x)) &

    z ε successor)]}]

The relation "less than or equal to" has a simpler description:

x ε less ≡ first (x)ε numeral & second (x) ε numeral &

   [{head (first(x))=lambda

   & (head (second(x))=lambda }

  or {head(first(x)) = head(second(x))

    & value (tail(first(x))=0}

  or (∃z) (first(z) = head(first(x)) & second(z)

              = head (second(x)) &

    z ε less)]

We shall use these descriptions as examples for the discussions in the rest of this paper. We believe that although our examples are from a very restricted area of application, they will point out the kinds of strengths and weaknesses that this and similar description languages can be prone to. We shall discuss three ways in which descriptions can be used. We will illustrate how the description can be used to recognize a given object as satisfying a given description, how a set of objects can be used to learn a description satisfied by them (induction) and how, given a description, an object satisfying the description can be constructed. It is this last capability which we want to emphasize

3

in this paper, since it is this one which enables us to consider a description as a program. Moreover, it increases the efficiency with which one can use a description with quantifiers for recognition and induction purposes. In most work with similar languages, a quantifier initiates a search in the existing data base. This can be done in our language by writing description in a certain way. However, if one can efficiently construct an object satisfying a statement instead of looking for it in the data base, one obviates the inefficiency of search when it can be avoided. It must be stated, in fairness to other work, that the search needed in their kind of application (recognition and induction of scenes or utterances by graph matching, for instance) cannot be avoided. The kind of application being used in our examples here has not been tried by other authors to the best of my knowledge.

III.   CONSTRUCTION OF OBJECTS

In this section we shall describe the construction process in some detail, relegating the other two processes to later sections. However, before anything can be done, we shall be better off if at least a semiformal definition be given for sentences. We shall ignore disjunctive sentences initially, merely noting that if we have to construct an object x to satisfy "A(x) or B(x)", then we shall construct x to satisfy A(x). Only if such a procedure fails will a construction be attempted to satisfy B(x).

We describe a process whose input is a sentence $\exists x P(x)$ where x is the only free variable in P(x) and produce a sentence of the form (x=t) where t is any object or the special identifier "impossible". Initially we shall consider only atomic sentences, calling the output its "reduced form". Then we shall describe a process called "merging" by means of which a conjunction of sentences in reduced form can be made to yield a single sentence (if the process succeeds). The presentation here is informal and incomplete. I intend to present a formal version at a future date.

Thus we start with atomic sentences of the form term=term, where, a term can be a symbol, a variable, an object or an expression of the form term (term). Terms of this last kind can be reduced to simpler terms if the term in the parenthesis reduces to an object and the term outside the parenthesis has a reduced form which is one of the properties of the object. Thus, the term 'Color ((color, blue))' has the reduced form 'blue'.

The term –

$$\text{Color ((color, blue)) (blue,red)}$$

has as reduced form, the reduced form of blue ((blue, red)) which is 'red'.

If the reduced form of the term inside the parenthesis is a symbol, then the term has the reduced form "impossible". Also, if either term inside or the term outside the parenthesis has reduced

4

form "impossible", so does the entire term. Objects yield reduced
forms if some of their properties or values have reduced forms.

Given an atomic sentence of the form (term=term), where each
term is in reduced form, a number of possibilities arise, of which
we shall only discuss a few important ones and then exemplify them
by a construction.

If the sentence is of the form (symbol=symbol) then any object satisfies this sentence if the two symbols are identical and
by no object when they are not. A sentence of the form (symbol=
object) is satisfied by no object. If it is of the form (x=symbol)
then it is satisfied by the symbol. Similarly if the sentence is
of the form (x=object), it is satisfied by the object.

These, of course, are elementary constructions. Problems occur only when one or both sides of the "equation" has the form
term (term), even after reduction, i.e. when variables are involved in either of the two terms. In this case the equation is
of the form $(term_1=term_2(term_3))$. Such an equation is replaced by
a new equation $(term_3=(term_2, term_1))$. The reader will notice
that this is a sort of "unreduction". This enables us to deduce
(x=(Color,blue)) from (Color(x)=Blue).

This method is only effective if $term_3$ above is a variable
or a symbol, since this changes the equation to one of the previous forms. If $term_3$ itself is of the form term (term) then the
equation can be looked upon as having the form $(term_1 = term_2)$.
In this case we choose a new variable z, which does not occur in
either term and replace the above equation with two equations

$$(z = term_1)$$

and

$$(z = term_2).$$

In most cases this allows the construction of many objects satisfying the equations - but the construction remains mechanical. As
an illustrative example a sentence like (Color(x) = Shape(x))
would be replaced by two sentences (z=Color(x)) and (z=Shape(x))
which would reduce to (x=(Color,z)) and (x=(Shape,z)). These
would merge to a single sentence by the process of merging of sentences described below. If one of the terms in an equation involved a variable then one uses a similar trick. For example (x=
(Shape, Color(x))) would give rise to two sentences, (x=(Shape,z))
and (z=Color(x)) which latter reduces to (x=(Color,z)).

The merging process occurs if there are two or more statements of the form (x=object) with the same variable on the left
hand side. The two objects are unioned as sets of property-value
pairs; e.g. (x=(Color, green)) and (x=Shape, square)) get "merged"
to (x=(Color, green; shape, square)).

Such a process can produce an object which has the same property with two distinct values. Then the object is replaced by
"impossible". Another phenomenon that may occur is exemplified by
the merging of (x=(Color, shape(x))) and (x=Color, green)). In
this case we obtain (x=(Color,z)), (z=green) and (z=shape(x)), the

5

last reducing to (x=(shape,z)). The first and last merge to (x= (Color,z; shape,z)).

As in the above case, repeated applications of these and other similar replacement rules finally yield a set of equations, each with as distinct variables on its left hand side. Now one substitutes for variables in equations. For example, with (x= (Color, z; shape,z)) and (z=green) we obtain (x=(Color, green, shape, green). Such substitution processes, of course, may have some variables unspecified in which case more than one object satisfy the equations.

A complete formal treatment of this process will have to a-wait a future publication. Meanwhile the process can be exempli-fied by an example. Let us consider the description of "successor" as a program i.e., one which constructs the successor of a numeral from the numeral. Consider the numeral --

$$(head, \ lambda; \ tail, \ (value,1))$$

and the sentence

$$(\exists y) \ ((first, \ (head, \ lambda; \ tail, \ (value,1)); \\ second,y) \ \varepsilon \ successor).$$

If we replace x by the object (first, (head, lambda; tail, (value, 1)); second, y) in the definition of successor we obtain a conjunction of three statements. The first statement first (x) ε numeral is satisfied (i.e., (head, lambda; tail, (value, 1)) is recognized as a numeral--a recognition process as we shall pre-sently describe). The next conjunct, y ε numeral, can be relega-ted to later consideration. Considering the third conjunct we find it to consist of three disjuncts. The first disjunct is false since

$$value \ (tail \ ((head, \ lambda, \ tail, \ (value, 1)))$$

is 1 and not 0. The second disjunct has four conjuncts of which -

$$value \ (tail \ (first(x)))=1 \ is \ satisfied \ and$$

$$[head \ (first(x)) \ = \ lambda] \ is \ satisfied \ also.$$

The two which remain to be satisfied are

$$value \ (tail \ (y)) \ = \ 0$$

and

$$head \ (y) \ =(head, \ lambda; \ tail, \ (value,1)).$$

The first one reduces to

```
        tail (y) = (value, 0)
```

and then to

```
        y = (tail, (value, 0)).
```

The second one reduces similarly to

```
        y = (head, (head, lambda; tail, (value, 1))).
```

Merging the two sentences yield

```
        y = (tail, (value, 0)); Head, (head, lambda;
            tail, (value,1))
```

representing 10, the successor of 1.

This "call" to the construction used the "escape clause" of the definition since the parameter was a simple "1". The successor of 11, however, would have to get the successor of 1, the head of 11 and recursively invoke the last disjunct in the last conjunct

```
    [(∃z) (first (z) = (head, lambda; tail, 1) & second (z) -
          head (second (y)) and z ε successor)]
```

which would construct the second z as shown above and obtain second (y) from it. The details are left to the imagination of the reader.

IV.   RECOGNITION AND LEARNING

Given a description and an object it is a straight forward procedure to verify that the object satisfies the statement. One can look upon the process as follows. If x ε C≡S(x) is the description and t the object, one has to see if the construction of an object satisfying S(x) and (x=t) is possible. The process is very simple if S(x) does not have a quantified variable. Consider, as an example the description of numeral and the object:

```
        X = (head, (head, lambda; tail, (value, 1));
            tail, (value, 1)).
```

If one considers the first disjunct of numeral

```
        tail (x) ε digit
```

or in reduced form

```
        (value, 1) ε digit.
```

On replacing y by (value, 1) in the description of digit we obtain after reducing value (y) = 1

$$1 = 1$$

satisfying the first disjunct. The second conjunct has two disjuncts. Of these head (x) = lambda yields

(head, lambda; tail, (value, 1)) = lambda

patently false! But the second disjunct yields after reduction

(head, lambda; tail, (value, 1)) ε numeral

which is now seen to be true after one more recursion.

Learning is a much more difficult process. The process has as its input two disjoint sets of objects; the output is a description satisfied by all objects in the first set and not satisfied by any in the second set.

A lot of difficult problems of statistical [6,7] and computer theoretic [8] variety occur when we study the basis of this learning or "induction" process. This is hardly the place to enter such discussions. Suffice it to say that one encounters in literature two ways of processing the sets. One way is to process them in their entirety as sets. The other way is to consider their elements sequentially. Our algorithm will be of the second variety. As a matter of fact, it will be of a variety with feedback i.e. when the algorithm will construct an element on its own and test to see in which of the two sets it is. The importance of this feedback has been discussed elsewhere. In what follows we shall euphemistically assume that the feedback occurs in the form of a question and answer session between the algorithm and a "trainer".

The algorithm is shown schematically in the flow chart (Fig.1). The basic motivation behind the design can probably be gleaned by the following discussion and example.

The algorithm is given one object in the set to be described (which we shall call the "upper set"). The algorithm constructs from it all the statements that it can about the object. This would range from such trivia as value (tail (x)=1) to $(\exists z)$ (z ε successor & first (z) = head(x)). We are desisting here from a complete discussion of the pointer system which would enable these constructions.

The algorithm then constructs another object which violates one of the resulting statements, leaving the rest unchanged. The construction process has been described before. The technique for violating one statement without violating others is a somewhat tricky process when the statements imply one another in conjunction. However, that is another detail I am not covering here. The construction of this violating object enables the program to

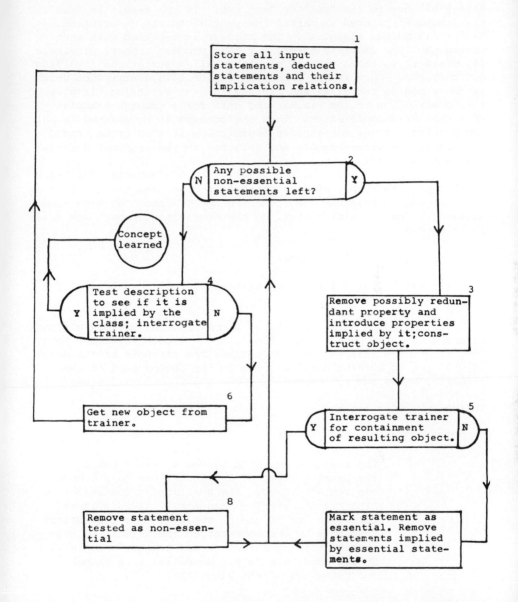

1. Store all input statements, deduced statements and their implication relations.

2. Any possible non-essential statements left?

Concept learned

4. Test description to see if it is implied by the class; interrogate trainer.

3. Remove possibly redundant property and introduce properties implied by it; construct object.

6. Get new object from trainer.

5. Interrogate trainer for containment of resulting object.

8. Remove statement tested as non-essential

Mark statement as essential. Remove statements implied by essential statements.

exhibit this object to the trainer and ask him whether this new object belongs to the "yes" or "no" set. If the result is "yes", the statement changed is marked inessential to the description. Else it is marked essential. The process is repeated with each statement. The complete theory for this process appears elsewhere [9] where it is shown that it can learn all descriptions involving conjunctions. Once it has found the conjunctive description which is contained in the class and has the largest extension, it gives this description to the trainer and asks for a counter-example. If a counter-example exists, then the concept to be learned is not conjunctive. A new conjunctive description is then grown around the positive counter-example and attached to the previous description with an "or".

An example of learning the description of "numeral" follows. Some steps with complicated justification have been taken out of the dialogue between the algorithm and the trainer. We have also violated a few rules of syntax, so the descriptions which are really being learned are

$$w \ \varepsilon \ \text{digit} \equiv (w=0) \text{ or } (w=1)$$

$$w \ \varepsilon \ \text{num} \equiv (\text{tail}(w) \ \varepsilon \ \text{digit}) \ \& ((\text{head}(w)=\text{null}) \text{ or } (\text{head}(w) \ \varepsilon \ \text{num}))$$

The following is a scenario of a conversation between a trainer and a computer based on the flow chart. Though the first part (digit) is essential to the explication, the strength of the method will not be evident until we come to the second part of the scenario, where num is learned.

TRAINER: 0 ε digit

COMPUTER: $(w=0) \equiv (w \ \varepsilon \ \text{digit})$?

> The question is asked by box 4, since box 1 (at the present level of knowledge) can only deduce one sentence, w=0. The question is tantamount to 'is this description adequate?' If this looks like cheating it can be replaced by a statistical test done by the computer on the trainer by generating various objects x and asking 'x ε digit?' To our mind this is not essential to a proper understanding of the algorithm.

TRAINER: No.

COMPUTER: Please show another.

TRAINER: 1 ε digit.

COMPUTER: (w=0) or (w=1) ≡ w ε digit?

TRAINER: Yes.

COMPUTER: Thanks, now I know.

> This is a case of 'rote learning.' This is the
> best that can be done at this level of pre-pro-
> cessing. In the next scenario we shall show how
> this initial 'rote' simplifies the learning of
> more difficult concepts.

TRAINER: (hear, lambda;tail,1) ε num.

> Now the computer deduces not only (head(w)=null)
> and (tail(w)=1) but also something that is implied
> by the latter, namely, (tail(w) ε digit). It is
> beginning to use its "knowledge base" in box 1.
> The tree of implications looks like:

head(w) = null   tail(w) = 1
                                      |
                                      |
                                  tail(w) ε digit

COMPUTER: (tail, 1) ε num?

> Result of perturbing head(w)=lambda in box 3.
> Question at box 5.

TRAINER: No.

> head(w)=lambda becomes essential.

COMPUTER: (tail, 0; head, lambda)εnum?

> Removal of tail (w)=1 introduces tail(w) ε digit
> as a possibly essential statement. "tail, 0"
> replaces "tail, 1" to perturb the statement within
> digit - the construction process helps here.

TRAINER: Yes.

COMPUTER: (head, lambda) ε num?

> Trying tail(w) ε digit for inessentiality.

TRAINER: No.

Back to box 2. head(w)=lambda and tail(w) ε digit are now both essential.

COMPUTER: head(w)=null & tail(w) ε digit ≡ w ε num?

TRAINER: No.

Computer now knows that the description must have an "or" in it. A little rote is needed, even with tail(w) ε digit having introduced some simplification.

COMPUTER: Please show another.

TRAINER: (head, (head, null; tail, 0) ε num

Now the knowledge base allows not only that tail(w) ε digit but also a deduction from the partial knowledge of num, namely head(w) ε num. The deduction tree (somewhat simplified):

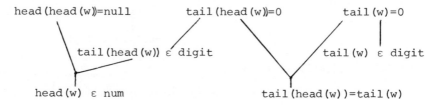

head(head(w))=null   tail(head(w))=0   tail(w)=0

tail(head(w)) ε digit   tail(w) ε digit

head(w) ε num   tail(head(w))=tail(w)

The rest of the scenario is based on this tree.

COMPUTER: (head, (head,lambda;tail,0); tail,1) ε num?

TRAINER: Yes.

tail(w)=0 as well as tail(head(w))=tail(w) is inessential.

COMPUTER: head(w) εnum & tail(w) ε digit → w ε num?

TRAINER: Yes.

Both head(head(w))=null and tail(head(w)) ε digit could be inessential as long as the statement implied by their conjunction in the knowledge base implied w ε num. So changing any part of the head is tantamount to asking this question.

COMPUTER: tail(w) ε digit & (head(w)=null or head(w) ε num) ≡ w ε num?

12

TRAINER: Yes.

> This test makes it unnecessary to test for further
> "or" terms. Notice that in this question the →
> to the left of w ε num has been replaced by ≡.
> This leads to the description of num given at the
> beginning of the training dialogue.

V. SUMMARIZING COMMENTS

The language and algorithms briefly described in this paper
are designed to emulate certain parts of the activities of an
artificially intelligent system.

Ideally an artificially intelligent system should be able to
look at a situation and classify it as needing a specific action
if a certain goal is to be reached. We are looking here at the
process of classification. We are assuming that a situation can
be exhibited as an object. The representation of a real object
in the format shown by us is obviously very much dependent on the
properties we choose. Obviously also, the description of the
class being learned will vary in complexity depending on the initial representation - *unless new representations can be found* according to the purpose. Because of this, it is essential that the
statements in the language be allowed to have the form x ε name in
addition to (property (x) = value) - the former allows one to use
previous knowledge to learn new descriptions. I hope the example
has adequately brought out the importance of this. Any language
for learning must allow this capability of growth in vocabulary.

Of the three algorithms described in this paper, recognition
and construction are very efficient, being based on the concept of
a search-tree rather than that of graph matching. However, if
some of the objects to be constructed have to be constructed essentially through table look-ups (a process not exemplified here,
but possible within the set-up described here), the efficiency
naturally drops to something comparable to the matching techniques.

The learning algorithms cannot be easily compared--since the
sequential question technique used here often is inapplicable in
the circumstances (self-imposed or otherwise) under which many
authors have worked. Since our system depends heavily on the existence of growth, an important source of inefficiency may stem
from the need for continually accessing a growing knowledge base:
a phenomenon not encountered by workers who work with fixed languages. It would be interesting to see what kind of bind we get
into as simulation proceeds.

ACKNOWLEDGEMENTS

I thank my friend and colleague, Prof. Elliot Koffman for
many suggestions which, I believe, helped me in improving my presentation.

13

REFERENCES

1. Michalski, R. S., "Discovering Classification Rules by the Variable Valued Logic System VL", Proc. Third International Jt. Conf. on Artificial Intelligence, Stanford, California, August 20-24, 1973.
2. Vere, S. A., "Relational Production Systems", Report from Department of Information Engineering, University of Illinois at Chicago Circle, January, 1976.
3. Hays-Roth, F., "An Optimal Network Representation and other Mechanisms for Recognition of Structured Events", Proc. Second International Joint Conference on Pattern Recognition, Copenhagen, 1974.
4. Banerji, R. B., "A Language for Pattern Recognition", Pattern Recognition, 1, 63 (1968).
5. Comfort, J. C., "A Flexible Efficient Computer System for Answering Human Questions", Birkhaser-Verlag, Basle, 1975.
6. Cover, T., "Generalizations on Patterns Using Kolmogorov Complexity", Proc. First International Joint Conference on Pattern Recognition, Washington, D. C. 1973, p. 551.
7. Banerji, R. B., "Some Linguistic and Statistical Problems in Pattern Recognition", Pattern Recognition, 3, 409 (1971).
8. Feldman, J. A., "Some Decidability Results on Grammatical Inference and Complexity", Information and Control 20, 244(1972).
9. Banerji, R. B., "Theory of Problem Solving", American Elsevier Publishing Co., N. Y. 1969.
10. Rosenschein, S. J., "Structuring A Pattern Space with Applications To Lexical Information and Event Interpretation", Moore School of Electrical Engineering, University of Pennsylvania, Dec. 1975.
11. Srinivasan, C. V., "The Architecture of a Coherent Information System; A General Problem Solving System", Proc. of the Third International Joint Conference of Artificial Intelligence, Stanford, 1973.

TIME/SPACE TRADEOFF FROM THE VIEWPOINT
OF GRAMMATICAL SIMILARITY*

Eberhard L. Bertsch
FB Informatik
Universität des Saarlandes
Saarbrücken, West Germany

I. INTRODUCTION

Any kind of pattern recognition may be regarded as comprising at least two methodologically distinct parts: a part referring to the constituents of a given pattern, and a part referring to the relationships between such constituents. The two parts may be called lexical and grammatical description, respectively.

It is by no means easy to define a borderline between these two areas, however. In general, syntactic methods can only be employed when an appropriate pre-pass is available. The pre-pass finds out which lexical item should be assigned to a given input signal. This part of the analysis may be quite complicated when noise has to be filtered out, or input signals are unreliable for some other reason such that the assignment of lexical items has to be performed in terms of probability distributions.

Even when all input signals are elements of a well-defined set of mutually distinct characters whose individual recognition presents no problem, a separation between lexical and grammatical descriptions may be advantageous. The translation of programming languages is usually separated into scanning, parsing, and code-generation. Scanning and parsing are analogous to lexical and grammatical analyses, respectively. Although the distinction is somewhat less obvious in a programming language like PASCAL (which has a so-called one-pass compiler), Niklaus Wirth's own implementation contains a specific procedure to recognize and identify such entities as keywords, labels, and programmer-defined names.

In the present paper, we are going to concentrate on the syntactic parts of pattern recognition systems. More specifically, we will assume that the recognition process has to be performed on a typical time-shared computer, where runtime and storage space are expensive but potentially unlimited (one may always add another disk pack). Accordingly, our main results will be concerned with time- and/or space-minimization of grammatical procedures, complexity estimates, and practical methods for improving a parser in terms of either time or space.

It is readily admitted that a programmer may improve his code by means of dirty machine-dependent tricks without appealing to

---

* The author is a member of SFB 100 "Electronische Sprachforschung" which is fully supported by the German Research Society (DFG).

abstract insights into the nature of computing. This type of
thinking will be disregarded for two reasons: first of all, the
effect of "tricks" with respect to portability, reliability, and
documentability of programs has again and again been shown to be
nothing less than catastrophic. A programmer may be incapable of
understanding his own program after one such "improvement" and an
additional period of two weeks' vacation. Secondly, it is quite
clear that local improvements can only subtract a negligible factor from the order of complexity that a problem possesses. Thus
it is necessary to capture the parsing problem in sufficiently
general terms, and then to work down to the level of applicability.

Section 2 below presents a definitional framework for Chomsky
grammars, monoidal categories, and Lindenmayer systems which were
originally motivated by some phenomena in theoretical biology. In
section 3 these definitions are used to show some theorems in
space reducibility. The main result of that section has not been
officially published before. For that reason an outline of the
proof is added. Some ramifications of the theory, including a
connection to translative processes, are also discussed. Section
4 contains an important paragraph about the relationship between
runtime efficiency and the kind of space reduction mentioned in
section 3. In addition to that, we indicate how and why certain
restrictions on the control devices of matrix and indexed grammars
can lead to sensible runtime bounds. Section 5 deals with an extremely practical, compiler-oriented technique for coming to grips
with the space requirement and error-detection facilities of simple parsers. As a matter of fact, one gets the impression that
space- and time-complexity can almost be turned on and off like
the volume-button on a radio.

All definitions and proofs are kept on a medium level of de-
tailedness. All significant steps are preceded by a short motivation and, if possible, an appropriate illustration. An extensive bibliography has been added to lead the reader to the more
technically written papers in the field.

II. DEFINITIONAL PRELIMINARIES

Grammatical structures are often described in terms of rewriting systems. A word is said to belong to a language, if it
can be obtained by means of repeated rewriting from some distinguished starting symbol. The specification as to how a string
may be rewritten is called the grammar of the language.

The following definition, which is due to Noam Chomsky of
MIT, is generally taken as *the* foundation for work in formal language theory.

Definition: Let A be an alphabet, and let P be a set of
pairs of words over that alphabet. We say that a word w *directly
derives* a word y (for short: $w \longrightarrow y$), if there are decompositions
$w_1 w_2 w_3 = w$ and $y_1 y_2 y_3 = y$ such that (w_2, y_2) is in P. w *derives*

y if there is a sequence of words $x_1, \ldots , x_n$ with $w \longrightarrow x_1 \longrightarrow x_2$
$\ldots \quad x_n \longrightarrow y$ (for short: $w \overset{*}{\longrightarrow} y$). By distinguishing a subset
T of A (the terminal symbols), and an element S of A, we say that
G= (A,T,P,S) is a *grammar*, and we call the set $\left\{ w \mid w \text{ is a word} \right.$
over T and $\left. S \overset{*}{\longrightarrow} w \right\}$ the *language* generated by the grammar G.

The clause "w is a word over T" can be abbreviated as "w in
T*". Furthermore, a set L of words is called a *contextfree* language if there exists a grammar G= (A,T,P,S) such that L is generated by G and all (u,v) in P have the property that u is a one-
letter word. G is called a *context-free grammar*.

We shall now consider an example of such a rewriting system.

Example:

Let A= {S,t,a,b} , T= {a,b} ,

    P = { (S,ata), (ta,ab), (aa,bbb)}

bbbb can be derived from S in the following way:

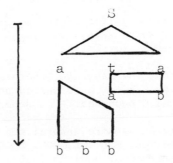

    S $\longrightarrow$ ata $\longrightarrow$ aab $\longrightarrow$ bbb is the rewriting sequence. Thus
bbbb is an element of the language.

In contrast to Chomsky grammars, Lindenmayer systems are
characterized by the necessity to derive *each* symbol at *each* step
of the generation process. Lindenmayer systems have been applied
to biology, in particular to the growth behavior of certain fila-
mentous fungi. The formal apparatus allows for a moderate amount
of nondeterminism as well as a strict dependency on time-variant
conditions such as cold, warm, dark, light. The following definitions are due to Rozenberg and his colleagues who have tried to
cast L-systems into the precise formalism of grammar theory.

The funny abbreviation ETOL stands for "extended time-variant
zero-context Lindenmayer system".

Definition: An *ETOL-system* is a 4-tuple G= (N,T,F,w) such
that:

N is a finite alphabet (of nonterminal symbols).

17

T is a finite nonempty alphabet (of terminal symbols) with $N \cap T = \emptyset$.

w is an element of $(N \cup T)*$ called the *axiom* of G.

F is a finite nonempty family, each element of which is a finite nonempty set of productions $a \longrightarrow v$ where a is in $N \cup T$ and v is in $(N \cup T)*$.

Each element P of F (called a production table of F) satisfies the condition:

For every a in $N \cup T$ there exists at least one v such that $a \longrightarrow v$ is in P.

Let G be an ETOL-system. Suppose that $x = b_1 \ldots b_t$ where $b_1, \ldots, b_t$ are in $N \cup T$. We say that x *directly derives* y (for short: $x \Longrightarrow y$), if there exists a P in F and a sequence $P_1, \ldots, P_t$ of productions in P such that for every i in $\{1, \ldots, t\}$ $p_i = b_i \longrightarrow v_i$ and $y = v_1 \ldots v_t$.

We say that x *derives* y (for short: $x \overset{*}{\Longrightarrow} y$) if for some $n > 0$ there is a sequence of words $x_0, x_1, \ldots, x_n$ in $(N \cup T)*$ such that $x_0 = x$, $x_n = y$ and $x_{i-1} \Longrightarrow x_i$ for $1 \leq i \leq n$.

We can now say that the *language* generated by G is the set $L = \{x \text{ in } T* \mid w \overset{*}{\Longrightarrow} x\}$. A set L is called an *ETOL language* if there is an ETOL-system G such that L is generated by G.

The above definition is more general than most others in the literature. There are TOL, EOL, OL, DOL, DPOL and other classes, all of which can be defined by obvious restrictions

Example:

Let $N = \{1\}$, $T = \{c, d\}$, $F = \{P_{warm} , P_{cold}\}$ where

$P_{warm} = \{(1 \longrightarrow 11), (1 \longrightarrow c), (c \longrightarrow d), (d \longrightarrow d)\}$

$P_{cold} = \{(1 \longrightarrow 1), (1 \longrightarrow d), (c \longrightarrow c), (d \longrightarrow c)\}$

Then the following derivation is possible:

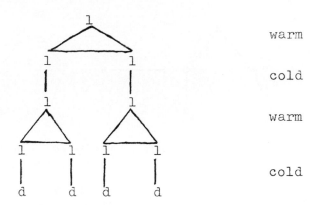

For our minimization results in section 3, we are going to
need a formal calculus describing relationships between *different*
grammars and/or L-systems. Monoidal category theory has been
shown to be particularly useful for that sort of thing. Derivations are considered as being instances of planar networks. Thence
it is possible to provide a natural (one might say "geometric")
notion of a mapping from one network to another network. Fundamental papers in this area were written by Hotz and Schnorr.

The present set of definitions is just another example of the
usefulness of categorial thinking in computer science.

Definition: Let $G = (A,T,P,S)$ be a contextfree grammar. By M
we denote the set of derivations corresponding to G. By $s(m)$ for
m in M we mean the source of m, by $t(m)$ we mean the target of m.
(All these notions are essentially the same for Lindenmayer systems.) As in the extant literature, we write $m_1 \times m_2$ for parallel
derivations m_1, m_2 and have $s(m_1 \times m_2) = s(m_1)s(m_2)$, $t(m_1 \times m_2) = t(m_1)t(m_2)$.

If $s(m_2) = t(m_1)$, we may compose m_1 and m_2 to $m_2 \circ m_1$ with
$s(m_2 \circ m_1) = s(m_1)$, $t(m_2 \circ m_1) = t(m_2)$.

For two grammars $G_1 = (A_1,T_1,P_1,S_1)$ and $G_2 = (A_2,T_2,P_2,S_2)$, an
x-functor $f : G_1 \longrightarrow G_2$ is a pair of mappings (f_1,f_2) where $f_1 : A_1^* \longrightarrow A_2^*$, $f_2 : M_1 \longrightarrow M_2$ such that

$$f_1(w_1 w_2) = f_1(w_1)f_1(w_2) \quad \text{for } w_1, w_2 \text{ in } A_1^*$$

$$\left.\begin{array}{l} f_2(m_1 \circ m_2) = f_2(m_1) \circ f_2(m_2) \\[2ex] f_2(m_1 \times m_2) = f_2(m_1) \times f_2(m_2) \end{array}\right\} \quad \text{for } m_1, m_2 \text{ in } M_1$$

and $\quad s(f_2(m)) = f_1(s(m))$ for all m in M_1.

The above conditions guarantee that the mapping is homomor-
phic.

Example:

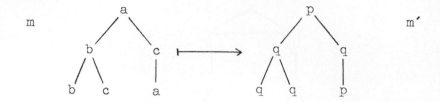

Here $s(m)= a$, $t(m)= bca$, $s(m')= p$, $t(m')= qqp$. f_1, f_2 are clear.

III.   SPACE REDUCIBILITY

The problem of space reducibility can be defined in simple
terms: Given a recognition mechanism for a set of syntactic patterns, find out whether there is a different mechanism which recognizes the same set of patterns with less internal storage space
for program and data.   The usual approach works as follows:

Construct a set of candidate mechanisms, any of which might
fulfill the above condition.   Then apply a decision procedure to
each candidate in order to find out whether the condition holds or
not.

The set of grammars up to a certain space bound can easily be
constructed.   Thus the critical point is whether a decision procedure is available.

It has been shown (by means of Post's correspondence theorem)
that it is undecidable whether two given context-free grammars
generate the same language.   To find decidable relations between
equivalent grammars, one must therefore search for stronger criteria.   It is natural to consider the existence of some sort of
mapping from the set of derivations of one grammar into the set of
derivations of another grammar as such a criterion.   As was shown
by Hotz, two grammars G_1 and G_2 generate the same language if
there is a surjective x-functor between G_1 and G_2 which leaves the
terminal symbols unchanged.   The decision whether a given functor
is surjective, turns out to be another difficult problem, however.

Using our formalism of the preceding section, we can sum up
the extant results:

For linear grammars, i.e. context-free grammars whose production rules generate no more than one derivable symbol, Hotz
showed in 1968 that the surjectivity problem is generally solvable.
In a subsequent paper by Schnorr, decidability was explicitly demonstrated for length-reducing functors between context-free grammars.   Schnorr even proved that the existence of a *chain* of functors:

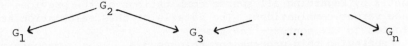

is algorithmically decidable. This notion happens to coincide
with the kind of structural equivalence studied by Knuth and Mc-
Naughton.

The problem of finding a decision procedure for the class of
functions which map the set of derivation trees of a grammar G_1 on
the set of derivation trees of a grammar G_2, remained open for
several years. In 1973/74, papers by H. Walter and myself showed
that it can be solved. This led to the following minimization result.

Theorem: Let C be any complexity measure for the class of
context-free grammars with the property that for any grammar G the
set of grammars G' with $C(G') < C(G)$ can be effectively constructed. Then there exists an effective procedure to find to any grammar G a grammar G' such that G' is minimal (according to C) among
all grammars for which there is a functor from G onto G'.

Although the relevant notions are similar, minimization results for Lindenmayer systems are harder to obtain, because:

      a)   time-dependency,

      b)   parallel derivation, and

      c)   derivability of terminals

are nontrivial features. We will now present a previously unpublished theorem which indicates that (at least) some results can
be carried over.

    Theorem: It is decidable whether a length-preserving functor
f: $G_1 \longrightarrow G_2$, where $G_1 = (N_1, T_1, F_1, w_1)$ and $G_2 = (N_2, T_2, F_2, w_2)$ are
ETOL-systems, is surjective or not.

Of course this result is much weaker than any hypothesis
about linguistic equivalence of two L-systems. We feel, however,
that functorial equivalence is more interesting than linguistic
equivalence, because two descriptions of e.g. mushroom growth can
only be compared when both generate the same *set* of mushrooms in
essentially the same *way*. In that case (and only in that case) a
"smaller" description may be preferable.

    Outline of the proof: Without loss of generality, we may as-
sume that $f^{-1}(w_2) = \{w_1\}$. For each production p_2 in G_2, check whether
there is a production p_1 in G_1 which is mapped on p_2 (p_1 is called
a pre-image of p_2).

If that is the case, assign the set of source symbols of all
pre-images to each rule p_2 in G_2.

In the next step, try to build pre-images for all trees of height 2 by regarding all source combinations of the previous step as new target combinations. The details of this calculation are analogous to the context-free case.

Continuing this process for heights 3,4 ... ,n , we obtain for each production p_2 a family of sets Fam(p_2) such that all elements of Fam(p_2) are sets of pre-image tops. Combinatorial arguments guarantee that this sequence will either terminate or run into an infinite loop. Both cases can be tested.

This leaves the problem of time-dependency. If the previous pass has been successful, we start all over again, this time grouping all set families by their time-conditions. As the process continues, we have to separate all families belonging to a certain *sequence* of time-conditions T_1, T_2, ... , T_n from those belonging to a different sequence. Again we can show that the decision process may be forced to terminate.

Example:

Let a,p be in N_1, b,q in N_2, r in N_1. Suppose that p and r are mapped on q, a on b.

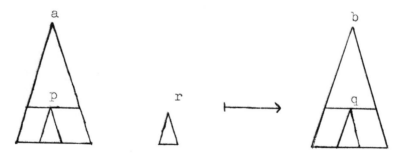

In this case the subtrees governed by b and q have pre-images.

In 1972, Hotz observed that the kind of syntax-directed translations studied by Lewis and Stearns are actually simple forms of x-functors plus permutations. In my doctoral thesis which appeared in October, 1973, I took account of this connection and developed some decision procedures for translatability and the word problem of transformational grammars. A subsequent master's thesis by J. Hertel dealt with the automata-theoretic aspects of the subject.

One word of caution must be added. In spite of (or maybe because of) the general applicability of the above algorithms, their runtimes for medium-sized examples would be in the order of days or weeks. It is well known that most good decision algorithms in computer science are subject to what has been called "combinatorial explosion". The only way out is to develop approximations which will work for useful subsets of the class of grammars or

ETOL-systems.

Someone who works in automatic pattern recognition or artificial intelligence should be quite meticulous about savings in runtime. For this reason, I will now turn to questions of time complexity.

IV. RELATIONSHIPS BETWEEN TIME, SPACE, AND DESCRIPTIVE POWER

Our first major result in this section is that a decrease in size along the lines suggested in section 3 can never entail an improvement in efficiency. More precisely: A more refined recognition mechanism will not be beaten in terms of runtime requirements. We formulate the theorem:

Theorem: Let f: $G_1 \longrightarrow G_2$ be a length-preserving functor, where G_1 and G_2 are context-free grammars and G_2 is unambiguous. Suppose there is an algorithm which will construct a parse for any w generated by G_2 and reject any w not generated by G_2 in less than t(length(w)) steps, where t is an integer-valued function. Then there is a constant c and an algorithm which will accept w generated by G_1 and reject w not generated by G_1 in less than ct (length(w)) steps.

While a detailed proof is beyond the scope of this paper, we can summarize the idea as follows.

Let w be the word to be analyzed. If there is a derivation of w in G_1, then there is a derivation of the image of w in G_2. By the unambiguity of G_2, f(w) cannot be parsed in more than one way. So we take the fastest parsing technique available for G_2 and get either a parse tree for f(w) or else an error message. If there *is* a parse, our next job is to find a pre-image. Making use of results by Ginsburg and Harrison, we see that this adds no more than a linear factor to the overall parsing time.

Let us now consider a few connections between time complexity and descriptive power. In the 1960's, dozens of new language families were invented, most of which had a context-free base component and some additional control structures. Many of them turned out to be rather short-lived. The classes of indexed grammars and matrix grammars are still of considerable interest, however.

Definition: An indexed grammar G is a 5-tuple G= (A,T,P,S,F) where (A,T,P,S) is a context-free grammar and F is a set of *flags*. To each rule p= (a, $a_1 \ldots a_k$) in P there is a corresponding flag rule f(p)= (f, $f_1 \ldots f_k$) where f,$f_1, \ldots, f_k$ are either a flag or the empty word.

Derivations are performed as follows: A flag string is assigned to every letter at each rewriting step. The initial symbol S carries the empty flag string. If a letter a carries the flag string $fw_1 \ldots w_n$, the replacing letters $a_1 \ldots a_k$ carry the flag strings $f_1 w_1 \ldots w_n, \ldots, f_k w_1 \ldots w_n$ respectively. A word of the language is any sequence in T* generated by G, regardless of the associated flags.

Note that a production can only be applied if the symbol to be rewritten has a flag string starting with a certain f (where f may be empty).

Example:

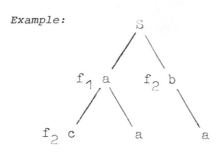

The productions are
$$((S,ab),(e,f_1f_2))$$
$$((a,ca),(f_1,f_2e))$$
$$((b,a),(f_2,e)   )$$

where e stands for the empty word.

We observe that a flag string may become arbitrarily long. It is mainly for that reason that no parsing time bounds better than exponential functions of the word length have been found so far. In a paper which appeared half a year ago, we could show the following result, however:

Theorem: Let G= (A,T,P,S,F) be a tree-unambiguous indexed grammar, i. e. an indexed grammar whose underlying context-free grammar derives unambiguously. Then there is an algorithm which will recognize any w generated by G in time cn^2 where c is a constant and n is the word length.

As unambiguous context-free grammars are also parsed in n^2 steps, any improvement of this bound for indexed grammars would be revolutionary. Indexed grammars are of practical interest because their concept of derivability is close to Van Wijngaarden's two-level grammars that were used for the programming language ALGOL 68.

Matrix grammars, which were introduced by S. Abraham in 1965, exploit the possibility of permitting only fixed sequences of context free productions.

Definition: A matrix grammar is a 5-tuple G= (A,T,P,S) where (A,T,P,S) is a context-free grammar and M is a finite set of sequences of productions in P. If $p_1...p_n$ is such a sequence, then a step-by-step application of $p_1, ... ,p_n$ to a word w yields a *direct derivation* of w. All other notions are the same as for Chomsky grammars.

Up to now, very little is known about the time complexity of matrix grammars or the mutual inclusion of matrix and indexed classes. Dealing with the problem of time complexity, we can only present the following result:

Theorem: Let L be a matrix language with the property that all words in L need no more than k derivable symbols at every step of their derivation. Then the time complexity of the word problem (parsing problem) has an upper bound which is given by a polynomial function of the word length.

While a time complexity of n^{10} may not be very comforting (even in terms of microseconds), we have at least avoided the sort of "explosion" mentioned earlier.

V. TABLE SIZE AND ERROR DETECTION TIME
FOR PRECEDENCE LANGUAGES

Precedence tables have been used and extensively studied as aids for syntax-directed compiling. The universal list-processing language EULER is only one (though prominent) example of the application of precedence techniques. Given a grammar G with alphabet A, a precedence table M contains exactly one entry for each pair of symbols in A. The entry $M(a,b)=-1$ means that when a and b occur together, b is the start of a "handle", i.e. a sequence of letters which can be reduced to one symbol.

The entry $M(a,b)=0$ means that ab are both parts of the same handle, and $M(a,b)=+1$ implies that a is the end of a handle. Obviously, many grammars will not permit unique entries for every pair (a,b). Floyd's opinion has been, however, that most *practical* (non-pathological) languages can be parsed by means of an appropriate precedence table.

Example:

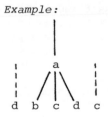

A table for this grammar would contain

$M(d,b)=-1, M(b,c)=0, M(c,d)=0, M(d,c)=+1$

In some cases, a precedence table may be even more simplified, if there are integer-valued functions f and g defined on A such that

$$M(a,b)= -1 \text{ implies } f(a) < g(b)$$

$$M(a,b)= 0 \text{ implies } f(a) = g(b)$$

$$M(a,b)= +1 \text{ implies } f(a) > g(b)$$

There are quite a few efficient algorithms which will test whether a given precedence table can be transformed into a pair of *precedence functions* f and g. The corresponding decrease in storage requirement is tremendous. While card $(A)^2$ storage cells are

25

necessary for a table, only 2card(A) cells are required for a pair
of functions.

This sort of thinking neglects a significant part of the
problem, however. In a precedence table, it is convenient to mark
all impossible pairs (a,b), i.e. pairs that will never occur together, by some unique error entry, say M(a,b)=+2. A more refined parser will even give the address of a textual error message
as the value of M(a,b). If integer-valued functions are used, one
of the relations "smaller", "equal", or "greater" must hold between
f(a) and g(b). Thus the occurrence of an error message (not to
speak of the quality of the message) is delayed.

As the primary purpose of precedence parsers, in contrast to
more sophisticated techniques, is *fast* recognition of permissible
and impermissible patterns, this disadvantage should not be overlooked. Using a graph-theoretic algorithm which was first published by J. Bell, we were able to show that intermediate forms
can be designed such that both storage space *and* detection time
stay within the desired bounds.

Definition: Let M be a precedence table with alphabet A.
Let $c,d,f_1, \ldots ,f_k,g_1, \ldots ,g_l$ be integer-valued functions on A
with $1 \le c(a) \le k, 1 \le d(a) \le l$ for all a in A.

If $M(a,b)= \text{sign}(f_{c(b)}(a) - g_{d(a)}(b))$ for all a,b in A for
which M is defined, we say that the ordered (k+1)-tuple $(f_1, \ldots ,$
$f_k,g_1, \ldots ,g_l)$ is a precedence value-table with k+1 rows.

A value-table may first of all contribute to a substantial
reduction in storage space, if no pair of precedence functions can
be found. Moreover, even when a pair of functions *can* be constructed, the error detection capacity of a value-table may be clearly
superior to that of the corresponding functions f and g. In a
paper which is going to appear in one of the next issues of Comm.
ACM, we have demonstrated that the table for arithmetic expressions used by Aho and Ullman can be reduced to 35 percent of its
original size, with a loss of no more than 10 percent in immediate
error detection.

Some of these ideas are currently being implemented for the
linguistics-oriented programming language COMSKEE.

BIBLIOGRAPHY

1. Abraham, S., Some questions of phrase structure grammars.
    Computational Linguistics, 4 (1965), 61-70.
2. Aho, A., Indexed grammars - an extension of contextfree
    grammars. JACM 15 (1968), 647-671.
3. Aho, A., and J. Ullman, Error detection in precedence parsers.
    Math. Systems Theory 7 (1973), 97-113.
4. Bell, J., A new method for determining linear precedence
    functions for precedence grammars. CACM 12 (1969), 567-569.
5. Bertsch, E., Existenz- und Entscheidbarkeitsfragen der Uber-
    setzungstheorie. Dissertation. Saarbrücken (1973).

6. Bertsch, E., Surjectivity of functors on grammars. Math. Systems Theory 9 (1975/76), 298-307.

7. Bertsch, E., An observation on relative parsing time. JACM 22 (1975), 493-498.

8. Bertsch, E., Two thoughts on fast recognition of indexed languages. Information and Control 29 (1975), 381-384.

9. Bertsch, E., On matrix languages with finite control. In preparation.

10. Bertsch, E., On the storage requirement in precedence parsing. Appearing in Communications of the ACM.

11. Bertsch, E., and Angelika von Brochowski, COMSKEE - eine Sprache für Linguisten. 4th GI-conference on programming languages. IFB 1 (1976), 166-174.

12. Chomsky, N., Formal properties of grammars. In: Handbook of Mathematical Psychology. Wiley, New York (1963), 325-418.

13. Chomsky, N., Contextfree languages and pushdown storage. MIT Res. Lab. Electron. Quarterly Progress Report 65 (1962).

14. Ehrenfeucht, G., and G. Rozenberg, Nonterminals versus homomorphisms in defining languages for some classes of rewriting systems. Acta Informatica 3 (1974), 265-283.

15. Fu, K. S., Syntactic (linguistic) pattern recognition. In: Digital pattern recognition. Springer-Verlag (1975), 95-134.

16. Ginsburg, S., The mathematical theory of contextfree languages. McGraw-Hill, New York (1966).

17. Ginsburg, S., and M. Harrison, Bracketed contextfree languages. Journal of Computer and System Sciences 1 (1967), 1-13.

18. Grau, A., U. Hill and H. Langmaack, Translation of ALGOL 60. Springer-Verlag 1967.

19. Hertel, J., Transductors for linearized representations of trees (in German), unpublished diploma thesis. Saarbrücken (1974).

20. Hotz, G., Eindeutigkeit und Mehrdeutigkeit formaler Sprachen. Elektronische Informationsverarbeitung und Kybernetik 2 (1966), 235-246.

21. Hotz, G., Reduktionssätze über eine Klasse formaler Sprachen mit endlich vielen Zuständen. Mathematische Zeitschrift 104 (1968), 205-221.

22. Knuth, D., A characterization of parenthesis languages. Information and Control 10 (1967), 269-289.

23. Lindenmayer, A., Mathematical models for cellular interaction in development. J. Theor. Biology 18 (1968), 300-315.

24. McNaughton, R., Parenthesis grammars. JACM 16 (1969), 490-500.

25. Schnorr, C., Transformational classes of grammars. Information and Control 14 (1969), 252-277.

26. Walter, H., Einige topologische Aspekte der syntaktischen Analyse. Research Rept. AFS-1, TH Darmstadt (1972).

27. Wijngaarden, A. van et al., Draft report on the algorithmic language ALGOL 68. Supplement to Algol Bulletin 26. Math. Center Amsterdam (1968).

28. Wirth, N., On the design of programming languages. Proc. of
     the IFIP Congress. Stockholm (1974), 386 ff.
29. Wirth, N., The programming language PASCAL (Revised Report),
     Lecture Notes in Computer Science 18. Springer-Verlag (1974).

SOME MULTIDIMENSIONAL GRAMMAR INFERENCE METHODS*

J. M. Brayer
Dept. of Electr. Engin. &
   Comp. Science
University of New Mexico
Albuquerque, NM

K. S. Fu
School of Electrical Engineering
Purdue University
W. Lafayette, IND.

I. INTRODUCTION

One of the most difficult and most intriguing problems associated with the linguistic approach to pattern recognition is that
of constructing a grammar which adequately describes the patterns
being considered. Many researchers have tackled the problem of
trying to find automated schemes for finding a grammar from a subset of a language. Considering the difficulty that researchers
themselves have in finding good grammars for non-trivial problems,
it is not too surprising that these efforts have been of little
practical value. Nevertheless these attempts are important because
they yield insight into the detailed mechanisms of learning, and
because they may eventually lead to successful results.

A grammatical inference algorithm is an algorithm whose input
is a sequence of training sample webs (or strings or trees) and
whose output is a grammar. Each input web is accompanied by the
information of whether or not this web belongs to the language
which the output grammar is supposed to generate. There may also
be some input information on the internal structure of a given
sample. An inference algorithm works adequately when it yields a
grammar which generates all of the training samples which belong
to L and none of the training samples which do not belong to L.
But the situation is more complicated as is illustrated by Figure 1. The samples which belong to L are called positive training
samples. Those samples which do not belong to L are called negative training samples. In general the set of positive samples, P,
does not contain all of the webs which belong to L. Also the inference algorithm has no information about the set $S-\{N \cup P\}$. Therefore the approach usually tried is to use the internal structure
of the sets N and P to infer information about $S-\{N \cup P\}$. There
have been several approaches to this idea but the most successful
one consists of looking for substructures which occur more than
once in the training set. Supposedly these repetitive substructures indicate recursive rules in the grammar. These recursive
rules then generate webs which belong to $S-\{N \cup P\}$. Unfortunately,
since no information exists about $S-\{N \cup P\}$, there is usually no way
of checking the accuracy of the inference.

---

* This work was supported by the National Science Foundation
   Grant ENG 74-17586.

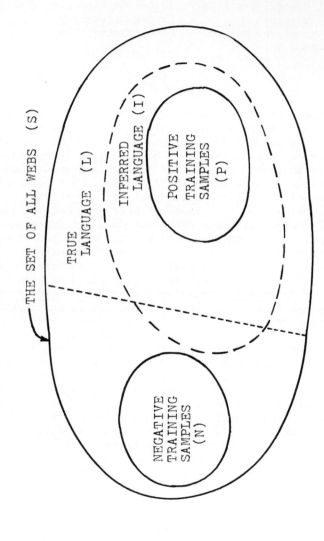

Figure 1   A Venn Diagram Illustrating Grammatical Inference

In the following sections, methods proposed for multidimensional grammatical inference are discussed. These are called multidimensional methods because they were originally proposed in that context. However, as will be shown, there is little fundamental difference about inferring multidimensional grammars. The reason is that the inference process is simply trying to discover the structure of the derivation diagram. This structure is independent of the dimensionality of the grammar and only dependent on the power of the grammar. Thus, multidimensional inference methods will be very similar to those for string grammars. A review of previous work in grammatical inference is given in two papers by Fu and Booth [1,2].

II. VARIABLE-VALUED LOGIC INFERENCE

This learning system has been proposed for picture description by Michalski [3,4] and reviewed in a grammatical inference context by Baskin [5]. It is a system which, when supplied with a set of primitives and their relations, will find a minimally complex description for a finite set of patterns. The description is a logical expression (string) in a variable-valued logic system. The basic method for minimization is the enumerative approach using the idea of covering ([6] section 5.2.2). This method is only feasible in rather simple cases and Michalski has developed a quasi-minimal cover method. However, the details of this method have not been reported in a grammar inference context. The advantage of the method is that it produces a measure of how far from optimal a calculated description is. The major limitations of this method seem to be that (1) a reasonable set of primitives and relations must be known a priori and (2) the descriptions only apply to finite sets, a subclass of finite state languages.

III. TREE GRAMMAR INFERENCE

Two papers on the inference of regular tree grammars were recently published by Bhargava and Fu [7] and by Gonzalez and Thomason [8]. The two methods are very similar and can be interpreted as an extension of the k-tail method of Biermann and Feldman for the inference of finite-state grammars [9]. However, as defined in the above paper, their method is restricted to k = 1 where k represents the depth of a tree. Recall that in the inference of finite-state grammars, as k varies from 0 to the length of the longest string, the inferred grammar varies from the universal language to the given sample set. Thus, any method restricted to k = 1 will infer grammars which generate languages that are very "loose" in their fit of the sample set.

It is possible to extend these methods to general k. The method is as follows:

1. Form the following collection:

$$C_t = \left\{ (\tau_1, \tau_2, \ldots \tau_m) \mid t\tau_1\tau_2 \ldots \tau_m \text{ is a tree in the training set and } |\tau_\ell| \leq k \right\}$$

where t is a tree with a single special frontier node,

$t\tau_1\tau_2 \ldots \tau_m$ is the tree formed by concatenating τ_ℓ at

the ℓ th position of the special frontier node of t,

$|\tau_\ell|$ is the depth of τ_ℓ +1,

m is the number of descendants of t and is not fixed to any particular interger.

2. The collection C_t of tuples of trees can be partitioned into subcollections, C_{tm}, of m-tuples where m is a fixed integer for all elements of each subcollection.

3. Each subcollection of i-tuples of trees must be divided into groups in which any member of a specified set may be used in a given position of the i-tuple. Thus C_{ti} may be written:

$$C_{ti} = C_{ti1} \cup C_{ti2} \cup \cdots C_{tin}$$

where $C_{tij} = \{ (\tau_1, \tau_2, \cdots \tau_i) \mid \tau_1 \in S_{j1}, \tau_2 \in S_{j2}, \cdots \}$

That is, each C_{tij} is characterized by i sets, $S_{j\ell}$ of trees from which the ℓth member of an i-tuple must be selected.

4. Now the rules for the grammar can be constructed. Equivalent S_{j1} sublanguages are combined and a nonterminal is assigned corresponding to each distinct sublanguage. A rule $A_i \rightarrow xA_{j1}A_{j2} \cdots A_{jm}$ is produced if there is a tree t

32

such that:

(1) A_i is the nonterminal corresponding to the sub-language $S_{j\ell}$,

(2) There exists a C_{tij} that contains the sublanguage $S_{j\ell}$ in the ℓth position of its specification.

(3) tx is a tree with x concatenated at the ℓth position of t.

(4) There exists a C_{txin} which is specified by the sublanguages $S_{n1}, S_{n2}, \cdots S_{nm}$.

(5) $A_{j1}, A_{j2} \cdots A_{jm}$ are the nonterminals corresponding to the $S_{n1}, S_{n2}, \cdots S_{nm}$ sublanguages respectively.

(6) Either

$$\overset{\textstyle x}{\underset{\alpha\ \beta\cdots\lambda}{\bigwedge}}$$

is a tree in S_j

where $\alpha \in S_{n1}, \beta \in S_{n2}, \cdots \lambda \in S_{nm}$

or

$$\left|\ \overset{\textstyle x}{\underset{\alpha\ \beta\cdots\lambda}{\bigwedge}}\ \right| > k$$

A rule $A_i \to x$ is produced if conditions (1),(2) and (3) above are satsified and tx is in the training set.

This procedure is illustrated in detail in a report to be published. The results of its use are shown in the following example.

Example 1. Consider the following regular tree grammar:

(1) $S \to$ $\overset{\textstyle \$}{\underset{B\ \ B}{\bigwedge}}$

(2) $B \to$ $\overset{\textstyle b}{\underset{B\ \ B}{\bigwedge}}$

(3) $B \to$ $\overset{\textstyle b}{\underset{a\ \ b}{\bigwedge}}$ $\overset{}{\underset{A\ \ B}{\bigwedge}}$

(4) $A \to a$

(5) $B \to b$

The training set is the following:

33

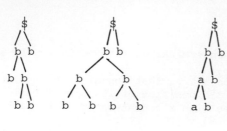

Applying the procedure with k=2 results in the following grammar:

(1) S → $
         /\
        B B

(2) B → b
        /\
       B B

(3) B → b
        /\
       A C

(4) C → b
        /\
       A B

(5) B → b

(6) A → a

Note that with this training set, the procedure of Bhargava and Gonzalez would have produced the following grammar:

(1) S → $
          /\
         B B

(2) B → b
        /\
       B B

(3) B → b
        /\
       A B

(4) B → b

(5) A → a

This is the same as would be produced by the above procedure with k=1. Note that $L_{k=2} \subset L_{k=1}$. For any given training set, there is no way to tell which is the better grammar unless some other information (e.g. some negative samples) is available. However, choice of the parameter k gives the designer some flexibility in how "close" to fit the training set.

IV. INFERENCE BY APPLICATION OF KNOWN PREDICATE FORMS

The method discussed in this section was proposed by Evans[10] and applied to the inference of context free grammars. Evans applied his method to several examples including some simple pictures.
The general procedure for constructive inference is given below:

(1)   Discover the syntactic structure of the strings
(2)   Generate nonterminals for each sublanguage
(3)   Combine equivalent nonterminals

Evans' procedure accomplishes step (1) by assuming a set of predicates is given which can be applied to the pictures to generate structural descriptions. The procedure then uses a set of heuristic rules to identify and then combine nonterminals. The procedure is "tuned" by picking the values of two thresholds, one for "predicate-weakening" and another for "object-weakening". Loosening each threshold independently loosens the fit of the grammar to the sample set. However there is no way to tell how the two are related or to pick their values.

It seems that the assumption of a given set of predicates is a very strong one. In fact, if these predicates are known, it is not necessary to merge nonterminals heuristically. The predicates can be used to develop the derivation trees for the sample set. It is a well-known result in tree grammar theory that the set of derivation trees of a context free string grammar can be generated by a regular tree grammar. Thus the predicates convert the sample set of patterns to a sample set of trees. The regular tree grammar which describes this set of derivation trees can be learned with the k-tail procedure discussed in section three. This regular tree grammar can then be very simply transformed back into a context free grammar in the original topology. The existence of this procedure reduces the inference problem to two basic issues:

(1)   What are the necessary characteristics of the a-priori known predicates and how are these predicates to be chosen?
(2)   What are the necessary characteristics of the training set?

To clarify the above ideas the notion of adequacy is introduced. This concept is not defined formally but rather is used to simplify the discussion accompanying the following examples.

A set of predicates or production rules will be called "adequate" for a language if all of the recursiveness of the grammar can be contained internal to the rules themselves. This means that recursive rules like $A \rightarrow X_1 X_2 \cdots A \cdots X_n$ are allowed but sets of rules such as $A \rightarrow B$, $B \rightarrow C$, $\cdots X \rightarrow A$ where the recursiveness spans over several rules are not allowed. Another way of viewing this is by noting that when there is recursiveness the derivation tree may contain multiple examples of the same nonterminal along a given path from root to frontier. If the grammar rules are adequate for the language, all of the examples of a given nonterminal will be adjacent in such a path.

Now this definition is used to introduce the concept of adequacy of a set of predicate or production *forms*. A production form is an expression, $N \rightarrow NtNN$ where the N and t are "place holders" for nonterminals and terminals respectively. In other words the form tells how many and where a nonterminal or a terminal appears in the rule but does not tell which specific nonterminal or terminal appears. Finally, a set of production forms will be called adequate for a language if when the proper terminals and nonterminals are substituted into the forms, a set of adequate productions results.

The definition of a "structurally adequate" training set is more complex. Certainly the training set must be at least structurally complete (i.e. each production of the grammar must be used at least once to generate some sample in the training set). But the definition of structurally adequate also depends on the predicates being used and on whether or not the shortest strings are in the training set. As the following examples will show, it is possible to find any predicate of the form:

$$S=\text{Pred}\{S_1,S_2,\ldots S_n\}$$

where $\forall i$: $S_1 \overset{*}{\Longrightarrow} x_i$ and x_i is in the training set and $S \overset{*}{\Longrightarrow} x$ and x is also in the training set. The procedure cannot discover predicates for patterns shorter than are in the sample set. This seems to define the notion of structurally adequate. That is, a training set is structurally adequate if all of the x and x_i samples are present such that all of the predicates of the grammar can be learned. It should be noted at this point that this definition helps to clarify the discussion but it is not helpful practically because in order to test if a training set is structurally adequate, the grammar must already be known. To illustrate these ideas, the following examples are given.

Example 2 Consider the following string language:

L $=\{x \mid x \in (0,1) * \&$ the number of 1's and 0's are equal$\}$

The first few strings in L are:

L:		
	01	001110
	10	010011
	1001	010101
	0011	010110
	0101	011001
	0110	011010
	1010	011100
	1100	100011
	000111	100101
	001011	100110
	001101	

Now assume that the following *forms* are all that are necessary in the grammar G:

$A \rightarrow tt$

$B \rightarrow tCt$

$D \rightarrow EF$

where A,B,...F can be any arbitrary nonterminals, and t can be any terminal. The actual nonterminals to be placed in each slot will be learned by the procedure. In this case, all the strings of length < 4 will be a structurally adequate sample set and the given forms of the rule are adequate. Apply the forms to the strings to derive all possible derivation trees:

For 01:

For 10:

For 1001:

For 0011:

For 0101:

For 0110:

For 1010:

For 1100:

Now apply the k-tail procedure for k=1 to these trees. The result:

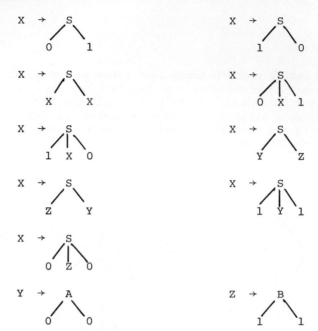

Now these tree rules can be converted back to string rule form and since A and B only generate finite sublanguages, the grammar can be converted to:

$$S \rightarrow 01|10|SS|0S1|1S0$$

Example 3 Consider the same language as in Example 2

Now assume the predicates:

A → tB

C → t

In this case the predicates are not adequate but the strings of length ≤ 4 are structurally adequate. Apply the forms to derive all possible derivation trees.

For 01:   For 10:

For 1001: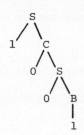

For 0011: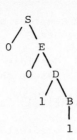

For 0101: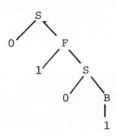

For 0110: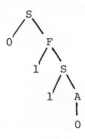

For 1010: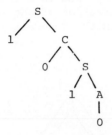

For 1100: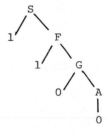

The grammar resulting would be:

S → OB	A → 0	F → 1S
S → 1A	B → 1	G → OA
S → 1C	C → OS	
S → OE	D → 1B	
S → OF	E → OD	

It seems that if there is a string in the sample set such that there exists recursiveness in some of its trees but there is no derivation tree for which all recursiveness is within one predicate, then the predicates are not "adequate". (See for example string 1010 above.) This corresponds to needing a higher value of k to detect all recursiveness. Note that the highest value of k that could possibly be needed if the sample set is structurally adequate would be k=the length of the longest string in the sample

set. Now consider an example where the sample set is not structurally adequate.

Example 4 Consider the same language as in Examples 2 and 3, and
assume the adequate set of predicates used in Example 2.

L={x|x∈{0,1}* and has equal number of 1's and 0's}

The set of predicates (which are adequate) is:

A → tt

B → tCt

D → EF

Consider the sample set: {011001,001011,11010100}

This set is structurally complete for L in the sense that there
exists a grammar for L (in fact the one of Example 3) that uses
each production at least once in the generation of the sample set.
Also that grammar uses each rule twice in the generation of a
string.

Consider all possible derivation trees:

For 011001:

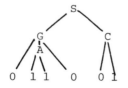

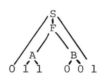

For 001011:

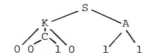

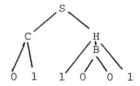

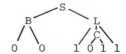

For 11010100:

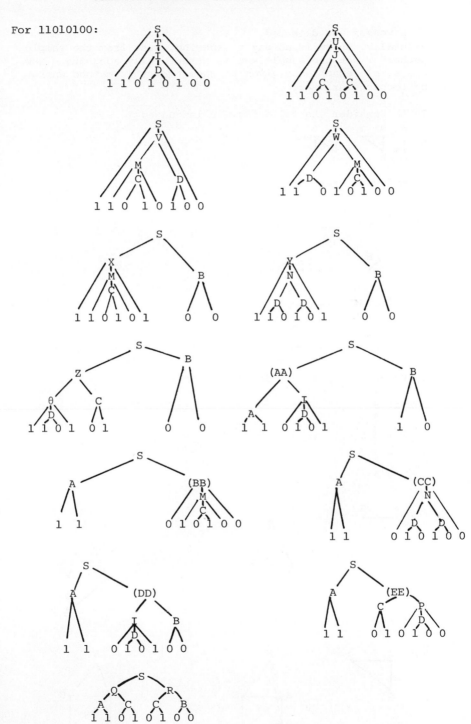

No recursiveness was detected.

Naturally, there is no way of knowing, just from the sample set whether or not the sample set is structurally adequate. Now one more simple example is given to show that this method works for any topology grammar.

Example 5 Consider the following web language:

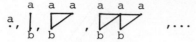

The assumed web forms are:

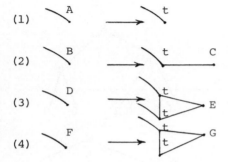

Now construct some possible derivation trees:

For a: S

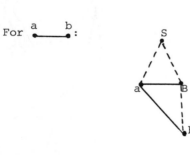

For a ────── b :

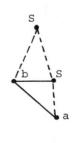

For

For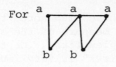

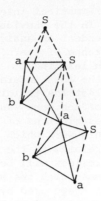

The dotted lines show the trees that are generated. The process can easily distinguish between similar rules with different embedding function by detecting whether or not a particular predicate is satisfied. For the last web above, it could not be derived using a rule of type (3) because if it had there would have to be more edges connected to the second b node as follows:

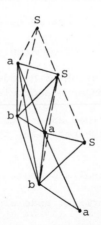

There are two conclusions which can be drawn from this investigation. First the ideas proposed in the examples and informal definitions should be formalized and proofs should be given. Second, if these proofs can be found, then any time there is a-priori information about the *form* of the predicates, the grammar can be inferred by using the k-tail method on its derivation trees.

V. INFERENCE BY SELECTED EXAMPLE

In his work on identification in the limit, Gold [11] noted the importance of correctly ordering the information sequence.

Most other grammatical inference researchers have also noted this importance. In the previous section, a large measure of the success was dependent on analyzing the short samples first. Certainly the importance of learning "first things first" is very important in human learning.

One of the most interesting demonstrations of the need to carefully select the training sequence is the work by Winston [12]. The purpose of the work was to develop a system which could learn structural descriptions of scenes by analyzing specially selected examples. This work which was largely heuristic will now be formalized and related to the grammar inference problem.

The basic idea will be to correlate the derivation diagram of a web grammar with the semantic net used by Winston. Then by following the steps used by Winston on the semantic net and finding equivalent steps for the derivation diagram, the method can be translated into web grammar terminology. The result will be a grammatical inference procedure for web grammars which can be applied more generally than in the specific block world considered by Winston. A brief review of the theory of web grammars will be required to support this discussion.

The following definitions introduce the necessary concepts of web grammars [6].

A *directed graph* is an ordered pair (N,E) where:

    N is a finite set of *nodes*

    E is a finite set of ordered pairs of nodes called *edges*.

A *web* is a directed graph with nodes and edges labelled to identify the respective objects and relationships they represent.

A *web grammar* is defined as a 4-tuple, $G = (V, V^t, S, P)$ where:

    V is the web alphabet (i.e. the set of node and edge labels).

V^t is the terminal alphabet.

$S \in V_N^n$ (the nonterminal node alphabet) is the initial web.

P is a finite set of 3-tuples, $\pi = (\alpha, \beta, \phi)$ called rewriting rules.

The language, L(G) of the grammar G is the set of terminal webs which can be derived from the initial web by repeated application of the rewriting rules. The web grammar defined above is called a type 0 or unrestricted web grammar. Just as in the case of string languages, some more interesting classes of web languages can be defined by placing certain restrictions on the rewriting rules. In particular, a rewriting rule is called *context free* if α, the web being replaced, has only a single node and ϕ the embedding does not depend on the context.

The Derivation Diagram

Study of the context free class of web languages reveals that many of the formal language properties of string languages also hold for the corresponding web languages. One example is the existence for context free web grammars of a structure similar to a derivation tree for context free string grammars. The definition of this structure, called a derivation diagram is now given and an example is given in Figure 2.

A new unique relation called the direct descendant relation is introduced. For a pair of nodes (n_1, n_2) connected by this relation, n_2 is called the direct descendant of n_1. n_1 is called the direct ancestor of n_2. A node n_k is called a descendant of n_1 if there is a sequence $n_1 \ldots n_k$ such that n_{i+1} is a direct descendant of n_i. n_1 is called an ancestor of n_k.

Definition   D, a web, is a derivation diagram for a context free web grammar $G = (V, V^t, I, P)$ if:

(1) There is one node called the root with no ancestors whose label is I, the initial symbol of G.

(2) All other nodes have exactly one direct ancestor and every node is a descendant of the root.

(3) Every node has a label which is a symbol in V_N.

(4) If a node n has at least one descendant and has label Λ, then A must be in V_N^n.

(5) If nodes $n_1, n_2, \ldots n_k$ are the direct descendants of node n with labels $A_1, A_2, \ldots A_k$ respectively, $A \to \beta$ must be a production in P of G where $N_\beta = n_1, n_2, \ldots n_k$ and the A_i are the labels of the n_i in β.

(6) n_i and n_j are connected by relation r if and only if
   a) one is the direct descendant of the other and r is the direct descendant relation or
   b) n_i and n_j are both direct descendants of $\overset{A}{\underset{\bullet}{}}$, $\overset{A}{\underset{\bullet}{}} \to \beta$ is a rule in P and

$$A_i \xrightarrow{\ \ r\ \ } A_j$$
$$n_i \qquad\qquad n_j$$

   is a subweb of β or
   c) n_j and some node n_k are connected by relation r and n_i is the direct descendant of $\overset{A}{\underset{n_k}{\bullet}}$ through the rule $\overset{A}{\underset{\bullet}{}} \to \beta$, a rule in P and the r between n_i and n_j results from the embedding mapping ϕ of A.

There are two kinds of sub-diagrams which are of interest. The first, called the *skeleton* of the derivation diagram, is obtained by keeping all nodes and all direct descendant relations and erasing all other relations. The result shown in Figure 2 c nicely illustrates the basic structure of the *derivation*.

The second sub-diagram of interest is called a *section*. If m_i is a frontier node of the skeleton (i.e. has no descendants), let $n_o, \ldots m_i$ be a path to m_i from the root node, n_o along descen-

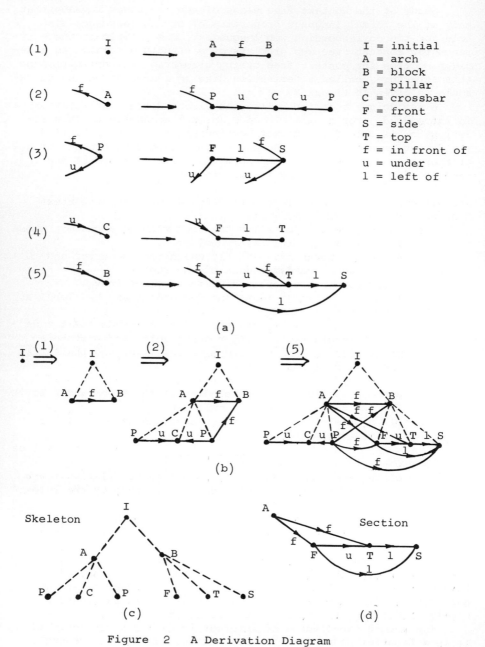

Figure 2   A Derivation Diagram

dent edges. Let $m_1, m_2, \ldots m_k$ be all of the frontier nodes. Then a set C of nodes of the derivation diagram is a crosscut set if C $[n_o, \ldots m_i]$ is a singleton for all $1 \leq i \leq k$. A crosscut set, C, together with all of the edges of the derivation diagram between nodes of C is called a *section*. Naturally only those edges are kept which are connected to two nodes which are both kept. A section, illustrated in Figure 2 d, nicely illustrates the basic structure of *sentential forms*.

The proofs of the following two theorems may be found in [10]

Theorem 1 The skeleton of any derivation diagram for a context free web grammar is a tree.

Theorem 2 Let $G = (V, V^t, S, P)$ be a context free web grammar.

Then for $w \neq \epsilon$, $S \stackrel{*}{\Longrightarrow} w$ if and only if there is a derivation diagram in grammar G with result w. Note that by "result" w is meant that w is a section of a derivation diagram G and all of the nodes of w are frontier nodes of that derivation diagram.

Winston's System

An example of the type of scene Winston's system analyzes is shown in Figure 3. The sequence of examples Winston found necessary to train the system is shown in Figure 4. Notice that Winston's method uses negative samples in the form of near misses as shown in scene 2 and scene 3. The description that is finally learned is shown in Figure 5. It is assumed that all of the concepts illustrated (except ARCH) have already been learned. Thus the learning system works its way up from the bottom in the same way the k-tail method in the last section did. Each example in the training sequence is constructed so that it has only one difference from the already learned description. Scene 2 illustrates that the supports of the arch must not abut. Scene 3 illustrates that A must be supported by B and C. Scene 4 illustrates that a more general object than a BRICK may be used as a top.

The description in Figure 5 can be interpreted as a hierarchical graph model and as a derivation diagram of a web grammar. As such it can be converted to a web grammar. Some of the rules of this grammar are shown in Figure 6. These rules are created from Figure 5 by generating a rule when a relationship such as "a-kind-of" or "one-part-is" is encountered in the diagram. Thus the grammar will have a derivation diagram similar to Figure 5.

In this case, the system is learning one rule. That is, it is trying to find the predicate which describes the right side of rule (1). If this predicate can be learned, it can then be used to analyze higher order patterns containing it. An example illustrating how a higher order recursive rule might be learned is shown in Figure 7.

Many important nonterminals in a web grammar will not occur in recursive rules. These nonterminals will be important because

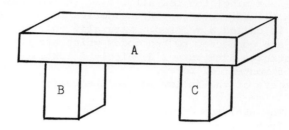

Figure 3   An Example of an Arch

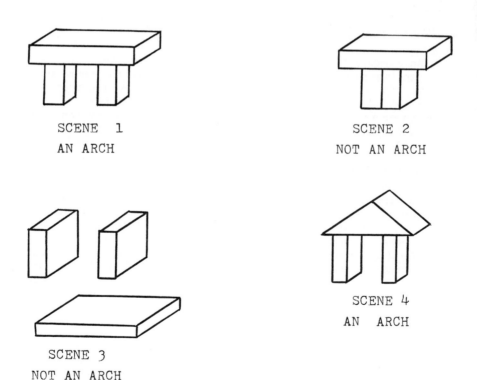

SCENE 1
AN ARCH

SCENE 2
NOT AN ARCH

SCENE 3
NOT AN ARCH

SCENE 4
AN   ARCH

Figure 4   A Training Sequence for an Arch

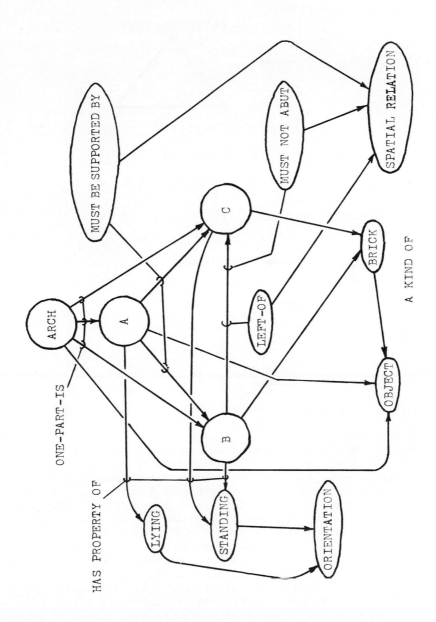

Figure 5   Derivation of an Arch

49

they represent important semantic concepts which give "meaning" to the structural descriptions.

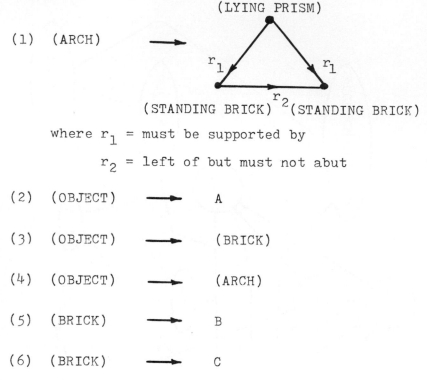

(1)　(ARCH)

where r_1 = must be supported by

r_2 = left of but must not abut

(2)　(OBJECT) ⟶ A

(3)　(OBJECT) ⟶ (BRICK)

(4)　(OBJECT) ⟶ (ARCH)

(5)　(BRICK) ⟶ B

(6)　(BRICK) ⟶ C

Figure　6　Some Web Grammar Rules Describing an Arch

　　To learn an individual rule in a web grammar, the system must be able to learn the most general description possible for each object on the right hand side. Assuming the form of the rule is known (This is generally learned from the first example), then learning the exact rule becomes a matter of finding how much each object may be generalized. In this case, the original description of ARCH might contain the objects, A, B and C, that is, an exact description of this particular scene. This description would be of little general use because no slightly different arch could be identified. Even the appropriate parse of this scene is not known because grammars describing it might be ambiguous.

　　In a general formalism an object like A is described by properties like orientation and shape. These properties allow successive generalization to occur according to what values of a particular property are important. The structure which describes and systematizes the generalization process is called the property lattice.

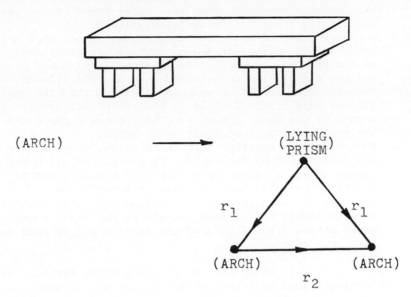

Figure 7 Example of a Scene Generating a Recursive Web Grammar Rule

A set of elements $\mathcal{C} = \{c_1, c_2, \ldots\}$ is said to be *partially ordered* (hierarchical) if there exists a relation ($\leq$) defined on the elements of $\mathcal{C}$ which is:

(1) Reflexive: $c \leq c$
(2) Antisymmetric: $c_1 \leq c_2$ and $c_2 \leq c_1$ implies $c_1 = c_2$
(3) Transitive: $c_1 \leq c_2$ and $c_2 \leq c_3$ implies $c_1 \leq c_3$

If $\mathcal{C}$ is a partially ordered set and X is any subset of $\mathcal{C}$, then $a \in \mathcal{C}$ is a *lower bound* of X if $a \leq x$ for all $x \in X$ and a is an upper bound of X if $x \leq a$ for all $x \in X$. A lower bound b of X is called the *greatest lower bound* (g.l.b) of X if for every a that is a lower bound of X, $a \leq b$. Similarly, an upper bound d of X is called the *least upper bound* if for every e that is an upper bound of X, $d \leq e$. A partially ordered set of $\mathcal{C}$ in which any two elements have a least upper bound and a greatest lower bound is called a *lattice*.

In the case of concept learning here, the elements of $\mathcal{C}$ are called *concepts* and consist of subsets of examples containing certain property values. The partial order relation considered is set inclusion. The purpose of the learning procedure will be to find that concept which contains all of the examples showing allowed property values and none of the examples having disallowed property values. The procedure to be used in learning a concept will be as follows:

(1) Whenever a set of positive examples are given, then all lower bounds of the set in the lattice are *allowed* as

the possible concept. The least upper bound of the set
and all its lower bounds are also allowed.

(2) Whenever a set of negative examples are given, then all
upper bounds of the set in the lattice are disallowed
as the possible concept. The greatest lower bound of
the set and all its upper bounds are also disallowed.

(3) Whenever a new positive example is given, then the new
allowed part of the lattice is the set of all lower
bounds of the least upper bound of the new example and
the previously learned least upper bound.

(4) Whenever a new negative example is given, then the new
disallowed part of the lattice is the set of all upper
bounds of the greatest lower bound of the new example
and the previously learned greatest lower bound.

(5) When all of the points in the lattice are either allowed
or disallowed, the correct concept is the least upper
bound of the allowed part of the lattice and is said to
have been *learned*.

The purpose of this study will be to see how the lattice can
help in selecting a good training set and to see how grammars can
help in setting up the lattice.

In many practical cases, properties are neither all independent nor all dependent. In these cases, the property lattice is
more non-uniform. Fortunately, the property lattice can be constructed from the grammar if the grammar is in the right form as
is shown in Figure 8. Note in this case that a (STANDING TRIAN-
GULAR PRISM) is not allowed by the grammar so the higher order
concepts (STANDING) and (TRIANGULAR PRISM) are also not present.
Now the number and selection of examples necessary to learn a concept in this lattice can be investigated. To generalize to the
concept, (PRISM), 2 + examples, (STANDING BRICK) and (LYING TRIA
PRISM) must be given. To generalize only to (BRICK) or (LYING),
all three examples (2+ and 1-) must be given. To generalize to
(STANDING BRICK) only, two examples must be given.

Thus, by using the grammatical formalism for lower order concepts, such as (PRISM), a more efficient lattice structure can be
set up. If this lattice is big enough, there is less necessity
for a "near miss" to be so near because examples which are more
different will still have a least upper bound and greatest lower
bound in the lattice. This lattice structure can help in the selection of proper training examples for higher order concepts such
as (ARCH).

In terms of formal grammatical inference as studied in the
previous sections, Winston's procedure as just formalized can be
viewed as a method which is an extension of Evan's method without
the heuristics. The method can be stated as follows:

(1) Assume a given set of properties and predicate forms
are known to be appropriate from a priori information
about the application.

Given the Grammar:

(PRISM) ⟶ (BRICK)

(PRISM) ⟶ (LYING)

(BRICK) ⟶ (LYING BRICK)

(BRICK) ⟶ (STANDING BRICK)

(LYING) ⟶ (LYING BRICK)

(LYING) ⟶ (LYING TRIA PRISM)

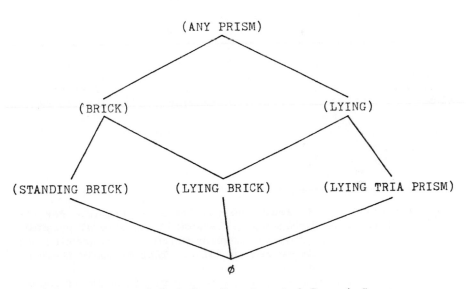

Figure 8   A Lattice Constructed From A Grammar

(2) Given a scene, get all possible parses of it with these
forms and arrange the parse nonterminals in a property
lattice.

(3) Then, by giving a sequence of appropriate positive and
negative examples, and using least upper and greatest
lower bound operations in the lattice, converge to the
correct parse common to all + examples and including no
- examples.

(4) Construct the grammar rule reflecting this parse. An example of applying this procedure to a Winston-like problem is now given.

Example 6

(1) Assume we are given a problem in which the only objects
are rectangular prisms and the only properties detectable are size, shape and color. Furthermore assume that
green cubes do not exist. A lattice illustrating these
properties is shown in Figure 9. The objects, properties
and relations are summarized below in Table 1.

Table 1.
Objects, Properties and Relations for Example 6.

Objects	Properties	Values	Relations
Rectangular Prisms	Size	Larger	Supported by
		Smaller	Larger-smaller
	Shape	Cube	Same color
		Rectangular Prism	
	Color	Red	
		Green	

(2) We now wish to learn the concept of a pyramid. For illustrative purposes it is assumed that a legal pyramid
can have cubes or rectangular prisms but supporting objects can only be red in color. That is, only the top
object can be green.

To begin, an example of a pyramid (shown in Figure
10) is presented and the example pattern is parsed. It
is possible to parse because all of the objects in the
pyramid have already been learned. The only information
supplied by the teacher in this case is that this is indeed a pyramid.

The parse or derivation diagram or semantic net resulting is shown in Figure 11.

(3) Now by presenting an appropriate sequence of (+) and (-)
examples, the teacher must illustrate the most general

54

Object Lattice

P = (P1,P2)

P1 = Color, 0 = RED, 1 = GREEN

P2 = Shape, 0 = Cube, 1 = Rectangule

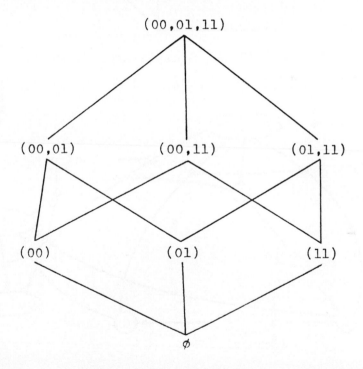

Figure 9   Lattice for Properties of Example 5.8

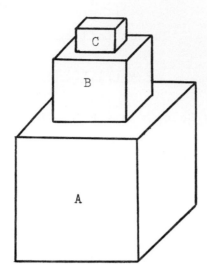

Figure 10   An Example of a Pyramid

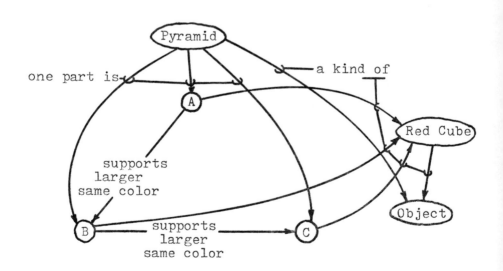

Figure 11   Parse of Figure 10

object or relation which is allowed in each position.
This example will concentrate just on the objects and
for the moment ignore the fact that the relations must
be learned also.

The supporting objects in the pyramid can be any
shape but must be red. This is illustrated by the (00,01)
entry in the lattice. This can be illustrated by three
examples: 00 and 01 as (+) examples and 11 as a (-) example. The top object can be green. Since a cube cannot
be green, this is illustrated by the (00, 01, 11) entry
in the lattice. This state in the lattice can be learned
by presenting 00, 01 and 11 as (+) examples. Thus for
each individual object, three examples must be given.
But since these can occur in various combinations with
the other objects, a total of 27 combinations must be
presented to completely learn the definition of the pyramid. The examples are shown in Figure 12. Note that
if the objects can be considered independent only seven
examples need to be given. These examples are shown
with asterisks in Figure 12.

The derivation diagram which is finally learned is shown in
Figure 13. The grammar rule learned is extracted from this diagram by putting the ancestor of the "one-part-is" relation on the
left hand side and the descendants on the right hand side. This
rule is shown in Figure 14. The embedding of this rule is somewhat arbitrary.

Several conclusions can be drawn from this example. First,
if there are several properties involved and these properties take
on several values and it is necessary to learn a pattern containing
several objects, then many examples must be used in training unless
some heuristic assumption is made. Second, if one part of the pattern can be assumed independent of other parts, the number of examples needed to learn it can be greatly reduced. Third, this
method as shown does not specify the embedding.

VI. CONCLUSIONS

The results of the methods studied here may now be summarized
with the following recommendations:

(1) If the predicate forms are known, they may be used to
     develop derivation trees. Then the k-tail method can
     be employed to infer the tree grammar. This tree gram-
     mar can then be converted back to the original topology.

(2) If the predicate forms are not known, try to use a
     "semantic teacher" in the sense of Winston to learn the
     meaningful nonterminals one level at a time.

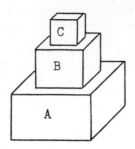

Example
```
         Code for C       00
         Code for B  =  00
         Code for A       00
```

Examples which must be presented:

(+) examples:

```
00*  00*  00*  00   01*  01   01   01
00   00   01   01   00   00   01   01
00   01   00   01   00   01   00   01

11*  11   11   11
00   00   01   01
00   01   00   01
```

(-) examples:

```
00*  00   00*  00   00    01   01   01   01   01
00   01   11   11   11    00   01   11   11   11
11   11   00   01   11    11   11   00   01   11

11   11   11   11   11
00   01   11   11   11
11   11   00   01   11
```

Figure 12   Training Examples

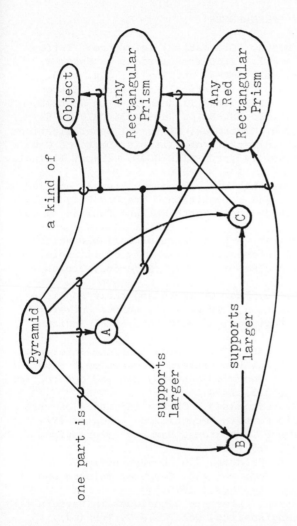

Figure 13   Final Derivation Diagram

Figure 14   The Resulting Grammar Rule

Finally, note that the methods studied here are by no means exhaustive. Many inference methods (e.g. stochastic methods) have not been discussed (see 1,2). The above methods are representative of the few of these string grammar methods which have been applied to multidimensional grammars.

REFERENCES

1. Fu, K. S. and T. L. Booth, "Grammatical Inference: Introduction and Survey-Part I," *IEEE Transactions on Systems, Man, and Cybernetics,* Vol. SMC-5, pp. 95-111, Jan. 1975.
2. Fu, K.S. and T. L. Booth, "Grammatical Inference: Introduction and Survey-Part II," *IEEE Transactions on Systems, Man, and Cybernetics,* Vol. SMC-5, pp. 409-423, July 1975.
3. Michalski, R.S. and B.H. McCormick, "Interval Generalization of Switching Theory," University of Illinois, Dept. of Computer Science Report No. 443, c00-2118-0008, Urbana, Illinois, May 1971.
4. Michalski, R.S., "A Variable-valued logic system as applied to picture description and recognition," *Graphic Languages,* F. Nake and A. Rosenfeld (eds), North-Holland Publishing Company, London, 1972.
5. Baskin, A.B., "A Comparative Discussion of Variable Valued Logic and Grammatical Inference," University of Illinois, Dept of Computer Science Report UIUCDCS-R-74-663, Urbana, Illinois, July 1974.
6. Brayer, J.M. and K.S. Fu, "Web Grammars and their Application to Pattern Recognition," TR-EE 75-1, Purdue University, School of Electrical Engineering, West Lafayette, Indiana, 1975.
7. Bhargava, B. K. and K.S. Fu, "Transformations and Inference of Tree Grammars for Syntactic Pattern Recognition," *Proc. of 1974 International Conference on Systems, Man and Cybernetics,* Dallas, Texas, pp. 330-333, 1974.
8. Gonzalez, R.C. and M.G. Thomason, "On the Inference of Tree Grammars for Syntactic Pattern Recognition," *Proc of 1974 International Conference on Systems, Man and Cybernetics,* Dallas, Texas, pp. 311-315, 1974.
9. Biermann, A.W. and J.A. Feldman, "On the Synthesis of Finite-State Acceptors," A.I. Memo No. 114, Computer Science Department, Stanford, University, April 1970.
10. Evans, T.G., "Grammatical Inference Techniques in Pattern Analysis," *Software Engineering,* Vol. 2, J.T. Tou (ed), Academic Press, 1971.
11. Gold, E.M., "Language Identification in the Limit," *Information and Control,* Vol. 10, pp. 447-474, 1967.
12. Winston, P.H., "Learning Structural Descriptions from Examples," Ph.D. Thesis, TR-76, Dept of Electrical Engineering, M.I.T., September, 1970.

FINDING STRUCTURE IN OUTDOOR SCENES*

Bruce L. Bullock
Hughes Research Laboratory
Malibu, CA.

I. INTRODUCTION

The problem of generalizing current scene analysis capability
to deal with complex outdoor scenes has been under consideration
by a number of researchers for several years [1-5]. A program of
this type has been underway at the Hughes Research Laboratory for
the past four years. The specific goal of this program has been
to develop the technology to derive useful information from real
scenes in a realistic system context. Within this framework,
"useful information" means that the system should be able to answer the following questions: is there an object of interest in
the scene, and if so, what is its position and orientation; and
what is a description of the object itself? The term "real scene"
implies that the scenes are complex outdoor scenes with natural
backgrounds and man-made objects. Finally, a "realistic system
context" implies that the analysis strategy should be governed
both by the user's current goal and by the scene at hand, and that
the imagery should not be limited to a particular type of sensor.
Progress towards these general goals resulted in an evolutionary
sequence of complex system organizations and analysis strategies
[6-7].

Presently, an attempt is being made to apply the analysis
strategy developed in this general context to several specific ap-
plication-related problems. The resulting system is best described
as a "stripped down" scene analysis system in which many of the
general capabilities have been omitted to achieve a simple, working system. It is the purpose of this paper to describe the tradeoffs and ideas that resulted from this application exercise.

II. APPLICATION CONTEXT

The application under study is the problem of finding a specific structure or object in an outdoor scene, and if it is found,
to specify its position and orientation. Although this is a highly restricted problem, it is very important because of its frequent occurrence. A successful scheme that deals with this problem

---

*   This research was partially supported by DARPA and monitored
    by RADC Contract F30602-76-0074 and by the Air Force Office
    of Scientific Research (AFSC), United States Air Force, under
    Contract F44620-74-C-0054.

could be used to implement solutions to the more general problem categories of cueing, navigation, and change detection. Cueing is simply notifying a user that an object of interest is in the scene and of its location; navigation is the use of a reference image to derive position error signals; and change detection is the comparison of a previous reference image with the current image to determine what parts of the image are new or absent. These three solution categories, limited as they are, cover many important applications dealing with military, medical, industrial inspection, automation, and resource monitoring imagery. The major difference between these application domains is not the particular solution, but the complexity of the specific objects of interest.

III. SYSTEM PHILOSOPHY

Initially, the solution for this restricted structure finding problem was viewed as a direct mapping of the general approach then under development, complete with general control structures, representations, and organization. After some early attempts along this line it was decided to adopt a quite different philosophy. The new philosophy consisted of looking for simplifications that could be made to the general approach that would make a solution practical with existing technology. Thus the system should be constructed using very simple control, simple models and simple matching. Further, because only one object is looked for at a time and a nearly perfect model for it exists a-priori, it can be assumed that the system is completely goal-guided. The approach in this study is to identify the simplifications that could be made in a tradeoff of available technology, and to see how far a system based on these guidelines could be pushed in the outdoor environment.

IV. TRADEOFFS

The first tradeoff is in the overall system organization. Rather than the very general structures with complex control that have evolved in previous scene analysis programs, a very straightforward, minimal system as shown in FIG. 1, is used.

Note that the sensor and reference paths are identical up to the matching step. Then because we are assuming that the goal does not change during the operation of the system, the goal model is then constructed by the same analysis processes as the sensor image, and simply stored as a fixed model data structure.

From this organization it is obvious that the available tradeoffs are in the feature extraction process, the construction of the scene model, and in the model matching process. The next few sections will describe the tradeoffs and resulting simplifications for each of these three components.

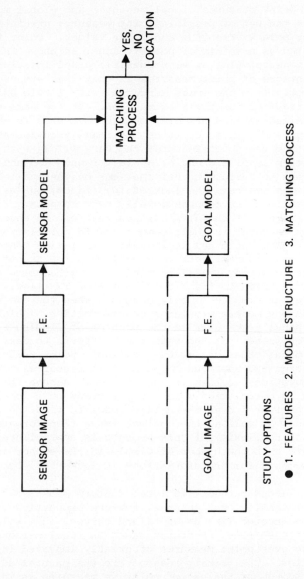

STUDY OPTIONS

● 1. FEATURES 2. MODEL STRUCTURE 3. MATCHING PROCESS

FIG. 1: SYSTEM ORGANIZATION

V.   FEATURE EXTRACTION ALTERNATIVES

A careful examination of image features shows that they are derivable from image measures that fall into three general categories: point measures, local measures and global measures. Included in the set of possible point measures are intensity values at one or more wavelengths and range values. Point features are represented as a matrix of point values, as shown in FIG. 2, with a point measure value at each possible pixel location. One of the big advantages of point measures is that they are usually available directly from the image sensor(s) with little additional processing required for their extraction. At the same time, one of the big disadvantages of point feature measures is that they have poor invariance characteristics for image transformations. This implies that the point features can vary wildly with changes in illumination level and angle, scale, translation and rotation. It is possible to perform transformations on the available point feature data to overcome the lack of invariance, but as a rule these transformations are computationally very complex.

An example of the difficulties that can be encountered in using point features is their common use in correlation image processing. Experience has shown that correlation based processors, using point features, work very well when the transformations from reference to sensor image are minimal. Such a case exists, for example, in frame-to-frame correlation of TV imagery. On the other hand, the performance is only marginal when the two images are different by any moderately large transformation. Unfortunately, this is usually the case in the problem of finding a structure in an outdoor scene. At the same time, efforts to deal with the necessary transformations of the available point features, have typically required enormous computational resources. The source of the computational burden is easy to see. Assume that the form of matching is correlation which is performed on a local window. It must be evaluated over the entire image to find the optimal correlation peak as well as the optimal image transformation. The computational complexity of this process is approximately $3[n**2]\log(n)$, where n is the number of pixels in the sensor image [9] and the 3 accounts for transformations in intensity, range, and rotation.

The second category is local feature measures. These include average intensity over an area, texture properties over an area, locally connected line segments and curves, and isolated line and curve intersections. Features based on local measures have the advantage over point measures of greatly improved invariance characteristics. The primary reasons are the natural advantage of local averaging, or the use of relative measures as in the detection of edges. The improved invariance is not without cost, however, as a moderate amount of processing is required to extract the local feature measures from the more primitive point feature values.

The third category of feature measures is global measures.

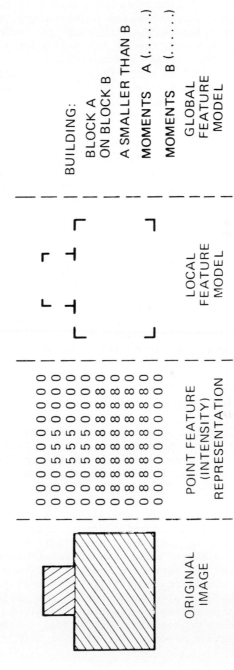

ORIGINAL IMAGE

POINT FEATURE
(INTENSITY)
REPRESENTATION

LOCAL
FEATURE
MODEL

BUILDING:

BLOCK A
ON BLOCK B

A SMALLER THAN B

MOMENTS   A (.......)

MOMENTS   B (.......)

GLOBAL
FEATURE
MODEL

FIG. 2:   IMAGE FEATURE EXAMPLES

Global features are usually shape descriptions based on completely connected segmented boundaries. These include the description of object shapes, as shown in FIG. 2, and the relations between the objects. The extraction of global features requires even more processing than local features, but because of the added constraint of demanding completely connected segmentation, global feature extraction is nearly impossible with existing techniques on complex outdoor scenes. Two examples of the difficulties are shown in FIGS. 3 and 4. FIG. 3 shows a simple blocks world scene of the type that has consumed so much effort in past scene analysis research. There are two missing edges in the processed scene due to low contrast across the front surfaces. It is true that these errors could be corrected by goal direction from a model, but it illustrates that even simple scenes present unexpected difficulties when the demand is made for completely connected segmentation. The second example, in FIG. 4, shows a camouflaged aircraft on a high contrast desert background. Again, the resulting line fit from the edge point data is in great error and would cause the next phase of processing to fail unless the interpretation is cleaned up by model-directed reinterpretation.

The results of this feature tradeoff are shown in TABLE 1. A number of conclusions are obvious from this table. First, there is a little utility in pushing the use of point features for finding objects in ourdoor scenes. Second, the impossibility of extracting good global features in complex outdoor scenes also makes their use of little utility at this stage of development. Thus, the best available alternative is the use of local features. Also, because one of the primary differences between local and global features is the demand for completely connected segmentation, then the more this condition can be relaxed, the better the chances for success.

VI. MODEL FORMATION ALTERNATIVES

Once the features have been derived from the image, they are used to form an abstract representation, or model, of the scene. Currently there are very few models of the complex information found in outdoor scenes [6,10]. For that reason, a number of hypotheses are put forward here about features in outdoor scenes. The first assumption is called the sensory richness hypothesis. This assumes that if enough information is provided from a rich enough variety of features and sensors, then a particular image can be represented uniquely by a small collection of simple features. This is a direct extension of Tenenbaum's use of "distinguishing features" to represent complex office scenes in terms of a small set of simple features [1]. Note that this assumption may not hold for the general representation and analysis of outdoor scenes. But, because the application is only to find a specific object, it appears reasonable. The second assumption is called the isolated feature hypothesis. This is simply a statement of

ORIGINAL GRAY SCALE

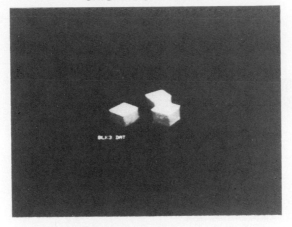

AFTER EDGE DETECTION

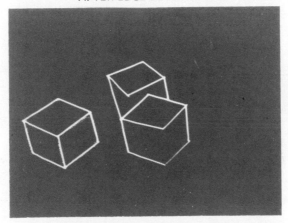

NOTE MISSING EDGES AT
BOUNDARIES OF LOW CONTRAST

3: BLOCKS WORLD GLOBAL FEATURE EXTRACTION

a) ORIGINAL

b) EDGE POINTS

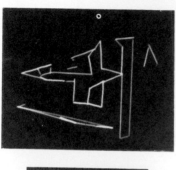

c) RESULT OF LINE FITTING

FIG. 4: AIRCRAFT GLOBAL FEATURE EXTRACTION

CHARACTERISTIC CATEGORY	INVARIANCE RANK	EXTRACTION DIFFICULTY	ASSOCIATED COMPLEXITY OF OPERATION	NO. ELEMENTS IN MATCH (100 x 100 IMAGE)	ACTUAL EVALUATION COMPLEXITY	TRANSFORMS TO CORRECT FOR INVARIANCE ERROR
POINT FEATURES	POOR	TRIVIAL	$3i^2 \log i$	$i = 10^4$	$\sim 10^9$	DIFFICULT
LOCAL FEATURES	GOOD	MODERATE	$2(n \log n)$	$n \sim 10^3$	$\sim 10^4$	NOT NECESSARY
GLOBAL FEATURES	EXCELLENT	EXCEEDINGLY DIFFICULT	$n^2 + n^3$	$n \sim 10^2$	$\sim 10^8$	NOT NECESSARY

TABLE 1: FEATURE COMPARISON

the demand that it is not necessary to get completely connected segmentation of objects and that the features need not be strongly connected. The importance of this assumption was stated in the description of local vs. global features. The final assumption is that a complex outdoor scene is a mixed feature environment. This is based on the simple observation that every outdoor scene contains both resolvable structure and unresolvable structure. The resolvable structure is represented by local features based on resolvable edges, such as line and curve segments and their possible intersections (all of which are assumed by the previous hypothesis to be isolated). At the same time, the unresolvable structure is represented by local texture features (again isolated).

An outdoor scene is then representable, using the above assumptions, as a collection of local edge and texture features and a description of their relative positions in the scene. A collection of feature descriptions and location descriptions of this type is called a rich isolated feature model. An example of such a model for a simple scene is shown in FIG. 5. The actual model is stored as a data structure containing the feature descriptors and a description of their relationship.

The usual approach for storing this information as a data structure involves using a general graph structure. In such a representation the nodes are associated with the feature descriptors and the links with the relations between the features. For the rich isolated feature model, the nodes can be of several types. The nodes for an isolated edge or curve segment point to a description of the orientation (slope), length (number of edge points), and center position. The nodes corresponding to intersections or vertices of edges point to a description of the number of intersecting edges, their angles, the position of the intersection, and the relative contrasts between the areas enclosed by the edges. The nodes corresponding to texture features point to a description of the center of the prominence and the value of the texture measure. The links in the rich isolated feature model correspond to spatial relations such as: in front of, above, below, and beside.

The representation structure used in this application is slightly simpler. Instead of a graph structure, a minimal spanning tree is used [11]. This simplification allows the matching process to be slightly easier, and the relations are represented exactly by the Euclidean distance between the feature nodes instead of deriving spatial relations. The use of the minimal spanning tree seems appealing as it only preserves the minimal amount of information necessary to represent the feature relations, and avoids the choice of possibly redundant relation links. Also note that any of the more general spatial relations can be derived trivially from the minimal spanning tree representation. Again, no claim is made as to the optimality of such a representation for a more general scene analysis process.

The complexity of the graph versus the minimal spanning tree representations can be estimated approximately. It is assumed that the process of deriving graph node relations is done in $k**2$

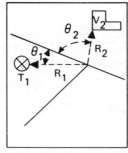

(T_1, θ_1, R_1)

(V_2, θ_2, R_2)

$(V_1, \ldots)$

$(T_1, \ldots)$

c) STORED MODEL

a) LINE DRAWING   DERIVED FEATURES

FIG. 5: RICH ISOLATED FEATURE MODEL EXAMPLE

operations, where k is the number of feature nodes (smaller than
n, the number of pixels, by perhaps two orders of magnitude), and
that the graph matching process is done in k**3 operations. On
the other hand, the minimal spanning tree is generated in klog(k)
operations [12], and the matching is performed in klog(k) operations. In reality, however, the strongest appeal of the minimal
spanning tree representation is intuitive, as the difference   in
performance for these two alternatives is not computationally significant as long as the number of nodes stays small (approximately
1000).

VII.   FEATURE EXTRACTION PROCESS

Now that it has been determined that the features are to be
based on edges and texture and the form of the model representation has been decided, the next step is to determine the technique
to extract the edge and texture features. After considering several alternatives, the system shown in FIG. 6 was chosen. The justi-
fications for this choice are described below. The components of
the process are shown in FIG. 6.

Edge points are first extracted from the scene by an edge detector. The output from the edge detector is the location of
points in the scene that lie along edges, the magnitude of the edge
strength, and the edge direction. A qualitative study of the performance of edge detectors has been performed previously [13]. A
sample of the results from this report is shown in FIG. 7. The
conclusions from this qualitative comparison are shown in TABLE 2.

Based on these results the decision was made to use the
Hueckel operator [14]. Although the complexity of this operator
is the highest of those evaluated, the performance benefits on low
contrast edges make the cost worthwhile. Additionally, real time
processors for Hueckel-like operators are now being investigated
with good promise.

Once the edge points are found, the next problem is to find
the line structure. There are many approaches to the structure
finding problem, including line and curve fitting [15], dynamic
programming [16], heuristic search [17], and transform techniques
[15]. When the goal is to mechanize complete global segmentation
in terms of connected boundaries, then the fitting and searching
techniques produce good results. Unfortunately, as mentioned
earlier, the complexity and noise in outdoor scenes usually prevents the practical application of global segmentation. At the
same time these operations are computationally very complex, usually requiring at least m**2 operations, where m is the number of
detected edge points. An attractive alternative is the use of
transform techniques. Although it might be possible to use the
Fourier transform for such a purpose, a much more effective transform is called the Hough transform [18]. The Hough transform has
been used successfully to find isolated line and curve segments

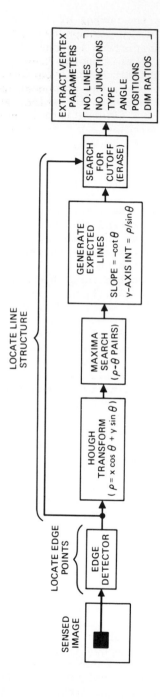

FIG. 6: EDGE FEATURE EXTRACTION PROCESS

72

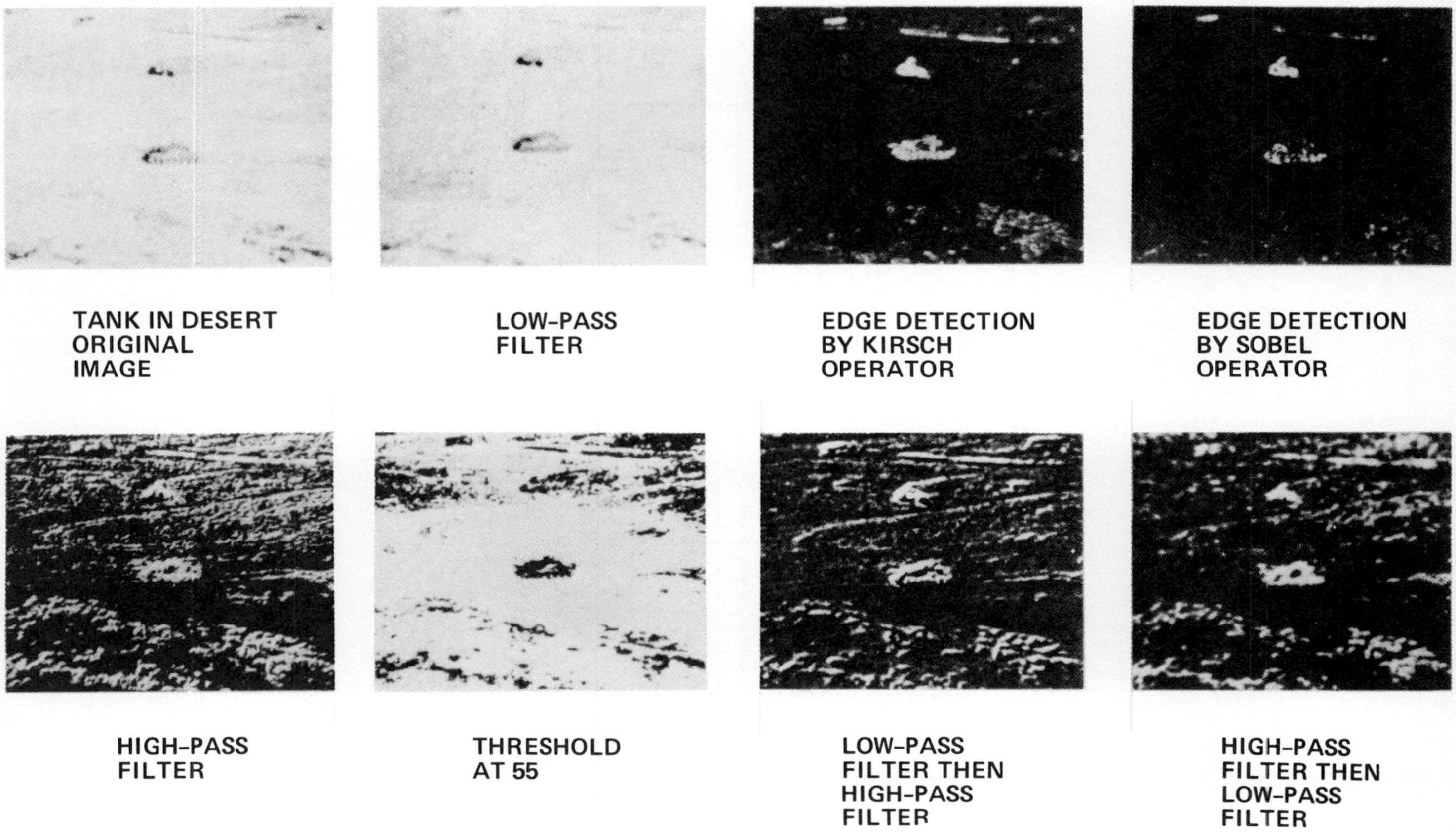

TANK IN DESERT
ORIGINAL
IMAGE

LOW-PASS
FILTER

EDGE DETECTION
BY KIRSCH
OPERATOR

EDGE DETECTION
BY SOBEL
OPERATOR

HIGH-PASS
FILTER

THRESHOLD
AT 55

LOW-PASS
FILTER THEN
HIGH-PASS
FILTER

HIGH-PASS
FILTER THEN
LOW-PASS
FILTER

NOTE: ALL FROM TECH REPORT B. BULLOCK, OCTOBER '74

FIG. 7: EDGE DETECTOR RESULTS

73

EDGE OPERATOR	PERFORMANCE RANK	COMPUTATIONAL COMPLEXITY
ROBERTS CROSS	4	N (3a)
HIGH PASS FILTER	4	N (9a)
LAPLACIAN	4	N (9a)
SOBEL	3	N (14a)
KIRSCH	2	N (72a)
HUECKEL	1	54 (a+m) = 270a

N = NUMBER OF IMAGE ELEMENTS
a = MACHINE ADD CYCLE TIME
m = MACHINE MULTIPLY CYCLE TIME
   (ASSUME m ~ 4a)

TABLE 2:   EDGE DETECTOR COMPARISON

[18,19] and has a complexity of order m.

The basic notion of the Hough transform is to map edge points in the image space into curves in the transform space on the basis of the normal parameterization of the line (curve). A simple example is shown in FIG. 8. Concurrent edge points generate curves in the transform space that intersect at a common point which corresponds to the slope and y-intercept of the corresponding line. The transform space information is deposited as a two-dimensional accumulator array, then the important slopes and intercepts are found by searching for maxima. The actual line segments are then efficiently found by searching in a goal-guided way along the predicted trajectory. Finally, possible line intersections are found from the line segment position data by solving sets of simultaneous equations. Thus, the information provided by this process about edge features in the scene is the position, length and orientation of isolated line segments. For intersecting lines it provides the position, number of intersecting lines, and their angles. This information is stored in the model as nodes with the correct image space coordinates and with labels on the nodes as to the details of the features.

The texture features are found in a quite different manner. First, remember that based on both the principles of sensory richness and isolated features mentioned earlier, the goal is to only look for the most prominent texture features in the scene. This is mechanized by the process shown in FIG. 9.

The first step in the process is to produce a texture-transformed version of the scene [20]. The purpose of this transform is to map areas of equal texture micro-structure into equal numerical value. To find the most prominent areas this transform is performed over sample windows, such that each window is assigned a single transform value. Then local maxima of the window values are found and tagged as the prominent areas [21]. The information supplied to the model is then the location of the texture prominences and their texture transform value.

The use of the local maxima suppresses the tagging of texture edge and only passes highlight areas. Thus a natural transition between edges and texture is provided in the model, such that edge features are only found in areas where there is resolvable structure and texture features are only found in areas with unresolvable edge structure.

VIII. MATCHING PROCESS

The final process is the matching process. This process is somewhat locked-in by the decision to use the minimal spanning tree as the modeling structure. The final choice is a slightly modified algorithm for matching noisy minimal spanning trees [22], shown in FIG. 10.

The operation is described briefly as follows. The nodes of the minimal spanning trees in the sensor and reference model are

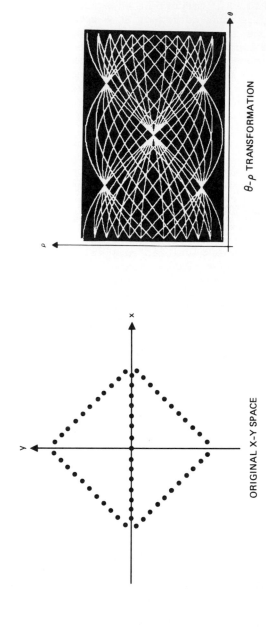

θ-ρ TRANSFORMATION

ORIGINAL X-Y SPACE

FIG. 8: HOUGH TRANSFORM EXAMPLE

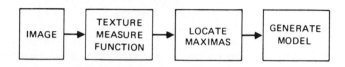

FIG. 9:   TEXTURE PROMINENCE DETECTION PROCESS

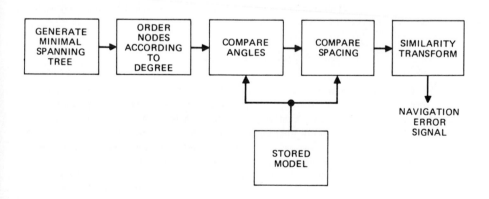

FIG. 10:   NOISY MINIMAL SPANNING TREE MATCHING

first ordered by degree (number of lines meeting at the node). A local match is first performed on nodes between the two models of similar highest degree. Once this is found, a Waltz filtering operation is performed to check the consistency of the node labelings. Then a global match is made to check the angles at the matching nodes. If a similar angle is located, the links generating the angle are traced and a new local match is then performed at the two new nodes. Once a match of this type is established, the ratio of the lengths of the matching links in the two models is used to determine the scale difference. Finally, the appropriate coordinate transformation is derived by doing a least squares fit of the matching points to determine the coefficients of the transformation.

The nice quality of this matching process is its tolerance to noise. Even though the presence or absence of new nodes can cause the minimal spanning trees to look different between the sensor and reference models, the use of local matching assures that as long as some part has remained noise-free, the match can be determined.

IX.   FINAL SYSTEM CONFIGURATION

The previous sections of this paper have provided the details of a study to simplify and tradeoff the components of a "stripped down" scene analysis system to be applied to the problem of finding a given structure in an outdoor scene. When possible an attempt has been made to choose the optimal subprocesses in terms of performance and computational complexity. The final path through the maze of choices is shown in FIG. 11.

X.   EXPERIMENTAL RESULTS

At the time this paper was written, results from the edge-line-vertex process have been obtained, and results have been obtained from the texture prominence processor. As yet, however, no mixed models have been derived using both edge and texture features. The result of the edge-line-vertex processing on a noisy road scene is shown in FIG. 12. The frames (from left to right) show the original image, the output of the Hueckel operator, and the locations of the maxima in the Hough transform space. The second row shows the predicted line trajectories, the detected vertices (overlaid on the line image for verification), and finally the extracted model information. The second result, shown in FIG. 13, shows the ability of the edge-line-vertex processor to find the lines corresponding to road boundaries in a particularly cluttered scene. The third edge-line-vertex result, shown in FIG. 14, shows a very complex and noisy building scene. This example shows several correctly discovered vertices and several that would probably not have been tagged as important, by a human viewer. It should be noted that for the problem of finding a specific object

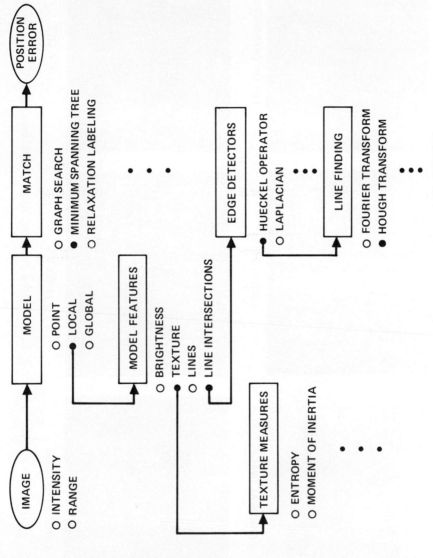

FIG. 11: FINAL SYSTEM TRADEOFF CHOICES

79

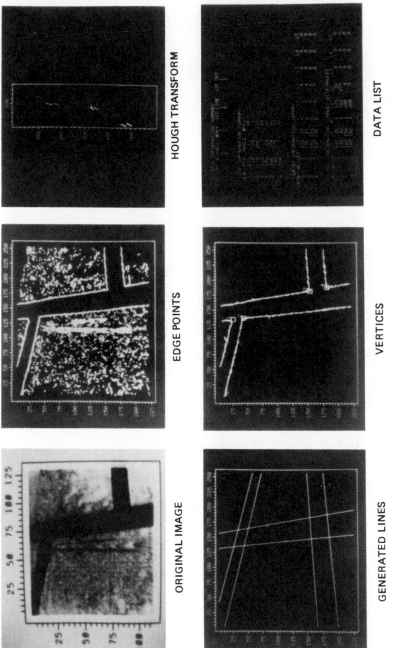

HOUGH TRANSFORM

DATA LIST

EDGE POINTS

VERTICES

ORIGINAL IMAGE

GENERATED LINES

FIG. 12: EDGE–LINE–VERTEX FEATURE EXTRACTION PROCESS

80

ORIGINAL IMAGE

EDGE POINTS

HOUGH SPACE (THRESHOLD)

GENERATED LINES

FIG. 13: ROAD LINE FINDING

81

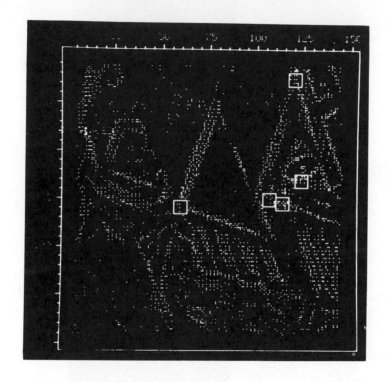

FIG. 14: COMPLEX SCENE VERTICES

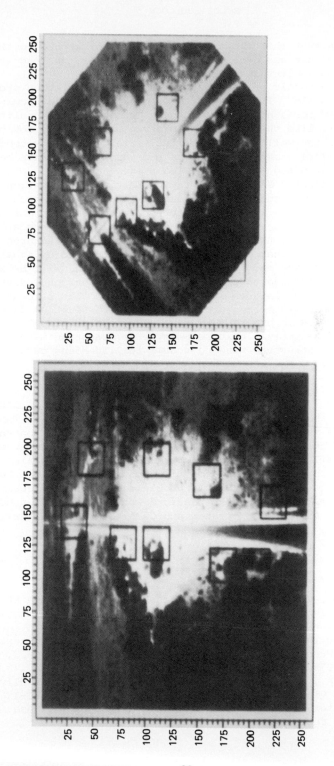

FIG. 15: TEXTURE PROMINENCE PROCESSOR RESULTS

it is not important that the tagged locations correspond to the same locations that would be tagged by an observer, as long as the tagging process remains invariant.

Finally, a result of the texture prominence detection process is shown in FIG. 15. The first frame shows the texture prominences that were found for a noisy road scene. The invariance qualities of an operator, like the texture prominence process, may not be as obvious as for the well known edge-line-vertex case. A second frame is therefore shown in which the same prominences have been found on a rotated and slightly scaled scene.

The four results shown here provide initial verification of the sensory richness and isolated feature assumptions stated earlier. It is encouraging that the features are quite invariant to the transformations that have caused so much trouble for correlation-based systems. Also, the sparseness of the detected features provides encouragement that when a system is constructed using mixed models, the resulting model and therefore the macth, will be unique, even for very complex outdoor scenes. Although not conclusive, the success of these initial results has verified the basic ideas used to construct this system and provided a basis for further development. Work is now in progress to develop more sophisticated, and hopefully more selective, texture prominence detection methods, and an improved structure finding scheme for lines and curves.

ACKNOWLEDGMENTS

I would like to acknowledge valuable discussions with Tom Binford of the Stanford A.I. Lab, and Ram Nevatia of USC on the use of the Hueckel operator and line finding, and Hans Moravec of the Stanford A.I. Lab on detecting texture prominences. Also I would like to thank Joe Jenney for his encouragement, Sahib Dudani for anticipating and solving early problems before they became problems, and making the Hough transform work, Jacquie Stafsudd who programmed the original system and Carol Clark for later improvements.

REFERENCES

1. Tenenbaum, J., "On Locating Objects By Their Distinguishing Features in Multisensory Images", Stanford Research Institute, A.I. Center, Tech. Note 84, September, 1973.
2. Bajcsy, R., and M. Tavakoli, "Image Filtering - A Context Dependent Process", IEEE Trans. on Computers, vol. CAS-22, no. 5, May 1975.
3. Hanson, A., and E. Riseman, "The Design of a Semantically Directed Vision Processor (revised)", Tech. Rept. 75C-1, Dept. of Computer and Information Science, University of Mass. at Amherst, Feb. 1975.

4. Ohlander, R., "Analysis of Natural Scenes", AD-A012-857, Dept. of Computer Science, Carnegie-Mellon Univ., April 1975.
5. Marr, D., "Analyzing Natural Images", M.I.T. A.I. Memo 334, June 1975.
6. Bullock, B., "Real World Scene Analysis in Perspective", ACM 75: Proceedings of the National ACM Convention, Minneapolis, 1975, (also Hughes Research Lab. Tech Report).
7. Bullock, B., "Unstructured Control Concepts in Scene Analysis", Proc. Eighth Annual Southeastern Symp. on Systems, University of Tenn., 1976, (also Hughes Research Lab. Tech. Report).
8. Lilestrand, R., "Change Detection", IEEE Trans. on Computers, vol. C-21, no. 7, July 1972.
9. Barnea, D., and H. Silverman, "A Class of Algorithms for Fast Digital Image Registration", IEEE Trans. on Computers, vol. C-21, Feb. 1972.
10. Bullock, B., "Footprints: A Representation for Restricted Motion in Outdoor Scenes", Third International Joint Conf. on Pattern Recognition, San Diego, Nov. 1976.
11. Zahn, C., "Graph Theoretical Methods for Detecting and Describing Gestalt Clusters", IEEE Trans. on Computers, vol. C-20, no. 1, Jan. 1971.
12. Bentley, J., and J. Friedman, "Fast Algorithm for Constructing Minimal Spanning Trees in Coordinate Spaces," SALC PUB. 1665, Stanford Linear Accelerator Center, 1975.
13. Bullock, B., "The Performance of Edge Operators On Images With Texture," Hughes Research Laboratory Tech. Report, Oct. 1974, (submitted to Computer Graphics and Image Processing).
14. Hueckel, M., "A Local Visual Operator Which Recognizes Edges and Lines", Journal of the ACM, vol. 20, no. 4, Oct. 1973.
15. Duda, R., and P. Hart, Pattern Classification and Scene Analysis, Wiley, 1973.
16. Montanari, U., "On Optimal Detection of Lines in Noisy Pictures", Comm. ACM, vol. 14, no. 5, May 1971.
17. Martelli, A., "An Application of Heuristic Search Methods to Edge and Curve Detection", Comm. ACM, vol. 19, no. 2, Feb. 1976.
18. Duda, R., and P. Hart, "Use of the Hough Transform to Detect Lines and Curves in Pictures", Comm. ACM, vol. 15, no. 1, Jan. 1972.
19. Ballard, D., and J. Sklansky, "Tumor Detection in Radiographs", Computers and Biomedical Research, vol. 6, 1973.
20. Haralick, R., and J. Bissell, "Texture Tone Study with Applications to Digitized Imagery", Tech Rept. 182-1, CRES, University of Kansas, Dec. 1970.
21. Moravec, H., Thesis Proposal, A.I. Lab., Stanford University, 1974.
22. Zahn, C., "Noisy Template Matching", IFIPS Congress Proceedings, 1974.

MOLDING COMPUTER CLAY -
STEPS TOWARD A COMPUTER GRAPHICS
SCULPTORS' STUDIO*

B. *Chandrasekaran*
Richard E. Parent
Department of Computer and Information Science
and Computer Graphics Research Group
The Ohio State University
Columbus, Ohio 43210

ABSTRACT

One of the biggest bottlenecks in 3-D computer graphics is the
inputting of complex object descriptions. This paper describes our
current attempts to provide one solution to the problem: creation
of a sculptor's studio-like environment in which the "sculptor" can
create complex three-dimensional objects in the computer, as if
moulding a piece of clay in the machine. This calls for an array
of techniques to be implemented and available at call to the user:
scaling, slicing, gouging, joining objects, cutting one object with
another, 3-D warping, and smoothing. The emphasis throughout will
be on naturalness and habitability. The paper discusses the issues
involved in designing such a system, especially in a minicomputer
environment. A fast, efficient hidden-line routine is discussed.
Almost all sculpting operations call the basic intersection algorithm, which is described in some detail.

I. INTRODUCTION

A major problem in three-dimensional computer graphics is that
of making available to the computer descriptions (or "models") of
complex objects in a form suitable for various graphics manipula-
tions. This paper discusses some of the issues involved in the design of an interactive minicomputer-based 3-D data generation system. We also describe our current attempts at the creation of a
sculptor's studio-like environment, in which the "sculptor" can
create complex 3-D objects in the computer, as if moulding a piece
of clay in the machine. We will attempt to give a general feeling
for the design issues, with less emphasis on purely graphics details.

There are two typical approaches to the 3-D data generation
problem. In one, a straightforward, if laborious, process is em-

---
* B. Chandrasekaran's work partially supported by AFOSR Grant 72-
2351. R. E. Parent's research supported by NSF Grant DCR 74-
00768 A01 to Professor Charles Csuri.

ployed to read in, point by point, the coordinates of the various points constituting the surface of the object. In the other approach, the object may be directly "created", or synthesized, in the machine. Of course, in practice, one might adopt stances intermediate to these polarities, such as reading in some "primitive" objects and then synthesizing more complex objects out of the primitive ones.

It has become increasingly apparent that artificial intelligence (AI) techniques should play an important role in reducing the labor involved in working with computer graphics systems. For instance, the various hidden-line elimination techniques have an AI flavor to them due to their heuristic features. The habitability of graphic systems can be improved by incorporating knowledge-based interaction on the part of the computer. One particular form of this would be the incorporation of features such as "understanding" sketches, or more generally, possessing a good model of how the 3-D and 2-D representations interact in the human. We discuss later in the paper ways in which 3-D graphics systems may use some of these abilities.

Our work in data generation is heavily influenced by the fact that, historically, the Computer Graphics Research Group (CGRG) at The Ohio State University, has had as one of its aims for its graphics systems ease of use by artists and other nonprogrammers. Thus the graphics language *Graphics Symbiosis System*, or GRASS [1], could be learnt by persons with little computer background in a short time to create two-dimensional figures of nontrivial complexity. The WHATSISFACE system [2], developed at the CGRG, enabled nonartists and nonprogrammers to draw on the CRT a facial image with remarkable likeness to a target photograph. In this historical context, we were naturally led to the notion of opening up the possibilities of the computer as a medium of expression for sculptors and "clay" animators.

In the next section, we take a brief look at some previous work in 3-D data generation.

II. APPROACHES TO 3-D DATA GENERATION

Conceptually, the simplest method is perhaps that of having the physical object, whose description has to be read in, available, selecting a number of points on the surface of the object (the number depending upon the degree of approximation desired in representation), and, by means of some digitizer, reading in the three-dimensional coordinates of the points. In fact, in our group, we currently have operational a sonic pen which is used for this purpose. This device contains an acoustic transducer which is placed at the particular location whose coordinates have to be digitized and read in. Three linear sensors located at the three axes pick up the acoustic energy, on the basis of which the coordinates of the transducer are calculated. This method is reasonably accurate. However, it is a laborious process, and the labori-

ousness is exacerbated by the fact that when a point is being digitized, the object may have to be removed in order to avoid absorp-
tion of the acoustic energy by the object and consequent loss of
accuracy.

An example of the synthesis approach is the work of Davis,
Nagel and Guber [3], which generates 3-D data using what is called
"Combinatorial Geometry" or "Computational Geometry". The idea is
that one class of complex objects can be synthesized by combining
simpler objects such as boxes, wedges, cylinders and cones. The
operators used to generate a new object O_1 from two more elementary
objects O_2 and O_3 are: +, -, and OR, where points in O_1 are points
in both O_2 and O_3, points in O_2 and not in O_3, and points in either O_2 or O_3, respectively. By a suitably nested sequence of
primitive objects and operations, objects of greater complexity
can be described to the machine. Note that this requires a generative algorithmic viewpoint on the part of the user. Further, the
system was not interactive, and the user had to carefully specify
the location and orientation of the primitive objects beforehand.
More recently, Braid [4] has used a similar approach, and he displays pictures of machine components synthesized in this manner.
While appropriate for some engineering applications, this method
would impose severe hardships on the user in our environment, where
interactive generation of free-form objects is the goal. However,
Brooks et al. [5] have recently used the combinatorial geometry
approach to model descriptions of vegetations, such as bushes and
trees. While this application seems to extend the range of possibilities in the use of combinatorial geometry techniques, it still
does not provide the fine 'sculpting' capabilities in 3-D for precise object specification.

Yoshimura, Tsuda and Hirano [6] treat 3-D objects with curved
surfaces, and construct them by a building block approach. The
user describes rigid tubular elements by providing properly spaced
latticed curves which roughly represent the surface of the element.
These are connected by flexible portions. The program fits curves
to elements given, generates flexible portions and extracts outlines of the figure. This approach is not quite adequate for the
purposes of 3-D data generation, but is useful for the purpose for
which it was intended: animation of objects that can be approximated by tubular elements.

Shirai and Tsuji [7] describe a method for constructing a
description of a polyhedral scene by photographing the scene with
sequential illumination from several directions. As might be expected, this involves an array of picture-processing techniques
such as spatial differentiation, filtering, thinning, tracking,
and finally AI-type operations such as line-fitting, and detecting
the edges. The image-processing techniques are applied to four
images of the same scene, corresponding to four orthogonal angles
of illumination. Note that a video or half-tone image can be input to the machine quite straight-forwardly by means of a scanner.
The problem dealt with in [7] is the construction of a model of
the object, the only available representation of which is 2-D. Of

course, in the case of polyhedral scenes, if the 2-D representation
is a line drawing (without errors), the problem is simplified somewhat. In general, however, the image is noisy, full of extraneous
details and ambiguities caused by varying illumination, if the input is via video or other scanners. Hence the need for picture-
processing and AI techniques.

An interesting geometrical-modeling approach to scenes which
are not basically polyhedral in nature (like, say, toy horses) and
which are input to the computer by a video interface is the GEOMED
system developed by Baumgart [8]. In the preprocessing stage, it
uses a variety of image processing techniques similar to [7]. Then
it proceeds to obtain a polyhedral approximation of the surface of
the object. Hence the term, "geometrical modeling". The system
uses different views of the same scene.

Still another approach that has been pursued is that of giving
the machine orthogonal projections of the object, and letting it
construct the 3-D representation. This is most useful in cases
where the object has an engineering or architectural flavor to it.
Sutherland [9] describes a technique which requires placing two orthogonal views of the object in two different digitizing tables,
and the two styluses are placed on corresponding points in the two
drawings. Thus actually two pairs of coordinates are read in, and
the program computes from it a three-coordinate representation of
the point in question. This is repeated for all vertices, and the
machine constructs the polyhedral representation. This reduces
the labor somewhat from 3-D digitization by a sonic pen or other
device, but requires different, precisely drawn orthogonal views
of the object.

The program described in Lafue [10] reconstructs 3-D objects
from two or three orthogonal projections of wire-frame drawings.
Only one tablet is used, and the reader draws on the tablet the
wire-frame projections of the object. In case a face obscures
faces producing identical outlines, as in the case of the top view
of a cube, the user is required to draw the face as many times as
the number of coincidences of faces. Lafue's program has many AI-
features to it in that it uses some heuristics based on properties
of three-dimensional objects and a mini-theorem-prover.

The programs of [9] and [10] require precision in the line
drawings of orthogonal views. Negroponte [11] is concerned with
what he calls computer sketch recognition, one aspect of which is
to enable the computer to accept orthogonal projections which are
drawn free-hand, and to "clean" them up in order to construct 3-D
representations. This requires computer "understanding" of line
drawings and "graphical gestures". The complexity of objects constructed in this manner is not very high yet, but it represents an
interesting use of AI-techniques in computer graphics.

The reader has probably realized by now that there can be no
one solution to the 3-D data generation problem. Having to input
description of a particular object one has at hand requires different techniques from having to synthesize objects in the machine.
Objects occurring in engineering applications could use simpler

techniques than free-form objects occurring in art contexts. Computer understanding of free hand drawings require techniques more sophisticated than those for the case where precise drawings are available. Constraints on the user could range all the way from having to write a batch-mode program in a highly algorithmic language using special mathematical notation, requiring visualization of the object in advance, to being able to feel as if he is "sculpting" something creatively and interactively (our aim).

III.   REPRESENTATION

A central decision in 3-D computer graphics is the internal representation of the object in the computer. Baumgart [8] presents an excellent survey of the different representations that have been proposed and their relative advantages and disadvantages. He classifies the representations, or "models" as they are sometimes called, into two classes: space-oriented and object-oriented. An example of space-oriented representations is a 3-D space array, which simply represents, in a digitized 3-space, all the cells that are in the object. In addition to being impractical due to the rather large memories required, the space array makes it difficult to access objects and surfaces as entities, i.e., that cells are held together as parts of the same mass is not readily apparent. The idea of *recursive cells* can be used to eliminate some of the disadvantages of space array representations. In this technique, at first the whole space is a cell. Then, if it is not homogeneous, it is subdivided into a number of subcells, and this is done recursively until all cells are homogeneous. This technique permits treating objects as entities. The memory requirements are much less. A certain price is still paid in the form of increased complexity in addressing. Other space-oriented models include 3-D spatial density functions or two-dimensional surface functions. Generally, such functions are impractical for representing real-world objects. However, they can be useful for generating very complex and esthetically interesting mathematical objects.

Object-oriented representations are more common in computer graphics. One such representation consists of a sufficiently large set of cross sections of the object. The representation used in [6], referred to earlier, is a version of this. A generalization of the cross section representation is that of skeletal models. The object is represented first as a stick figure and then sets of cross-sections are associated with the sticks. Agin [12] and Nevetia [13] have used this representation, which is useful for recognition purposes, but less so for representing arbitrary shapes in a computer graphics environment. The most common object-oriented representation in computer graphics, however, is that of polyhedral approximation of the surface of the object. The data structures can be designed to maintain object coherence in this representation in a straightforward fashion. This representation is especially convenient for hidden-line elimination

routines, shading algorithms, and many other types of processing
in graphics. Further, as Baumgart [8] has demonstrated, it is also
very useful for automatic acquisition of models, i.e., automatic
construction of the representation, given, say, a video input of
the object.

We have chosen the polyhedral representation for our work because of the above-mentioned advantages. However, since our aim
is to be able to "sculpt" interactively, even objects which are
only moderately complex in a conceptual sense can begin to take on
highly complex polyhedral representation. (Imagine a sphere, which
is a rather simple object conceptually, represented in this manner;
the number of edges goes up quite rapidly, as the degree of approximation gets reasonably close to the real thing.) This fact places
great demands on the efficiency of all the underlying routines.
For instance, the standard implementations of hidden line elimination routines become quite inefficient. As a result, we have had
to write a powerful, fast, extremely efficient hidden-line elimination routine, which is briefly described in Section V. In the
next section, we outline the various aspects of the graphics sculptor's studio environment.

IV. COMPUTER GRAPHICS SCUPTOR'S STUDIO

A) *Hardware*

The CPU is a PDP 11/45 with 96K 16-bit words of memory, out
of which 64K is magnetic core and 32K is MOS. In addition, several disks of 2 megabytes each are abailable. The display is a Vector General Scope, with 4096X4096 addressable points. In addition,
the peripherals include a joystick, 16 function buttons, sonic pen
and 10 dials, all of which are used to interact with the system.

B) *Command Language*

When he is sculpting, a sculptor's natural mode of thinking
is in terms transforming the lump of clay in front of him by operating on it by means of various tools. It is possible to design
a command language in which the graphics sculptor can specify what
transformations he wants done on the object on the screen. We believe that for our aims, viz., to give maximum opportunities for
the sculptor to be creative by letting him operate in a mode most
compatible to his thinking, this kind of command language is unnatural. We should not force him to think in terms of numerical
coordinates etc., but rather to feel as if he is operating on the
object as directly as possible. For this reason, we make extensive use of the dials and function buttons. Operations of scaling,
rotating, translating, joining, intersecting, choice of "tools"
etc., will be done by the sculptor by means of these analog devices or function buttons. The system still provides the sculptor

with a "language" to communicate with it, but this is not a conventional command language.

C) *Primitive Object Input*

Rather than begin with the primitive objects supplied by the system, the sculptor might desire to generate his own primitive object. In our system, two ways of doing this currently exist. In one of them, a cross-section is drawn by means of the sonic pen and an object with that as the cross-section is generated by the machine. The other mode begins by specifying two orthogonal views, again by means of the sonic pen. The orthogonal views are really silhouttes, or outlines, rather than ones that show edges inside the views. The system used a "quick and dirty" procedure to construct the object having these silhouttes for the orthogonal views. The procedure simply consists of generating two objects which are "cylindrical" extensions of the given silhouttes and then intersecting the two objects at right angles to produce the primitive object. We will describe the intersection routine in some detail later on.

D) *The Scenario*

The scenario we envision can be described as follows. The sculptor either starts with a polyhedral object provided to him by the system, or a primitive object created by him by the methods described in the previous section. Then by means of dials he can rotate and position this. He can call for a tool to cut this object, and this tool again can be positioned at the appropriate place by means of a dial. The object can be rotated and cut a number of times, in a number of places and orientations. Temporarily, he might want to put this object away, sculpt another object, and then these two objects can be positioned at desired locations and orientations, and they can be joined, overlapped or intersected. The excess objects can be thrown away or stored for later use. He can shape the object further by a 3-D warping routine, which gives him a movable cursor to be attached to any point on the surface of the object and "pulled" or "pushed". An interpolation routine pulls the neighboring edges proportionately to give this warping ability. The surfaces of the object can be "smoothed" at any point. These warping and smoothing routines are straightforward 3-D generalization of the corresponding 2-D routines described in [2]. At any stage, any of the objects can be scaled in any of the three axes. This is one aspect in which the graphics sculptor is ahead of his clay cousin, since the latter is constrained by the law of conservation of mass.

The sculptor can also, if necessary, fashion his own tools to do specific kinds of cutting, because, after all, all the tools are "objects", and all operations of one object on another can be executed by the intersection routine.

It should be noted that as these operations are being done,

the objects appear in the wire-frame mode (i.e., with hidden lines
not deleted). This is due to the fact that the data structures
for the input to the hidden-line processing routines are generated
by a preprocessing routine which is not part of the intersection
algorithm. In order to increase speed, we have opted to do the
sculpting operations in the wire-frame mode, since the basic intersection algorithm does not need this preprocessing. However, at
any time, the sculptor can have the hidden-line-eliminated version
on the screen to increase his perceptual comfort before deciding
on where to cut or how to shape the object. Another aspect of the
system is that the sculptor, after a sequence of shapings, can go
back to an earlier part of the sequence, if he happens not to be
satisfied with any part of the sequence.

The system is not yet fully implemented, and as such the realization of the scenario as outlined in all its details is not yet
possible. However, many of the basic routines are implemented and
working.

We next give brief descriptions of two of the basic algorithms.
Hidden-line processing in a minicomputer environment has been generally slow, if not out of reach, and fast, efficient hidden-line
implementations are essential for many applications. Our hidden-
line processing routine is described in Section V. From the scenario, it should be clear that the intersection routine is fundamental to our sculpting system. The intersection routine is the
subject of Section VI.

V. HIDDEN-LINE PROCESSING IN A MINICOMPUTER ENVIRONMENT

Sutherland et al. [14] and Encarnacao [15] give surveys of
available hidden-line elimination algorithms. Our hidden-line
routine is based on Loutrel's algorithm [16] which employs what is
called the path-of-edges technique. Though some changes have been
made to the algorithm, mainly in the handling of special cases and
the treatment of boundary vertices, we omit a detailed discussion
of the algorithm, in view of the easy availability of [16]. Instead, we discuss the special considerations arising out of the
fact that the implementation was to be close to real-time (real-
time here means less than one second per frame) in a minicomputer
environment.

In our system, clipping in the X and Y directions is provided
and, if desired, the scene can be displayed in perspective. All
transformations are done by software. In addition, the following
features are noteworthy. First, it is interactive. The user is
provided with the joystick, various dials and buttons for inter-
acting with the program. Dials control rotation, placement of the
picture plane (for perspective calculation) and scaling. The joystick is used for three-dimensional translation. Function buttons
provide for, among other things, transformation speed changes, temporary halt, specification of scene or object for transformation

and exit. The second feature is the speed of processing, obtained by programming in assembler and doing all computations in integer arithmetic. Third is the ability to transform (rotate and translate) independently each object in the scene as well as transforming the entire scene. This ability, especially if implemented under program control, could be very useful for filming animation sequences.

The limitations are two-fold. First, because of the size of the data structures used, the routine is restricted to handling less than nine-hundred edges. This still allows for reasonably complex models. Second, due to the use of integer arithmetic on a 16-bit word machine, overflow and underflow errors occur at times. These, however, are usually few and far between, and appear only as occasional flashes in normal operation.

The routine resides in a 32K partition and consists of two parts. The first part, the preprocessor, builds the data structures which are needed by the second part to efficiently calculate the visible edge segments. These data structures are built separately for each object and an object list is maintained. The requirement of real-time or close to real-time operation when the objects are being manipulated imposes the requirement that the preprocessor output should be basically independent of the vertex position data. Thus the data structures have information about faces, edges and objects with respect to one another, and not with respect to the user, and refer to the vertices not by their coordinates, but by pointers to them. Further, in order to minimize cumulative inaccuracies because of integer arithmetic, the position data are recomputed for each dial setting. An arbitrarily chosen "initial" position and size are operated on by transformation matrices whose parameters are set by the dial information.

Figures 1 through 3 give an idea of the results obtainable by the program. Figure 1a represents a 615-edge scene with hidden lines drawn, while Figure 1b is the same scene with hidden lines removed. Processing time was approximately nine seconds. Figure 2 shows an 81-edge scene with four objects, the time taken for this being about 0.1 second. Figures 3a and 3b show a 168-edge scene with and without hidden lines, the calculations in this case taking less than one second. This compares favorably with a time of five seconds required by Loutrel's implementation on a CDC 6600 for a 200-edge object.

VI. THE INTERSECTION ALGORITHM

The intersection algorithm, as noted earlier, is fundamental to all of the sculpting operations, with the exceptions of warping and smoothing. It operates on two overlapping closed polyhedra, say O_1 and O_2, and can calculate any of the four resulting polyhedra: the object defined by the intersection of O_1 and O_2, that defined by their union, and either of the two objects formed when using one polyhedron to cut into the other. In each case the cal-

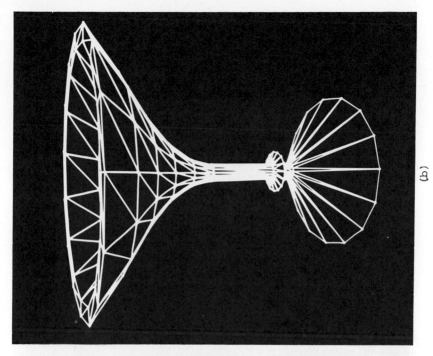

(b)

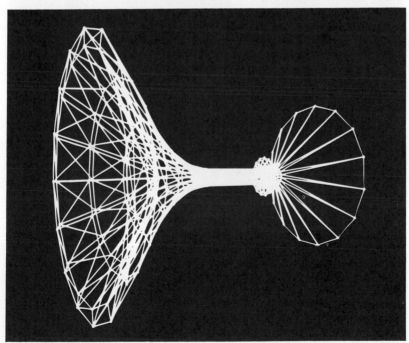

(a)

Figure 1. A 615-edge scene with and without hidden lines.

Figure 2. A 4-object, 81-edge scene without hidden lines.

(b)

(a)

Figure 3. A 2-object, 168-edge scene with and without hidden lines.

culations performed are identical, but the results are combined differently depending upon the object desired.

Baumgart [8] describes an intersection algorithm which seems to be based on geometric principles similar to ours, but the data structures and algorithms are different. Further, his algorithm imposes the restriction that the objects intersected have convex polygons for faces. Our algorithm has no such restrictions and is quite general.

The algorithm uses the fact that the resulting object will have faces which are either portions of faces or entire faces of either 0_1 or 0_2. In order to simplify the description of the algorithm, let us define by F_{ij}, the j-th face of object 0_i, and by e_{ij}^k the k-th edge of face F_{ij}. The algorithm can now be informally described as follows:

A1: Given edge e_{ij}^k and face F_{uv}, $u \neq i$, this returns the coordinates of the point of intersection between the two, if such a point exists, and sets up an information structure relating the edge, the intersection point and an indication of which vertex of the edge is in "front" of the face.

A2: Given faces F_{ij} and F_{uv}, $i \neq u$, this performs A1 1) for e_{ij}^k and F_{uv}, for all k, and 2) for e_{uv}^ℓ and F_{ij}, for all ℓ. All the intersection points generated, say $p_1, \ldots, p_n$, are sorted. (They will be collinear and n even.) Pairs (p_i, p_{i+1}), i odd, define edges that belong to the new object. At the conclusion of A2, the algorithm will have available new edges as well as information that will be used by A3 to generate segments of edges of the original objects.

A3: Given face F_{ij}, this performs A2 for F_{ij} and F_{uv}, $u \neq i$, for all v. The type of operation specified (intersection, join etc.) together with the information associated with the edges e_{ij}^k in A1 determine the segments of the edges to be included in the resulting object.

MAIN: For i=1,2 and all j, this gives A3 face F_{ij}, and information about the type of operation desired. At the conclusion of MAIN, all the faces belonging to the resulting object will have been generated.

Figures 4 through 9 demonstrate the performance of the intersection algorithm. Figures 4a and 4b show two views of a wedge (0_1) and a rectangular block (0_2) positioned and oriented before the intersection algorithm is actuated. Figure 5 shows the object which is the intersection of 0_1 and 0_2. Figure 6 corresponds to the two objects consisting of points in 0_1 but not in 0_2. Figure 7 is the result of joining 0_1 and 0_2, i.e., the object consists of points both in 0_1 and 0_2. Figure 8 shows, in perspective and with hidden lines removed, an object "gouged" in one part. Figure 9 shows a more complex object: a cylinder joined to a block which has also been gouged.

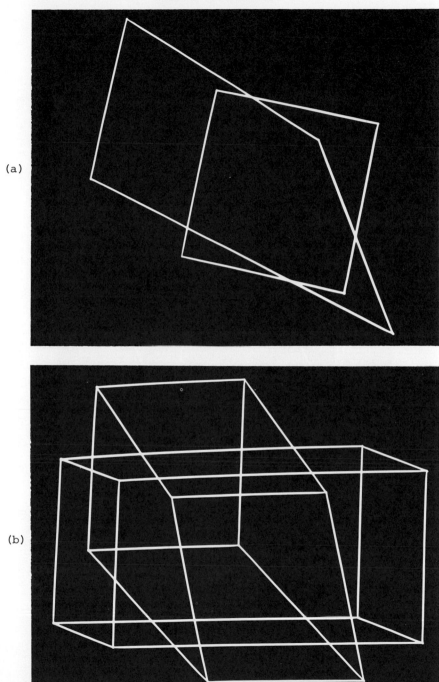

(a)

(b)

Figure 4. Two views of scene with wedge and rectangular block.

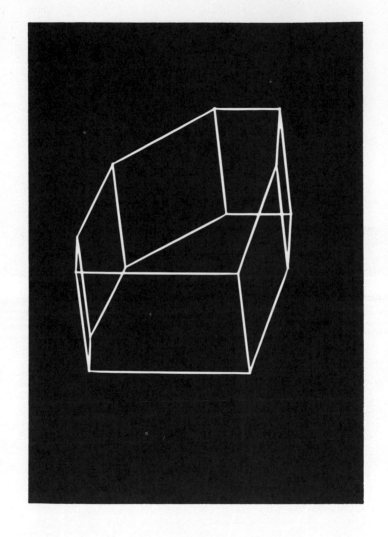

Figure 5. Object produced by intersection of wedge and rectangular block.

Figure 6. Object containing points in wedge, but not in rectangular block.

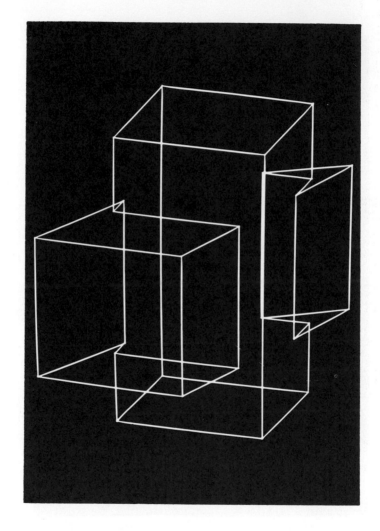

Figure 7. Object produced by joining wedge and rectangular block.

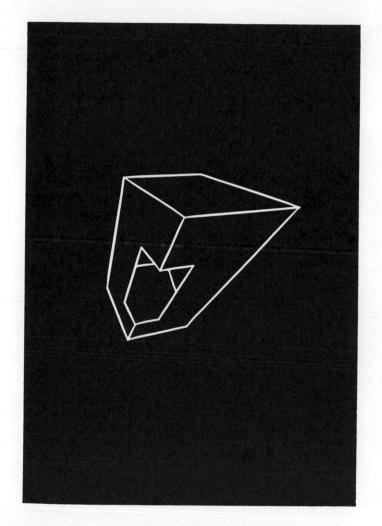

Figure 8. An Object after "gouging".

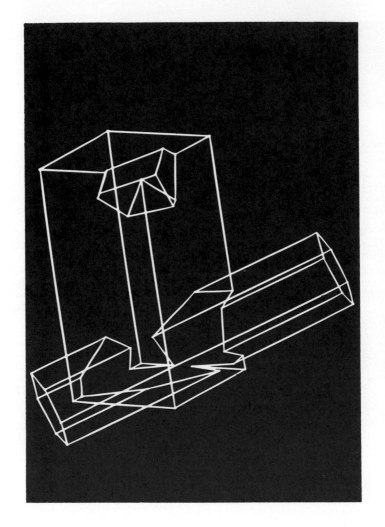

Figure 9. Cylinder joined with a block which has also been gouged.

The implementation of the algorithm, as it currently stands, can handle scenes with up to 4000 edges. Thus significantly more complex objects can be sculpted than can be handled by the hidden-line processing routine.

VII. CONCLUDING REMARKS

It is hoped that the preceding sections give the reader a fair idea of the underlying viewpoint, the design issues and criteria and the outlines of the workings of our sculptor's studio environment. The reader should especially note the kinds of human interaction permitted and called for, and thus be able to judge the naturalness and habitability of the system. While mainly intended for free-form objects the system could also be used for interactive synthesis of engineering-type objects. It is a relatively straightforward matter to modify the data structures so that the artist using the system for 3-D animation can specify independent movements for the subparts of the sculpted object. In systems which build 3-D models directly from images of different views of the object, this kind of independent control would be hard to do.

A few remarks about the limitations of our implementation are in order. A CPU with greater word length (currently it is 16 bits/ word) would be a better choice for various reasons, not the least of which is easy addressability of larger memory partitions, and consequent liberation from the constraint of a 32K partition. This will reduce the number of core/disk swaps, increase speed, and also increase the complexity of scenes that can be handled by the hidden-line processing routine. In addition, the longer word would reduce errors in integer arithmetic, an occasional problem in our current implementation.

Every sculpting operation inevitably produces edges. While this effect might be used to advantage in some artistic contexts, generally the sculpted objects may be deemed to have too many edges for perceptually satisfying images. However, use of efficient shading algorithms [17], when these edges are not desired, would create a more pleasing display.

Usefulness of such object-synthesis systems could be improved by incorporating aspects with strong AI-content to them. For instance, ability on the part of the system to understand "graphical gestures" as suggested by Negroponte [11] would enhance the value of such systems. As another example, consider the synthesis of engineering-type objects. We plan, at a later stage, to develop a capability for the machine to automatically generate blue-print type sketches, with dimensions added, hidden lines dotted, and so on, once the synthesis is completed.

ACKNOWLEDGMENTS

The authors wish to thank Professor Charles Csuri and the
Computer Graphics Research Group for providing the facilities and
a stimulating environment. We are indebted to Ron Hackathorn for
some of the data generation and photography.

REFERENCES

1. Defanti, T. A., "The Graphics Symbiosis System - An Interactive Minicomputer Graphics Language Designed for Habitability
and Extensibility", Ph.D. Thesis, The Ohio State University,
1973. Also technical report, Computer Graphics Research
Group.
2. Gillenson, M. L. and B. Chandrasekaran, "A Heuristic Strategy
for Developing Human Facial Images on a CRT", *Pattern Recognition,* Vol. 7, pp. 187-196, 1975.
3. Davis, J. R., R. Nagel, and W. Guber, "A Model Making and Display Technique for 3-D Pictures", *Proc. Seventh Annual Meeting of UAIDE,* pp. 46-72, San Francisco, October 1968.
4. Braid, I. C., "The Synthesis of Solids Bounded by Many Faces",
Comm. Association for Computing Machinery, Vol. 18, No. 4,
April 1975.
5. Brooks, J., R. S. Murarka, and D. Onuoha, "An Extension of
the Combinatorial Geometry Technique for Modeling. . .",
Available as AD-782883 from NTIS.
6. Yoshimura, S., J. Tsuda, and C. Hirano, "A Computer Animation
Technique for 3-D Objects with Curved Surfaces", *Proc. Tenth
Annual Meeting of UAIDE,* pp. 3-140 to 3-161, Los Angeles,
October 1971.
7. Shirai, Y., and S. Tsuji, "Extraction of the Line Drawings of
3-D Objects by Sequential Illumination from Several Directions",
*Proc. II International Joint Conference on Artificial Intelli-
gence,* London, September 1971.
8. Baumgart, B. G., "Geometric Modeling for Computer Vision",
Ph. D. Thesis, Stanford University, 1974. Available as AD/A-
002261, from NTIS.
9. Sutherland, I. E., "Three-Dimensional Data Input by Tablet",
Proc, IEEE, Vol. 62, No. 4, pp. 453-461, 1974.
10. Lafue, G., "Computer Recognition of Three-Dimensional Objects
from Orthogonal Views", Research Report No. 56, Institute of
Physical Planning, Carnegie-Mellon University, September 1975.
11. Negroponte, N., "Recent Advances in Sketch Recognition", *Proc.
National Computer Conference,* pp. 663-675, 1973.
12. Agin, G. J., "Representation and Description of Curved Objects", Ph. D. Thesis, Stanford University. Available as
Memo No. AIM-173, 1972.
13. Nevetia, R., "Structured Descriptions of Complex Objects for
Recognition and Visual Memory", Ph. D. Thesis, Stanford University, 1974.

14. Sutherland, I. E., R. F. Sproull, and R. A. Schumacker, "A Characterization of Ten Hidden-Surface Algorithms", *ACM Computing Surveys*, Vol. 6, No. 1, pp. 1-55, 1974.
15. Encarnacao, J. L., "A Survey of and New Solutions to the Hidden Line Problem", *Proc. Interactive Computer Graphics Conference*, Delft, Holland, October 1970.
16. Loutrel, P., "A Solution to the Hidden Line Problem for Computer-Drawn Polyhedra", *IEEE Trans. Computers*, March 1970.
17. Myers, A. J., "An Efficient Visible Surface Program", Technical Report, Computer Graphics Research Group, The Ohio State University, July 1975.

DEDUCE --- A DEDUCTIVE QUERY LANGUAGE
FOR RELATIONAL DATA BASES

C. L. *Chang*
IBM Research Laboratory
San Jose, CA.

ABSTRACT

In this paper, a language called DEDUCE for relational data
bases is given. This language allows one to state *queries, axioms,*
preferences, and *heuristics.* Queries having existential and/or
universal quantifiers can be handled quite *uniformly.* Axioms are
used to define views of a relational data base. A user can make a
query against views and original base relations. The query is e-
valuated in two steps: First, use axioms to transform the query
into a query containing only base relations. Second, evaluate the
transformed query by using a data base system such as SEQUEL. Preferences can be stated in a query. They are fuzzy formulas that are
preferred to be satisfied. Heuristics are also fuzzy formulas which
are used to select some particular values over others. Examples are
given to illustrate how DEDUCE could be used in relational data bases. Comparisons between DEDUCE and other AI languages and some related topics such as inferencial completeness will also be discussed.

I. INTRODUCTION

Relational model given by Codd [6,9] has been shown to be a
convenient and powerful tool for describing a data base. In this
model, the data base is viewed as a collection of time-varying relations of assorted degrees. For simplicity, a relation can be
viewed as a table of a finite number of columns and rows. Such a
table is called a normalized relation [4,5]. The table name is the
relation name. Column names of the table are called *attributes.*
Entries of the table are called *values.* A row of the table corresponds to a record. Orders of rows and columns of the table are
immaterial. A row is actually a ground atomic formula in the first-
order logic [5].

Very often we need inferences [14] for a relational data base,
because some information may not be explicitly stored. If we want
to know information which are not stored, we may have to infer that
information from those stored in a computer. For example, we may
have the relation FATHER(x,y), which denotes that x is the father
of y. An extension of this relation is given in Table 1.

Table 1

FATHER	NAME 1	NAME 2
	John	Smith
	Smith	Mary
	Smith	Robert
	Robert	Carl

Now, suppose we want to know who is an ancestor of whom. We can answer this type of question by introducing a new concept ANCESTOR(x,y), which denotes that x is an ancestor of y. Clearly, we can construct Table 2 for the ANCESTOR relation from Table 1.

Table 2

ANCESTER	NAME 1	NAME 2
	John	Smith
	John	Robert
	John	Carl
	John	Mary
	Smith	Robert
	Smith	Carl
	Smith	Mary
	Robert	Carl

However, this approach of building an explicit table for ANCESTOR introduces the following objections:

Objection 1. We need to provide spaces for storing Table 2.

Objection 2. When we insert a new row into or delete an old row from Table 1, appropriate rows have to be inserted into or deleted from Table 2.

Objection 3. Even Objection 1 and Objection 2 are tolerable, we still have to make sure that Table 1 and Table 2 are consistent. For example, if row (John, Smith) is missing from Table 1, then Table 1 and Table 2 will be inconsistent.

Objection 4. Sometimes we may not have enough spaces to store Table 2 because the size of Table 2 grows exponentially with that of Table 1.

In order to circumvent the above objections, we may just store Table 1, and define ANCESTOR(x,y) in terms of FATHER(x,y) by using the following axiom:

$$\text{FATHER}(x_1,x_2) \ \& \ \dots \ \& \ \text{FATHER}(x_{m-1},x_m) \rightarrow \text{ANCESTOR}(x_1,x_m)$$

In this paper, we shall propose a language named DEDUCE for expressing queries and axioms. DEDUCE also provides facilities for expressing preferences in a query and heuristics in an axiom. In addition, we shall discuss some related topics such as inferential completeness, and other AI languages.

II.   QUERY REPRESENTATIONS IN THE DEDUCE LANGUAGE

In this section, we first consider how to represent queries in DEDUCE.

DEDUCE is based upon symbolic logic [5]. Basically, there are constant (value) symbols, variable symbols, function symbols and predicate (relation) symbols. There are also logical connectives &, v and $\sim$. Using these symbols, we can build terms and formulas in the following:

Definition. A *term* is defined recursively as follows:
(1)   A variable or a constant is a term;
(2)   If f is an n-place function symbol, and $t_1, \ldots, t_n$ are terms, $f(t_1, \ldots, t_n)$ is a term;
(3)   Any term can always be constructed by repeated applications of the above two rules.

If P is an n-place predicate symbol, and $t_1, \ldots, t_n$ are terms, $P(t_1, \ldots, t_n)$ is an *atomic formula*. However, if P is a relation, the atomic formula will be written as $P(a_1=t_1, \ldots, a_n=t_n)$, where $a_1, \ldots, a_n$ are some attributes of P, and $t_1, \ldots, t_n$ will be either constants or variables. The reason for this is that attributes of the relation P in a relational data base may not be ordered, and the atomic formula may contain only some (not all) attributes of the relation. The interpretation of $P(a_1=t_1, \ldots, a_n=t_n)$ is that the atomic formula will be true if there is a row of P whose corresponding part can be matched with $(t_1, \ldots, t_n)$. Otherwise, it is false.

Definition.   (Quantifier free) formulas are defined recursively as follows:
(1)   An atomic formula is a formula;
(2)   If A and B are formulas, so are (A & B), (A v B), and $\sim$ A;
(3)   Any formula can always be constructed by repeated applications of the above two rules.

In DEDUCE, there are also some key words such as INSERT, DELETE, UPDATE, QUERY, SUBQUERY and AXIOM, and some facilities for deleting and updating axioms. In this paper, we shall discuss QUERY, SUBQUERY and AXIOM.

A query is always started with the key word QUERY and followed by a condition. A simple condition is a formula in conjunctive normal form [3]. A more complicated query can allow SUBQUERY inside the query.

In addition, there are two special symbols * and #. The user inserts a symbol * before any data he wishes to be outputted. The

symbol plays the same role as 'P.' in QUERY BY EXAMPLE [23]. DE-
DUCE queries which do not contain SUBQUERY is similar to the linearized form of QUERY BY EXAMPLE. However, DEDUCE queries which have
SUBQUERY are quite different from representations given in QUERY BY
EXAMPLE. The symbol # is the same as the symbol * except it is
used inside SUBQUERY. The BNF grammar of DEDUCE is given in Appendix.

Every QUERY or SUBQUERY has a scope. A QUERY (SUBQUERY) acts
like a do-loop. Conditions inside the QUERY are sequentially executed in the order given in the QUERY. When the last condition in
the QUERY is executed, control goes back to the beginning of the
QUERY and the conditions are executed again. This process is repeated until no more new values can be found for variables marked
by *. Then control goes to the next statement after the QUERY
(SUBQUERY) block. Of course, the above is a straightforward way
of interpreting the DEDUCE queries. Any other optimal and efficient interpretations that will result in the same answers as ones
obtained by the above method are allowed. When control exists from
a SUBQUERY, a bag of vectors of values indicated by the symbol #
that satisfy the conditions in the SUBQUERY is returned. This bag
will then be referred to by the variable or a list of variables
that are marked by the symbol #. Note that a bag is an unordered
collection of elements, where the elements may be duplicated.

There are some system-provided functions such as count, max,
min, avg, sum, set, etc. that can be applied to a bag and return,
respectively, the number of elements in the bag, the maximum value,
the minimum value, the average value, the sum of values in the bag,
and the set of distinct elements in the bag, etc. Sometimes, if
we want to perform computations on distinct values in the bag, the
system could provide functions such as count', avg', sum', etc.

We shall use examples to illustrate DEDUCE in detail. The
queries we shall give are divided into different classes according
to some informal criterion of query complexities. These classes
are restriction, computation, join, group-by on relations, nestings
of group-bys, group-by on restrictions, group-by on joins of relations, group-by on joins of restrictions, there-exit-for-all queries, for-all-there-exit queries, and other difficult queries.
The relational data base we consider and some of queries we use in
this paper are taken from [2]. This data base consists of the relations EMP(NAME, SAL, MGR, DEPT), SALES(DEPT, ITEM, VOL), SUPPLY
(COMP, DEPT, ITEM, VOL), LOC(DEPT. FLOOR), and CLASS(ITEM, TYPE).
The EMP relation has a row for every store employee, giving his
name, salary, manager, and department. The SALES relation gives
the volume (yearly count) in which each department sells each item.
The SUPPLY relation gives the volume (yearly count) in which each
department obtained various items from its various supplier companies. The LOC relation gives the floor on which each department
is located, and the CLASS relation classifies the item sold into
various types.

The DEDUCE queries will be written in Polish notation. Since
DEDUCE was implemented in LISP, we can use many built-in LISP

predicates such as greaterp, lessp, etc., and use any user-defined
LISP predicates. In addition, since query conditions are represented in a conjunctive normal form, we usually drop the conjunctive sign &. In the following, we declare only x, y, z, u, v, and
w as variables. Each query is expressed first in English and then
in DEDUCE.

(A)   Restriction

A restriction involves only one relation. The following
examples are the restriction type of queries:

(1)   Find the names of employees in the TOY department.

```
(QUERY
(emp *name=x dept=toy))
```

In the above query, since the attribute NAME is marked by *,
the QUERY will return all values of the attribute NAME in those
rows that satisfy the query condition. Mathematically, it means
to find the set $\{x|$ (emp name=x dept=toy)$\}$. Since x appears in on-
ly one atomic formula, without ambiguity, we may drop x and simply
represent the query as

```
(QUERY
(emp *name dept=toy)).
```

When the system interprets this query, it will automatically
fill in a variable for the attribute NAME. We note that to check
whether (emp name=x dept=toy) is true or not, the system goes to
the EMP table, and matches (x toy) with the corresponding part of
every row. If there is a match, then it is true. A value a of x
is said to satisfy (emp name=x dept=toy) if (emp name=a dept=toy)
is true. The QUERY means to find all values of x that satisfy
(emp name=x dept=toy).

(2)   Find the volume of guns sold by the toy department.

```
(QUERY
(emp *vol dept=toy item=gun))
```

The query is to find the set

$\{x|$ (emp vol=x dept=toy item=gun)$\}$.

(3)   List the names and managers of employees in the
shoe department with salary greater than 10000.

```
(QUERY
(emp *name *mgr sal=x dept=shoe)
(greaterp x 10000))
```

The query means to find the set

$$\{(u,v) \mid (emp\ name=u\ mgr=v\ sal=x\ dept=shoe)\ \&$$
$$(greaterp\ x\ 10000)\}$$

(B) Join
A join involves at least two relations, and has common
variables linking through some relations.

   (1) Find those items sold by departments on the second
        floor.

        (QUERY
        (sales *item dept=x)
        (loc dept=x floor=2))

In the above query, x is a linking variable. The query means
to find the set

$$\{y \mid (sales\ item=y\ dept=x)\ \&\ (loc\ dept=x\ floor=2)\}.$$

   (2) Find the salary of Anderson's manager.

        (QUERY
        (emp name=anderson mgr=x)
        (emp name=x *sal))

   (3) Find the names of employees who make more than their
        managers.

        (QUERY
        (emp *name sal=x mgr=y)
        (emp name=y sal=z)
        (greaterp x z))

(C) Computation

   (1) Find the average salary of employees in the toy or
        shoe department.

        (QUERY
           (SUBQUERY
           (emp #sal=x dept=y)
           (or (eq y toy) (eq y shoe)))
        (compute *(avg x)))

In the above query, since x is marked by #, when control exists from the SUBQUERY, a bag of all values of x that satisfy the
condition (emp sal=x dept=y) & (or (eq y toy) (eq y shoe)) in the
SUBQUERY is returned. This bag of values will be referred to by

x in the subsequent statements after the SUBQUERY block. Therefore, (avg x) is an application of the function avg on the bag.
To avoid considering x outside the scope of the SUBQUERY as a single value, it will be helpful that the reader mentally thinks that
avg is a function defined on a bag, and read (avg x) as average
all such x, or average all such x that satisfy the conditions specified in the SUBQUERY. The statement (compute *(avg x)) will be
true if (avg x) is computable; otherwise, it will be false. The
symbol * indicates printing the value of (avg x), i.e., the average salary. Therefore, the whole query means to evaluate the
statement,

avg([x|(emp sal=x dept=y) & (or (eq y toy) (eq y shoe))]),
where we use a pair of brackets instead of braces to indicate the
bag.

   (2)   How many type A items?

```
(QUERY
    (SUBQUERY
    (class #item=x type=A))
(compute *(count' x)))
```

The above query is similar to the one in (1) except that
(count' x) is to count all such *distinct* x that satisfy the conditions specified in the SUBQUERY.

(D) Group-by on relations

   (1)   List the name and salary of each manager who man-
         ages more than 10 employees.

```
(QUERY
(emp *name=x *sal)
    (SUBQUERY
    (emp #name=y mgr=x))
(greaterp (count' y) 10))
```

In the above query, control starts at QUERY and then goes to
the next statement (emp *name=x *sal). First, the system fills in
a variable, say u, for SAL. Thus, we have (emp *name=x *sal=u).
The system then goes to the EMP table and tries to match (x u)
with the corresponding part of every row of the EMP table. Whenever there is a match, variables x and u are bound to the matched
values, and control then goes to the SUBQUERY. In the SUBQUERY,
first, variable x is substituted for the matched value and then
the system tries to execute the statement (emp #name=y mgr=x).
This means that the system goes to the beginning of the EMP table
and tries to match (y x) with the corresponding part of every row
of the EMP table. Whenever there is a match, y is assigned to the
matched value. Since y is marked by #, the matched value of y is
put into a bag. Since there are no other conditions in the SUB-
QUERY, control goes back to the first statement in the SUBQUERY

and tries for another match. The process is repeated until no new matches are possible. Then control exits from the SUBQUERY block and the system returns the bag. This bag is the bag of all employees managed by the first matched value of x. The bag is referred to by y. Control then goes to the statement (greaterp (count' y) 10), and tests whether or not the number of distinct elements in the bag y is greater than 10. If yes, since x and u are marked by *, the pair of the matched values for x and u are put into a set, and all the variables are unbound. If no, every variable is unbound. Then, control goes to the first statement of the QUERY and tries another match for x and u. This is repeated until no new matches for x and u are possible. When this is the case, control exits from the QUERY block, and the system returns the set of all the pairs of the matched values of x and u that satisfy the conditions. The above is the semantic of DEDUCE. Of course, any equivalent interpretations will be allowed. One efficient way to interpret this query is first to group rows of the EMP table by manager, and count the number of employees managed by each manager, and then print those managers and their salaries where the countings are greater than 10. This is why this query is called a query of the type of group-by on relations. The remaining queries can be understood by following the same semantic we have for the above query.

(2) Find the names of those employees who make more than any employee in the shoe department.

```
(QUERY
      (SUBQUERY
      (emp #sal=y dept=shoe))
   (emp *name sal=x)
   (greaterp x (max y)))
```

(3) Find those companies, each of which supplies every item.

```
(QUERY
      (SUBQUERY
      (supply #item=z))
   (supply *comp=x
      (SUBQUERY
      (supply comp=x #item=y))
   (equal (set y) (set z)))
```

(4) Find companies, each of which supplies every item of type A to some department on the second floor.

```
(QUERY
      (SUBQUERY
      (class #item=u type=A))
```

```
(supply dept=x *comp=y)
(loc dept=x floor=2)
    (SUBQUERY
    (supply comp=y #item=z))
(contain (set z) (set u)))
```

(E)   Nestings of group-bys

(1)   List all companies that supply at least two departments with more than 100 items.

```
(QUERY
(supply *comp=x)
    (SUBQUERY
    (supply comp=x #dept=y)
        (SUBQUERY
        (supply comp=x dept=y #item=z))
    (greaterp (count' z) 100))
(ge    (count' y) 2))
```

In the above query, there is a SUBQUERY within another SUB-
QUERY. This is like a do-loop within another do-loop in a programming language. The interpretation of this query is similar to
the one given in (D). That is, we sequentially execute the statements, and treat each QUERY or SUBQUERY as a loop. The matching,
binding, and unbinding for variables are as the same before. An
equivalent efficient way to interpret this query is through first
grouping rows of the SUPPLY table by company, and then for each
company grouping rows by department. After these groupings, counting the number of departments in each company, and the number of
items in each department within the company can be done easily.

(F)   Group-by on restrictions

(1)   Among all departments with total salary greater
than 1m, find those departments which sell dresses.

```
(QUERY
(sales *dept=x item=dress)
    (SUBQUERY
    (emp dept=x #sal=y))
(greaterp (sum y) 1m))
```

The above query is similar to the query of the type of group-
by relations given in (D), except that for easy countings we need
to group by department *only* rows which have 'dress' in the ITEM
column of the EMP table, instead of grouping all rows of the EMP
table.

(G)   Group-by on joins of relations

(1)   Find all items that are sold on more than 2 floors.

```
(QUERY
(sales *item=x)
    (SUBQUERY
    (sales  dept=y  item=x)
    (loc  dept=y  #floor=z))
(greaterp  (count' z)  2))
```

Since locations and items are not in any table of the relational data base, the relation between them has to be obtained through the join, (sales dept=y item=x) & (loc dept=y #floor=z), as it appears in the SUBQUERY. Once this join is obtained, then we can group by item rows of the join for an efficient counting of the number of floors for each item.

(H)   Group-by on joins of restrictions

(1)   Among all pairs of departments that sell dress, find two departments that sell at least 3 items in common.

```
(QUERY
(sales  *dept=x  item=dress)
(sales  *dept=y  item=dress)
(not  (equal x y))
    (SUBQUERY
    (sales  dept=x  #item=z)
    (sales  dept=y   item=z))
(ge  (count' z)  3))
```

For this query, an efficient interpretation requires that we first form a subtable that consists of rows of the SALES table that have 'dress' in the ITEM column, next obtain a join, (sales dept=x #item=z) & (sales dept=y item=z), as indicated in the SUBQUERY, and then finally group rows of the join by pairs of distinct departments. After this, counting the number of items for each pair of departments will be easy.

(I)   There-exist-for-all queries

(1)   Find all the floors where a department sells all items.

```
(QUERY
    (SUBQUERY
    (class #item=u))
(loc  *floor=x  dept=y)
    (SUBQUERY
    (sales  dept=y  #item=z))
(equal  (set z)  (set u)))
```

This query is also a query of the type of group-by on relations.

(J)   For-all-there-exist queries

(1)   List all floors each of which has all departments on the floor selling a type A item.

```
(QUERY
(loc *floor=x)
    (SUBQUERY
    (loc floor=x #dept=y)
    (sales  dept=y  item=z)
    (class  item=z  type=A))
    (SUBQUERY
    (loc  floor=x  #dept=u))
(equal  (set y)  (set u)))
```

This query is also a query of the type of group-by on joins of relations. The join is specified by (loc floor=x #dept=y) & (sales dept=y item=z) & (class item=z type=A), as it appears in the first SUBQUERY.

III.   REPRESENTATIONS OF PREFERENCES

In a DEDUCE query, we also allow preferences to be stated. Preferences can be represented by fuzzy formulas [13] as well as non-fuzzy formulas. These are conditions that the user would like, but not necessarily, the data to satisfy. That is, if no data satisfy the preference conditions, the system will not be necessarily prevented from generating some answers. For example, the user may be interested in TV sets, and he may prefer they are made by Zenith. He wants to know which floors he should go. In this case, the query will be represented by

```
(QUERY
(loc  dept=x  *floor)
(sales  dept=x  item=TV)
$(supply  comp=Zenith  dept=x  item=TV)).
```

The first two statements are query conditions as we discussed in Section II. These two conditions must be satisfied. However, the last statement, $(supply comp=Zenith dept=x item=TV), is a preference condition. We note that a preference condition is always preceded by the symbol $. When the system sees this query, it will find all values of floor that satisfy the condition (loc dept=x *floor) & (sales dept=x item=TV), and then will list the values by putting those floors which have Zenith TV before the others.

In the above query, the preference condition is not a fuzzy

formula. In general, we allow fuzzy formulas to be preference
conditions. As query conditions, preference conditions will also
be expressed in a conjunctive normal form. In order to drop the
conjunctive sign &, we put a dollar sign $ in front of every pref-
erence condition. The interpretation of a fuzzy formula is based
on Zadeh's fuzzy set concept [21]. That is, a membership function
of the preference of each atomic formula will assume values in the
interval [0,1], and the membership value of a compound fuzzy formula is evaluated through the operations of min, max and difference.
If a DEDUCE query contains a fuzzy formula as a preference condition, the system will sort the values (in the descending order)
that satisfy the query conditions by their associated values of
the fuzzy formula.

DEDUCE was partially implemented in LISP. We shall discuss
some of the queries we have tested. The relational data base consists of the following two tables:

Table 3

JOB	NAME	AGE	JOBTITLE
	Smith	32	mathematician
	John	29	engineer
	Richard	25	programmer
	Judy	40	chemist
	Mike	55	engineer
	Anna	45	physicist
	Taylor	60	mathematician
	Jame	22	programmer
	Victor	19	programmer
	Frank	36	engineer
	Mary	33	mathematician
	Lucy	51	mathematician
	Allen	47	programmer
	Carl	50	engineer
	Peter	38	chemist
	Martin	46	physicist
	Susan	42	programmer
	Eva	37	chemist
	Raymond	21	engineer
	Ted	53	physicist

Table 4

SENIORITY	NAME	YEAR-OF-SERVICE
	Anna	20
	Allen	30
	Ted	18
	Martin	12
	Judy	19
	Frank	9
	Smith	10
	Carl	18
	Peter	15
	Jame	5
	Richard	6
	John	8
	Mike	30
	Eva	5
	Victor	1
	Mary	10
	Taylor	18
	Raymond	4
	Susan	9
	Lucy	25

The following is a listing of a session we have tried with DEDUCE on the IBM LISP 1.5 system. Those letters in the lower case were typed by the user, while those in the upper case were responded by the system. We see that in the first query, we have $(around y 50) as a preference condition, where (around y 50) is a fuzzy formula. That is, we prefer persons whose ages are around 50. Thus, in the answer, the names are listed in the order whose ages are 51, 47, 55 and 60. However, in the second query, we prefer old persons, i.e., large ages. Thus, in the answer, the names are listed in the order whose ages are 60, 55, 51 and 47. In the third query, we have a non-fuzzy formula $(eq z programmer) as a preference condition. Then, in the answer, programmers are listed before non-programmers.

A LISTING OF A SESSION WITH DEDUCE

```
deduce ()
DEDUCE NIL
 *** PROCEED
(query (job  * name = x  * age = y)
      $(around y 50)
      (seniority  name = x  year-of-service = u)
      (greaterp  (plus y u)  75))
THERE ARE 4 ANSWERS.  DO YOU WANT TO PRINT YOUR ANSWERS?
yes
```

```
(ANSWER   (NAME AGE)     (LUCY 51)    (ALLEN 47)   (MIKE 55)   (TAYLOR 60))
 ***  PROCEED
(query (job  * name = x  * age = y)
      $(large y)
       (seniority  name = x  year-of-service = u)
       (greaterp (plus y u)  75))
THERE ARE 4 ANSWERS.  DO YOU WANT TO PRINT YOUR ANSWERS?
yes
(ANSWER  (NAME  AGE)   (TAYLOR 60)   (MIKE 55)   (LUCY 51)   (ALLEN 47))
 *** PROCEED
(query (job  * name = x  *age = y  * jobtitle = z)
      $(eq z programmer)
       (sensiority  name = x  year-of-service = u)
       (greaterp (plus y u) 75))
THERE ARE 4 ANSWERS.  DO YOU WANT TO PRINT YOUR ANSWERS?
yes
(ANSWER   (NAME AGE JOBTITLE)   (ALLEN 47 PROGRAMMER)
(LUCY 51 MATHEMATICIAN)   (TAYLOR 60 MATHEMATICIAN)   (MIKE 55 ENGI-
    NEER))
 *** PROCEED
end
VALUE =   *** GOOD BYE |
```

IV.   REPRESENTATIONS OF AXIOMS

In DEDUCE, we define new relations through axioms. We shall call a relation that is explicitly stored in a computer a *base relation,* and call a relation defined by axioms a *view.* We shall use axioms which have the following form

$$A_1 \ \& \ \ldots \ \& \ A_n \rightarrow B_1 \ \& \ \ldots \ \& \ B_m \ ,$$

where each of $A_1 , \ldots, A_n$ is either an atomic formula or the negation of an atomic formula, and $B_1 , \ldots, B_m$ are atomic formulas. In order to handle many views in a simple fashion, we allow n in the axiom to be a fixed integer or a variable integer. In addition, we also allow a predicate or a function to take a variable number of arguments. The advantages of these extention of the first-order logic can be illustrated in the following examples, where x, y and the subscript x, y are declared as variables.

Example A.

Consider the following base relation

Table 5

FATHER	NAME 1	NAME 2
	a	b
	a	c
	b	d
	b	e
	e	f
	e	g

where FATHER(x,y) denotes that x is the father of y. For simplicity, let us assume the order of arguments in the relation is fixed, and any atomic formula that uses the relation contains all the attributes of the relation. Therefore, instead of writing FATHER (NAME1=x, NAME2=y), we simply write FATHER(x,y).

To insert every row of Table 5 into the data base, we use the following six DEDUCE statements:

(1)   (INSERT   (father a b))
(2)   (INSERT   (father a c))
(3)   (INSERT   (father b d))
(4)   (INSERT   (father b e))
(5)   (INSERT   (father e f))
(6)   (INSERT   (father e g))

To define a view ANCESTOR1(x,y) which denotes that x is an ancestor of y, we use the following DEDUCE axiom:

(7)   (AXIOM a1 (father x1 x2) ...
                (father xn-1 xn)
                imply
                (ancestor1 x1 xn)).

Note that (7) is the DEDUCE representation of the axiom given in Section 1, where a1 is a name for the axiom. A user can now make queries against this view and the base relation. For example, to find all descendents of a, the user can enter the query

(8)   (QUERY (ancestor1 a *x)).

When the system sees this query, it recognizes that ANCESTOR1 is a view. Therefore it unifies (ancestor1 a *x) in the QUERY with (ancestor1 x1 xn) in the AXIOM, and generates the query

(QUERY (father a x2) ... (father xn-1 *x)).

To interpret this query, it first let n be 2,3,4..., and generates the following sequence of queries

(QUERY (father a *x))
(QUERY (father a x2)   (father x2 *x))
(QUERY (father a x2)   (father x2 x3)   (father x3 *x))

.
.
.

Each of the above queries can then be evaluated by a data base management system such as SEQUEL [3]. Of course, the system *should not* evaluate the above sequence of queries *independently*. It should recognize that the result obtained from evaluating the

second query, and so on. Also, it should be able to decide when
to terminate the evaluation of queries. For the above sequence of
queries, the system can terminate the evaluation when it encounters
a query in the sequence which has no answers.

On the other hand, to find all the ancestors of f, the user
can enter the query

(9)   (QUERY (ancestor1 *x f)).

The evaluation of this query is the same as the one given
above.

Example B.

Consider the following table

Table 6

FATHER	NAME1	NAME2	DEGREE OF RELATIONSHIP
	a	b	1
	a	c	2
	b	d	2
	b	e	2
	e	f	3
	e	g	1

where the degree of relationship is a number that indicates how
good the relationship between a father and a child is. Now, we
want to define a special view ANCESTOR2 which has consistently the
same degree of relationship for all persons related by ANCESTOR2.
That is, ANCESTOR2 is defined by the following axiom

(AXIOM a2   (father x1 x2 y) ...
            (father xn-1 xn y)
             imply
            (ancestor2 x1 xn)),

where a2 is a name for the axiom. Similar to the queries in Example A, we can have the following queries

(QUERY (ancestor2 a *x)) and
(QUERY (ancestor2 *x f)).

Example c

In this example, we shall define a view ANCESTOR3. The definition
of ANCESTOR3 is the same as the one of ANCESTOR2, except the dis-
persion among all degrees of relationship for all persons related
by ANCESTOR3 is less than a certain number, say 1.5. The disper-
sion may be defined as a standard deviation. The axiom for ANCES-
TOR3 is given as

123

```
(AXIOM a3 (father x1 x2 y1) ...
          (father xn-1 xn yn-1)
          (lessp (disperse y1 ... yn-1) 1.5)
           imply
          (ancestor3 x1 xn)).
```
If we want to find all ancestors who have more than 4 descendents,
we could write a query as
```
(QUERY
(father   *name1=x)
   (SUBQUERY
   (ancestor3 x #y))
(greaterp (count' y) 4)).
```
To evaluate this query, the SUBQUERY has to be evaluated by using
the axiom for ANCESTOR3 in the way as it was discussed in Example A.
We note that it will be very clumsy to express AXIOM a3 in MICRO-
PLANNER. This is because it is impossible to recursively express
the function (disperse y1 ... yn-1) in terms of a function of (disperse y1 ... yn-2) and yn-1. Thus, it is impossible to recursively
define ANCESTOR3. Therefore, to compute (disperse y1 ... yn-1),
we need that all y1,...,yn-1 appear in the same axiom. This is
exactly why DEDUCE allows an indefinite number of atomic formulas
in an axiom. We believe this approach is natural and straightforward.

Example D.

In an axiom, we also allow preference conditions. For example, we
may define ANCESTOR4 as

```
(AXIOM a4 (father x1 x2 y1) ...
          (father xn-1 xn yn-1)
        $(almost-same y1 ... yn-1)
           imply
          (ancestor4 x1 xn)).
```

Here, $(almost-same y1 ... yn-1) is a preference condition,
where ALMOST-SAME is a fuzzy predicate. It indicates that the ancestor relation which has *more or less uniform* degrees of relationship among all persons related by ANCESTOR4 is preferred over the
others. The preference condition can serve for several purposes.
First, when there are many instances of (ancestor4 x1 xn) that can
be derived by using AXIOM a4, these instances will be sorted according to their degrees of preference. Second, if we want to
choose an instance of (ancestor4 x1 xn), we will choose the one
with a high degree of preference over others. Therefore, this
preference condition acts like a heuristic function in tree-search-
ing. However, since we allow different preference conditions for
different axioms, our approach is quite flexible. This will be
discussed in more detail in Section V.

Example E.

Now, we consider a well-known example in robot-planning. The problem is depicted in Fig. 1.

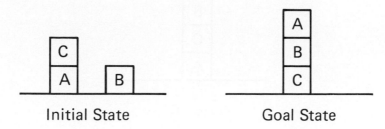

Initial State   Goal State

Figure 1.

    There are three blocks A, B, C, and a table. In the initial state, C is on A and B is on the table. The goal is to achieve a new configuration, where A is on B and B is on C. This example has been considered by many persons [10,15,16,18,19,26]. They all used the first-order representation. For example, one may use the predicate ON(x,y) which indicates that x is on y, and represent the goal state as a conjunction of two atomic formulas, i.e., ON (A,B) & ON(B,C). However, this representation leads to many kinds of problems such as the problems of anomalous situation, presence of bugs, producing non-optimal solutions, etc. To see this, let us try how some of their systems may do for this example. Suppose a system tried to achieve the subgoal ON(A,B) first. This can be done by putting C on the table and putting A on B, thus obtaining a state shown in Fig. 2.

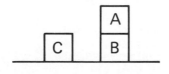

Figure 2.

    Now, to achieve the second subgoal ON(B,C), block A will have to be put away, thus undoing the subgoal ON(A,B) it achieved first. On the other hand, suppose the system tried to achieve the subgoal ON(B,C) first. This can be done by putting B on C in the initial state, thus obtaining a state shown in Fig. 3. But now when the system tries to achieve the subgoal ON(A,B), it finds it is even further from its goal than it was in the initial state.

    This problem is also familiar in a resolution system [5]. In the resolution system, we usually need a state variable. Suppose we use the predicate ON(x,y,s) to denote that x is on y in state s. Then, the goal can be represented as ON(A,B,s) & ON(B,C,s).

125

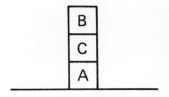

Figure 3.

Since the two subgoals ON(A,B,s) and ON(B,C,s) share the same variable s, they are dependent subgoals. That is, they *cannot* be proved *independently*. In resolution, there are splitting strategies [4,11,17] that try to prove subgoals independently, *provided* that any substitutions for shared variables must be made *consistently*. The methods used to handle conjunctive goals in some non-resolution systems are also similar to the splitting strategies.

In this paper, we shall try to avoid the above problem. We realize that the problem is caused by trying to solve conjunctive goals, and this is unavoidable if we restrict ourselves to the first-order logic representation. Therefore, we shall relax this restriction and allow us to use predicates which can have indefinite numbers of arguments. We shall see that our approach simplifies the representation tremendously, and in the same time avoids the problem discussed above.

We use a predicate STACK which can have any number of arguments. The block problem is represented in DEDUCE as follows:

(1)   (INSERT   (stack b table))
(2)   (INSERT   (stack c a table))

(3)   (AXIOM al   (stack x1 ... xn)
                  (stack y1 ... ym)
                  (in-right-sequence x1 y1 ... ym)
               @ (puton x1 y1)
                 imply
               / (stack x1 ... xn)
               / (stack y1 ... ym)
                 (stack x2 ... xn)
                 (stack x1 y1 ... ym))

(4)   (AXIOM a2   (stack x1 ... xn)
                  (not (in-right-sequence x1 ... xn))
               @ (puton x1 table)
                 imply
               / (stack x1 ... xn)
                 (stack x1 table)
                 (stack x2 ... xn))

126

(5)   (QUERY (stack a b c table)).

There are two stacks in the initial state. Statements (1) and (2) are used to insert these two stacks into the data base. Statements (3) and (4) are used to represent the knowledge of solving the problem. In the axioms, IN-RIGHT-SEQUENCE is a defined LISP predicate that will be true if a sequence of blocks is conformed to the sequence of blocks desired in the goal. For example, since the sequence in the goal is a, b, c, table, the sequence c, a, table is not in right order. In the axioms, the formulas @(puton x1 y1) and @(puton x1 table) that are preceded by the symbol @ are *action* formulas. These are expressions that tell the system what actions to take when the antecedents of the axioms are true, or when the axioms are applied successfully. The expressions that preceded by the slash symbol / tell the system to delete them from the data base. Statement (5) is a goal statement. The goal can be solved by a forward method. That is, it starts from the initial state. Since the two stacks in the initial state are not in right order, only axiom a2 can be applied. To match (stack c a table) with (stack x1 ... xn) in AXIOM a2, n is first set to 3 because the former has 3 arguments. Then, (4) becomes

(6)   (AXIOM a2   (stack x1 x2 x3)
                  (not (in-right-sequence x1 x2 x3))
               @(puton x1 table)
                imply
               /(stack x1 x2 x3)
                (stack x1 table)
                (stack x2 x3)).

We note that (6) is a first-order expression. Therefore, applying (6) to (stack c a table), we obtain a state shown in Fig. 4.

Figure 4.

Now, applying AXIOM a1 twice to the state of Fig. 4 by putting B on C, then A on B, we can successfully achieve the goal. We think that the above approach is more natural and straightforward than the first-order approach. In addition, we do not have the problem of conjunctive goals. Our approach exactly did what a person might do when he tries to solve this simple block problem.

V.   REPRESENTATIONS OF HEURISTICS

When evaluating a query or applying an axiom, the basic problem is to find values from a data base to satisfy a set of condi-

tions, where the conditions are represented by formulas. Assume
that {C1 ,..., Cn} is the set of conditions, and C1 ,..., Cn are
evaluated sequentially, then we basically have a decision tree
shown in Fig. 5.

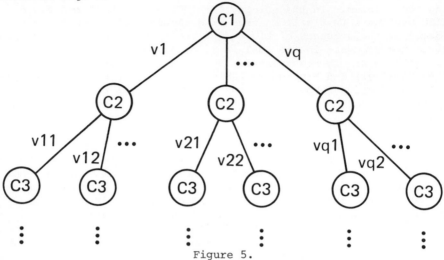

Figure 5.

That is, C1 is evaluated first, and, say, there are q values
v1,...,vq for variables in C1 that satisfy C1. Then, for each i,
vi is substituted into C2 ,..., Cn, and C2 is evaluated. Assume
there are values vi1, vi2, ... that satisfy C2. Again, each vij
is substituted into C3 ,..., Cn, and so on. Eventually, a value
or a set of values that satisfies all C1,...,Cn can be found. However, the above tree can be very large. Sometimes, it may pay to
sort the values at every node. This is especially true when we
are interested in only *one* value, instead of *all* values, that satisfies C1,...,Cn. To order values, we may insert a preference condition P, say, between Ci and Ci+1, and have the following sequence,
C1,...,Ci,$P,Ci+1,...,Cn. Then, we find all values that satisfy
C1,...,Ci, and order these values by the preference condition P.
After the values are sorted, the first value is chosen. This value is substituted into Ci+1,...,Cn which in turn is then evaluated.
In general, we can have more than one preference condition as follows:

    C1, $P1, C2, $P2, ... , Cn-1, $Pn-1, Cn,

where P1,...,Pn-1 are preference conditions some of which may be
empty. This sequence of conditions are evaluated as follows:
First, sort all values that satisfy C1 by P1. The first value is
chosen and substituted into C2, $P2, ... , Cn. Sort all values
that satisfy C2 by P2, and so on. Usually, the preference conditions are provided by a user. Of course, it would be nice if the
system could learn to find good preference conditions for a given
data base.

We now give an example to illustrate how heuristics can be used. Consider the following table:

Table 7

FATHER	NAME1	AGE1	NAME2	AGE2
	a	60	c	38
	a	60	d	42
	a	60	e	46
	c	38	h	7
	c	38	i	5
	b	70	f	45
	b	70	g	48
	f	45	j	20
	f	45	k	24
	k	24	m	1
	k	24	n	2

where FATHER(n1, a1, n2, a2) indicates that n1 whose age is a1 is the father of n2 whose age is a2. Suppose we define ANCESTOR by the following axiom:

```
(AXIOM a1 (father  name1=x1   name2=x2) ...
          (father  name1=xn-1  name2=xn)
          imply
          (ancestor x1 xn)).
```

Now, we want to find a person who has more than 5 descendents. One heuristic is this: The older the person is, the more descendents he might have. Therefore, we might incorporate this heuristic into the following query:

```
(QUERY
(father  *name1=x  age1=y)
$(large y)
      (SUBQUERY
      (ancestor x  #z))
(greaterp (count' z) 5)).
```

When the above query is evaluated, x will be first assigned to b, instead of a, thus the system can speed up the evaluation.

VI.   RELATED TOPICS: INFERENCIAL COMPLETENESS AND AI
      LANGUAGES

In this section, we shall first prove a theorem in resolution systems [5], and then discuss some implications of the theorem. In a resolution system, a clause is called a *Horn clause* iff it has at most one positive literal. Kuehner [12] and Henschen and Wos[11]

independently prove a theorem which says that there is a unit refutation from an unsatisfiable set of Horn clauses. In this section, we shall prove a stronger theorem.

Let an ordered Horn clause be a Horn clause where any negative
literals in the clause are put before (if any) a positive literal.
A *first-literal unit resolution* is a resolution in which a resolvent is obtained by resolving a positive unit clause upon the *first
literal* of an ordered Horn clause. A *first-literal unit deduction*
is a deduction in which every resolution is a first-literal unit
resolution. A *first-literal unit refutation* is a first-literal
unit deduction of the empty clause. First, we prove the following
Lemma.

Lemma 1. There is a first-literal unit refutation from an unsatisfiable set S of ordered Horn ground clauses.

Proof. Lemma 1 is proved by induction. Let A be the set of all
atomic formulas occurring in S. If A consists of a single element,
say Q, then among the elements of S, there exist unit clauses Q
and $\sim$Q. Clearly, the resolvent of Q and $\sim$Q is the empty clause.
This deduction is a first-literal unit refutation. Hence, Lemma 1
holds for this case. Assume Lemma 1 holds when A consists of i
elements, $1 \leqslant i \leqslant n$. To complete the induction, we consider A
such that A consists of exactly n+1 elements. By the theorem of
Kuehner [12] and Henschen and Wos [11], there is a unit refutation
from S. Therefore, there must be a unit positive clause L in S.
Let S' be that set obtained from S by deleting those clauses containing L and by deleting $\sim$L from the remaining clauses. Clearly,
S' is an unsatisfiable set of ordered Horn clauses. But S' contains n or fewer than n atoms. By the induction hypothesis, there
is a first-literal unit refutation D' from S'. From D', we can
obtain a first-literal unit refutation from S by modifying each
node of D' as follows: For each initial node N1 of D', if the
clause attached to N1 is obtained from an ordered Horn clause C in
S by deleting $\sim$L, add $\sim$L, in its proper place, back to C. If $\sim$L
is the first literal of C, replace node N1 by the first-literal
unit resolution of C and L. Otherwise, node N1 is left unchanged.
Then, for each non-initial node N2 of D', if its immediate predecessor nodes have been modified or unmodified in this way, obtain
the resolvent R attached to node N2. If R contains $\sim$L, and $\sim$L
happens to be the first literal of R, replace node N2 by the first-
literal unit resolution of R and L. In this fashion, eventually
we shall obtain a final deduction which is a first-literal unit
refutation from S. This completes the proof of Lemma 1.

Now, using Herbrand's theorem, Lemma 1 and the lifting lemma
[5], we can easily obtain the following theorem:

Theorem 1. There is a first-literal unit refutation from an unsatisfiable set S of ordered Horn clauses.

We note that every ordered Horn clause is either of the following three forms:

(i)   B
(ii) $\sim$A1 v ... v $\sim$An v B
(iii) $\sim$A1 v ... v $\sim$An,

Where A1, ... , An and B are atomic formulas. Cases (i), (ii) and
(iii) are equivalent to the following cases (i)', (ii)' and (iii)',
respectively:

(i)'   B
(ii)'   A1 & ... & An $\rightarrow$ B
(iii)' $\sim$(A1 & ... & An).

In a relational data base, case (i)' corresponds to facts (e.g.,
rows of a table,) case (ii)' to axioms, and case (iii)' to the
negation of conjunctive goals. Therefore, the implication of Theorem 1 is this: In AI languages [1], if axioms are in the form of
(ii)', facts are positive, and goals are represented by a conjunction of atomic formulas, then the first-literal method that are
used in most AI languages by sequentially evaluating A1,...,An in
an axiom is complete. However, for other cases, the first-literal
method does not guarantee to find a proof. For example, consider
the set,

$$S = \{\sim A \text{ v } B, A \text{ v} \sim C, \sim B, C\}.$$

S is a set of Horn clauses. However, the clause A v$\sim$C is not an
ordered Horn clause. Therefore, there is no first-literal unit
refutation from S. If we represent the clauses in S as

(1)   C
(2)   A $\rightarrow$ B
(3) $\sim$A $\rightarrow \sim$C
(4)   B,

then we cannot prove that (4) is a consequence of (1), (2) and (3)
by using any AI language such as MICRO-PLANNER, because (3) is not
in a correct form. However, if we represent the clauses in S as

(1)'   C
(2)'   A $\rightarrow$ B
(3)'   C $\rightarrow$ A
(4)'   B,

then we can use, say, MICRO-PLANNER to prove that B is a consequence of (1)', (2)' and (3)'. Therefore, to guarantee MICRO-
PLANNER can obtain a proof, no negative goals are allowed. However, in DEDUCE, we do not have this restriction because DEDUCE
does not use the first-literal method. In fact, in DEDUCE, a query
that may contain both base relations and views is evaluated in two
steps: First, use axioms to transform the query into a query containing only base relations. Second, evaluate the transformed
query by using a data base system such as SEQUEL [3].

ACKNOWLEDGMENTS

I wish to thank Dr. E. F. Codd of IBM Research Laboratory and

Professor L. A. Zadeh of University of California, Berkeley for
their unforgettable encouragements. I am particularly indebted to
Drs. E. F. Codd; W. F. King, III; J. M. Cadiou; S. Zilles of IBM
Research Laboratory, and Dr. D. Ribbens for their valuable critical discussion, especially during the development of the query
representation part of DEDUCE.

REFERENCES

1. Bobrow, D. G., and Raphael, B., 'New programming languages
   for artificial intelligence research', Computing Surveys,
   Vol. 6, No. 3, September 1974, pp. 153-174.
2. Boyce, R. F., Chamberlin, D. D., King, W. F., III, and Hammer,
   M. M., 'Specifying queries as relational expressions: SQUARE',
   Comm. of the ACM, 18(11):621-628, November 1975.
3. Chamberlin, D. D., and Boyce, R. F., 'SEQUEL: A structured
   English query language', Proc. of 1974 ACM-SIGFIDET Workshop
   on Data Description, Access, and Control, ACM, New York, 1974.
4. Chang, C. L., 'The decomposition principle for theorem proving systems,' Proc. the Tenth Annual Allerton Conference,
   University of Illinois, Urbana, Ill., Oct. 4-6, 1972.
5. Chang, C. L., and Lee, R. C. T., Symbolic Logic and Mechanical
   Theorem Proving, Academic Press, 1973.
6. Codd, E. F., 'A relational model for large shared data banks',
   Comm. of the ACM, 13(6):377-387, June 1970.
7. Codd, E. F., 'Further normalization of the data base relational model,' In Data Base Systems, Courant Computer Science Sym-
   posia Series, Vol. 6, pp.33, Prentice-Hall, 1971.
8. Codd, E. F., 'A data base sublanguage founded on the relational calculus,' Proc. of 1971 ACM-SIGFIDET Workshop on Data Description, Access, and Control, ACM, New York, 1971.
9. Codd, E. F., 'Recent investigations in relational data base
   systems', Information Processing 74, North-Holland Publishing
   Co., 1974, pp.1017-1021.
10. Fikes, R. E., and Nilsson, N. J., 'STRIPS: A new approach to
    the application of theorem proving to problem solving,' Arti-
    ficial Intelligence, Vol. 2, pp. 189-208 (1971).
11. Henschen, L. and Wos, L., 'Unit refutation and Horn sets',
    J. ACM, 21(4):590-605, October 1974.
12. Kuehner, D., 'Some special purpose resolution systems,' Ma-
    chine Intelligence, Vol. 7, B. Meltzer and D. Michie, Eds.,
    American Elsevier, New York, 1972, pp. 117-128.
13. Lee, R. C. T., 'Fuzzy logic and the resolution principle',
    J. ACM, vol. 19, pp. 109-119,1972.
14. Minker, J., 'Performing inferences over relational data bases',
    Proc. of 1975 ACM-SIGMOD International Conference on Manage-
    ment of Data, pp.79-91, 1975.
15. Sacerdoti, E. D., 'Planning in a hierarchy of abstraction
    spaces', Artificial Intelligence, Vol. 5, No. 2, pp. 115-
    135 (1974).

16. Sacerdoti, E. D., 'The nonlinear nature of plans', Proc. of the 4th International Joint Conference on Artificial Intelligence, 1975.
17. Slagle, J. R., and Koniver, D., 'Finding resolution proofs and using deuplcate goals in AND/OR trees', Information Science, Vol. 4, No. 4, pp.315-342, 1971.
18. Sussman, G. J., 'A computational model of skill acquisition', Technical Note AI TR-297, Artificial Intelligence Laboratory, MIT, Cambridge, Mass, August 1973.
19. Tate, A., 'INTERPLAN: A plan generation system which can deal with interactions between goals', Memorandum MIP-R-109, Machine Intelligence Research Unit, University of Edinburgh, Dec. 1974.
20. Warren, D. H. D., 'WARPLAN: A system for generating plans', Memorandum No. 76, Department of Computational Logic, University of Edinburgh, June 1974.
21. Zadeh, L. A., 'Fuzzy sets', Information & Control, Vol. 8, pp.338-353, 1965.
22. Zadeh, L. A., 'Fuzzy logic and approximate reasoning', Memo. No. ERL-M479, Electronics Research Laboratory, Univ. of Calif., Berkeley, November 1974.
23. Zloof, M. M., 'QUERY BY EXAMPLE', Proc. National Computer Conference, Anaheim, Calif., May 1975.

APPENDIX. DEDUCE SYNTAX

```
 1. <string>::=  char
              |  char<string>
 2. <constant>::=<string>
 3. <variable>::=<string>
 4. <relation>::=<string>
 5. <attribute>::=<string>
 6. <predicate>::=<string>
 7. <function>::= <string>
 8. <tuple1>::=<constant>
              |<variable>
              |<tuple1>,...,<tuple1>
              | (<function>,<tuple1>)
              |<tuple1>, <tuple1>
 9. <term>::=<constant>
            |<variable>
            |(<function>,<tuple1>)
10. <tuple2>::=<attribute>=<term>
             | *<attribute> <term>
             | *<attribute>
             | <tuple2>,<tuple2>
11. <atom>::= (<predicate>,<tuple1>)
            | (<relation>,<tuple2>)
12. <conjunction>::=<atom>
                  | (not <atom>)
```

```
                       | <atom>,...,<atom>
                       | $<atom>
                       | @<atom>
                       | /<atom>
                       | <conjunction>,<conjunction>
13.  <insert>::  ( insert<atom>)
14.  <delete>::= (delete<conjunction>)
15.  <update>::= (update<conjunction>/<conjunction>)
16.  <query>::= (query<conjunction>)
17.  <name>::= <string>
18.  <axiom>::= (axiom<name><conjunction>imply<conjunction>)
```

ON STATISTICAL AND STRUCTURAL
FEATURE EXTRACTION*

C. H. Chen
Department of Electrical Engineering
Southeastern Massachusetts University
North Dartmouth, MA. 02747

I. INTRODUCTION

The problem of extracting effective features has played a major role in pattern recognition studies. Most effort, however, has been limited to the selection of statistical or mathematical features. The statistical methods "extract" features by evaluating a number of features according to some performance measures, such as the error probability, information function, and distance criteria (see e.g. [1]). Although features so chosen may not have physical meaning, they are usually effective and computable. Examples of these features are the orthogonal transforms of vector measurements. Many unresolved problems remain in statistical feature extraction, such as the finite sample size effect, the learning sample selection, etc. The main drawback with the statistical feature extraction is that it is difficult to take contextual dependence into consideration. In many patterns such as the imagery data or the speech waveform, there is a close relationship among various parts or segments of a pattern. Such relationship representing the structural properties must be taken into account to achieve the best recognition performance. It also represents the a priori knowledge which is often difficult to be incorporated in the statistical framework. On the other hand, there has not been any general mathematical approach for structural feature extraction. Finding a small but effective set of primitives or features still requires much human ingenuity. The task of searching for better features appears to be endless. To equip the machine (computer) with some intelligent capability to automatically search for the best feature set within reasonable computational complexity remains now to be a challenging problem as it was twenty years ago. The past development has clearly indicated the limitation of a single approach whether it is statistical or structural. Therefore, the idea of a mixed model which uses both statistical and structural information should be explored. Sections II and III discuss the problems associated with the statistical and structural feature extraction respectively. Section IV shows some experimental results on feature extraction with real data. Section V examines the mixed model.

*Research supported by Grant AFOSR 71-2119 and Grant AFOSR 76-2951. Lt. Colonel George W. McKemie is the project monitor.

II. STATISTICAL FEATURE EXTRACTION

The number of initial feature measurements available is usually large. For example, a vector measurement based on 1024 sampled points of a biomedical waveform requires an excessive amount of computation when pattern classification is performed. By considering the patterns as random in nature, a small set of features with good average performance may be chosen from the available feature set. In statistical framework, features can be evaluated and selected by computing the average quantities such as the probability of error, mutual information, and divergence, etc. In addition to providing low error probability, desirable features should also lead to a simple classifier. The two requirements usually are not met simultaneously.

The statistical description information on a pattern is entirely provided by the probability density or distribution which is very much dependent on the samples available. The statistical averages can be accurate and reliable when the number of samples is large. However, the available number of learning samples is very much limited in most applications. The required number of features for a specified performance depends on the number of samples available. The evaluation of discriminating capability provided by a given feature may not be accurate with a small number of samples. As a result best features may not be selected. The finite sample size effects must be taken into account in feature extraction and classification. The finite sample size is a fundamental problem and limitation in statistical pattern recognition [2]. Examples of the finite sample size effect on the distance measure computation are given in Appendix. Another practical consideration with the learning sample is that the quality of the learning samples is not uniform. Sample estimate of the error probability or distance and information measures may vary considerably with different set of learning samples. Thus it may be necessary to select learning samples which are most representative of the pattern classes considered.

Among the statistical feature extraction techniques, multidimensional rotations or the orthogonal transforms are computationally most efficient except the Karhunen-Loeve transform. The resulting number of features can still be large and further reduction in the number of features may be necessary. The theoretical performance differences among various transforms do not always materialize in practice. For example, the simplicity in obtaining the Fourier transform may outweigh the slight performance advantage with the Karhunen-Loeve transform. Of course the periodicity implied by the Fourier analysis may not be valid in one-dimensional (waveform) or two-dimensional (image) patterns. The transforms derived from Fourier such as the cepstrum still have unknown performance characteristic as a feature set. The incorporation of nonlinear signal processing methods in feature extraction, however, provides an excellent potential for the most effective statistical feature extraction particularly when the noise effect cannot be

overlooked. In fact, the statistical methods are more useful than
the structural approach in the presence of noise.

In statistical feature extraction, attempt is made to *decor-
relate* the features so that the resulting features provide non-
overlapping discriminating information and to *compress* features so
that most discriminating information is contained in a small set
of resulting features. Most decision functions are designed for
independent samples and independent features. Vector samples corresponding to various parts of an imagery pattern or various segments of a speech waveform are highly correlated. It is difficult
to take into account such correlation or dependence in deriving
the optimal decision procedure except for the special cases such
as the Markov dependence. Even if all statistical dependence could
be considered, the local shapes and other structural information
are still missing in statistical framework. Also, the problem of
how to divide an image into parts or a speech signal into segments
is a difficult one if statistical approach is used. Thus, the limitation of statistical feature extraction is quite evident here.

III. STRUCTURAL FEATURE EXTRACTION

It is now apparent to researchers in pattern recognition and
artificial intelligence that knowledge representation is the key
to future progress in both areas. Understanding the structure of
patterns is essential for knowledge representation. Primitives
which can be put together to describe pattern structure should be
derived for classification. Primitives alone may not be distinguished from the features discussed earlier. In fact, "the feature extraction and selection problem in the decision-theoretic
approach and the primitive extraction and selection problem in syntactic approach are similar in nature except that the primitives
in the syntactic approach represent subpatterns and, on the other
hand, the features in the decision-theoretic approach may be any
set of numerical measurements taken from the patterns" [3]. However the primitives are usually small in number than the numerical
measurements. Since a structural pattern is described by primitives and multi-level relations, both primitives and a lowest level
of relations (or constraints) among primitives are needed in structural feature extraction.

Careful selection of primitives requires good understanding
of the pattern such as the geometrical, physical, psychological or
physiological factors involved. Examples of structural features
are: (1) primitives with emphasis on boundaries or skeletons, (2)
stroke sequences for handwriting, (3) phonemes and syllables in
speech, (4) characters and mathematical symbols in two-dimensional
mathematical expressions, and (5) peaks, zero-crossings, inflection points, etc. in a biomedical waveform. Obviously the structural information may be more readily available for some patterns
than the others. For examples, the bubble chamber pictures,

chromosome patterns, fingerprints, Chinese characters, Italian spoken words, chemical diagrams, etc. clearly have structures that syntactic recognition methods are particularly suitable. However, the structures of seismic waveform, natural scenes, etc. are much less evident. In general it is more difficult to select a small set of primitives which truly constitute the basic structure of a pattern than the numerical measurements such as the sampled points in waveforms and pictures for statistical approach. Distortions and noises which are statistical in nature also complicate the structural analysis and even make the structural features ineffective.

IV. EXPERIMENTAL RESULTS

In this section, experimental results on feature extraction with teleseismic data and aerial reconnaissance imagery are presented.

For the seismic study, comparative evaluation has been made on various features for discrimination between the nuclear explosion and the natural earthquake. The seismic data sets were provided by Colonel R. B. Ives [4]. There are equal numbers of explosion and earthquake events in each data set. Figure 1 shows a typical plot of seismic records. If the epicenter and depth of the seismic event can be determined accurately, feature extraction techniques may not be needed. Since this is not the case, features with some physical significance such as the energy ratio, spectral ratio, third moment of frequency and Alpha-C spectral ratio estimator, and strictly mathematical features such as the Markel coefficient, autocovariance, entropy, and cepstrum have been considered [5,6] for seismic discrimination. The best recent results show an 89.32% correct recognition by using 16 autocovariance features, 7 best learning samples from each class, and the nearest-neighbor decision rule. An increase in the number of features and learning samples does not improve the performance. Performance may degrade with the addition of lesser quality learning samples. The autocovariance features perform better than all other features mentioned above and the orthogonally transformed features. The bodywave magnitude which has a good physical meaning is an insignificant feature. Although no general conclusion can be made from the experimental study, mathematical features have been shown to be very effective. Performance improvement is much needed however. The structure of the seismic wave should be exploited. This includes the determination of the onset of the waveform; the segmentation of the wave and the structural/statistical relations among the segments; the detection and separation of component waves and the relation among the components; etc.

For the imagery recognition study, much effort has been made to locate the man-made volatile object from the background of irrelevant details [7]. Figure 2 shows a typical image studied along with some processing results. Comparative evaluation of tex-

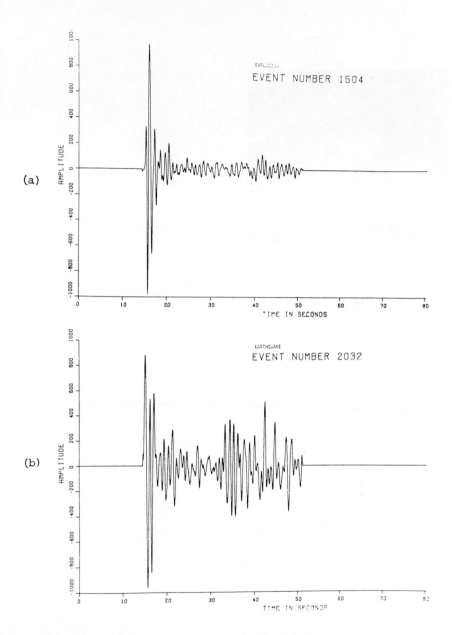

Fig. 1. Typical teleseismic waveforms: (a) explosion and (b) earthquake. The sampling rate is 20 samples per second.

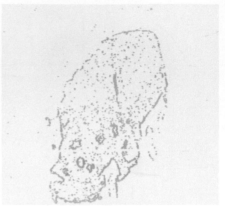

Fig. 2a   The image studied.

Fig. 2b   The gradient picture
of the object (truck)
in Fig. 2a.

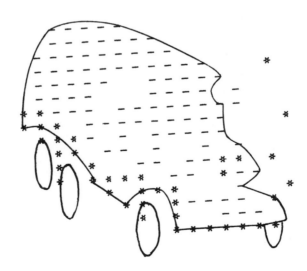

Fig. 2c   Object extraction by using textural measure . The
textural feature of a subimage is displayed as
*, -, or blank. A sketch of boundary is also shown.

tural features and gradient features was made [8] by using the subpictures of the image. The following textural measure has been
proven to be most effective,

$$\sum_i \sum_j (|i - j|)^3 \log (n_{ij} + 1)$$

where each summation is taken over 8 requantized gray levels from
the original 256 levels, and n_{ij} is the number of joint occurrence
of the ith and jth levels at two adjacent picture elements. The
relation among subpictures is useful to determine the region of
subpictures corresponding to the object of interest (Fig. 2C).
Again no general conclusion about the feature extraction should be
made. The textural measure which is a statistical feature, however, is very useful for the images studied where the pattern
structure is not evident other than the object boundary itself.

V.   THE STATISTICAL-STRUCTURAL MIXED MODEL FOR FEATURE
     EXTRACTION

     The discussion in the previous sections has clearly pointed
out the fact that structural and statistical features are each
more suitable for certain class of patterns. So far most effort
made has been to use one kind of feature extraction exclusively.
In syntactic approach we need grammars or formal language theory,
while in decision-theoretic approach we need mathematical statistics. For patterns which are rich in structure with little or no
noise, structural feature extraction should be used. For noisy
patterns with almost no structure present, statistical feature extraction is the clear choice. However, most patterns are in between these two extremes. Thus techniques based on a combination
of both statistical and structural approaches should be used. A
formalism which attempts to combine the linguistic and statistical
aspects of pattern analysis and recognition was proposed in [9].
Attempt was also made in [10] to show that hybrid linguistic-sta-
tistical techniques are more relevant for practical problem than
the pure statistical and linguistic models.
     The question now is how does the mixed model work. Among the
statistical, heuristic programming, and linguistic approaches, the
pattern recognition system as a whole and the feature extraction
in particular should have much *flexibility* to apply whichever approach or approaches that can best solve the problem or subproblem
at hand. Several examples of the mixed model are as follows. The
primitives in structural approach can be probabilistic to take into account the distortions. Both local textural (statistical) features and global structural features can be used in image recognition. Structural relation may be used as a guide in segmenting
the pattern so that mathematical features derived from each segment can be more effective. Experimental results reported in the
previous section indeed suggest that this is a direction for better
feature extraction. The basic idea being emphasized here is that

full advantage of each approach should be taken at each stage of problem solving. A possible disadvantage with the mixed model is that it is pattern dependent. Furthermore the choice of which approach to take may not be unique and could be difficult. Unless such choice is provided, the machine must learn from experience in making such choice. However, in view of the limited capability with purely statistical or structural approach it is worthwhile to equip the machine with more intelligence or flexibility by using the mixed model in feature extraction.

REFERENCES

(Note: Items 11 to 16 are additional references not quoted in the text.)

1. Chen, C. H., *Statistical Pattern Recognition,* Hayden Book Co., Rochelle Park, N.J., 1973.
2. Chen, C. H., "Statistical pattern recognition, review and outlook", Technical Report No. EE-75-4, SMU, N. Dartmouth, Mass., June 1975.
3. Fu, K. S., *Syntactic Methods in Pattern Recognition,* Academic Press, Inc., New York, 2nd edition, 1976.
4. Ives, R. B., "Feature and decision function selection for the detection of nuclear detonations from seismic signatures", presented at the Joint Workshop on Pattern Recognition and Artificial Intelligence, Hyannis, Mass. June 1-3, 1976.
5. Chen, C. H., "Feature extraction and computational complexity in seismological pattern recognition", Proc. of the Second International Joint Conference on Pattern Recognition, August, 1974. IEEE Catalog Number 74CHO 885-4C.
6. Chen, C. H. and I. C. Lin, "Pattern analysis and classification with the new ACDA seismic signature data base", Technical Report No. EE-75-7, SMU, N. Dartmouth, Mass., August 1975.
7. Chen, C. H., "Theory and applications of imagery pattern recognition", Proceedings of the Fourth International Congress for Stereology, September 1975, National Bureau of Standards Special Publication 431, January 1976.
8. Chen, C. H. and P. C. Chen, "A comparative evaluation of texture measures", Technical Report No. EE-75-9, September 1975.
9. Grenander, U., "A unified approach to pattern analysis", Technical Report, Brown University, Center for Computer and Information Sciences, May 1969.
10. Kanal, L. and B. Chandrasekaran, "On linguistic, statistical and mixed models for pattern recognition" in *Frontiers of Pattern Recognition,* S. Watanabe, ed., Academic Press, Inc., New York, N. Y. 1972.
11. Levine, M. D., "Feature extraction: a survey", Proceedings of the IEEE, Vol. 57, No. 8, pp. 1391-1407, August 1969.
12. Macleod, I. D. G., "On finding structure in pictures", in

Picture Language Machines, S. Kaneff, ed., Academic Press, Inc., New York, New York, 1970.
13. Blesser, B., R. Shillman, T. Kuklinski, C. Cox, M. Eden and J. Ventura, "A theoretical approach for character recognition based on phenomenological attributes", International Journal of Man-Machine studies, Vol. 6, pp. 701-714, 1974.
14. Hanakata, K., "Feature selection and extraction for decision theoretical approach and structural approach", presented at the NATO Advanced Study Institute on Pattern Recognition Theory and Application, Bendor, France, September 1975.
15. Fu, K. S., ed., *Digital Pattern Recognition*, Springer-Verlag, New York, N. Y. 1976.
16. Blackwell, F. W., "Combining mathematical and structural pattern recognition", Proc. of the Second International Joint Conference on Pattern Recognition, August 1974. IEEE Catalog Number 74CHO 885-4C.

APPENDIX

The Finite Sample Size Effect on Distance Measure Computation

To examine the finite sample size effects, consider first the case of two univariate Gaussian densities with means m_1 and m_2 and the same variance σ^2. Let "^" denote the quantity evaluated by using the sample estimates. Then the difference in divergence between infinite sample and finite sample sizes is

$$J - \hat{J} = \frac{1}{\sigma^2} \left[(m_1 - m_2)^2 - (\hat{m}_1 - \hat{m}_2)^2 \right] \tag{A1}$$

where we have assumed that σ^2 is known in both cases. The expected value of the difference can be shown as

$$E(J - \hat{J}) = -\frac{1}{N_1} - \frac{1}{N_2} < 0 \tag{A2}$$

where N_1 and N_2 denote the numbers of samples for classes 1 and 2 respectively. It is also assumed that all samples are statistically independent. Equation (A2) indicates that the expected error is inversely proportional to the sample sizes. The negative error further indicates that the divergence evaluated by using finite number of samples can lead to an over optimistic estimate of the error probability.

As a second example, consider the above Gaussian case again with zero means instead and the variances σ_1^2 and σ_2^2 are estimated from samples in the finite sample case for which the divergence is

$$J = \frac{\hat{\sigma}_1^2}{2\hat{\sigma}_2^2} + \frac{\hat{\sigma}_2^2}{2\hat{\sigma}_1^2} - 1 \tag{A3}$$

The ratio $\omega = \hat{\sigma}_1^2 / \hat{\sigma}_2^2$ has the F-distribution, with (N_1, N_2) degree of freedom, given by

$$p(\omega) = \begin{cases} C\omega^{N_1/2-1} \dfrac{\sigma_2^{N_1} \sigma_2^{N_2}}{(N_2\sigma_1^2 + N_1\sigma_2^2)^{N/2}} & ; \quad \omega \geq 0 \\ \\ 0, \omega < 0 \end{cases} \tag{A4}$$

where $N = N_1 + N_2$, and

$$C = \frac{\Gamma(\frac{N}{2}) \, N_1^{N_1/2} N_2^{N_2/2}}{\Gamma(\frac{N_1}{2}) \Gamma(\frac{N_2}{2})}$$

The expected error due to the finite sample size is

$$E(J - \hat{J}) = J + 1 - \frac{1}{2} \int (\omega + \frac{1}{\omega}) p(\omega) d\omega$$

$$= \frac{1}{2} \frac{\sigma_1^2}{\sigma_2^2} (1 - \frac{N_2}{N_2-2}) + \frac{1}{2} \frac{\sigma_2^2}{\sigma_1^2} \left[1 - \frac{N_1(N_2 + 2)(N_2 + 4)}{(N_1 - 2)(N_1 - 4)(N_1 - 6)} \right];$$

$$N_1 > 2, \; N_2 > 2 \tag{A5}$$

which approaches zero as N_1, N_2 approach ∞. However, for small sample size the error is always negative when $N_1 \leq N_2 + 8$. Equations (A2) and (A5) indicate that the sample estimates of divergence are always biased. It may also be proved that the estimates are consistent.

Although the above discussion is based on very simple and special cases, it does indicate the ineffectiveness of the distance measures when the sample size is small. To obtain more useful results for recognition system design use, the above discussion must be extended to vector sample case as well as other measures and distributions.

ON THE RECOGNITION OF HIGHLY VARIABLE LINE DRAWINGS
THROUGH USE OF MAXIMUM LIKELIHOOD FUNCTIONS

David B. Cooper
Division of Engineering
Brown University
Providence, RI

ABSTRACT

We describe a formalism for the construction of probability
distributions for distorted line drawings. We model those pictures
as stochastic perturbations of straight line segments and quadratic
curves containing unknown parameters. These curves are quadratic
polynomials in x and y. Pattern recognition is then composite hypothesis testing which is realized through use of maximum likelihood functions. Recognition involves recursive linear regression
using apriori parameter distributions for fitting lines and quadratic curves to the data. Even though continuous parameter estimation is involved, the methodology is computationally attractive,
effective for data segmentation, and effective for sequential recognition.

I.   INTRODUCTION

A much used and effective approach to some types of line drawing picture recognition is the method of "analysis by synthesis"
where the pattern is sequentially approximated by a sequence of
templates from a set of fixed line and curve templates. Prior
structural knowledge of the patterns in the various classes can be
readily used here, and a variety of models, probabilistic and non-
proabilistic, have been developed for describing pattern generation. Among the former are probability distributions for the templates in a class, and, for more complex problems, the use of finite state Morkov chains or more generally probabilistic grammars
for the sequential generation of templates and hence pictures.
Recognition usually involves sequential template matching often
treated as search within a state space. With each new template
match, the system moves to a new state in the statespace. A certain amount is known about efficient state space search methods,
both forward and backward procedures. There is also some understanding of the relative merits of making hard decisions about individual template matches, thus incurring the necessity of a certain amount of backtracking, versus carrying along a number of
states with some measure for each of its likelihood of being correct.

There are cases, however, where patterns are highly variable and it becomes desirable to use finer template quantization and hence a very large set of templates in order to better approximate the patterns and hopefully achieve lower error recognition. This can result in an overwhelming computational burden on the recognizer, for even if the size of the set of straight line templates is manageable, good coverage of an interesting range of curves can result in a set of templates which is too large. Or an unduly large computational burden can be incurred if highly variable curves are represented as long sequences of primitive templates such as straight line segments from a small set of templates. *Algebraic structure* in the form of parameterized variable templates then becomes attractive, and has been used in an interesting way in [1] and other papers. However, questions such as the *optimal* global use of prior structural knowledge, the proper use of the same fitted templates in eliminating pattern classes as not likely represented in the data, the fitting of *nonlinear curves* to *highly variable* data with a reasonable amount of computation, computationally efficient refitting of variable templates in order to resegment the data--these are important questions which are as yet not completely treated in the published literature. An interesting approach to the use of prior information for the efficient global fitting of straight lines to boundaries in noisy pictures appears in [2], and the effective use of prior information in globally directing analysis and recognition for other types of pattern classes appears in [3], [4] and [7] and a number of other papers.

II. DESCRIPTION OF THE PROBLEM TREATED

In this paper, we treat the use in pattern recognition of parameterized *arbitrary* straight lines and quadratic curves and partially answer some of the questions posed. A probabilistic framework is used. Data is modeled as having been generated by first generating an underlying pattern of straight lines and quadratic curves. A data point is then treated as a Gaussian perturbation of a point on one of these arcs. For the moment, the perturbation can be considered to be taken perpendicular to the arc and only one data point generated for a point on the underlying arc. This results in a model for thin highly-variable straight lines or quadratic curves; an arc can appear as a scatter of points as in figures 1 and 2. We show at the end of the paper that the methodology will handle thick lines or, with modification, some noise.

Since a line can be specified by 4 parameters and a quadratic curve by 7 parameters, an underlying line-curve pattern can be specified by a parameter vector α. Two endpoints, or a slope, a y axis intercept, and x values at the two end points specify a line. We describe the curve parameterization shortly. Let w be a vector of n data points, $(x_1,y_1,x_2,y_2,\ldots,x_n,y_n)^T$, with the points

(x_i, y_i) independent Gaussian perturbations for each arc*.

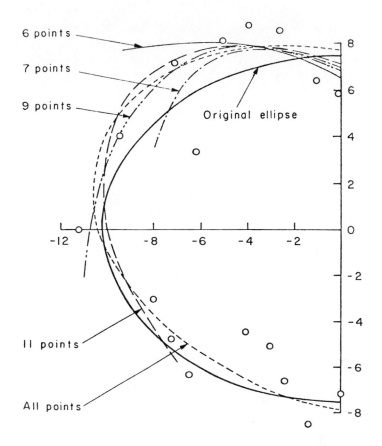

Figure 1. Sequential Curve Fitting Using a Penalty Function to Force Single Branch Hyperbolic Fits in the Initial Stages

Let $p(\alpha|H_m)$ be an apriori probability density function (p.d.f.) for the parameter vectors for the mth pattern class (hypothesis). *This embodies prior structural knowledge of the underlying patterns in a class.* Denote by $f(w|\alpha)$ the p.d.f. of w given α. Then with $P(H_m)$ the apriori probability of an observation coming from pattern class H_m, we are interested in the maximum likelihood of w and H_m, i.e.,

$$P(H_m) \max_{\alpha_{H_m}} p(\alpha_{H_m}|H_m) f(w|\alpha_{H_m}) \qquad (1)$$

* A T superscript denotes vector or matrix transposition.

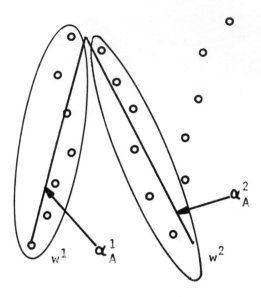

Figure 2. Possible Data for One Character and
Maximum Likelihood Line Fits Assuming Another.

If there are M pattern classes, the recognition of the pattern represented by the data w is determined by the largest of M maximum
likelihoods such as (1). Note that $P(H_m) \, p(\alpha_{H_m}|H_m) \, f(w|\alpha_{H_m})$ is
the joint likelihood of the observed data, of the hypothesis H_m,
and of an underlying line-curve pattern given pattern class H_m.
The maximization in (1) results in an underlying pattern for which
this likelihood is largest. Hence, recognition here involves *global optimization realized through arc fitting*--but the arc fitting
uses variable lines and quadratic curves and is guided *optimally*
by prior structural knowledge of the pattern classes. *The approach
can be applied to any--however complex--classes of line drawings.*
        Solely to illustrate various points, we use a simple version
of the hand printed character recognition problem in a number of
sections of this paper. We will assume the underlying pattern for
an "A", e.g., consists of three straight lines--two legs and a
cross bar. The parameter vector for the "A" has 12 components.
With the underlying pattern for an "R" consisting of two straight
lines and one quadratic curve, the associated α has 15 components,
etc. See figure 3.

Figure 3.   Possible Letters.

Before discussing results in detail, we briefly comment on
the significance of a number of assumptions and results.   A prior
p.d.f. $p(\alpha|H_m)$ is assumed for the underlying line-curve patterns
for the pattern classes H_m.   Is this realistic?   If there are only
a few lines and curves per pattern, then $p(\alpha|H_m)$ can reasonably be
a p.d.f. over Euclidean N-space. $p(\alpha|H_m)$ would most likely be a
cluster type distribution and be determined by a combination of
prior knowledge and measurements on prototypes.   It could be piecewise constant over a few regions bounded by hyperplanes.   Suppose
these hyperplanes were orthogonal to various coordinate axes.
Then the regions of constant probability density would be hyper
rectangular parallelapipeds.   Furthermore, a conditional p.d.f.,
such as that for the rightmost leg of an "A" given a specific left-
most leg, would be constant over rectangular regions for the two
endpoints of the leg.   This is the usual type of structural specification made in non-probabilistic approaches to the problem!
Other clustering models such as mixtures of Gaussian distributions
might also be useful.   For more complex situations where many lines
and curves specify an underlying pattern, conditional p.d.f.'s for
one is more lines and curves given one or more lines and curves
would be used.
        Line and curve fitting is carried out recursively.   The arc
fit to n data points is used to predict the location of the n+1 st
data point, which, when found, is used to compute an arc fit to
the enlarged set of n+1 data points.   This provides for meaningful
data segmentation, i.e., the grouping and association of data
points with appropriate lines and curves.   The recursive curve-
parameter estimation algorithms are based on *linear* methods and

are simple and fast. Whereas parameterizing x and y as sinusoidal functions of a parameter "t" in order to represent quadratic curves can result in nonlinear estimation in order to match appropriate values of t with corresponding values of x and y, we represent quadratic curves as quadratic polynomials in x and y, and avoid the complications inherent in the nonlinear estimation problem.

Recursive least square error estimation of arc parameters oc-curs within the computation which must be carried out for maximum likelihood arc fitting and pattern recognition. It is the basis for the computational feasibility of our recursive arc fitting, it permits resegmentation of the data at a reasonable computational cost, and it is the basis for the use of the same computational results in the maximization of the likelihoods of many of the hypothesis. An interesting conclusion drawn from the expressions for maximum likelihood arc fitting is that these arcs differ from those minimizing the least square error--because of the influence of the structural information--the $p(\alpha_{H_m}|H_m)$. The maximum likelihood approach to recognition also leads to interesting interpretations or algorithms for early determination of whether data represents a line or a quadratic curve.

Some peculiarity in quadratic curve fitting algorithm behavior occasionally results, but this is easily treated with a modest amount of computation, as we point out.

The usefulness of recursive curve fitting in data resegmentation has been exploited in [5] where a recursive algorithm (different from those in this paper) was used in generating least squares polygonal approximations to arbitrary thin curves.

We say little in this paper about where to look for lines and curves and in what order. The conditional distributions of remaining underlying arcs given the data already processed contains all the available information on the locations of these arcs. Some use of this type of information is made in the references previously cited, and [6] is devoted to the topic of where to look for the next arc.

Of course there are problems for which the methods of this paper would constitute only a portion of the processing used. For example, there are problems for which $p(\alpha)$ or the conditional distributions containing equivalent information would be much simpler if one or more global transformations (perhaps parameterized) such as rotation were first applied.

III. RECURSIVE LEAST SQUARE ERROR LINE AND CURVE FITTING

Straight lines and quadratic curves are fit to possible highly variable data using equations of the same form and the same methodology. We first discuss the least square error arc fitting solution and then in the following section treat the modification resulting from use of prior information.

An arc can be fit recursively with the best fit determined

for n data points. This arc can then be used to predict the location of the n+1 th data point, and the n+1 th data point searched
for starting from the predicted point, and then incorporated to
provide the best arc fit based on the n+1 data points. Or the best
fit to n+1 data points can be determined by processing all n+1 data
points once. *The advantage of recursive fitting is that it permits
intelligent data search and hence segmentation based on accumula-
ting information.*

Line: We use the parameterization $y = c_o + c_1 x$ if the slope magnitude is less than 1 and x as a function of y otherwise. Denote
the estimated coefficient vector based on n data points by $c^n \equiv$
$[c_o{}^n, c_1{}^n]^T$, and let $z^i \equiv [1, x_i]^T$. Then c^n is the coefficient vector for which

$$\sum_{i=1}^{n} [y_i - c_o - c_1 x_i]^2 \quad \text{is a minimum, equivalently,}$$

for which

$$\sum_{i=1}^{n} [y_i - c^T z^i]^2 \quad \text{is a minimum.} \tag{2}$$

The error measure used here is the square of the difference between
the line and the y component of the data point for each x_i. See
figure 4.

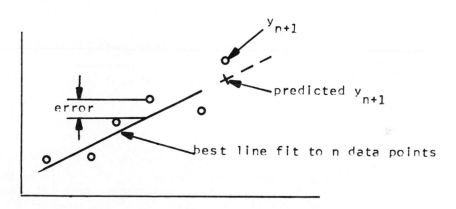

Figure 4. Sequential Line Fitting.

Quadratic Curve: We parameterize a quadratic curve as $c_1 x^2 +$
$c_2 xy + c_3 y^2 + c_4 x + c_5 y - 1 = 0$. Let $z^i \equiv [x_i{}^2, x_i y_i, y_i{}^2, x_i, y_i]^T$
and $c^n \equiv [c_1{}^n, c_2{}^n, c_3{}^n, c_4{}^n, c_5{}^n]^T$. Then the optimum coefficient
vector c^n based on n data points is that which minimizes

$$\sum_{i=1}^{n} [1 - c^T z^i]^2 \tag{3}$$

The error measure involved here is explained shortly.

Upon defining A_n to be the matrix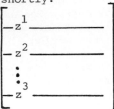

b^n to be the n-vector $[y^1,\ldots,y^n]^T$ or $[1,1,\ldots,1]^T$, depending on whether line or curve fitting is involved, z^n to be the vector $A_n^T b^n$, and B_n to be the matrix $A_n^T A_n$, the well-known solution is

$$c^n = B_n^{-1} z^n \tag{4}$$

B_n is a 2 x 2 matrix for a line and is a 5 x 5 matrix for a quadratic curve: Hence, c^n can be computed by a matrix inversion and then a vector-matrix multiplication. However, the important point here is that B_{n+1}^{-1} and z^{n+1} can be computed simply in terms of the last data point (x_{n+1}, y_{n+1}) and B_n^{-1} or Z_n, respectively, without any time consuming direct matrix inversions. From [7], the recursions are

$$B_{n+1}^{-1} = (\sum_{i=1}^{n+1} z^i z^{iT})^{-1} = B_n^{-1} - \frac{B_n^{-1} z^{n+1} z^{n+1T} B_n^{-1}}{1 + z^{n+1T} B_n^{-1} z^{n+1}}$$

and $\tag{5}$

$$z^{n+1} = \sum_{i+1}^{n+1} z^i b_i = z^n + z^{n+1} b_{n+1}$$

Hence, both c^{n+1} and the least square error $||A_n c^n - b^n||^2$ in the approximations (2), (3) are recursively updatable. From [7], theoretical cpu times per recursion for computing c^n are roughly 120μ sec. and 880μ sec. for a straight line and quadratic curve, respectively.* If the additional cpu times for predicting the location of the n+1 th data point and computing the contribution of the last data point to the least square error in the arc fit to the data are included, the total cpu times per recursion for straight lines and quadratic curves are roughly 155μ sec. and 985μ sec. respectively. Experimental results for lines are about 35% higher.

* Programs are written in assembly language for the IBM 360/67. Instruction execution times were taken from [8].

An additional cost is the search cost for a data point starting from the predicted location. For *highly* variable lines, this can be close to the parameter estimation time. Though this search time does not contribute significantly to the cpu time for fitting quadratic curves, the curve fitting algorithm does exhibit peculiarities. This is due to (1) the some-time fitting of two branches of a hyperbola to the data instead of one branch or an elliptic curve, and (2) some slight limitation on the hyperbolic or elliptic curves which can be fit. Both of these limitations are easily overcome, but the required computation could increase by up to 100% [7]. We comment further on these points later. We see that quadratic curve fitting requires about 6 times as much cpu time per recursion as does straight line fitting. Quadratic curves are therefore relatively expensive to fit even though the algorithm used here is a linear one.

The error measured by (3) is interesting. If c defines an ellipse as shown in figure 5, the error

$$(c_1 x_d^2 + c_2 x_d y_d + c_3 y_d^2 + c_4 x_d + c_5 y_d - 1)^2 \qquad (6)$$

involving the ellipse and data point $v_d = (x_d, y_d)$ is $[\delta(\delta+2)\rho]^2$ where δ is the signed distance from v_e to v_d divided by the distance from v_o to v_e and ρ is a constant depending on c.

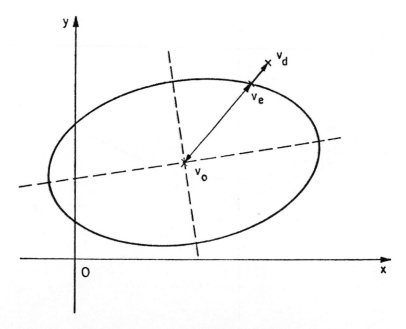

Figure 5. Ellipse for Interpreting the Error Measure in (6).

Note that δ is positive if v_d is in the exterior of the ellipse and is negative if in the interior region. If, e.g., v_d were a distance ϵ outside the ellipse along the ellipse major axis, δ would be positive and would be ϵ divided by the distance from the ellipse center to the ellipse along its major axis.

(6) can be rewritten as

$$[(v_d - v_o)^T C (v_d - v_o) - v_o^T C v_o - 1]^2 \qquad (7)$$

with C and v_o defined in terms of the components of c. For $|\delta| \ll 1$, (6) is approximately $4\delta^2\rho^2$, and for v_o near the origin, this becomes roughly

$$4\delta^2 \qquad (8)$$

It should always be simple to choose an appropriate origin for this data (either before or during experimentation) such that $\rho \approx 1$.

(7) should be as satisfactory as the square of the perpendicular distance from v_d to the ellipse for just about any application. When c defines a hyperbola, the solid curve in figure 6, the interpretation of (7) is the same with v_e replaced by v_h if v_d is in region I, and v_e replaced by v_c if v_d is in region II. The dashed curve is the conjugate hyperbola.

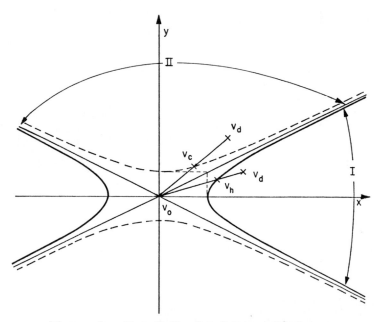

Figure 6. Hyperbola for Interpreting the Error Measure in (6).

In view of the preceding, when (8) is true there is a convenient Gaussian model for $v_d - v_e$ and for $(1-z^Tc)$, which we discuss shortly.

The quadratic curve representation can also be used for a line as

$$c_1y + c_2x - 1 = 0 \qquad (9)$$

Then the error to be minimized is

$$\sum_{i=1}^{n} (c_1y_i + c_2x_i - 1)^2 \qquad (10)$$

Since (10) can be rewritten as

$$\sum_{i=1}^{n} k^2 [y_i \sin \theta + x_i \cos \theta - (1/k)]^2 \qquad (11)$$

with k a constant, we see that the error minimized is not

$$\sum_{i=1}^{n} [y_i \sin \theta + x_i \cos \theta - 1/k)]^2 \qquad (12)$$

which is the sum of the squares of the perpendicular distances from the data points to the line, but rather is this multiplied by k^2. Hence, the optimum line fit here differs from that resulting from minimization of (12) *unless* the origin of the data is shifted during experimentation in order that the line pass within a distance of roughly 1 of the origin and k is therefore roughly 1. However, for most cases, minimization of (11) would probably result in a line close to that obtained through minimization of (12).

Since in recursive arc fitting the association of a data point with an arc may be terminated and the data point assigned to some other arc, an important capability is that c^n can also be recursively modified as data points are removed. For example, suppose the contributions of (x_n, y_n) to Z^n and B_n^{-1} are to be removed. Then $Z^{n-1} = Z^n - z^n b_n$, and from $B_{n-1}^{-1} = (B_n - z^n z^{nT})^{-1}$ we see that

$$B_{n-1}^{-1} = B_n^{-1} + \frac{B_n^{-1} z^n z^{nT} B_n^{-1}}{1 - z^{nT} B_n^{-1} z^n}$$

IV. RECURSIVE LINE (OR CURVE) FITTING THROUGH LIKELIHOOD MAXIMIZATION

We assume the prior structural information for curve fitting is available in the form of an apriori p.d.f. for the underlying arc parameters. Then maximum likelihood curve fitting proceeds as follows. Let c denote arc parameters, p(c) an apriori p.d.f.

for c, (x_i, y_i) the ith data point, and w the data vector for n data points. Then the optimum fit to w is defined to be

$$\max_{c} p(c) \, f(w|c) \tag{13}$$

Line: (13) can be written as

$$\max_{c} \; p(c) \, (2\pi\sigma^2)^{-n/2} \exp[-(2\sigma^2)^{-1} \sum_{i=1}^{n} (y_i - c_o - c_1 x_i)^2$$

$$= (2\pi\sigma^2)^{-n/2} \max_{c} p(c) \exp \left[-(2\sigma^2)^{-1}(c^n-c)^T \begin{bmatrix} n & \sum\limits_{i=1}^{n} x_i \\ \\ \sum\limits_{i=1}^{n} x_i & \sum\limits_{i=1}^{n} x_i^2 \end{bmatrix} (c^n-c) \right]$$

$$\times \exp[-(2\sigma^2)^{-1} \sum_{i=1}^{n} (y_i - c_o^n - c_1^n x_i)^2 . \tag{14}$$

Note that the second exponential in (14) is a function of the data and of c^n, the parameters of the line resulting in the least square error fit, but is not a function of c. *The only function involved in the optimization with respect to c is the first line of (14).* The optimization is most easily handled through maximization of the natural logarithm, i.e.,

$$\max_{c} \left\{ \ln p(c) - (2\sigma^2)^{-1} (c^n - c)^T \begin{bmatrix} n & \sum\limits_{i=1}^{n} x_i \\ \\ \sum\limits_{i=1}^{n} x_i & \sum x_i^2 \end{bmatrix} (c^n - c) \right\} \tag{15}$$

We see that in general, c is not c^n!

If c takes only a finite number of values--corresponding to a finite number of possible line segments--then the c maximizing (14) or (15) is easily determined. Note that only (15) need be calculated for the various values of c in order to determine the optimum. If p(c) is continuous or piecewise continuous, then (14) can be easily maximized. For example, if p(c) is constant over a few regions bounded by hyperplanes, then (15) is a quadratic maximization problem with linear constraints. As was the case for least squares processing, the estimate of c can be computed recursively. c^n in (14) is computed recursively, the matrix in the quadratic form (15) is trivially recursively updatable and (15) can therefore be maximized recursively with n.

There are two interesting interpretations of (14). When appropriately normalized, the first line of (14) might be viewed as the maximum likelihood of a permissible line given the best least square error line fit. The other interpretation of course is simply the maximum likelihood of the data and of the permissible lines.

Intelligent recursive data search, i.e., data segmentation and fitting here would involve guiding the search for (x_{n+1}, y_{n+1}) based on the c which maximizes (15) for n data points rather than on c^n. *Hence, the resulting segmentation may be greatly influenced by p(c)*!

More generally, if c is the vector of parameters appearing in (6) for a quadratic curve (say an ellipse), and if (8) holds, a plausible model for $f(w|c)$ which can be decomposed using c^n, as in (14), can be constructed. Two interpretations for one such model are the following. (1) Assume each (x_i, y_i) is obtained by choosing an angle θ_i and then proceeding from the origin along a ray making angle θ_i with the x-axis until a data point (x_i, y_i) is found. (This is equivalent in the straight line model to finding a data point by choosing x_i and then searching for the corresponding y_i.) Then model the amplitude of (x_i, y_i) (i.e., distance from the origin) as a Gaussian random variable with p.d.f. roughly $\eta(||u_{ei}||, \sigma^2||u_{ei}||^2/4)$ where v_{ei} is the intersection of the ray with the underlying ellipse and $u_{ei} \equiv v_{ei} - v_o$. (Equivalently, take δ_i to be $\eta(0, \sigma^2/4)$.) More generally, for $||v_o|| << ||u_e||$ but $v_o \neq 0$ and for ρ not quite 1, model the amplitude p.d.f. of $(x_i, y_i) - v_o$ as $\eta(||u_{ei}||, \sigma^2||u_{ei}||^2/4 \rho^2)$. Note, this variance is a function of ellipse diameter and it's angle ϕ_i. For $v_o \approx 0$, $\phi_i \approx \theta_i$. The variance is an increasing function of ellipse diameter, but this is not an unreasonable dependence. For interpretation (2), let $(x_i, y_i) - v_o$ be a random vector with angle ϕ_i uniformly distributed over the angular range subtended by the underlying arc and amplitude p.d.f. given in interpretation (1). Let the angle and amplitude be statistically independent random variables.

With the preceding, (13) is maximized as

$$\max_c p(c) \ (2\pi\sigma^2)^{-n/2} \ [\text{Var}]^{-1/2} \ \exp[-(2\sigma^2)^{-1} \sum_{i=1}^{n} (1 - z_i^T c)^2]$$

$$= (2\pi\sigma^2)^{-n/2} \max_c p(c) \ [\text{Var}]^{-1/2} \ \exp[-(2\sigma^2)^{-1} (c^n - c)^T B_n (c^n - c)]$$

$$\times \exp[-(2\sigma^2)^{-1} ||b^n - A_n c^n||^2] \tag{16}$$

where $[\text{Var}] = \prod_{i=1}^{n} \sigma^2 ||u_{ei}||^2/4\rho^2$

which can be expressed explicitly in the parameters $\{c_1, c_2, \ldots, c_5\}$ using $v_{d_i} = (x_i, y_i)$,

$$|| u_{ei} ||^2/\rho^2 = || v_{d_i} - v_o ||^2/[1 + v_o^T C v_o](v_{d_i} - v_o)^T C(v_{d_i} - v_o)$$

$$C = \begin{bmatrix} c_1 & c_2/2 \\ & \\ c_2/2 & c_3 \end{bmatrix} \quad, \quad v_o = -(1/2)C^{-1} \begin{bmatrix} c_4 \\ \\ c_5 \end{bmatrix} \quad.$$

Again, $|| u_{ei} ||^2/\rho^2$ is well approximated by $|| v_{d_i} ||^2 / v_{d_i}^T C v_{d_i}$

for $v_o \approx 0, \rho \approx 1$.

V. SEQUENTIAL MAXIMUM LIKELIHOOD DETERMINATION AND DATA SEGMENTATION

The considerable advantages of recursive arc fitting show up in data segmentation and in sequential recognition. Suppose, for example, the system is to fit a line to the left-most data in figure 2 in order to maximize the likelihood of the data and the "A" hypothesis. Data points are picked up until the rate of increase of the maximum likelihood of the data and the "A" hypothesis drops below some threshold. The result is the maximization

$$P(A) \max_{\alpha_A^1} p(\alpha_A^1) f(w^1|\alpha_A^1)$$

where w^1 is the data subset used (circled in figure 2) and α_A^1 is the parameter vector for the fitted line. The system then performs the second maximization to obtain

$$P(A) \max_{\alpha_A^1} p(\alpha_A^1) f(w^1|\alpha_A^1) \max_{\alpha_A^2} p(\alpha_A^2|\overline{\alpha_A^1}) f(w^2|\alpha_A^2).$$

where $\overline{\alpha_A^1}$ results from the first maximization.

At this point or later, as necessary, the system can resegment the data, changing the association of one or more data points among w^1 and w^2 in order to improve the maximization. The re-estimations of α_A^1 and α_A^2 in order to fine tune the global maximum likelihood estimation are computed efficiently because of the linear recursive estimation. This is a very useful capability when the maximum likelihoods for two or more hypotheses do not differ greatly, and accurately determining which is larger is therefore important!

VI. SEQUENTIAL RECOGNITION USING SHARED COMPUTATION

Maximum likelihood recognition involves recursively including more data and determining the maximum likelihoods of this data and the appropriate line and curve fits under the possible pattern classes. As various maximum likelihoods increase at both a slower rate than some predetermined numbers and at a significantly slower rate than does the maximum among the pattern classes, they are e-liminated as classes under which the data could have occurred. The significant result discussed in this section is that certain calculations are made only once and then used in computing the maximum likelihoods for two or more classes. This arises because for two or more pattern classes, essentially the same data set may often be segmented as being associated with a line (or with a curve). Since arc fitting then involves first determining the least square error arc fit, *this calculation need be performed only once and then used in determining the maximum likelihoods for a number of classes.* For example, consider the data in figure 2 and the fitting of left-most lines under hypotheses "A" and "N". The maximum likelihood of the "A" hypothesis and the data w^1 is

$$P(A) \quad \max_{\alpha_A^1} \quad p(\alpha_A^1) \ f(w^1 | \alpha_A^1) \qquad (17)$$

with

$$f(w^1 | \alpha_A^1) = h(\alpha_A^1, \ \hat{\alpha}^1) \ g(w^1, \ \hat{\alpha}^1) \qquad (18)$$

where $\hat{\alpha}$ denotes the least square error line fit to w^1, and $h(.,.)$ and $g(.,.)$ are the functions appearing in the first and second lines, respectively, of (14). $g(.,.)$ does not depend upon the "A" hypotheses--though the segmentation resulting in w^1 may very well be different than for another hypothesis with a line on the left. If the segmentation under hypothesis "N" results in the same w^1, then the associated likelihood maximization involves the function

$$f(w^1 | \alpha_N^1) = h(\alpha_N^1, \ \hat{\alpha}^1) \ g(w^1, \ \hat{\alpha}^1) \qquad (19)$$

Note that both $\hat{\alpha}^1$ and the function $g(w^1, \ \hat{\alpha}^1)$ are identical to those appearing in (18). $h(\alpha_N^1, \ \hat{\alpha}^1)$ differs from $h(\alpha_A^1, \ \hat{\alpha}^1)$ only in the variables α_N^1 and α_A^1. Hence, much of the computation involved in the maximizations, such as (17), can be shared by a number of hy-

potheses. If it happens that the data segmentations differ slightly for the various hypotheses having a straight line (or curve) on
the left, then not all but *much* of the computation involved in the
determination of the least squares curve fits and the h and g functions can be shared by the various hypotheses.

VII. HOW MANY DATA POINTS ARE ENOUGH?

For real data, obviously as data points along an arc are taken
closer together, they become statistically dependent. Little improvement in arc fit can result by using increasing numbers of increasingly dependent data points. The usefullness of data points
for each arc is determined by their effects on the pattern class
maximum likelihoods and their consequent contributions to pattern
class recognition. Data points are most useful when taken of arcs
which are most effective in discriminating among pattern classes.
The behavior of the maximum likelihood of the correct hypothesis can be fairly well characterized if the data segmentation
is good. This is true because the square of the error in the
least squares arc fit in such a case is a chi square random variable. It is difficult to say much about the behavior of the maximum likelihoods for the incorrect hypotheses.
For an individual arc fitting, we can say more. One interesting simple case for which there is an explicit solution is the
following. Assume there is an underlying linear function $y =
c_o + c_1x$ or parabolic function $y = c_o' + c_1'x + c_2x^2$, and for vari-
ous values of x, y perturbed by independent Gaussian noises can be
observed. Assume the line parameters are unknown and arbitrary
and this is also true of c_o' and c_1' for the parabola. Take c_2 to
be known--set at some value which represents what is felt to be
the minimum quadratic content in order to characterize a function
as being parabolic. No apriori p.d.f.'s for the parameters will
be used here. Then we can devise a sequential decision procedure
for deciding whether the data is that for the linear or the parabolic function and which has the following properties: the probabilities of the two possible types of decision errors will not exceed values arbitrarily specified by the designer, and this performance is achieved by processing the minimum average number of data
points. The interesting point here is that the maximum likelihood
ratio test used reduces to a test involving the cross-correlation
of n data points with a deterministic function of n and comparison
with two n-dependent thresholds for each n. If the upper threshold
is exceeded, the decision is "parabola". If the lower threshold
is exceeded, the decision is "line". If neither threshold is exceeded, no classification is made and another data point is taken.
The function used in the correlation is shown in figure 7. It is
the difference of the parabola c_2x^2 at n values of x, and the line
which approximates this parabola best in a least squares sense.
(Mathematical details can be found in [7].)

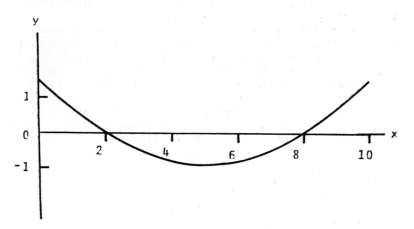

Figure 7. Optimum Reference Function for Cross-
correlation in Order to Differentiate Between a
Line and a Parabola When $c_2=0.1$ and the x_i's Take
Values 0,1,2,...,10.

VIII. PECULIARITIES OF THE QUADRATIC CURVE FITTING ALGORITHM

The useful curve types which can be produced by the quadratic
curve fitting algorithm are an elliptic arc or a single branch hyperbolic arc. Unfortunately, on occasion the algorithm fits arcs
from two branches of a hyperbola. In [7] we discuss the use of a
penalty function to force a single branch hyperbolic arc fit. This
can be realized using linear equations and at a modest increase in
the required computation. Quadratic curve fits were made sequentially to 6,7,9,11 and then all points in figure 1. The data
points there are perturbations of an elliptic curve. The use of
the penalty function is required for the first three fits.
A second problem is that the fitted quadratic curve is sensitive to the origin of the data. For example, the same data con-
stellations near the origin and far removed from the origin result
in somewhat different elliptic fits because of the effect of ρ on
the minimization of (6) when the data is far removed from the origin. If this poses a problem for the user, it can be overcome by
choosing a new origin located near the data.

IX. THICK LINES

The arc fitting algorithms can be used as they are to handle
some thick arc models or extended to handle lines and additive
noise, as follows:

161

1. Thick arcs having little variability in line thickness can be treated by taking slices across an arc and applying the theory to the mid points of these slices.

2. Thick arcs which are noisy and have the appearance of a point scatter about an underlying thin arc can be treated by applying the developed arc fitting algorithms to all of the thick arc data present. This procedure is optimum for the following data generation model, among others. Assume the field is quantized into cells and that for each point on an underlying thin arc, black cells are generated in the perturbation direction by a random mechanism. Let i be an integer valued random variable taking positive and negative values and specifying cell location with respect to the underlying point on the thin line, positive values in one direction and negative values in the other. Let the probability that the jth cell is black be given by a quantized Gaussian distribution and assume the probabilities of such cells being black are independent. Then the observed line thickness will be highly variable, there will be missing black points within a thick line, and the probability of a cell being black will fall off as a Gaussian function of distance from the underlying thin arc.

3. One model for thin lines plus additive noise can be treated as follows. Assume the line is represented with y as a function of x. For each value of x, there is one black cell which is a perturbation of a point on the underlying straight line. Suppose other cells can be black due to an additive noise which leaves a cell as is or changes it to black with probabilities $(1-P)$ and P, respectively. We assume the noise phenomena for the different cells are statistically independent. Suppose there are J_i+1 black cells in the column of x_i and assume these cells are numbered 1 through J_i+1. (J_i of these cells are due to noise.) With y_{ij} the y location of the jth cell, the likelihood of the J_i+1 cells is

$$\text{constant} \times \sum_{j=1}^{J_i+1} (2\pi\sigma^2)^{-(1/2)} \exp\left[-(y_{ij} - c_o - c_1 x_i)^2\right] \quad (20)$$

The products of these functions for all i constitutes the likelihood function to be maximized with respect to (c_o, c_1). The required calculation is now more extensive. An initial suboptimal solution can be obtained by finding an optimal line for a class of subsets of the y_{ij}--one cell for each i--and then modifying this solution through maximization of the product of the i functions shown in (20). Note that an optimal solution does contain contributions from all the y_{ij}, and this happens because the Gaussian perturbation p.d.f. has tails running off to ∞.

ACKNOWLEDGMENTS

The derivations of many of the mathematical results discussed in this paper are in a joint work with Nese Yalabik [7]. Experimental results on the performance of the arc fitting algorithms can be found there as well.
This work was partially supported by NASA Grant NSG5036.

REFERENCES

1. Yashida, M. and M. Eden, "Handwritten Chinese character recognition by an analysis by synthesis method", Proceedings of the First International Joint Conference on Pattern Recognition, October 30-November 1, 1973, Washington, D.C., pp. 197-204.
2. Griffith, A. K., "Edge detection in simple scenes using apriori information", IEEE Transactions on Computers, Vol. c-22, No. 4, pp. 371-381, April, 1973.
3. Martelli, A., "An application of heuristic search methods to edge and contour detection", Communications of the acm, Vol. 19, No. 2, pp. 73-83, February, 1976.
4. Stockman, G., L. Kanal, M. Kyle, "Design of a waveform parsing system", Proceedings of the First International Joint Conference on Pattern Recognition, October 30-November 1, 1973, Washington, D.C., pp. 236-243.
5. Pavlidis, T.,and S. L. Horowitz, "Segmentation of Plane Curves", IEEE Transactions on Computers, Vol. c-23, No. 8, pp. 860-870, August, 1974.
6. Koppelaar, "Ontwerp van optimalisering van letterherkennende komputerprogramma's", Technical Report of the Laboratorium voor Technische Natuurkunde, Technische Hogeschool Delft, March, 1974.
7. Cooper, D. B., and N. Yalabik, "On the cost of approximating and recognizing a noise perturbed straight line or a quadratic curve segment in the plane", Technical Report NASA NSG 5036/1, Brown University, March, 1975.
8. IBM System/360 Model 67 Functional Characteristics Manual, 2nd Edition, January 1970, File No. S360-01, Form GA27-2719-1.

A MINICOMPUTER BASED REAL TIME EYE TRACKING
SYSTEM FOR PATTERN RECOGNITION APPLICATIONS*

Nelson Corby
Lester A. Gerhardt
Electrical and Systems Engineering Department
Rensselaer Polytechnic Institute
Troy, N. Y.

"...Indeed, it is well said that 'in every object
there is inexhaustible meaning; the eye sees in it what
the eye brings means of seeing'...To Newton and to
Newton's dog Diamond, what a different pair of Universes,
while the painting on the optical retina of both was,
most likely, the same."

Thomas Carlyle, "The French Revolution" Vol I

I. INTRODUCTION

The human eye or rather the whole human visual system is perhaps the most elegant, most sophisticated, most fascinating but
least understood system for the processing of spatial data. While
it is true that for tasks that are well characterized, specialized
computing systems may be able to deliver results faster and analyze masses of data with more ease, no system yet devised by man
can challenge the versatility, flexibility, or complexity of the
eye. Many areas of modern study have attempted to discover the
secrets of visual perception. Anatomical and psychological studies have yielded much data on the structure and response (spatial,
spectral and temporal) of the eye, of the optical tract and finally of the brain itself. More is known now, physiologically, about
the human optical system than ever before. Mathematics, systems
analysis and various branches of engineering have combined to attempt to model and study the processes at work in the tasks of human visual perception.
    The field of pattern recognition has yielded much insight in-
to the nature of visual sensory and perceptual processes in humans.
Much of the early work in pattern recognition was unsystematic.
For specific tasks, such as recognizing handwritten characters,
sorting and counting blood cells, classifying chromosomes, a list
of salient features was heuristically generated, suited to the
task at hand. Once features have been extracted, then a classification algorithm may be applied. Initially, this classification
procedure was not very well characterized. Thus a new algorithm

* Research sponsored by the Air Force Office of Scientific Research, Air Force Systems Command, USAF, under grant no. AFOSR-
  73-2486. Lt. Col. George McKemie is the project monitor.

was needed for each task. Modern mathematics in the form of statistical decision theory has yielded some universal characteriza-
tions of the pattern recognition process. By deriving a set of
selected features as a vector in a multi-dimensional feature space,
all recognition problems have virtually the same structure: first,
processing to yield feature vectors and then classification by
multi-dimensional decision rules to yield a classification. Classification algorithms use mathematical decision theory which operates on the features extracted to choose one of a set of possible
outcomes as in Figure 1.

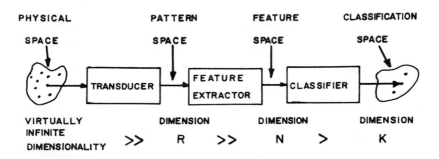

Figure 1. Structure of the Pattern Recognition Process[1]

The classification algorithm consists basically of finding
separating surfaces in N-space that will, according to some performance measure and set of rules, correctly separate known samples and which will, with some degree of confidence, sort the unknown samples. The essence of the pattern recognition problem
presently lies in the area of feature extraction.

How are features chosen? With the exception of relatively
few techniques, such as direct global transform theory (Hadamard,
Fourier transforms, etc.) together with filtering operations in
the transform domain, most feature extraction is done by examing
the performance of a human assigned a classification task. The
person's report of his method or procedure is the basis for determining the feature extraction technique being used. The main
source of feature extraction rules, especially for complex tasks,
is introspection, (namely the reports of subjects recalling their
performances). Appropriately designed tests are subsequently used
to refine the initial guess as to the choice of important features.

Such introspection to determine features is, by its very nature, complex and imprecise, since many decisions and rankings are of a subconscious nature which reflect the introspector's past experiences and learning. Furthermore, having a subject dwell on the nature of his search strategy tends to inhibit his normal scanning regime.

Of particular interest then, are methods for perceiving the observer's train of thought when attempting to classify or search. Attempts to fathom the thought process are usually not successful due to the largely subconscious nature of feature extraction and pattern discrimination in humans. However, knowledge of eye physiology gives some clue as to the thought processes at work, when applied to imagery, the subject of this paper.

II. EYE PHYSIOLOGY

The eye is known to orient itself so as to place upon the area of maximum resolution (the fovea), that part of the total image about which the observer seeks more detailed data[2].

The retina of the human eye is composed of two types of photo receptors, rods and cones, as well as the neural layers needed to interconnect them and carry the outputs to the brain. It has been found [6] that the densities and arrangements of photo receptors in the retina are such that the circular zone of maximum visual acquity is about one to one and half degrees in diameter. Visual acquity drops precipitiously outside this zone. The portion of the retina responsible for this high acquity vision is called the fovea.

Only a tiny portion of the retina has the capacity for high resolution, high acquity vision. The remainder of the retina gives only a low resolution rendition of the scene imaged on the retina. Even though resolution is low in the extra foveal areas, much information is still extracted. Groups of rods in these areas are interconnected in various ways and act cooperatively to enhance movements, edges, etc.

Given that only an insignificant fraction of the retina is responsible for high resolution, high luminance vision, how is one able to perceive a total image? Two basic factors contribute to our perceptions. First, a visual cortex with a high degree of linear magnification of the fovea compared with that of the rest of the retina. Second, a set of six extraocular muscles and a neurological control system giving the eye great mobility, pointing the sensitive area of the fovea in rapid succession at one point of regard after another. Unfortunately little is known about how the observer assembles the sequence of radically different, high resolution "patches", to perceive the total image in the context of the task assigned.

When studying a photograph, experiments show that the human observer does not try to assimilate all the information in the image immediately. Rather, he sequentially and selectively links small areas and details (or features) of the image in an attempt to interpret the image. This idea of sequential adaptive scanning procedure is further supported by noting that the nature of the scan changes as different questions are asked [2]. It seems reasonable to assume that the sequences of eye fixations (or pauses) has relationship to the content of the cerebral processes of the subject. It would be desireable to be able to measure and record the point of regard of the subject as he views a stimulus scene. In this way it would be possible to infer the nature of the feature extraction and feature ranking processes at work.

III. PREVIOUS RESEARCH

Numerous attempts over the years have been made, since the turn of the century, to accurately measure and record the point of regard of the eye during the time the eye observes an image. Early attempts used direct live observation [2], sequences of still photographs were used [3], as well as mechanical methods. There was very little success with these methods because of the extreme discomfort to the subject and the change in mechanical properties of the eyeball, induced by attachments to the eye. Most of the subsequent work from 1915 to the present involves the principal of reflecting a light beam from the eye onto a photographic film or photosensor [3]. In these methods, a small mirror is, in principle, affixed to the eyeball. Except for some technical innovations, these methods have not changed much over the years. Early attempts with contact lenses were disappointing due to the tendency of the lens to float on the eye, which rendered the system inaccurate. Work with rubber suction cups and scleral contact lenses led to the use of tiny suction cups with attached optical systems the size of an aspirin, which were attached to the eye and used to measure point of regard. This direct approach, while quite accurate and precise (eye movements of the order of 20-30 minutes of arc are detectable) is (1) uncomfortable (2) unnatural (due to the apparatus on the eye and the taped eye lid) and (3) usable only for limited periods due to eye discomfort as the eye dries out. All of these factors distract the subject from the normal pattern of movements that would be executed in scanning the target of interest.

Non-contact methods of determining eye positions are far more valuable, since the normal pattern of eye movements are uninfluenced by externally imposed constraints. Non-contact methods can generally be used with any subject, with very little instruction or supervision, and with no danger to the subject.

There are two or three methods which determine, in a non-contact manner, the point of regard of the subject. The one which was chosen for the system to be described, is the pupil center-corneal reflex center distance method.

IV. CORNEAL HIGHLIGHT - PUPIL CENTER DISTANCE METHOD

What is usually desired regarding eye position sensing is to determine the fixation point of the subject, in space, not the orientation of the eye relative to the head. In most other approaches, the actual point of regard is derived from eye position by carefully stabilizing the head, illuminators, optics and sensors. Nevertheless, lateral head motions can generate in these methods, the same effects as rotations of the eye. To overcome such problems, either the head must be stabilized (using a bite board and heavy solid apparatus) or else head position must be sensed and the head motion signals used to cancel the errors induced in the eye position signal by head movements. These errors are of the order of 1 degree for each 50 mils of lateral head movement.

Features of the eye that vary only with rotation and not with translation can be used to sense eye rotation directly. Alternatively, features that behave differently under translation than under rotation allow rotary movements to be deduced.

A point source of illumination is placed in the visual field of the subject. This point source is fixed with respect to the scene material. The point source illuminates the eye resulting in a white or "backlighted" pupillary disk. The point source also generates a corneal reflection (or reflex) of the point source due to the convex front surface of the cornea. If the point source of illumination is fixed with respect to the visual scene material, the point of regard of the eye can be shown to be proportional to the relative separation of corneal highlight center and pupil center. The image of the eye with the point highlight, is projected onto the sensor plane. The x and y distances between the pupil center and the highlight center are proportional to the coordinates of the point of regard of the eye.

The two points of the eye that are used in this measurement technique are the pupil center and the center of corneal curvature. It can be shown that measurements of the movements of the corneal reflex are equivalent to measurements of the center of corneal curvature, provided that the point source of illumination is at optical infinity and the axis of the imaging system is coaxial with the axis of the illumination system. The apparent displacement of the center of the corneal reflection from the pupil center on the plane of the sensor, is equivalent to the spatial orientation of the center of corneal curvature from the center of the pupil. Figure 2 demonstrates how the eye image on the sensor plane appears as the eye undergoes rotations and translations.

Thus to implement the pupil center - corneal highlight techniques, using a point in the visual field, all that is needed is to image the eye and calculate the distance between the center of the pupillary disk and the center of the corneal reflex as shown in Figure 3.

This method permits large head movements (eye translations) which do not interfere with the measurements of interest. But

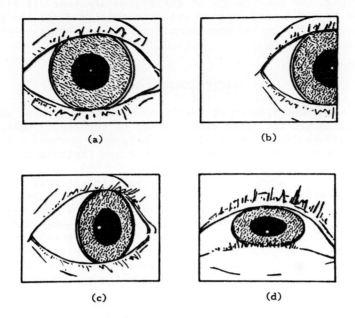

(a) (b)

(c) (d)

Figure 2. Image of Eye, Pupil and Reflex for a Variety of Conditions [5]

    a) normal undeviated gaze-reflex at center of pupil
    b) eye translated - reflex still at center of pupil
    c) eye rotated left - reflex displaced from center of pupil
    d) eye rotated up - reflex displaced from center of pupil

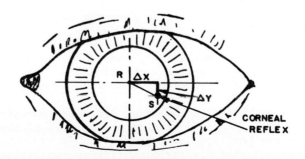

Figure 3. Image of Eye Showing Distance to be Measured to Determine Point of Regard

nevertheless, the constraints of the system are that (1) illumination must be maintained coaxial with the pupil and (2) the pupil image must be kept on the photosensitive (planar) surface of the imaging device.

V. SYSTEM DESIGN GOALS

The major shortcoming of most past work in eye point of regard research was the stand alone nature of the sensor combined with the inconvenient nature of most instrument outputs. Most results of eye position measurement devices was photographic in nature.

For pattern recognition research, the time history of the point of regard is of vital importance. Where did the subject look first and for how long? Where next? These are important questions. Even the best work done has failed to give easily studied instantaneous time histories of eye movements. Most reflected light (photographic) methods inherently give time integrated histories which indicate on the average, the most important areas of regard. Of more importance is where the eye looked, for how long and in what order.

The use of a specialized eye coordinate preprocessing system, interfaced directly (on-line and in real time) with a powerful, graphics computer, can generate a detailed sequence of eye movements driven directly by the eye. Such a system (1) overcomes the failure of previous work in generating time histories, (2) does not impose mechanical constraints on the eye (thereby not altering the sequence of normal scan stops), (3) allows for building and accessing data files easily, (4) speeds analysis by easy retrieval and correlation with source data, and (5) permits (by virtue of the system's on-line, real-time operation) interactive testing and study of free and task oriented examination.

Thus far, the processing power of an on-line computer has not generally been linked with an eye position measurement device in any readily available systems.

Primary goals for an on-line computer based eye-track collection and analysis system include the following:

1. Accurate, non-mechanical, non-contact, sensing of eye position in real-time with the minimum possible interference with the subject. The subject should be permitted moderate head movements.
2. On-line interface to a fast dedicated computer to allow for collection and complex processing, if necessary, of the eye position data.
3. Sophisticated display capabilities, specifically an on-line graphics processor and video controller.
4. A convenient system for storage and retrieval of eye-track time history data along with source imagery.

5. Opportunity for "feedback", i.e. by having the parameters of the subject's display controllable by the processing computer, there exists a fascinating range of real time sensory and visual processing experiments.
6. Data reduction programs should be available so that the raw data can be reduced to its essentials. These programs should have parameters which can be varied by the experimenter and produce annotated, easily understood graphical output.
7. Rapid calibration (either manual or computer assisted) should be provided for.

By combining a specialized high speed pre-processor to determine eye position, with an interactive, disk based mini-computer system, experimental results are available more rapidly. Also, the range of studies that can be undertaken is greatly enlarged. In addition, the graphics processor allows for sophisticated display not only of the basic track, but also of statistical parameters of the track along with the ability to view the results of various filtering algorithms which operate upon this basic eye-track data.

The system described herein allows for on-line acquisition of sequential instantaneous positions of the eye and thus generates the time history of eye position (the eye" track" or "trace"). Data, not only about where the subject looked, but in what sequence and for how long, are readily available via the graphical display. The software operating system in the host computer allows a variety of data to be displayed in various formats. The program also executes powerful filtering operations which analyze and reduce the raw data. Also, various combinations of original scenes and their corresponding eye traces can be viewed simultaneously and studied to better advantage.

VI. SYSTEM TECHNICAL DESCRIPTION

An on-line eye position tracking and analysis system, in its simplest form, would perform the following basic tasks.

The sensor must generate the (x, y) point of regard relative to the scene. These coordinates of eye position are read in by a central computer. The programs in the computer are responsible for calibration of the experimental apparatus, input and storage of data points, filtering and analysis of data with subsequent output in a form that is easily interpreted on a system output monitor. The computer may also have control over the scene being presented to the subject.

The specific system which has been built at R.P.I. is the Eye Motion Analysis and Tracking System (EMATS).

Figure 4 illustrates some of the key points of the EMAT system. To free the host computer from dedicated processing of the raw video eye image and extraction of eye point of regard, a spe-

171

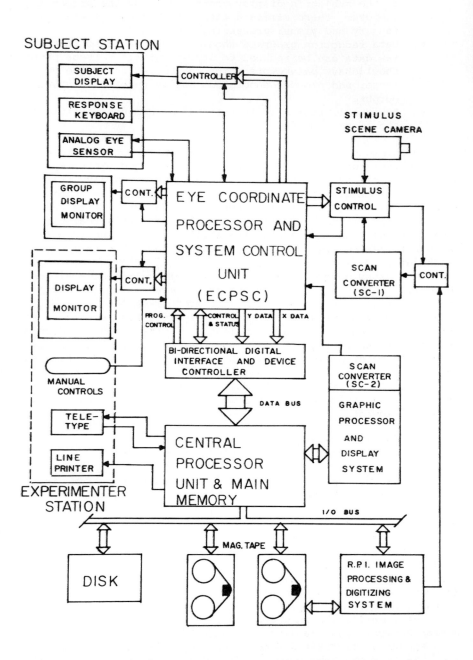

Figure 4. The Eye Motion Analysis and Tracking System (EMATS)

cial digital preprocessing computer system, the Eye Coordinate Processor and System Control unit (ECPSC), has been built. This pre-processor, explained later, is the heart of the system. It operates on the analog video image of the eye from the eye sensor, to yield the coordinates of the point of regard, 30 times a second. The ECPSC also is responsible for control of system visual resources under manual control or central processor control.

The subject station consists of the viewing hood, subject monitor (to display the selected stimulus scene), the illumination and imaging optics, television camera and a subject response board. The subject display controller of the ECPSC is responsible for synchronizing and routing the proper video outputs to the subject. Additionally, if it were desired to test many subjects simultaneously, all subject station outputs could be time-multiplexed onto the basic ECPSC by suitable multiplexing circuitry.

The experimenters station provides for manual control of the ECPSC and of the executive operating system program running in the central processor. The experimenter can view any system video input or output, along with processing information produced by the ECPSC. All system functions are controlled by the ECPSC via manual experimenter control or by commands issued by the host computer.

Since many devices are connected to the central processor I/O bus in parallel, the device controller is responsible for interpreting only the commands directed to the ECPSC and for routing the desired data out onto the common data bus at the proper time.

The central processor is a Varian 620/i, 16 bit general purpose mini-computer with 32K of core and a basic cycle time of 2.4 microseconds. Attached to it are a 50 Mbit disk, two 9 track magnetic tape drives, high speed paper tape reader and punch, as well as high speed line printer, and the basic system control device, a teletype.

An important peripheral attached to the central processor is the RPI Image Processing and Digitizing system [7]. It runs online or off-line, and can digitize images and record them on tape or on disk as well as display them on a precision display. Thus, the digitizing system can generate and process images which can then be shown to the subject.

The unique, powerful processing and display capability of the graphic display processor separates this eye tracking system from others. The graphic processor operates in conjunction with the central processor to generate graphical displays on a 21" CRT with 1024 by 1024 addressable points and 4 levels of brightness. This graphic processor output is a random scan display which, as noted before, must be converted to a 525 line, raster scan format with a repetition rate of 30 frames/sec. This is accomplished by scan converter SC2. The output of the graphic processor scan converter is combined with the stimulus scene to create a superimposed image. This superimposed image can consist of the original stimulus scene together with graphical output such as eye position, raw track, filtered track, alphanumeric characters or statistical data.

Alternatively, this graphical output may be fed back to the subject, thereby allowing "closed loop" operation. The subject views
a scene whose parameters are variable. The changer made in the
scene depend on the eye motions of the subject.

Another scan converter, SC_1, is used as a bulk video storage
device to store individual video frames generated by the scene
camera or the RPI image processing system. These frames are used
as stimulus scenes for the subject. Finally, direct live video inputs are provided for, via a standard monochrome television camera.

In summary, the subject can be caused to view static or moving scenes, live images, as well as static or moving graphical images. The track data can be stored in core or in bulk storage
devices. The experimenter has complete control over all modes of
operation of both the ECPSC and the executive program, as well as
being able to view or preview any system resource. Output displays consisting of multiple overlays of visual and graphical data
are available instantaneously, thus allowing for elaborate, sophisticated display capabilities. In addition, isolated remote monitors under system control, are provided for group viewing.

The purpose of EMATS is to make possible the study, in real-
time, of the sequence of points of regard of the eye of a human
observer engaged in a viewing task. To this end, EMATS consists
of an integrated array of hardware and software assemblies which
measure the instantaneous point of regard of the eye, collect
those points sequentially, allow for their display, storage, and
retrieval, as well as for complex analysis of the sequence of
points and subsequent re-display. All of these functions are under the control of the experimenter in a real-time interactive
manner.

Subject Station and the Optical Subassembly

The subject station provides support and mounting facilities
for the subject stimulus monitor, as well as for the eye space il-
luminating and imaging optics (used for generating the image of
the subject's eye). The enclosure also provides a comfortable
physical framework in which the subject can perform his viewing
tasks.

Description of the Eye Coordinate Processor
and System Control Unit

This section deals with the Eye Coordinate Processor and System Control unit, (ECPSC), the hardware unit that has been built
specifically to analyze the image of the subject's eye and determine its point of regard. The processor, operating upon the eye
image, deduces the coordinates of the point of regard of the eye.

The image of the eye that is generated by the silicon matrix

image tube of the television camera in the subject station is processed by the ECPSC. By using collimated illumination aligned co-
axially with the axis of the imaging tube, the retinal reflex (pupillary disk) appears bright, rather than dark. The corneal reflex appears as a bright white point which is even brighter than
the bright pupillary disk. The following discussion of the operation of the ECPSC unit refers to Figure 5.

The feature extractor section is responsible for analyzing
V_1 and from it, determining those parameters, points, and features
that can be used to determine the x and y coordinates of the point
of regard as referenced to some coordinate system. Data extracted
from V_1 is used to control the actions of the x and y digital computation channels. The control signals are used to develop x and
y data from the image for analysis, to control storage of these
points in memory, to control the digital arithmetic units of each
channel and to control the updating of the digital value of the
coordinate. This digital value represents the latest estimate of
the point of regard of the eye.

The digital representations of the coordinates of the point
of regard (x and y) are then converted to analog form ($\hat{x}$ and $\hat{y}$)
so that real-time smoothing and interpolation can be performed.
It is more convenient to do this filtering in the analog domain,
rather than in the digital domain because of the rather complex
hardware that would be necessary to implement the operations in
the digital domain. The adjustable integrating filters act over
varying numbers of the past data points to weight the present data
point. The number of points used, as well as the weighting, can
be varied.

After smoothing, $\hat{x}_f$ and $\hat{y}_f$ are then linearly transformed,
independently, by their respective channels. The form of the transformation allows for scaling and translation of $\hat{x}_f$ and $\hat{y}_f$ to yield
the final estimated value of the coordinate of the point of regard.
The scaling and translation are necessary to calibrate the ECP so
that its output is isomorphic to the scene image coordinate system. Also, anisotropic corrections which may be necessary due to
geometric distortions etc., can be carried out. The analog values
of the point of regard coordinate are available in buffered form
on the rear apron of the ECP.

In order for the host computer to be able to read in the coordinates, they are converted to digital form by the analog to
digital converters. After conversion, they are transmitted by
line drivers to the Device Controller and ultimately onto the I/O
bus of the host computer. The Device Controller is responsible
for isolating only those commands that are of interest to the
ECPSC. The computer I/O bus is a parallel bi-directional bus and
as such, all devices connected to the host computer send signals
over it. Each Device Controller has a unique device code associated with it and as such can isolate those commands of interest
to its device. The Device Controller is also responsible for placing data from the ECPSC on the I/O bus.

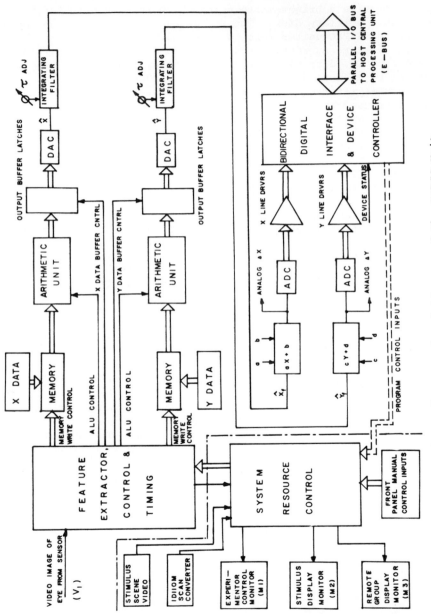

Figure 5. Functional Diagram of the ECPSC Unit

VII. GENERAL OPERATING SYSTEM SOFTWARE

The operating system or system executive, that is resident in the host computer, should be designed to allow for control of all functions and running modes via easily understood commands entered from the teletype. An integrated software structure should allow for control in the areas of calibration, data gathering, data filtering, track display, data compression and replay. The stored data should be available for review at speeds suited for analysis, once initial capture is made. This means that provision must be made for slow motion and incremental replay of either the original raw track data or the filtered data.

An additional area that the system executive should be responsible for is the actual running of an experiment, insofar as this can be automated. Sequencing of stimulus slides for the subject, timing functions etc. could all be under the control of the executive. The following diagram illustrates software responsibilities:

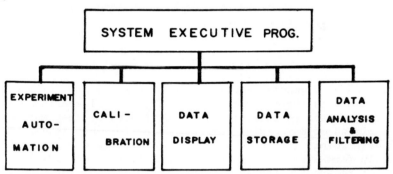

Figure 6. Structure of the Operating System

Calibration Functions

The calibration routine establishes a function or set of functions, which can be used to relate measured eye position to actual eye position. Typically, an m by n array of points with known coordinates is fixated point by point by the subject, while measured coordinates are stored.

A two dimensional mapping can be formulated to map the measured point (X_m, Y_m), into the estimated actual point of regard $(\hat{X}, \hat{Y})$. This mapping function correct for cross-coupling between axes, non-linear and multiplicative effects and time varying system parameters if necessary. Alternatively, instead of extimating the fixation point using estimation equations, a table look-up procedure can be implemented to arrive at an estimate of eye position, by interpolation within this table.

Eye Position Recording Software

Due to the sophisticated processing performed by the ECPSC, as well as the packed data format and low word rate, a polling interface is implemented in this design. Between processing functions within the main program, periodic branches are made to a sense routine to determine the status of the eye position sensing device regarding computation of a new point. Thus, the interface works asynchronously, with control assured by hand-shaking protocol. The service routine, initiated by a sense true condition, will be responsible for input and storage in core of the new data word.

Approximately two minutes of real-time data can be internally stored, filtered and displayed. Software drivers for core to magnetic tape or disk transfers are responsible for transfer of blocks of data to the bulk storage devices at appropriate times. Generally, storing the original raw data is preferred to storing processed or filtered data, since once the data is compressed, the original sequence of points is generally no longer available for post-experimental processing.

VIII. CLUSTERING

The data is generally compressed by the use of a clustering algorithm and is stored in a variety of ways. Clustering algorithms can be based on intuition and experience, or they may be based on minimizing or maximizing some chosen performance index. Eye track data points (the sequential points of regard of the subject) spatially form a two-dimensional distribution. The individual points of regard however are functions of three variables, two coordinates (x and y) and a temporal coordinate (time). In normal clustering procedures, the clustering is done on all points in parallel. Domain boundaries are established to minimize the performance index. The data points can be grouped at will. In eye track data however, the points have to be grouped with their temporal component in mind. Points may be deleted but not interchanged. Thus, for eye track data, a clustering algorithm must proceed in a sequential manner. Most standard approaches to clustering, such as nearest neighbor algorithms as well as minimum mean squared error clustering must be modified to work with sequential data.

It is difficult to define a performance measure which can be minimized by a sequential algorithm. However, intuition and knowledge of physical parameters do point towards a solution in this case as in many other practical cases. The approach uses a distance metric together with threshold testing based on physical processes. In general, this type of procedure yields a suboptimal but generally very useful solution.

Consider the schematic representation of a typical eye track shown in Figure 7a. The track in Figure 7a is shown in its entire-

178

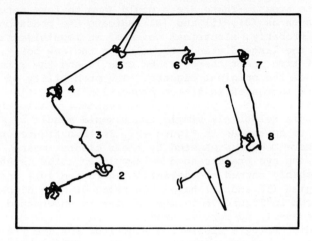

Figure 7a.   Representative Eyetrack

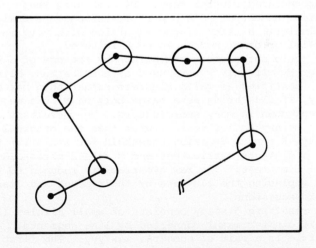

Figure 7b.   Filtered Eyetrack Corresponding to Figure 7a

ty for ease of presentation. The action of the filter actually
proceeds sequentially on a point by point basis. A number of features are immediately apparent. There are some areas of concentration, such as regions (1), (2), (4), (6) and (7) that indicate
tentative cluster centers. The large concentration of points in a
relatively small area imply that the subject is locally investiga-
ting those areas. These areas would seem to form natural clusters.
Regions such as (3), (5) and (8) indicate the presence of a blink
(or less probably, electrical noise of an impulsive nature) because of the large distance traveled to the new point, the small
amount of time spent there (33-66 msec.), and the return to the
vicinity of the original cluster. The probability of the occurance
of a blink increases in direct proportion to the time spent in a
given area because of physiological reasons. Easier interpretation of this relatively simple track would result if Figure 7a were
filtered to appear as in Figure 7b. In this figure, the cluster
domains have been represented by their cluster means. The variations in the eye track caused by impulsive noise (such as that
which probably caused the deviation in region (9)) and blinks (such
as in region (5) and (8) have been removed. The display of the eye
track shown in Figure 7b is much easier to understand and lends itself more easily to further study.

In discussing a clustering algorithm for eye track filtering
there are two key parameters. One can be called minimum dwell time
within a cluster domain and the second the maximum size of a cluster. Regarding minimum dwell time, a certain lower limit usually
exists, below which the subject has no opportunity to gether significant data. The dwell time (N), is proportional to the number of
points included in the cluster, since points arrive at a constant
rate of 30 per second. The other parameter, cluster radius (R),
sets a maximum deviation that a new data point can have relative
to the accumulated cluster mean. By combining these two criteria
(the minimum number of points per cluster and the maximum radius
of the cluster), a blink (large excursion with very short (1/30
sec.) dwell) or other noise can be eliminated.

One could not cluster the points by the use of a single parameter R or N. If only R were used as a criterion, blink excursions
would be identified as valid clusters rather than being suppressed.
Similarly, if clustering were based only on N, the major clusters
would break down in many sub-clusters. The resultant display
would not be any easier to interpret than the original eye track.
In summary, R sets a decision threshold for a similarity measure
based on a distance metric test and N sets a threshold for a minimum dwell time test. The raw eye track is reduced to its essentials by replacing the clusters by their means and discarding noise
and blink excursions.

The resulting display consists of small circles (located at
each valid cluster mean) connected by line segments. Next to each
small circle is a pair of numbers, xxx/yyy. The first (xxx) is
the fixation point number (0, 1, 2, 3,...) while the second (yyy)
is the number of points which were averaged into the cluster.

Since points occur at a rate of 30 per second, yyy gives the dwell time in units of 33.3 msec. This annotated eye track overcomes the difficulty of most past eye track analysis systems, in that the track can be seen in its entirety, viz. the sequence of the fixation points can be identified along with the fixation dwell time.

This graphical image is then overlayed electronically on the experimenter's monitor with the stimulus scene being viewed by the subject. The operating system allows replay of the eye track in real-time or in slow motion. The operating system also allows for interactive clustering by allowing the experimenter to run the clustering filter with parameters entered from a teletype console. The results are available instantaneously. An example of an un-processed eye track together with the results of processing by the clustering algorithm for a given set of parameters, are shown in Figure 8a and Figure 8b.

Notice that the extraneous excursions (caused by system noise as well as physiological "noise") are mostly eliminated. If the clustering used did not appear adequate, then new parameters for R and N could be re-entered and the results viewed instantaneously.

IX. SUMMARY

With the completion of the EMAT system, Figure 9, in October 1975, there now exists a unique, elaborate real-time, on-line in-teractive system for the measurement, collection, storage, analy-sis, retrieval, and re-display of point of regard time histories (eye tracks). The system provides for variable speed replay of the original data, as well as for building easily indexed librar-ies of eye tracks with their corresponding stimulus scenes. The subject data can be viewed and interpreted as it occurs or it may be reaccessed and reviewed at a later time at a more leisurely speed of replay. The data can be interactively filtered and the results viewed immediately and directly compared with the scene they are superimposed upon.

Various other data analysis programs are now being formulated, which will aid in evaluating the eye track. Typical examples are displacement distribution as well as velocity distribution. Once the data is stored in immediately accessible form by EMATS, many types of rapid processing that would have been impossible previ-ously can be easily carried out.

A few potential areas of application are listed below:

1) Pattern recognition and feature extraction.
   (a) Determination of the nature of the evoked response adaptive scan.
   (b) Study feature extraction and ranking.
   (c) Study effectiveness of image enhancement techniques.
   (d) Study change detection and target tracking by humans.

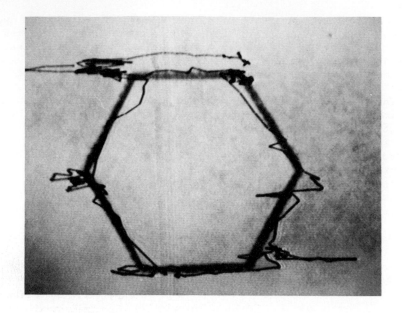

Figure 8a.   Sample Eye Track

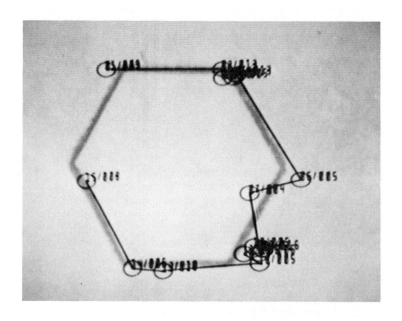

Figure 8b.   Result of Filtering
Eye Track of Fig. 8a

Figure 9.   R.P.I. Computer Graphics and Image Processing
            Laboratory

2) Medical uses for diagnoses of brain dysfunction as well as visual system disorders. Evaluation of learning disorders.
3) Human factors and safety engineering.
4) Visual communication studies.
5) Control of systems based on eye position data.

Of particular interest to researchers at R.P.I. are areas one, two and five.

As part of the formal presentation of this paper, a video tape was shown which illustrated the operation of and some results produced by the EMAT system. This video tape is a one-half inch, helical scan tape, 17 minutes in length and can be made available by contacting Dr. Lester A. Gerhardt, Electrical and Systems Engineering Dept. Rensselaer Polytechnic Institute, Troy, NY.

REFERENCES

1. Andrews, H. C., *Introduction to Mathematical Techniques in Pattern Recognition*, Wiley and Sons, New York, 1972.
2. Yarbus, A. L., *Eye Movements and Vision*, Plenum Press, New York, 1967.
3. Davison, H., *The Eye*, Vol. 1-4, Academic Press, New York and London, 1962.
4. Fukunaga, K., *Introduction to Statistical Pattern Recognition*, Academic Press, New York, 1972.
5. Technical Report No. RADC-TR-71-194, "The Viewing Hood Oculometer", Mason, K. A., Merchant, J., Honeywell Radiation Center, 1971.
6. Geldard, F. A., *The Human Senses*, Second Edition, John Wiley and Sons, New York, 1972.
7. Corby, N., Sims, E., Gerhardt, L., "An Interactive System for Digital Image Processing and Pattern Recognition:, EIA/AIPR Conference, April 1975.
8. Corby, N. R., "The Design and Development of a Real-Time, Online, Interactive, Minicomputer Based Eye Motion Measurement Analysis System", Doctoral Thesis, R.P.I., Troy, NY, 1976.

DESIGN OF OPTIMAL FEATURE EXTRACTORS BY
MATHEMATICAL PROGRAMMING TECHNIQUES*

Rui J. P. de Figueiredo
Rice University
Houston, Tex.

I.   INTRODUCTION

The "feature extraction" operation plays a very significant
role in the functioning of a pattern recognition system. For this
reason, considerable attention has been devoted to the feature extraction problem in the pattern recognition literature (see, for
example, [1] and [2] and the references therein). However, most
of the existing techniques for feature extractor design rely on
the maximization of some average distance measure amongst pattern
classes in the "feature (transformed) space."

More recently, it was proposed by the author [3] that the performance of the entire pattern recognition system ought to be taken
into account when selecting the optimal feature extraction transformation. According to this point of view, the structure of the
desired feature extractor would be tuned to the classification
strategy adopted in a given problem. In particular, if the classification strategy were Bayes, the optimal feature extraction transformation would be the one that would minimize, over a suitable
class of admissible transformations the Bayes risk (probability of
misclassification) in the feature space. The problem thus posed
becomes essentially a mathematical programming problem.

In what follows, we formulate precisely the above problem in
a framework sufficiently general to permit the use of statistical
and/or linguistic considerations. Then, for the case in which the
classification strategy is Bayes, we discuss the important design
considerations and cite some specific results.

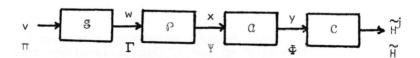

Fig. 1.   Block Diagram of a Pattern Recognition System.

* Supported by the AFOSR Grant 75-2777.

II. MATHEMATICAL FORMULATION

The general configuration of a pattern recognition system is depicted in Fig. 1. It consists of four blocks representing respectively a system S of sensors, a preprocessor P, a feature extractor Q, and a classifier C. In an actual hardware implementation, some of these blocks may overlap or be combined into a single unit.

The sensing system S converts the excitation from a "pattern" v being perceived by S into some form of raw data w. This data is usually contaminated by "distortion" and "noise" introduced by the sensing devices and the environment. The preprocessor P simply removes, to the extent possible, this distortion and noise from w by means of some "cleaning" (filtering, enhancement, restoration, . . .) operation. Thus the output x from P is what may be called "clean data" or "preprocessed signal". The feature extractor Q then measures the values of a set of variables pertaining to x called "features". Hopefully these variables contain most of the information needed for recognition purposes. Finally, if y denotes the output of Q, the classifier C assigns y to some pattern class H^j, and thus the recognition operation is completed.

It may be remarked in passing that, in some pattern recognition literature (see, for example, [1], p.7), the preprocessor P and the feature extractor Q are considered to be one and the same entity. Here, we make the distinction between P and Q, in the sense that P performs a "signal processing" operation on the raw data with the objective of essentially optimizing the signal-to-noise ratio without necessarily taking the ultimate use of the signal into account (many of the so-called "picture processing" papers deal with this problem); on the other hand, the objective of Q is to provide measurements on the (filtered) signal solely for the purpose of recognition.

Let us now attempt to formulate precisely the problem under consideration.

Let π denote the set of all patterns v to be sensed by S. Assume that π may be partitioned into M pattern classes H^1, ..., H^M, and let the set $\{H^1, \ldots, H^M\}$ be denoted by H. Each member of H is to be classified as belonging to some H^j.

Let Γ, Ψ, Φ and $\tilde{H}$ denote the sets of outputs from respectively S, P, Q, and C.

As done earlier in this section, members of Γ, Ψ, and Φ will be denoted respectively by w, x, and y. Any given output from C is a statement saying that a pattern v being perceived by S belongs to some class H^j. We will denote such a statement simply by $\widetilde{H}^j$. The set of all $\widetilde{H}^j$, j=1, ..., M, constitutes the set $\widetilde{H}$ mentioned above.

In order to describe the operation of S, P, Q, and C we introduce respectively the maps

$$S: \quad \pi \to \Gamma, \tag{1}$$

$$P: \quad \Gamma \to \Psi \tag{2}$$

$$A: \quad \Psi \to \Phi \tag{3}$$

$$C: \quad \Phi \to \tilde{H} \tag{4}$$

The operation of the pattern recognition system may now be expressed by

$$\tilde{H}^j = C(A(P(S(v)))) \tag{5a}$$

$$\overset{\Delta}{=} K(v) \tag{5b}$$

It ought to be noted that in (5a) the superscript j on $\tilde{H}^j$ is generic, that is, depending on v, $\tilde{H}^j$ could be any one of the statements $\tilde{H}^1, \ldots, \tilde{H}^M$.

In terms of the above notation then, we will call a given set $\{\pi, H\}$ a "pattern structure". Also, given any "pattern recognition system", we will refer to it by the set of maps $\{S, P, A, C\}$ or simply by the corresponding composition map K, which describes it.

In our formulation, we will assume, as in most practical cases, that S is fixed because of hardware constraints, and so is P since the design of P is conditioned by the structure of S, as we pointed out earlier.

The same is not true with regard to the two remaining maps A and C. Clearly, A is not fixed since our very objective is to select a $A^* \in \chi$ which is optimal with respect to all maps A belonging to an admissible class χ.

Usually the classification strategy is selected beforehand. However, since the domain of C depends on A, the structure of the classifier itself will vary with A. To signal this fact we will replace the symbol C by C_A.

One final consideration is the inclusion of training sets in our problem formulation. Such sets constitute the main source of information on a given pattern structure, on the basis of which a recognition system for that structure can be designed. We will denote by Λ^j the available training set pertaining to the pattern class H^j, $j=1, \ldots, M$. Elements of Λ^j will be denoted by u^j, and when necessary to distinguish these elements among themselves we will number them with subscripts, thus $u^j_1, u^j_2, \ldots, u^j_{N_j}$, where N_j is the total number of training samples in Λ^j.

In a conventional way, we will assume that the elements in Λ^j, $j=1, \ldots, M$, are independent (with respect to some underlying probability measure), and that each Λ^j is partitioned into two subsets: a subset Λ^j_C is used in the construction of the structure of the classifier, and a subset Λ^j_A used in the design of the map A. Let

$$\Lambda = \Lambda^1 \cup \Lambda^2 \cup \ldots \cup \Lambda^M \tag{6}$$

and define the partition of Λ into Λ_C and Λ_A where

$$\Lambda_C = \Lambda^1_C \cup \Lambda^2_C \cup \ldots \cup \Lambda^M_C, \tag{7}$$

$$\Lambda_A = \Lambda^1_A \cup \Lambda^2_A \cup \ldots, \cup \Lambda^M_A. \tag{8}$$

To indicate that the structure of the classifier is based on Λ_C we will replace C_A by $C_{A\Lambda_C}$.

Let a function ξ from $\tilde{H} \times \tilde{H}$ to the reals be defined by

$$\xi\,(\tilde{H}^j,\ \tilde{H}^k) = 1 - \delta_{jk}, \quad j,k = 1, \ldots, M, \tag{9}$$

where δ_{jk} = Kronecker delta.

Then the total cost (risk or probability) of misclassification when all the training samples in Λ are presented to a pattern recognition system $\{S, P, A, C_{A\Lambda_C}\}$ is

$$Q(A) = \sum_{j=1}^{M} \sum_{u_i^j \in \Lambda^j_A} \alpha_{jk(i)} \xi(\tilde{H}^j, C_{A\Lambda_C}(A(P(S(u_i^j))))), \tag{10}$$

where the nonnegative constants $\alpha_{jk(i)}$ are suitable "cost" weights. The subscript $k(i)$ on $\alpha_{jk(i)}$ is the superscript on the output $\tilde{H}^k$ of the pattern recognition system with u_i^j as input, i.e. $\tilde{H}^k =$

$$C_{A\Lambda_C}(A(P(S(u_i^j)))). \tag{11}$$

The optimal feature extractor design problem now reduces to the following:

Problem. Let all the symbols be defined as above. For the purpose of finding a system $\{S, P, A, C\}$ to recognize a pattern structure (π, H), suppose that you are given S, P, Λ, a classification strategy C, a set of weights α_{jk}, $j,k=1, \ldots, M, j \neq k$, and a class χ of admissible maps A. Find a $A^* \in \chi$ which minimizes $Q(A)$ defined by (10) over all $A \in \chi$.

At this point, the following observations about our formulation are in order:

(i) In selecting the feature extraction map, we are considering the performance of the entire pattern recognition system.

(ii) Except for the mild measurability condition assumed on the training sets needed to justify our criterion functional (10), no restrictions have been imposed on the ranges and domains of the four maps constituting our pattern recognition system. So our formulation may be used when the pattern recognition system under consideration is described either by operators in linear vector spaces as in statistical pattern recognition [1], or by the formal language approach [4].

(iii) We have developed our general formulation to the point where, with the addition of details pertaining to a specific application, the feature extractor design problem becomes a very well-defined nonlinear programming problem which can be readily solved by any one of the standard algorithms available in the literature [5].

III. SPECIFIC CONSIDERATIONS AND RESULTS

3.1. *The structure of* π, Γ, Ψ *and* Φ .

A given pattern recognition application would determine the structures of the sets π, Γ, Ψ, and Φ. In many applications, Γ, Ψ, and Φ are linear spaces, the dimensions of Γ and Ψ being high and that of Φ low. For this reason, the selection of A is sometimes called the "dimensionality reduction" problem.

From now on, we will assume that Φ and Ψ are linear spaces.

3.2. *The characterization of* χ.

One important consideration in the design of the optimal A* is the characterization of the class χ of admissible transformations A. A very general class that we propose is that of continuous functions from Ψ to Φ. We denote such a class by χ_C. Provided the domain of each $A \in \chi_C$ is assumed compact, any member of χ_C can be represented to any desired degree of accuracy by a polynomic operator [6] [7]. In particular, if Ψ and Φ are finite-dimensional with dimensions n and m respectively, a member of χ may be approximated by m multivariate polynomials p_i, i = 1, ...,m, expressing the components of y = $(y_1, ..., y_m) \in \Phi$ in terms of the components of x = $(x_1, ..., x_n) \in \Psi$, thus

$$y_i = A_i(x) = p_i(x_1, ..., x_n), \quad i = 1, ..., m. \qquad (12)$$

A subclass of such χ_C is the class χ_{CL} of linear transformations consisting of all m×n matrices.

The various discrete transforms (e.g. Fourier, Walsh, ...)

that have been used in digital data processing are linear transformations and may be used as intermediate vehicles in composing
a subclass of χ_{CL}.
For example, suppose we pick for this purpose the discrete
Fourier transform which we denote by D. Then D is a linear transformation from Ψ to $\tilde{\Psi}$, the span of an appropriate discrete Fourier
transform basis elements. The dimension of $\tilde{\Psi}$ is the same as that
of Ψ and hence equal to n. It is well-known that in some pattern
recognition problems, events pertaining to different pattern classes are better separated in the transformed domain Ψ. For the purpose of dimensionality reduction then, one would follow the transform operation by some other appropriate linear operation L. For
example, L could select m of the spectral components of the transformed data vector, the choice of these components being such that
those m components containing the maximum amount of information
needed for recognition are selected. In this case, we would construct a subset of χ_{CL} consisting of all maps A = LD, different A's
corresponding to different L's (different choices of m spectral
components).

3.3. *The Bayes risk as Criterion Functional*

If the pattern structure to be recognized is modeled probabil-
istically, then the criterion functional (10), with appropriate
interpretation, may be viewed as the Bayes risk (probability of
misclassification).
Thus in the probabilistic case, for j=1, ..., M, let $f_Y(y/H^j$,
A) denote the probability density function for the random vector
$Y = (Y_1, \ldots, Y_m)$ conditioned on the pattern class H^j and on the
transformation A. Here we consider the elements $y = (y_1, \ldots, y_m)$
$\in \Phi$ as realization of the random vector Y conditioned on one of
the pattern classes. Also, let P_j denote the prior probability
for H^j and β_{ij} the cost of classifying a y arising from H^j as pertaining to H^i. Then the *Bayes risk* is:

$$Q(A) = \sum_{\substack{i=1}}^{M} \sum_{\substack{j=1 \\ j \neq i}}^{M} P_j \beta_{ij} \int_{\Omega_i(A)} f_Y(y, H^j, A) \, dy, \tag{13}$$

where $\Omega_i(A)$ is the Bayesian decision region in Φ for H^i.

If

$$\beta_{ij} = 1 - \delta_{ij}, \quad i, j=1, \ldots, M, \tag{14}$$

(13) reduces to the *probability of misclassification*

$$Q(A) = \sum_{\substack{i=1 \\ j=1 \\ j\neq i}}^{M} \sum_{j=1}^{M} P_j \int_{\Omega_i(A)} f_Y(y/H^j, A) \, dy. \tag{15}$$

Under (14), the decision regions $\Omega_i(A)$ appearing in (15) are defined by

$$\Omega_i(A) = \{y \in \Phi : g_{ij}(y,A) > 0 \ j\neq i, \ j=1, \ldots, M\}, \ i = 1, \ldots, M, \tag{16}$$

where

$$g_{ij}(y, A) = P_i f_Y(y/H^i, A) - P_j f_Y(y/H^j, A). \tag{17}$$

We assume that the functions f_Y satisfy conditions that allow $\Omega_i(A)$ to be well defined (see [3]).

A number of ways of estimating the probability of error from the training samples have been reviewed by Toussaint [8].

However, a new way of estimating the error in the feature space has been proposed and studied by Sagar and the author [9]. This approach essentially considers the discriminant functions g_{ij}, $i = 1, \ldots, M-1$, $j = 2, \ldots, M$, $j>i$, as random variables.

For given $f_Y(y/H^j,A)$, $j = 1, \ldots, M$, we define the conditional distributions F_j, $j = 1, \ldots, M$, as follows: For any given (M-1) real numbers $\gamma_1, \ldots, \gamma_{M-1}$, we have*

$$F_1 (\gamma_1, \gamma_2, \ldots, \gamma_{M-1}/A)$$

$$= \text{Prob } \{y : g_{12}(y,A) \leq \gamma_1, \ldots, g_{1M}(y,A) \leq \gamma_{M-1} / y \in H^1\},$$

$$F_2 (\gamma_1, \ldots, \gamma_{M-1} / A) \tag{18-1}$$

$$= \text{Prob } \{y : -g_{12}(y,A) < \gamma_1, g_{23}(y, A) \leq \gamma_2, \ldots, g_{2M}(y,A) \leq \gamma_{M-1}$$

$$/ y \in H^2\}, \tag{18-2}$$

$$\cdots$$

$$F_M (\gamma_1 \ldots, \gamma_{M-1} / A)$$

$$= \text{Prob } \{y : -g_{1M}(y,A) < \gamma_1, -g_{2M}(y,A) < \gamma_2, \ldots, -g_{M-1,M}(y,A) < \gamma_{M-1}$$

$$/ y \in H^M\}. \tag{18-M}$$

It now follows that the expression (15) for the probability of misclassification is equivalent to**

---

*$y \in H^j \longleftrightarrow y$ arises from a pattern belonging to H^j.

**Strictly speaking, some of the arguments, of F_j, $j\neq1$, in (19) should be written 0- instead of 0, to show that we are referring to left-hand limits corresponding to the strict inequalities in equations (18).

$$Q(A) = \sum_{j=1}^{M} P_j \, F_j \, (\, 0, \, 0, \, \ldots \, , \, 0/ \, A).$$ (19)

In writing an estimate $\hat{Q}$ (A) of (19) on the basis of training samples, we first use the samples in Λ_C to obtain estimates $f_Y(y/H^j,A)$ of the functions $f_Y(y/H^j,A)$ by means of the Parzen kernel [10], [11]. This in turn leads to estimates $\hat{g}_{ij}$ (y,A) of $g_{ij}(y,A)$ via equation (17). We use the training samples in Λ_A to obtain the estimates $\hat{F}_j(., \ldots, ./A)$ of the distributions $F_j(., \ldots, ./A)$ defined by equations (18-1) through (18-M) and hence the estimates $\hat{F}_j$ (0,...,0/A), appearing in (19).

By means of the Kiefer-Wolfowitz [12] generalization of the Kolmogorov [13] and Smirnov [14] theory, one can derive bounds on the error in the estimate $\hat{Q}(A)$ of the probability of error $Q(A)$. Details of this study will appear elsewhere [9].

3.4. *Optimal Dimensionality of the Feature Space*

The optimal dimension m of the feature space Φ is intimately related to the size of the training set Λ. This is because, for sets Λ_A and Λ_C of fixed sizes, the errors in the estimates $\hat{g}_{ij}$ and $\hat{F}_j$ of the functions g_{ij} and F_j decrease with m(that is, the lower the m the closer the $\hat{g}_{ij}$ and $\hat{F}_j$ to g_{ij} and F_j); on the other hand, the probability of error increases with decreasing m, because of the loss of information by reduction of dimensionality. This indicates that the optimal dimension m should be the one that corresponds to the best compromise between the aforementioned two competing effects.

While some papers have appeared previously [15-17] on the dimensionality-versus-sample-size problem, we have studied this problem in the context of the feature extraction problem using the developments mentioned in the preceding section, and these results appear in [9] and [18].

3.5. *The Mathematical Programming Approach*

From all the preceding considerations it is clear that the problem of optimal feature extractor design stated at the end of section 2 is a well-defined nonlinear programming problem with the criterion functional given by (10) or (19) to be minimized, and the constraints specified by the properties of the given pattern structure to be recognized, and by the class χ over which the optimization is to be carried out.

Typically, in any given application, a complete study and implementation of this approach would require: (a) the study of conditions for the existence and uniqueness of the optimal A*; (b) development of efficient convergent algorithms for the determination of A*; (c) programming and testing of these algorithms on a computer with simulated and real data bases.

All these phases have been carried out by the author and his associates for Gaussian pattern structures and for the class of linear feature extractors in [3, 18-20]. Also, phases (a) and (b) of the study of the general non-Gaussian nonlinear case has nearly been completed by A. Sagar and the author, and these results will appear in future.

IV. CONCLUSION

A mathematical programming approach has been described for the design of a processor for feature extraction in pattern recognition.
The main consideration in the development of the design algorithm is the optimization of the recognition capability of the system taking into account the realistic constraints appearing in a particular application.

REFERENCES

1. Meisel, W. S., Computer-Oriented Approaches to Pattern Recognition. Academic Press, New York, 1972.
2. Chen, C. H., "On Information and distance measures, error bounds, and feature selection", *Information Sciences*, 10, 159-173 (1976).
3. de Figueiredo, R.J.P., "Optimal linear and nonlinear feature extraction based on the minimization of the increased risk of misclassification," Rice University Institute for Computer Services and Applications Technical Report #275-025-014 (June, 1974) and Proceedings of the Second Joint International Conference on Pattern Recognition, Copenhagen, Denmark, August, 1974.
4. Fu, K.S., Syntactic Methods in Pattern Recognition. Academic Press, New York, 1974.
5. Luenberger, D.G., Introduction to Linear and Nonlinear Programming. Addison-Wesley, Reading, Mass., 1973.
6. Prenter, P.M., "A Weierstrass theorem for real normed linear space", *Bull. Amer. Math. Soc.*, 75, 860-862 (1969).
7. Prenter, P.M., "On polynomial operators and equations" in *Nonlinear Functional Analysis and Applications*. (L. Rall, Editor). Academic Press, New York, 1971.
8. Toussaint, G.T., "Bibliography on estimation of misclassification", *IEEE Trans. on Info. Theory*, IT-20, 472-479 (1974).
9. Sagar, A. and de Figueiredo, R.J.P., to be published.
10. Cacoullos, T. "Estimation of a multivariate density", *Annals of the Institute of Statistical Mathematics* (Tokyo), *18*, 179-189 (1966).
11. Bennett, J.O., de Figueiredo, R.J.P., and Thompson, J.R., "Classification by means of B-spline potential functions with application to remote sensing", in *Proc. of the Sixth South-*

eastern Symposium on System Theory, Louisiana State University, Baton Rouge, La., February, 1974.

12. Kiefer, J. and Wolfowitz, J., "On deviations of the empirical distribution functions of vector chance variable", *Trans. Am. Math. Soc.*, *87*, 173-186 (1958).

13. Kolmogorov, A.N., "Determinazione empirica di una legga di distribuzione", *Giornale Instit. Ital. Attuari*, 4, 83 (1933).

14. Smirnov, N., "Sur les ecarts de la courbe de distribution empirique", *Mat. Sbornik*, *48*, 3 (1939).

15. Highleyman, W.H., "The design and analysis of pattern recognition experiments," *Bell Syst. Tech. Journal*, *41*, 723-744 (1962).

16. Hughes, G.F., "On the mean accuracy of statistical pattern recognizers", *IEEE Trans. on Information Theory*, *IT-14*, 55-63 (1968).

17. Kanal, L.N. and Chandrasekaran, B., "On dimensionality and sample size in pattern recognition", *Pattern Recognition*, *3*, 225-234 (1971).

18. Starks, S.A., de Figueiredo, R.J.P., and Van Rooy, D.L., "An algorithm for optimal single linear feature extraction from several Gaussian pattern classes", To appear in the *Intl. Journal of Computer and Information Sciences*, vol. 6, No. 1.

19. de Figueiredo, R.J.P., "Feature extraction techniques for classification and identification of spectral signatures", *Proc. of the 1976 Milwaukee Symposium on Automatic Computation and Control*, pp. 303-304, 1976.

20. de Figueiredo, R.J.P., Pau, K.C., Sagar, A.D., Starks, S.A. and Van Rooy, D.L., "An algorithm for extraction of more than one optimal linear feature from several Gaussian pattern classes", Rice University ICSA Technical Report No. 275-025-026 (EE Tech. Report No. 7604), April 1976. (To appear in the Proc. of the 3rd. Joint Intl. Conference on Pattern Recognition, Coronado, California Nov. 1976).

TYPOLOGICAL SELECTION
OF PARAMETERS

E. Diday
University of Paris 9, Paris
and IRIA, Le Chesnay, France

SUMMARY

Given a set of objects E characterized by two groups of parameters J_1 and J_2, the problem is to detect simultaneously the
parameter(s) of J_1 and the partition of E (into a number of classes
given beforehand) that optimize a certain criterion W. This criterion expresses the association between the selected parameters
of J_1, the partition that has been obtained and the parameters of
J_2. Algorithms are introduced that provide a good approach to this
type of problem. Their properties are studied in the case of nominal data for quadratic distances. Finally, local regression and
typological discrimination analysis are introduced.

1. INTRODUCTION

From a practical standpoint, the user is faced increasingly
with large-scale *tables* of data; one of his major concerns is trying to select those parameters that provide the best "explanation".
The purpose of this study is to facilitate the construction of a
set of programs to help the user make his selections both in the
case of certain highly significant mathematical criteria and of
large tables.

All these programs require as *input* the giving of a set E of
objects characterized by two groups of parameters J_1 and J_2. The
problem is to select the parameters of J_1 that best "explain" J_2.
One must use the term "explain" carefully. In fact, the methods
referred to here, make it possible to show certain numerical occurrences between the selected parameter(s) of J_1 and the parameters
of J_2. It will then be up to the user to interpret this discovery
by justifying -or not- the term "explain" with a complementary
study.

From the point of view of pattern recognition (cf. [6],[7])
the problem is generally to select a set of parameters among a set
J_1 which explains as well as possible patterns given a priori (for
example, characterized by a nominal, qualitative parameter). Here
we assume that we are given a field of fuzzy, imprecise patterns
characterized by the parameters of J_2. We then look simultaneously
for the parameters of J_1 and the patterns of J_2 such that these
patterns are significant and that these parameters explain them
the best.

From the point of view of data analysis the formalism stated here includes classical segmentation as a special case, (cf. [1], [2],[3]) and to some extent, discrimination; the main difference being that the partition obtained is imposed neither by the explanatory variables (as in segmentation) nor by the variables to explain (as in discrimination).

2. NOTATIONS

E   :the set of objects

J   :the set of parameters characterizing the elements of E

J_1 :the set of explanatory parameters.

C   :the set $[J_1]^k = J_1 \times \ldots \times J_1$, k times.

J_2 :the set of parameters to explain.

B   :is a set depending on J_2 (for example the set of the elements of E characterized by the parameters of J_2 or else $B \equiv \mathbb{R}^{\text{card}(J_2)}$).

$\mathbb{P}$:the set of the parts of E.

$\mathbb{P}_k$:the set of the partitions into k classes of E.

3. THE PROBLEM

We must optimize the following criterion W : W is an application $C \times \mathbb{P}_k \to \mathbb{R}^+$ such that:

$$W\ (j,P) = \sum_{\ell=1}^{k} \sum_{i \in [P_\ell]} \left[\mu_t(X_i)\ d_{j\ell}\ (h_{j\ell}\ (P_\ell),\ x_{ij_\ell}) + \mu_s\ (X_i)\ d\ (h(P_\ell),\ X_i) \right]$$

- $j = (j_1, \ldots , j_k)$, in this vector one may have j_i identical to j_ℓ.
- $P = (P_1, \ldots , P_k)$
- X_i is the ith element of E.
- $[P_\ell]$ is the set of indices of the elements of E that belong to P_ℓ.
- $h_{j\ell}$ is an application $\mathbb{P}$ (E) $\to \mathbb{R}^+$ such that $h_{j\ell}$ (P_ℓ) yields the kernel of P_ℓ for the parameter j_ℓ (the kernel is a representation of P_ℓ for instance, the center of gravity of P_ℓ restricted to the parameter j_ℓ).
- h is an application of $\mathbb{P} \to \mathbb{R}^+$ such that h (P_ℓ) yields the kernel for the set of parameters to explain (J_2).
- μ_t and μ_s are two applications E $\to \mathbb{R}^+$ which verify the property
  $$\mu(A) = \sum_{a \in A} \mu(a)\ \forall\ A \in E$$
- x_{ij_ℓ} is the coordinate j_ℓ of the element X_i.
- d_{j_ℓ} is a measure of resemblance associated to the parameter j_ℓ.

It allows us to measure the resemblance of the j_ℓ coordinate of an element of E to a given kernel.

- d allows us to measure the resemblance between a kernel and an element of E characterized by the parameters of J_2.

The problem consists in looking for the couple (j*,P*) that minimizes W among all the elements of CxP.

So as to provide an intuitive idea of what W expresses, we may for instance want to discover $j* = (j_1*, \ldots, j_k*)$ and $P* = (P_1*, \ldots, P_k*)$ such that $\forall \, \ell \in \{1,2, \ldots, k\}$, $P_\ell*$ be the "least dispersed possible" in J_2 *and* for the parameter $j_\ell*$.

4. COMPARISON WITH CLASSICAL SEGMENTATION AND DISCRIMINATION

4.1. *Segmentation*

One can decompose the criterion W into two parts W_1 and W_2 such that:

$$W_1 \, (j,P) = \sum_{\ell=1}^{k} \sum_{i \in [P_\ell]} \mu_t \, (X_i) \, d_{j_\ell} \, (h_{j_\ell} \, (P_\ell), \, x_{ij_\ell})$$

$$W_2 \, (P) = \sum_{\ell=1}^{k} \sum_{i \in [P_\ell]} \mu_s \, (X_i) \, d \, (h(P_\ell), \, X_i)$$

We thus have $W = W_1 + W_2$. Here we consider that d and d_ℓ are quadratic and that $h_{j_\ell} \, (P_\ell)$ (resp. h (P_ℓ)) is the center of gravity of P_ℓ for the parameter j_ℓ (resp. the parameters J_2). If we fix K = 2 and if we consider that all the parameters of J_1 are dichotomous, then classical segmentation consists in minimizing first W_1 then W_2 in the following way:

any solution $Y_\ell = (j*,P*)$ such that $j* = (j_\ell, j_\ell)$ and such that $P* = (P_1, P_2)$ is the dichotomy associated with the parameter j_ℓ and means that $W_1 \, (j*,P*) = 0$. Trying to minimize W_2 among the set of partitions P* induced by the solutions $Y_\ell (\ell = 1, 2, \ldots,$ card $J_1)$ obtained in the preceding stage is exactly the problem of classical segmentation (cf. [1],[2],[3]).

4.2. *Discrimination*

For discrimination (cf. [4],]5]), the problem is to find the most discriminating parameters of a given partition. The problem we pose here is different since we are looking for the partition *and* for the most discriminating parameters at the same time. Both problems, however, are alike if J_2 is reduced to a single qualita-

tive parameter. This means trying to minimize W_2 which yields P*
(the partition induced by this parameter), then minimize $W_1(j,P*)$
with P* fixed which yields j* the most discriminating explanatory
parameter(s).

5. THE FUNCTIONS OF REPRESENTATION, AND OF IDENTIFICATION AND THE NEW EXPRESSION OF THE CRITERION.

- let $D_t : J_1 \times \mathbb{P} \times \mathbb{P} \to \mathbb{R}^+$ a measure of resemblance of j_ℓ to
P_2 "conditioned by" P_1, in other words, such that:

$$D_t (j_\ell, P_1, P_2) = \sum_{i \in [P_2]} \mu_t (X_i) d_{j\ell} (h_{j_\ell} (P_1), x_{ij\ell})$$

- let $D_s : B \times \mathbb{P} \to \mathbb{R}^+$ a measure of resemblance such that:

$$D_s (a,P_1) = \sum_{i \in [P_1]} \mu_s (X_i) d (a, X_i)$$

- Calculation of the kernels: we introduce the two following
applications R_1 and R_2.

. $R_1 : J_1 \times k] \times \mathbb{P} \times \mathbb{P}_k \to \mathbb{R}^+$ is defined by:

$$R_1 (j_\ell, m, Q, P) = D_t (j_\ell, Q, P_m)$$

$$= \sum_{i \in [P_m]} \mu_t (X_i) d_{j\ell} (h_{j\ell} (Q), x_{ij\ell})$$

. $R_2 : B \times]k] \times \mathbb{P}_k \to \mathbb{R}^+$ is defined by:

$$R_2 (a, m, P) = D_s (a, P_m) = \sum_{i \in [P_m]} \mu_s (X_i) d (a, X_i)$$

- let $\mathbb{C}_k = [J_1 \times B \times \mathbb{P}]^k$ the set of kernels.

The application $g : \mathbb{P}_k \to [J_1 \times B \times \mathbb{P}]^k = \mathbb{C}_k$ is defined by
$g (P) = A$ where $A = (A_1,...,A_k)$ with $A_i = (j_i, a_i, P_i)$ where j_i
is the element that minimizes $R_1 (.,i, P_i,P)$ among $j_\ell \in J_1$; a_i
is the element that minimizes $R_2 (.,i,P)$ among $a \in B$.
Calculation of the partitions:

- let the kernel $A_i = (j_i, a_i, Q_i) \in J_1 \times B \times \mathbb{P}$ then
$D:E \times \mathbb{C}_k \to \mathbb{R}^+$ which measures the resemblance between an element
of E and a kernel is defined by:

$$D (X_\ell, A_i) = \mu_t (X_\ell) d_{j_i} (h_{j_i} (Q_i), x_{\ell j_i}) + \mu_s (X_\ell) d (X_\ell,a_i)$$

The application $f : \mathbb{C}_k \to \mathbb{P}_k$ is such that $f (A) = P$ where

$P = (P_1, \ldots, P_k)$ with $P_i = \{ X \in E / D(X, A_i) \leqslant D(X, A_j) \}$ in a case of equality X is affected to the class with the smallest index.

With the notations thus introduced, we can express the criterion by means of a more general function:

$W_G : \mathbb{C}_k \times \mathbb{P}_k \to \mathbb{R}^+$ such that:

$$W_G(A,P) = \sum_{i=1}^{k} [R_1 (j_i, a_i, Q_i, P) + R_2 (a_i, i, P)]$$

where $A = (A_1, \ldots, A_k)$ with $A_i = (j_i, a_i, Q_i)$, $Q = (Q_1, \ldots, Q_k)$ is a set of k parts of E where $P = (P_1, \ldots, P_k) \in \mathbb{P}_k$.

We can find the criterion W introduced in section 3 again by taking $A_i = (j_i, a_i, P_i)$ $\forall$ i we have $W_G (A,P) = W (A,P)$.

6. THE ALGORITHM

It is based upon the construction of two sequences v_n and u_n which we are now going to give:

We assume that $P^{(n)} = (P_1^{(n)}, \ldots, P_k^{(n)})$, $A^{(n)} = (A_1^{(n)}, \ldots, A_k^{(n)})$ with $A_i^{(n)} = (j_i^{(n)}, a_i^{(n)}, P_i^{(n-1)})$, $v^{(n)} = (A^{(n)}, P^{(n)})$.

We define v_n on v_{n-1} as follows: $v_{n-1} = (A^{(n-1)}, P^{(n-1)})$ allows first to define $A^{(n)}$ with the help of g as follows:

$A^{(n)} = g (P^{n-1})$; more specifically:

(1)
$j_i^{(n)}$ is the element of J_1 that minimizes

$R_1 (.,i,P_i^{(n-1)}) = D_t (.,P_i^{(n-1)}, P_i^{(n-1)})$

$= \sum_{\ell \in [P_i^{(n-1)}]} \mu_t (X_\ell) \, d. \, (h.(P_i^{(n-1)}),x_\ell).$

$a_i^{(n)}$ is the element of B that minimizes $R_2 (.,i,P^{(n-1)}) = D_s (.,P_i^{(n-1)}).$

We deduce $P^{(n)}$ from $A^{(n)}$ with the help of f by posing $P^{(n)} = f(A^{(n)})$; in other words: $P_i^{(n)} = \{X \in E / D(X,A_i^{(n)}) \leqslant D (X,A_\ell^{(n)})\}$ with $D (X_\ell, A_i^{(n)}) = \mu_t (X_\ell) \, d_{j_i (n)} \, (h_{j_i (n)} (P_i^{(n-1)}), x_{\ell_{j_i}} (n))^+$

$\mu_s (X_\ell) \, d (X_\ell, a_i^{(n)}).$

Initialization:

Thus we see that the datum of $P^{(o)}$ (estimated or drawn at random) allows us to initialize the algorithm; thus with the help of (1) we can construct $j_i^{(1)}$ and $a_i^{(1)}$. So we have $A^{(1)}$ hence $P^{(1)} = f(A^{(1)})$.

Definition of the sequence u_n : we assume $u_n = W(v_n)$.

PROGRAM

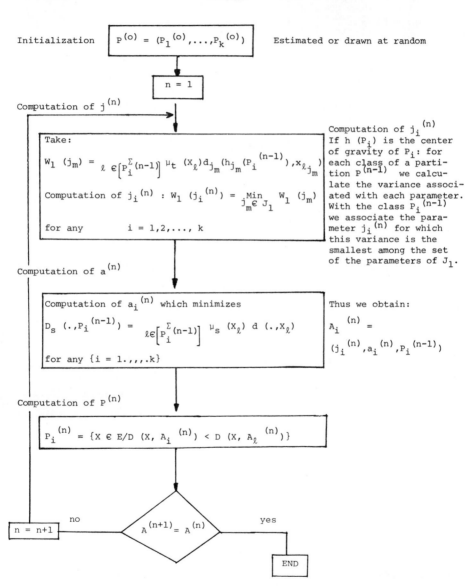

Initialization $\quad P^{(o)} = (P_1^{(o)}, \ldots, P_k^{(o)})$ $\quad$ Estimated or drawn at random

$n = 1$

Computation of $j^{(n)}$

Computation of $j_i^{(n)}$
If $h(P_i)$ is the center of gravity of P_i: for each class of a partition $P^{(n-1)}$ we calculate the variance associated with each parameter. With the class $P_i^{(n-1)}$ we associate the parameter $j_i^{(n)}$ for which this variance is the smallest among the set of the parameters of J_1.

Take:

$$W_1(j_m) = \sum_{\ell \in [P_i^{\Sigma(n-1)}]} \mu_t(x_\ell) d_{j_m}(h_{j_m}(P_i^{(n-1)}), x_{\ell_{j_m}})$$

Computation of $j_i^{(n)}$: $W_1(j_i^{(n)}) = \min_{j_m \in J_1} W_1(j_m)$

for any $\quad i = 1, 2, \ldots, k$

Computation of $a^{(n)}$

Computation of $a_i^{(n)}$ which minimizes

$$D_s(., P_i^{(n-1)}) = \sum_{\ell \in [P_i^{\Sigma(n-1)}]} \mu_s(x_\ell) d(., x_\ell)$$

for any $\{i = 1.,,,.k\}$

Thus we obtain:

$A_i^{(n)} = (j_i^{(n)}, a_i^{(n)}, P_i^{(n-1)})$

Computation of $P^{(n)}$

$$P_i^{(n)} = \{X \in E/D(X, A_i^{(n)}) < D(X, A_\ell^{(n)})\}$$

$n = n+1$ $\quad$ no $\quad$ $A^{(n+1)} = A^{(n)}$ $\quad$ yes

END

7. STUDY OF THE CONVERGENCE

Theorem 1:

If $h = (h_{j_1}, \ldots, h_{j_k})$ is such that:

$$R_1 (j_\ell, \ell, Q_\ell, P) > R_1 (j_\ell, \ell, P_\ell, P) \ \forall \ j_\ell \in J_1, Q_\ell \in P$$

$P = (P_1, \ldots, P_\ell, \ldots, P_k) \in \mathbb{P}_k$, then the sequence u_n decreases while converging.

Demonstration:

We have:

$$u_{n-1} = W (A^{(n-1)}, P^{(n-1)}) = \sum_{\ell=1}^{k} \left[R_1 (j_\ell^{(n-1)}, \ell, P_\ell^{(n-2)}, P^{(n-1)}) + R_2 (a_\ell^{(n-1)}, \ell, P^{(n-1)}) \right]$$

Take $y_n = W (A^{(n)}, P^{(n-1)})$

$$= \sum_{\ell=1}^{k} \left[R_1 (j_\ell^{(n)}, \ell, P_\ell^{(n-1)}, P^{(n-1)}) + R_2 (a_\ell^{(n)}, \ell, P^{(n-1)}) \right]$$

As it is hypothesized in the theorem, we have:

$$R_1 (j_\ell^{(n-1)}, \ell, P_\ell^{(n-2)}, P^{(n-1)}) \geqslant R_1 (j_\ell^{(n-1)}, \ell, P_\ell^{(n-1)}, P^{(n-1)})$$

Hence

$$u_{n-1} \geqslant \sum_{\ell=1}^{k} \left[R_1 (j_\ell^{(n-1)}, \ell, P_\ell^{(n-1)}, P^{(n-1)}) + R_2 (a_\ell^{(n-1)}, \ell, P^{(n-1)}) \right] \geqslant y_n$$

By merely constructing $j_\ell^{(n)}$ and $a_\ell^{(n)}$, we obtain the second inequality.

We must still show that $y_n \geqslant u_n$. Now:

$$y_n = \sum_{\ell=1}^{k} \left[D_t (j_\ell^{(n)}, P_\ell^{(n-1)}, P_\ell^{(n-1)}) + D_s (a_\ell^{(n)}, P_\ell^{(n-1)}) \right]$$

$$= \sum_{\ell=1}^{k} \left[{}_{i\in}\Sigma \left[P_\ell^{(n-1)} \right] \mu_t (X_i) d_{j_\ell(n)} (h_{j_\ell(n)} (P_\ell^{(n-1)}), x_{ij_\ell(n)}) + i^\Sigma_\in \left[P_\ell^{(n-1)} \right] \mu_s (X_i) d (a_\ell^{(n)}, X_i) \right]$$

(2) $\quad y_n = \sum\limits_{\ell=1}^{k} \left[\sum\limits_{i \;\in\; \left[P_\ell\right]^{(n-1)}}\right] D\;(X_i,\;A_\ell^{(n)})$

On the other hand:

$u_n = \sum\limits_{\ell=1}^{k} \left[\sum\limits_{i \;\in\; \left[P_\ell\right]^{(n)}} \mu_t\;(X_i)\;d_{j_\ell}\;(n)\;(h_{j_\ell}\;(n)\;(P_\ell^{(n-1)}),x_{ij_\ell}(n)) + \right.$

$\left. \sum\limits_{i \;\in\; \left[\Sigma P_\ell\right]^{(n)}} \mu_s\;(X_i)\;d\;(a_\ell^{(n)},\;X_i) \right]$

(3) $\quad u_n = \sum\limits_{\ell=1}^{k} \left[\sum\limits_{i\in\; \left[P_\ell\right]^{(n)}}\right] D\;(X_i,\;A_\ell^{(n)})$

Let's take any term of the sum (2), or D $(X_i, A_\ell^{(n)})$ for instance as $P^{(n)}$ and $P^{(n-1)}$ are partitions, X_i appears equally in (3); or $D(X_i,\; A_{\ell_{(n)}}^{(n)})$ the term where X_i appears in (3) by merely constructing $P_i^{(n)}$ we have D $(X_i,\; A_\ell^{(n)}) \leqslant$ D $(X_i,\; A_\ell^{(n)})$. As the same reasoning holds $\forall\; X_i \in E$, we have indeed $y_n \geqslant u_n$.

8. CASE OF QUADRATIC DISTANCE

8.1. *Expression of the criterion in the case of quadratic distances.*

Reminders about quadratic distances:

We suppose that E is embedded in $\mathbb{R}^n$.
We note X_i for i = 1, ..., card E the elements of E with
$X_i = (x_{i1}, \ldots, x_{im})$.
Let P = $(P_1, \ldots, P_k)$ a partition of E.
Let μ a measure on E such that $\mu\;(P_i) = \sum\limits_{a\in P_i} \mu\;(A)\;\forall\; P_i \in E$
and assume that: D $(x,P_i) = \sum\limits_{a\;\in\; P_i} \mu(a)\;d\;(x,a)$; $G(P_i) =$
$\dfrac{1}{\mu\;(P_i)} \sum\limits_{a\in P_i} \mu(a)\;a$; var $P_i = \dfrac{1}{\mu\;(P_i)} \sum\limits_{a\in P_i} \mu(a)\;d\;(a,G(P_i))$

According to the Koenig-Huygens theorem, we have

(4) $\quad$ var $(\bigcup\limits_{i=1}^{k} P_i) = \sum\limits_{i=1}^{k} \mu(P_i)$ var $P_i + D\;(P_1,\;\ldots\;P_k)$

where D $(P_1,\;\ldots,\;P_k) = \sum\limits_{i=1}^{k} \mu(P_i)\;d\;(G(P_i),\;G\;(\bigcup\limits_{j=1}^{k} P_j))$

In addition we have the following properties:

(5) $D(x,P_i) = \mu(P_i) \left[\text{var } P_i + d(x, G(P_i)) \right]$ and

$$D(P_i, P_j) = \frac{\mu(P_i)\ \mu(P_j)}{\mu(P_i) + \mu(P_j)}\ d(G(P_i), G(P_j))$$

Remark:

Let $S_j(y) = \sum\limits_{i \in [P_\ell]} \mu_t(X_i)\ d_j(y, x_{ij})$

We can easily show that if $h_{j\ell}(P_\ell) = \inf\limits_{y \in \mathbb{R}^+} S_j(y)$, then

$R_1(j, Q_\ell, P) > R_1(j,\ell,P_\ell,P)$. It follows that if the d_j are quadratic distances and if $h_{j\ell}(P_\ell)$ is the center of gravity of P_ℓ for the parameter j_ℓ, then the hypothesis of the theorem is verified.

General expression of the criterion:

Let $A = (A_1, \ldots, A_k)$ with $A_\ell = (j_\ell, a_\ell, Q_\ell)$

$$W(A,P) = \sum_{\ell=1}^{k} \left[R_1(j_\ell, \ell, Q_\ell, P) + R_2(a_\ell, \ell, P) \right]$$

$$= \sum_{\ell=1}^{k} \sum_{i \in P_\ell} \left[\mu_t(X_i)\ d_{j_\ell}(h_{j_\ell}(Q_\ell), x_{ij_\ell}) + \mu_s(X_i)\ d(a_\ell, X_i) \right]$$

We suppose that d and d_j are quadratic $\forall j$. We note $\text{var}_j(P_\ell)$ is the variance of P_ℓ for the parameter j, $G_j(P_i)$ the center of gravity of P_i for the parameter j.

According to (5) the criterion can be written as:

(6)
$$W(A,P) = \sum_{\ell=1}^{k} \left[\mu_t(P_\ell)\ (\text{var}_{j_\ell}(P_\ell) + d_{j_\ell}(h_{j_\ell}(Q_\ell), G_{j_\ell}(P_\ell)) + \mu_s(P_\ell)\ (\text{var}(P_\ell) + d(a_\ell, G(P_\ell))) \right]$$

Here we are led to suppose that $j = (j_1, \ldots, j_k)$ is such that $j_1 \equiv j_2 \equiv \cdots \equiv j_k$ (in other words the j_i all express the same parameter), which can be obtained by adding this constraint at the time of the computation of $j^{(n)}$ in the algorithm without changing the properties of convergence. If the parameters of J_1 are sufficiently homogeneous, we can choose the d_{j_ℓ} all identical and create a new parameter $\tilde{j}$ that assumes the values of j_i for the class P_i. *From now on we shall consider one or the other case and we shall write this parameter $\tilde{j}$.*

Another expression of the criterion can be obtained by using (4). According to this formula we obtain:

$$\sum_{\ell=1}^{k} \mu_t (P_\ell) \, \text{var} \, \tilde{j} (P_\ell) = \text{var} \, \tilde{j} \, E - D_{\tilde{j}} (P_1, P_2, \ldots, P_k) \text{ where}$$

$$D_{\tilde{j}} (P_1, \ldots, P_k) = \sum_{\ell=1}^{k} \mu_t (P_\ell) \, d_{\tilde{j}} (G_{\tilde{j}}(P_\ell), G_{\tilde{j}}(E))$$

By using similar formulas for the second part of the criterion we have:

$$W (A,P) = \mu_t (E) \, \text{var} \, \tilde{j} \, E + \mu_s (E) \, \text{var} \, E$$

(7)
$$- \sum_{\ell=1}^{k} \left[\mu_t(P_\ell) d_{\tilde{j}}(G_{\tilde{j}}(P_\ell), G_{\tilde{j}}(E)) + \mu_s (P_\ell) \, d (G(P_\ell), G(E)) \right]$$

$$+ \sum_{\ell=1}^{k} \left[d_{\tilde{j}}(h_{\tilde{j}}(Q_\ell), G_{\tilde{j}} (P_\ell)) + d (a_\ell, G(P_\ell)) \right]$$

8.2. *Variant of the center of gravity.*

For this variant we consider that $h_j(P_i)$ is the center of gravity of P_i and that B is identical to $R \, \text{card} \, J_2$, in other words (cf. demonstration of theorem I) :

$$y_n = \sum_{\ell=1}^{k} \left[\sum_{i \in \left[P_\ell \right]^{(n-1)}} \right] \left[\mu_t (X_i) \, d_{\tilde{j}(n)} (h_{\tilde{j}(n)} (P_\ell^{(n-1)}), x_{\tilde{j}(n)}_{ij}) + \right.$$

$$\left. \mu_s (X_i) \, d (a_\ell^{(n)}, X_i) \right]$$

$$y_n = \sum_{\ell=1}^{k} \left[\sum_{i \in \left[P_\ell \right]^{(n-1)}} \right] \left[\mu_t (X_i) \, d_{\tilde{j}(n)} (G_{\tilde{j}(n)} (P_\ell^{(n-1)}), x_{\tilde{j}(n)}_{ij}) + \right.$$

$$\left. \mu_s (X_i) \, d (G(P_\ell^{(n-1)}), X_i) \right]$$

Because of the very definition of "var_j" and "var" we obtain

$$y_n = \sum_{\ell=1}^{k} \left[\mu_t (P_\ell^{(n-1)}) \, \text{var}_{\tilde{j}(n)} (P_\ell^{(n-1)}) + \mu_s (P_\ell^{(n-1)}) \text{var} (P_\ell^{(n-1)}) \right]$$

Hence according to (4) :

$$Y_n = \mu_t \ (E) \text{var}_{\nu(n) \atop j} (E) + \mu_s \ (E) \ \text{var} \ E - \sum_{\ell=1}^{k} \left[\mu_t (P^{(n-1)}) d_{\nu(n) \atop j} \right.$$

$$\left. (G_{\nu(n) \atop j} (P_\ell^{(n-1)}), G_{\nu(n) \atop j} (E)) + \mu_s (P_\ell^{(n-1)}) \ d \ (G(P_\ell), \ G \ (E)) \right]$$

In the course of the demonstration of theorem 1 we saw that $\forall$ n we have $u_n \leqslant y_n \leqslant u_{n-1}$; as the sequence u_n converges while decreasing after lemma I (choice of C_j), the method of the center of gravity tends to maximize the following quantity:

$$(8) \quad y(\overset{\nu}{j},P) = \sum_{\ell=1}^{k} \left[\mu_t \ (P_\ell) \ d_{\overset{\nu}{j}} (G_{\overset{\nu}{j}} (P_\ell), G_{\overset{\nu}{j}} (E)) + \right.$$

$$\left. \mu_s \ (P_\ell) \ d \ (G(P_\ell), \ G \ (E)) \right]$$

8.3. *Case of qualitative nominal data: maximization of the* χ^2

Let us pose n = card E

We have written the elements of E as $X_i = (x_{i1},..., x_{im})$; in the case of nominal data the variables can assume a finite number of integer values; in other words x_{ij}^{ν} for $i \in \{1, ..., n\}$ assumes an integer value.

The variable j is characterized by the vector

$$Y_{\overset{\nu}{j}} = \begin{pmatrix} x_{1\overset{\nu}{j}} \\ \vdots \\ \vdots \\ x_{n\overset{\nu}{j}} \end{pmatrix}$$

We can transform this vector $Y_{\overset{\nu}{j}}$ into a matrix n x $\tilde{m}$ (in which $\tilde{m}$ is the number of the modalities of the variable $\tilde{j}$) by replacing each x_{ij}^{ν} by the vector with $\tilde{m}$ coordinates $(0,...0, 1, 0, ...0)$ which contains only zeros except for the coordinate of rank x_{ij}^{ν} which is worth 1. Let us write this vector as $(z_{i1},...,z_{i\tilde{m}})$.

Example:

$$Y_{\overset{\nu}{j}} = \begin{pmatrix} x_{1\overset{\gamma}{j}} \\ x_{2\overset{\nu}{j}} \\ x_{3\overset{\nu}{j}} \\ x_{4\overset{\nu}{j}} \end{pmatrix} = \begin{pmatrix} 3 \\ 1 \\ 2 \\ 3 \end{pmatrix} \quad z_{\overset{\nu}{j}} = \begin{pmatrix} z_{11} & z_{12} & z_{13} \\ z_{21} & z_{22} & z_{23} \\ z_{31} & z_{32} & z_{33} \\ z_{41} & z_{42} & z_{44} \end{pmatrix} = \begin{pmatrix} 0 & 0 & 1 \\ 1 & 0 & 0 \\ 0 & 1 & 0 \\ 0 & 0 & 1 \end{pmatrix}$$

Let us consider the following quadratic distance

$$d(X_i, X_{i'}) = \sum_{q=1}^{\overset{m}{m}} \frac{1}{z_{.q}} (z_{iq} - z_{i'q})^2 \text{ where } z_{.q} = \sum_{i=1}^{card\ E} z_{iq}$$

On the other hand from a partition $P = (P_1, \ldots P_k)$ and for a fixed variable Y_j we can construct the following contingency table:

Y_j P	P_1	P_2		P_k	E
1	n_{11}	n_{12}	$\cdots$	n_{1k}	$n_{1.}$
2	n_{21}	n_{22}	$\cdots$	n_{2k}	$n_{2.}$
.	.	.		.	.
.	.	.		.	.
.	.	.		.	.
.	.	.		.	.
m	n_{m1}	n_{m2}	$\cdots$	n_{mk}	$n_{m.}$
sum	$n_{.1}$	$n_{.2}$		$n_{.k}$	$n_{..}$

Let us assume that $\mu_t (X_i) = \mu_s (X_i) = 1 \ \forall \ i.$

Let us consider the table Z; according to the formulas given here, we have:

$$G_j (P_i) = \frac{1}{card\ P_i} \sum_{z \in P_i} z = \frac{1}{n_{.i}} (n_{1i}, \ldots, n_{mi})$$

$$G_j (E) = \frac{1}{n_{..}} (n_{1.}, n_{2.}, \ldots, n_{m.}) \text{ in addition } \frac{1}{z_{.q}} = \frac{1}{n_{q.}}$$

$$d_j (G(P_i), G(E)) = \sum_{q=1}^{m} \frac{1}{n_{q.}} (\frac{n_{qi}}{n_{.i}} - \frac{n_{q.}}{n_{..}})^2$$

New expression of y (j,P):

we have $\sum_{\ell=1}^{k} \mu_t (P_\ell) d_j (G_j (P_\ell), G_j(E)) = \sum_{\ell=1}^{k} \sum_{q=1}^{m} \frac{n_{.\ell}}{n_{q.}} (\frac{n_{q\ell}}{n_{.\ell}} - \frac{n_{q.}}{n_{..}})^2$

By multiplying this quantity by $n_{..}$ we obtain exactly a χ^2 of a $(k-1)(\tilde{m}-1)$ degree of freedom

If J_2 is reduced to a single nominal variable with m modalities taking $d \equiv d_j$ we reach a similar result:

$$n_{..} \sum_{\ell=1}^{k} \mu_s \, (P_\ell) \, d \, (G(P_\ell), \, G(E)) = \chi^2_{(k-1)\,(m-1)} \, .$$

Finally, the method tries to discover the partition $P = (P_1, \ldots, P_k)$ and the parameter j that maximize the sum of two χ^2; the first one of $(k-1)$ $(\tilde{m}-1)$ order, if it is large enough, allows us to reject the hypothesis of independence between the partition P and the parameter $\tilde{j}$; the second one, of $(k-1)$ $(m-1)$ degree of freedom, if it is large enough, allows us to reject the hypothesis between the parameter to explain J_2 and the partition P_k.

One can extend the result to the case when J_2 contains several qualitative parameters $y_1, y_2, \ldots, y_q$ of $m_1, m_2, \ldots m_q$ modalities; we then obtain χ^2 of $(k-1)$ $(\sum_{\ell=1}^{q} m_\ell - 1)$ order. (See 11).

9. PROBLEMS OF CLASSIFICATION WITH MULTIPLE CONSTRAINTS

Let us recall that J, the set of the parameters, is the union of J_1 and J_2. Let us call (E_1, E_2) a partition of E; take J^ℓ a package of parameters contained in J_1.

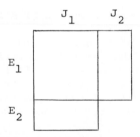

We write $I = (J^1, J^2, \ldots J^n)$. We can then define the criterion:

$$W(P, I) = \sum_{\ell=1}^{n} \sum_{i=1}^{k} \left[\alpha_1 \, F(P_i, \, J^\ell) + \alpha_2 \, F(J^\ell, \, P_i) \right]$$

$$+ \, \alpha_3 \sum_{i=1}^{k} F \, (P_i, \, J_2) + \alpha_4 \sum_{\ell=1}^{n} F(J^\ell, \, E_2)$$

Where $P = (P_1, \ldots P_k)$ is a partition of E_1, W is an application of $\mathbb{P} \, (E) \times \mathbb{P} \, (J_1) \to \mathbb{R}^+$

Posing $F \, (x, y) = \mathrm{var}_x y$ we have:

$F \, (P_i, \, J^\ell) = \mathrm{var}_{P_i} J^\ell, \; F \, (J^\ell, \, P_i) = \mathrm{var}_{J^\ell} P_i$ (where $\mathrm{var}_x y$ is the variance of y with, as parameters, the elements of x) and: $\alpha_2 = \alpha_3 = 0$ the algorithm that we have studied here, allows us to improve the criterion:

$$W(P,J^\ell) = \sum_{i=1}^{k} \alpha_1 F(P_i, J^\ell) + \alpha_3 \sum_{i=1}^{k} F(P_i, J_2) \text{ with } P \in P_k$$

$J^\ell \in J_1$ and card J^ℓ fixed.

G. Govaert* has suggested an algorithm whenever the J^ℓ s form a partition of J allowing us to improve the criterion

$$W(P, I) = \sum_\ell \sum_i (\alpha_1 F(P_i, J^\ell) + \alpha_2 F(J^\ell, P_i)).$$ In this case, the question is to find the partition of the individuals and the partition of the parameters such that the contingency tables of the classes associated with these partitions tend to maximize the χ^2 of contingency associated with this table with $(n-k)(k-1)$ degrees of freedom.

If we pose the same problem with $\alpha_3 \neq 0$ and $\alpha_4 \neq 0$, we must then find the partitions P and I yielding the best contingency under the constraint E_2 and J_2.

In all these cases, the simultaneous representation of the $F(P_i, J_\ell)$ for any i and ℓ can be interesting namely in the case of large tables.

10. CODING UNDER CONSTRAINT

When the parameters of J_1 are all ordinal (qualitative or quantitative) variables, the partition obtained at the convergence point of the algorithm, induces a coding**of the selected parameter that has taken into account the constraint imposed by the parameters of J_2. Thus, if all the parameters are continuous no preliminary coding is necessary; one has an adaptive coding of the selected parameters.

In case one wanted to code a fixed parameter j under the constraint J_2, the criterion to optimize would then be written as

$$W(j,P) = \sum_{i=1}^{k} (\text{var}_j P_i + \text{var}_{J_2} P_i)$$

---

* IRIA report to be published.

** Coding a parameter means that each class of the partition obtained corresponds to a given integer.

One can obtain a good local optimization of such a criterion by using the dynamic clusters methods [11] over the population characterized by the parameters $j \in J_2$.

When j is an ordered variable, Y. Lechevallier* gives an algorithm that allows the *optimal* minimization of $W(P) = \sum\limits_{i=1}^{k} \text{var}_{J_2} P_i$

with the constraint: "for any i, any two individuals of P_i are part of the same contiguous interval of j".

11. LOCAL LINEAR MODELS

1. *The Problem**:*

The data are given in a table of m lines written $z \in E$ and n + 1 columns written x^1, x^2, ..., x^p, y.

The ith object of E is written

$$z_i = (x_i^{\ 1}, x_i^{\ 2} \ldots x_i^{\ p}, y_i)$$

The space of the kernels is $\mathbb{L} = \mathbb{R}^p$. We write $\mathbb{L}_k = (\mathbb{L})^k$ the space of the k kernels:

$B \in \mathbb{L}_k \Longrightarrow B = (B_1, \ldots, B_k)$ with $B_j \in \mathbb{R}^p$.

We write $\mathbb{P}_k$ the space of the k partitions:

$$P \in \mathbb{P}_k \Longrightarrow P = (P_1, P_2 \ldots, P_k).$$

We write:

z_i^j the ith element of the class P_j; the corresponding coordinates are

$$z_i^j = (x_i^{1,j}, \ldots, x_i^{p,j}, y_i^j).$$

We assume that $n_j = \text{card } P_j$, $z^j = \begin{pmatrix} z_1^j \\ \cdot \\ \cdot \\ z_{n_j}^j \end{pmatrix}$, $x^{\ell,j} = \begin{pmatrix} x_1^{\ell,j} \\ \cdot \\ \cdot \\ x_{n_j}^{\ell,j} \end{pmatrix}$

$x_i^j = (x_i^{1,j}, x_i^{2,j}, \ldots, x_i^{p,j})$ represents the P first coordinates of the ith element of P_j.

---

* IRIA report to be published.

** A recent bibliography on this problem can be found in [8].

$$x^j = \begin{pmatrix} x_1^{1,j} & \cdots & x_1^{p,j} \\ x_i^{1,j} & \cdots & x_i^{p,j} \\ x_{n_j}^{1,j} & \cdots & x_{n_j}^{p,j} \end{pmatrix} \qquad B_j = \begin{pmatrix} b_j^1 \\ \vdots \\ b_j^p \end{pmatrix} \qquad y^j = \begin{pmatrix} y_1^j \\ \vdots \\ y_{n_j}^j \end{pmatrix}$$

2. *The criterion to optimize:*

$$W : \mathbb{L}_k \times \mathbb{P}_k \to \mathbb{R}^+ \qquad W(L,P) = \sum_{j=1}^{k} \left\| y^j - x^j B_j \right\|^2 = \sum_{j=1}^{k} \sum_{i=1}^{n_j} (y_i^j - x_i^j B_j)^2$$

We must find (L*,P*) such that :

$$W(L^*, P^*) = \min_{(L,P)\, \in\, \mathbb{L}_k \times \mathbb{P}_k} W(L,P)$$

3. *The method :*

3.1. *The function of identification f :*

f is an application $\mathbb{L}_k \to \mathbb{P}_k$: f (B) = P where

$$P_i = \{z \in E/ \ d\ (z, B_i) \leqslant d\ (z, B_j)\}$$

where $d : E \times \mathbb{R}^p \to \mathbb{R}^+$

$d\ (z_i, B_j) = (y_i - X_i B_j)^2$ where $X_i = (x_i^1, \ldots, x_i^n)$ and $z = (X_i, y_i)$

3.2. *The function of representation g :*

g is an application $\mathbb{P}_k \to \mathbb{L}_k$: g (P) = $(B_1, B_2, \ldots B_k)$

where B_j minimizes $R\ (B,j,P) = \sum\limits_{z \in P_j} d\ (z, B)$

$R(B_j,j,P) = \text{Inf } \{R\ (B,j,P)\ /\ B \in \mathbb{R}^p\}$ $B_j = ((X^j)' X^j)^{-1} (X^j)' y^j$

(Normal equations, we suppose thus that X is injective.).

Construction of the sequences v_n and u_n.

The sequence v_n is defined in the following way: $v_o = (P^{(o)}, B^{(o)})$ where $P^{(o)}$ is estimated or taken at random. v_{n+1} is deduced from $v_n = (P^{(n)}, B^{(n)})$ as follows: $B^{(n+1)} = g\ (P^{(n)})$ and $P^{(n+1)} = f\ (B^{(n+1)})$.

The sequence u_n is defined by $u_n = W(v_n)$

Theorem : the sequence u_n decreases while converging.

Demonstration:
We must only show successively that $(B^{n+1}, P^n) = w_n$ verifies $W(v_n) > W(w_n)$, then that $W(w_n) > W(v_{n+1})$.

We know that $B^{(n+1)} = g(P^{(n)})$ is defined by the normal equations hence

$$\sum_{i=1}^{n_j} (y_i^j - x_i^j B_j^{(n)}) > \sum_{i=1}^{n_j} (y_i^j - x_i^j B_j^{(n+1)}),$$ (the y_i^j and x_i^j

being fixed $B_j^{(n+1)}$ is the best possible solution in any case) and this for all the classes. We still have to show that $W(w_n) > W(v_{n+1})$. Let us take any given term in the development of $W(w_n)$ for instance

$$(y_i^j - x_i^j B_j^{(n+1)}) \; ; \; \text{two cases may occur:}$$

a) $d(z_i^j, B_j^{(n+1)}) < d(z_i^j, B_m^{(n+1)}) \forall m$, z_i^j does not change

class.

b) $m : d(z_i^j, B_j^{(n+1)}) > d(z_i^j, B_m^{(n+1)})$, then by construction

of v_{n+1}, z_i^j belongs to the class m and the term $(y_i^j -$

$x_i^j B_j^{(n+1)})$ of $W(w_n)$ is replaced by the term $(y_i^m -$

$x_i^m B_m^{(n+1)})$ of $W(v_n)$; as $(y_i^m - x_i^m B_m^{(n+1)}) < (y_i^j -$

$x_i^j B_j^{(n+1)})$ and as one can apply the same reasoning for

all the terms of $W(w_n)$, we obtain the result.

3.3. *Selection of the parameters:*

The classical methods for the selection of parameters in the framework of the linear model must be adapted to the local linear model : examination of all the possible regressions, then selection of the best one ; descending eliminations : we start with the full regression and we remove the parameter that causes the largest increase in error, and we start again with n-1 remaining parameters. We can also use the ascending introduction of the parameters (cf. [9] and [10]).
Problems of convergence arising in the framework of the local linear model would call for developments well beyond the limits of this article.

12. TYPOLOGICAL DISCRIMINATING FACTOR ANALYSIS

12.1. *The problem*

Given a population of n objects characterized by p parameters, the question is to look simultaneously for the best aggregated and separated k classes of objects and the most discriminating factorial plan (or hyper-plan) for these classes.

The typological discriminating factor analysis *under constraint* is expressed in the same way, with the additional condition that the classes obtained will have to be at a minimum variance over J_2.

12.2. *Mathematical formulation*

Take $\mathbb{C}_{\eta_k} = (\mathbb{R}^q)^k \times \mathbb{R}^p$ $\quad p = \text{card } J_1, \quad q = p + \text{card } J_2$

If W is the application $\mathbb{P}_k \times \mathbb{C}_{\eta_k} \rightarrow \mathbb{R}^+$

$$W(P,L) = \sum_{\ell=1}^{k} \left[\sum_{i\in[P_\ell]} \left[\sum_{j\in J_1} b_j (x_{ij} - a_{\ell j}) \right]^2 + \alpha \text{ var}_{j_2} P_\ell \right]$$

where $P = (P_1, \ldots, P_k)$ and $L = (a,b)$ with $a = (a_1, \ldots, a_k) \in (\mathbb{R}^q)^k$

and $b = (b_1, \ldots, b_j) \in \mathbb{R}^p$ plays the role of the first axis of the

typological discriminating factor analysis.

$$\text{var}_{J_2} P_\ell = \sum_{i\in P_\ell} \sum c_j (x_{ij} - a_{\ell j})^2 , \quad a_{\ell j} \text{ is the center of gravity}$$

of the class P_ℓ for the parameter j; x_{ij} is the coordinate j of the element i. $c = (c_1, \ldots, c_{q-p})$ is a ponderation of the parameters of J_2 to be defined by the user.

The mathematical formulation of the problem is the following:

We must find P and b that minimize W (P,L) in $\mathbb{P}_k \times \mathbb{C}_{\eta_k}$.
Minimizing W (P,L) when P and a are fixed is identical to minimize

$$\sum_{\ell=1}^{k} \sum_{i\in[P_\ell]} \left[\sum_{j\in J_1} b_j (x_{ij} - a_{\ell j}) \right]^2$$

$$= \sum_{\ell=1}^{k} \sum_{i\in[P_\ell]} b' (x_i - a_\ell) ' (x_i - a_\ell) b = b' Hb = H (b,b)$$

where H is the sum of the within-class scatter matrix.
We avoid the trivial solution b = 0 by introducing the constraint $\sum_{\ell=1}^{k} m_\ell (\sum_{j=1}^{p} b_j a_{\ell j})^2 = 1$ or else $\quad B (b,b) = 1$

with $B = a\, D_m\, a'$ where $a = (a_1, \ldots a_k)$ and $D_m = \begin{pmatrix} m_1 & & 0 \\ & \ddots & \\ 0 & & m_k \end{pmatrix}$

with m_j = card P_j (to simplify).

The problem then consists in minimizing :

$\quad$ H (b,b) under the constraint B(b,b) = 1

We know that the solution is given by the proper vector of the largest proper value of $V^{-1}B$ where V is the scatter matrix of E.

The method:

$\quad$ We define two applications g and f:

$\quad$ 1) $g : \mathbb{P}_k \to \mathbb{L}_k$ $\quad$ L = g(P) is defined by:
$\quad$ $L = (a_1, \ldots, a_k, b)$ where a_i is the center of gravity of the class P_i and b is the proper vector of the largest proper value of $V^{-1}B$ with $B = a\, D_m\, a'$ and $a = (a_1, \ldots, a_k)$.

$\quad$ 2) $f : \mathbb{L}_k \to P_k$ is defined by f (L) p P $(P_1, \ldots, P_k)$ with

$P_\ell = \{X_k \in E / d_b\ (X_i,\ a_\ell) < d_b\ (X_i,\ a_j)\ \forall\ j \neq \ell\}$ in the case of equality, we attribute X_i to the class with the smallest index.

d_b is the application $E \times \mathbb{R}^p \to \mathbb{R}^+$:

$$d_b\ (X_i,\ a_\ell) = \sum_{j \in J_1} b_j\ (x_{ij} - a_{\ell j})^2 + \sum_{j \in J_2} c_j\ (x_{ij} - a_{\ell j})^2$$

Definition of the sequences u_n *and* v_n:

$\quad$ $u_n = W\ (v_n)$ where v_n is defined as follows:

$\quad$ $v_o = (P^{(o)},\ L^{(o)})$ where $L^{(o)} = (a^{(o)}, b^{(o)})$ with $a^{(o)} \in \mathbb{R}^p$ and
$\quad\quad$ $b^{(o)} \in \mathbb{R}^p$

$\quad$ $v_n = (P^{(n)},\ L^{(n)})$ where $P^{(n)} = (P_1, \ldots P_k)$ and $L^{(n)} = (a^{(n)}, b^{(n)})$

$\quad$ $v_{n+1} = (P^{(n+1)},\ L^{(n+1)})$ with $L^{(n+1)} = (a^{(n+1)}, b^{(n+1)}) = g\ (P^{(n)})$
$\quad\quad$ and $P^{(n+1)} = f\ (L^{(n+1)})$.

$\quad$ *Proposition:* under the constraint B(b,b) = 1 the sequence u_n converges while decreasing.

$\quad$ *Demonstration*

Let us first show that $W(P^{(n)}, L^{(n)}) > W(P^{(n)}, L^{(n+1)})$.

We first have $W(P^{(n)}, (a^{(n)}, b^{(n)})) > W(P^{(n)}, (a^{(n+1)}, b^{(n)}))$ since $a_\ell^{(n+1)}$ is the center of gravity of class $P^{(n)}$ (by definition of application g).
Which is not necessarily the case for $a_\ell^{(n)}$.
In addition:

$W(P^{(n)}, (a^{(n+1)}, b^{(n)})) \geqslant W(P^{(n)}, (a^{(n+1)}, b^{(n+1)}))$ for,

under the constraint $B(b,b) = 1$, we know that $H(b^{(n+1)}, b^{(n+1)}) \leqslant H(b,b) \; \forall \; b \in \mathbb{R}^p$ by construction of g.

We have indeed $W(P^{(n)}, L^{(n)}) \geqslant W(P^{(n)}, L^{(n+1)})$, we must still show that

$$W(P^{(n)}, L^{(n+1)}) \geqslant W(P^{(n+1)}, L^{(n+1)})$$

$$W(P^{(n)}, L^{(n+1)}) = \sum_{\ell=1}^{k} \sum_{X_i \in P_\ell^{(n)}} d_b(n+1)(X_i, a_\ell^{(n+1)}) \qquad (1)$$

$$W(P^{(n+1)}, L^{(n+1)}) = \sum_{\ell=1}^{k} \sum_{X_i \in P_\ell^{(n+1)}} d_b(n+1)(X_i, a_\ell^{(n+1)}) \; (2)$$

Let us take an individual X by the very construction of $P^{(n+1)}$ and let us suppose that it shows in the term $d_b(X, a_j^{(n-1)})$ in (1) and $d_b(X, a_\ell^{(n+1)})$, in (2), by construction $P^{(n-1)}$, we have necessarily $d_b(X, a_j^{(n+1)}) \geqslant d_b(X, a_\ell^{(n+1)})$; as we can use the same reasoning for all the individuals of this population we have the result.

13. CONCLUSION

As far as pursuing and extending the results obtained here, new pathways are open to research: in segmentation, the study of different types of coding (only the nominal case was studied in depth), heuristics for the selection of combinations of parameters, the choice of different types of distances; in local regression, the study of singularities, the introduction of pseudo-inverses, of the ridge regression. In typological discrimination, the introduction of stepwise methods, the search for the most discriminating k-hyperplans, the utilization of other affectation rules.

The problems we have raised are independent from the algorithms that have been proposed; it would be necessary to compare different types of algorithms and study techniques to improve on local optimization.

In terms of pattern recognition, the work that we have presented rests upon the following problem of perception as its basic theme: that is to say how to select the parameters that allow one to recognize and represent a set of objects in a given context.

BIBLIOGRAPHY

1. Baccini, A., (1975), "Aspect synthétique de la segmentation et traitement de variables qualitatives à modalités ordonnées" Thèse Université Paul Sabatier de Toulouse.
2. Morgan, J. N., and R. C. Messenger, (1974), "A sequential analysis program for the analysis of nominal scale dependant variable survey research center". Institute for Social research. The University of Michigan, USA.
3. Tenenhaus, M., and J. M. Bouroche, (1970). "Quelques méthodes de segmentation". RAIRO, vol V-2.
4. Romeder, J. M., (1969). "Méthodes de discrimination" Thèse de 3° Cycle - Faculté des Sciences de Paris - ISUP.
5. Sebestyen, G., (1962). "Decision - Making Process in Pattern Recognition" New York: MacMillan Co.
6. Kanal, L., (1974). "Patterns in Pattern Recognition: 1968-1974" I.E.E.E. on Inf. th. vol II-20, N° 6.
7. Dasarathy, B. V., (1974). "Feature selection and the concept immediate neighborhood in the context of clustering techniques" Proc. I.E.E.E. (Lett.) pp. 529-530 April 1974.
8. Guthery, B., (1974). "Partition Regression" J.A.S.A. Vol 69, N° 348.
9. Efroymson, M., (1962). "Multiple regression analysis" Ralston-Wilf Math. Meth. for dig. comp. Wiley. New-York.
10. Draper n. and H. Smith (1966) "Applied Regression Analysis" Wiley, New York.
11. Diday, E., (1974), "Classification séquentielle pour grands tableaux" RAIRO (9ème année mars 1975, B-1, p. 29 à 61).

REGION EXTRACTION USING
BOUNDARY FOLLOWING

Sahibsingh A. Dudani
Hughes Research Laboratories
Malibu, CA

ABSTRACT

In this paper the problem of extracting regions from a given
picture is discussed. A boundary following algorithm is first described which traces the outer boundary of the region. Based on
the number of boundary points encountered during the tracing, it
is determined whether the region is of desired size. A technique
to generate silhouette corresponding to the boundary found is presented. A silhouette is a binary picture with 1's corresponding
to cells belonging to the area inside the boundary. The concept
of *region-crossing* type of boundary points is used in the silhouette generation process. A combinatorial logic representation for
a region-crossing function is also derived. A region in a given
picture may be extracted with the help of the silhouette generated.
In context of the techniques discussed in this paper, a few illustrative examples of region extraction applications are given.

I. INTRODUCTION

There are numerous image processing applications for which it
would be desirable to extract certain regions in a given scene. A
region in a scene may be characterized with the help of a closed
boundary which separates it from the background or the rest of the
scene. The particular criteria used for separating regions from
its background may depend on the application in use. The three
most common picture properties used for the purpose of separating
regions are the pixel intensities, color, and local texture. For
example, intensity values may be used to separate or extract the
region representing an aircraft image from its light background.
Also, for this same example, color information may be used to extract the aircraft image from its blue background representing the
sky. Texture information is often used for classification of regions representing different types of vegetations in a terrain
map.[1] Once a region boundary is located, it may then be desirable to extract the complete region enclosed by the boundary from
given scene. This step may be necessary in situations where further processing is desired only on the region within the boundary.
For example, one may wish to compute certain picture statistics,
moments, texture, etc., based only on the region of interest in a
given scene.
Numerous techniques for handling boundary following or contour

tracing have been reported in literature. Few of the interesting
references on this subject are given here. In one of the earlier
applications of contour following for character recognition,
Greanias, Meagher, Norman and Essinger [2] used a flying-spot
scanner that progressed along the boundary between the light background and the dark numerals. Freeman [3,4] was first to suggest
the use of a string of integer code words or the directional codes
for contour tracing. An interesting contour follower based on directional codes is described by Polyakov. [5] A method due to
Sidhu and Boute [6] uses a containment code, a special case of the
more general property code, for following the boundary of the regions of a scene. Merrill [7] has proposed use of a novel computer-
searchable representation for a closed boundary. The representation, which has practical storage requirements, provides a rapid
means of searching large files for data associated with geometric
position as well as with attribute value. Based on the concepts of
connectivity, Rosenfeld [8] discusses the validity of certain contour following algorithms. A more detailed list of references on
the subject of boundary following appears in Refs. 8, 9, and 10.

In Section II a technique for tracing a closed boundary for a
region is described. Using certain properties of the closed boundary, an algorithm is developed in Section III to generate a binary
silhouette which corresponds to the entire area within the boundary. Using such a silhouette and the original given scene, the
desired region may be extracted for further processing. A combinatorial logic representation for the silhouette generation algorithm
is derived in Section IV. An extension of this basic algorithm is
presented in Section V for region extraction in more complex situations such as when the area within the boundary is composed of both
the desired region and the background. Section VI summarizes the
work reported in this paper.

II. BOUNDARY FOLLOWING

The first step toward region extraction is the location of its
outer boundary. The criteria used for defining region boundaries
may be based on picture properties such as pixel intensities, col-
or, or textural information. Based on the criteria selected, one
can determine easily whether a picture cell belongs to the desired
region. For example, a simple expedient of thresholding the picture may be used to extract the region from the background, i.e.,
by merely declaring that everything in the picture darker (or
lighter) than a fixed value is in the desired region and therefore
also a candidate for a boundary point. Thus, with the help of a
region criteria, a grey level picture may be reduced to a simple
binary case. It will be assumed here for simplicity that the given
picture has only two levels, dark (level 1) and light (level 0)
cells, and also that the region to be extracted is composed of only dark cells.

There are two main steps involved in the boundary following algorithm described below.

A) *The Search Strategy*

The picture is scanned left-to-right, top-to-bottom until a region cell (based on the region criteria selected) is found. This cell (I_S, J_S) is considered as the starting boundary point. The position of this cell (I_S, J_S) is saved in the first element of a boundary array.

B) *The follow Strategy*

From the starting point (I_S, J_S) found by search strategy, the boundary of the region is followed in such a manner that the region within the boundary is kept always to the left of the path being followed. Let the neighbors of a boundary cell be numbered as shown in Figure 1.

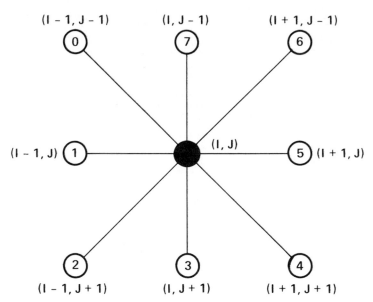

Figure 1. System of numbering the neighbors of a picture cell.

The neighbors of the currently considered boundary cell (I, J) are now checked for a region cell. The checking begins with neighbor $N-2$ (Modulo 8), where N is the number that indicates which of the neighbors of the preceding boundary cell the currently considered cell is. For the starting boundary point (I_S, J_S), N may be considered as being 4, i.e., the checking of neighbors begins with

number 2. When a neighboring region cell is found, it will become
the next currently considered boundary cell. The position of this
cell is saved in the boundary array. A count for the total number
of boundary points found is also kept.

This follow strategy is repeated until the starting point (I_S,
J_S) is again encountered. At this time, it is likely that the complete boundary has been traversed. To check this, the next boundary point is located and compared with the second point in the
boundary list. If the two points are identical, then one can say
that the complete closed boundary has been found. If the two boundary points differ, then it indicates the occurrence of a region for
which the deletion of the first boundary cell (I_S,J_S) would result
in the splitting of the region into two unconnected portions. An
example of such a region is illustrated in Figure 2.

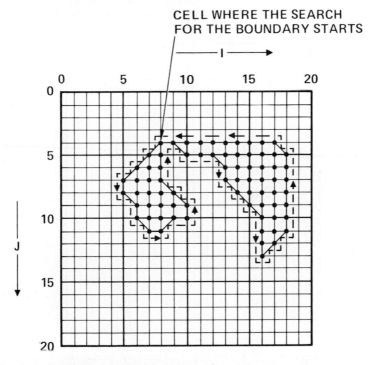

Figure 2. An example where the region has two parts connected by
a one-cell-wide path.

In such a case, the follow strategy is continued until the starting point (I_S,J_S) is once again encountered. Note that this method of following the boundary will prevent it from ever getting into the region within the outer boundary.

An example of a boundary following is illustrated in Figure 3. The boundary search begins at cell (7,4). Note that a region cell may appear more than once in the boundary list depending on the boundary path traversed. For example, the cell (5,5) appears twice, No. 3 and 5, in the boundary list shown in Table I. Also given in the table are the neighbor numbers for the preceding and next boundary cell with respect to the position of the current boundary cell. For example, boundary cell number 8 in the list is at position (5, 8) and the neighbor numbers for the preceding and next boundary cell are 6 and 2. The neighbor numbers for the preceding and next boundary cell are useful for a silhouette generation as will be discussed in the following section.

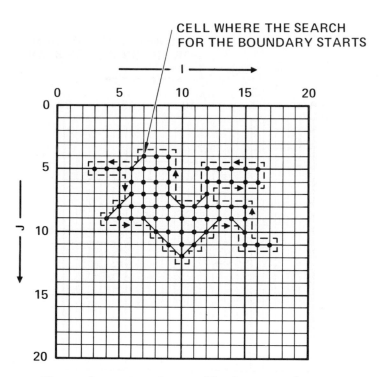

Figure 3. A Boundary Following Example

III. SILHOUETTE GENERATION

A silhouette corresponding to a given closed boundary is defined as a binary picture with 1's corresponding to cells present
within the area enclosed by the closed boundary. In order to extract a region enclosed by a given boundary, one must first identify all the cells which belong to that enclosed region. The silhouette corresponding to a given boundary serves to identify all
the cells belonging to the enclosed region.

An algorithm for silhouette generation based on the list of
boundary points located is presented below. The three steps in
this technique are as follows:

1. A binary silhouette picture with all cells set to 0 is
first generated. Next, for each of the points in the boundary
list, it is determined whether it is a region-crossing point. The
definition of a region-crossing point will be given later in this
section. If the boundary point under consideration is a region-
crossing point, then the corresponding cell in the silhouette picture is complemented, i.e., if it is already 0, then it is set to
1 and, if it is already 1, then it is set to 0. If the boundary
point under consideration is not a region-crossing point, then it
is ignored and the next point in the boundary list is considered.
This is repeated until all boundary points have been considered.
At the end of this step, a binary picture is obtained with certain
cells (corresponding to region-crossing points) set to 1.

2. This step fills in cells between the region-crossing
points present in the silhouette picture generated in Step 1. Each
line is scanned left-to-right. The cells between the region-
crossing point pairs first and second, third and fourth, fifth and
sicth and so on, are set to 1's in each line.

3. Cells in the silhouette picture corresponding to each
point in the boundary list are now set to 1's. At the end of this
final step, a complete silhouette corresponding to the given list
of boundary points is obtained.

Figure 4 shows all possible combinations between positions of a
preceding neighbor, a current neighbor and a next neighbor. Each
of these combinations may fall into one of the following categories:

a. Non-existing type: some of the configurations shown in
Figure 4 will never occur using the boundary following algorithm
discussed in Section II. These configurations are denoted by '-'
in Figure 5. These combinations will be considered as "don't-care"
terms in deriving a combinatorial logic representation for detecting region-crossing points. This is discussed in Section IV.

Table 1

List of Boundary Cells for Figure 1

No.	Position (I,J)	Neighbor Number** of Preceding Boundary Cell	Neighbor Number** of Next Boundary Cell	Region-Crossing Point (Y/N)
1	(7,4)	5*	2	Y
2	(6,5)	6	1	N
3	(5,5)	5	1	N
4	(4,5)	5	5	Y
5	(5,5)	1	4	N
6	(6,6)	0	3	Y
7	(6,7)	7	2	Y
8	(5,8)	6	2	Y
9	(4,9)	6	5	Y
10	(5,9)	1	5	N
11	(6,9)	1	5	N
12	(7,9)	1	4	N
13	(8,10)	0	4	Y
14	(9,11)	0	4	Y
15	(10,12)	0	6	N
16	(11,11)	2	6	Y
17	(12,10)	2	6	Y
18	(13,9)	2	5	N
19	(14,9)	1	4	N
20	(15,10)	0	3	Y
21	(15,11)	7	5	Y
22	(16,11)	1	5	N

222

	(I,J)			
23	(17,11)	1	1	Y
24	(16,11)	5	0	N
25	(15,10)	4	7	Y
26	(15,9)	3	7	Y
27	(15,8)	3	1	Y
28	(14,8)	5	1	N
29	(13,8)	5	0	N
30	(12,7)	4	6	Y
31	(13,6)	2	5	N
32	(14,6)	1	5	N
33	(15,6)	1	5	N
34	(16,6)	1	7	Y
35	(16,5)	3	1	Y
36	(15,5)	5	1	N
37	(14,5)	5	1	N
38	(13,5)	5	1	N
39	(12,5)	5	3	Y
40	(12,6)	7	3	Y
41	(12,7)	7	2	Y
42	(11,8)	6	1	N
43	(10,8)	5	0	N
44	(9,7)	4	7	Y
45	(9,6)	3	7	Y
46	(9,5)	3	7	Y
47	(9,4)	3	1	Y
48	(8,4)	5	1*	N

*The last boundary cell (8,4) is considered as the preceding boundary cell for the first boundary cell (7,4). Similarly, the first boundary cell (7,4) is considered as the next boundary cell for the last cell (8,4).

**The neighboring numbers given in this table are with respect to the corresponding position (I,J) for that entry.

b. Region-crossing points: loosely speaking, these configurations correspond to situations where there are two different regions on the two sides of the current boundary point along the horizontal line. A better feeling for the region-crossing points may
be obtained by studying the Figures 4 and 5. These configurations
are denoted by 'Y' in Figure 5.

c. Non-region-crossing points: this category includes the
remaining configurations that do not fall in the first two categories. These are denoted by 'N' in Figure 5.

The silhouette generation for the region of Figure 3 is now
considered. Table 1 gives a list of boundary points, their positions, corresponding neighboring numbers for the preceding and next
boundary cells, and whether they are region-crossing points. Figure 6 shows the intermediate result of silhouette picture with the
region-crossing points. Figure 7 is the final result of silhouette
generation.

The results shown for the simple example of Figure 3 seem very
trivial. This is because there is only a single region present in
the picture. The usefulness of this process of region extraction
lies in situations where there may be more than one region present
in the given scene. Some applications of boundary following and
silhouette generation are given in Section V.

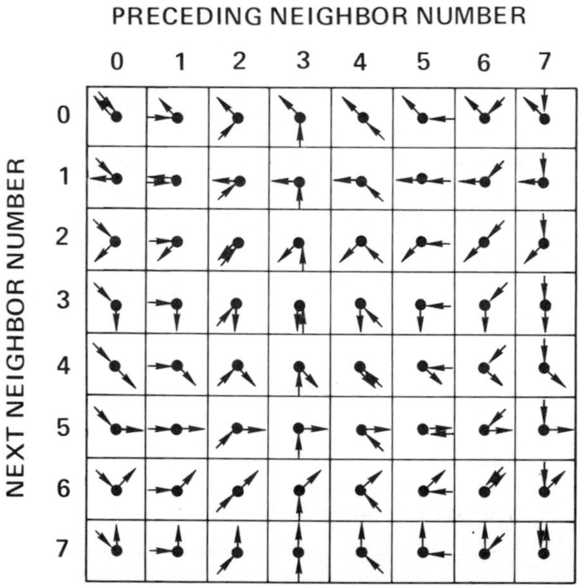

Figure 4. All possible boundary point configurations

PRECEDING NEIGHBOR NUMBER

	0	1	2	3	4	5	6	7
0	N	Y	Y	Y	Y	N	N	–
1	–	Y	Y	Y	Y	N	N	–
2	Y	–	N	N	N	Y	Y	Y
3	Y	–	–	N	N	Y	Y	Y
4	Y	N	N	–	N	Y	Y	Y
5	Y	N	N	–	–	Y	Y	Y
6	N	Y	Y	Y	Y	–	N	N
7	N	Y	Y	Y	Y	–	–	N

(Row labels, top to bottom: NEXT NEIGHBOR NUMBER)

Figure 5. Types of boundary point configurations. '-' represents the nonexisting type, 'Y' represents the region-crossing type, and 'N' represents the non-region-crossing type.

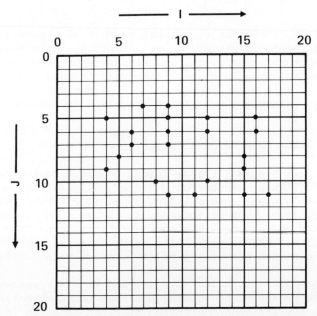

Figure 6. Intermediate results of silhouette picture with the region-crossing points.

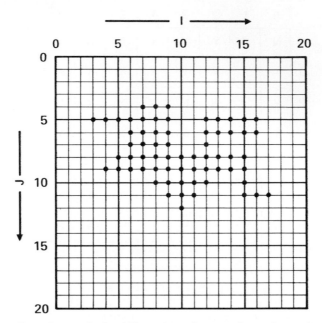

Figure 7.   Generated silhouette for region shown in Figure 3

The results shown for the simple example of Figure 3 seem
very trivial.   This is because there is only a single region present in the picture.   The usefulness of this process of region extraction lies in situations where there may be more than one region present in the given scene.   Some applications of boundary
following and silhouette generation are given in Section V.

IV.   COMBINATORIAL LOGIC REPRESENTATION

In the last section, the different possible configurations of
a boundary point were considered.   These configurations were divided into three groups: non-existing types (don't-care terms), region-crossing types, non-region-crossing types.   In Figure 5, the
classification for all possible configurations were shown.   In
this section, a combinatorial logic representation for a function
to detect the region-crossing type of boundary points will be derived.

Let the binary variables $(p_1p_2p_3)$ and $(n_1n_2n_3)$ represent the
neighbor numbers for the preceding and next boundary cells.   A
Karnaugh map for the region-crossing function is given in Figure 8.
Note that the entries '1' represent the existence of a region-

crossing point and the entries '-' represent the don't-care terms.
As is seen from Figure 8, the region-crossing function may be represented as follows.

$$f(p_1,p_2,p_3,n_1,n_2,n_3) = \bar{n}_1\ \bar{n}_2\ (\bar{p}_1p_3 + \bar{p}_1p_2 + p_1\bar{p}_2\bar{p}_3)$$

$$+ \bar{n}_1\ n_2\ (\bar{p}_1\bar{p}_2 + p_1p_2 + p_1p_3)$$

$$+ n_1\ n_2\ (\bar{p}_1p_3 + \bar{p}_1p_2 + p_1\bar{p}_2)$$

$$+ n_1\bar{n}_2\ (\bar{p}_1\bar{p}_2\bar{p}_3 + p_1p_2 + p_1p_3).$$

It should be mentioned that a different logic representation for
the region-crossing function may be obtained by using a different
numbering system for neighbors (see Figure 1).

V.   APPLICATIONS OF REGION EXTRACTION

In context of the algorithms discussed here, a few interesting
applications are given in this section.

A)   *Noise Removal*

Consider a situation where one is interested in extracting a
fairly large sized object image in a given picture. Also assume
that there are small pieces of noise present in the background.
An example of such a case is illustrated in Figure 9. First, a
boundary following algorithm is used to detect a region. Based on
the number of points encountered on the boundary of this region,
one can determine if it is of the size of the object image. If
not, it is considered to be noise and this region is extracted
from the given picture and discarded. These steps are continued
until the region corresponding to desired object image is obtained.

B)   *Multiple Object Images*

If in a given picture, there are more than one object images
of interest that need to be extracted, the boundary tracing followed by silhouette extraction technique may be used to obtain all
the object images of interest. This is similar to the noise removal process described.

C)   *Extraction of Regions with Holes Inside*

This is a more complex example where the area within the outer boundary is composed of both the desired region and the background. This is illustrated in Figure 10. First the outer boundary and its corresponding silhouette is computed. The silhouette
generated will correspond to the entire area within the outer

$n_1n_2n_3 \backslash p_1p_2p_3$	000	001	011	010	110	111	101	100
000		1	1	1		-		1
001	-	1	1	1		-		1
011	1	-		-	1	1	1	
010	1	-			1	1	1	
110		1	1	1			-	1
111		1	1	1	-		-	1
101	1		-		1	1	1	-
100	1		-		1	1	1	

$$
\begin{aligned}
f(p_1, p_2, p_3, n_1, n_2, n_3) = {} & \overline{n}_1\overline{n}_2\,(\overline{p}_1p_3 + \overline{p}_1p_2 + p_1\overline{p}_2\overline{p}_3) \\
& + \overline{n}_1n_2\,(\overline{p}_1\overline{p}_2 + p_1p_2 + p_1p_3) \\
& + n_1n_2\,(\overline{p}_1p_3 + \overline{p}_1p_2 + p_1\overline{p}_2) \\
& + n_1\overline{n}_2\,(\overline{p}_1\overline{p}_2\overline{p}_3 + p_1p_2 + p_1p_3)
\end{aligned}
$$

Figure 8. A Karnaugh mapping for the region-crossing function.

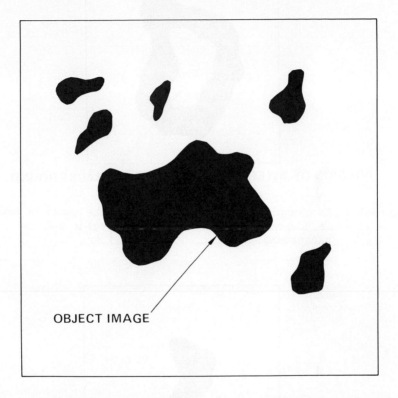

OBJECT IMAGE

Figure 9. An example of an object image with noise regions in background.

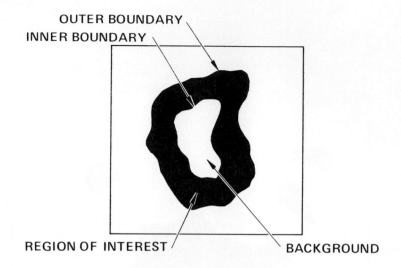

Figure 10. An example where the area within the outer boundary is composed of both the desired region and the background.

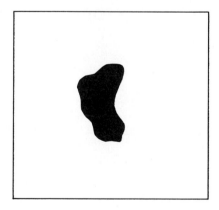

Figure 11. The background portion within the outer boundary of region shown in Figure 10.

boundary. Next, this complete area within the outer boundary is extracted, complemented and placed in a new picture. This is shown in Figure 11. Now, it is fairly simple to detect the inner boundary and a silhouette corresponding to the area within this inner boundary. By subtracting the silhouette for inner boundary from the silhouette for outer boundary, one obtains a silhouette corresponding to the region of interest alone. This basic technique may be extended to even more complex situations.

VI. SUMMARY

The problem of region extraction through boundary following and silhouette generation were considered. First, a boundary following algorithm was described to locate the regions in a picture. This consisted of two main steps - the search strategy and the follow strategy. The boundary of the region is followed in a manner that the region within the boundary is kept always to the left of the path being followed. A list of boundary points is obtained through this algorithm. Each boundary point is then checked to see if it is of a region-crossing type of configuration. If so, then it is used for the silhouette generation process. A silhouette is generated by filling the cells between the pairs of points corresponding to the region-crossing boundary cells. A derivation was presented for a combinatorial logic representation for the region-crossing function. A few illustrative examples of region extraction applications were also discussed.

ACKNOWLEDGMENTS

The author gratefully acknowledges the contributions of Ms. Jacqueline Stafsudd in development of the silhouette generation technique presented in this paper. The author also wishes to thank Mr. John Busch for his help in this study.

REFERENCES

1. Haralick, R. M.,K. Shanmugam, and I. Dinstein, "Textural Features for Image Classification", IEEE Transactions on System, Man and Cybernetics, Vol. SMC-3, No. 6, November 1973.
2. Greanias, E. C., P. F. Meagher, R. J. Norman, and P. Essinger, "The Recognition of Handwritten Numerals by Contour Analysis", IBM J. Res. Develop. Vol. 7, pp. 14-21, January 1963.
3. Freeman, H., "On the Encoding of Arbitrary Geometric Configurations", IRE Trans. Electron. Comput., Vol. EC-10, pp. 260-268, June 1961.
4. Freeman, H., "Techniques for Digital Computer Analysis of Chain-Encoded Arbitrary Plane Curves", in 1961 Proc. Nat. Electron. Conf., Vol. 18, October 1961, pp. 312-324.

5. Polyakov, V. G., "On Digital Techniques of Computation and Analysis of Contours", (in Russian), in Opoznania Ovrasov: Teoria Peredachi Informaisii. Moscow: Akad. Nauk. SSR Inst. Problem Peredachi.

6. Sidhu, G. S., and R. T. Boute, "Property Encoding: Application in Binary Picture Encoding and Boundary Following", IEEE Trans. on Comp., Vol. C-21, No. 11, November 1972.

7. Merill, R. D., "Representation of Contours and Regions for Efficient Computer Search", Comm. of the ACM, Vol. 16, No. 2, February 1973.

8. Rosenfeld, "Connectivity in Digital Pictures", J. Ass. Comput. Mach., Vol. 17, pp. 146-160, January 1970.

9. Rosenfeld, A., *Picture Processing by Computer*, New York: Academic, 1969.

10. Duda, R. O. and P. E. Hart, *Pattern Classification and Scene Analysis*, New York: John Wiley & Sons, 1973.

COMPUTER-AIDED DIAGNOSIS OF BREAST CANCER
FROM THERMOGRAPHY

S. J. Dwyer, III,[1] R. W. McLaren[2]
and C. A. Harlow[3]
University of Missouri-Columbia
Columbia, Missouri

ABSTRACT

This paper concerns the application of image analysis techniques to the detection of breast cancer, with emphasis on the
screening of thermograms in a clinical setting. The need for early
detection of breast cancer is stressed. Thermography is then introduced and its advantages and disadvantages are summarized. Next,
the goals and potential uses in applying image processing to the
detection problem are discussed in the context of using thermography for a screening tool in a clinical environment. Finally,
some essential needs crucial to the effective use of image processing for this problem are identified and discussed.

I. INTRODUCTION

Breast cancer is the leading cause of cancer deaths in American women - 21% of all cancer deaths are of the breast. There
were an estimated 33,000 deaths and 90,000 new cases in the United
States in 1974[1].   It is particularly common among certain high
risk groups. The current rate of incidence is about 7/10,000,
with a mortality rate of 26/10,000. This paper tries to achieve
three goals: (1) Emphasizing the need for solving the problem of
early detection of breast cancer; (2) Establishing the potential
use of image analysis in the diagnosis of breast cancer, using the
thermogram as the basic image; and (3) Identifying and emphasizing the significant, unsolved problems relevant to detecting
breast cancer through the application of image analysis as a
screening tool. Thus, rather than presenting here a solved problem, this paper tries to establish the potential uses and problems
relative to the goal of detecting breast cancer through the use of
image analysis.

1. Director, Bioengineering and Advanced Automation Program, University of Missouri-Columbia.

2. Department of Electrical Engineering, University of Missouri-
   Columbia.

3. Bioengineering and Advanced Automation Program and Electrical
   Engineering, University of Missouri-Columbia.

II. PROBLEM OF EARLY DETECTION

As with most types of cancer, early detection of breast cancer is a significant factor in its successful treatment and an improved survival rate. However, the early detection of breast cancer is hampered by several basic factors. The smallest tumor which is clinically detectable is about 1 cm; 1 cm contains on the order of 10^9 cells, which require some 150-300 days to develop. Thus, the very early stage will be missed. In addition, some 85-90% of all detectable breast cancer is discovered by the patients themselves before clinical methods of detection can be effective; this means that early detection is not being effective as part of or as a result of a regular physical examination. There are several detection methods which have proved their effectiveness under specific conditions.

III. METHODS OF DETECTION

Current principal techniques for the detection of breast cancer are radiography-based techniques, primarily mammography (soft-tissue roentgenography) and thermography. More detailed descriptions of these and others can be found in the literature [2,3], for example. The accuracy of mammography has been 80-85% while, for thermography, it has been 72-74%. With the early detection of breast cancer by the use of image analysis as the main objective, the following guidelines or constraints are imposed. (1) The method is to be used "universally" as a clinical tool in conjunction with other methods in screening for breast cancer not only, hopefully, for establishing an early diagnosis, but to establish a record for each patient for periodic follow-up with minimum risk, and (2) the method is to be amenable to pattern recognition techniques, particularly computer-aided feature extraction and ordering as well as applying a decision scheme, with emphasis on the interactive mode with a trained observer so as to control performance characteristics, such as minimizing false negatives. The particular methods reported here emphasize the use of thermography; also, the techniques and results discussed are presented not as a finished project but as work in progress.

IV. THERMOGRAPHY

Thermography, a method for producing an infrared image of the surface of an anatomic section, is based on the principle that the amount of radiation emitted by an object depends on its absolute temperature. If an infrared sensitive detector is made to scan a patient, an image representing surface temperature variation is produced; the result is a pictorial representation of the temperature on the surface of the skin. In 1956, it was noted [4] that the temperature of the skin in the vicinity of palpable mammary cancers was generally higher than the corresponding area of the opposite breast. In fact, cancer and other pathological mammary conditions increase surface temperature. Its advantages include (1) although initial equipment costs may be relatively high, the technique is inexpensive to perform, (2) because the technique is simple, it can be repeated at frequent intervals, (3) it is non-invasive - no radiation hazard, (4) abnormal thermograms indicate that a breast requires further examination, (5) thermography may indicate a lesion too small to be seen on a roentgenogram, and (6) each woman has a unique thermogram, useful in follow-up analysis. Its disadvantages include (1) all cancers are not "hot" if they are of low grade activity at the time of the examination, (2) thermograms need not have a spatial relationship to cancer, (3) simultaneous, bilateral cancer could be considered as negative, (4) all thermographic signs can occur in benign conditions, and (5) occasionally, anatomical aberrations can cause false positives. The use of thermography in screening for breast cancer has had mixed results and reactions. Various studies have supported the view that thermography is not sufficiently reliable to be used as a single diagnostic tool, but rather that it would be used in conjunction with other screening tools. Some such studies appear to support the use of thermography [5,6,7] in conjunction with mammography and manual palpation as reliable and useful in the detection of breast cancer. They demonstrate that an effective mass-screening system should include thermography because of its safety and because it can detect some cancers which are not detected by mammography and manual palpation; overall, its use would increase the probability of early breast cancer detection. With the use of thermography, mammography, requiring radiation exposure and further expense, could be limited to patients with positive thermograms, which, in turn, could then be used to further select patients for breast biopsy.

V. POTENTIAL USES OF IMAGE PROCESSING

A) Introduction

In the use of thermographic images for the detection of breast cancer, common normal patterns can be described as follows: (1) avascular or cool, (2) vascular with inner vessel markings sharply defined, (3) mottled or patchy patterns lacking linear configurations, and (4) tendency toward symmetry. Common abnormal patterns are as follows: (1) a localized area of increased heat (temperature differences of $1.5^{\circ}C$ are significant), (2) localized increased vascularity with more numerous dilated vessels, (3) a generalized increase in temperature, (4) increased heat in the areolar area, and (5) changes in the thermographic breast pattern in a follow-up is a "warning" sign. Some examples of normal thermographic breast patterns and abnormal patterns are shown in

Figure 1.   These thermograms were generated on a General Electric
Spectrum 2000.

B)   Goal of Image Processing

Ideally and eventually, the goal of applying image processing
to breast thermograms through screening in a clinical setting is
the early detection of breast cancer with a high degree of confidence in the results.   To achieve this, it would be used in conjunction with other screening tools.   For example, there have been
several significant efforts devoted to breast thermograms [7,8,9].
However, apparent problems are: (1) non-consistent results in
some cases as compared with other methods, (2) a feature selection
problem, (3) small sample sets, and (4) results obtained are often
achieved in a non-screening environment.   Achieving this ideal
goal is viewed as not attainable in the near future.   Some particular problems that support this view will be discussed in the
next major section.   A more reasonable goal for the near future is
considered here; it is two-fold.   Image processing applied to
thermographic breast patterns can go a long way in assisting with
the normal/abnormal problem in the screening of an event which
occurs in only 7/10,000 observations.   In general, this can involve image inhancement, especially of the breast areas, delinea-
tion of particular areas, computer-generated features, breast sym-
metray comparisons, and processing of man-extracted features. One
of the most potentially useful aspects of image processing applied
to this problem is to apply it in an interactive mode; this allows
direct control of the processing by a trained observer, in terms
of selecting features to be utilized in a subsequent decision
scheme, emphasis or "outlining" of significant areas, comparison
with past imagery, and control of performance.   This could be accomplished through direct coupling of the scanner and the image
processing system, i.e., no film.   In order to provide these functions in assisting with the normal/abnormal separation, a few general methods which are potentially useful in this regard will now
be discussed.

C)   Signature Analysis

A significant factor in breast thermography is the comparison
of opposite sections of the pattern as well as an overall view of
the temperature pattern, using one breast as a "control" for the
other.   Spatial signature analysis is a technique which can be
employed to develop symmetry criteria.   In general, an image signature refers to some calculated function of the image element amplitudes which distinguish one classification from another and often can be interpreted directly by an observer - such as, a frequency signature could be one or more coefficients of the spatial
Fourier transform of the image, the mean or variance of amplitudes
over a designated area, and the like [10].   Here, three separate

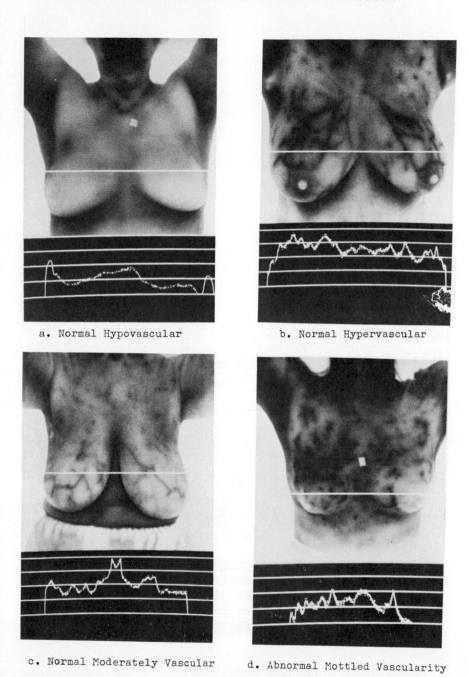

a. Normal Hypovascular

b. Normal Hypervascular

c. Normal Moderately Vascular

d. Abnormal Mottled Vascularity

Figure 1. Examples of Normal and Abnormal Breast Thermograms

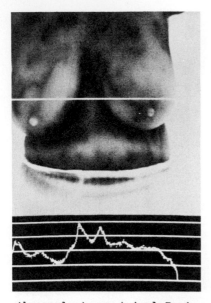 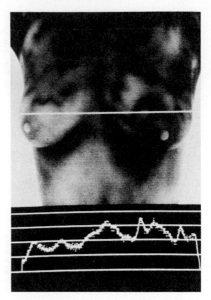

e. Abnormal, Asymmetrical Periareolar
    Heat Focus

f. Abnormal, Unilateral
    Hypervascularity;
    Asymmetrical

g. Abnormal, Unilateral
    Hypervascularity

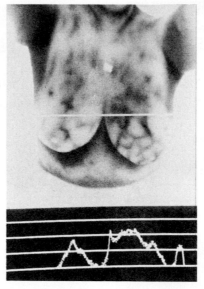

Figure 1 (continued).

spatial signatures can be computed: a horizontal signature, and right and left signatures (see Figure 2). Each point of the hori-

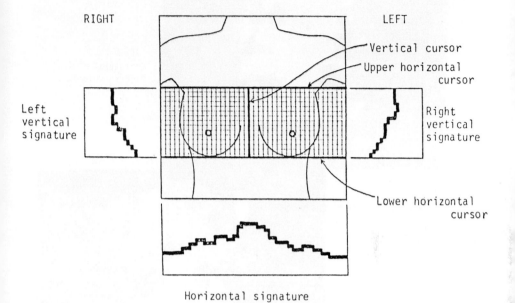

Fig. 2 Signature arrangement.

zontal spatial signature represents the projection of the mean temperature of the corresponding column of the image between speci- fied upper and lower horizontal cursors. Each point of a vertical signature represents the projection of the mean temperature of the corresponding row between the proximal edge of the image and the vertical cursor. The potential use of this measure is based on the expectation that a specific abnormailty ("hotspot") may be cross-localized by matching horizontal and vertical signature peaks. Figure 3 is an example of unilateral hypervascularity of the left breast, which proved to be a carcinoma. The horizontal signature follows bilateral asymmetry and the right vertical sig- nature shows two elevated temperature peaks corresponding to the abnormal region. Figure 4 illustrates the focal heat of fibro- cystic disease. An elevated temperature plateau in the horizontal signature directs attention to the hotspot located low in the right breast. However, a corresponding elevated temperature is not visually apparent in the left vertical signature, although quantization correctly distinguishes the left signature from the corresponding one on the right. The asymmetrically elevated tem- perature of the upper right breast is projected as a peak high on the left vertical signature. Figure 5 demonstrates the broadly elevated temperature signature indicative of diffuse heat. Cysto- sarcoma phyllodes is suspected.

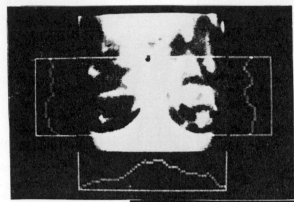

Fig. 3
Unilateral
hypervascularity.

Fig. 4
Fibrocystic
disease.

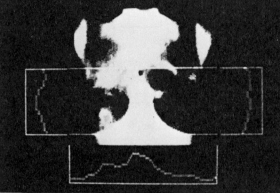

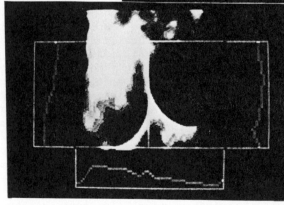

Fig. 5
Asymmetric diffuse
heat. Enlarged
right breast.

Asymmetry of the breast patterns due to disease can be examined more directly by overlapping the breast images digitally as if "folding" a thermogram along the vertical midline; this may involve registration of the two breast images. Then it is relatively easy to compute the differences between digital representations of the breast patterns, excluding bilateral symmetries and enhancing differences. A signature plot will show this differential image. A projection of signatures from axes other than horizontal or vertical needs examination. As for example, bilateral signatures projected from temperature paths joining the suprasternal notch and breast nipples may prove meaningful. Different variations in the computed signature (projections) may be useful, such as average value (per line or column), maximum value, variance, or maximum minus average.

D)   Texture Analysis

The nature of thermograms appear to fit the use of texture. Intuitively, texture is subjective and refers to a random pattern of image element amplitudes over a defined region of an image; such a pattern may consist of a repeated "small" pattern and can be described by well-defined statistics. It is a property of a region in an image modelled as a discrete random process which is assumed to be stationary to some order k with respect to translation (spatial). Two textures would be considered to be different if, for at least one sampling geometry, the resultant joint probability density functions for each texture are different [11,12]. The simplest sampling geometry is that of a single point, (x_1, y_1). The probability density function, $p(i)$, $i = 0$, $,..., N-1$, where N is the number of gray levels, is given by the normalized histogram of the image. Four important parameters are estimated from this distribution - mean, variance, skewness, and kurtosis [11]. These represent the first-order probability distribution; these are called first-order texture statistics.

Not all textures can be distinguished on the basis of first-order distributions; the next level involves sampling geometry of the form, $[(x_1 y_1), (x_2, y_2)]$, two points. Here spatial relationships are very flexible. The result is essentially a texture defined as a discrete random process with N gray levels defined by an NxN probability matrix. From this, one can derive the heuristic quantities - energy, entropy, correlation, local homogeneity, and moment of inertia. Emphasis here is placed on determining the characteristics and dependencies of second-order statistics relative to the images. It is necessary to establish the ability of second-order statistics to discriminate various thermographic textures. Experience with these on radiography indicates that first-and second-order statistics contain sufficient discriminating information to match or exceed the diagnostic accuracy of trained observers. Thus, for thermograms, the use of such statistics to describe texture in the breast region is potentially use-

ful because of the lack of great detail in these images and because of the intuitive appeal.

E) Edge Sign Detection

In separating normal/abnormal breast thermograms, a potentially useful indicator is the edge sign [13]. This visually appears as an alteration of the smooth arc that defines a normal
breast edge. Often, it may occur in a local "hot" infrared region.
The edge sign may be due to skin retraction after fibrosis occurs,
causing abnormal traction upon Cooper's ligaments [14]. The edge
sign can be demonstrated thermographically most conveniently with
the patient in a particular position and may be easily seen in the
oblique view. Image analysis can be employed to display this edge
sign. The method involves constructing isothermal images from the
original infrared thermogram to separate the cooler breast tissue
from the hotter underlying inframammary areas. This requires selection of isothermal levels, giving the trained observer a deci-
sion/control effect on the result. Edge sign detection can make a
positive contribution overall to the seaparation of normal/abnormal
thermograms. One image analysis technique which has promise involves a computer-automated edge detector. The image is initially
displayed on a color display (3 primary colors with addressable
coordinates). The edge is then traced on the display using an interactive Graf Pen device to record the coordinate locations of
the edge curve. The "smoothness" of the arc thus traced may be
measured in the following ways. (1) Compute perpendiculars to
the curve to distinguish large changes in slope magnitude and po-
larity, giving edge inflection points. (2) Extract Fourier descriptors or Walsh coefficients of the curve and compare them with
either corresponding coefficients describing the curve for the
other breast or with stored values representing a "standard" normal breast curve.

The decision process itself may, for example, (1) use the edge
measurements in a one-dimensional threshold detection scheme; the
threshold would be established on the basis of a large data base
of normal and abnormal thermograms (training data). (2) Another
variation is to group the edge measurements into graded classes to
be used with other classification parameters at a subsequent step
in the decision process; the breast curve, for example, could be
graded from -1 to +1, with -1 indicating a gross edge defect and
+1 indicating an obvious normal contour.

VI. PROBLEMS IN APPLYING IMAGE PROCESSING TO THERMOGRAMS

A) Introduction

In this section, six basic problems are identified which must
be dealt with in order that the potential advantages of image analysis in the detection of breast cancer from imagery generated

through screening in a clinical environment can be fully realized.
The first three are most closely related, the next two deal with
the decision process and instrumentation, and the last one deals
with hardware.

B) Data Base Problem

Before image analysis techniques as applied to images, particularly thermograms, for the purpose of detecting breast cancer
can be proven with the necessary high reliability or level of confidence consistent with a clinical setting, it is absolutely essential to develop a "library" of confirmed cases of sufficient
size. This, in general, is not an easy task, for several reasons.
These reasons include obtaining such cases from different places,
cooperation of appropriate personnel, maintaining different forms
(films, tape, slides, etc.), maintaining files (security, loss,
etc.), and the like. Another problem in this connection is obtaining a sufficient sample; with the incidence rate of breast
cancer at 7/10,000, a very large number of cases must be available
to obtain even a moderate-sized set of "typical" abnormals, without even differentiating between cancer and other abnormalities
showing up in the thermograms. It is difficult to obtain such a
sample from one source; when obtained from several sources, some
of the previously indicated concerns arise, as well as problems
concerning uniform images in terms of quality and calibration
(temperature), especially when images are generated from different
machines. These considerations lead one to the strong need for
information management.

C) Information Management System

The problem of managing all of the data required to satisfy
the establishment of high reliability when testing image analysis
techniques as previously indicated must be solved. The information management problem concerns the following major tasks. (1)
Establishing a long-term accessible data storage/retrieval system
(e.g., tapes, films, or what). (2) What code or codes should be
used if images are to be stored on tape, or disk, for example.
(3) Establish a procedure for converting different forms of the
thermograms to a common form, including images obtained from different scanners, calibrations, and the like. (4) Establish a
protocol for applying an (interactive) image processing facility
for screening thermograms in a clinical environment in the detection of breast cancer. Some of these problems become particularly
crucial when one considers an objective in using thermograms for
screening in a clinical setting - not only for early detection
but for establishing a history for later comparison; this latter
factor intensifies the need for the previously mentioned factors.
In addition to maintaining long-term security in the sense as
previously indicated, careful examination must be given to the

storage and retrieval of the processed images and the associated diagnosis assigned to each image. In building up such a system, it is important to continuously provide medical evaluation of results.

D) Medical Evaluation

In establishing and maintaining a useable data base containing "confirmed" normals and abnormals as well as results regarding their features, say based on machine processing, it is essential to (1) evaluate the stored images based on agreement of experts in the field of thermographic imagery, agreeing to a common set of relevant findings defining breast abnormalities, as well as a grading of thermograms, i.e., definite normals, definite abnormals and the like on a scale, and perhaps differential diagnosis with respect to specific abnormalities other than cancer, and (2) evaluate conclusions made through the use of computer-aided techniques - i.e., consistent probability of breast cancer, temperature variations, associated characteristics, and the like. These problems can be very difficult to solve in themselves.

E) Pattern Recognition Problem

The techniques for feature extraction and ordering as well as for the decision or pattern classification process as applied to image analysis are readily available; they vary from relatively simple to complex, sometimes involving image preprocessing before application of the decision process [10,15], for example. There is encouragement in that many of these techniques have been successfully demonstrated as applicable to the image recognition problem, especially in regard to medical data. A major problem is the data base; in [8], for example, some 23 computed features are used and the performance is based on only 85 cases, while in [7], three image processing techniques are applied to a smaller sample. However, the sample size is not the main problem here; this can be solved in time. The main question here is, if a pattern recognition technique, perhaps in conjunction with a feature selection and ordering procedure, is successfully demonstrated (say, in terms of percent correct recognition) when applied to a data base consisting of say, 50% normal/abnormal or 2/3 normal, 1/3 abnormal, etc., how reliable will it be when applied in a clinical setting when one class (abnormals) has a probability of occurrence of .0007. It is desired to obtain a workable pattern classification scheme which can demonstrate high reliability (high confidence in the decision) with this type of class partition, especially if false positives or false negatives are to be controlled and if the normal/abnormal partition is biased for each patient, as it generally is for thermograms. A related problem deals with the measurement selection problem to effectively distinguish between two classes with one of them occuring with a probability of .0007; what features or measurements should be made, considering differences in patient thermograms. This problem is compounded when considering follow-ups, i.e., multiple (periodic) processing of thermograms, looking for features and their changes, trying to establish a flexible set of features, perhaps conditioned to each patient or a group of patients. Another related problem is that of calibration of the thermogram, both in terms of temperature (absolute value and range) and geometric measurements which may be significant in computing some features. Direct temperature calibration of the thermographic instrument can be handled since the temperature signal is available in electrical form directly from the thermographic equipment; one needs absolute temperature calibration and the range of variation for each patient for more effective image processing. The physical calibration could be treated by joining this image output with computed tomography (CT) for accuracy.

F) Computer Interface

In general, thus far, the physician's diagnostic abilities exceed those of current computer-aided techniques relative to thermography, especially when visual interpretation is required. The computer can provide assistance in the diagnostic effort, especially in a clinical setting, where a highly repetitive screening operation is performed. Breast thermograms are a logical choice for applying computer-aided image processing techniques because of their relative simplicity (low resolution and narrow dynamic range) compared with other radiological images; criteria for detection are based essentially on measures of symmetry and relative temperature. Relatively few features may be required and only a relatively basic knowledge of anatomy and pathology is necessary for thermographic interpretation. Thermographic images do not contain the overlapping objects present in radiographic images [7], and are inherently quantitative in nature. The role of the computer for such imagery can be satisfied by an interactive, man-machine interface perhaps directly coupled from output of scanner, with no intervening film. In this case, relevant questions pertain to: (1) what display medium should be used, (2) what should be the form of the hardcopy (processed or non-processed, for example), and (3) what should be the form or mode of the interaction, i.e., how much control should the system operator have over the decision or measurement extraction procedures, etc.

G) New Infrared Technology

Finally, it often happens that a new technology emerges that renders its use inevitable in a certain situation or application. Here, the previous statement refers to the new infrared CCD devices to be used as a scanner. However, such a device must be evaluated and validated in application to thermographic images with respect to such factors as ease of use, calibration, accuracy, and the like.

VII. SUMMARY AND CONCLUSIONS

This paper has briefly discussed the use of thermography in the detection of breast cancer. The potential uses of image processing in this task have been emphasized. In particular, some difficulties are contributed to by some reluctance on the part of medical people to accept the use of thermograms as well as computer-aided detection. Problems directly associated with thermographic imagery can be traced to the interpretation of temperature variations - the modeling of disease progression in terms of surface temperature and its changes. Finally, difficulties encountered in the application of pattern recognition techniques are based on the need for a screening tool for detecting a very low probability event.

ACKNOWLEDGEMENTS

The direct aid of members of the Bioengineering and Advanced Automation Staff in contributing information and photographic examples for this paper is gratefully acknowledged.

REFERENCES

1. Moore, D. H., and J. Charney, "Breast Cancer: Etiology and Possible Prevention", *American Scientist,* vol. 63, pp. 160-168, March - April, 1975.
2. Bjurstam, N., et al., "Diagnosis of Breast Carcinoma", *Progr. Surg.,* vol. 13, pp. 1-65, 1974.
3. Evans, K. T., K. H. Gravelle, *Mammagraphy, Thermography, and Ultrasonography in Breast Disease,* Butterworth, London, 1973.
4. Lawson, R. N., "Implications of Surface Temperatures in the Diagnosis of Breast Cancer", *Can. Med. Assoc. J.,* vol. 75, pp. 309-310, Aug., 1956.
5. Gershon-Cohen, J., et al., "Thermography in Detection of Early Breast Disease", *Cancer,* vol. 26, pp. 1153-1156, Nov., 1970.
6. Ishard, H. J., et al., "Breast Thermography After Four Years and 10,000 Studies", *Amer. J. of Roentgenol.,* vol. 115, pp. 811-821, 1972.
7. Winter, J. and M. A. Stein, "Computer Image Processing Techniques for Automated Breast Thermogram Interpretation", *Comp. and Biomedical Res.,* vol. 6, pp. 522-529, 1973.
8. Ziskin, M. C., et al., "Computer Diagnosis of Breast Thermograms", *Radiology,* vol. 115, pp. 341-347, May, 1975.
9. Jones, C. H., et al., "Thermography of the Female Breast: A Five-Year Study in Relation to the Detection and Prognosis of Cancer, *British J. of Radiology,* vol. 48, pp. 532-538, July, 1975.

10. Hall, E. L., et al., "A Survey of Prepreocessing and Feature Extraction Techniques for Radiographic Images", *IEEE Trans. on Computers*, vol. C-20, pp. 1032-1044, September, 1971.

11. Ausherman, D. A., "Texture Discrimination with Digital Imagery", Ph. D. Thesis, Electrical Engineering, University of Missouri - Columbia, December, 1972.

12. Lipkin, B. S., A. Rosenfeld, Editors, *Picture Processing and Psychopictorics*, Academic Press, N. Y., 1970, pp. 289-308, 287, 175-183.

13. Isard, H. J., "Thermographic Edge Sign in Breast Carcinoma", *Cancer*, vol. 30, pp. 957-963, 1972.

14. Isard, H. J., and B. J. Ostrum, "Breast Thermography--The Mammatherm", *Radiologic Clinics of N. Amer.*, vol. 12, April, 1974.

15. Preston, K., Jr., "Computer Processing of Biomedical Images", *Computer*, vol. 9, pp. 54-68, May. 1976.

STRUCTURAL ISOMORPHISM OF PICTURE GRAPHS

Eugene C. Freuder
Artificial Intelligence Laboratory
Massachusetts Institute of Technology
Cambridge, MA.

ABSTRACT

A notion of structural isomorphism of line drawings is presented which serves as the basis for model matching. Structural
isomorphism employs a concept of structural description that captures in a linear string the order in which vertices and regions
surround each other in a line drawing.

1. Structural Isomorphism Captures the Concept of Order
   Missing from Graph Isomorphism.

Visual recognition is often treated as a matching problem:
matching a description of an object with a description of a stored
model. These descriptions are often based on a line drawing or
"picture graph" representation.

Graph isomorphism has been used to express the basic structural similarity between two picture graphs.[1] Graphs are isomorphic if there is a 1-1 vertex mapping between them which preserves
edges (lines); i.e. if f is a graph isomorphism from G to H, and
p and q are connected in G, f(p) and f(q) are connected in H.
However, the picture graphs in figure 1 are graph isomorphic while
intuitively they are not an acceptable match.

Figure 1

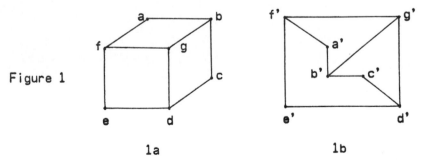

1a   1b

This paper will present a concept of "structural isomorphism"
which captures more of our intuitive idea of structural similarity
of picture graphs. In particular, it allows us to express formally the distinction between the picture graphs in figure 1. Structural isomorphism also has the advantage of being relatively efficient as a basis for model matching. Essentially, I will extend

the notion of graph isomorphism by adding another constraint: *order*.

The use of order constraints was somewhat anticipated by Roberts in his classic recognition program.[2] Roberts used matrix transformations to verify a match; however, he employed an initial "topological" search to obtain sets of corresponding points in object and model upon which to base the transformation attempts. A primary topological test involved finding vertices in object and model whose surrounding regions matched in order, to the extent that they had the same number of sides. Roberts commented on the difficulty of implementing on a computer what he called "topology tests and matching". The techniques of this paper address that difficulty.

Structural isomorphism is defined in section 2, along with the notion of structural description upon which it is based. The connection between structural isomorphism and the problem raised in figure 1 may not be immediately obvious. In section 3, I introduce a concept of region isomorphism which clearly captures the ordering constraint that distinguishes the two graphs in figure 1. I then go on to demonstrate the equivalence of this region order isomorphism and structural isomorphism. (These in turn are equivalent to a natural extension of graph isomorphism.) In section 4, I describe how an object can be matched rather easily against models to determine structural isomorphism, a process which I have implemented as a LISP program. Finally section 5 discusses possible extensions of the structural description concept.

I might observe that the techniques discussed here could prove to be of use in domains other than picture graphs where a network representation also includes an ordering constraint. Graph isomorphism techniques have been applied to semantic network matching problems.[3]

2. Structural Isomorphism Preserves Structural Descriptions.

A *partial structural description* of a (connected, planar) picture graph G at a point p on a region R, S(G,p,R), consists of a list of boundary lists. Each boundary list contains the boundary vertices of a region of G in counterclockwise order. There is one list for each region (not including the background). (I will generally omit one or both of the modifiers in "partial structural description" for brevity; extended notions of structural description are discussed in section 5.) The order of the boundary lists and of the vertices within the boundary lists is uniquely specified by G, p and R.

Basically we begin with R, then include the regions which surround R in counterclockwise order, then the regions surrounding those in turn, and so on; except we only include each region once. The boundary list for R begins with p; each new region is first encountered as bordering some vertex in the boundary list of a previous region, and we use that vertex as the starting point in the counterclockwise listing of the new boundary. The following is $S(G,p,R)$ for G, p and R as shown in figure 2:

$$S(G,p,R) = ((p\ g\ f\ h\ i\ j)\ (p\ j\ b\ a)\ (f\ e\ d\ h)\ (h\ d\ c\ i)\ (i\ c\ b\ j))$$

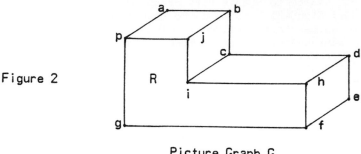

Figure 2

Picture Graph G

I will express more precisely the procedure for generating $S(G,p,R)$, given any picture graph G with point p on the boundary of region R:

1) Set CURRENT-REGION to R, STARTING-POINT to p, $S(G,p,R)$ to the empty list, set up NEXT as an empty queue.
2) List the vertices surrounding CURRENT-REGION in counterclockwise order beginning with STARTING-POINT.

For each vertex v in turn, consider the regions surrounding v (excluding the background) in counterclockwise order following CURRENT-REGION. If any of these regions are not yet included in $S(G,p,R)$ or the queue NEXT, enter them, each together with v, successively onto the queue.

When complete, add the boundary list for CURRENT-REGION at the end of $S(G,p,R)$.
3) If the queue NEXT is empty, $S(G,p,R)$ is complete.

If not, the top entry will consist of a region and a vertex. Set CURRENT-REGION to the region, STARTING-POINT to the vertex, and go to step 2.

A *(partial) structural isomorphism* f of G and H is a 1-1 mapping from the vertices of G onto the vertices of H which preserves structural descriptions. If

$$S(G,p,R) = ((p_1 \ldots p_n) \ldots \ (q_1 \ldots q_m))$$

then

$$S(H,f(p),R') = ((f(p_1) \ldots f(p_n)) \ldots (f(q_1) \ldots f(q_m))$$

where R' is a region of H whose boundary is $(f(p_1) \ldots f(p_n))$.

G and H in figure 3 are structurally isomorphic, under the

isomorphism f which takes p_i into q_i.

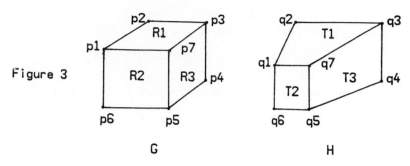

Figure 3

G   H

For example:

$$S(G,p_1,R_1) = ((p_1\ p_7\ p_3\ p_2)\ (p_1\ p_6\ p_5\ p_7)\ (p_7\ p_5\ p_4\ p_3))$$

$$S(H,q_1,T_1) = ((q_1\ q_7\ q_3\ q_2)\ (q_1\ q_6\ q_5\ q_7)\ (q_7\ q_5\ q_4\ q_3))$$

On the other hand the two objects in figure 1 are not structurally isomorphic.

3. Structural Isomorphism is Equivalent to a Natural Concept of Region Isomorphism.

I define a concept of region isomorphism which embodies the ordering constraint that figure 1 calls for. A *region order isomorphism* f of G and H is a 1-1 mapping from the regions of G onto the regions of H which preserves the regions surrounding a given region. That is, if $(S_1...S_n)$ is an ordered list of the regions around R in counterclockwise order, then $(f(S_1)...f(S_n))$ is a counterclockwise ordered list of the regions around f(R). Furthermore if S_i and R share n vertices, $f(S_i)$ and f(R) share n vertices.

Proposition: Picture graphs are region order isomorphic if and only if they are structurally isomorphic.

A structural isomorphism f from G to H naturally induces a region mapping f*, by applying the vertex mapping f to the set of boundary points for each region; f* is a region order isomorphism. A boundary segment of a region A consists of (counterclockwise) consecutive vertices on the boundary; we write "$p_1...p_n$ in A". Observe that f preserves boundary segments: $p_1...p_n$ in A implies $f(p_1)...f(p_n)$ in f*(A). Thus it is obvious that f* preserves the number of vertices in a shared boundary. To see that it preserves the order of surrounding regions observe that C follows B around A if and only if there exists p, q such that p in A, qp in B and pq in C (figure 4).

251

Figure 4

These boundary segments will be preserved by f, thus f*(C) follows
f*(B) around f*(A).

A region isomorphism f induces a vertex mapping f*, which is
a structural isomorphism. Vertices with more than two edges are
uniquely identified by the ordered (circular) list of surrounding
regions. If v is surrounded by $(R_1 \ldots R_n)$, f*(v) is defined as the
vertex surrounded by $(f(R_1) \ldots f(R_n))$. Sequences of vertices between only two regions are mapped onto each other in order starting from an already defined vertex. To see that f* preserves
structural descriptions we observe that if q follows p around the
boundary of R, f*(q) follows f*(p) around the boundary of f(R).
Note first that q follows p around the boundary of R if and only
if there exists R, S such that S follows R in a counterclockwise
ordered listing of regions surrounding q, and R follows S around
p (see figure 5).

Figure 5

Then f(R) follows f(S) around f*(p) and f(S) follows f(R) around
f*(q) by definition of f*. Thus f*(q) follows f*(p) around f(R).

A vertex order isomorphism may also be defined, as a natural
extension of graph isomorphism. Graph isomorphism requires that
if p is surrounded by q_1, lll, q_n in G, f(p) is surrounded by $f(q_1)$,
$\ldots, f(q_n)$. Thus Guzman in an early recognition program[1] used connection lists as the basis for his descriptions of objects and
models, listing each vertex, followed by a list of its neighbors.
"Vertex order isomorphism" requires that not only are the neighbors of a vertex preserved, but that their order is preserved as
well. If $(q_1 \ldots q_n)$ is a counterclockwise ordered list of the
neighbors of p, $(f(q_1) \ldots f(q_n))$ is a counterclockwise ordered list
of the neighbors of f(p).

Vertex order isomorphism is a nice intermediate notion between region and structural isomorphism, and may be shown equivalent to both, by arguments similar to those used above. Thus if
two picture graphs are structurally isomorphic they will be graph
isomorphic, though not necessarily vice versa, of course. (An

alternative equivalent form of structural description may also be
defined based on traversing the vertices surrounding a vertex in
order, as opposed to the vertices surrounding a region.)

Another way of viewing structural isomorphism is to consider
attempting to describe a single vertex in a picture graph. To
fully identify it we might start by describing its immediate
neighborhood, the regions which surround it. However this would
not necessarily specify it fully and uniquely; we would want to
include the next regions further away, and then beyond those until
finally to fully describe the single vertex we would end up by describing the entire graph from the point of view of that vertex.
This is essentially what a structural description does.

4. Structural Isomorphism Forms a Basis for Model Matching.

If a function preserves one structural description, it will
preserve them all, thus it is sufficient when testing for structural isomorphism of object O and model M, to determine if one
structural description of O can be preserved. There are basically
two ways to proceed.

All the structural descriptions of M can be stored away ahead
of time, and a single one computed for O when recognition is
sought. The structural description of O is then matched against
those for M until a successful match is found; if none is found
the match of O and M fails. On the other hand, we can store a
single structural description for M, and compute the structural
descriptions for O, stopping when a match is found, or all fail.
If we match each structural description with the model piece by
piece as it is computed, we will rarely have to complete computing
a full description; failure will occur earlier.

Matching two structural descriptions is a trivial bit of
string matching. Consider S_1 and S_2:

$$S_1 = ((a\ b\ c)\ (b\ c\ d))$$

$$S_2 = ((v\ w\ x)\ (w\ z\ y))$$

If the number of boundary lists were unequal we could quit immediately. We start matching: a with v, b with w, c with x. New
boundary lists begin. Now b must again match w; it does. However,
c must match x; its second occurence matches z. The match of S_1
and S_2 fails; no function can map c onto both x and z. If the
string matching process does succeed, it will define the structural isomorphism mapping from the vertices of S_1 onto those of S_2.

We have thus decomposed the problem of matching two graph
structures into the relatively easy processes of computing structural descriptions and performing string matches. The additional
constraint of order which essentially transfers a two dimensional
description into a linear one, makes operating with structural

descriptions straightforward.

The number of descriptions which need to be considered (computed or stored, and matched) can be cut down considerably by some simple heuristics. For example, we need only store one structural description for a cube model (figure 1a), and still not have to consider all the possible structural descriptions for objects we want to match against it. We store one description for the central fork type vertex (g in figure 1a), and indicate that all the descriptions for this vertex are the same because of symmetry. We perform a simple preliminary check of the object vertices to identify the forks. (If our matcher is part of a larger machine vision system, vertex type[4] may well have already been determined.) Only these forks need be matched, and only one structural description for each needs to be computed. Other properties that distinguish vertices, such as number of edges or presence on the background, can be used to restrict the vertices considered. (Of course, these heuristics may be implicitly adding further constraints to the match; see section 5.)

If we know the background, or the vertex is of an unsymmetric type, we can specify one region to choose at the vertex and thus compute only one structural description rather than one for each of the surrounding regions. Thus for arrow vertices, e.g., b, d, f in figure 1a, we could specify that the only structural descriptions to be considered were those begin-ing with the region at the "head" of the arrow (or if that region is the background, the next region counterclockwise around the vertex). For a vertex bordering the background, we could specify that the only structural description considered would be that beginning with the region following the background in counterclockwise order around the vertex.

A simple program has been written to compute and match structural descriptions, in particular matching objects with stored descriptions for models. It includes some initial experimentation with the possibility of extending the approach to imperfect matching, caused e.g. by occlusion. The program was prepared as a possible addition to the M.I.T. Robot Copy Demo system [Winston 1972], but never substantially tested or developed.

5. A Primitive Structural Description Should Include the Elementary Structural Properties Specified by all Models.

The partial structural description I have defined clearly does not capture all the structural properties of a picture graph. The two objects in figure 6 indicate that a notion of convexity and concavity might be desirable.

Figure 6

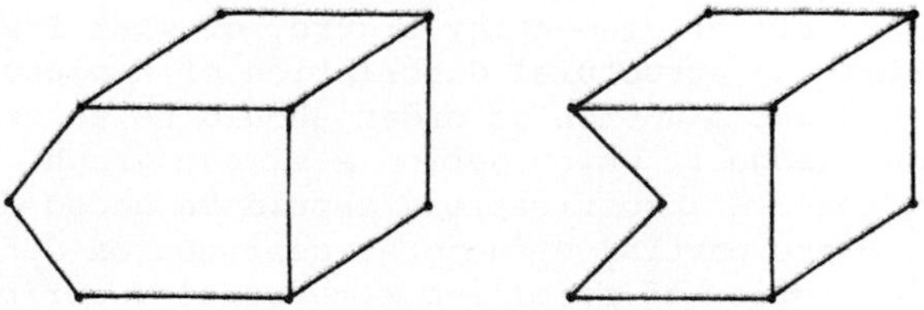

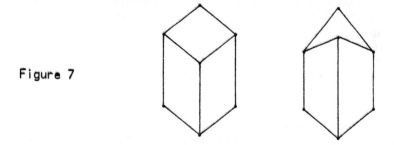

The angle of a vertex, convex or concave (or 180 degrees), with respect to each region the vertex borders, can be included as a marker in the structural description, without basically altering either the form of structural descriptions, or the procedure for matching them. This information would have the effect of specifying many vertex types and distinguishing, for example, the two objects in figure 7, which are graph isomorphic, and structurally isomorphic, as defined above.

Figure 7

There are, of course, numerous other properties which may need to be included in matching object and model. More precise constraints on angles may be imposed, in absolute or relative terms. Line lengths may also be specified. Regions can also have properties; many of these are less structural in nature, e.g. color. Many additional properties can be simply added as markers in the ordered sequence of the structural description. If necessary, others can be hung onto the "skeleton" given by the structural description.

Guzman[1] made a distinction between that part of a description which always was present, for every model, and those properties which might or might not be specified in a given case. The former he called an "elementary figure"; it consisted of a connection list, indicating vertex connections. Upon this framework he hung other properties, like parallelism, as required.

I believe that this distinction is a useful one conceptually. If the elementary descriptions are also easy to match, the distinction might also profitably partition the recognition process; elementary descriptions could be quickly matched to determine if success were possible and to determine precisely where additional properties should be matched.

The question remains how much information should be considered part of the elementary figure, or what I would like to call the primitive structural description of a picture graph. I feel that at least a notion of order should be added to the vertex connections (edges), which define a simple graph. Most likely the convex/concave specifications should be added as well. Adding these to the partial structural description defined above gives us a formal notion of *primitive structural description*. To this we can add other constraints as a particular model or recognition task may require.

ACKNOWLEDGMENT

This report describes research done at the Artificial Intelligence Laboratory of the Massachusetts Institute of Technology. Support for the laboratory's artificial intelligence research is provided in part by the Advanced Research Projects Agency of the Department of Defense under Office of Naval Research contract N00014-75-C-0643.

REFERENCES

1. Guzman, A., Some Aspects of Pattern Recognition by Computer, *AI TR-224*, Artificial Intelligence Laboratory, M.I.T., Cambridge, Massachusetts, February 1967.
2. Roberts, L., Machine Perception of Three-Dimensional Solids, *Technical Report 315*, Lincoln Laboratory, M.I.T., May 1963.
3. Barrow, H. G., Ambler, A. P., and Burstall, R. M., Some Techniques for Recognizing Structures in Pictures in *Frontiers of Pattern Recognition*, Academic Press, New York, 1972.
4. Guzman, A., Computer Recognition of Three-dimensional Objects in a Visual Scene, *MAC TR-59. Project MAC*, M.I.T., 1968.
5. Winston, P. H., *The M.I.T. Robot*, in Machine Intelligence 7, B. Meltzer and D. Michie, Eds., John Wiley and Sons, New York, 1972.

TREE LANGUAGES AND SYNTACTIC
PATTERN RECOGNITION*

K. S. Fu
School of Electrical Engineering
Purdue University
West Lafayette, Ind.

I. INTRODUCTION

In syntactic approach to pattern recognition, patterns are
represented by sentences of a language which is then characterized
by a grammar [1]. Most results in syntactic pattern recognition
are based on one-dimensional string grammars. Each pattern is represented by a string of primitives and relations. The recognition
of a pattern string is realized through a syntax analysis or parsing procedure. Naturally, if the patterns under study are one-
dimensional, representing patterns by strings is an effective and
efficient way of pattern description. On the other hand, if the
patterns under study are high-dimensional, we must first convert a
pattern into a one-dimensional description ("linearization" process)
which is then represented by a string. A typical example is to
trace the boundary of a two-dimensional object and then to represent the (one-dimensional) boundary by a string. The resulting
string becomes a linguistic representation of the object. However,
in many applications, such an approach appears to be quite cumbersome and inefficient. The use of high-dimensional languages has
recently been proposed. High-dimensional patterns can be represented by webs [2], arrays [3], graphs [4], and trees [5]. Gips
has recently used a formal syntactic technique in the analysis of
line drawings of three-dimensional objects [6]. There has been an
increasing interest in the study of properties and parsing algorithms for high-dimensional languages [7 - 9].
A natural way to extend one-dimensional strings to high-dimensional representations is to generalize strings to trees. Tree
grammars and the corresponding recognizers, tree automata, have
been studied recently by a number of authors [10, 11]. If a pattern can be conveniently described by a tree, it will easily be
generated by a tree grammar. For example, in Figure 1, patterns
and their corresponding tree representations are listed in (a) and
(b), respectively [5, 12]. For a given tree grammar, a tree automaton can be easily constructed to recognize the trees generated
by the grammar. Thus, the recognition procedure of tree patterns
is readily available. In this paper, after a brief review of tree
grammars and tree automata, we describe a simple tree grammar inference procedure and several applications of tree grammars to syntactic pattern recognition.

* This work was supported by the AFOSR Grant 74-2661.

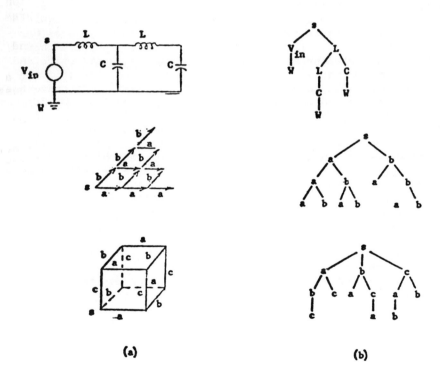

Figure 1. (a) Patterns and
(b) Corresponding Tree Representations.

II. TREE GRAMMARS AND TREE AUTOMATA

Definition 1: A (regular) tree grammar G_t is a four-triple

$$G_t = (V, r', P, S)$$

where $<V, r'>$ is a finite ranked alphabet such that $V_T \subseteq V$ and $r'|_{V_T} = r$. $V = V_T \cup V_N$, and V_T and V_N are the set of terminals and nonterminals, respectively. P is a finite set of productions of the form $\Phi \to \psi$ where $\Phi, \psi \in T_V$. $S \subseteq T_V$ is a finite set of axioms and T_V is a set of trees over $<V, r'>$.

A generation or derivation $\alpha \Rightarrow \beta$ is in G_t if and only if there is a production $\phi \to \psi$ in P such that $\alpha|a = \phi$ and $\beta = (a \to \psi) \alpha$. That is, ϕ is a subtree of α at "a" and β is generated by replacing ϕ by ψ at "a". $\alpha \overset{*}{\Rightarrow} \beta$ is in G_t if and if there exist trees $t_0, t_1, ---, t_m \in T_V$, $m \geq o$ such that

$$\alpha = t_0 \Rightarrow t_1 \Rightarrow --- \Rightarrow t_m = \beta$$

in G_t. The sequence $t_0, t_1, ---, t_m$ is called a derivation of β from α.

Definition 2: The language generated by tree grammar G_t is

$$L(G_t) = \{t \in T_{V_T} \mid \text{ there exists } Y \in S \text{ such that } Y \overset{*}{\Rightarrow} t \text{ is in } G_t\}.$$

Example 1: The tree grammar

$$G_t = (V, r, P, S)$$

where

$$V = \{S, a, b, \$, A, B\}$$

$$V_T = \{\overset{a}{\longrightarrow}, \uparrow b, \bullet\$\}$$

$$r(a) = \{2, 1, 0\}, \quad r(b) = \{2, 1, 0\}, \quad r(\$) = 2$$

and P:

generates such patterns as

259

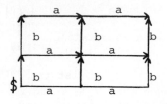 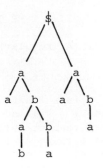

Definition 3: A tree grammar $G_t = (V, r^\prime, P, S)$ over $< V_T, r>$ is expansive iff each production in P is of the form

$$X_o \rightarrow \overset{x}{\diagup\diagdown}_{X_1---X_{r(x)}}$$

or $\qquad X_o \rightarrow x$

where $\quad x \in V_T$ and $X_o, X_1, ---, X_{r(x)} \in V_N$.

Theorem 1: For each regular tree grammar $G_t = (V, r^\prime, P, S)$ over $< V_T, r>$ one can effectively construct an equivalent expansive grammar [10].

Definition 4: Let $< \Sigma, r>$ be a ranked alphabet and $\Sigma = \{\sigma_1, \sigma_2, ---, \sigma_k\}$. A tree automaton over Σ is a system

$$M_t = (Q, f_1, ---, f_k, F)$$

where $\quad Q$ is a finite set of states:

$\qquad f_i$ is a relation on $Q^{r(\sigma_i)} \times Q$, $1 \leqslant i \leqslant k$;

and $\qquad F \subseteq Q$ is a set of final states.

If each f_i, $1 \leqslant i \leqslant k$, is a function,

$$f_i : Q^{r(\sigma_i)} \rightarrow Q$$

then M_t is deterministic. Otherwise, M_t is nondeterministic.

Definition 5: The response relation ρ of a tree automaton M_t is defined as follows. Let $\Sigma_n = r^{-1}(n)$.

   (i)   If $\sigma \in \Sigma_o$, $\rho(\sigma) \sim X$ iff $f_\sigma \sim X$.

   (ii) If $\sigma \in \Sigma_n$, $n > 0$, $\rho(\sigma\alpha_o ---\alpha_{n-1}) \sim X$ iff there exists

$\qquad X_o, ---, X_{n-1}$ such that $f_\sigma(X_o, ---, X_{n-1}) \sim X$ and

$\rho\ (\alpha_i) \sim X_i,\ 1 \leqslant i \leqslant n.$

Note that if M_t is deterministic,

$\rho: T_\Sigma \rightarrow Q$

(i) If $\sigma \in \Sigma_o$, $\rho(\sigma) = f_\sigma$.

(ii) If $\sigma \in \Sigma_n$, $n > o$, $\rho\ (\sigma\alpha_o\text{---}a_{n-1}) = f_\sigma\ (\rho(\alpha_o),\text{---},\rho\ (\alpha_{n-1}))$.

Definition 6: The language accepted by tree automaton M_t is

$T(M_t) = \{\alpha \in T_\Sigma |$ there exists $X \in F$ such that $\rho\ (\alpha) \sim X\}$.

Theorem 2: For every regular tree grammar $G_t = (V,r\acute{}\,,P,S)$, one can effectively construct a deterministic tree automaton M_t such that $T(M_t) = L(G_t)$ [10].

The construction procedure of tree automaton from a regular tree grammar is summarized as follows:

Step 1: To obtain an expansive tree grammar $G_t^\acute{} = (V\acute{}\,,r,P\acute{}\,,S)$ from the given tree grammar $G_t = (V,r,p,S)$ over alphabet V_T.

Step 2: The tree automaton M_t accepting $L(G_t)$ is $M_t = (V^\angle V_T,\ f_1,\text{---},f_k,\ \{S\})$

where $\qquad f_x(X_1,\text{---},X_n) \sim X_o$ if $X_o \rightarrow$ ⋀ is a production in $P\acute{}$.

Example 2: The following tree grammar generates trees representing directed triangles.

$\qquad G_t = (V,r,P,S)$

$\qquad V = \{S,A,B,a,b,\$\},\ V_T = V\{\bullet\$,\ \overset{a}{\rightarrow},\ \nearrow b\}$

$\qquad r(a) = \{2,0\}$

$\qquad r(b) = \{2,0\};\ |a| = |b|$

$\qquad r(\$) = 2.$

P:

$\qquad S \rightarrow$

261

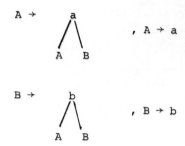

$$A \rightarrow \qquad , \ A \rightarrow a$$

$$B \rightarrow \qquad , \ B \rightarrow b$$

A tree generated by this grammar is

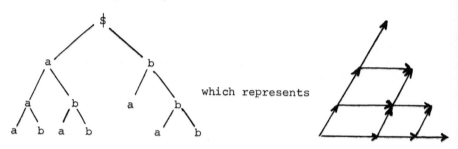

which represents

The tree automaton which corresponds to the preceding tree grammar and also accepts the "directed triangles" is as follows:

$$M_t = (Q, f_a, f_b, f_\$, F)$$

where

$$Q = (q_a, q_b, q_F)$$

$$f_a = q_a$$

$$f_b = q_b$$

$$f_a(q_a, q_b) = q_a$$

$$f_b(q_a, q_b) = q_b$$

$$f_\$(q_a, q_b) = q_F$$

$$F = \{q_F\}$$

III. INFERENCE OF TREE GRAMMARS

In the use of a tree grammar to describe a class of patterns, it would be nice to have the grammar directly inferred from a set of trees representing sample patterns. Only heuristic inference

procedures are available at present. We briefly summarize a tree
grammar inference procedure in this section. The procedure consists of the following steps [13]:

Step 1: Attempt to discover the syntactic structure of given
samples.

Step 2: Determine the sublanguages making up the language
which is being analyzed.

Step 3: Look for equivalence between the various sublanguages.

Step 4: Produce the inferred tree grammar.

The syntactic structure of a given set of sample trees can be
found through the prefix codes [14]. For a given tree, the structure is contained in the "repetitive sub-structure" (RSS) found in
the tree. In the case that the tree does not contain RSS, it is
partitioned into subtrees which may contain RSS. Initially, a tree
grammar is inferred for each sample tree. Then a final tree grammar is obtained by merging all the tree grammars inferred from the
given set of sample trees.

The procedure to infer a tree grammar for a given sample tree
α_i is as follows:

(i)   Represent α_i as

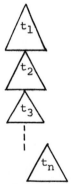

where any of the subtrees $t_1, t_2, ---, t_n$ may contain RSS.

(ii) Find subtrees with depth one in α_i excluding the subtrees having RSS (consider only RSS), starting from the
root.

(iii) Associate nonterminals to nodes of the subtrees and construct an expansive tree grammar $G_{\alpha_i} = (V_{Ni}, V_{Ti}, P_i, S_i)$
for α_i.

For a given set of sample trees $\{\alpha_1, \alpha_2, ---, \alpha_n\}$, the inferred
tree grammar is obtained by

$$G_t = \bigcup_{i=1}^{n} G_{\alpha_i}$$

G_t can then be simplified by eliminating redundant nonterminals and merging duplicate production. The tree grammar so obtained is usually in expansive form which is convenient for the construction of its equivalent tree automaton.

Example 3: The given set of sample trees consists of

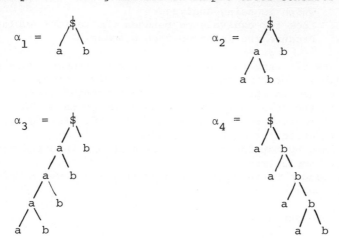

Represent the sample trees in the following form:

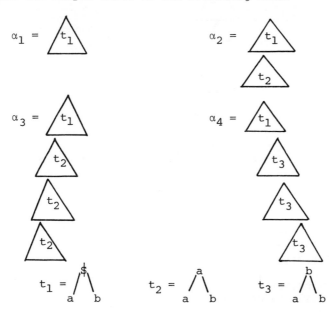

The expansive tree grammar for α_1 is G_{α_1} where

P_1: $S \rightarrow \overset{\$}{\underset{A_1 \quad A_2}{\diagup\diagdown}}$, $A_1 \rightarrow a$, $A_2 \rightarrow b$.

For α_2, P_2: $S \rightarrow \overset{\$}{\underset{A_3 \quad A_4}{\diagup\diagdown}}$, $A_3 \rightarrow \overset{a}{\underset{A_5 \quad A_6}{\diagup\diagdown}}$, $A_4 \rightarrow b$

$A_5 \rightarrow a$, $A_6 \rightarrow b$

For α_3, P_3: $S \rightarrow \overset{\$}{\underset{A_7 \quad A_8}{\diagup\diagdown}}$, $A_7 \rightarrow \overset{a}{\underset{A_7 \quad A_9}{\diagup\diagdown}}$, $A_7 \rightarrow a$

$A_8 \rightarrow b$, $A_9 \rightarrow b$

For α_4, P_4: $S \rightarrow \overset{\$}{\underset{A_{10} \quad A_{11}}{\diagup\diagdown}}$, $A_{10} \rightarrow a$, $A_{11} \rightarrow \overset{b}{\underset{A_{12} \quad A_{11}}{\diagup\diagdown}}$

$A_{11} \rightarrow b$, $A_{12} \rightarrow a$

Let $G_t = \bigcup\limits_{i=1}^{4} G_{\alpha_i}$, we obtain $G_t = (V, r, P, S)$

where $V = \{S, A_1, A_2, V_T\}$, $V_T = \{\$, a, b\}$

and P: (1) $S \rightarrow \overset{\$}{\underset{A_1 \quad A_2}{\diagup\diagdown}}$, (2) $A_1 \rightarrow \overset{a}{\underset{A_1 \quad A_2}{\diagup\diagdown}}$, (3) $A_2 \rightarrow \overset{b}{\underset{A_1 \quad A_2}{\diagup\diagdown}}$

(4) $A_1 \rightarrow a$, (5) $A_2 \rightarrow b$.

This grammar generates the set of all two-branch trees with a on the left branch and b on the right branch.

It has been intended to interpret the inference procedure as an extension of the k-tail inference procedure for finite-state grammar for k=1 [15,16]. Nevertheless, such an interpretation has not yet been rigorously proved.

IV. APPLICATION TO THE CLASSIFICATION
OF BUBBLE CHAMBER EVENTS

The aim of high-energy physics research is to understand the composition of matter by studying the properties of subnuclear particles and by determining the forces that govern their interaction. The experimental techniques used involve directing a beam of high energy particles of known kind and energy onto a target of known nuclei and observing the secondary particles produced within the target volume. A typical experiment requires the recording, measurement, and analysis of hundreds of thousands of such nuclear interactions or events. An event is said to have occurred if an incoming track interacts with an atomic nucleus in the liquid. Events must satisfy two conditions.

Condition 1: The 4-momentum of an incoming particle is equal to the sum of 4 momenta of all secondary particles generated at the point of interaction called vertex.

Condition 2: The charge on the particles associated with the event is conserved. Because the events take place in a chamber under the influence of a magnetic field, the trajectories of positively and negatively charged particles are concave or convex, respectively, and their curvature is a function of their moments. Since most of the information needed is contained in the trajectories of incident and secondary particles, photographs of the bubble chamber from three views are taken. Three views are necessary for space reconstruction since the trajectories of particles are three-dimensional curved tracks. In addition to particles tracks, a photograph contains identifying information such as frame number, view number, and a set of "fiducials," which are marks on the chamber and required for reconstruction of three-dimensional curved tracks.

A typical bubble chamber photograph is shown in Fig. 2. With the given knowledge of the incident particle momentum and chamber target liquid (usually H_2) and such a photograph, it is required to know the following.

1) How many secondary particles were associated with an event (topological information)?

2) What is the exact position of vertex where the event occurred?

3) What is the secondary particles (proton, antiproton, K-Meson, and π-Meson, etc.)?

The complete system of analyzing bubble chamber photographs, giving position of vertex and topology of an event is described in Fig. 3. The point set representing a possible event obtained by a manual system or automatic scanner is divided into different classes representing points on different tracks of the event. This procedure is called track element linking. Vertex and type of curvature for each track is found by fitting first- or second-order polynomials that are reasonably good approximations of the tracks. The data set is represented by trees and each tree repre-

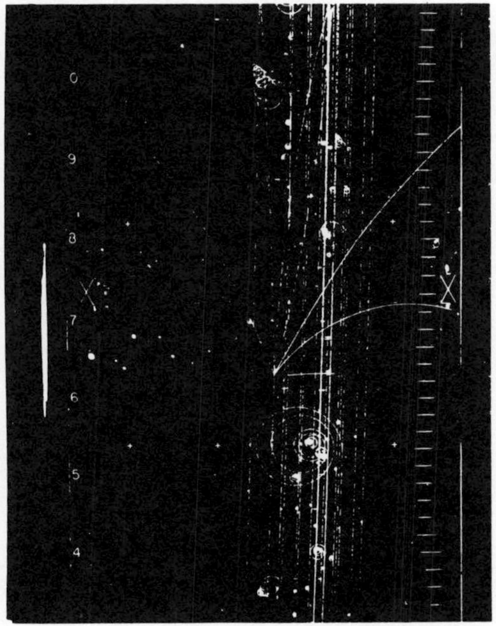

Picture

50-750 digitizing/track by Operator

Filtering to 2 to 40 digitizing/track

100,000 co-ordinate pairs from Flying Spot Digitizer

Track Filtering

Track Element Linking yielding 2-40 digitizing/track

co-ordinates of vertex

Polynomial Fitting Vertex Finding Type of Curvature? Concave or Convex

Tree Representation of event

Tree Automata

Reject → Decision: non event

Accept → Decision: Event type?

Figure 3.   Bubble Chamber Photographs Classification System

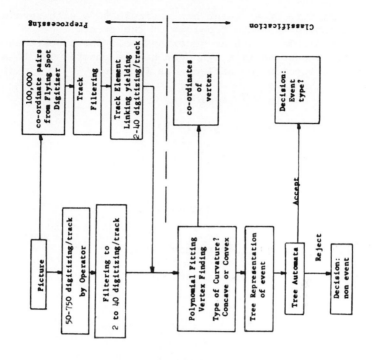

Figure 2.   Typical Bubble Chamber Photograph

267

senting the picture of an event has a single node with several branches depending upon the topology of the event.

The tree grammar G_{tb} that generates only the trees that represent events occurring in a hydrogen bubble chamber due to a positively charged incoming particle is as follows:

$$G_{tb} = (V, r, P, S)$$

$$V = \{S, c_p, c_n, A, B\}$$

$$V_T = \{c_p, c_n\}$$

where

c_p: convex arc,

c_n: concave arc,

and curvatures of c_p and c_n are variable.

r: $r(c_n) = \{0,1\}$, $r(c_p) = \{0,1,2,4,6\}$

P: (1)   S →

$$
\begin{array}{c}
c_p \\
| \\
S
\end{array}
$$

(2)   S →

$$
\begin{array}{c}
c_p \\
/ \quad \backslash \\
A \quad\quad B
\end{array}
$$

(3)   S →

$$
\begin{array}{c}
c_p \\
/ / \backslash \backslash \\
A \ A \ A \ B
\end{array}
$$

(4)   S →

$$
\begin{array}{c}
c_p \\
A\ A\ A\ A\ B\ B
\end{array}
$$

(5)   A →

$$
\begin{array}{c}
c_p \\
| \\
A
\end{array}
$$

(6)   A → c_p

(7) $B \to$
$$\begin{array}{c} c_n \\ | \\ B \end{array}$$

(8) $B \to c_n$.

The branching in production (2) – (4) represents the number of prongs that is usually not greater than 6.

In a hydrogen chamber, if the incoming particle is positively charged, an event with six prongs looks like

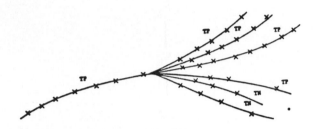

This event can be represented by a tree as shown in Fig. 4. Obviously the tree in Fig. 4 is generated by tree grammar G_{tb}. The tree automaton for the tree grammar G_{tb} is as follows:

$$M_{tb} = (Q, f_{cn}, f_{cp}, F)$$

where

$$Q = \{q_1, q_2. q_R, F\}, \quad F = \{q_{F_2}, q_{F_4}, q_{F_6}\}$$

$$q_R = \text{rejection state}$$

and

$$f_{cp} = q_1$$

$$f_{cn} = q_2$$

$$f_{cp}(q_1) = q_1$$

$$f_{cn}(q_2) = q_2$$

$$f_{cp}(q_{F_i}) = q_{F_i} \qquad \text{for } i = 2, 4, 6.$$

$$f_{cp}(q_1, q_1) = q_{F_2}$$

$$f_{cp}(q_1, q_1, q_1, q_2) = q_{F_4}$$

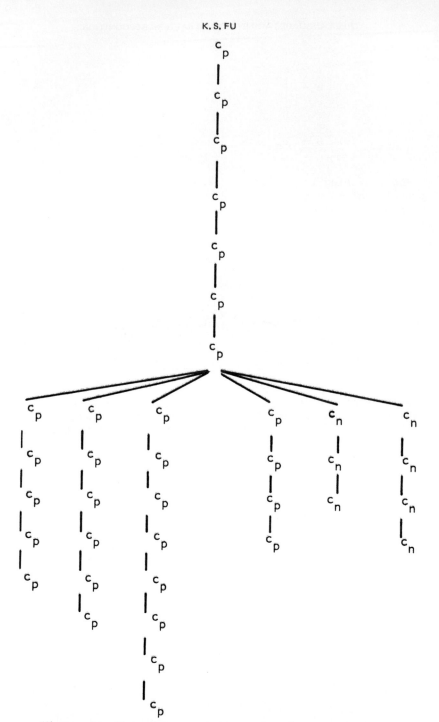

Figure 4.   Tree Representation of a 6-prong Event.

$$f_{cp}(q_1, q_1, q_1, q_1, q_2, q_2) = q_{F_6}$$

All other transitions lead to q_R.

Thus, if the tree automaton is in state q_{F_i}, the picture under inspection represents an event with i-prongs. In the case that the tree automaton reaches the state q_R, the program stops and classifies the picture as nonevent. Here the decision of a trained operator can help the computer in case the event is of a typical complex type. (Two tracks may be so close that they cannot be i-dentified as separate by the computer with the given resolution, but they can be seen by the human eye.)

The same scheme is employed for all the three views and cor-related results for identifying events to give their exact topol-ogy and the position of vertex are obtained. Sometimes in one of the views two tracks are so close that events cannot be identified correctly. If the event was correctly identified in the other two views, a decision about the type of event can still be made.

The results obtained using the tree grammar for classification of bubble chamber photographs were very encouraging. Since the data obtained for each event from the High Energy Physics Labora-tory of Purdue University were only for events of known topology, we were able to verify our results by checking back. All programs were written in Fortran language and were implemented on the CDC 6500 computer at Purdue University, Computer Science Center. The computation time for complete analysis on preprocessed data were about 0.30 s for each event. There were 99 percent of events for prongs 2 and prongs 4 correctly classified. For 6-prong events the classifications were 96 percent correct. In all, 300 events were tested. The causes of misclassification were insufficient data from the scanner and the high degree of resolution required for events with very close tracks. Details of the programs and computer results can be found in [17].

V. APPLICATION TO FINGERPRINT PATTERN RECOGNITION

An early attempt of applying syntactic approach to finger-print pattern recognition uses context-free string grammar to de-scribe various classes of fingerprint patterns [18]. The grammars used have the potential of generating about forty classes. A com-plete identification system for fingerprint requires a technique which utilizes the features of fingerprint patterns, called minu-tiae, such as abrupt ridge ending, short ridge, branches, and mer-gers. The relationship of the minutiae are so unique that although each fingerprint pattern has about 100 minutiae, as many as a dozen is considered sufficient to identify an impression [19].

In this section, we briefly describe a tree grammar approach to fingerprint pattern recognition [20]. A 4 x 4 sampling matrix is superimposed on a fingerprint impression which is then divided into 16 windows. Typically, we have 16 windows for each finger-

print pattern with each window containing 48 x 48 binary pixels.
Fig. 5 shows a sampling window for tree grammar approach. After
certain preprocessing steps (e.g., thinning, gap-filling, etc.),
each ridge becomes a line pattern and is coded by a chain code.
Fig. 6 shows the chain coded window corresponding to that shown in
Fig. 5.

The minutiae of fingerprint impressions define the patterns
so uniquely that if 50 minutiae are considered in each pattern and
if it is assumed that each minutia can be either a branch or termination, then 2^{50} or about 10^{15} unique fingerprints can be expected. Therefore, if all variations of minutiae and their location
within the pattern area are taken into account, the number of unique
fingerprint impressions can reasonably be considered infinite for
all practical purposes. The primitive set shown in Fig. 7 has been
selected based on the type of information associated with the ridge
configuration within each window.

It is true that the goal of the classifier is to generate as
many classes as needed; however, the generation of all the tree
grammars is a very cumbersome task, unless an inference procedure
is available to infer new grammars or their recognizers whenever un-
classified fingerprint patterns are found. The inference procedure
described in Section 3 was used in the construction of tree grammars.

Example 4: The grammar G_{t3} is a typical tree grammar which
generates all windows with a set of continuous ridges along with
one ridge having a branch minutia [20]:

$$G_{t3} = (V,r,P,S)$$

where 　　　　　　$S = \text{starting symbol} = \{N3\}$

$$V = \{N3,T1,R,L,A,B,C,D,s,T3,Rs,L3,X\}$$

$$r(s)=r(L)=r(R)=r(A)=r(B)=r(C)=r(D)=r(R3)=r(L3)=\{1,2\}$$

$$r(X)=2$$

and P:

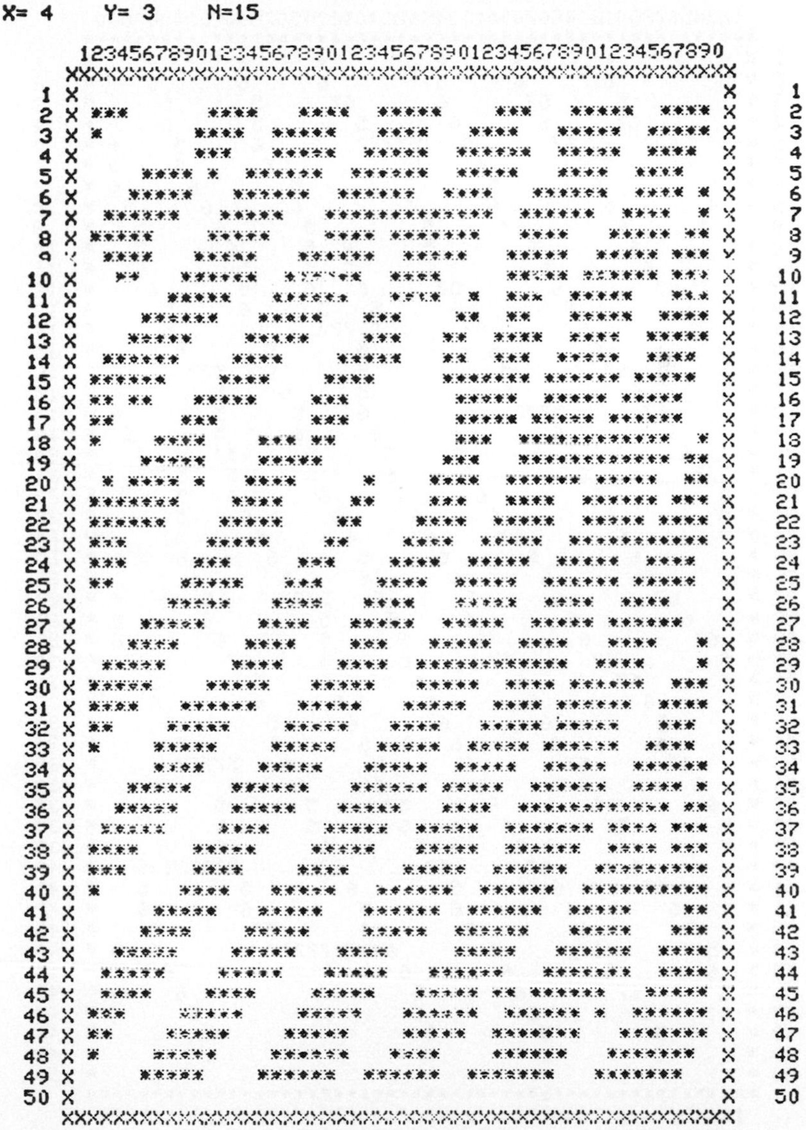

X= 4   Y= 3   N=15

Figure 5.   A Sampling Window of Fingerprint Pattern.

273

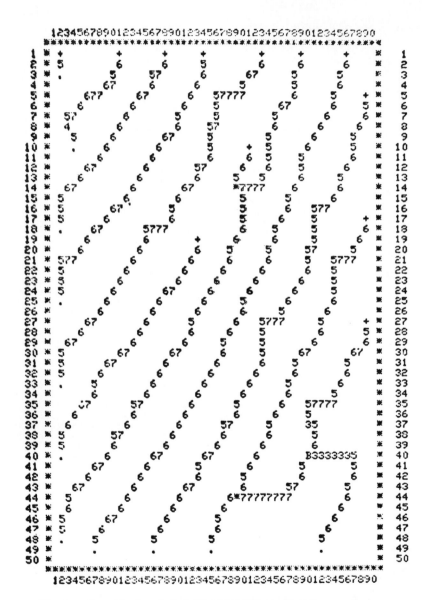

Figure 6. Chain Coded Window After Preprocessing.

Terminal Primitives	Code	Name
	A	Directional code
	B	Directional code
	C	Directional code
	D	Directional code
	X	Branching point
	*	Merging point
	-	Loop
	$	Sudden-ending
	$ $	Segment
Left-side	L	Left
Right-side	R	Right
Starting-point	s	Starting ridge

Figure 7. The Set of Primitives.

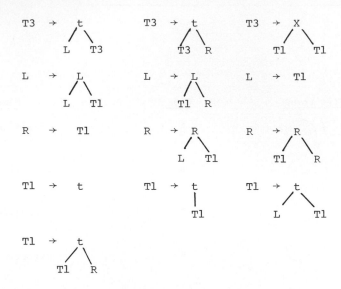

Where $t = \{A, B, C, D\}$. The tree automaton corresponding to this grammar accepting windows of continuous ridges with one ridge having a branch minutia is:

$$M_{t3} = (Q, f_A, f_B, f_C, f_D, f_R, f_L, f_S, f_X, F)$$

$$Q = \{q_{T1}, q_{T3}, q_{N3}, q_R\}$$

$$F = \{q_{N3}\}$$

and

$$f_X(q_{T1}, q_{T1}) = q_{T3} \qquad f_t(q_{T1}, q_{T3}) = q_{T3}$$

$$f_L(q_{T1}, q_{T3}) = q_{T3} \qquad f_R(q_{T1}, q_{T3}) = q_{T3}$$

$$f_L(q_{T1}, q_{T1}) = q_{T1} \qquad f_R(q_{T1}, q_{T1}) = q_{T1}$$

$$f_t(q_{T1}, q_{T1}) = q_{T1} \qquad f_s(q_{T1}, q_{T3}) = q_{N3}$$

$$f_s(q_{T3}) = q_{N3} \qquad f_t(q_{T3}) = q_{T3}$$

$$f_t(q_{T1}) = q_{T1} \qquad f_t = q_{T1}$$

where $t = \{A, B, C, D\}$. All other transitions lead to q_R the rejecting state. Depending on the final state of the tree automaton, the window is classified as continuous ridges with one ridge having a branch minutia or is rejected as a member od these classes.

An experiment was conducted on the basis of 92 fingerprint samples. The computer programs were written in Fortran Language on the CDC-6500 Computer at Purdue University. The grammars of the first 10 classes were generated manually while the rest of the

grammars were inferred through the simulation by the tree grammar
inference procedure. Although the 92 fingerprint patterns may
generate as many as 1472 classes for each window, however, many of
the window configurations are similar to each other and a small
group of tree languages may be sufficient to describe all the fingerprint impressions. To limit the number of classes in this study
the differentiation between left and right position of the features
and their type of curvature were ignored, while these primitives
may be used to generate a more balanced system.

The experiment showed that the inference rate of the new classes was high at the beginning of the study and it decreased as more
patterns were considered. The system generated totally 193 classes.
If all 16 windows of the sampling matrix have the same probability
to be classified into any of the 193 classes, then a total of 193^{16}
or approximately 2×10^{34} classes of fingerprints may be generated
which is much greater than all the fingerprints already collected.
However, the fact is that many of these classes have zero probability of occurrence such as a fingerprint whose 16 sampling windows
all consist of two loops and a merging ridge.

About 4.2% of the windows were classified as misconnected
which indicated that the preprocessing algorithm made improper connection of the ridges. The erroneous results have mainly been
found in the windows with the ridges having a high degree of curvature. It seems that this type of misconnection may be eliminated by developing different algorithms for different windows or
may be by considering different sizes of windows. Also, about
11.9% of the windows were found too noisy for feature extraction.
Windows which were too dark or too light due to excessive or insufficient use of ink when the fingerprints were taken, were classified as too noisy. Some of the fingerprint impressions with
scars, which interrupted the normal flow of the ridges, were also
found too noisy for classification. The computer time for a complete processing, including preprocessing, encoding, feature extraction and parsing, is about 50 seconds per fingerprint [20].

VI. APPLICATION TO THE LANDSAT DATA INTERPRETATION

As the ability of satellites to gather data for the purpose
of survey and monitoring of earth resources grows, the need to fully automate the recognition process of a large number of pictures
obtained by satellite photography is also becoming more evident.
In the past, the use of pattern recognition techniques has been
very successful in the classification and interpretation of the
data taken from agriculture fields, vegetation, water, soil, etc.
However, these methods usually employ only spectral and/or temporal properties of the objects and neglect the spatial relationships among classes in the picture. Difficulties could then arise
when one is dealing with smaller objects such as bridges, highway,
river, etc. because the surrounding environment changes greatly
the expected reflectance of those objects due to the resolution

size. For instance, the spectral measurements of a segment of the highway is obtained from a combined reflectance of concrete surfaces, grasses, trees, etc. Sometimes it is impossible to distinguish this class from, say, suburban scenes where similar features dominate. In cases like this, one has to extract a certain geometric feature from the data in order to interpret them more accurately. In other words, properties such as shape, size, and texture must be used to delineate one from the other among classes of similar spectral properties. Often, the spatial relationships such as "surrounded by," "near by," and directional references can also be explored to locate classes of large areas where no definite shapes exist, such as those found in land use classification. For instance, in the study of land use classification of the Marion County (Indianapolis), Indiana, an overall accuracy of about 87 percent is reported using only the spectral information from LANDSAT data [21]. Difficulties were encountered in the spectral separation of grassy (open country, agriculture) area and multi-family (older) housing. One solution to this problem consists of spatially dividing the data into urban and rural land use prior to classification. Over 95 percent accuracy of recognition may be achieved by this manual preprocessing step [21].

The use of syntactic methods to describe the spatial relationship has recently been suggested [22]. As an example, an earth scene of a metropolitan area can be modelled as consisting of downtown area surrounded by inner city area with near-by suburban area and a system of highways. These classes can be classified by utilizing their spatial relationships expressed in terms of syntactic rules. Brayer and Fu have applied web grammars to the description of cloud-shadow pair, urban complex, and highways [23]. In this section, we briefly described some preliminary results obtained from the use of tree grammar approach to determine highways and rivers from LANDSAT data [24].

The LANDSAT data of Lafayette, Indiana was selected as training data. Seventeen clusters were detected in the feature space of four spectral signals. The 17 clusters were further combined into seven ground cover types. They are general agriculture areas, pastures with wheat dominant, forests, commercial areas, residential areas, highways and rivers. We use highways and rivers to demonstrate the effectiveness of syntactic approach in utilizing spatial information. Our purpose would be to separate lakes or ponds from rivers and highways from other classes with similar spectral features. In terms of spatial characteristics, highway and river are similar, although from spectral characteristics highway consists of primarily concrete and river consists of water. For simplicity, we use the same grammar for both highways and rivers. The inference procedure described in Section 3 was used to construct the tree grammar.

The pointwise classified data of the Lafayette area is shown in Fig. 8.

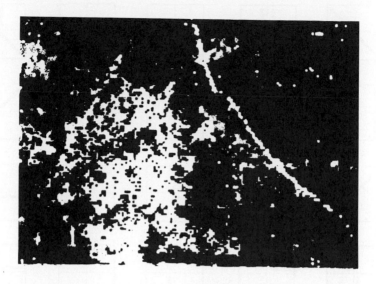

Figure 8.   Pointwise Classified Results of
the Lafayette Area.

The primitives selected for both river and highway are based on a
2x2 pixel window. This low level extraction will eliminate all
isolated points. Its main purpose, however, is to generate the
terminals for further learning. The next step is to find the most
probable combinations of primitives which occur as neighbors of
each other in the river and highway data samples. For the sake of
convenience, we chose a set of 4-tuple patterns which are more representative of suburban highways than, say, streets in commercial
areas or any other features which reflect like a mixture of concrete and grass, like those appearing quite extensively in the new
residential area in south Lafayette. Those 4-tuple patterns are
shown in Fig. 9.

After a series of trials and errors, we deduce a set of 26
combinations which give us a good result in terms of showing the
Wabash River and Interstate Highway 65 in the Lafayette area.
Since the 4-tuples can be applied in both directions, we really
learn the highway and river structures from the 13 combinations
shown in Fig. 10.

The next step is to discover what subtrees make up the tree
language and generate nonterminals for each subtree. We can divide those 13 patterns into three categories; they are shown as
the three rows in Figure 10. If we denote a → (horizontal line
segment), b ↘ (diagonal line segment), and c ↓ (vertical line segment), then the tree representation of the following highway pat-

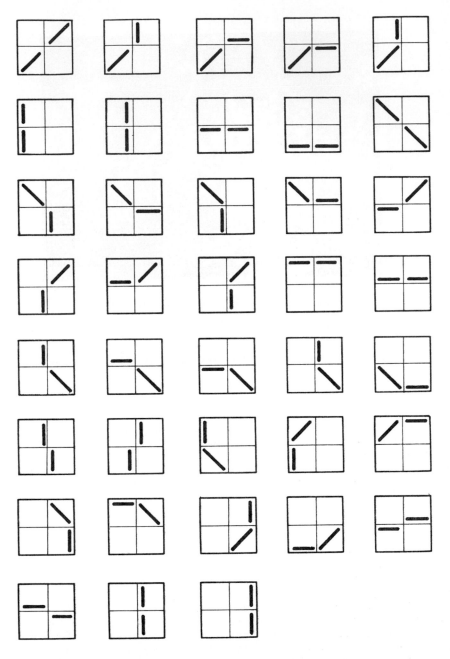

Figure 9.   4-Tuple Patterns.

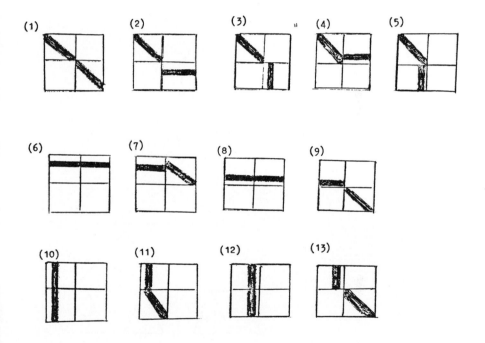

Figure 10. Basic (First Level) Highway Patterns.

tern within a 6x6 pixel window

will be

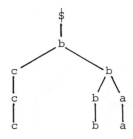

The subtrees of depth one within this tree can be expressed in terms of the following representation

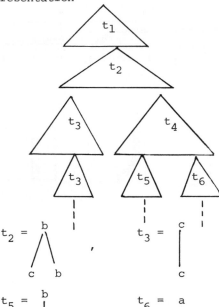

where

$t_1 = \begin{array}{c} \$ \\ | \\ b \end{array}$, $t_2 = \begin{array}{c} b \\ \diagup \backslash \\ c \quad b \end{array}$, $t_3 = \begin{array}{c} c \\ | \\ c \end{array}$

$t_4 = \begin{array}{c} b \\ \diagup \backslash \\ b \quad a \end{array}$, $t_5 = \begin{array}{c} b \\ | \\ b \end{array}$, $t_6 = \begin{array}{c} a \\ | \\ a \end{array}$

Following the inference procedure described in Section 3, we obtain the following tree grammar for highway (or river) patterns:

$$G_t = (V, r, P, S)$$

$$V = \{s, a, b, c, \$, A_1, A_2, A_3, A_4, A_5, A_6\}$$

$$V_T = \{a, b, c\}$$

$$r(a) = \{2, 1, 0\}, \ r(b) = \{2, 1, 0\}, \ r(c) = \{2, 1, 0\}$$

$$r(\$) = \{2, 1\}$$

P:

Presumably, each tree generated by the tree grammar G_t represents a highway (or river) segment within a 6x6 pixel window.

Corresponding to this tree grammar, we can then construct a

tree automation

$$M_t = (Q, f_\$, f_a, f_b, f_c, F) \quad \text{over } V_T$$

$$Q = \{A_1, A_2, A_3, A_4, A_5, A_6, q_F\}, \quad F = \{q_F\},$$

$$V_T = \{\$, a, b, c\}$$

$$f_\$ (A_1, A_2) = q_F$$

$$f_\$ (A_2, A_3) = q_F$$

$$f_\$ (A_1, A_3) = q_F$$

$$f_\$ (A_1) = q_F$$

$$f_\$ (A_2) = q_F$$

$$f_\$ (A_3) = q_F$$

$$f_a (A_4, A_5) = A_1$$

$$f_a (A_4) = A_1$$

$$f_a (A_1) = A_1$$

$$f_b (A_4, A_5) = A_2$$

$$f_b (A_5, a_6) = A_2$$

$$f_b (A_4, A_6) = A_2$$

$$f_b (A_4) = A_2$$

$$f_b (A_5) = A_2$$

$$f_b (A_6) = A_2$$

$$f_c (A_5, A_6) = A_3$$

$$f_c (A_5) = A_3$$

$$f_c (A_6) = A_3$$

$$f_a = A_4$$

$$f_b = A_5$$

$$f_c = A_6$$

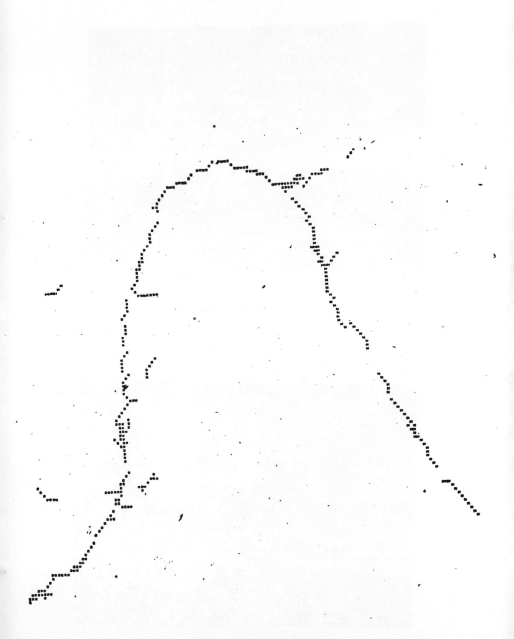

Figure 11. Syntactically Classified Results of
Rivers and Highways - Lafayette Area.

Figure 12. Pointwise Classified Results of
Grand Rapids (Suburban Area).

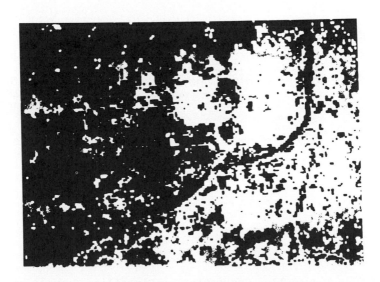

Figure 13. Pointwise Classified Results of
Grand Rapids (Urban Area).

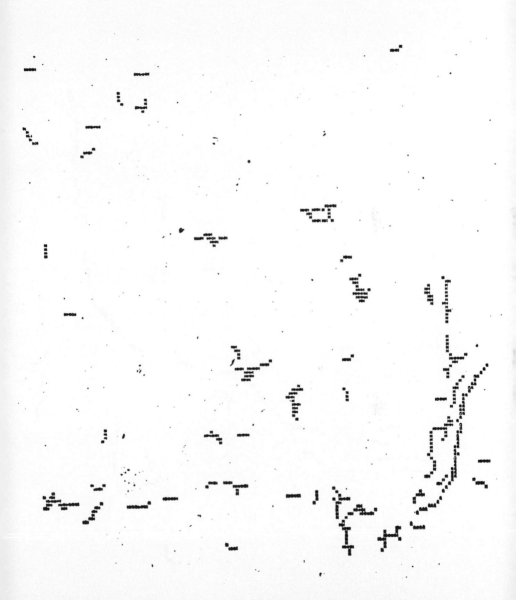

Figure 14. Syntactically Classified Results of Rivers and
Highways - Grand Rapids (Suburban Area).

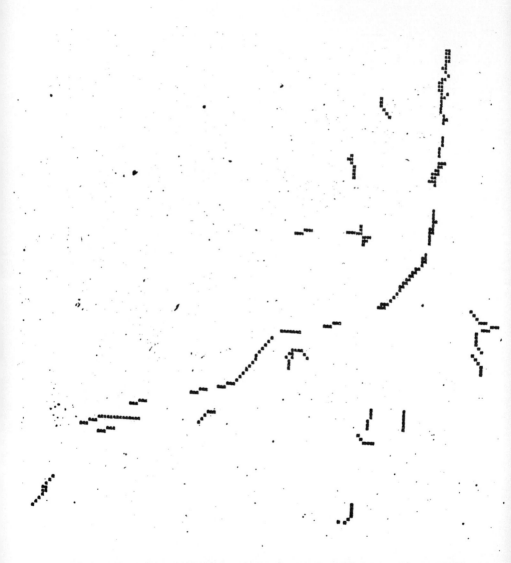

Figure 15.   Syntactically Classified Results of Rivers and
Highways - Grand Rapids (Urban Area).

After an input tree extracted from a picture window is applied, if the tree automaton is in q_F then the picture contains a highway (or river) pattern. If the tree automaton reaches any other state we conclude that this particular picture does not have what we are looking for.

Using the tree automaton as recognizer, the result of highway and river patterns in the Lafayette area is shown in Fig. 11. The tree automaton is also tested on a new data set, that of Grand Rapids, Michigan. The results on Grand Rapids, Michigan show that the highways in suburban areas can be detected as a road-like feature. In urban areas, there are too many streets and concrete parking lots confused as highways. On the other hand, the river, which is usually easier to find due to good resolution, is not so obvious in the lower portion of the urban-area data set due to the confusion with the shadow class. However, these rivers have been successively traced out in our syntactic approach. Figs. 12, 13, 14, and 15 give the pointwise classification and the syntactic interpretation of highways and rivers, respectively, in the Grand Rapids area.

VII. CONCLUSIONS AND REMARKS

In this paper, tree grammars and tree automata are briefly reviewed and several application examples to syntactic pattern recognition are described. Tree languages can be used to effectively describe high-dimensional patterns. For a given tree grammar, a tree automaton can be conveniently constructed to recognize the language generated by the tree grammar. The operation of the tree automaton is, in general, deterministic, and, hence, can be efficiently implemented as a pattern recognizer.

Depending upon the node labelling, tree representation of a pattern may not be unique. The final choice is, of course, also based on the pattern primitives selected. The tree grammar inference procedure described in the paper, though heuristic, is very convenient for practical applications. The resulting grammar is often in expansive form which can be directly used to construct the recognizer (tree automaton). For the analysis of noisy and distorted patterns, stochastic tree languages and error-correcting tree recognizers have been proposed [1], 25]. Their effectiveness and efficiency still need to be evaluated.

REFERENCES

1. Fu, K. S., *Syntactic Methods in Pattern Recognition,* Academic Press, 1974.
2. Pfaltz, J. L. and A. Rosenfeld, "Web Grammars," Proc. Joint International Conference on Artificial Intelligence, Washington, D.C., 1969.

3. Siromoney, G., R. Siromoney, and K. Kristhivasam, "Picture Languages with Array Rewriting Rules", *Information and Control,* Vol. 22, 1973, pp. 447-470.

4. Pavlidis, T., "Linear and Context-Free Graph Grammars," *Journal of ACM,* Vol. 19, January, 1972.

5. Fu, K. S. and B. K. Bhargava, "Tree Systems for Syntactic Pattern Recognition," *IEEE Trans. on Computers,* Vol. C-22, pp. 1087-1099, December, 1973.

6. Gips, J., *Shape Grammars and Their Uses,* Interdisciplinary Systems Research Monograph, Vol. 10, Birkhauser-Verlag, Basel Stuttgart, 1976.

7. Ota, P. A., "Mosaic Grammars," *Pattern Recognition,* Vol. 7, 1975, pp. 61-65.

8. Williams, K. L., "A Multidimensional Approach to Syntactic Pattern Recognition," *Pattern Recognition,* Vol. 7, 1975, pp. 125-137.

9. Ng, P. A. and S. Y. Bang, "Toward a Mathematical Theory of Graph Generative Systems and Its Applications," *Information Sciences,* to appear.

10. Brainerd, W. S., "Tree Generating Regular Systems," *Information and Control,* Vol. 14, pp. 217-231, 1969.

11. Doner, J. E., "Tree Acceptors and Some of Their Applications," *J. Comp. Syst. Sci.,* Vol. 4, October, 1970.

12. Bhargava, B. K., "Tree Systems for Syntactic Pattern Recognition," Ph.D. Thesis, Purdue University, May, 1974.

13. Bhargava, B. K. and K. S. Fu, "Transformations and Inference of Tree Grammars for Syntactic Pattern Recognition," Proc. IEEE International Conf. on Systems, Man, and Cybernetics, Dallas, Texas, October 2-4, 1974.

14. Lassez, J. L., "Prefix Codes, Trees and Automata," Information Sciences, Vol. 8, April, 1975

15. Brayer, J. M. and K. S. Fu, "Some Multidimensional Grammar Inference Methods," These proceedings, pp. 29-60.

16. Fu, K. S. and T. L. Booth, "Grammatical Inference - Introduction and Survey," Part II, *IEEE Trans. in Systems, Man, and Cybernetics,* Vol. SMC-5, July, 1975.

17. Bhargava, B. K. and K. S. Fu, "Application of Tree System Approach to Classification of Bubble Chamber Photographs," Tech. Rept. TR-EE 72-30, Purdue University, November, 1972.

18. Moayer, B. and K. S. Fu, "A Syntaction Approach to Fingerprint Pattern Recognition," *Pattern Recognition,* Vol. 7, January, 1975.

19. Eleccion, M., "Automatic Fingerprint Identification," *IEEE Spectrum,* Vol. 10, September, 1973.

20. Moayer, B. and K. S. Fu, "A Tree System Approach for Fingerprint Pattern Recognition," *IEEE Trans. on Computers,* Vol. C-25, March, 1976.

21. Todd, W. J., and M. F. Baumgardner, "Land Use Classification of Marion County, Indiana by Spectral Analysis and Digitized Satellite Data," LARS Information Note 101673, Purdue University, 1973.

22. Fu, K. S., "Pattern Recognition in Remote Sensing of the Earth's
     Resources," *IEEE Trans. on Geoscience Electronics,* Vol. GE-14,
     January, 1976.
23. Brayer, J. M. and K. S. Fu, "Application of a Web Grammar Model
     to an Earth Resources Satellite Picture," Proc. Third Interna-
     tional Joint Conference on Pattern Recognition, November 8-11,
     1976, Coronado, California.
24. Li, R. Y. and K. S. Fu, "Tree System Approach for LANDSAT
     Data Interpretation," Proc. Symposium on Machine Processing
     of Remotely Sensed Data, June 29-July 1, 1976, Purdue Univer-
     sity, West Lafayette, Indiana.
25. Lu, S. Y. and K. S. Fu, "Error-Correcting Syntax Analysis for
     Tree Languages," Tech. Rept. TR-EE 76-24, Purdue University,
     July, 1976.

ACQUISITION AND UTILIZATION OF ACCESS PATTERNS
IN RELATIONAL DATA BASE IMPLEMENTATION*

Michael Hammer
Arvola Chan
MIT Laboratory for Computer Science
545 Technology Square
Cambridge, Massachusetts, 02139.

ABSTRACT

The efficient performance of a relational data base depends
heavily on the matching of the data base's physical organization
to the way that the data base is used. This can be accomplished
by monitoring the use of the data base, recognizing patterns of
usage, and synthesizing storage and access structures most appropriate for the evidenced mode of use. We describe in this paper
the principles of the automatic index selection facility of a prototype self-adaptive data base management system currently under
development. Statistics gathering mechanisms capture the essential parameters of a usage pattern, and exponential smoothing
techniques are used to project future access requirements. The
cost model used to evaluate proposed index sets is accurate and
flexible enough to incorporate the overhead costs of index maintenance, creation, and storage. An heuristic algorithm is used to
select a near-optimal index set without an exhaustive enumeration
of all possibilities.

I. INTRODUCTION

The development and utilization of large integrated data
bases promises to be one of the most important data processing activities of the next decade. By an integrated data base, we mean
one which contains all the data used by an enterprise in a variety
of applications. There are many reasons for the incorporation of
heretofore separate but related data bases with a high degree of
duplication into a single integrated one. The reduction of storage and updating costs, and the elimination of inconsistencies
that may be caused by different copies of the data in different
stages of updating, are among the more important ones.
In order for these data bases to be truly effective, the data
management systems which support them will have to manifest two
important characteristics: data independence and non-procedural

---
* This research was supported by the Advanced Research Projects
   Agency of the Department of Defense and was monitored by the
   Office of Naval Research under contract no. N00014-75-0661.

access. By data independence we mean that users and their application programs are shielded from knowledge of the actual physical
organizations used to represent their data, concentrating instead
on a *logical* view of the data. This makes the data base easier to
use and avoids the need for application programs to change when
the data base's physical structure is reorganized. Non-procedural
access also makes the data base easy to use; this means the provision of access languages which allow the specification of desired data in terms of properties it possesses rather than in
terms of the search algorithm used to locate it in the data base.
    The relational model [1] of data has been proposed as a means
of achieving these two goals. The user of a relational data base
is provided with a simple and uniform view of the data, a logical
view which is completely independent of the actual storage structures used to represent this data. The simplicity of this logical
data structure lends itself to access by means of easy-to-use languages, which provide associative referencing (content addressing)
of the data base contents.
    Specifically, a relational data base consists of a collection
of relations - a relation is a named two-dimensional table, which
has a fixed number of (named) columns and an arbitrary number of
(unnamed) rows (called tuples). Each tuple $(t_1, t_2 \ldots, t_m)$ represents an entry in the relation; t_i, the ith component of a tuple,
is a member of D_i, the domain associated with the ith column. The
relation EMP depicted in Figure 1 has four columns; for each tuple
of the relation, the corresponding columnar values represent the
name, age, sex, and salary of the particular employee. Figure 1
represents a snapshot of the relation at a particular point in
time; relational data base languages provide users the ability to
selectively retrieve or modify individual tuples, as well as insert and delete tuples.

EMP:	NAME	AGE	SEX	SALARY
	Smith	30	M	16000
	James	25	M	12000
	Black	28	F	14000
	Brown	35	M	20000
	Jones	20	F	10000
	—	—	—	—
	—	—	—	—
	—	—	—	—

Figure 1.

    The table of Figure 1 is purely the user's logical view of
the data base; there are no stipulations as to how this data would
actually be stored on the computer.

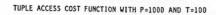

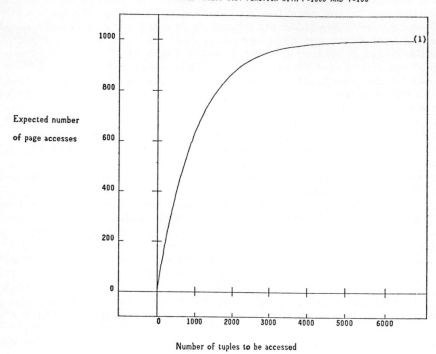

Number of tuples to be accessed

Figure 2

In order to find the names of all male employees making more than $15,000, the user might express a query [2] such as:

```
SELECT    NAME
FROM      EMP
WHERE     SEX = 'M'
AND       SAL > 15000.
```

The query language processor would translate this specification of the desired information into searches on the data base that utilize the precise storage structures and auxiliary access mechanisms used to store the data.

Because of the distance of the user's view of a relational data base (and of his queries against it) from the realities of the data base's physical organization, more responsibility is placed on a relational data base system than on a conventional system. This responsibility takes two forms: choosing the physical representation for a relation; and optimizing the execution of queries against a relation, making optimally efficient use of the available access structures. Relational data base systems must possess "intelligence" in order to make decisions in these areas, which have heretofore been the province of human decision-makers.

We believe that the selection of good storage structures is the primary issue in relational data base implementation, since the efficiency that can be achieved by a query optimizer is strictly delimited by the available storage structures. Furthermore, the efficient utilization of a data base is highly dependent on the optimal matching of its physical organization to its access requirements as well as to other of its characteristics (such as the distribution of values in it). (For example, certain data base organizations are suitable for low update - high retrieval situations, while others yield optimal performance in opposite circumstances.)

Hence, the usage pattern of a data base should be ascertained and utilized in choosing its physical organization. In addition, when viewed as the repository of all information used in managing an enterprise, an integrated data base can no longer be considered as a static entity. Instead, it is continually changing in size, and its access requirements gradually alter as applications evolve and users develop familiarity with the system. Accordingly, the tuning of a data base's physical organization to fit its usage pattern must be an ongoing process.

In current relational data base systems, the data base administrator (DBA) may make recommendations to the system about desirable auxiliary access structures, but his judgements are based largely on intuition and on a limited amount of communication with some individual users. For large integrated data bases, a more systematic means for acquiring information about data base usage, and a more algorithmic way of evaluating the costs of alternative configurations, will be essential. A minimal capability of data base management system should be the incorporation of monitoring mechanisms that collect usage statistics while performing query processing. A more sophisticated system would sense a change in access requirements, evaluate the cost/benefits of various reorganization strategies, and choose an optimal structure to be recommended to the DBA; eventually, such a system might itself perform the necessary tuning.

This paper describes a research effort that seeks to develop a facility that monitors the use of a relational data base and chooses near-optimal physical storage and access structures based on the evidenced pattern of use; furthermore, shifts in usage pattern will be detected and will result in timely reorganization of the data base. At its heart, this is a problem in pattern recognition and artificial intelligence: first, to extract from a mass of statistics relating to data base performance a succinct pattern which characterizes its mode of use; second, since an exhaustive consideration of all possible structures is computationally infeasible, to develop efficient heuristics that can use the usage pattern to synthesize a near-optimal structure.

II. INDEX SELECTION IN AN ADAPTIVE DATA BASE SYSTEM

We are currently developing a self-adaptive data base management system which monitors the access patterns and the data characteristics of a data base, and uses this information to tune its physical organization. We operate in the environment of a relational data base system, which provides a level of physical data independence that facilitates physical reorganization. Continuous monitoring of the usage of a relational data base provides many opportunities for its reorganization, and we expect to experiment with a variety of alternatives and study their costs and tradeoffs. As a first cut at the problem, we have concentrated on the problem of index selection. A secondary index (sometimes referred to as an inversion) is a well-known software structure which can improve the performance of accesses to a relation (file) [3]. For each domain (field) of the relation that is inverted, a table is maintained, which for each value of the domain in question contains pointers to all those tuples (records) whose contents in the designated domain is the specified value. Clearly, the presence of a secondary index for a particular domain can improve the execution of many queries that reference that domain; on the other hand, maintenance of such an index has costs that slow down the performance of data base updates, insertions, and deletions. Roughly speaking, a domain that is referenced frequently relative to its modification is a good candidate for index maintenance. The choice of which (if any) domains to invert must be done with care; a good choice can significantly improve the performance of the system, while a bad selection can seriously degrade it. The goal of our system is to make a good choice of those domains for which secondary indices are to be maintained, based on how the data is actually used.

The operation of the initial version of our prototype system can be described as follows. The specifications of data base interactions, by both interactive users and application programs, are expressed in a non-procedural language; these are first translated into an internal representation made up of calls to system level modules. The language processor has available to it a model of the current state of the data base, which contains, among other things, a list of the currently maintained set of secondary indices, plus various information about these indices. Using this information, the language processor can choose the best strategy for processing each data base operation in the current environment. Statistics gathering mechanisms are embedded within the system modules that interpret the object code of the language processor; they are used to record data concerning the execution of every data base transaction. The statistical information gathered for a run is deposited in a collection area and is summarized from time to time. When the reorganization component of the system is invoked (which will occur at fixed intervals of time) the statistical information collected over the preceding interval is combined with statistics from previous intervals and is used to obtain a forecast of the access requirements of the upcoming interval; in addition, a projected assessment of various characteristics of the data in the data base is made. A near-optimal set of domains for which indices should be maintained is then determined heuristically; optimality means with respect to total cost, taking into account the expense of index storage and maintenance. This minimal cost is compared with the projected cost for the existing set of indices. Data base reorganization is performed only if its payoff is great enough to cover its cost as well as that of application program retranslation.

In this paper, we stress our approach to the problems of acquiring an accurate usage model and estimating data characteristics, by means of continuous monitoring and the application of forecasting techniques. We have considered the reduced problem of choosing indices for a single relation, but we expect our approach to be extendible to more complex situations once we have developed a model for the costs of different strategies for processing multi-relation queries. We believe that an accurate interaction and cost model is essential for a practical environment, and that the use of problem-oriented heuristics to cut down the index search space is needed to achieve near-optimum solutions with acceptable efficiency.

III. ORGANIZATION OF THE PAPER

The remainder of this paper is organized as follows. We begin with a summary of our view of the data base organization: the file model, the storage and index organizations, and the data base operations. Next, a procedure for determining the strategy (whether or not to use existing indices) for processing the qualification part of a query is presented. We then describe the statistics that are to be gathered during query processing, and explain the use of exponential smoothing techniques in the derivation of parameters needed by the cost model. This is followed by a discussion of the need for heuristics in solving the index selection problem, and the presentation of the heuristics that we have devised. Finally, we include a brief comparison with previous related work.

IV. FILE MODEL

We have chosen the relational model [1] of data as the logical interface between application programs or interactive users and the data base system, since it provides the level of physical data independence needed to facilitate physical reorganization. The totality of formatted data in the data base consists therefore of one or more relations. However, we address here the reduced problem of selecting indices for a data base made up of a single relation. Herein, the data base consists of a single relation (file) R with n tuples (records) $T = (t_1, t_2, \ldots, t_m)$ where each $t_i \in D_i$, the ith domain, i.e. R is a subset of the cartesian product of the domains $D_1, D_2, \ldots, D_m$. Even though insertion and deletion of tuples are permitted, we assume that the cardinality (number of tuples) of the relation remains relatively unchanged between two consecutive points at which index selection is considered.

Following Rothnie [4], we assume a paged memory environment for tuple storage. More specifically, the n tuples in the relation R are stored on p pages of t tuples each, where n, t, and p are approximately constant. Every tuple in the relation possesses a tuple identifier (TID), a logical address which enables the tuple to be located with only one page access. The accessing cost of a page is assumed to be independent of the sequence of page accesses, and dominates all other internal processing costs. Hence, the processing cost for a query is measured solely in terms of the number of pages that have to be accessed to resolve the query. If a query is resolved by sequentially scanning all tuples in the relation, then the total number of pages that are accessed is just p. If an index is available for a domain referenced in a query, it may significantly reduce the number of tuples that need to be examined to resolve the query. These tuples may correspondingly reside on fewer than p pages. We shall assume that such a restricted set of tuples will be randomly distributed over the memory space, but that, given their TIDs, it is possible to access them in such a way that each page is touched at most once. Yue and Wong [5] have derived an exact formula for the expected number of pages that have to be touched in order to access r tuples which are randomly distributed over the file.

Let $b(r;p,t)$ be the expected number of page accesses for referencing r randomly distributed tuples in a file of p pages each containing t tuples, and let

$$f(0) = 0,$$

$$f(i+1) = \frac{t(p-1)-i}{pt-i} * f(i) + \frac{pt}{pt-i} ;$$

then it has been shown in [5] that $b(r;p,t) = f(r)$. We make use of the above formula in determining if it is profitable to use indices to resolve a query. Since the above formula is defined recursively on r for given values of t and p, (which are assumed to be roughly constant between two consecutive reorganizational points), f can be precomputed and tabulated for a number of values of r. When it is necessary to evaluate this function for an arbitrary value of r, the recursive computation can begin with the tabulated result for the closest smaller r value.

For a fixed value of p (say 1000), and for a typical realistic value of t (say 20), the shape of the function $f(r)$ is indicated in Figure 2. Observe that the curve is nearly linear to start, and asymptotically approaches the value of p. It is instructive to note that for values of r close to, but less than, p, the value of $f(r)$ is roughly $.6p$, which is substantially different from the value given by a linear cost function. In addition, the value of $f(r)$ never exceeds p, in contrast to some linear cost models.

Most previous studies of index selection have utilized linear cost functions for tuple accessing. That is, they have assumed that the cost of accessing a set of tuples, given their TIDs, is directly proportional to the size of the set. As we shall see in a subsequent section, this leads to a simple analysis for the utility of indices. However, a linear cost function is only applicable when all tuples are equally accessible (for example, if they all reside in primary memory) or equally inaccessible (e.g., if each tuple is stored on a separate page and so requires a separate access for its retrieval). In realistic data bases where individual tuples are not excessively large, it is standard to store a number of tuples together on secondary storage and transfer them in unison to primary memory. This so-called "blocking effect" must be taken into account in evaluating the utility of an index.

V. INDEX MODEL

An index on a domain of a relation is a mapping from values of the domain to tuples in the relation with those values. We assume that indices, just like tuples in the relation, are stored in a paged memory, with the usual two-level hierarchical organization, i.e. the domain values and their associated TID lists are

assumed to be on separate levels [6]. Each domain value is stored
together with a pointer to the head of its associated TID list,
and the length of that list. We assume that only those domain
values that are associated with existing tuples in the relation
are stored in the index. To further simplify our discussion here,
we will assume that the values and the associated list pointers
and list lengths are organized as a B-tree [7], each node of which
is stored on a page. One or more TID lists may be stored on the
same page. The use of an index to obtain the TID list for those
tuples which have a given value in the indexed domain involves
searching for the value in the B-tree to obtain the beginning address of the TID list, and the subsequent retrieval of that list.
When a tuple is inserted, deleted or updated, each of the indices
that are currently maintained also requires some modification.
(The maintenance to an index caused by an update is essentially
equivalent to a delete followed by an insert.) In most cases,
this maintenance will cause a single node in the B-tree to be updated. In rarer cases, a domain value may have to be inserted into or deleted from the B-tree, possibly resulting in a node overflow or underflow, which may in turn propagate through the tree.
As for the TID list involved in an insertion, it is possible in
many cases to write back a lengthened version of it onto the same
page on which it was stored before the insertion, by utilizing
empty spaces in the original page. Occasionally, though, the empty space may run out, and it becomes necessary to allocate a new
page. Similarly, occasional garbage collection may be necessary
to recompact the TID lists, and recover wasted space caused by deletions.

VI. TRANSACTION MODEL AND PROCESSING

Our transaction model allows for the retrieval, insertion,
updating, and deletion of tuples in a relation. Data selection
(the specification of some subset of a relation by means of its
properties) is the fundamental component of all these operations.
In choosing data selection operators to be included in our transaction model, we have limited ourselves to those for which the u-
tility of using indices can readily be determined. These include
conjunctions of equality conditions and disjunction of equality
conditions. (By an equality condition, we mean a predicate of the
form A = k, where A is some domain name and k is a constant or a
program variable). The use of indices and list processing techniques for resolving these kinds of queries is well known [2], and
will not be reiterated here. However, our tuple access cost model
implies that it may not always be desirable to resolve a conjunction or a disjunction of equality conditions using indices. (This
will occur when the set of qualified tuples is expected to reside
on close to p pages; we say "close to", because utilizing the in-
dex(es) also entails some page accesses.) Therefore, we need a

means whereby the number of tuples that can be expected to qualify for such a query can be estimated. We can define a selectivity measure for a domain as the average fraction of the set of tuples under consideration that have historically satisfied an equality condition involving that domain. We will, furthermore, assume that the values specified in conjunctive/disjunctive selection predicates are uncorrelated. Hence the joint conjunctive selectivity of a set of domains D each with selectivity S_i is

$$\Pi_{i \in D} S_i .$$

Similarly, the joint disjunctive selectivity of the set of domains D is

$$1 - \Pi_{i \in D} (1-S_i) .$$

Thus, given the selectivities of the domains involved in a set of equality predicates, the number of tuples that can be expected to satisfy a conjunction or disjunction of these predicates can be readily estimated. This can be translated into expected page accesses by the formulae of an earlier section.

The average cost of using an index to obtain the TIDs of the tuples that satisfy an equality condition involving the indexed domain can also be readily estimated, given the number of values in the domain (which determines the height of the B-tree) and the lengths of the associated TID lists. Thus, given a query and an existing set of indices, the query processor can determine the cost of using the indices to resolve the query; it will use them only if the cost of doing so is less than the cost of a sequential search of the entire tuple space.

VII. STATISTICS GATHERING

An important component of our adaptive system is the monitoring mechanisms that collect usage statistics as data base operations are performed. The statistics gathered over a time period are summarized and then "averaged" with summaries from previous periods. The statistics to be gathered for the purpose of index selection fall into three general classes.

(1) update related statistics - This class has several components. First of all, there are the total numbers of tuples that are deleted from (inserted into) the relation in the current time period. (We assume that each insertion or deletion of a tuple will require some maintenance for each active index.) In addition, for each domain of the relation, we record the number of updates made to that domain in the tuples (because each such update involves some maintenance of the index for that domain). Finally, we record the actual difficult-to-parameterize costs of the maintenance of each active index (node splitting and merging, garbage

collection, etc.), measured in terms of the actual number of page
accesses expended for such overheads.

(2) domain selectivity statistics - For each domain, we maintain its average selectivity over all uses of the domain in equality conditions in the current interval. This is accomplished by
recording the number of times the domain occurs in equality conditions and the selectivity of the domain in each of these predicates. The selectivity of the use of a domain in an equality condition is measured as follows:

(a) If an index for the domain is used to resolve the particular equality condition, then the precise selectivity of the domain for this query can be calculated as the fraction of tuples in
the relation with the domain value in question.

(b) Suppose the equality condition appears in a conjunction
of conditions that is resolved by sequential scanning. (This scan
may be of a reduced set of tuples obtained via an index.) Let the
total number of tuples scanned be N_0. Let the conjunction be of
the form $C_1 \wedge C_2 \wedge \ldots \wedge C_n$ where each of the C_i is an equality condition involving domain D_i. Let $N_1, N_2, \ldots, N_n$ be the number of
tuples that satisfy C_1, $C_1 \wedge C_2$, $\ldots$, $C_1 \wedge C_2 \wedge \ldots \wedge C_n$ respectively.
(Note that these values are readily available). The selectivity
of domain D_i for this query is then approximated as N_i / N_{i-1}.

(c) Suppose the equality condition appears in a disjunction
of conditions that is resolved by sequential scanning. Let the
total number of tuples scanned be N_0. Let the disjunction be of
the form $C_1 \vee C_2 \vee \ldots \vee C_n$ where each of the C_i is an equality condition involving domain D_i. Let $N_1, N_2, \ldots, N_n$ be the number of
tuples that satisfy C_1, $\sim C_1 \wedge C_2, \ldots, \sim C_1 \wedge \sim C_2 \wedge \ldots \wedge C_n$ respectively. (Note that these values are readily available). The selec-
tivity of domain D_i for this query is then approximated as $N_i / (N_0 - \Sigma_{1 \leq j < i} N_j)$.

(3) query type statistics - The type of a query is determined by the set of domains it utilizes and by whether it is a
conjunction or disjunction of equality predicates. We record the
number of queries of each type that are processed in the current
time interval.

The foregoing statistics comprise our model of the usage pattern of the data base. We observe that our measure of domain selectivity serves as a succinct yet precise indication of how a domain is actually used in queries. By averaging the selectivities
of the actual occurrences of a domain, we can detect both skewness
in the distribution of domain values over the tuples as well as
non-uniform use of domain values in the equality predicates. This
measurement of selectivity is more accurate than its conventional
estimate as the reciprocal of the number of distinct values in the
domain.

The frequency count of the query types, together with the update statistics, constitute the record of transactions with the data base. By recording the types of the queries that actually occur, we detect any correlations (positive or negative) that may exist between the occurrences of different domains in a query; it may happen that some combinations of domains are always used together, while others never are. Thus we avoid making the strong (and often inaccurate) assumption that the simultaneous occurrences of domains in a query are mutually independent events. Previous studies have made this assumption, and so have recorded access history merely as the frequency of each domain's occurrence in queries.

Finally, we note that all of the foregoing statistics can be collected and maintained with very little overhead, either in execution time or in storage requirements. All of the required information can be easily obtained during query or transaction processing, and requires little space for its recording.

VIII. ACCESS PATTERN FORECASTING AND PARAMETER ESTIMATION

We assume that the index selection problem is to be reconsidered at fixed intervals. At each reorganizational point, we forecast a number of characteristics for the period up to the next reorganizational point. Specifically, we predict the following:

(1) the number of occurrences of each query type;
(2) the selectivity of each domain of the relation;
(3) the number of distinct values in each domain (if a domain is not indexed in the current interval, then the current value for this number is approximated as the reciprocal of the observed selectivity);
(4) the number of tuples (hence the number of pages) in the entire relation at the end of the period;
(5) the expected cost (in terms of page accesses) of maintaining an index for each domain and the expected cost of such an index in obtaining the TIDs of those tuples that satisfy an equality condition involving the domain.

We could do these projections solely on the basis of statistics collected during the latest time period, or we could combine together the statistics collected over all previous periods. However, neither alone would be satisfactory for the purpose of a stable and yet responsive adaptive system. In the former case, the system would be overly vulnerable to chance fluctuations in access requirements and data characteristics, whereas in the latter case, it would be too insensitive to real changes. Intuitively, a weighted moving average of observations over previous periods should be more satisfactory. We utilize the technique of exponential smoothing [8,9] for our forecasting and estimation procedures because of its simplicity of computation, its flexibility, its minimal storage requirement, and its generalizability to account for trends and cycles. The basic formulation of exponential smoothing in making a forecast of a discrete time series is as follows:

new forecast = α * (observation from last period) + (1-α) *
(previous forecast),

where α is called a smoothing constant and takes on values between 0 and 1. In essence, this is a weighted average of all previous observations with the weight decreasing geometrically over successively earlier observations. The rate of response to recent changes can be adjusted simply by changing the smoothing constant: the larger the smoothing constant, the more sensitive is the forecast to recent changes and chance fluctuations. (The value of α can be selected by the DBA or can be adaptively chosen by the system itself to minimize the difference between observed and predicted data.) The compactness of the scheme lies in the fact that only two parameters need to be maintained for each time series: the current observation and the previous estimate. This scheme is used for the estimation of domain selectivity.

Since both the file size and the level of activity in a data base system can generally be expected to change over time, we use a modified version of exponential smoothing, which takes trends into account, in order to forecast query frequencies, index maintenance cost, and file size. Its formulation is as follows [8].

new average = α * (current observation) + (1-α) * (old average),

current trend = new average - old average,

new trend = α * (current trend) + (1-α) * (old trend),

new forecast = new average + ((1-α)/α) * (new trend).

In this form, it is necessary to store only the previously calculated values for the (new) average and for the (new) trend, and the calculation of the forecasted values is still simple.

IX.   INDEX SELECTION AT A REORGANIZATION POINT

As we have said, at each reorganizational point, a number of forecasts are made. A projection is made of the file size at the end of the upcoming interval. The average file size over the next interval can then be approximated as the average of its current size and this projected size. A prediction is made of the selectivity of each domain in the relation, together with the expected costs of accessing and maintaining an index on that domain during

the next interval. In addition, the expected size, and hence the
storage requirement, of an index for each domain is estimated.
Then the cost of creation for each index that is not currently
maintained is approximated. Finally, the expected number of queries of each type can be estimated. Thus we possess all the information needed to project, for any proposed set of indices, a
total cost for the next time period. (This cost includes retrieval processing; index creation, maintenance and storage; and application program recompilation.)

For example, the costs of retrieval processing are computed
as follows. For each query type, we can determine, using the selectivities of the domains that occur both in the query and in
the proposed index set, how many tuples will need to be scanned to
resolve this query type, with the full use of the indices. Our
non-linear cost function translates this into an expected number
of page accesses. To this is added the expected number of page
accesses that are involved in accessing the indices themselves;
this is determined by the number of values in each of these domains. This then gives us the total processing cost for this
query type, if the proposed indices are used. We then know if
the query processor would, given the proposed index set, use them
to resolve this query type, or would process it by means of a sequential scan. In any event, we thus know the projected cost of
processing this query type in the presence of the proposed set of
indices. We multiply this cost by the expected frequency of this
query type, and repeat the process for all the query types. This
gives the projected total query processing cost.

Predicting the cost of index maintenance is not so straightforward. Index maintenance costs can be separated into two components. The first reflects basic maintenance to the B-tree and
TID lists, and depends on the frequencies of updates/deletes/
inserts for the domain in question, the cost of updating a node
in the B-tree, and the cost of reading and writing an average TID
list. Therefore, this component can be readily estimated. The
second, which accounts for node splitting/merging in the B-tree
and garbage collection in the TID lists, depends heavily on the
pattern of updates, as well as on their frequencies. Consequently,
this component is difficult to forecast for a currently non-indexed
domain, given the information available to us. Instead, we explicitly record these costs for currently indexed domains, and use
their normalized average for those domains that are not indexed.
This is not a very precise measure, and is one we hope to refine
in the future.

Using the foregoing techniques, we are able to predict total
cost for any proposed index set. Therefore, we should be able to
choose that set whose indexing in the next time interval will minimize this total cost.

A straightforward approach to the index selection problem
would be to evaluate the total cost for each possible index set,
and then select that set of domains which gives the smallest cost.

With m domains in the relation, there are 2^m possible choices of index sets. For small m, this enumerative approach is probably the best strategy, as the optimal combination of domains to be indexed is guaranteed to be found. But for moderate m, the cost of repeated application of the cost evaluation procedure becomes very expensive, and for large m, it is prohibitive. It is not uncommon to find single-relation data bases with tens of domains. Therefore, it is appropriate to look for ways whereby the search space of potential index sets can be systematically reduced. One possible approach is to look for properties of the cost function that will allow it to be minimized without exhaustive enumeration, such as through a depth-first search, as exemplified in Schkolnick's index selection study [10]. This approach often requires simplifying assumptions on the data base environment, which may not always be realistic.

For example, in [10], it is assumed that the tuple accessing cost is linear, and that the probability of a domain being specified in the qualification part of a query is independent of the other domains being specified. This greatly reduces the number of parameters in the cost model and simplifies the procedure for evaluating the utility of an arbitrary set of domain indices. The cost function for accessing the set of tuples identified through the use of indices for an typical query is there assumed to be proportional to

$$N * \Pi_{i \in D}(P_i * S_i + (1 - P_i)),$$

where with probability P_i, domain i in the index set D is specified in the query, and reduces the number of tuples that have to be accessed by S_i, the selectivity of the domain; and with probability $(1-P_i)$, domain i is not specified, in which case the index on domain i does not reduce the number of tuples to be accessed.

Even with the above simplifying assumptions, the associated upper bound of $2m^{0.5}\log m$ index sets to be tested is not enough of a reduction to enable the inexpensive selection of the optimal index set for a relation with a moderate number of domains.

When we remove the somewhat unrealistic assumptions of linear tuple access cost and independent domain occurrence probabilities, and extend the transaction model to include retrieval specifications involving disjunction of equality conditions as well as conjunctions, the tuple accessing cost component of a projected set of queries, given the index set D (and assuming that indices will be used to reduce the number of tuples that have to be examined whenever possible) becomes, as we have seen,

$$\Sigma_{q \in Q} F_q * C_q, \text{ where}$$

$$Q = \text{the set of query types forecasted,}$$

$$F_q = \text{the projected number of occurrences of query type q,}$$

C_q = the expected cost of accessing the set of
tuples that must be individually inspected
in order to resolve q.

Thus the cost of evaluating the utility of a set of indices
is dependent on the number of distinct query types forecasted.
(All told, there are $(2^m - 1)$ possible conjunctive query types
(which specify 1 or more domains) and $(2^m -m-1)$ disjunctive query
types (which specify 2 or more domains for a total of $(2^{m+1}-m-2)$
possible query types.) Except in cases when only a few of the
large number of potential query types actually occur, the evaluation of the cost-effectiveness of a particular potential index set
is quite expensive. Hence, we have a strong incentive for systematically reducing the search space. Yet, because of our lack of
simplifying assumptions, the hope of finding an algorithmic way to
explore a reduced search space of practical size is dim. Therefore, it is appropriate to draw on the experience of artificial
intelligence researchers working in areas where formal mathematical structures are computationally impractical [11,12], and use
heuristic methods that significantly prune down the search space
and that work towards obtaining a near-optimal solution.

X.   INDEX SELECTION HEURISTICS

In our index selection procedure, we make use of five problem-oriented heuristics.

(1) A near optimum choice of the index set can be made incrementally. This heuristic permits analysis of the problem as a
stepwise minimization, each time adding to the index set that domain which will bring the best improvement to the cost function.
There have been two previous suggestions regarding the incremental
selection of domains to be indexed. Farley and Schuster [13] suggest that the incremental selection process can be terminated once
no single domain in the non-indexed set can be chosen that will
yield incremental cost/benefits. This is insufficient for our
choice of query and tuple access models; there are two reasons why
it may be necessary to consider the incremental savings brought by
considering two or more indices together. First, it may happen
that for a query involving a conjunction of conditions, the selectivity of any one domain may not be sufficient to reduce the number of pages to be accessed to be less than the total number of
pages in the relation, whereas the joint selectivity of two or
more domains might. Secondly, a disjunction of conditions can be
resolved via indices only if all of the domains involved in the
disjunction are indexed. An alternative strategy has been suggested by Held [14], who, at any stage of the incremental index
selection procedure, considers the incremental savings of each of
the possible subset of domains in the candidate set with less than
or equal to some fixed number of domains in it. This, of course,

may be very inefficient. We have taken an intermediate approach.
We consider the adjoining of multiple domains to the index set
only if no single domain that will yield positive incremental savings can be found.

(2) Not all queries can use indices profitably. If the expected set of tuples that satisfy the query is so large that they
are likely to reside on close to p pages, then no set of indices
can possibly be useful in processing this query. The expected
number of tuples that will satisfy each query type can be estimated using the selectivity of the domains involved. Those queries
that cannot profitably make use of indices are eliminated from the
projected query set whose processing cost is to be minimized.
This eliminates some unnecessary cost calculations. Similarly,
only queries that involve domains still in the candidate set need
to be retained in the query set for incremental savings calculation. (This heuristic does not cut down the search space, but
does speed up the cost evaluation at each step.)

(3) Some domains can be eliminated from the initial candidate set by virtue of their low occurrence frequencies in queries.
This effectively reduces m, the initial number of domains in the
candidate set. From the forecasted frequency of each query type,
and the projected selectivity of each domain in the relation, we
can compute an upper bound on the number of page accesses that an
index on a domain can save in the processing of the forecasted set
of queries. If this upper bound is less than the projected cost
of maintaining an index on the domain, then this domain can safely
be excluded from the initial candidate set, i.e., the domain is so
unselective or is used in retrievals so infrequently relative to
its being updated, that it cannot possibly be profitable to index
it.

The upper bound on the utility of an index for an arbitrary
domain i is computed as follows. Let q be a conjunctive query
type that involves domain i, and let S_q be the joint selectivity
of all the domains of q. Then the tuples that satisfy q are expected to reside on $f(S_q*N)$ pages, where N is the total number of
tuples in the relation and f is our non-linear function for expected page accesses. So the maximum benefit that an index on i
could possibly bring to the evaluation of q would be to reduce the
number of pages to be accessed from p to $f(S_q*N)$. A similar formula holds as well for the maximal reduction where q is a disjunctive query, but with S_q now representing the joint disjunctive selectivity of the domains used in q. Thus the upper bound on the
utility of an index for i is:

$$\Sigma_{q \varepsilon Q} F_q * (p - f(S_q)), \text{ where}$$

Q_i = set of forecasted query types that use domain i.
F_q = projected number of occurrences of q,
N = total number of tuples in the relation,

f = non-linear tuple access cost function for the
relation,

S_q = joint selectivity of all domains used in q
(conjunctive or disjunctive, depending on
type of q).

(4)   Only a small subset of all possible candidate domains
need be considered in determining the next domain or set of domains to be adjoined to the index set at each stage. We can rank
the domains with respect to the above described upper bound and
then consider only the top ranking M domains, and combinations of
them, for detailed incremental savings calculation. Furthermore,
a bound M' (M'≤M) can be imposed on the number of domains that will
be considered together.

(5)   An upper bound can be put on the total number of cost
evaluations that are performed in the entire selection procedure.
The procedure is terminated when this bound is exceeded.

To illustrate the above heuristics, we present the details of
our index selection procedure. Our procedure can be divided into
two stages. During the first, a tentative set of domains to be
indexed is chosen in an incremental fashion. It is possible to
put a bound on the cost of this phase by adjusting the parameters
M and M'. An alternative (or additional) constraint is to bound
the total number of sets of indices for which cost evaluation is
performed.

(1)   Rank the domains in the relation using the procedure
described above and let S be the set of domains that occur so infrequently that indexing them cannot be profitable.

(2)   Partition the set of domains D in the relation into three
disjoint subsets: D_i - the index set, D_c - the candidate set, and
D_n - the non-index set. Initialize D_i to null, D_n to S, and D_c to
$D - D_n$.

(3)   Consider in turn the incremental savings gained by indexing each of the M top ranking domains in the candidate set. Adjoin to D_i the one that will give the best improvement to the cost
function. If one cannot be found, then consider larger-sized combinations (up to M') of these M domains. Consider combinations of
the next larger size only if it is not profitable to adjoin any of
the combinations less than or equal to the current size. Remove
the domain(s) from D_c as they are adjoined to D_i. After an adjoinment to D_i, resume considering individual domains for further
adjoinment.

(4)   Terminate the first phase of the procedure if:

(a)   no subset (of size less than or equal to M') of the
M top ranking domains in the candidate set can be
chosen such that its adjoinment to the index set
will improve the index set's cost function; or

(b)   the upper bound on the total number of cost evaluations is reached.

The second stage may be called the bump-shift phase [11]. Domains that have been adjoined to the index set early in the first stage may turn out to be uneconomical as the result of later addition of other domains to the set, and thus should be removed from the index set. Only individual domains will be considered for removal from the tentatively chosen index set. This is accomplished by comparing, for each domain d tentatively assigned to D_i, the total costs for D_i and for D_i - d. That d for which the difference between these two is the largest is then removed from D_i, and the process continues until no domains remain in D_i, whose removal would improve its cost function.

XI. INDEX SELECTION COST

The main thrust of the above heuristic algorithm has been towards reducing the search space for potential index sets, by making the selection process an incremental one. Since we consider adjoining a combination of domains to the index set only if no adjoinment of an individual domain improves the cost function, the total number of potential index sets examined depends heavily (and in an unpredictable way) on the query patterns, data characteristics, and page size, and consequently does not admit of a formal analysis. We intend to assess the optimality of the above algorithm experimentally. Our guess is that under most circumstances, most of the adjoinments will consist of single domains, and the number of index sets examined will essentially be proportional to the number of domains in the relation.

We have performed a limited amount of experimentation with this heuristic algorithm, applying it to a number of access histories, and comparing its results to those obtained by an exhaustive consideration of all possible index sets. (Both procedures utilize the cost model described above.) In the cases considered so far, the heuristic has almost always found the optimal index set, at a small fraction of the cost of the exhaustive procedure. We are currently embarking on a program of extensive experimentation with our heuristics, attempting to assess their performance for a wide range of access histories and data characteristics.

Aside from the need to cut down the search space of potential index sets, it is also important to minimize the cost in assessing the cost/benefits of each potential index set. By making forecasts of query type occurrence frequencies based on past observation, we have thus far avoided the strong assumption that the individual domain occurrence probabilities in a query are independent. In consequence, however, our scheme requires that in considering each possible increment to the index set, we evaluate the costs of processing each of the projected query types that involves any of the domains in the increment. The number of possible query types is an exponential function of the number of domains in the relation; so the number of query types that actually occur is also likely to increase quite rapidly with the number of domains. There may be as many as $2^m - 2^{m-k}$ conjunctive query types that will require individual projection, where k is the size of the increment under consideration; these are those queries that use at least one of the domains in the proposed increment. By contrast, under the independence assumption, only $2^n - 1$ different conjunctive query types need be considered, where n is the size of the current index set plus the increment; this is true because it is possible to lump together all conjunctive queries that involve the same set of domains that are in the proposed index set. (Both with the independence assumption, and without it, the number of disjunctive query types that need consideration is $2^n - n - 1$.)

Therefore, it is desirable to use heuristics to limit the number of queries that we have to consider in evaluating a potential increment to the index set. Eliminating some queries from consideration because they cannot possibly benefit from any indices, as we have done above, will be of some help; but other simplifications will be necessary as well.

One approach would be to partition the set of conjunctive query types into two classes: those that occur frequently, and those that do not. (However, the aggregate of infrequent queries may constitute a significant fraction of the total observed query set.) For those queries involving the increment that occur frequently, we proceed as usual, with an individual cost projection for each one. However, we might relax our non-independence assumption for the infrequent queries, and process them in classes. That is, we would lump together all queries that involve the same domains from the proposed index set, and compute the projected cost of each class as in [10]. In this way, we would utilize the accurate measurement of domain correlation for the (presumably few) frequently occurring queries, but sacrifice it for the mass of infrequent queries (where it would have little impact anyway).

XII. COMPARISON WITH PREVIOUS WORK

We have presented an experimental and heuristic approach to the index selection problem that is different in many respects from recent studies on index selection by Stonebraker [14], King [15], Schkolnick [10], Farley [13], and Held [16]. These other studies have either been formal analyses, which have made many simplifying assumptions in order to obtain an analytic solution, or else system designs that have been incomplete or unrealistic in various ways. Our work attempts to go farther than these by utilizing more complete and accurate models of cost and access, and by emphasizing important aspects of realistic data base environments. The novel aspects of our approach are as follows. We have stressed the importance of accurate usage model acquisition and data characteristic estimation in a dynamic environment where access acquirements are continually changing. We believe it necessary to apply forecasting techniques to predict future access requirements based on past observations, in order to capture and

respond to the dynamic and changing nature of data base usage.
Our scheme endeavours to obtain a precise model of data base usage
by recording actual query patterns, thereby avoiding the strong
assumption that the probabilities of two domains appearing in a
query are mutually independent. We also take into consideration
the facts that values of a domain are not equally likely to be
used in queries, and that they are not evenly distributed among
tuples of the relation, by monitoring the actual selectivities of
domain values that are used in queries.

The size of actual data bases is reflected in our concern for
efficient heuristics to speed up the index selection process. Our
cost models account for such real overheads as the expense of index accessing and the costs of key insertion/deletion and garbage
collection in index maintenance, and are based on reasonable models of data b se storage. Our approach of minimizing the total
processing cost for the upcoming time interval, rather than the
expected cost for a single query, is flexible enough to account
for the overhead costs of index creation, index storage and application program recompilation.

XIII. CONCLUSIONS

We have presented a high-level description of our approach to
the problem of index selection in an adaptive data base management
system that we are developing. This has been done, however, only
in the restricted environment of a single-relation data base accessed through a restricted interface with limited capabilities
for the selection of data. To fully realize the flexibility of a
relational data base, it is necessary to consider a multi-relation
environment together with a high-level non-procedural language
interface that permits queries with arbitrary interconnection between relations in the qualification part and high level operators
on the qualified data. In such an environment, it is necessary to
consider the utility of indices for more complicated operations
(such as restriction, projection, division, join, etc. [1]) and to
select indices for all the relations in the data base as a whole.
This is where the recording of detailed access history is necessary for optimal index selection, and where the use of heuristics
should be fruitful for cutting down the search space and for selecting richer index structures (such as combined indices). Our
heuristic index selection procedure should be readily extendible
to such an environment, once a cost evaluation procedure has been
defined to estimate the cost of processing an arbitrary query in
the presence of a particular set of indices. Our plan is to experimentally assess the optimality of our heuristic index selection algorithm in a reduced environment, before embarking on the
more ambitious project of index selection in a more general environment. More fundamentally, our long-range intent is to experimentally study the needs for, and capabilities of, a self-adaptive

data management system in realistic data base environments.

REFERENCES

[1] E. F. Codd, "A Relational Model of Data for Large Shared Data Banks", CACM, Vol. 13, No. 6, June, 1970.

[2] M. M. Astrahan, D. D. Chamberlin, "Implementation of a Structured English Query Language", Proceedings of the ACM-SIGMOD International Conference on Management of Data, May, 1975.

[3] J. Martin, "Computer Data-Base Organization", Prentice Hall, Inc., Englewood Cliffs, New Jersey, 1975.

[4] J. B. Rothnie, T. Lozano, "Attribute Based File Organization in a Paged Memory Environment", CACM, Vol. 17, No. 2, Feb., 1974.

[5] P. C. Yue, C. K. Wong, "Storage Cost Considerations in Secondary Index Selection", International Journal of Computer and Information Sciences, Vol. 4, No. 4, 1975.

[6] A. F. Cardenas, "Analysis and Performance of Inverted Data Structures", CACM, Vol. 18, No. 5, May, 1975.

[7] R. Bayer, E. McCreight, "Organization and Maintenance of Large Ordered Indexes", Acta Informatica, Vol. 1, Fasc. 3, 1972.

[8] R. G. Brown, "Statistical Forecasting for Inventory Control", McGraw-Hill Book Company, 1959.

[9] R. G. Brown, "Smoothing, Forecasting and Prediction of Discrete Time Series", Prentice Hall Inc., Englewood Cliffs, New Jersey, 1962.

[10] M. Schkolnick, "Secondary Index Optimization", Proceedings of the ACM-SIGMOD International Conference on Management of Data, May, 1975.

[11] A. A. Kuehn, M. J. Hamburger, "A Heuristic Program for Locating Warehouses", Management Science, Vol. 9, No. 4, July, 1963.

[12] R. C. Meier, W. T. Newell, H. L. Pazer, "Simulation in Busineww and Economics", Prentice Hall Inc., Englewood Cliffs, New Jersey, 1963.

!131 J. H. G. Farley, S. A. Schuster, "Query Execution and Index Selection for Relational Data Bases", Technical Report CSRG-53, University of Toronto, Mar., 1975.

[14] M. Stonebraker, "The Choice of Partial Inversions and Combined Indices", International Journal of Computer and Information Sciences, Vol. 3, No. 2, 1974.

[15] W. F. King, "On the Selection of Indices for a File", IBM Research RJ 1341, San Jose, Jan., 1974.

[16] G. D. Held, "Storage Structures for Relational Data Base Management Systems", Memorandum No. ERL-M533, University of California, Berkeley, Aug., 1975.

PATTERNS OF INDUCTION AND ASSOCIATED
KNOWLEDGE ACQUISTION ALGORITHMS*

Frederick Hayes-Roth
Computer Science Department
Carnegie-Mellon University
Pittsburgh, Pa. 15213

ABSTRACT

The common need of both Artificial Intelligence and Pattern
Recognition for effective methods of automatic knowledge acquisition is considered. A pattern of induction is defined as a framework which relates a theory of behavior generation, underlying
knowledge structures, and a learning methodology. One particular
learning theory, called interference matching, suggests that knowledge structures which underlie behavior descriptions can be directly abstracted from those descriptions. Because of the close connection between descriptions and inferences in such a framework,
the strengths and weaknesses of several types of descriptions are
considered. Algorithms which exploit this theory are presented
for three classes of problems: pattern learning and classification; induction of quantified production rules; and the induction
of syntactic categories and phrase structure rules. Preliminary
results are presented and directions for future research are outlined.

I.   INTRODUCTION

Despite many impressive advances in the areas of knowledge
representation and engineering, Artificial Intelligence (AI) has
made virtually no progress on general learning problems in the
last 20 years. Both AI and Pattern Recognition (PR) currently experience a pressing need for automatic methods of knowledge acquisition, but their problems are somewhat different. Current efforts
in AI aimed at building large-scale knowledge-based systems (e.g.,
for speech, vision, text understanding) are virtually overwhelmed
by the task of *knowledge engineering*. The goal of this task is
the implementation of all potentially valuable "knowledge sources".
problem solving modules which exploit the known physical, syntactic, contextual, and semantic relations to constrain the search
for solutions. The cost--in terms of people, time, and machine
resources--of translating this human knowledge into computer programs is nearly insupportable. Furthermore, even after these

*   This research was supported in part by the Defense Advanced Re-
    search Projects Agency under contract no. F44620-73-C-0074 and
    monitored by the Air Force Office of Scientific Research.

handcrafted knowledge sources are developed, they are difficult
to evaluate comparatively because each tends to be "one-of-a-kind",
a body of code specially tailored to operate in one specific system and to employ only one particular subset of the many potentially relevant problem solving techniques. Thus, to a large extent,
the immediate need for general learning procedures in AI is to automate much of the work of knowledge programming. The field of PR,
on the other hand, needs general learning procedures because the
conventional methods of pattern description and learning do not
perform well in most complex environments. The inadequacy of the
well known dimensional, parametric, and syntactic techniques of
representation and classification is made apparent by their inability to contribute significantly to modern AI understanding
systems. In short, the field of PR has reached a point where its
principal tools no longer seem sufficiently suited to the recognition problems being encountered. The development of general learning procedures which can generate symbolic pattern representations
and facilitate improved classification in such domains is a goal
of great importance for the PR field.

This paper considers three types of general learning problems
related to pattern classification, rule induction, and syntax
learning. Each of these is approached within the theoretical
framework of a related *pattern of induction* or *learning paradigm*.
A pattern of induction is an analytical framework which relates
and organizes the various components of a learning problem and its
solution. The first three components of the induction pattern are
as follows: (1) a *model* of a knowledge-based system which defines
a body of knowledge or information (K) and a behavior generating
function (B) which operates on the knowledge to produce observable
behaviors (training data); (2) a collection of observed behaviors
which constitute the training data (I) for the induction algorithm;
and (3) a learning algorithm (L) which operates on the training
data to infer the knowledge K which produces or "causes" the observations I. If we assumed that the behavior generating function
B were known and invertible, the ideal knowledge acquisition algorithm L would be its inverse, such that $L(I) = B^{-1}(I) = K$; that
is, we would simply apply the inverse function B^{-1} to I to identify K. This view gives rise to the last component of the induction
pattern, which is: (4) an *induction theory* which relates a learning algorithm L to a presumed behavior generator B.

All three learning problems considered in thie paper are approached uniformly by means of the same induction theory, which is
called *interference matching (IM)*. Basically, this theory holds
that the knowledge underlying many training examples of the same
pattern or rule may be directly identified by producing a representation (an *abstraction*) of the examples which emphasizes their
commonalities and attenuates their differences. This theory is an
extension of a primitive notion of Galton [4] called the composite
photograph theory, which suggests that people learn to identify
different views of the same object by developing a pattern template (a "composite photograph" transparency) by superimposing

in memory many descriptions (transparencies) of varying training
views of the object. Under this theory, the resulting template
would retain only the essential features, those common to all examples. Any novel view of the same object would then be expected
to exhibit (match) all criterial properties of the template. Of
course, Galton's conception is completely dependent upon the presumed capacity to superimpose the multiple views in such a way as
to preserve all criterial commonalities. Even the slightest difference in size or orientation would nullify the effectiveness of
direct, physical superimposition as a method of producing abstractions. Interference matching generalizes the process of extracting
commonalities of pattern descriptions to feature and relational
representations. It is considered in detail in section 4, after
the various types of representations are introduced in section 3.

The three types of learning problems considered in this paper
are: *symbolic pattern learning,* the discovery of disjunctive and
conjunctive formulae of the predicate calculus which characterize
diverse examples of one pattern class and distinguish that class
from other classes; *rule learning,* the identification of universally quantified [condition=>action] productions derived from
training data consisting of before-and-after pairs of events which
have been transformed by an unknown rule; and *category learning,*
the formation of sets of functional substitutes or alternatives
which constitute the domain of choices allowable within particular
syntactic behavior rules. Each of these problems is described in
more detail in section 2. Section 3 discusses a number of alternative knowledge representation schemes in terms of their capacity
to facilitate learning from examples. The representations considered include simple feature codes, topologically organized feature manifolds which facilitate generalization and discrimination
of patterns over noisy and continuous attribute values, complementary feature codes for missing (negative) attributes which facilitate discovery of disjunctions, and relational descriptions which
facilitate learning of structured patterns, production rules, and
categories. Section 4 explains interference matching and two of
its products, the abstraction and the residuals of compared representations. Abstractions produced by IM provide the solution to
the first two types of learning problems, and residuals provide
the solution to the category learning problem. Related algorithms
for knowledge acquisition are described in section 5, and directions for future research are considered in the last section.

II. THREE LEARNING PROBLEMS

Three learning problems of considerable generality and wide
applicability are considered here. The first is the pattern learning and classification problem: Given descriptions of an unclassi-
fied test item and several examples of each of a number of mutually exclusive pattern classes, identify the most probable class to
which the test item can be assigned. The basic approach followed

in solving this problem is to hypothesize that any set of properties (a *characteristic*) manifested by the test item might reliably
distinguish the training exemplars of one class from all other
classes. Each such hypothesis is more or less plausible depending
on the empiricial likelihood that the associated characteristic
occurs primarily among examples of a single class. The likelihood
that a characteristic is matched only by examples of one class is
called the *diagnosticity* of the characteristic with respect to the
class. To the extent that a characteristic is diagnostic with respect to some class, it is plausible to suppose that a test item
matching the characteristic is actually an example of that class.
The method used for determining classifications is simply to assign each test item to the one class which is indicated by the
most diagnostic characteristic which the test item manifests [6,7].
    The second learning problem is that of rule induction and re-
sponse selection: Given a description of a novel stimulus and
training descriptions of previously experienced antecedent-consequent event pairs (or condition=>action sequences), choose the
most plausible response to the current test stimulus. A special
case of rule induction and response selection is that of classifying a test item as belonging to one or several alternative pattern
classes. More generally however, we may wish to respond to a
stimulus by transforming the stimulus description by adding or deleting relations (asserting or denying predicates). Examples of
the kinds of rules which might be induced are the problem solving
rules of STRIPS [3] which relate conditions of a problem domain to
actions taken on related objects, the rules of transformational
grammar which relate before-and-after deep structures of sentences,
and the premise-conclusion rules of inferential reasoning systems
such as MYCIN [15].
    The basic approach taken to this type of problem is to hypothe-
size that each [condition=>action] pattern which is a characteristic of some [antecedent consequent] training sequences defines a
plausible rule. Those hypothetical rules whose inferred action
components are most realiably supported by the training data are
considered most plausible. Maximally reliable support for a hypothetical [condition=>action] rule can be claimed whenever all
training data whose antecedent events satisfy (match) the condition component of the rule are associated with consequent events
which also satisfy the hypothesized action or response component.
This is equivalent to extending the notion of diagnosticity to apply to the measurement of the degree to which the presence of a
certain condition indicates that a particular response pattern will
follow (in the training data). The learning methods which are developed to handle the first learning problem (pattern learning and
classification) can be extended in a straightforward manner to
solve these rule induction and response selection problems too.
    The third learning problem considered is the category and syn-
tax learning problem: Given training descriptions of behaviors
generated by a system which arbitrarily selects and systematically
relates elements chosen from specific classes of alternatives,

317

identify the unknown classes and the systematic ways in which they are related. The classes are called *categories;* systematic constraints on the use of categories are called *syntax.* An example of this sort of problem is to infer from a corpus of natural language in which one class of words (adjectives) systematically precedes another class (nouns), the categories *adjective* and *noun* and the relationship that an element of the class of adjectives is usually followed by an element of the class of nouns. As another example, consider learning the category of *animate noun* from the fact that only such nouns are regularly used as agents of instrumental and reflexive actions and, also, as the objects of verbs expressing affect (such as "love," "admire," etc.). The approach taken to this problem is to hypothesize that several objects which reliably occur in identical relationships with some other objects constitute a category. It may be inferred that membership in that category is a necessary and sufficient condition for objects to participate in the observed relationships. Thus a reliably occurring relationship is inferred as a syntactic pattern (e.g., the adjective→noun sequence pattern) at the same time as the actual objects which play consistent functional roles (e.g., the adjectives "big," "brown," "cute," ... reliably precede nouns) enumeratively define related syntactic categories.

Obviously, the approaches outlined above to all three of these learning problems are combinatorial in nature. In every case, it was superficially suggested that each possible hypothesis (characteristic, rule, or category) be considered as a potential solution to the corresponding induction problem. Two separate issues of feasibility must be considered. First, if the combinatorics of this hypothesize-and-test method could be sufficiently controlled, would the proposed method produce good results? That is, would such a method be an effective learning algorithm. Both theoretical arguments and some preliminary experimental data suggest that the answer is yes. Secondly, given that such an exhaustive evaluation of plausible inferred knowledge (patterns, rules, categories) is an effective learning procedure, can heuristic methods be devised which can adequately control the combinatorics of the search? The answer to this question is approached in two ways in this paper. Firstly, a number of alternative knowledge (data) representation schemes have been studied with respect to their providing a feasible basis for induction algorithms. Some surprisingly simple representations make possible quick, effective solutions to seemingly complex pattern learning problems. These alternative representations are considered in some detail in the next section before the related learning algorithms are presented. The second avenue of approach, development of specific heuristics to constrain the amount of computing of the learning algorithms themselves, is discussed in section 5.

III. DATA AND KNOWLEDGE REPRESENTATIONS
AS BASES FOR LEARNING

Because the computational complexity of learning algorithms is likely to be exponential, the choice of data representation may significantly affect its feasibility. Four alternative types of representations are considered in this section. Each entails a different combination of desirable and undesirable properties, and these are briefly considered. The four types of representations, ordered in increasing completeness of representational power, are based on (1) simple feature or property lists, (2) topologically organized feature manifolds, (3) enumerated complementary feature code manifolds, and (4) general relational descriptions. Each of these representation schemes is now considered in turn.

Simple feature descriptions are well known. This sort of representation employs the concept of an exogenously identified object which is described by a list of features (i.e., properties, unary predicates or attribute-value pairs). As in all of the four representation schemes considered, the segmentation and identification of objects as well as the feature coding processes are exogenous to the representation itself. The inability of feature list descriptions to express general relationships among several objects in a single event is their chief weakness. This limitation is shared by all of the representation schemes except relational coding. Conversely, it is just because they are so simple that property list descriptions are attractive. While only simple combinations of attributes can be abstracted from training descriptions and employed for pattern recognition, such processing can be performed with great efficiency. Each feature can be associated with a single value in a bit vector--the value being one if the feature is present and zero if not--and matching operations performed by simple bit comparison operations [7,10]. Specifically, the bit-wise logical product ($\wedge$) of two feature bit vectors is their maximal abstraction, the set of all features common to both of them. Furthermore, if a pattern template is represented by a bit vector of criterial features, the determination of whether any event description matches the template can be performed by a simple bit-wise masking operation.

The attractiveness of bit operations to effect learning (abstraction) and pattern recognition in the framework of feature list descriptions is seriously diminished by the fact that such matching operations are fundamentally all-or-none. Each bit in a feature vector represents an attribute that *is* or *is not* present and provides no basis for *fuzzy* comparisons of two objects. In this context, the term *fuzzy* refers to a graded measure of the degree to which the values of the same attributes of two objects are similar. The capacity to retain the information that two objects are fuzzily equal is important in many learning problems involving continuous, ordinal, or noisy data. In these tasks, it is often necessary to infer from examples of a pattern an exact range of

values on each attribute dimension which is characteristic of the
pattern to be learned. While feature list matching is inherently
all-or-none, special organizations of features have been identified which enable the efficient production of graded comparisons
in such domains. A collection of features organized to facilitate
particular learning tasks is referred to as a feature manifold,
and two special manifolds which are well suited to the fuzzy match
problem are now discussed.

Two general principles of organization for fuzzy match feature
manifolds have so far been identified. First, values on any ordinal dimension may be described by features which are organized in
an *overlapping receptive field (ORF)* manifold to facilitate, simultaneously, maximum generalization and discrimination during learning. Consider the problem of representing sampled values of a continuous attribute (e.g., amplitude, frequency, duration) to facilitate the discovery of the range of variability exhibited by successive pattern examples. Many sophisticated approaches to similar
problems (e.g., the mixture problem) have been developed which depend upon an a priori parametric model of the data (Cf., [2]).
While such an approach may be very efficient in some domains, ORF
representations provide an efficient basis for the generation of
non-parametric inferences.

Basically, the maximum possible range of attribute values [A,
Z] on any dimension of interest is divided into adjacent overlapping intervals. Each interval $[Q,Q+G]$ is assigned to a single
feature which represents a range of values in which an observed
value may be contained. The term *receptive field* is borrowed from
the psychology of vision. In that context, the receptive field of
an individual neuron refers to the specific retinal pattern which
causes it to fire. In a similar way, the receptive field of a
feature is just the range of possible attribute values which cause
it to be true. Adjacent receptive fields overlap so that their
ranges include common values. The largest range of values of any
feature, G, is the maximum generalizability of any single conjunctive pattern description. The amount of separation between adjacent overlapping fields, D, is the maximum amount of discriminability between any two patterns and corresponds to the psychophy-
sical concept of a just noticeable difference (JND). The values of
A, Z, G, and D are the basic parameters of the ORF manifold representation [1, 11]. With only minor modifications needed if D
does not evenly divide G or G does not evenly divide (Z-A), the
feature manifold F of the simplest ORF representation is defined
to be G = {[A, A+D],[A,A+2D], ..., [A,A+G-D],[A,A+G],[A+D,A+G+D],
[A+2D,A+G+2D], ..., [Z-G-D,Z-D],[Z-G,Z],[Z-G+D,Z], ..., [Z-D,Z]}.
The data representation of any attribute value h in the manifold
F is $R_F(h)$ = {[a,b] : h ε [a,b] and [a,b] ε F}. As a result of
such representation, two data values h and h' may be fuzzily compared by simple set intersection of $R_F(h)$ and $R_F(h')$:$R_F(h) \cap R_F(h')$
= {[a,b] : h ε [a,b] and h' ε [a,b] and [a,b] ε F} ≡ [$\min_F(h,h')$,
$\max_F(h,h')$], where $\min_F(h,h')$ is the minimum of h and h' modulo

the precision specified by D and $\max_F(h,h')$ is the corresponding maximum. For example, if A=1, Z=10, D=1, G=4, F={[1,2], [1,3], [1,4], [1,5], [2,6], [3,7], [4,8], [5,9], [6,10], [7,10], [8,10], [9,10]}, h=4 and h'=6, then $R_F(h) \cap R_F(h') = \{[2,6],[3,7],[4,8]\}$. This set comprises just those features which would all be true of data values in the range [4,6]. Such a maximally informative abstraction (range generalization) from the data values h=4 and h'=6 is what was desired. Notice that this intersection can be achieved by the same bit-wise logical product that was suggested for the all-or-none simple feature comparison problem. ORF organization thus is an effective representational basis for abstracting fuzzy commonalties from ordinal (temporal, spatial, amplitudinal, etc.) data.

The second principle for the organization of fuzzy match feature manifolds is that of a *radius of generalization* for value coding. Essentially, any observed value h of an attribute is generalized so that it is treated as if it were actually a range of values, $[h-\varepsilon, h+\varepsilon]$. For example if some scalar attribute had features for each of the values in F' ={1,2,...,10} and $\varepsilon=3$, and any data value h were represented as $R_{F',\varepsilon}(h) = \{f : f\varepsilon F'$ and f ε $[h-\varepsilon, h+\varepsilon]\}$, then the data values h=4 and h'=6 would be represented $R_{F',3}(h) = \{1,2,3,4,5,6,7\}$ and $R_{F',3}(h') = \{3,4,5,6,7,8,9\}$ and the common abstraction would be $R_{F',3}(h) \cap R_{F',3}(h') = \{3,4,5,6,7\}$. Thus, the radius of generalization ε provides a basis for fuzzy matching of data like that previously considered with ORF manifolds. Here, however, the manifold consists of simple feature values organized so that whenever the feature h is directly matched, all adjacent features within radius ε of h are also excited. This organization of features for value representation is referred to as a *radial generalization* (RG) manifold. The organization of an RG manifold provides a suggestive basis for interpretation of the observation that perceptual system ganglia and cortex are organized so that physically adjacent neurons have approximately equal receptive field values. As a result, the excitation of any neuron is likely to occur only if adjacent neurons are also excited to some extent.

Interestingly, both the ORF and RG manifolds produce equivalent representations and abstractions. This can be seen by comparing the abstractions $R_F(4) \cap R_F(6)$ and $R_{F',3}(4) \cap R_{F',3}(6)$ of the preceding examples. The first represented all data values in the range [4,6]. The second abstraction, which was {3,4,...,9} , contains features that would all be true only of values in the range [4,6]. Thus, the generalization parameter G of the ORF manifold corresponds to the ε of the value generalization manifold. In either case, this radius of generalization corresponds to the amount of variability of data values which may be tolerated as perturbation or noise in evaluating the difference between an observed (measured) data value and the "true" underlying value. Alternatively, the radius of generalization can be interpreted as the maximum difference between the values of the same attribute

which can be viewed as fuzzily equal. Given the equivalence of
the two organizational principles, it is apparent that if ε is a
function of the data value (for example, the error of measurement
is often an increasing function of its magnitude), the corresponding generalizability parameter G of the ORF manifold must also vary
accordingly. The choice of a particular organization between
these two types of manifold is largely arbitrary. Functionally,
the ORF and RG manifold representations are not identifiably different, although it seems that RG representations may actually be
easier to implement since all feature coding may be completed without comparisons between the observed data values and the boundaries
of the receptive field intervals. The common strength of both
representations is their ability to compensate for error of measurement and accomplish fuzzy comparisons of data values, up to a specified precision or JND, in ordinal or continuous scales by intersection of bit-vectors corresponding to discrete features.

While abstractions derived from any of the preceding representations will reflect only common, conjunctive characteristics
of compared data, the third type of data representation, *enumerative complementary coding*, provides a basis for abstracting disjunctive characteristics of patterns through simple bit matching
operations. The organizing principles of *complementary feature*
manifolds are two: first, mutually exclusive attribute values are
organized into sets called *categories*; and second, one feature is
defined for every attribute which *is* and one is defined for every
value which *is not* a property of the data to be coded. For example, in speech learning, the category of vowels might be V =
{AH,AX,AO,EH,ER, ..., UH}. One feature might be assigned to represent the presence of each vowel in each example of an unknown
pattern. Under enumerative complementary coding, features would
also be assigned to represent the absence of each possible vowel
type. Let the "positive" features be defined by the set V, and
let the special feature εV represent that at least one vowel was
detected. Let the complementary set of "negative" features be W =
{¬AH,¬AX,¬AO, ...,¬UH}. Now consider comparing two data examples
(B, AH, G) and (B, AX, G) of some unknown phonetic sequence pattern. If only positive feature codes were used, the two examples
would exhibit features AH and AX, respectively, as well as the
common feature εV. *The comparison of these two des*criptions would
be just {εV}, representing only that each datum contained some
vowel. Alternatively, suppose each of the examples were also described by complementary features. The data (B, AH, G) and (B,
AX, G) would be described as $C_V(B,AH,G) = \{εV, AH,¬AX,¬AO, ...,$
¬UH} and $C_V(B,AX,G) = \{εV, AX,¬AH,¬AO, ...,¬UH\}$. A feature comparison would be $C_V(B,AH,G) \cap C_V(B,AX,G) = \{εV,¬AO,¬EH, ...,¬UH\} =$
{εV}∪(W - {¬AH,¬AX}) ≡ AH ∨ AX. That is, the result of forming the
intersection of complementary codes of data based on a category V
is to produce a set of negative features which exactly represents
the disjunction of common positive features. It is interesting
again to speculate upon the relationship between such feature

manifolds and neural organizations. It is a well known fact that much of the perceptual system is organized in *paired opponent processes,* consisting of two or more mutually inhibitory assemblages of neurons whose receptive fields are complementary (e.g., represent the mutually exclusive alternatives of light on vs. light off at the same locus). Simply stated, a complementary manifold may be conceived of as a set of mutually inhibitory detectors, where the "excitation state" of one feature in a category causes the "inhibited state" of all the others to be registered. Both types of detector states are considered as elements of the pattern description.

The last type of representation used is *relational coding,* which provides a basis for describing events in terms of objects, attributes, and relationships among objects. The basic elements of a relational representation are *parameters, properties,* and *case frames.* A parameter is a unique symbol which represents a constant or names an object in one or more relations. A property is a feature or attribute of an object. A case frame is a set of property:parameter terms which represents a relationship among the objects named by the parameters. A case frame is a generic type of relation and thus corresponds to an n-ary predicate. Instances of case frames, produced by substituting constants or object names for the generic parameters, are called *case relations.* Entire events are described by sets of case relations called *parameterized structural representations* (PSRs). A PSR is normally interpreted as a conjunction of the corresponding constituent predicates [6,7,9,10].

A simple example will illustrate these concepts. Consider the problem of representing the pronunciation of the word "America". Using the ARPA speech understanding project phonetic alphabet, one pronunciation is (AX, M, EH", R, IH, K, AX'). This may be easily described in terms of the case frame {phone:x, begin:t_b, end:t_e, stress:k} meaning that the phone between times t_b and t_e is of type x and its stress is level k (0, 1, or 2). A PSR for the preceding "America" pronunciation would then be:

$$
\begin{aligned}
T = \{&\{\text{phone:AX, begin:}t_1,\text{end:}t_2,\text{stress:0}\}, \\
&\{\text{phone:M, begin:}t_2,\text{end:}t_3,\text{stress:0}\}, \\
&\{\text{phone:EH, begin:}t_3,\text{end:}t_4,\text{stress:2}\}, \\
&\{\text{phone:R, begin:}t_4,\text{end:}t_5,\text{stress:0}\}, \\
&\{\text{phone:IH, begin:}t_5,\text{end:}t_6,\text{stress:0}\}, \\
&\{\text{phone:K, begin:}t_6,\text{end:}t_7,\text{stress:0}\}, \\
&\{\text{phone:AX, begin:}t_7,\text{end:}t_8,\text{stress:1}\}\}
\end{aligned}
$$

This PSR is interpreted as follows: The word "America" is described by T as a pattern in which the unstressed phone AX spans the time interval t_1 to t_2, the unstressed phone M spans the time interval t_2 to t_3, the maximally stressed phone EH spans the interval t_3 to t_4, etc. It should be noticed that the parameters $t_1, \ldots, t_8$ may be interpreted either as constants or variables. In the former case, T would be a description of some sequence of phones from a particular time t_1 to a time t_8 containing the word "America." If these parameters are considered as variables, on the other hand, T represents a template for the word "America." If the description of some stimulus event S is given such that correspondents (parameters) in S can be found to bind to the variables $t_1, \ldots, t_8$ which insure that all case relations in T are true of S, S matches the template T and contains the word "America."

While it is usually true that pattern templates can be described by conjunctive sets of case relations as in the preceding example, it is sometimes desirable to represent disjunctive or negated case relations. In the framework of PSRs, this is done by augmenting the PSR to reflect component weights and overall thresholds for matching. For example, the series-parallel network of Fig. 1 represents the eight alternative pronunciations of "America" used in our speech work.

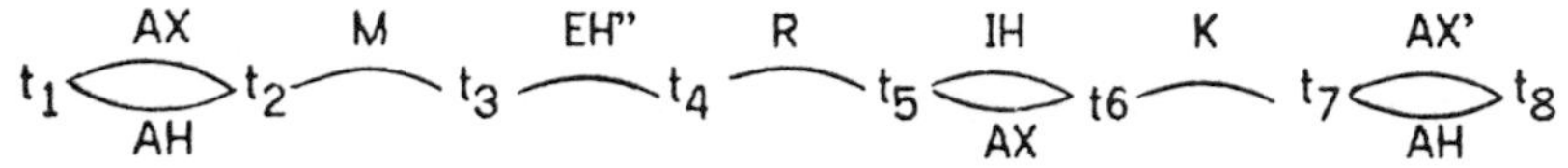

Figure 1. A network representation of eight pronunciations of "America"

Parallel paths represent acceptable phone alternatives at any point, while the left-to-right sequence of arcs represents a conjunctive set of necessary phones. The fact that either AX or AH may occur between t_1 and t_2 is represented by the PSR:

$$S_1 = \{\{phone:AX, begin:t_1, end:t_2, stress:O\}=>+1,$$
$$\{phone:AH, begin:t_1, end:t_2, stress:O\}=>+1\}\geq 1$$

This subtemplate asserts that if an unstressed AX occurs between times t_1 and t_2, +1 is to be added to the *match count* of S_1. Similarly, +1 is to be accumulated if AH occurs. The total match count is then checked to see if it is $\geq$ the specified PSR threshold of 1; if the threshold is equalled or exceeded, S_1 is matched, otherwise not. By convention, each case relation which is matched increments the match count of the containing PSR by 1 and the default threshold of a PSR with n case relations is n. Recursively, any matched PSR nested within another PSR counts as a single matched case relation and by default contributes 1 to the match count. Negated relations can be similarly represented by adding -1 to the match count for conditions that *are* matched but are intended not to be matched. Thus, the PSR corresponding to the template in Fig. 1 is just:

$$T' = \{\{\{phone:AX, begin:t_1, end:t_2, stress:O\},$$
$$\{phone:AH, begin:t_1, end:t_2, stress:O\}\}\geq 1,$$
$$\{phone:M, begin:t_2, end:t_3, stress:O\},$$

$$\{phone:EH, begin:t_3, end:t_4, stress:2\},$$
$$\{phone:R, begin:t_4, end:t_5, stress:0\},$$
$$\{\{phone:IX, begin:t_5, end:t_6, stress:0\},$$
$$\{phone:AX, begin:t_5, end:t_6, stress:0\}\}^{\geq}1,$$
$$\{phone:K, begin:t_6, end:t_7, stress:0\},$$
$$\{\{phone:AX, begin:t_7, end:t_8, stress:1\},$$
$$\{phone:AH, begin:t_7, end:t_8, stress:1\}\}^{\geq}1\}$$

The default threshold for T' is the sum of immediately nested PSRs or case relations which is 7. Thus, if each of the seven conditions is satisfied by some stimulus data description S, S contains the word "America." For example, noting that corresponding parameters in T and T' have been identically named, the pattern T which describes one particular pronunciation is seen to satisfy all the conditions of T'. Furthermore, it will be true that all specific occurrences of the word "America" will match T' and, thus, it would be conceivable to abstract the definition of T' directly from the common elements of the descriptions of such examples. Such comparisons of relational event descriptions require a general interference matching procedure that can identify which objects correspond and which case relations are true of corresponding objects in two compared events. One such procedure, SPROUTER [12], has been implemented, and it is discussed in the next section.

In summarizing the current section, it should be noted that a variety of methods exist for representing training data to facilitate the discovery of the criterial characteristics of patterns by noting the common properties of several examples of the same pattern. Feature representations permit comparison operations through bit matching operations, but relational representations apparently necessitate more complex matching procedures. Interestingly, some problems which at first view appear to require relational coding and matching can be solved by appropriate application of the feature manifold techniques. In particular, the complex pronunciation template T' can be directly inferred from examples which are simply described using an ordinal feature manifold and a complementary feature manifold for the temporal positions of phone labels [11]. Specifically, if the set of possible phone labels is P, let the ordinal feature manifold $F = \{(p,t) : p \in P$ and $t = 1,2,...,7\}$, where any feature (p,t) represents the occurrence of a phone p in temporal position t in an input sequence. Let the complementary manifold be $F' = \{(\varepsilon P,t), (\neg p,t) : p \in P$ and $t = 1, 2,...,7\}$, where $(\neg p,t)$ means p is not a phone in temporal position t. If every example of the word "America" is represented by all appropriate features in F and F', the maximal abstraction of these examples will be a feature list equivalent to the PSR template T' (ignoring stress properties). This may be easily seen by considering just the abstraction of two examples, $E_1 = (AX, M, EH, R, IH, K, AH)$ and $E_2 = (AH, M, EH, R, AX, K, AX)$ whose representations are denoted $R(E_1)$ and $R(E_2)$. The abstraction $E_1 * E_2 = R(E_1) \cap R(E_2) = \{(\varepsilon P,1), (\neg p,1) : p \in (P-\{AX,AH\})\} \cup \{(M,2), (\varepsilon P,2), (\neg p,2)$

:p ε (P - {M})}∪ ...∪{(εP,7), (¬p,7) : p ε (P - {AH,AX})}} ≡ ((AX,1)
∨ (AH,1)) ∧ (M,2) ∧ (EH,3) ∧ (R,4) ∧ ((IH,5) ∨ (AX,5)) ∧ (K,6) ∧ ((AX,7)
∨ (AH,7)) ≡ ((AX∨AH), M, EH, R, (IH∨AX), K, (AX∨AH)). If this
abstraction were matched to any of the other six pronunciations,
the result would be equal to $E_1 * E_2$. In this case, just two examples and simple bit-wise intersections would suffice to produce
learning of a symbolic pattern equivalent to the seemingly complex
PSR T'.

Thus, it is apparent that some learning problems are made
particularly simple by applying the IM procedure to an appropriately organized feature-based description of examples. The main
objective of the current section has been to develop a familiarity
with the variety of representation schemes available and to suggest
the importance of choosing a representation which is as simple as
possible for any particular induction problem. Later in this paper, several more examples will be given of the use of feature
manifolds as bases for description and learning.

IV. INTERFERENCE MATCHING:
ABSTRACTIONS AND RESIDUALS

Interference matching is the process of comparing two event
descriptions to identify their commonalities and differences. Any
set of properties which are common to two compared representations
is an *abstraction* of them. A *maximal abstraction* comprises all
properties common to the two. Properties which are true of one
description but not the other constitute the *residual* of the first.
Interference matching of any of the feature based representations
can be performed by computing the set intersection of the property
list descriptions. More simply, each attribute-value pair can be
associated with a particular bit in a bit vector, and the abstraction of two descriptions is simply the set of features corresponding to the bits in the logical product of the two bit vectors. If
E and F are the two bit vectors, $E*F = E \wedge F$ is the maximal abstraction, and the residual of E with respect to $E*F$, $E/E*F = E \wedge (\neg F)$.
In the next section, several results of using maximal abstractions
of feature-based representations to learn patterns and syntactic
categories are reported.

To perform interference matching of relational descriptions
is far more difficult. Basically, since PSRs can describe graphs,
the production of a maximal abstraction of two PSRs is at least as
difficult as finding a maximal subgraph of two graphs. Such problems are NP-complete, meaning that it is widely believed that this
problem cannot be solved in an amount of time which is less than
an exponential function of the number of case relations in the two
compared PSRs. However, a heuristic program called SPROUTER has
been implemented which performs interference matching and nearly
always finds optimal abstractions in limited time and space [12].

The simplest way to understand interference matching in the framework of relational descriptions is as follows. Let E and F be two PSRs in which all parameters are variables.[1] Suppose E = $\{R_1, \ldots, R_m\}$ and F = $\{S_1, \ldots, S_n\}$ where each R_i and S_j is a case relation, and let the parameters of E and F be $P_E = \{e_1 \ldots e_V\}$, $P_F = \{f_1 \ldots f_W\}$ respectively, where it is assumed that $|P_E| \geq |P_F|$. A maximal abstraction of E and F can be computed by forming a 1-1 binding function B: $P_E \to P_F$ such that each element $e \in P_E$ from the event E has the parameter f = B(e) $\in P_F$ as its correspondent in F. Ignoring alphabetic differences between corresponding parameters, the maximal abstraction of E and F under the binding function B is $E_{*_B}F$, the set of case relations common to both E and F when corresponding parameters are treated as identical. As an example, if the events "Mary is a tall, dark, female" and "John is a tall, fair, male" are represented, respectively, by E = {{name:m, word:p}, {sex:m, value:s}, {female:s}, {height:m, value:g}, {complexion:m, value:j}, {"Mary":p}, {tall:g}, {dark:j}} and F = {{name:n, word: q}, {sex:n, value:t}, {male:t}, {height:n, value:h}, {complexion: n, value:k}, {"John":q}, {tall:h}, {fair:k}} and the binding function B = { (m,n),(p,q),(s,t),(g,h),(j,k)}, then E $_{*_B}$ F = {{name:v_1, word:v_2}, {sex:v_1, value:v_3}, {height:v_1, value:v_4}, {complexion: v_1, value:v_5}, {tall:v_4}}. The residuals of E and F with respect to E $_{*_B}$F are E/E$_{*_B}$F = {{female:v_3}, {"Mary":v_2}, {dark:v_5}} and F/E$_{*_B}$F = {{male:v_3}, {"John":v_2}, {fair:v_5}}.

From this simple example, it is possible to see how the residuals of IM can be used to identify the elements of a category. Consider the parameters v_2, v_3, and v_5 which occur in both residuals. v_2, for example, is associated with the attribute values "John" in F/E$_{*_B}$F and "Mary" in E/E$_{*_B}$F. The comparability of "John" and "Mary," which is indicated by the fact that they serve similar descriptive functions in E and F and results in their attribution as different properties of the same parameter in the abstraction E$_{*_B}$F, suggests that they are both elements of the same syntactic category (say N). Thus, the hypothesis that there is a category N such that {"Mary","John"}$\in$N represents an inference that properties which play comparable roles in different event descriptions are syntactically substitutable for one another. While at the outset of learning the only category known may be the set of all words, W = {"a", "be", ..., "Joe", "John", ..., "Mary", ..., "zoo"}, the use of similar assertions (e.g., {name:v_i, word:v_j} where {"Joe": v_j} or {"John":v_j} or ... {"Mary":v_j} supports the inference that a particular subset of W is the category of names, N = {"Joe", "John", ..., "Mary"}. More complex bases for category induction are discussed in [9] and also in the next section.

This section concludes with a brief description of the relational interference matching program SPROUTER (see [12] for more details). The program accepts as inputs (1) a lexicon of case

---

[1] One may convert any constant c into a variable in a term such as attribute:c by replacing the term by the variable term, attribute:x, and adding a unary relation {c:x} to the PSR.

frames which specify the types of properties and case relations which are used to describe events and (2) two descriptions, E and F, which are sets of parameterized case relations (PSRs). It is presumed that preprocessing has been done so that all relevant properties are present in E and F and all parameters are variables. SPROUTER computes a number of distinct binding functions $B_1, \ldots, B_k$ and, for each, outputs (1) a PSR corresponding to the maximal abstraction E $*_{B_i}$ F and (2) a special recognition network called an ACORN [13] which can be used to decide, for any other PSR S, if S matches E $*_{B_i}$ F. This is particularly valuable if we are hypothesizing classification rules and must evaluate a rule's diagnosticity by determining how many training examples of each class match it.

The method SPROUTER employed is as follows. Suppose the PSR E has the smaller cardinality of E and F. One node in the ACORN is generated ("sprouted") for each generic abstraction of E which is also an abstraction of F. Originally, (terminal) nodes are created for each generic case frame present in both E and F. Iteratively, case relations A_E and B_E from two nodes A and B are selected and are conjoined to form a tentative higher-order binary node. This node represents the abstraction of E corresponding to the set of case relations $\{A_E, B_E\}$. If at least one corresponding pair of case relations in F can be found, the new node is permanently added to the sprouting ACORN. Otherwise, the tentative node is deleted. The process is limited by a best-first search of alternative binding functions after a breadth-first growth process has generated a pre-specified number of nodes. When the process terminates, the maximal nodes in the ACORN correspond to maximal abstractions of E and F.

Hayes-Roth and McDermott discuss the strengths and weaknesses of this particular method of IM and suggest directions for further improvements. The major issues considered are: (1) methods for increasing the amount of real-world knowledge that can be brought to bear in specific abstraction problems to increase SPROUTER's appreciation of the relative utilities of the various commonalities it finds; and (2) the need which arises in some contexts to generalize the concept of a binding function to permit one-many mappings between parameter sets. These issues, while very important, are simply beyond the scope of this paper.

V.   KNOWLEDGE ACQUISITION PROCEDURES

In this section, algorithms are described for the three learning problems introduced in section 2 and, where possible, empirical results obtained using these methods are presented.

A)   Pattern Learning and Classification

The algorithm used to solve these problems is called SLIM

(Space Limited Interference Matching, [7]). Briefly, SLIM compares the examples of each pattern class using IM to develop maximal abstractions. Each abstraction is evaluated for its diagnosticity, and those which are expected to produce the greatest net (weighted) number of correct less incorrect judgments are given highest priority in the competition to persist in the limited memory space. Subsequently, novel test items are classified according to the most diagnostic abstraction they match. If a test item T matches no stored abstraction, a new abstraction T*A is generated from T and each stored abstraction A. Since T does match each T*A, T is classified in the class indicated by the most diagnostic T*A.

The example used to illustrate pattern learning through SLIM is taken from [11]. The problem is to classify speech syllable types from training examples which are sequences of sets of machine generated alternative labels for a series of acoustic segments. The difficult aspects of this problem include: (1) the syllable types are theoretical clusters of confusable speech patterns which do not necessarily share a close relationship with characteristics of the machine generated data themselves; (2) even if a theoretical syllable type consisting of n acoustic segment labels were valid, the machine segmentation of a spoken syllable frequently contains errors of insertion and deletion; and (3) in addition to the fact that the machine segmentation often inserts or deletes some segments compared to a theoretically perfect segmentation, the segmenter-labeller which generates hypothetical phonetic labels for each segment of speech makes many errors, including both assignments of multiple, incorrect labels and failures to assign the correct label to each segment. Thus, the type of training examples one might receive for the syllable corresponding to the theoretical sequence (M,EH,R) in "America" would be as follows (where multiple labels within column i represent alternative phonetic hypotheses for the i-th segment):

	SEGMENTS				
	1	2	3	4	5
Theoretical:	M	EH	R		
Example 1:	T	N	AX	AX	M
	B	M	EL	EL	M
	–	V	ER	EH	R
		F		IH	N
Example 2:	M	AX	B		
	N	ER	R		
	–	IH	G		
			H		

The basic approach taken to this learning problem is to develop a method of description which relates the training data to the presumed underlying behavior generator. The model posits that the underlying knowledge is the sequence pattern (M,EH,R) and the result of applying the behavior generating function (the effect of speech plus the effect of machine segmentation and labelling) is to insert and delete segments as well as add incorrect additional labels and delete proper labels from the segments that remain. Thus, interference matching (SLIM) will be an effective learning procedure only if the feature coding employed is robust with respect to the sources of variability. Only in that case will an abstraction of training data retain criterial properties of the underlying pattern (knowledge).

The data representation employed in this case is a composition of both the ORF and the enumerative complementary coding feature manifold techniques. Each training example $E = (A_1, ..., A_k) = (\{a_{11}, ..., a_{1n_1}\}, \{a_{21}, ..., a_{2n_2}\}, ..., \{a_{k1}, ..., a_{kn_k}\})$, where $A_i = \{a_{i1}, ..., a_{in_i}\}$ contains the n_i alternative machine generated hypothetical labels assigned to the i-th segment, is coded as having the following features: $\{(a_{ij}, i) : a_{ij} \in A_i, i = 1, ..., k\} \cup \{(-b, i)$: b is a possible label not in $A_i\}$. To compensate for the expected error $|i-i'|$ between the theoretical position of the i-th segment and the position i' of the corresponding machine generated segment in the sequence $(A_1, ..., A_k)$, overlapping receptive fields are used. Because the expected error is an increasing function of i, the features used are $(a, [i-G_i, i+G_i])$ where the radius of generalization G_i is the smallest integer which is at least i/2. The labels used were the 44 acoustic labels of the Hearsay II speech understanding system [5].

SLIM was used to search for diagnostic abstractions of the training examples of the 12 most frequent syllable types. There were between 4 and 16 training examples of each class and five novel test items per class (total test set size = 60). The segmenter-labeller used performs at about 60% accuracy at labelling and about 80% at segmentation (by a number of measures, see [5]). SLIM's performance in this task was 85% correct classifications of novel test items on the basis of the most diagnostic matched abstraction. A performance of 98% was achieved when SLIM was applied in its "filtered classification mode," in which the abstraction process is re-performed for each item to be classified and all intermediate abstractions are masked by the features which are present in the test item. These results can be compared to the performance of a refined, theoretically motivated syllable classifier which was specially designed and hand-tuned to perform the syllable recognition task in the Hearsay II system [16]. On exactly the same task, using the best matched syllable network template, the handcrafted knowledge source module achieved 68% correct. We think that this test provides impressive evidence of the capacity of the proposed techniques to achieve effective learning even in very noisy problem domains.

B)   Rule Learning.

The algorithm used to induce quantified production rules from before-and-after examples of situations where the rule was applied is called SPROUTER [12]. Basically, as previously described, SPROUTER computes maximal abstractions of any two relational descriptions. In particular, if A_i is a PSR describing an antecedent situation which was transformed into a consequent situation described by the PSR C_i $(i=1,...,n)$, SPROUTER compares the two-tuples (A_i, C_i) and (A_j,C_j) to produce the abstraction (A_i*A_j, C_i*C_j). The procedure used for rule induction is, roughly, to compute $(A_1*...*A_n,C_1*...*C_n)$ and infer that $A_1*...*A_n =>C_1*...*C_n$.
As an illustration, consider the problem of inducing an unknown rule of transformational grammar from the following three antecedent-consequent example pairs.

(1) "The little man sang a lovely song."-->
    "A lovely song was sung by the little man."
(2) "A girl hugged the motorcycles."-->
    "The motorcycles were hugged by a girl."
(3) "People are stopping friendly policemen."-->
    "Friendly policemen are being stopped by people."

The relational descriptions of these sentence pairs consist of three types of components: (1) syntactic phrase structures and markers (e.g., NUMBER:SINGULAR, TENSE:PRESENT); (2) a property which distinguishes elements of the antecedent sentence from elements of the consequent sentence (EVENT:e1 and ANTECEDENT:e1 as opposed to EVENT:e2 and CONSEQUENT:e2); and (3) *same-type* relations joining any pair of antecedent and consequent syntactic components which are identical types (i.e., are distinct tokens of the same type or, equivalently, are the roots of identical directed phrase structure graphs). The PSR for the first sentence pair is shown below.

```
{{ANTECEDENT:e1,CONSEQUENT:e2},
 {S:s1,NP:np11,VP:vp1,EVENT:e1},
 {S:s2,NP:np21,VP:vp2,EVENT:e2},
 {NP:np11,DET:the1,ADJ:little1,NOUN:noun11,EVENT:e1},
 {NP:np21,DET:a1,ADJ:lovely1,NOUN:noun21,EVENT:e2},
 {NOUN:noun11,NST:man1,NUMBER:n11,EVENT:e1},
 {NOUN:noun21,NST:song1,NUMBER:n12,EVENT:e2},
 {SINGULAR:n11,EVENT:e1},
 {SINGULAR:n12,EVENT:e2},
 {VP:vp1,AUX:aux11,VERB:verb11,NP:np22,EVENT:e1},
 {SAME!NP:np21,SAME!NP:np22},
 {NP:np22,DET:a2,ADJ:lovely2,NOUN:noun22,EVENT:e1},
 {SAME!NOUN:noun21,SAME!NOUN:noun22},
 {NOUN:noun22,NST:song2,NUMBER:n13,EVENT:e1},
 {SINGULAR:n13,EVENT:e1},
```

```
{VP:vp2,AUX:aux12,PB:pb1,VERB:verb12,PP:pp1,EVENT:e2},
{AUX:aux11,AUXST:have1,TENSE:t11,NUMBER:n15,EVENT:e1},
{AUX:aux12,AUXST:have2,TENSE:t12,NUMBER:n16,EVENT:e2},
{SAME!AUX:aux11,SAME!AUX:aux12},
{VERB:verb11,VST:sing1,TENSE:t21,NUMBER:n15,EVENT:e1},
{VERB:verb12,VST:sing2,TENSE:t22,NUMBER:n16,EVENT:e2},
{SAME!VERB:verb11,SAME!VERB:verb12},
{PB:pb1,PBST:be1,TENSE:t23,NUMBER:n16,EVENT:e2},
{SAME!TENSE:t11,SAME!TENSE:t12},
{SAME!TENSE:t21,SAME!TENSE:t22,SAME!TENSE:t23},
{SINGULAR:n15,EVENT:e1},
{SINGULAR:n16,EVENT:e2},
{PRESENT:t11,EVENT:e1},
{PRESENT:t12,EVENT:e2},
{PAST-PART:t21,EVENT:e1},
{PAST-PART:t22,PAST-PART:t23,EVENT:e2},
{PP:pp1,PREP:by1,NP:np12,EVENT:e2},
{SAME!NP:np11,SAME!NP:np12},
{NP:np12,DET:the2,ADJ:little2,NOUN:noun12,EVENT:e2},
{SAME!NOUN:noun11,SAME!NOUN:noun12},
{NOUN:noun12,NST:man2,NUMBER:n14,EVENT:e2},
{SAME!NUMBER:n11,SAME!NUMBER:n12,SAME!NUMBER:n13},
{SAME!NUMBER:n14,SAME!NUMBER:n15,SAME!NUMBER:n16},
{SINGULAR:n14,EVENT:e2},
{THE:the1,EVENT:e1},
{THE:the2,EVENT:e2},
{SAME!WORD:the1,SAME!WORD:the2},
{LITTLE:little1,EVENT:e1},
{LITTLE:little2,EVENT:e2},
{SAME!WORD:little1,SAME!WORD:little2},
{MAN:man1,EVENT:e1},
{MAN:man2,EVENT:e2},
{SAME!WORD:man1,SAME!WORD:man2},
{HAVE:have1,EVENT:e1},
{HAVE:have2,EVENT:e2},
{SAME!WORD:have1,SAME!WORD:have2},
{SING:sing1,EVENT:e1},
{SING:sing2,EVENT:e2},
{SAME!WORD:sing1,SAME!WORD:sing2},
{A:a1,EVENT:e1},
{A:a2,EVENT:e2},
{SAME!WORD:a1,SAME!WORD:a2},
{LOVELY:lovely1,EVENT:e1},
{LOVELY:lovely2,EVENT:e2},
{SAME!WORD:lovely1,SAME!WORD:lovely2},
{SONG:song1,EVENT:e1},
{SONG:song2,EVENT:e2},
{SAME!WORD:song1,SAME!WORD:song2},
{BE:be1,EVENT:e2},
{BY:by1,EVENT:e2}}
```

332

This corresponds to Fig. 2. The PSRs for all 3 sentence pairs were supplied to SPROUTER, which abstracted the structure illustrated in Fig. 3.

Here, same-type relations which were common to all examples have been retained and are represented by arrows linking subgraphs in the antecedent sentence structure with corresponding subgraphs in the consequent sentence structure. These correspondences represent identical quantified variables in the left and right-hand sides of the inferred production. When the rule is applied, the actual parameter in a stimulus event which matches the antecedent will be bound to the corresponding quantified variable and should be substituted into the corresponding locus of the consequent structure. If this is done, the inferred production will effect the active-to-passive transformation rule.

How general is such a rule learning paradigm? In my opinion, all rule learning will correspond, in part, to the preceding methodology. The basic elements of the induction procedure are: (1) a set of antecedent-consequent examples $I = \{(A_i, C_i)\}$; (2) instantiation of a set of predicates which can describe the criterial properties, relations, and common subpattern types of each exemplar pair; (3) an interference matching algorithm to identify the rule $F = [A_i * \ldots * A_n \Rightarrow C_i * \ldots * C_n]$; (4) a method for evaluating the goodness of the rule F by ascertaining the diagnosticity of the rule, i.e., the extent to which F is a reliable description of the way in which each A_i can be altered to produce the corresponding C_i; and (5) a method of implementing the inferred rules as universally quantified productions so that the most reliable rules execute first. The keystone of this framework is (2), the instantiation of criterial predicates. Of course, in any reasonably complex learning environment, either there may be an excessive number of potentially criterial properties to evaluate or, worse, the properties that are criterial to the rule may themselves be yet unknown (undiscovered, undefined). In the former situation, heuristics must be used to evaluate only the most promising properties first. In the latter case, discovery of criterial properties must precede or, at least, occur simultaneously with discovery of an unknown rule. Such a situation arises when, for example, one wishes to infer Newton's law F = ma and any of the concepts of *force, mass, acceleration* or *multiplication* is unknown. In the next subsection a similar problem, that of discovering syntactic categories, is considered in some detail.

C) Category and Syntax Learning.

The algorithm used to discover syntactic categories attempts to invert the assumed syntactic behavior generator. For the sake of simplicity, assume surface strings of words are generated by context free rules in Chomsky normal form, such as $D \rightarrow EF$. That is, words or phrases in category E precede words or phrases in category F when generated as respellings of category D. To induce categories of single words from a corpus of text $T = t_1 t_2 \ldots t_L$,

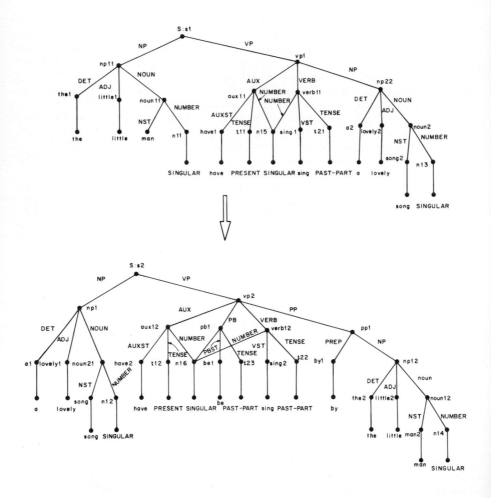

Figure 2. Graphical representation of the first example of the active-to-passive transformational rule.

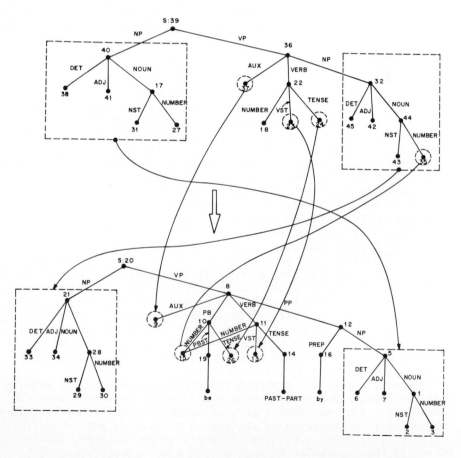

Figure 3.   Graphical representation of the induced active-to-passive transformational rule.

one must identify systematic sequential constraints on word sets.
Suppose two sets of words $W = \{w_1, \ldots, w_m\}$ and $Y = \{y_1, \ldots, y_n\}$
exist such that $(\forall i,j)$ $\Pr[t_{k+1} = y_j \ \varepsilon \ Y \ | t_k = w_i \ \varepsilon \ W]$ is significantly
better than chance. In that case, one may reasonably infer that
W and Y are subsets of some categories E and F such that, for some
$D, D \rightarrow EF$ is a rule of the language. (This may also be represented
as the probabilistic rule E => F.) If W and Y are maximal, in the
sense that the addition of any word to either one reduces the significance of the prediction of Y from W, a reasonable inference is
that $D \rightarrow WY$ is a rule of the language. Once such inferences are
made, the categories W and Y become unary predicates W(w) and Y(y);
i.e., the category name is a property of any word which is contained in the corresponding set. Subsequent inferences may depend
upon discovery of categories of categories, n-ary relations of
categories, or sequences of categories [9]. For example, if the
categories of *determiner* (words that precede adjectives, numbers,
and nouns), *adjective* (words that precede numbers and nouns and
succeed determiners), and *noun* (words that follow determiners, adjectives, and numbers and precede verbs) have been induced, the
rule NP $\rightarrow$ (*determiner*) (*adjective*) (*number*) *noun* can be inferred
from the fact that all eight possible sequences of these categor-
ies reliably precede relative qualifying pronouns (e.g., which, who,
that, ...) as well as precede and succeed verbs.

Three algorithmic approaches to this sort of induction problem are being pursued. First, Rich [14] showed that fairly effective categorizing of words could be accomplished simply by clustering words according to proximity in Euclidean N-space where
each word w_i was represented by a vector of N numbers $(v_1, \ldots, v_N)$
where v_j represented the probability that word w_j followed w_i in
the training corpus. This method has two chief problems. First,
clustering must be heuristically controlled either by some arbitrary proximity criterion or by some predetermined number of clusters. Secondly, the clustering can assign any word token to at
most one category (cluster). Thus, distinct syntactic roles or
senses of the same word token cannot be found. The second approach to this problem aims to correct these deficiencies by attempting to compute directly the probability that any two words
are in one of the same categories by computing the extent to which
the two words have significant concordances of predecessors and
successors. Once hypothesized subsets of size n are formed, the
algorithm is iterated to attempt to combine these into sets of
size n+1 which preserve the significant concordance of successors
and predecessors (n=2,3,...).

Finally, the third approach being pursued employs the enumerated complementary coding technique and IM to generate category
inferences. Each sequential pair of words $S = w_i w_j$ from the training corpus is represented by the set of properties $R(S) = \{(w_j, 1),$
$(w_j, 2)\} \cup \{(\neg w_i, 1), (\neg w_j, 2) : i' \neq i, j' \neq j'\}$ which, in turn, is efficiently represented by the bit string $B(S) = (b_{11}, \ldots, b_{1M}, c_{11},$
$\ldots, c_{1M}, b_{21}, \ldots, b_{2M}, c_{21}, \ldots, c_{2M})$, where $b_{hk} = 1$ only if (w_k, h) is
a feature and $c_{hk} = 1$ only if $(\neg w_k, h)$ is a feature of $R(S)$. Then,

the bit-wise logical product of B(S) and B(T) = S*T represents the common information about sequences S and T. For example, if S = (a,dog), T = (the,dog), then S*T represents ((a v the), (dog)). The statistical information relevant to assessing the goodness (diagnosticity) of the inference that the category {a,the} predicts the category {dog} includes F({a}), F({the}), F({dog}) and F({dog}| {a,the}) which are, respectively, the frequencies of the words "a", "the", and "dog" and the frequency with which the word "dog" follows the words "a" or "the". One possible measure of the goodness of the inference that some rule of grammar is X → {a, the} {dog} then is M({dog}| {a,the}) = F({dog}|{a, the})/expected F({dog}| {a,the}) where the expected F({dog}|{a,the}) = F({dog})F({a,the})/ N and N is the total number of words in the training corpus. Basically, this measure M(V|U) is the ratio of the observed *positive frequency* of the sets U followed by V divided by the expected (chance) frequency of such sequences.

If the goodness measure M replaces the expected net number of correct classifications (the performance) of hypothetical classificatory rules, if inferred syntax rules are represented by bit string products of the sort described above and ordered so that the best rules occur highest in the working list of intermediate abstractions, and if the observed positive frequency of a rule is conditionalized upon (reduced by) the positive frequency of the higher performing rules with which it is redundant (see [7]), the SLIM algorithm is effective for finding categories and related syntactic rules. As an illustration, the following corpus of partial sentences (noun phrases) were described using enumerative complementary codes and supplied for training of categories.

s_1	a dog ...
s_2	the dog ...
s_3	a cat ...
s_4	the cat ...
s_5	a big dog ...
s_6	a green cat ...
s_7	the yellow dog ...
s_8	the big cat ...

The following sequences of categories were inferred and are written here as prediction rules:

RULE	GOODNESS	INTERPRETATION
{big,green,yellow} => {dog,cat}	2.5	adjective => noun
{a,the} => {big,green, yellow,dog,cat}	1.67	determiner => adjective v noun

Note that these two rules account for all 12 sequential pairs of words in the training set. The first rule accounts for 4 pairs of words when a chance co-occurrence would yield 1.6 sequences of these words. The second rule accounts for 8 sequential pairs of words when 4.8 are expected. All other possible rules are lower performing and redundant with these.

A full investigation of such syntactic inference is beyond the scope of this paper. It would be necessary to augment training descriptions by properties corresponding to membership of words in inferred categories and then to reiterate this non-supervised learning procedure. This would facilitate discovery of rules based on higher-order syntactic relations as in transformational grammar. For the present purposes, it suffices to say that the outlook is bright for learning categories and rules of syntax by simple generalization of the methods which are proving so useful for the induction of patterns and rules from examples.

VI. FUTURE DIRECTIONS

Within the framework of the present paper, it is easy to understand where the chief obstacles and most promising applications of such learning techniques are likely to be in the near future. The most difficult problems remaining to be solved concern the combinatorics of relational matching and the need to restrict the evaluation of potential predicates to the most criterial ones first. The possibility of finding a feature manifold representation for general relational structures (like those found for disjunctions and sequences) must be considered a significant goal. The wide-scale application of the interference matching algorithm to many AI and PR learning problems is apparently warranted. Both in areas where much theoretical knowledge exists about potentially criterial properties and in areas where combinations of large numbers of primitive features need to be evaluated as possible bases for pattern description, interference matching provides an effective technique for abstracting patterns and rules from examples.

REFERENCES

1. Burge, J., and Hayes-Roth, F., A novel pattern learning and recognition procedure applied to the learning of vowels. *Proc. 1976 IEEE intl. conf. acoustics, speech, and Signal Processing,* 1976.
2. Diday, E., Schroeder, A., and Ok, Y., The dynamic clusters method in pattern recognition. *Proc. IFIP Congress,* 1974.
3. Fikes, R. E., and Nilsson, N. J.,STRIPS: A new approach to the application of theorem proving to problem solving. *Artificial Intelligence 2,* (1971), 189-208.

4. Galton, F., *Inquiries into Human Faculty and its Development*.
    Dent, London, 1907.
5. Goldberg, H., A comparative evaluation of parametric segmen-
    tation and labelling strategies. Unpublished doctoral dis-
    sertation, Department of Computer Science, Carnegie-Mellon
    University, 1976.
6. Hayes-Roth, F., A structural approach to pattern learning
    and the acquisition of classificatory power. *Proc. First
    Intl, Jt. Conf. Pattern Recognition,* 1973.
7. Hayes-Roth, F., Schematic classification problems and their
    solution. *Pattern Recognition 6,* 2(Oct. 1974), 105-114.
8. Hayes-Roth, F., An optimal network representation and other
    mechanisms for the recognition of structured events. *Proc.
    Second Intl. Jt. Conf. Pattern Recognition,* 1974.
9. Hayes-Roth, F., Uniform representations of structured pat-
    terns and an algorithm for the induction of contingency-
    response rules. *Information and Control,* (in press).
10. Hayes-Roth, F., Representation of structured events and ef-
    ficient procedures for their recognition. *Pattern Recognition*
    (in press).
11. Hayes-Roth, F., and Burge, J., Characterizing syllables as
    sequences of machine-generated labelled segments of connected
    speech: a study in symbolic pattern learning using a con-
    junctive feature learning and classification system. Working
    paper, Department of Computer Science, Carnegie-Mellon Uni-
    versity, 1976.
12. Hayes-Roth, F., and McDermott, J., Knowledge acquisition from
    structural descriptions. Working paper, Department of Com-
    puter Science, Carnegie-Mellon University, 1976.
13. Hayes-Roth, F., and Mostow, D. J., An automatically compilable
    recognition network for structured patterns. *Proc. Fourth
    Intl, Jt. Conf. Artificial Intelligence,* 1975.
14. Rich, E., Personal communication, 1975.
15. Shortliffe, E. H., *MYCIN: Computer-based medical consulta-
    tions.* New York: American Elsevier, 1976.
16. Smith, A. R., Word hypothesization in the Hearsay II speech
    understanding system. *Proc. 1976 IEEE Conf. Acoustics,
    Speech, and Signal Processing,* 1976.

PICTORIAL MEDICAL
PATTERN RECOGNITION

H. K. Huang
R. S. Ledley
Georgetown University Medical Center
3900 Reservoir Road N.W.
Washington, D. C.

ABSTRACT

This paper describes six different applications of pictorial
medical pattern recognition: electromicrographic tissue film,
chest X-ray film, chromosome analysis, Pap Smear analysis, three-
dimensional imaging and display from serial computerized tomo-
graphical (CT) scans, and a comparison between pre- and post- contrast CT scans. In each case, the problem is defined, the recognition procedure is explained, results and the current trends are
illustrated.

I.   GENERAL INTRODUCTION

Medical pictures can be recorded and displayed by different
media depending upon the nature and source of the information under consideration. Since the methods for performing medical pattern recognition vary according to these factors, there is, in
general, no unilateral rule governing the method of approach.
In this paper we have organized some methods used in medical
pattern recognition according to the two criteria of how the picture is recorded and the nature of the picture itself. In the
case of microscopy, the pictorial information is either contained
on a glass slide or recorded on conventional films. In radiography, the picture is recorded on X-ray film, and in computerized
tomography, the scan result is on magnetic tape or on a disk. For
film input, we have given two examples, one on electron micro-
graphic tissue film and the other on chest X-ray film. For glass
slide input, we used chromosome analysis and pap smear analysis as
illustrations, and for computerized tomography input, we utilized
the 3-dimensional reconstruction image from serial scans and a
comparison between contrast and noncontrast scans for our purposes.

II.   FILM INPUT

A)   Electron Micrography - Analysis of Synapses[1]

Introduction

In this section we describe a method for providing an automatic means of studying the morphology of synapses. (A synapse or a synaptic junction is the region of contact between processes of two adjacent neurons.) Figure 1 is a drawing of a typical synaptic junction.

Until now, the only attempted classification of synaptic junctions based upon morphologic criteria was that of Gray, who divided synaptic junctions in material fixed or stained with osmium on the basis of the apparent thickness of the post-synaptic specialization. Moreover, there has as yet, been no extensive study of the morphometric variability among several samples of similar or homologous synaptic contacts. The major drawbacks of studies of this sort have been the inability to recognize synapses to the exclusion of other similarly shaped organelles and the inaccuracy of manual measurements of morphological indices. Several different tissue staining techniques have been tried, but it has always been necessary for someone to visually inspect the electron micrograph to find the synapses present. Then if morphologic measurements are desired beyond counting the number of synapses, they must be made by hand, a method which usually proves inaccurate. The method we have developed overcomes these obstacles through computer controlled automatic recognition and measurement of the synaptic junctions.

Method

The major steps in the method are as follows: (a) preparing cytochemical tissue, a procedure which includes ethanolic phosphotungstic acid staining (the Bloom method); (b) putting the representation of the tissue into a computer for analysis; and (c) analyzing each field to locate the synapses and make the measurements on them. Figure 2 is an overall block diagram of the procedures for analyzing a synapse.

Input

After the tissue is stained (see Reference 1 which is for brain tissue preparation), thin serial sections of 800 Å are cut on a diamond knife microtone. Photographs are then taken with a Phillips EM200 electron microscope on 35mm roll film. This film serves as input to our automatic analysis method. Figure 3 shows a typical electron micrograph of stained tissue.

To put the micrographs of specially prepared brain tissue into the computer's memory, a flying spot scanner called FIDAC (Film Input to Digital Automatic Computer) is used. FIDAC is an on-line computer-input device, which can scan and store a picture directly into an IBM 360/44 computer memory at real time speed and with high resolution. For a detailed description of the

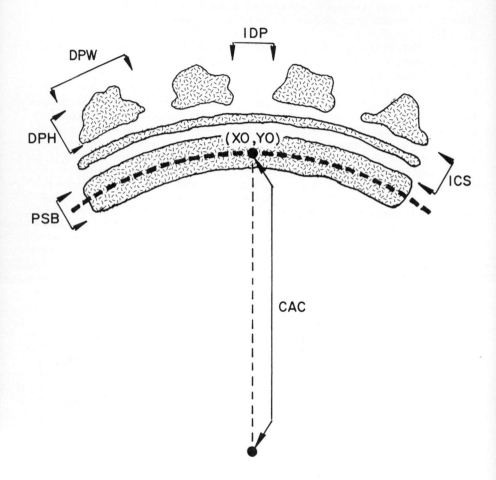

Fig. 1. A drawing of a typical synaptic junction
         PSB = The thickness of the post-synaptic band
         CAC = The curvature at the centroid of the post-synaptic
               band
         ICS = The intercleft space
         DPW = The dense projection width
         DPH = The dense projection height
         IDP = The space between dense projections

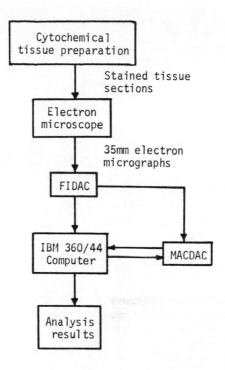

Fig. 2. An overall block diagram of the procedures for analyzing
a synapse.

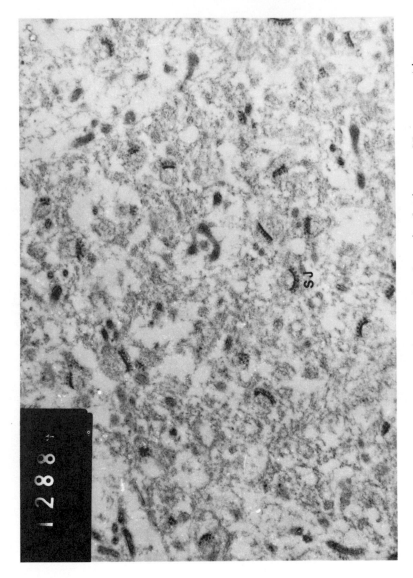

Fig. 3.   An electron micrograph of stained tissue, SJ representing a synaptic junction.

344

operation of this device, consult reference 2. Figure 4 is a
picture of the Pattern Recognition Laboratory of the National Biomedical Research Foundation at Georgetown University Medical Center, with the FIDAC Scanner at the far right. Figure 5 shows a
synaptic junction as digitized by the FIDAC with four grey levels.

Interactive Device

One part of the analysis system is an interactive computer
display called MACDAC[3] (MAn Communication and Display for an Automatic Computer) (Figure 4, center). This instrument is operated
on-line with the computer and in real time. It enables the operator to edit the pictures prior to their computer analysis, or to
monitor the stages of the computer analysis for possible manual
intervention.

MACDAC enters our analysis first after the electron micrograph has been scanned by FIDAC and before it is transmitted to
the computer. The scanned picture is displayed on the MACDAC
cathode-ray tube face and can be manually edited by means or a
"joystick" cursor. This editing consists of identifying artifacts
in the electron micrograph which are not synapses but are similar
in size. It also allows separation in the picture of those objects which should not be touching. The results of this editing
are transmitted to the computer based on the position of the cursor and a code, which is manually set with a group of switches on
the MACDAC panel. Then, after the editing, the digitized picture
is transmitted from FIDAC to the computer.

Analysis

Once the edited picture has been stored in the computer's
memory, the programs to detect and analyze the synapses take over.
First, each object in the picture is detected and the boundary
points are found. This is accomplished by scanning the raster of
points line by line, and when the gray-level value of a point is
found to exceed a previously determined minimum, the boundary of
that object is traced out and marked so that it will not be detected again. As each object is bounded, it is initially tested
for the number of boundary points and its area. If these two
values fall within certain limits, which are based on the magnification of the original micrograph and the actual size of a synapse
and the object has not been edited out by MACDAC, then this object
is marked as a possible synapse, and its boundary points are
stored for further analysis.

After the whole frame is scanned for all the objects, each
object marked as a possible synapse is further analyzed. The
first step in the analysis is to fit a parabola to the object
thought to be the post-synaptic band.

Using this parabola, the ratio of the average width to the
length of this band can be computed. Based on this value, the

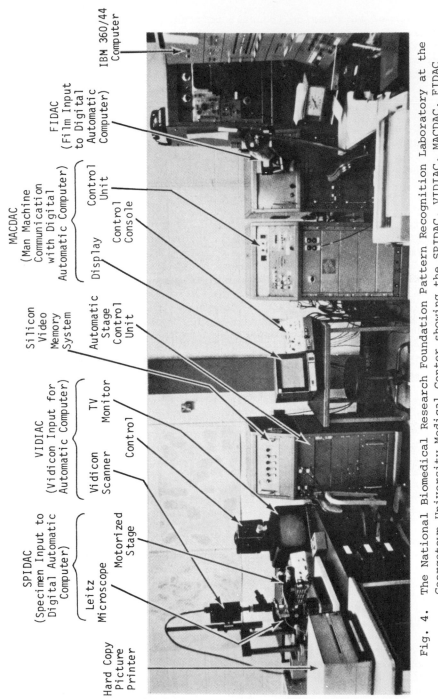

Fig. 4. The National Biomedical Research Foundation Pattern Recognition Laboratory at the Georgetown University Medical Center showing the SPIDAC, VIDIAC, MACDAC, FIDAC systems, and the IBM 360/44 computer.

346

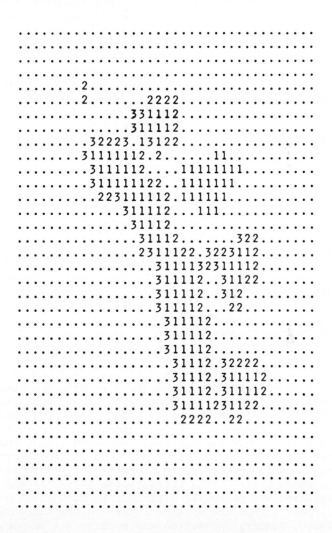

Fig. 5. A digital representation of a synapse in four grey levels as read into a computer by FIDAC.

object is again tested to determine if the ratio falls within certain calculated limits. If it does not, the object is discarded.
Otherwise, an area which is a predetermined distance from the parabolic axis is searched for the presence of objects with the shape and area of dense projections (Figure 1). This is the final criterion used to mark an object as a synapse. If there is an organized row of dense projections along one side of the proposed synaptic band, these objects are classified as a synapse. Finally, certain measurements are made upon all objects so classified.
These include the curvature of the post-synaptic band, along with its length and average width, the number of dense projections, the distance between their centroids, and their average area.

When all the synapses have been found in a frame, the results are displayed on the MACDAC screen for final editing. If any of the synapses have been analyzed poorly, the cursor and code switches can be used to correct the analysis. This might include altering the fitted parabola or excluding an object chosen as a dense projection. Then, after these changes are made, the final results are printed and labeled by frame on a high speed printer.

This automatic method, representing a typical procedure in medical picture pattern recognition, allows for recognizing and analyzing synaptic junctions in a more accurate and much faster way than the manual methods previously employed. Presently, an electron micrograph taken at a magnification of 6000x can be read and analyzed in 14 seconds.

The possible applications of such a method are many. With this system it is now possible to quantify the morphological features of a synaptic junction. It may be possible to determine that there are morphological differences among specific synaptic connections. Also, the possibility of some form of synaptic plasticity underlying long-term memory might be investigated.

B) Radiography--Coal Workers' Pneumonconiosis[4]

Introduction

In the previous section, the example we gave demonstrated a very delicate input preparation procedure, namely brain tissue preparation. The analysis phase is rather simple and straight-forward; only the elementary boundary detection technique is involved. This is because the carefully prepared tissue images make the structures of a synaptic junctions quite distinct from their background. In this section we have chosen X-ray film with coal workers' pneumoconiosis. This illustration is rather easy in its input preparation but extremely difficult to do through automatic analysis. Chest X-rays are a valuable aid in the diagnosis of pneumoconioses, tumors, pneumonias and occurrences of pleural fluid. Previous studies have included the evaluation from chest X-rays of cardiomegalies and specific heart-chamber enlargements.

Because of the large number of X-rays required to be processed each year, and the inconsistency among radiologists in e-
valuating the films, the design of an automatic system for mass
screening is desirable. Depending upon the types of applications,
different methods for automatic measurements have been proposed.
However, most of these automatic methods are primarily methods of
analyzing curvilinear boundaries rather than the qualities of the
objects. To analyze a chest X-ray automatically, it is important
for a person to recognize the texture of the areas in the image.
Other investigators have not been able to take this approach,
mainly because in order to evaluate the texture parameters of a
chest X-ray, each picture point of the image has to be evaluated
many times; as a result, the computation time consumed becomes
unfeasible for practical purposes. Here we first describe a software simulation for classifying a chest X-ray film automatically,
according to the UICC/Cincinnati standard, by using the texture
analysis method. Then we propose a completely automatic system
for the classification of a chest X-ray film.

Software Simulation

The subjects for discussion in this section are coal workers'
pneumoconiosis and the concept of texture analysis. The UICC/
Cincinnati classification of the radiographic appearances of pneumoconiosis is an international standard for classifying the disease according to its severity. It has foud categories (0,1,2,3)
for the sizes of small opacity, and, depending upon the number of
opacities each category is further divided into three subcategories. In addition, there are three categories (A,B,C) for extremely large opacities and an N category for normal cases. This
makes a total of 16 categories. Figure 6 shows 2 of these
categories.

The automatic analysis follows the radiologists' criteria in
order to identify a given chest X-ray with one of these categories. Since a chest X-ray contains many other tissue features in
attition to the pathology, which is complicated enough by itself,
it becomes obvious that boundary analysis would not be effective
in this type of pattern recognition.

The concept of texture analysis involves the evaluation of
the "texture" of various areas of a chest X-ray by going through
a number of smoothing and substracting cycles from the original
picture. During each smoothing and substracting cycle, texture
descriptors (for example, total area, contour length, annular
width and elongatedness spectra of opacities) are calculated.
Based on these calculations, the pattern recognition program
makes a decision about which category this chest X-ray should be
classified into. Our software simulation on examing 68 chest
X-ray films showed a very consistent comparison with that of
radiologists.[4]

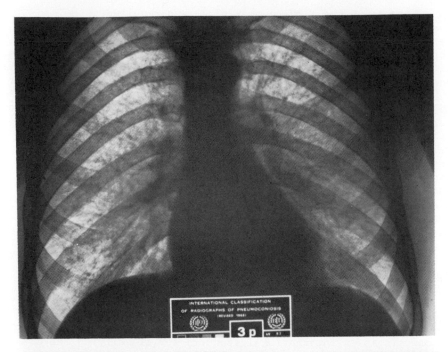

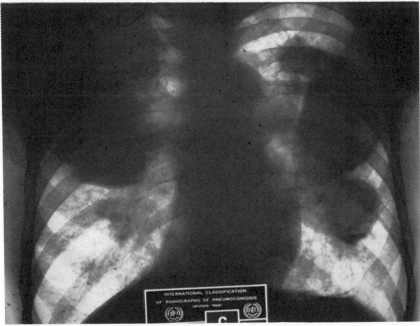

Fig. 6. Some UICC/Cincinnati standard films.

TEXAS--Texture Evaluation Auxiliary Computer

Texture analysis by the computer involves a type of computing that is extremely time consuming and, therefore, very expensive. This is because texture analysis involves the comparison of each point or a selected collection of points, with every other point (or every point in some neighboring region around the selected points) of the picture. Since a digital computer can work with only one point at a time (or at most, only the few points that can be packed in a word), the number of instructions that must be performed is of the order of a multiple of N^2, where N is the number of points in the picture. If the number of sampled points in the picture is, say, 500,000, this amounts to a multiple of 250 billion. If the computer performs 10^7 operations per second, the analysis time will be in units of 25,000 seconds, or units of about 7 hours. Fortunately, there is another approach to texture analysis. This approach utilizes a new development which has recently occurred, namely the silicon video-memory tube. Using a battery of these memory tubes, organized into a special-purpose texture-analysis computer, the texture analysis can be completed in a very short time, in approximately 3 seconds. The reason for this speed is that all the points of the picture are compared in the analog mode, and the effect is as if the operation were performed on all points in parallel fashion, not serially, as in a digital computer.

These analog operations performed by the special-purpose texture-analysis computer are under the control of the digital computer, and the digital computer itself contains the computer program that operates the texture-analysis computer.

Figure 7 illustrates in block diagram form the hardware required to carry out the analysis of X-rays. A film stacking and transport unit is required to systematically and rapidly handle the X-ray plates, presenting them sequentially to the scanner. The scanner unit converts the optical image into electronic form for temporary storage in the silicon video-memory unit. Then during the processing, the A-D (analog to digital) converters "digitize" the picture or selected parts thereof for input to the digital computer. The nondigitized image is transferred into the special-purpose texture-analysis computer for certain of the processing operations. The texture-analysis computing unit can also receive information directly from the digital computer, via the D-A converters, and send information to the digital computer through the A-D converter. The computer will of course print the report for each patient on its high-speed printer. A patient-identification unit is shown to indicate that in some manner each X-ray being analyzed must be identified.

The interactive-graphics unit should also be considered. It has been our experience that in handling real data for automatic processing, some form of human interaction is always required. It is difficult, and sometimes economically unfeasible, to program

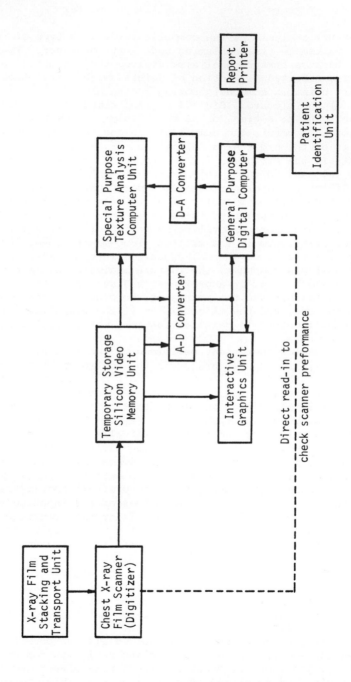

Fig. 7. A proposed TEXAC system.

352

the computer for all eventualities, and hence leaving the door open to some small amount of human interaction is always wisest. The digital-computer program controls the processing performed by the special-purpose texture-analysis computer unit. Because of the texture-computer unit, the digital computer need not have a particularly large core memory. About 32,000 16 bit words should be adequate.

In our device, the examination of chest X-rays of the lung would essentially be accomplished by a special-purpose, extremely high-speed digital computer. This computer has been designed to allow for the rapid examination of pictures where "texture" is the main feature to be utilized in the automatic pattern recognition.

The operation of the TEXAC unit is based on the use of the newly available scan-converter tubes previously described. In order to properly assess the texture of the chest X-ray pictures, it is estimated that at least 32 distinct "good" levels must be utilized; but present scan-converter tubes are good to only 10 grey levels. In addition, there can be bias problems depending on the immediate past history of the tube utilization. Therefore, our design utilizes a somewhat more complicated method for storing the picture and also handles the operations in a digital or binary format, thereby insuring the reliability of the result from an engineering-design point of view while still maintaining the 1/30 second operational speed per picture operation. For more detail about the TEXAC, consult Reference 5.

III. MICROSCOPIC SLIDE INPUT

This section of the paper contains a discussion of two applications using glass slides as input. The first example is chromosome analysis, in which hundreds of cells were analyzed and then compared with the results obtained using the manual method. A new unit based on the principle of the SPIDAC system (described below) is being designed for clinical use. The second example is the Pap smear analysis, which is at the trial stage, with recognition programs still being modified.

A) Chromosome Analysis[6]

Introduction

Chromosome analysis is of great importance in evaluating the frequency of the occurrence of genetic abnormalities and in instituting preventative measures. It has been observed, using only the classical staining and karyotyping methods, that one out of every two hundred people examined has a major chromosomal abnormality. This figure will surely be significantly increased when the chromosomes are analyzed using the banding techniques. A centralized mass-screening facility for automatic chromosome analysis will, therefore, be essential for clinical centers.

Procedure

Figure 8 summarizes the flow of processing in automatic chromosome analysis. The solid lines represent the processing of a
chromosome spread by the Giemsa type of stain directly from the
microscopic glass slide. The broken lines represent an alternative method for precessing chromosome spreads, using fluorescent
stain from photomicrographs of the chromosome spreads. Because of
the scope of this topic, we will concentrate only on the solid
lines.

After the patient material (e.g. blood sample), with patient
identification, has been received by the cytogenetic laboratory,
the cells must be cultured and the chromosome spreads prepared and
stained for banding analysis. Then the automatic computer analysis is performed and the resulting report delivered to the proper
recipient.

Assuming now that the microscopic slide is ready to be analyzed automatically, we can then turn to the system called SPIDAC
(SPecimen Input to Digital Automatic Computer, Fig. 4, left)[7].
this system operates in two successive modes: The search mode and
the analysis mode. In the search mode, the objects of interest
are detected under a low-power 22X oil-immersion objective lens,
and their centers are located. In the analysis mode, a high-power
100X oil-immersion objective lens is used, and the microscope
stage is automatically moved to center these detected objects in
the field for detailed analysis.

The complete operational procedure begins with the search
mode. The technician puts a slide on the stage, selects the original position (usually the left upper corner of the cover slip),
and turns to the 22X objective lens. He presses the "start" button, and the digital computer automatically directs the SPIDAC
system to move the stage continuously past field (260μ x 200μ)
after field and strip (260μ x 1cm) after strip until all the
strips have been searched. As the microscope slide is being
searched, the software program finds good metaphase cells and
saves the coordinates of each cell for the analysis mode. Figure 9 shows two metaphase cells being detected by the software
program. The system also includes an optional visual display,
which shows all the metaphase cells for each field on a TV screen
and on the MACDAC. The search mode terminates when all designated
strips have been searched.

The analysis mode starts with the technician switching the
objective lens from the low power to high power and pusing the
start button for the analysis mode. The computer then directs the
microscopic stage to move successively to the centers of metaphase
cells found in the search mode. The magnified image of each such
successively located metaphase cells is displayed on the TV screen.
The technician accepts or rejects a cell based on whether the cell

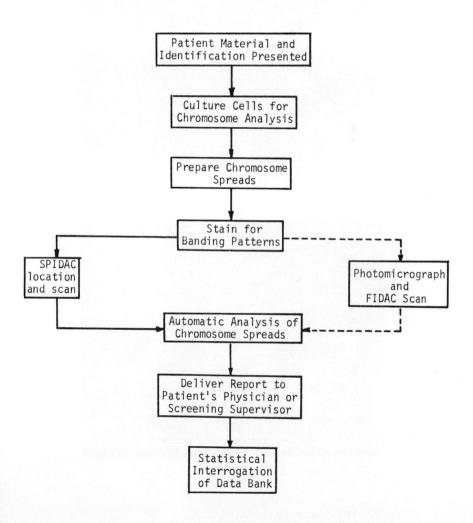

Fig. 8. The flow of processing for the chromosome-analysis.

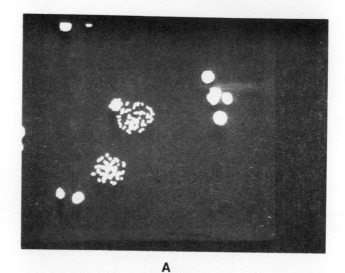

A

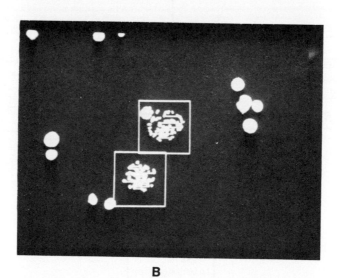

B

Fig. 9.   Metaphase cell detection
        a.   Two metaphase cells in a field
        b.   Software detecting these two cells

is analyzable or not. If the cell is rejected, the next cell is located; if the cell is accepted, the analysis program initiates a high-resolution scan and the detailed analysis of the cell. Figure 10 shows a metaphase cell with banding patterns, and Figure 11 illustrates the karyotyping with banding profile of a cell, which is the final product of the detailed analysis. For a detailed description of the chromosome analysis, consult Reference 6.

B) Pap Smear Analysis[8,9]

Introduction

The automatic chromosome analysis method described earlier is well accepted, and we are seeing the day when the complete system will be available for clinical use. In this section we are discussing pap smear analysis.

In the past few years, the importance of cervical and vaginal Papanicolaou smears as a diagnostic tool in the detection of cancer has rapidly increased. It is generally accepted that Pap smear analysis should be done annually on all women over 30 years old, and the demand for analysis is constantly growing. However, accompanying this growing demand is the problem of training individuals to perform the analysis accurately, for this training period may take up to two years of an individual working with a skilled pathologist. Therefore, the importance of automating the Pap smear procedure becomes apparent. However, the Pap smear analysis has remained at its infancy; both input preparation and data analysis are still at the trial and error stage.

In the following passages we will first define the problem and then show some elementary results.

Degree of Abnormality and Requirements for Automatic Analysis

The typing scheme now in use by pathologists to indicate the degree of visible abnormality refers to entire smears rather than to individual cells. It can be summarized as follows:

1. Normal
2. Slight atypia, perhaps hyperplasia (enlarged cells) or metaplasia (an inappropriate cell type produced by an abnormal environment)--cancer unlikely
3. Moderate atypia, more pronounced metaplasia or hyperplasia, perhaps anaplasia (loss of differentiated characteristics--typical of malignant cells), probably displasia (abnormal appearance and growth patterns), cancer possible
4. Severe atypia, displasia, anaplasia or diskaryosis (abnormal nuclei)--cancer probable
5. Severe atypia--cancer definitely present

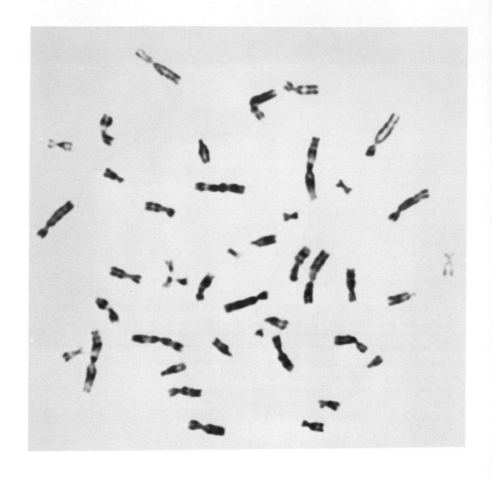

Fig. 10. A metaphase cell with bending patterns.

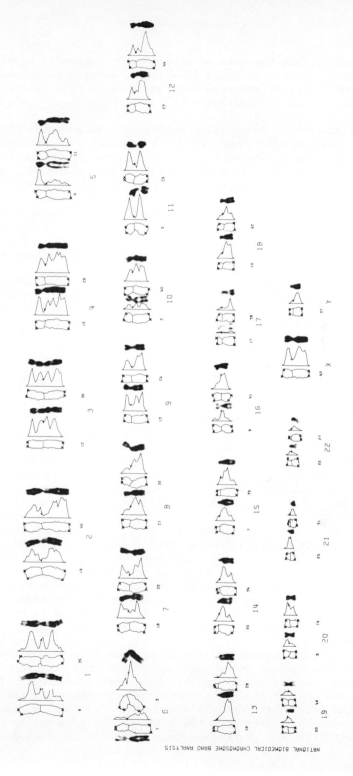

Fig. 11. The karyotyping of a metaphase cell with 46 chromosomes, each entity containing a chromosome (right) its computerized image (left) and its banding pattern (center).

Assuming that the goal of an automated system is to classify a Pap smear into one of these five types, several requirements must be met in order for automatic analysis to be a practical alternative to human evaluation:

1. There must be *no* false negatives. No abnormal cells, particularly those which are cancerous or pre-cancerous, must escape detection. Pathologists admit that human error permits 1-5% of slides containing abnormal cells to be given a lower classification than they should properly have.
2. There must not be an excessive number of false positives. It may be permissible for the machine to misclassify a few percent of the normal slides as abnormal or ambiguous; if this number is too large, the advantages of automation are lost.
3. The technician time required for sample preparation, machine operation, data analysis, etc., must be considerably less *per slide* than the time now spent by pathology laboratory technicians in direct examination.

Example of Normal and Abnormal Cells

The smear preparation for automatic analysis is quite complicated, and some of the methods have been tried and described in Reference 9. Here we are focusing on illustrating the cells detection method and showing some of the elementary results.

Assuming that a Pap smear is well prepared on a glass slide and the cells are nicely separated, then we can use the SPIDAC system to scan the slides field after field as in the search mode of chromosome analysis. (See III. A) Figure 12 shows some normal and abnormal exfoliative cells as seen in a field.

In analyzing each field, the first step is to locate every cell nucleus because of the extremely dark color in comparison with the cytoplasm and background. Thus, the boundary points of the nucleus are determined by searching the scan field horizontally until an object above a certain grey level cutoff is located. The tracing of its boundary is based upon this cutoff.

Locating the boundary of the cytoplasm is not so easily accomplished, since there is no distinct grey level cutoff which distinguishes it. Therefore, a grey level spectrum is calculated along numerous equiangular radial lines extending from the center of the nucleus, and the behavior of this spectrum is used to determine possible boundary points along each line. Once the boundaries of the nucleus and cytoplasm of each cell are known, certain parameters are calculated to characterize the cell. These include the perimeter length of both the cytoplasm and the nucleus, the area of the cytoplasm and of the nucleus, a shape factor for each cell based upon the ratio of the area to the perimeter squared, and the percentage composition of the cell divided

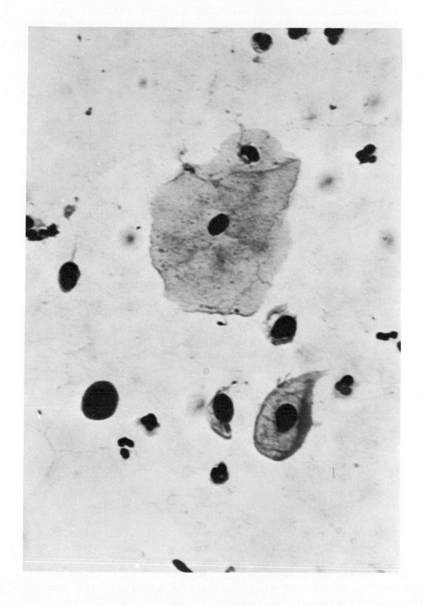

Fig. 12. Some normal and abnormal exfoliative cells as seen in a Pap Smear.

between the nucleus and the cytoplasm and so forth. These parameters are then used as input to a discrimination function, which
classifies each cell as either normal or malignant. Figures 13
and 14 are illustrations of some results based on the method described above.

IV. COMPUTERIZED TOMOGRAPHY INPUT

Introduction

Computerized tomography (CT), which was first used for medical purposes in 1974, is a recent advent in radiographical technology [10].   It blends the established tomographic technique with
new computer technology to form cross-sectional scans of patients;
and these scans reveal much more diagnostic information than a
conventional X-ray. The output of computerized tomography is a
digital picture of various sizes (from 160 x 160 to 320 x 320
pixels; see Figure 15), each picture representing a cross-sectional anatomy of the patient. The value of each pixel indicates the
X-ray attenuation of a tissue area of approximately 1.5 x 1.5 mm,
and it also relates to the tissue mass density.[11] At the present
time, any tissue abnormality of more than .5% in mass density
difference from its surroundings and of more than 5 x 5 mm^2 in
size can be detected by this type of scanner. Because of its excellent quality of instrumentation, its noninvasive nature, and
the output already in digital format, computerized tomography has
opened up a new avenue in medical picture processing. In the following paper, we shall describe two applications from these computerized tomographic scans, namely 3-dimensional imaging and display, and the comparison between contrast and noncontrast scans.
The scanner used was the ACTA-Scanner

A)   3-Dimensional Imaging and Display

CT scans can give only cross-sectional pictures of patients,
each scan representing one cross-sectional anatomy of the patient
under consideration. The thickness of each section varies depending on the type of scanner used. If a patient is scanned trans-
axially and in serial order, then the accumulated scan pictures
represent serial sections of the patient. These serial sections
can be read back into the computer storage device and aligned
properly; then an interpolation technique can be used to fill in
gaps among sections if they exist. As a result, the complete 3-
dimensional image of the patient is in the computer memory for
proper retrieval.[12] This 3-dimensional imaging is extremely useful for diagnostic purposes. Figure 15a shows two cross-sectional
scans through the neck of a patient who has syringomyelia. Figures 15b and c illustrate a sagittal and a coronal reconstruction
from sixteen of these cross-sectional scans.

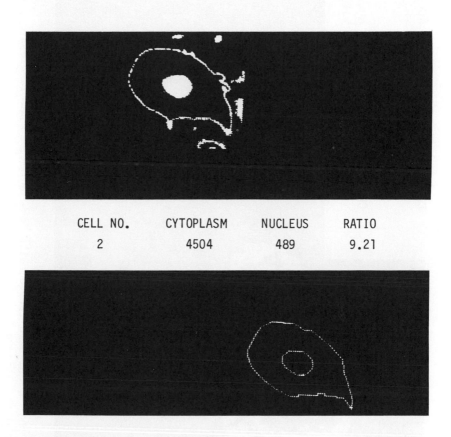

CELL NO.	CYTOPLASM	NUCLEUS	RATIO
2	4504	489	9.21

Fig. 13. An abnormal exfoliative cell, the upper picture showing the nucleus and the possible boundary of the cytoplasm, the lower picture showing the same cell with clear boundaries of both the cytoplasm and the nucleus.

CELL NO.	CYTOPLASM	NUCLEUS	RATIO
1-A	23359	360	64.88

CELL NO.	CYTOPLASM	NUCLEUS	RATIO
1-B	3999	181	22.09

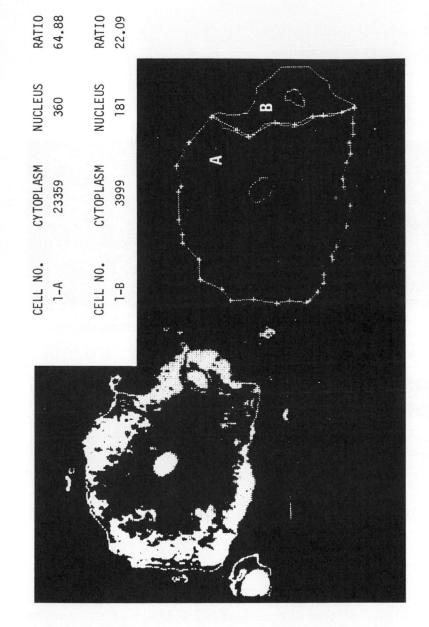

Fig. 14. Two normal exfoliative cells, the upper left before clean-up, the lower right after clean-up.

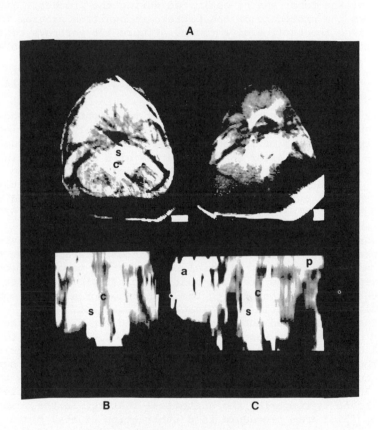

Fig. 15. 3-dimensional imaging in computerized tomography
    a. 2 cross-sectional scans through the neck of a
        patient (a patient of Dr. G. DiChiro of NIH).
        Showing the cervical spinal column (s), and the
        spinal cord (c)
    b. A cornoal reconstruction from sixteen of these
        cross sections
    c. A sagittal reconstruction from sixteen of these
        cross sections (A: anterior; P: posterior)

After the 3-dimensional information from a patient is stored
in the computer memory, it is sometimes advantageous to display
only the pathology, for example a tumor, on the display unit. This
requires highly sophisticated pattern recognition techniques; the
general flow diagram is shown in Figure 16.[13] After the tumor is
located in the 3-dimensional arrays, the isolated 3-D image can be
rotated and displayed in a contour-gram or in a shaded image,
which allows the clinician to have a 3-D morphology of the tumor.
In addition, in order to increase the diagnostic information, the
volume of the tumor can be estimated during the process. Figure
17a shows the procedure of the pattern recognition program for
recognizing the outline of a tumor. Figure 17b portrays contour-
grams of six sections of the same tumor at various rotation angles.

B) Comparison Between Contrast and Noncontrast Scans[14]

It has become increasingly evident that contrast enhancement
in computerized tomography often gives additional information
about certain types of intracranial pathology. Since the density
changes before and after the application of a contrast medium are
often rather subtle, they can best be imaged by subtraction techniques. The density changes observed over various time intervals
after contrast injection are even less distinguishable, and therefore subtraction methods are more important if tumors or infarct
are scanned sequentially at short time intervals.
Various manual methods of subtraction, designed to investigate pre- and post- contrast medium enhancement scans, have been
reported on by different clinical centers. The major difficulty
involved in comparing pre- and post- contrast pictures is that of
movement of the patient during the scanning, for a slight movement
in position will result in an inaccurate subtract.
The computerized subtraction technique can minimize the error
caused by movement. Furthermore, this method, as opposed to the
manual one, allows both qualitative and quantitative comparisons.
The procedure involved is to read both the pre- and post- contrast
scans into the computer memory. The computer program will then
shift the scan pictures for an optimal meaningful subtraction between scans by comparing the anatomical features in the scans.
The result of this procedure is a subtraction digital picture
which shows the enhancement because of the injection of the contrast medium. Figure 18 shows three different kinds of cranial
tumors in pre-, post- contrast and subtraction formats. It is
evident that the subtraction images complement the information of
the pre- and post- contrast images.

V. CONCLUSION

We have discussed six different applications in pictorial

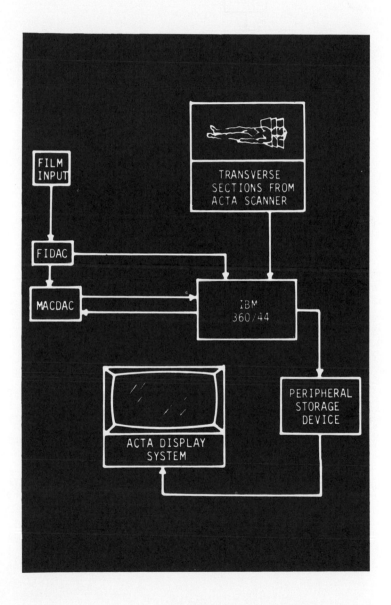

Fig. 16 a.

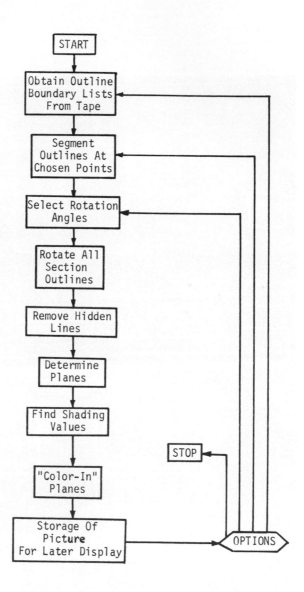

Fig. 16 b.

Fig. 16. The flow diagram of 3-dimensional imaging and display
  a. General
  b. Pattern recognition procedure

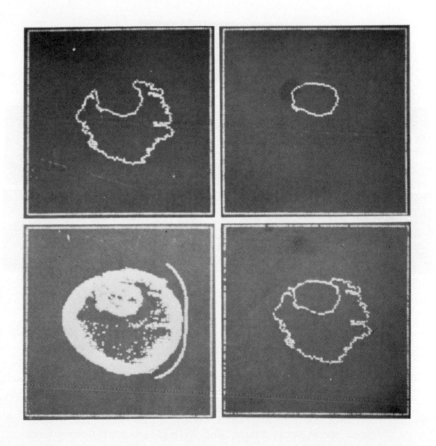

Fig. 17 a.

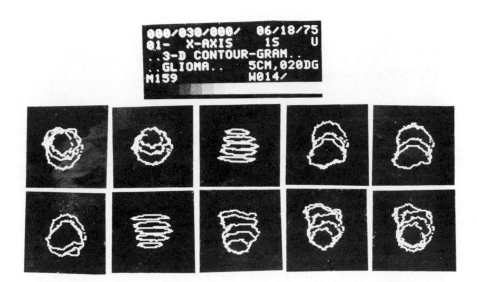

Fig. 17 b.

Fig. 17. A tumor in computerized tomographic scans (courtesy of
Drs. Mazziotta, Huang and Schellinger of Georgetown
University)
    a. Pattern recognition procedure in outlining the
        boundary of the tumor
    b. Contour-grams of six sections of the tumor at
        various rotation angles

pre   post   sub

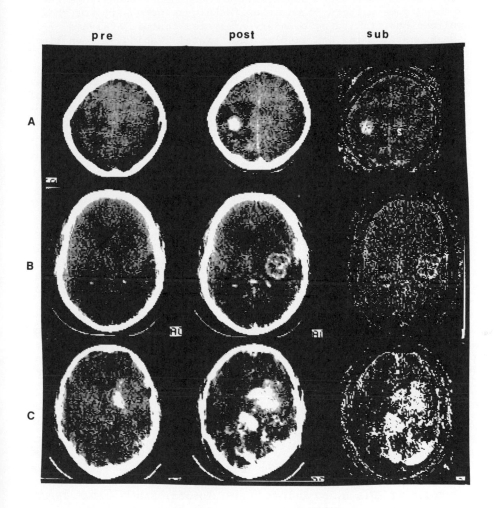

Fig. 18.   Pre-, post- contrast and subtraction images of cranial
           pathologies (courtesy of Drs. Chamberlin, Huang,
           Schellinger, Garnic)
           a.   Metastatic astrocytoma, only the subtraction image
                revealing the secondary metastsis (see S)
           b.   Glioma
           c.   A-V malformation, only subtraction image showing
                detailed structure of the AVM

medical pattern recognition. The input format of these applications varies from conventional film, microscopic slides to the more recently developed computerized tomographic scans. We have explored some pattern recognition techniques necessary for these applications, including boundary analysis, texture analysis, 3-dimensional imaging and display, rotational imaging, hidden line removal and shaded imaging. Also, the point has been stressed that there are no unilateral rules governing the operating procedure in pictorial medical pattern recognition; the nature of the problem always dictates the method used. At the present stage of development in the field of medical pattern recognition, the man-machine interaction is still essential, which is demonstrated in almost every application. Computerized tomography has given rise to a new type of medical pattern recognition, one that is potentially rich and requires further exploration.

ACKNOWLEDGMENT

This work was supported in part by NIH grants (GM 10797, GM 5192, HD 05361 and RR 05681), in part by a contract (HSM 99-72-29) from HEW to the National Biomedical Research Foundation, and in part by a grant from Pfizer Medical Systems, Inc., to the Georgetown University Medical Center, Department of Physiology and Biophysics, Division of Biomedical Computing.

The authors would like to thank the staffs of the National Biomedical Research Foundation and the Division of Biomedical Computing, Georgetown University Medical Center, for their contributions, and also Drs. John Mazziotta and Keith Chamberlin for their work in computerized tomography, as well as Dr. Sam Joseloff for reading the complete manuscript and offering his criticism.

REFERENCES

1. Ungerleider, J. A., R. S. Ledley, F. E. Bloom, *Automatic Recognition and Analysis of Synapses*, Comput. Biol. Med., Vol. 6, pp. 61-66, 1976.
2. Golab, T. J., R. S. Ledley, L. S. Rotolo, *FIDAC - FILM INPUT to Digital Automatic Computer*,Pattern Recognition, Vol. 3, pp. 123-156, 1971.
3. Ledley, R. S., T. J. Golab, R. G. Pence, *An Inexpensive On-Line Interactive Computer Display*, Proc. 9th Annual IEEE Region III Convention, pp. 369-373, 1971.
4. Ledley, R. S., H. K. Huang, L. S. Rotolo, *A Texture Analysis Method in Classification of Coal Workers' Pneumoconiosis*, Comput. Biol. Med., Vol. 5, pp. 53-67, 1975.
5. *Chest X-ray Analysis by Computer*, Final NBR Technical Report, HSMHA 99-72-29, 1975.

6. Ledley, R. S., H. A. Lubs, F. H. Ruddle, *Introduction to Chromosome Analysis*, Comput. Biol. Med., Vol. 2, pp. 107-128, 1972.
7. Ledley, R. S., H. K. Huang, et. al., *SPIDAC - Specimen Input to Digital Automatic Computer*, AFIPS Proc., Vol. 42, pp. 489-496, 1973.
8. Ledley, R. S., J. A. Ungerleider, *A Computerized System for Automatic Pap Smear Analysis*, Proc. 26th ACEMB, 1973.
9. Zimmerman, B. K., *Exfoliative Cytology: Automated Computer Analysis*, NBR Report 0376-01, 1976.
10. Ledley, R. S., et. al., *Computerized Transaxial X-ray Tomography of the Human Body*, Science, Vol. 186, pp. 207-212, 1974.
11. Huang, H. K., S. C. Wu, *The Evaluation of Mass Densities of the Human Body in Vivo from CT Scans*, to be published Comput. Biol. Med., Dec. 1976.
12. Huang, H. K., R. S. Ledley, *Three Dimensional Imaging Reconstruction from in Vivo Consecutive Transverse Axial Sections*, Comp. Biol. Med., Vol. 5, pp. 165-170, 1975.
13. Mazziotta, J. C., H. K. Huang, *THREAD (Three-Dimensional Reconstruction and Display) with Biomedical Applications in Neuron Ultrastructure and Computerized Tomography*, to appear in Proc. AFIPS, National Computer Conference, N. Y., June,1976.
14. Huang, H. K., K. Chamberlin, *A Subtraction Technique for Comparison of Pre- and Post- Contrast Medium Enhancement Scans from Computerized Tomography*, Submitted for Presentation and Publication, 62nd Annual Conference of the Radiological Society of North America, Chicago, Illinois, November, 1976.

DISTANCE MEASURES FOR SPEECH RECOGNITION -
PSYCHOLOGICAL AND INSTRUMENTAL

Paul Mermelstein
Haskins Laboratories
New Haven, CT.

ABSTRACT

Perceptual confusion among speech sounds can serve as a guide
to the selection of appropriate distance metrics for verification
of hypotheses in speech-recognition systems. Known results covering psychological representation of speech sounds are first reviewed. Desirable properties for distance measures for verification are stated, and previously proposed distance metrics for word-
recognition are evaluated in this light. The paper reports on one
experiment that demonstrates the need for assessing the significance of local differences for any distance metric to be used for
verification of syllable-sized hypotheses concerning the speech
signal.

I. INTRODUCTION

Analysis of the continuous speech signal to obtain a phonetic
transcription is a significant problem for any speech-understand-
ing system. Speech sounds undergo a complex reorganization of
their acoustic properties from their form when uttered in isola-
tion to their form in a sentence context. This reorganization is
generally accompanied by a loss of information--distinctive differences among sounds become reduced and sometimes disappear alto-
gether.
Analytic segmentation and labeling rules may be constructed
to extract the segments of speech that are characterized by un-
changing features [1].   Due to variations in context and speaker,
however, these rules are at best probabilistic in nature, they
select a highly likely hypothesis concerning the underlying segments. The rules are based on acoustic measurements pertaining
only to a short time interval of the signal in and around the hypothesized segment.
To utilize information from a somewhat larger context, one
attempts to verify the analysis-derived hypotheses at the syllable or word level. Word-boundaries are not readily apparent in
fluent speech; therefore, one wants to consider the verification
of syllable-sized units. By restricting our analysis to admissible syllables of the language, both those found within words and
those spanning word boundaries, we can immediately reject a large
number of hypotheses. Additionally, knowing the syllable context,

374

we can utilize predictions concerning the effects of neighboring sounds on each other to ascertain whether the data in fact support those hypotheses.

We first review some results concerning human perceptual confusions among speech sounds in order to select an appropriate representation on which to compute distance measures. Next, several desirable properties are cited for a distance metric appropriate for the verification of syllable-length hypotheses. Distance measures previously used for limited word-recognition systems possess these properties to a variable extent. Distance-based recognition is generally inappropriate for selecting one of more than a few hundred distinct patterns. For a fixed finite probability of error for any individual membership comparison, the recognition probability tends to zero as the number of patterns is increased. Therefore, we suggest that analysis be used to select only a few reasonable hypotheses concerning the phonetic content of a syllable, and conventional word-recognition techniques be limited to verification of such hypotheses. In order that a metric be appropriate for verification as well as recognition, we require not only that the distance to the correct category be a minimum but also that such minima lie below a fixed threshold and distances to incorrect categories lie above that threshold. Finally, we cite a simple experiment whose results emphasize the need for weighting the short-time spectral distances according to the significance of the local differences.

II. PSYCHOLOGICAL DISTANCE REPRESENTATION

Experimental data on confusion among speech sounds by human listeners are available from perception and recall experiments. Miller and Nicely [2] measured perceptual confusions among single initial consonants under various conditions of noise added to the speech signal. Wickelgren [3] measured confusion among consonants that were perceived correctly in a serial recall experiment. The confusion patterns were generally similar. Essentially the same feature system could explain the confusions in auditory perception as in short-term memory. Where confusion exists, it can be viewed as the result of selective substitution of features such as voicing, nasality, openness and place. Similarity among consonants was found to be a monotonic function of the number of features they share. Where confusion among consonant-vowel and vowel-consonant sequences was tested, the order was not significant for vowel errors but was a feature of consonant errors.

Shepard [4] derived a similarity matrix from the Miller-Nicely confusion data and obtained a spatial representation of the speech sounds. He assumes that similarity is an exponentially decreasing function of inter-class distance and minimizes the error between the similarity and its distance derived representation,

$$\sum_{i>j} \{S_{ij} - e^{-bD_{ij}} + c\}^2$$

Here $S_{ij} = (P_{ij} + P_{ji})/(P_{ii} + P_{jj})$, a function of the reported confusion matrix. D_{ij} is the distance between classes i and j in the spatial representation recovered, given by

$$\sqrt{\sum_k (X_{ik} - X_{jk})^2} \quad \text{where } X_{ik} \text{ is the}$$

projection of the coordinate of the ith class on the kth orthogonal dimension of the underlying perceptual space. b and c are parameters to be determined. Over 99% of the variance for confusion among 16 consonants was accounted for on the basis of two orthogonal dimensions. These dimensions corresponded roughly to the perceptual features of voicing and a combination of nasality and frication.

This spatial representation is shown in Figure 1. A hierarchical clustering procedure which sequentially clusters sound pairs in the order of their similarity yields the clusters indicated. These clusters roughly correspond to those one derives on the basis of confusions at decreasing levels of signal to noise ratio There appears to be a good correlation between the similarity values under different noise conditions--decreasing signal to noise increases the confusion among similar sounds.

It is significant to note that the sound-space is not uniformly populated. A distance sufficiently large to cross the boundary between /p/ and /k/ is probably not significant for variation among different tokens of /s/. The technique relies on confusion data; therefore, the distance between distinct tokens of members of the same phonemic category is assumed to be zero. Since any continuous instrumental measure must be sensitive to both inter-category and intra-category variation, these results can only be used as a guide to the construction of an appropriate distance metric.

A similar spatial distribution can be achieved for vowel sounds and is given in Fig. 2. Although the data are shown in three dimensions, which account for 99% of the variance, the first two dimensions account for 97%. While the principal dimensions correspond roughly to the first two formant frequencies of the vowels, the second dimension appears compressed roughly logarithmically with frequency. These results correlate well with known data concerning the spacing of critical bands in the human auditory system--the band within which noise effectively masks a signal of fixed frequency. These critical bands are roughly equally spaced with frequency below 1000 Hz and increase logarithmically thereafter. The mel frequency scale reflects that spacing.

Confusion between vowels and consonants seems quite rare; but no data are available. It is unfortunate that the semivowels and glides were not included in the Miller-Nicely confusion experiments since these would have yielded the most interesting consonant-vowel confusion data.

Compound consonants present additional problems. Despite the

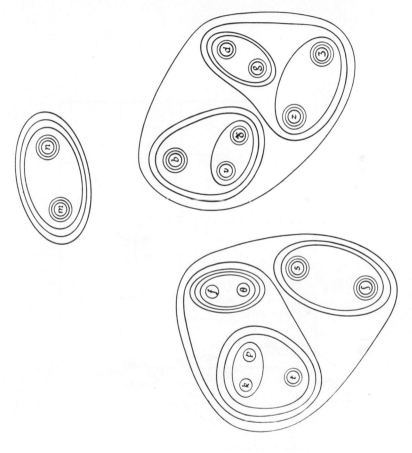

Figure 1. Spatial and hierarchical representation of the perceptual similarity between consonants. From Shepard (1972). Copyright 1972, McGraw-Hill, Inc. Used with permission of McGraw-Hill Book Co.

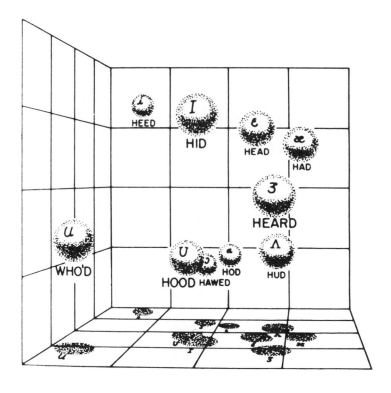

Figure 2 . Three-dimensional spatial representation for
10 vewel phonemes. From Shepard (1972).
Copyright 1972. McGraw-Hill, Inc. Used with
permission of McGraw-Hill Book Co.

close fusion in articulation between the component consonants of a compound, the confusions of the compounds can be explained in terms of the confusion of the components. [5] This result may be due to phonological constraints among the compounds. Since stops and fricatives are relatively rarely confused,the classes of compounds in which they participate will also be rarely confused. Confusion predominates among the stop-liquid compounds in initial and the nasal-stop group in final position.

According to Wickelgren [3] consonant similarity and vowel similarity can be considered as independent dimensions in syllable recall. However, co-articulation effects modify the acoustic cues for consonants depending on the syllabic vowel. Therefore the possibility of perceptual interactions between consonant and vowel must be recognized.

III. DESIRABLE DISTANCE MEASURE PROPERTIES

In view of the above results, a distance measure that models human performance should ideally recognize the phonemes, and construct the distance measure from phoneme confusability data. Failing such recognition, we can at best approximate the peripheral, precategorical aspects of human speech perception behavior.

Let us postulate a set of desirable properties for a distance measure for the verification of syllable-sized segments.

1. The measure should operate on time-aligned versions of the tokens to ensure consonant to consonant and vowel to vowel comparison. Since syllables have but one prominent vowel, the best-aligned tokens can be viewed as those that will minimize vowel-vowel differences as well as differences in the prevocalic as well as post-vocalic position.

2. If the final distance measure is a time-integral of some distributed distance function, an appropriate weighting function must be used that assesses the significance of the contributions from the individual short-time segments.

3. The distance measure between tokens should be symmetric, $D(X,Y) = D(Y,X)$.

4. The distance measure should be utilizable to determine phonetic equivalence. If X and Y are phonetically equivalent, but X and Z are not, the $D(X,Y) < D(X,Z)$.

5. Let A, B be parametric representations of two tokens, then $M(A,B) = M(B,A) = (A+B)/2$ is a template for the class (A,B) such that $D(A,M) \leq D(A,B)$ and $D(B,M) \leq D(A,B)$.

Templates are used as compact descriptors for equivalence classes. Consider the class of metrics defined as the weighted sum of elemental metric components for short-time segments. Let P be some space of time-warping transformations such as shown in Fig. 3.

$$D(X,Y) = \min_{p(\tau)\varepsilon P} \sum_\tau w(\tau) \; d[x(\tau),y(\tau)]$$

where $d(\tau) = d[x(\tau), y(\tau)]$ is an elemental metric component over a short-time segment of the path $p(\tau)$ that maps $1 \leq t_x \leq T_x$, and $1 \leq t_y \leq T_y$ onto τ and $w(\tau)$ is some positive semidefinite weighting function that assesses the significance of the contribution from each element of the path.

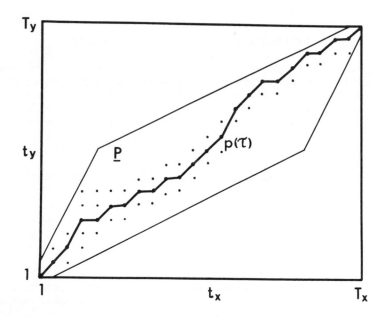

Figure 3.   Typical path in the space of time-alignment transformations between two speech segments.

Among requirements that we may want to impose on the elemental distance metric between any two short-time segments are:

1)   Positive semidefinite, $d(x,y) \geq 0$
This ensures that the global metric is also positive semidefinite.

2)   Symmetric, $d(x,y) = d(y,x)$

3) Satisfies the triangle inequality $d(x,y) + d(y,z) \geq d(x,z)$

4) Satisfies a perceptual weighting of the frequency components of the power spectra of the signals. If variation in $s(\omega_1)$, the energy at frequency ω_1, is perceptually more significant than that in $s(\omega_2)$, then $d[x,x + \Delta s (\omega_1)] > d[x, x + \Delta s (\omega_2)]$.

The need for careful assessment of the significance of spectral variations was realized when we carried out the following experiment. Human spectrographic pattern recognizers were asked to match the words of an unknown sentence, presented in spectrographic form, with the same words from a reference library of spectrographic patterns. The reference library was generated by the same speaker, stored in computer retrievable form, and displayed through specification of a list of required features. Since the phonetic transcription of the reference words was not made available, the subjects were discouraged from using syntax and semantics to assist the pattern matching operation. While the subjects had no problem in rejecting the phonetically dissimilar words, they encountered frequent confusions between similar words. Fig. 4 shows the two reference words "community" and "immunity" at left and the unknown word at the right. In the presence of some uncertainty concerning the word boundary, the disagreement in the unstressed syllable at the top just to the right of the first arrow was accepted by two observers in view of the wide agreement over the rest of the word. The region of significant spectral disagreement between the two extends for no more than 100 msec. Clearly,we need a rather sophisticated metric to resolve such distinctions.

IV. ACOUSTICS-BASED DISTANCE MEASURES

Let us now examine some distance measures proposed previously in the light of these requirements. Sakoe and Chiba [7] constructed a Euclidean distance metric on short-time spectral samples obtained from a bank of band-pass filters. When the words were aligned in time through use of a dynamic programming algorithm to minimize the total word-to-word distance, they achieved 99% recognition of the 100 two-digit Japanese numbers by five speakers. Klatt [8] has proposed weighting the spatial distance metric with a function that reflects the increased perceptual importance of differences near the spectral peaks and reduced perceptual importance of the differences near spectral minima. Itakura [9] suggested use of the minimum prediction residual as a distance measure for isolated word recognition. This measure computes the ability of the linear predictor that is optimum for the reference-word segment to predict the signal waveform of the target-word segment.

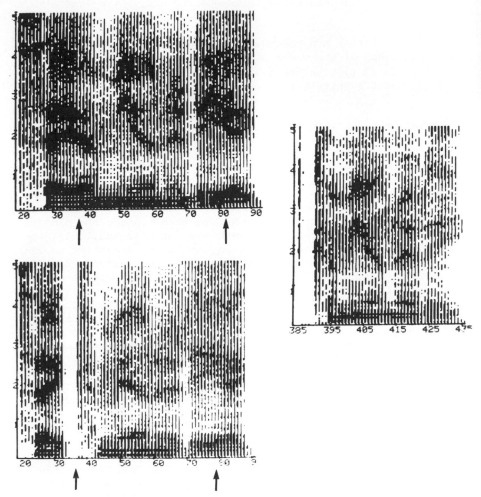

Figure 4. Spectrograms for the reference words "immunity" (top), "community" (bottom) and unknown (right). Frequency in kHz units, time in increments of 12.8 msec.

$$d(X/a) = \log\ (\underline{a}\ \underline{V}\ \underline{a}'/\hat{\underline{a}}\ \underline{V}\ \hat{\underline{a}}'),$$

i.e., the distance of the target segment characterized by process X from the reference segment having the optimum linear predictor vector $\underline{a}$ is given by the log-likelihood ratio where $\hat{\underline{a}}$ is the optimum linear predictor of X, and $\underline{V}$ is the vector of autocorrelation coefficients of X. While this measure can be computed rather quickly from the signal waveform, it is not symmetric between reference and target. To overcome this, Gray & Markel [10] have suggested a symmetric modification of the linear-predictor residual, namely

$$d_s(X/a) = d(X/a) + d(a/X)$$

The linear prediction residual is a measure of the unpredicted signal energy. There is no attempt to assess the significance of the suboptimum prediction of the signal waveform. For some signals even a rough spectrum approximation appears adequate, for others a finer representation is required.

White and Neely [11] performed a comparative evaluation of the Euclidean spectral distance measure and the one based on the linear-prediction residual. They found them roughly equivalent in terms of performance for recognition of a 36-word and a 91-word vocabulary by one speaker. They concluded that the major improvement over previous results arose from the use of the various dynamic programming algorithms for word-alignment. Use of the dynamic programming technique for word-recognition was first proposed by Velichko and Zagoruyko [12].

Atal [13] has used a non-Euclidean distance measure for speaker recognition, namely

$$d(\underline{\mu}_1, \underline{\mu}_2) = (\underline{\mu}_1 - \underline{\mu}_2)\overset{-1}{W}(\underline{\mu}_1 - \underline{\mu}_2)'$$

where the $\underline{\mu}_j$ are parameter vectors to be selected and W is the covariance matrix of $\underline{\mu}$. He explored representations in terms of linear predictor coefficients, impulse response coefficients, autocorrelation function samples, predictor derived area functions, and cepstral parameters. The cepstral coefficients C_k are related to the linear predictor parameters by

$$\sum_{k=-n}^{k=n} C_k e^{-jk\theta} = \ln \left[\sigma/|A(e^{j\theta})|\right]^2 ; \qquad (\sigma = \text{rms energy})$$

where $1/A(e^{j\theta})$ is the linearly predicted signal spectrum. Among the different parametric representations, the cepstral coefficients gave the highest speaker identification accuracy. Representation in terms of cepstral coefficients has the advantage that a set of coefficients of the same order can be averaged, and the result equals the cepstral representation of the average of the log power spectra (after normalization to unity gain). Use of the covariance matrix normalizes the contributions of the components of the parameter vectors independently of any linear transformations they may undergo.

Bridle and Brown [14] used a set of 19 weighted spectrum-shape coefficients given by the cosine transform of the outputs of a set of nonuniformly spaced bandpass filters. The filter spacing is chosen to be logarithmic above 1 kHz and the filter bandwidths are increased there as well. We will, therefore, call these the mel-based cepstral parameters. Pols [15] showed good word-recognition results using only the three shape variation components maximally contributing total spectral shape variation. These components resemble the mel-based ceptral parameters rather closely in terms of their variation with frequency. The mel-based cepstral parameters have the advantage that generally fewer parameters suffice for an adequate representation of the power spectrum than the linear-prediction coefficient series. A truncated cepstral representation corresponds to a frequency-smoothed power spectrum, one from which evidence concerning the individual harmonics of the speech signal is missing. To the extent that the spectrum of the excitation signal is invariant between successive voiced segments of the speech signal, the mel-based cepstral measure corresponds to a mel-weighted summation of the difference between the two smoothed vocal-tract transfer functions.

V.   EXPERIMENTS WITH A MEL-BASED CEPSTRAL DISTANCE MEASURE

I have been concerned with the adequacy of a mel-based cepstral distance measure to discriminate phonetically similar words and syllables. To evaluate the contribution of time-dependent significance functions to an integrated distance measure, I conducted the following experiment. Four speakers, two male, two female, recorded one production of each of the twelve phonetically similar words "stick", "sick", "skit", "spit", "sit", "slit", "strip", "scrip", "skip", "skid", "spick" and "slid" in a reference context "say -- again". The words were excised from the carrier by listening to a specifiable delimited segment of the signal. Spectra were computed for all the words and reduced to a two-dimensional cepstral representation. The respective inter-word distances were determined for all possible pairs of words by time alignment with Itakura's dynamic algorithm. The unweighted metric

$$d(a,b) = \frac{1}{N} \sum_{\tau=1}^{N} \sum_{k=1,2} [c_k^a(\tau) - c_k^b(\tau)]^2 \qquad \text{was used.}$$

$c_k^x(\tau)$, $\tau=1,\ldots,$ N;x=a,b; k=1,2 are the time-aligned two-dimensional mel-based cepstral coefficient vectors for the two words. Figure 5 shows histograms of the inter-word distances for the same word spoken by two different speakers, as well as for all other pairs comparing different words spoken by the same or different speakers. The complete overlap between the two comparison categories is surprising. Although the unweighted distance measure is useful to differentiate phonetically distant words, it is clearly not applicable to the discrimination of phonetically similar words.

I next generated templates for each of the words by time-warping the words of each speaker onto the one with longest duration using the same dynamic programming algorithm. The mean and variance of the first two cepstral parameters were next computed for the time-aligned versions and used as templates representative of the respective words. Next the weighted distance between each token x and template A was determined using the inverse of the variance for weighting each cepstral coefficient difference, i.e.,

$$d_w(x,A) = \frac{1}{N_A} \sum_{\tau=1}^{N_A} \sum_{k=1,2} [(c_k^x(\tau) - c_k^A(\tau))/\sigma_k^A(\tau)]^2$$

The time alignment path $\tau=1,\ldots N_A$ is now a function of the local cepstral variance, $[\sigma_k^A(\tau)]^2$.

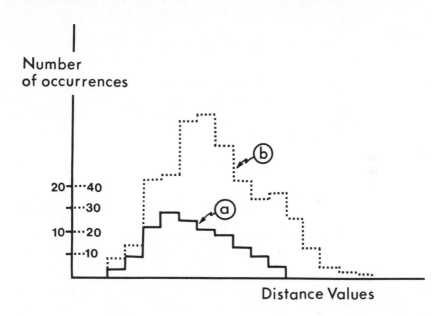

Figure 5. Histograms of computed inter-word distance values for
(a) words from the same category (different speakers),
(b) words from different categories (same or different speakers).

A fixed distance threshold allowed the correct assignment of all but 2 of the 48 tokens to the appropriate word class. The two confusions arose through incorrect assignment of one token of "slit" to "sit" and one token of "spit" to "spick". The same tokens were used to generate the template and to test them; therefore, this represents a biased test of discriminability. When I attempted to generate templates from fewer tokens, editing problems near the word edges, such as whether the release of the final stop was properly included, resulted in significantly poorer discrimination. Nevertheless, the dramatic difference underlines the necessity of including appropriate modeling of the significance of the encountered variation of the parameters.

One result of using the inverse of the parameter variance for the weighting function is to assign more significance to silent segments where the variance was actually zero (assigned a finite nominal value) than to the segments having finite energy. Since all our tokens began with the phoneme /s/, we could not explore the question of the relative weights to be assigned to fricatives and voiced sounds. Presumably, the relative cepstral distance among the class of unvoiced fricatives is larger than that among the vowels. Therefore one would want to tolerate larger differences in fricative regions than in vowel-like regions before rejecting a given hypothesis.

A further desirable property of a time-dependent weighting function appears to be the assignment of larger weights to regions of high spectral variation than to stationary regions. Otherwise, for steadystate segments the contributions to overall distance are proportional to the durations of the segments. Under those conditions vowel-differences would be overemphasized. No experimental results are as yet available on this point.

VI. DISCUSSION AND CONCLUSIONS

Synthesis represents an alternative technique for generating the reference templates. Klatt [16] and Cook [17] have proposed a word-verification procedure based on synthesis of the hypothesized word. Its use offers large potential savings in storage requirements at the costs of a small increment in processing requirements.

The prime motivation of using templates derived from actual productions at this point in time is the need to establish quantitatively the amount of speaker and context-dependent variation that verification techniques must provide for. While synthesis procedures generally give us a perceptually acceptable representative of the class to which the token may be assigned, they provide no information concerning the admissible variation in the individual parameters. As we gain more insight into the relative significance of short-time variations in speech spectra and achieve an ability to model the process adequately, synthesis will undoubtedly become a more cost-effective procedure for the generation of templates. Until that time, however, one must resort to the generation of templates from actual productions in the exploration of hypothesis verification techniques.

Our attempt to utilize insights from speech perception processes as an aid to improved speech verification techniques suffers from an inability to separate the peripheral and central processes in human speech perception. There remains a large gap in our knowledge concerning the transformations that the signal undergoes before the segmental information is extracted. We do not yet have an adequate model of the extent of acceptable variation among tokens that belong to a segmental equivalence class. Nevertheless, known properties of perception may be used to guide us toward perceptually relevant representations of the speech signal. We have some evidence that improved verification results are obtainable by focusing on those representations of the speech signal which have proven to be of interest for human speech perception.

ACKNOWLEDGMENTS

This work was supported in part by the Advanced Research Projects Agency, Department of Defense.

REFERENCES

1. Mermelstein, P., A Phonetic-Context Controlled Strategy for Segmentation and Phonetic Labeling of Speech, IEEE Trans. Acoustics, Speech and Signal Processing, *ASSP 23*, 79-82, 1975.
2. Miller, G. A. and P. T. Nicely, An Analysis of Perceptual Confusions Among Some English Consonants, J. Acoust. Soc. Am. *27*, 338-352, 1955.
3. Wickelgren, W. A., Distinctive features and errors in short-term Memory for English consonants, J. Acoust. Soc. Am., *39*, 388-398, 1966.
4. Shepard, R. N., Psychological Representation of Speech Sounds, in *Human Communication, A Unified View*, E. E. David, P. B. Denes editors, McGraw-Hill, N. Y., 67-113, 1972.
5. Pickett, J. M., Perception of Compound Consonants, Language and Speech, *1*, 288-304, 1958.
6. Nye, P. W., F. S. Cooper, and P. Mermelstein, Interactive experiments with a Digital Pattern Playback, J. Acoust. Soc. Am., *58S*, S105, 1975.
7. Sakoe, H. and S. Chiba, A Dynamic-programming Approach to Continuous Speech Recognition, Reports of the 7th Int. Congress on Acoustics, Budapest, 20-C-13, 65-68, 1971.
8. Klatt, D., A Digital Filter Bank for Spectral Matching, Conference Record, IEEE Int. Conference on Acoustics, Speech and Signal Processing, Philadelphia, 573-575, 1976.
9. Itakura, F., Minimum Prediction Residual Principle Applied to Speech Recognition, IEEE Trans. Acoustics, Speech and Signal Processing. *ASSP-23*, 67-72, 1975.
10. Gray, A. H., Jr., and J. D. Markel, COSH measure for speech processing, J. Acoust, Soc. Am., *58S*, S97, 1975.
11. White, G. M. and R. B. Neely, Speech Recognition Experiments with Linear Prediction, Bandpass Filtering and Dynamic Programming, IEEE Trans. Acoust. Speech and Signal Processing, ASSP-24, 173-188, 1975.
12. Velichko, V. M. and N. G. Zagaruyko, Automatic Recognition of 200 Words, Int. J. Man-Machine Studies, *2*, 223-234, 1970.

13. Atal, B. S., Effectiveness of linear prediction characteristics of the speech wave for automatic speaker identification and verification, J. Acoust. Soc. Am. *55*, 1304-1312, 1974.

14. Bridle, J. S., and M. D. Brown, An Experimental Automatic Word Recognition System, JSRU Report No. 1003, Joint Speech Research Unit, Ruislip, England, 1974.

15. Pols, L. C. W., Real-Time Recognition of Spoken Words, IEEE Trans. Computers, *20*, 972-978, 1971.

16. Klatt, D., Word Verification in a Speech Understanding System in *Speech Recognition* D. R. Reddy, ed., Academic Press, NY, 321-341, 1975.

17. Cook, C., Word Verification in a Speech Understanding System, Conference Record, IEEE Int. Conference on Acoustics, Speech and Signal Processing, Philadelphia, 553-556, 1976.

SYNTACTIC PATTERN RECOGNITION ON THE
BASIS OF FUNCTIONAL APPROXIMATION*

T. *Pavlidis*
Dept. of Electr. Engin. & Comp. Science
Princeton University
Princeton, N. J.

ABSTRACT

This paper discusses the use of syntactical analysis of polygonal approximations of contours. This allows the use of simpler
grammars than if one started with the raw data because most of the
noise is removed by nongrammatical means. The advantage of the approach is the simplicity of the grammars involved and its flexibility.

I. INTRODUCTION

Syntactic techniques have been used for shape recognition for
many years (for a review see [1]). Their best feature is that
they are able to produce "anthropomorphic" descriptions of the
data and therefore facilitate the development of recognition algorithms. This approach is best exemplified by the pioneering
works of Frischkopf and Harmon [2], Eden [3], Ledley [4] and more
recently of Fu [1,5,6]. Grenander [7,8] has developed a general
theory for pattern recognition based on the syntactical approach.
Two major problems in the application of such techniques to
real life data are the effects of noise and the need to develop
grammars of higher order than context free in order to take care
of global properties.
We have proposed in the past polygonal approximations as
means of eliminating the noise, while preserving local details [9-
11]. The choice of the error of approximation determines how
closely the approximation fits the original data. In the present
work we have concentrated on the external boundary and ignored the
shape of holes since this is not always a reliable feature. For
poorly written characters they are often either filled or "open".
The complete syntactic description often encounters problems
because it has to worry about closing boundaries etc. One way
around these difficulties is to process syntactically only up to
a certain level. An example of this approach can be found in the
work of Horowitz [11]. The starting symbols of the grammar were
PP(positive peak) and PN(negative peak). An initial string of
these symbols is assumed to be generated by nongrammatical means
or by a different grammar. The grammatical rules are then used

---

*   Research supported by NSF Grant ENG 72-04133.

for the generation of the final form of the waveform. Conversely
during parsing one proceeds only till he determines the occurence
of peaks. The final classification is not necessarily grammatical.
This approach is highly localized and therefore simple context free
or linear grammars can be used.

In this paper we describe such a parser for polygonal approximations of contours which has been implemented in the C language
under the UNIX operating system on a DEC PDP 11/45 machine [12,13].
Its output can be used for description and/or classification through
regular expressions using the UNIX software for the implementation.

The localization of boundary grammars can be seen by examining carefully some of the examples described by Swain and Fu [5]
and by Lee and Fu [6]. Thus the stochastic indexed grammars for
the production of the chromosome boundaries have four groups of
rules with the groups being very similar to each other. One might
choose only one group of rules and then put together the strings
generated by them by a nongrammatical algorithm.

II. THE BASIC PARSER

In the present approach we have used five starting symbols.
The convex boundary (0), the stroke (|), the corner (<), the convex
arc (^) and the concave arc (_). A stroke is defined as a long
protrusion from the boundary. For polygonal approximations it is
detected as a pair of sides which are close by and form a very
small angle or they are parallel. The corner is defined as a pair
of sides which are close by and form an angle less than 90 degrees
but greater than the size of the angle formed by the sides of the
stroke. Checking convexity of the whole boundary is trivial when
a polygonal approximation is available and it is done before any
other processing. During that check the first convex vertex after
a concave one is marked and used as the starting location for the
parsing of nonconvex boundaries.

The input to the parser is the description of the polygon
through the following attributes. The i(th) side is considered as
a vector forming an angle $a[i]$ with the horizontal, having length
$v[i]$ and ending at the i(th) vertex with coordinates $vx[i], vy[i]$.
The boundary is scanned in a clockwise direction. The i(th) vertex follows the i(th) side and it is characterized by the quantity
$c[i]=a[i+1]-a[i]$, the change in the direction of the sides at that
vertex. This is positive at concave vertices and negative at convex ones (Fig. 1). It is convenient to describe the polygon
through two strings in a manner somewhat similar to that used by
Horowitz for peak detection [11]. One string is that of the angles
$c[i]$, the *vertex string*. The other is that of the lengths $v[i]$,
the *side string*. It is easy to verify that the external perimeter
of the polygon can be reconstructed exactly from these two strings.

In the sequence we will refer to sharp or very sharp angles
and by this we will mean that $c[i]$ exceeds one given threshold or

another. Similarly we distinguish short lengths and long lengths of sides.

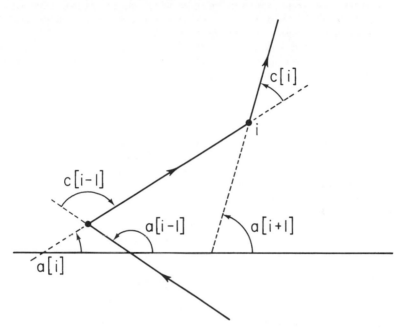

Figure 1. Illustration of the angle definitions given in the text.

The production rules for polygons are by necessity context sensitive since we want to avoid crossing lines, we want to have closed boundaries etc. However, the parsing problem is simplified if we assume that we see only strings which come from well-formed polygons. This is a reasonable assumption if all our inputs are from polygonal approximations of digitized contours. Therefore, we will not give a complete generative grammar but only local production rules. These apply to both strings but when a rule refers to only one of them, the effect on the other is arbitrary. Thus generation of a concave vertex implies that a side is also being generated but its length is arbitrary.

    STROKE ---> one sharp convex vertex.
    STROKE ---> two sides forming a very sharp corner which
                are either adjacent or with the sides in
                between having small total length.
    CORNER ---> one convex vertex less than 90 degrees which
                is not sharp.

391

```
CORNER ---> two sides forming a corner less than 90
             degrees, but not very sharp, which are
             either adjacent or with the sides in
             between having small total length.
CONVEX ---> one convex vertex and CONVEX.
CONVEX ---> one convex vertex.
CONCAVE --> one concave vertex with short first side and CONC2.
CONCAVE --> one concave vertex with long first side and CONC1.
CONCAVE --> one concave vertex.
CONC1 ----> one concave vertex with long first side and CONC3.
CONC1 ----> one concave vertex with short first side and CONC2.
CONC2 ----> one concave vertex and CONC2.
CONC2 ----> one concave vertex.
CONC3 ----> one concave vertex with a long first side.
```

A detailed description of an implementation of these rules is given elsewhere [14]. We may point out here a major difference between this and our earlier work [10]. There a sequence of concave vertices gave rise always to only one concave arc. Here a long side separates this into two concave arcs as shown in Figure 2a. Furthermore "sharp" convex vertices (or pairs thereof) introduce strokes or corners and thus produce a separation of convex arcs in the manner shown in Figure 2b. The present representation can be reduced to the earlier one by merging adjacent arcs. The detection of strokes is made in a simpler manner than that described by Feng and Pavlidis [15], although the ones detected in this way are only a subset of those detected by the more complex method.

The output of the parser is a sequence of nonterminals with their attributes. Each one of them is a string of six characters with the following meaning.

1: | for stroke, < for corner, ^ for convex arc, _ for concave arc.

2: A number 0-7 describing the orientation of the bisectrix of the arc. 0 stands for east, 1 for north-east, 2 for north etc. (see Figure 3).

3: s,t,r, or u depending on how sharp the angle (psi in Figure 2) formed by the first and last side of the arc is. However if the length of the arc is very large the angle information is ignored and the symbol U is used instead. In this case the arc direction is not always the same as the one expected intuitively since a long convex arc may spiral around.

4: l,h,c for low, high or center depending on the vertical location of the middle vertex (or two middle vertices) of the arc.

5: f,g,c for left, right or center depending on the horizontal location of the middle vertex (or two middle vertices) of the arc.

6: L or S depending on whether the arc length is long or short.

Convex boundaries result in a string of the form zn0 where z is | or ^ and n is the direction of the longest side using the notation defined in 2 above.

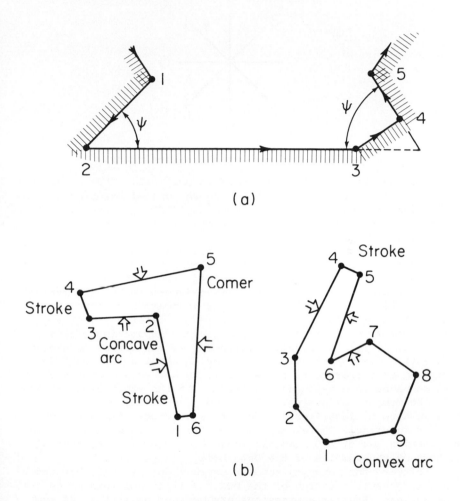

(a)

(b)

Figure 2.   Illustration of arcs defined by the parser.

III.   THE LINGUISTIC DESCRIPTION

The result of the previous parsing is to provide a linguistic description of the boundary in very much the manner discussed by Zadeh [16]. The assignment of the various descriptors is made through comparison of angles and lengths with thresholds and this introduces a possible discontinuity in the subsequent analysis. However this can be overcome by describing shape attributes not by a single descriptor value but by pairs of adjacent values, at least

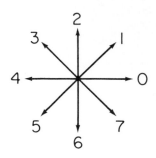

Figure 3.   Numbering of the orientations.

whenever the choice of the threshold is critical.   Thus we may describe an angle by r or s.   Table I shows typical examples of the
processing of handwritten numerals in the IEEE Data Base 1.2.2
which has been used previously for tests of pattern recognition
algorithms [10].

The entries of the table should be read in a cyclic way because we refer to representations of closed boundaries.   We shall
illustrate next an approach to classification through the detection of regular expressions.   One might expect to use grammatical
inference [1,17] to detect the regular grammars describing each
class.   However, classification requires to infer not just a grammar generating a class but rather a grammar *separating classes*.
This is a far more difficult problem and we are forced to use an
interactive design procedure.   One may think of a "typical" description of a character, translate it in a regular expression and
then use a pattern matching algorithm.   If the expression matches
only the members of a single class and does so for all of them
then we have a classifier.   In practice a number of iterations are
usually required.   The experiments described next were performed
on a design set of 370 numerals, one set of each of the first 37
authors of the samples of the Data Base.

Software for matching regular expressions is available under
the UNIX operating system of the DEC PDP 11/45 and this makes the
task easier.   Regular expressions are defined as strings of symbols with the following special provisions.   A dot (.) stands for
any symbol.   The star (*) denotes any number of repetitions of the
previous symbol, so that .* denotes any sequence.   The brackets([])
denote the union of the enclosed symbols.   Thus [abc] means anyone
of a,b or c.   Using this notation we may now give a description
for the numeral "2".   The string of a "2" contains:

"_[01].1"

it does not contain

"|1.h" or "|6.1"

Encodings of boundaries of "2"

|4shfS|0shqL_0slfS|0slqS<5slfL_5shqS
|4shfS^0shqS_0slfS|0slqS|4slfL_5shqS
|0slqL^5tlfL_5shfS|5shfS^1shqS_0slfS
|5shfS^1shqL_1tltS|0slqS_6ulcS<5tlfS^3ulfS_5shqS
|4shfS^1thqS_1tlcS^2rlqS<0tlqS<5slfL_5thqS
<3rhfL_0rlcS|7slqS_6rlfS<4slfS_3tcfS_5thfS
|5shfS<1shqL_1tlcS|0slqS<5tlfL_5shqS
|3rhcL_1tlfS|0slqL<5slfS_3ulfS_5thcS
|5shfS^1shqL_1tlfS|0slqS^4slfS_4shqS
|7slqS_6rlcS<5tlfS^3rlfS_3rlfS_5shcS<3rhfL_1rlqS
|4shfS^1shqS_0tlfS|0slqS<5tlfL_5shqS
^7rlqL_5thfS|4shfS^0thqS_1tlqS
<3uhqL_0tlfS<7slqS_5rlfS^4slfS_5shqS
|0slqS_6ulqS^4slfS_3tlfS_5thfS|5shfS^2thfS_1rlqS
|0slqS<5tlfL_5shqS|5shfS^1shqL_1tlfS

Encodings of boundaries of "5"

^4shfL|0shqS_0thfS^7slqS|4slfS_4slcS
^7slqS<3tlfS_4slfS^4thfL|1shqL_0thfS
^7tlqL|3tlfS_4slqS|4shfL|0shqS_0shfS
^4shfL|0saqS_7rhqS_1rcfS^0slqS|4slfS_4slcS
^4rhfS|1shqL_7rhfS^6slfL<3tlfS_3tlfS
^4shfL|0shqS_0shfS^0slqS|4slfS_4slfS
^4shfS|0shqS_7thfS^7tlcS|3slfS_3slfS_5rcfS
^7tlcS<5tlfS_4rlfS^3thfL|0shqL^6rhfS_7shfS
|2shqS^7rhqS_0shfS^1tcqS|5slqS_5tlqS^4shfS_3rhqS
^4thfS<1thcS_1rhcS|0shqL_7rhfS^6slfS<3tlfS_3slfS
^5rcfS<3thfS_2uhfS|0shqS_7thfS^7slqL|3slfS_3slfS
^4shfS|0shqS_7thfS^7slqS|3slfS_3slcS
^5tlfS<3thfS_2uhfS|0shqS_7thfS^7slqS|4slfS_4slfS
<4shfL|0shqS_0shfS^7slqS|3slfS_4slcS
^4thfS<0shqS_7thqS^5ulfL_3slfS
<5tlfS^3rhfS|0shqS_0shfS^7tlfS<3tlfS_4slcS

Table I

and it contains at least one of the following expressions:

$$|[701].1[gc]$$

or

$$\_[45].h \quad \text{and not } |4.1$$

This can be verbalized as following:

"A concave arc facing E or NE at the lower part and no strokes pointing NE at the upper part or pointing South at the lower part. Also one of the following: A stroke pointing SE to NE at the lower part and not in the left part. Or a concave arc facing West to SW at the upper part and no stroke pointing West at the lower part."

Note that most samples contain both of the two alternate features even though either one is sufficient for description. It is this redundancy which allows recognition of greatly distorted figures.

The string of a "5" contains:

$$[^<|][345].1.._[2345].[1c]$$

it does not contain

$$[^<|]..hg.*|[01]shg$$

and it contains at least one of the following:

$$[<|]0shg.*\_[07]$$

or

$$\_[701].hf$$

This can be verbalized as following:

"A convex arc (possibly a stroke or a corner) pointing SW to NW at the lower part immediately followed by a concave arc facing SW to N and not located in the upper part. It does not contain a stroke and a convex arc both in the upper right part and it contains at least one of the following: A stroke or a corner pointing East and located at the higher part and to the right followed by a concave arc facing East or SE. Or, a concave arc pointing NE and located at the higher left part."

It is obvious that we have reached descriptions of the numerals which are similar to those that a person might give if he is asked for a generic description of a "2" or a "5".

In the design set 35 out of 37 "2"s and 36 out of 37 "5"s were characterized in this way. No other character matched these descriptions.

IV. CONCLUSIONS

The examples of the previous section show that the local syntactic analysis can detect features useful for both pattern recognition and description in linguistic or even fuzzy terms. The methodology should be applicable not only on the polygonal approximations derived by the split-and-merge algorithm [9] but also on the results of other polygonal or functional approximations [18-21].

One major advantage of the hierarchical approach is its flexibility. If one wants to treat different problems he has to do modifications only at the higher level. Thus one must derive different regular expressions for the description of alphabetic characters but he does not need modify the basic parser or the polygonal approximation routines. Such flexibility is not present in an integrated approach [22].

The current multicomputer implementation can be translated as following for an eventual "on-line" application: The boundary tracing and approximation are performed by special purpose digital hardware. Since these steps are common to a wide variety of applications the development of such a device may be economically feasible. Since these processes are also far more time consuming than the rest, it is the logical point to use hardware implementation. The parser can also be implemented in hardware or at least in assembly language. The descriptor - classifier which is the one which depends more heavily on the specific application can be implemented in a high level language.

V. ACKNOWLEDGMENTS

This research was supported by NSF grant ENG72-04133 of the Control and Automation Program of the Engineering Division. Its completion would have been impossible without the use of the interactive computing facilities of the Dept. of Electr. Engineering and Computer Science. In particular it made extensive use of the graphics and a link between the DEC 11/45 and IBM 360-91 machines developed by P.A.Eichenberger.

VI. REFERENCES

1. Fu, K. S., *Syntactic Methods in Pattern Recognition*, Academic Press, 1974.
2. Frischkopf, L. S. and L. D. Harmon, "Machine Reading of Cursive Script", *Proceedings of the Symposium on Information Theory*, (C. Cherry, editor) Butterworth, 1961, pp. 300-316.
3. Eden, M., "Handwriting and Pattern Recognition", *IRE Trans. Inform. Theory*, vol. IT-8(1962), pp. 160-166.
4. Ledley, R. S., "High Speed Automatic Analysis of Biomedical Pictures", *Science*, vol. 146 (Oct. 1964) pp. 216-223.

5. Swain, P. H. and K. S. Fu, "Stochastic Programmed Grammars
    for Syntactic Pattern Recognition", *Pattern Recognition,*
    vol. 4 (1972) pp. 83-100.
6. Lee, H. C. and K. S. Fu, "A Stochastic Syntax Analysis Pro-
    cedure and its Application to Pattern Classification", *IEEE
    Trans. on Computers,* vol. C-21 (1972) pp. 660-666.
7. Grenander, U., "Foundations of Pattern Analysis", *Quarterly
    of Applied Mathematics,* vol. 27, 1969, pp. 1-55.
8. Grenander, U., *Pattern Recognition,* Springer-Verlag, 1976.
9. Pavlidis, T. and S. L. Horowitz, "Segmentation of Plane Curves",
    IEEE Transactions Computers, vol. C-23, (Aug. 1974) pp. 860-
    870.
10. Pavlidis, T. and F. Ali "Computer Recognition of Handwritten
    Numerals by Polygonal Approximations", *IEEE Trans. Systems,
    Man, Cybernetics,* vol. SMC-5, (Nov. 1975) pp. 610-614.
11. Horowitz, S. L., "A General Peak Detection Algorithm with Ap-
    plications in the Computer Analysis of Electrocardiograms",
    Com. ACM vol. 18 (May 1975) pp. 281-285.
12. Richie, D. M., "C Reference Manual", *Tech. Report,* Bell Tele-
    phone Laboratories, Jan. 1974.
13. Thomson, K. and D. M. Richie, "UNIX Programmer's Mannual",
    Tech. Report, Bell Telephone Laboratories, Sixth edition,
    May 1975.
14. Pavlidis, T., "Syntactic Feature Extraction for Shape Recog-
    nition", *Tech. report No. 213,* (April 1976) Computer Science
    Laboratory, Princeton University.
15. Feng, H. Y. and T. Pavlidis, "Decomposition of Polygons into
    Simpler Components: Feature Extraction for Syntactic Pattern
    Recognition", *IEEE Trans. on Computers,* vol. C-24 (June 1975)
    pp. 636-650.
16. Zadeh, L. A., "The Concept of a Linguistic Variable and its
    Application to Approximate Reasoning", *Information Sciences.*
17. Fu, K. S. and T. L. Booth, "Grammatical Inference: Introduc-
    tion and Survey", *IEEE Trans. on Systems, Man and Cybernetics.*
    vol. SMC-5(1975), pp. 95-111(Part I) & pp. 409-423(Part II).
18. Sklansky, J., R. L. Chazin and B. J. Hansen, "Minimum-Perime-
    ter Polygons of Digitized Silhouettes", *IEEE Trans. on Com-
    puters,* vol. C-21 (1972), pp. 260-268.
19. McClure, D. E., "Nonlinear Segmented Function Approximation
    and Analysis of Line Patterns", *Quarterly of Applied Mathe-
    matics,* vol. 33 (April 1975) pp. 1-37.
20. Davis, L. S., "Understanding Shape I: Angles and Sides",
    TR-376, Univ. of Maryland, Computer Science Department (May,
    1975).
21. Cooper, D. B. and N. Yalabik, "On the Cost of Approximating
    and Recognizing a Noise Perturbed Straight Line or a Quadratic
    Curve Segment in the Plane", *Tech. Report,* Brown Univ. March
    1975.
22. Stockman, G. C., L. N. Kanal and M.C. Kyle "Design of a Wave-
    form Parsing System", *Proceedings First International Joint
    Conference on Pattern Recognition* (Oct.1973) pp.236-243.

A PROGRAM FOR LEARNING
TO PLAY CHESS

Jacques Pitrat
C.N.R.S.
Paris, France

I. INTRODUCTION

1.1. Game playing learning programs.

1.1.1 - What are they learning? A learning program can
learn many different things. It can first learn to find directly
the move which it has to play. The program developed by Waterman
[6] learns to play poker. It acquires a set of rules, each of
them indicates that, if certain conditions are fulfilled in the
real situation, the program must take the corresponding decision.
This is good for games where there are few possible moves and
where it is unnecessary to develop a tree. But for games like
chess, it seems necessary to generate a tree and it is not possible to use the former, simpler method. The program generates a
tree and learns only some of the procedures which are used for
finding out from this tree what move it will play.

A possibility is to learn the function necessary to evaluate
a board. This function is used for giving values to the leaves of
the tree; these values are backed up from the evaluated board positions through the tree. Carrying the minimax procedure back to
the root results in the selection of a move. Samuel [4] uses such
a method for checkers. The program learns the values of the coefficients of the linear polynomial which scores the board positions.
The parameters of this polynomial are not learned; they are given
by the author.

But the main problem for realizing a game playing program is
not to find this evaluation function. It is to control the growth
of the tree. Experiments made by de Groot [1] on human chess play-
ers show that one of the most important reasons for the strength
of the grandmaster is not that he generates larger trees, but that
he chooses very well the moves that he considers at every level in
the tree. Chess playing programs are very inefficient in that way:
they cannot accurately judge the value of the moves, so they consider too many moves. Although computers are faster than the human brain, they cannot go as deep as a grandmaster in the tree.
It would be interesting to have a program learning to choose the
moves which have to be considered in the tree.

The first approach is to learn a function scoring the moves
(instead of the boards). If the program has such a function, it
generates all the legal moves, evaluates them and keeps the best
ones. It would be possible to learn this function with methods
similar to those developed by Samuel [4]. The program must gener-

ate all the moves, something which is not necessary for a human player. Also experience shows that it is difficult to define, even without learning, a function which gives good results.

Another approach is that the program learns procedures which investigate if a certain characteristic is present on the board. If so, the procedure indicates that some set of moves has to be considered. An example of such a procedure could be: "If the enemy king and an enemy knight are on the same file or on the same rank, if there is no man on the squares between them, generate all the moves where a friendly rook can move to this line". We wrote a learning program to find such procedures. Learning is used only for improving the choice of the branches of the tree. When the tree has been developed, the choice of the move played by the program is made by classical methods, with the minimax procedure. The function scoring the boards is not learned. In the present experiment, this function was only the balance of the captures, but it would be possible to use any other function.

1.1.2 - What is used for learning? It is possible to learn with a teacher. For instance, Samuel [4][5] gave two examples of this: in one of them the program assumed that his opponent was playing well, in the other that the move given in a book was the best one. It is also possible to learn without a teacher. Waterman [6] studied this. His method was based on the fact that, when a game of poker is completed, in some cases we can see the opponent's cards. Then it is easy to find what we could have played for winning more or losing less. This information was used for learning. But at chess where each player has the total game information available, it is not easy to know what is the best move, that is just what the program has to learn. So, it is more difficult to define a piece of information which can be found by the program. The result of the game: win, loss, draw occurs once in a game and if only this information was used, the learning would be very slow. In our case, the program will detect combinations in real games. It finds a combination when a player has, for some subset of moves, a positive balance of the captures. The program uses the usual piece values: Pawn = 100, Knight = Bishop = 300... We could also define positional advantages like the opening of a file, and the program could detect combinations for getting such advantages; but this has not been implemented. The program receives real games. This is not essential, and it would be possible for the program to learn from games played against itself. But the learning would be slower.

When the program detects a combination winning a material advantage in a game, it tries to understand the reasons for the success of this combination and, if it succeeds, generates a procedure generalizing this combination. We could think that there are not many combinations in a game. This is not true. Let us take an example. It is frequent to have exchanges in a game. Suppose that four moves in sequence M1, M2, M3, M4 are capture moves, and that the value of the men captured in moves M1 and M2 are the same, and

that the captures M3 and M4 have the same value. The program can
find two possible combinations. The first one begins at move M2.
After the first capture, the second player has a real combination
where he wins the value of the man captured in move M2. The second combination includes moves M1, M2, M3. If we had exactly the
same situation, but without the man which moves in M4, we would
have a combination. In this particular game, it does not succeed,
but it would succeed in another position.

Let us give an example, with an imaginary position (Figure 1).
Let us suppose that the following moves were played:

Nf2xg4[1]   Nf6xg4

Qa1xh8   Qc7xa5

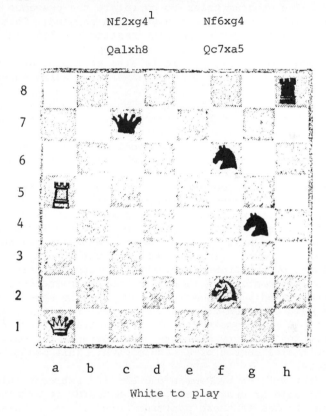

White to play

Figure 1

The balance of the captures is zero. But after the first
move: Nf2xg4, there is a combination for Black, where they win a
knight. The idea is that a pinned man can capture if the pinning
piece has also to protect one of his men which is attacked. The
program would generate a procedure, not so general, but advising
the consideration of such moves if the situation is of this type.

But we could have the same board without a queen on c7. Then
there would be a combination for White. The corresponding proce-

dure would mean that if the opponent has a pinned man M, we can try to capture the men protected by M. When the program uses this method, it can find several procedures in one game. As we will see later, it is even possible to learn procedures from parts of the game where there are no capture moves, but only threats. If the program was also able to detect a positional advantage, it would also learn procedures which may eventually win this advantage.

1.1.3 - How can a program learn? The first idea is a statistical method. The program tries to correlate the presence of a characteristic with the fact that a position is good. This method, used by Samuel [4], has given some interesting results; but we do not always have 100 000 positions or the computer time needed for these statistical computations. It is also evident that, in some cases, human beings can learn from an experience which occurs only once.

The second idea is rote learning. When the program receives a position, it keeps some data on this position; it uses these data if it has to consider exactly the same position again later. Unfortunately there are many possible positions for games like chess; it is unlikely to have the same board several times, except for openings and endgames.

An improvement is to generalize the situations. It is easy to generalize if the situations are described by continuous parameters. If a decision was good for a situation, it is likely that the same decision is also good for all the situations for which the parameters have almost the same value. Waterman [6] succeeded with this idea for poker. In this game the parameters are continuous (measure of the probability that the opponent can be bluffed) or almost continuous (amount of money in the pot, value of the program's hand). We nearly always take the same decision if we have a pair of nines or a pair of tens. But it is different for chess; it is necessary to play completely different moves in positions which are very similar: for instance the only difference could be the placement of a single pawn. This method does not apply there.

The program written by Newman and Uhr [2] extracts interesting patterns (desirable or undesirable) from a board; it examines the new situations to see if these patterns occur or not. This method is well suited to games like tic-tac-toe or go bang, but is difficult to adapt to chess: there are too many such patterns and the relationships between men are logical rather than geometric.

Our program learns from one example. It tries first to understand the reasons for the success of a combination. A program has understood a combination if it has generated a tree beginning with the first move of the combination so that the minimax procedure gives a positive value. If it succeeds, it generalizes the tree and generates a procedure: if certain characteristics are present in a position, consider certain moves.

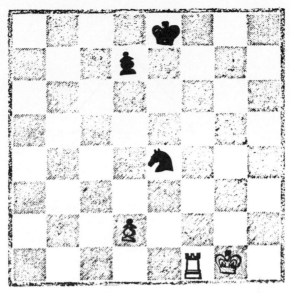

White to play

Figure 2

Let us quickly look at an example of how the program works. We suppose that the following moves have been played in a real game, starting from Figure 2.

Rf1-e1   d7-d5

d2-d3   Ke8-f8

d3xe4

For the first move, the program generates the tree of Figure 3; Ø stands for a no-move. We do not indicate the move d7-d5 at this stage, because it could be possible that in other positions there would be no pawn on d7. In that case, this combination would succeed immediately, which was not the case for Figure 2. Next this tree is generalized, and finally we will have the following procedure: if the enemy king and an enemy piece P are on the same rank or the same file, and if there is no man between the king and P, let S_i be an empty square, the opposite side of P to the king, such as there is no man between P and S_i; then the program must consider (but not always play) the moves where a friendly rook can move to S_i.

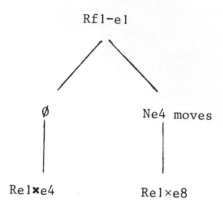

Figure 3

1.2. The plans.

In fact, the program does not learn which moves, but which plans it has to consider. Plans are sequences of moves. For the preceding example, the end of the procedure would become: then the program must consider the moves where a friendly rook can move to S_i. If then the enemy piece P moves, rook takes king. If P does not move, consider: rook on S_i takes P.

We have developed another program where the combinations were found by use of such plans. Using plans has several advantages:

- positions other than the initial one are quickly analyzed. If the opponent plays one of the foreseen moves, we have at once a good reply, and no analysis is performed.

- if a plan fails, we can improve it. We analyze why it fails and generate a new plan with a first part correcting what is wrong.

With this method, the program considers very few moves: only the moves which it is natural to consider. If the initial plans fail, they are modified, and other moves will become natural. For instance sacrificing a piece for removing some disturbing enemy man. But it is unnatural to consider a priori all the possible sacrifices. The program is limited to considering a few moves at each level of the tree, and however it has generally among them the best moves. So it can find combinations where it is necessary to develop a tree to a depth of 20 ply. As the learning program was written before the program using the plans efficiently, the program described here does not fully use this possibility. It would be possible to use the learning program for finding which plans have to be considered by the second program. The use of plans, by the part of the learning program which develops a tree to try to understand a combination, is far from optimal.

II. DESCRIPTION OF THE PROGRAM

The program was written in FORTRAN for CDC 3600. Some possibilities of list processing had been added to FORTRAN. Particularly, there is a garbage collector. We will see:

- how the program understands the reasoning of a combination in building a tree.

- how the program generalizes a combination.

- how the program generates a procedure which indicates that, if some characteristics occur on a board, such a plan must be considered.

For understanding a move, the program uses the procedures already learned. It is essential for understanding the examples to know what procedures have already been learned. For the sake of simplicity, we suppose that it has learned only two procedures:

- if there are capture moves, consider them.

- if a man is threatened, consider the moves which involve moving the man.

We call TREE (Position, Player), the function which generates a tree for Player to play in Position. For this it uses the procedures already learned, in our case the two preceding procedures at the beginning. This function will be described in 2.4. Its value is the tree. If we use this function in a tree, we do not specify the Position: it is the position immediately after the move before.

Let C the move of the given game which the program tries to understand. Then D is the enemy move following C, B the enemy move played just before C and A the friendly move played before B. So we have the succession of moves: A - B - C - D, A and C being friendly moves and the program tries to understand move C.

2.1. Understanding a combination.

The program has understood a combination, beginning with move C (or how to parry a threat with move C), if it has developed a tree with move C at his root and such that the minimax procedure gives a satisfactory value. For developing the tree, the program uses the procedures already learned.

We say that an enemy man is "unnecessary" if it is not necessary to the combination to capture this man. For instance in Figure 2, the pawn on d7 is unnecessary; but the king and the knight are necessary. If there were no pawn on d7, there would still be a combination. In the tree beginning with move C, the program erases the moves played by one unnecessary man of the player who does not play at the first level of the tree.

There are three main cases:

2.1.1 - C is a capture move. Let P be the position of the board just before move A (the friendly move played just before C). The program examines if C is a legal move in position P. If it is, the program generates a tree with two branches at the first level. The first branch leads to move C, followed by the tree generated by the program which supposes that the opponent has to play: TREE (Opponent). The other branch leads to move A followed by TREE (Opponent) and by the enemy move B actually played in the game after A. After B, there is the friendly move C, then the result of the function TREE (Opponent) which is applied to the position after move C has been played (see Figure 4). Let us give an example (Figure 5). The following moves were played in the game:

A   Bb5xc6   B   d7xc6

C   Nf3xe5

The Figure 5 gives the situation before move A. We try to understand move C.

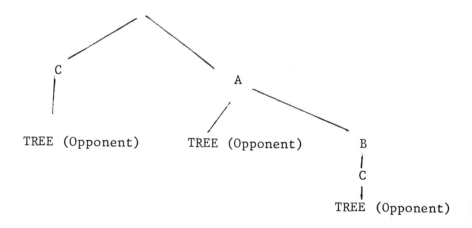

Figure 4

White to play

Figure 5

We will have the tree of Figure 6. In reality there will be more capture moves, but we will see later that the simplifying sub-routine erases them. This tree will be used for generating a procedure which indicates: if we want to capture a man protected by a knight, try first to exchange the knight, then capture the man.

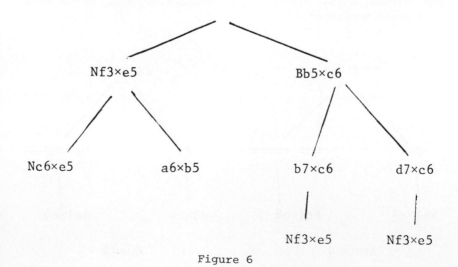

Figure 6

2.1.2 - C is a threat. The program tries to see if C is a threatening move. For this it generates the tree of Figure 7. If, after erasing enemy moves played by an unnecessary man, the minimax procedure gives a satisfactory result, the program considers that there is an interesting threat.

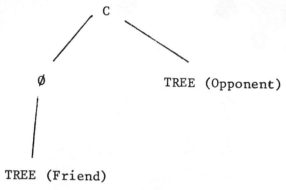

Figure 7

When the program tries to understand the move Rf1-e1 played in the position given Figure 2, it generates the tree of Figure 8. When, after Rf1-e1, d7-d5, it studies d2-d3, it generates the tree of Figure 9. Re1xe4 and Re1xe8 are generated because they are capture moves. Ne4 moves, because, as the knight is threatened, we must consider moving it. If we know also that we can save a threatened man by protecting it, we would still have the tree of Figure 8. The move d7-d5 would be generated after Rf1-e1, and, after Re1xe4, d5xe4. But d7 is an unnecessary man, so the move d7-d5 would be erased.

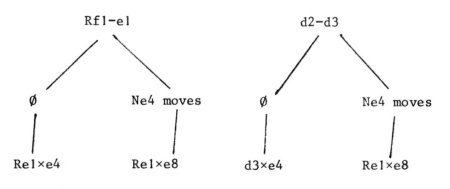

Figure 8   Figure 9

If the minimax procedure gives a satisfactory result when applied to this tree, the tree is kept to try to find a new procedure. With this method, the program may find a procedure when, in the real game, the threat fails. This happens with Rf1-e1 in Figure 2 which does not succeed immediately.

2.1.3 - C parries a threat. If a player has tried to parry a threat, the program tries to understand his method. Let D be the move played after the threatening move C. The program generates the tree of Figure 10. If the minimax procedure applied to this tree does not give an unsatisfactory value for the player who played D, the program supposes that it has understood a way of destryoing the threat and it keeps the tree. This is done after removing after D the moves where unnecessary man of the threatening player moved.

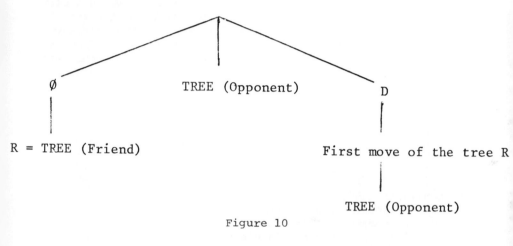

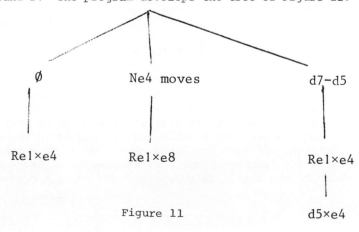

Figure 10

For Figure 2, if C is Rf1-e1, D is d7-d5. Let us try to understand D. The program develops the tree of Figure 11.

Figure 11

With these methods, the program can find, from the five moves given with Figure 2, three procedures which are after generalization:

- if the enemy king and an enemy piece are on the same rank or file move a rook to a square of this line, on the opposite side of the piece to the king.

- if an enemy piece is pinned, attack it with a pawn.

- if a knight is threatened and pinned by a rook or a queen, protect it with a pawn.

2.2 Simplification and generalization of trees.

The same position is unlikely to occur twice. We must eliminate what is not essential: then it is possible for the useful part of this position to recur several times. We have already seen that we remove the moves played by unnecessary men from the trees. This simplifies the tree and is equivalent to generalization by removing men from the board. More generally, the program acts as if none of the men which do not occur in a move of the tree exist. This is a first generalization which is very powerful. But there are other simplifications and generalizations.

2.2.1 - Simplifications. The program keeps only the best friendly move in the trees generated by the function TREE (friendly refers to the player at the first level of the tree). For instance in Figure 11, after d7-d5, Relxe4 gives a check. The program considers Ke8-f8 to avoid this threat. But the value of this move is not so good as that of d5xe4, so the move Ke8xf8 is removed. We remove also the enemy moves which do not give a satisfactory value. For instance in Figure 9, after d3xe4, the move d5xe4 is removed because Black has already lost a knight and it is not sufficient to win a pawn.

Another method is to keep, among the terminal nodes of the trees, only the capture moves. The other moves are only kept if they create a move further down the subtree or if they destroy an enemy move elsewhere in the tree. We say that a move creates another move if it creates one of the conditions necessary for this move. For instance in Figure 8: Rfl-el creates Relxe4 and Relxe8. On the same way "Ne4 moves" creates Relxe8. A move destroys another move if it destroys at least one of the conditions necessary for this move. Still in Figure 8, "Ne4 moves" destroys Relxe4. We see that we have to keep all the moves of Figure 8. This is useful for removing moves which are played in the middle of a combination, but have nothing directly to do with this combination. If the opponent plays a check move or an exchange in another area of the board, this move and our reply are erased.

2.2.2 - Generalization.

1. On the player. The player is called friend, and his opponent: enemy. Further, when the program examines a position, the player is called friend.

2. On the squares. The program replaces the designations of the squares by variables. If there is, for a move of the tree, a condition on a square which is used elsewhere on the tree, the symbol for this square is also kept with the move. For instance in Figure 12 the tree on the left becomes the tree on the right. Relxe8 becomes Rb-cxd, c representing the square e4, because the move Relxe4 uses also the square e4. But we do not specify the squares e2, e3, e5, e6, e7 which must be empty for the move Relx e8, but are not used as departure or arrival squares of other moves. This generalization includes translations and rotations, if they are possible, but also many other transformations.

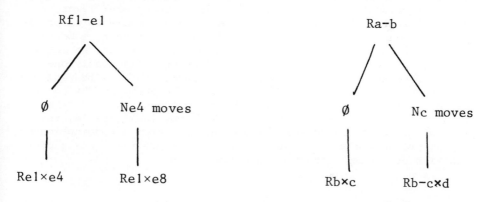

Figure 12

3. If a man of type T plays only in one move (this move may occur several times), if this man is not captured and if there is no condition on an intermediary square in this move (after generalization), the program estimates that the type of this man has no interest and it is erased. Only the side (enemy or friend) is kept. We write F for friend and E for enemy without indicating the type of man. For instance in Figure 1, we would have, if we want to understand Qc7xa5, the tree of Figure 13 which begins after White has played Nf2xg4. We must retain the fact that there is a queen on a1: there are two moves for her, Qa1xa5 and Qa1xh8. We must also retain the fact that there is a queen on c7: she plays Qc7xa5 and then is captured by Qa1xa5. But the knight on f6 is used only once for capturing the knight on g4. The combination would also be good if we replace this knight by any other man.

This is naturally possible only when the names of the squares are replaced by letters: only a knight can move from f6 to g4, but any piece can go from a to b. We have learned a procedure for a pinned man instead of just a procedure for a pinned knight.

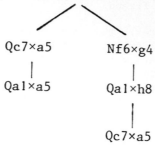

$$
\begin{array}{cc}
\text{Qc7}{\times}\text{a5} & \text{Nf6}{\times}\text{g4} \\
| & | \\
\text{Qa1}{\times}\text{a5} & \text{Qa1}{\times}\text{h8} \\
& | \\
& \text{Qc7}{\times}\text{a5}
\end{array}
$$

Figure 13

4. If a man plays only one move and if this man is captured (in one or several moves), we replace its designation by that of a man of value greater or equal if it is an enemy man; lower or equal if it is a friendly one. The minimax procedure which previously gave a satisfactory value would give, after that, a better one. From the tree on the left-hand side of Figure 14, we obtain the tree at the right. The friendly queen on b plays only one move: Qb×d and then she is captured in Pe×d. She may be replaced by a rook, a bishop, a knight or a pawn. The enemy knight on c may be replaced by a bishop, a rook or the queen. We indicate this by $\leq$Q or by $\geq$ N in the trees. We give, in Figure 14, the initial state of the squares in both cases. From a combination on a pawn protecting a bishop and a knight, the program finds a combination on a pawn protecting any two pieces.

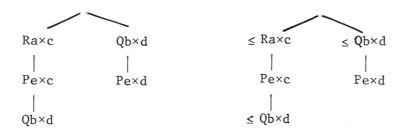

$$
\begin{array}{cccc}
\text{Ra}{\times}\text{c} & \text{Qb}{\times}\text{d} & \leq \text{Ra}{\times}\text{c} & \leq \text{Qb}{\times}\text{d} \\
| & | & | & | \\
\text{Pe}{\times}\text{c} & \text{Pe}{\times}\text{d} & \text{Pe}{\times}\text{c} & \text{Pe}{\times}\text{d} \\
| & & | & \\
\text{Qb}{\times}\text{d} & & \leq \text{Qb}{\times}\text{d} &
\end{array}
$$

Initial situation of squares.

a. Friendly rook   a. Friendly rook,bishop,knight or pawn

b. Friendly queen   b. Friendly queen,rook,bishop,knight or pawn

c. Enemy knight   c. Enemy knight,bishop,rook or queen

d. Enemy bishop   d. Enemy knight,bishop,rook or queen

Figure 14

5. If the move at the first level of the tree is a capture, the program examines whether or not the minimax procedure would still give a satisfactory result if there were no capture at this level. If so, the square occupied by this enemy man is considered as being empty. This capture is not necessary.

2.3. Generation of procedures.

A procedure consists of three parts.

- the name of some squares with their state at the beginning of the combination. The names are variables. (Their state may be: friend, enemy, empty, enemy queen, friendly man of value less or equal to the value of the rook ...). This is useful for finding in a given situation, where we apply the procedure, what squares may be given as values for each variable.

- a numbered set of generalized moves. In a generalized move, we have the name of the man which moves, a variable designating the departure square, possibly some variables for intermediary squares, and a variable for the arrival square.

e.g. EB a-b   an enemy bishop moves from a to b.

FR c-d×e the friendly rook on c captures on e. There
is at least one intermediary square d.

$\overset{>}{-}$ER f×g   an enemy rook, queen or king on f captures on
g.

We will see later why it is important to put the moves in order.

- a tree which indicates the plan that the program has to consider, if we can find values for the variables such that all the generalized moves become legal moves. In the nodes of the tree there are numbers, and we put in their places the move which has the same number.

2.3.1 - Use of a procedure. Before showing how procedures are generated, we will see how the program uses them. We take the procedure of Figure 15 (which is in fact generated by the program when it understands the first move of Figure 2). We apply this procedure to the imaginary position of Figure 16.
The program looks first if the first move: FR a-b×c is possible on the board. In the initial situation a is empty, b is occupied by an enemy piece and c is occupied by the enemy king. So the program knows that c is h2 and b is h1, c2 or g5. As the move is played by a rook, g5 is erased. a is an empty square on the opposite side of the white piece to the king. If b is h1,

413

Initial state of squares   Moves   Tree

a : empty

b : enemy ≥ knight

c : enemy king

d : friendly rook

1. FR a-b×c

2. E ≥ N a moves

3. FR a×b

4. FR d-a

```
          4
         / \
        ∅   2
        |   |
        3   1
```

Example of a procedure

Figure 15

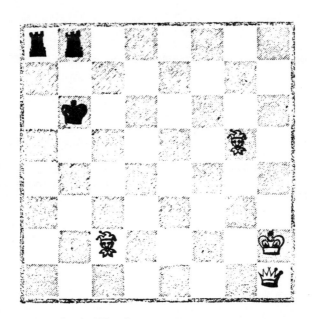

Black to play

Figure 16

414

there is no such square. So h1 is also erased and we get c=h2 and
b=c2. a may be b2 or a2. So there are two possible legal moves
for the first generalized move. Let us take first a=b2. There is
no problem for the second and third move. For the fourth one, we
must find d. d is occupied by a friendly rook: d=a8 or b8. But
Ra8-b2 and Rb8-b2 are not legal (b6 is not empty for the second
move). So there is a failure and we try a=a2. Rb8-a2 is not legal, but Ra8-a2 is. We have defined the four moves and we get the
tree of Figure 17.

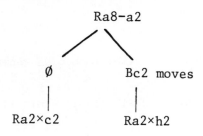

Figure 17

We can notice that the generalization is not sufficient for
finding the combination beginning with Rb8-h8. We see also that
it is important to put the generalized moves in order. If we began with Rd-a, there would be 14 possible couples (d,a) on this
board. For most of them, we would see later that we cannot find
values for b and c.

2.3.2 - Ordering the moves. The idea is to find which moves
are the most unlikely. We give each square, occuring in a generalized move, a value which is a function of its occupation in the
initial situation, used for locating the squares. Two functions
will be used, I and J. We take the following values for the function I (square):

square already known	1
empty square	32
square occupied by a king, a queen	1
square occupied by a rook, a bishop, a knight	2
square occupied by a pawn	8
square occupied by a rook or the queen or the king	4
square occupied by a piece	8

....

415

For the function J(man), we have:

Pawn   2

Knight 6

Bishop 8

Rook   10

Queen   15

King   6

The evaluation of the likelihood of a generalized move on some board is:

$$\min_{i} [I(a_i) \times J(P) , I(a_i) * \min_{j \neq i} I(a_j)]$$

a_i are the squares occuring in the generalized move and P is the man which moves.

e.g. With the initial values of the squares given in Figure 15, we have:

Ra-b×c   8   8 for I(b) and 1 for I(c)

Ra×b   80   10 for J(R) and 8 for I(b)

Rd-a   20   2 for I(d) and 10 for J(R)

So the first move of the procedure will be Ra-b×c. When a move has been chosen, we suppose that all the squares which occur in it are known and the program re-calculates all the values. In this case the new value of Ra×b will be 1 (a and b are known) and that of Rd-a will be 2 (1 for I (a) and 2 for I (d)). So Ra×b will be considered before Rd-a, although in the first computation the order was the inverse.

This method was used because a move may be defined by two squares, or by a square and the type of the man moving. This last possibility is mainly useful for pawn moves, because a pawn has few possible moves. The best order of moves is not always found, the definition of functions I and J is approximate, but it does not give a bad order.

The program numbers the moves as soon as it chooses them. It does this for all the moves of the tree. When it has chosen a move, it replaces it in the tree by its number. When all the moves have been chosen, the tree is the third part of the procedure. When we use this method with the tree of Figure 12, we get the procedure of Figure 15.

2.4. Use of procedures.

The function TREE (Position, Player) generates a tree for the Player in the Position given. For this it uses the procedures already found. This is useful for learning when the program generates the tree used for understanding a combination. It is also useful when the learning is completed; if we want the program to play a move, it calls the function TREE and it applies the minimax procedure to the generated tree.

The function TREE begins with the initial position and looks at what procedures may be applied. This gives a set of trees which are merged. The program applies minimax to this composite tree. If the value is not positive, there is no combination and the output of the function is the empty tree. If it is positive, the program uses the procedures which parry threats for the opponent. If it succeeds the new subtrees are added, and the function TREE is applied to the intermediary positions which are unfavourable for the player.

We do not develop the description of the method, because we improve it later in a program finding combinations without learning. Such as it is described, the method is too rough to give good results, and the trees grow too fast once the program has found many procedures. It is not a problem of learning, and the difficulties encountered here show that we must first write an efficient program without learning before we can write a learning program.

Some other details on the program, such as the method used for storing the procedures are given in Pitrat [3].

III. RESULTS AND CONCLUSION

Several combinations were given to the program, it also studied the beginning of a game. For every example, it found several procedures which were useful. But it would be possible to improve this learning method in the following ways:

- it is difficult to eliminate superfluous moves from a combination. It may be that these moves use squares also used for moves in the combination. In which case the program does not see that these moves are diversions and retains them. The procedure has too many moves and it is unlikely to be applicable later on. It is necessary to improve the mechanism which simplifies the tree.

- when the program executes a procedure, it looks for the existence of moves, but not for the absence of moves. It would be better to have this capability in order to decrease the number of times that the procedure can be applied, and consequently the width of the tree. A solution would be to examine what happens when a procedure has given a plan which does not succeed. The program would search for an enemy move which prevents success. It would generalize it and add it to the procedure, indicating that it is useless to try the plan if the move is legal. With this improvement, the program could find that it must avoid capturing a protected rook with a queen: consider Qa×b provided the opponent cannot reply c×b.

None of these improvements have been implemented because the main problem was not the learning method, which seems good, but how to use the plans found by the program using the procedures discovered by the learning program. The real problem was to write a good chess program for finding combinations, and for that reason, we later developed such a program.

The program learned from games which were given to it. But it would be also possible to learn without these games: the program could play against itself and learn from these games. We would then have learning without teacher. But this learning would be slower because interesting possibilities of combination would appear only by chance: if the program does not know them, it does not try to play them.

The program is indifferent to bad moves in a game. That is the reason why learning without teacher is feasible. What is a bad move? Perhaps a move which is not the best one: there was a combination, and the player did not see it. The program does not learn, because nothing appears in the game. This slows down the process, but does not disturb it. Perhaps there was a combination better than the one which was played. But as soon as there is a combination, the program learns, and in another situation this combination may be the best one. Also the move may be bad because the opponent may play a combination after it. This is good for learning, since the program can learn the opponent's combination.

The reason for this insensibility to bad moves is that the program learns only when it has understood. The program does not learn a procedure for each move: the move may be incoherent, or purely positional. A move may be a part of a combination already known. It occurs also that the program does not know a sufficient number of procedures for understanding a clever move. If, later, it receives exactly the same game, it would possibly understand moves which it could not understand the first time because it had not enough procedures. At the beginning, it is better not to give games played by grandmasters, because their moves are more difficult to understand.

NOTES

[1] We use the algebraic notation. The eight files counting from left to right are lettered consecutively a to h. The eight ranks counting from the side of the board initially occupied by the white men are numbered consecutively 1 to 8. Each square is named by the combination of the letter of the file and the number of the

rank in which it occurs. A move will be recorded by the designation of the man moved (not being a pawn: K for King, Q for Queen, R for Rook, B for Bishop, N for Knight) followed by the designation of the square it occupied and then the square to which it has been moved. × indicates a capture. ∅ is the representation of a no-move.

REFERENCES

1. De Groot, A. D., *Thought and choice in chess*. Mouton, The Hague (1965).
2. Newman, C. and Uhr, L., BOGART: a discovery and induction program for games. *ACM 20th National Conference*, 1965, p.176.
3. Pitrat, J., Realization of a program learning to find combinations at chess. *Computer oriented learning processes*. Nato advanced study institute. Bonas, 1974, p.273.
4. Samuel, A. L., Some studies in machine learning using the game of checkers. *Computers and thought*. Feigenbaum and Feldman eds, McGraw Hill, New York, 1963, p.71.
5. Samuel, A. L., Some studies in machine learning using the game of checkers. II - Recent progress. *IBM Journal,* 11, p.601, 1967.
6. Waterman, D. A., Generalization learning technique for automating the learning of heuristics. *Artificial Intelligence,* 1, p.121, 1970.

INTERACTIVE SCREENING OF
RECONNAISSANCE IMAGERY*

George C. Stockman[1]
Laveen N. Kanal[2]
Department of Computer Science
University of Maryland
College Park, MD

ABSTRACT

Following an assessment of the current needs and practices of
the Air Force in reconnaissance imagery screening, an interactive
system is proposed to accomplish the imagery screening operation
in a manner more efficient and reliable than either a completely
manual system or completely automatic system. Even the proposed
semi-automatic system requires the existence of completely automatic screens that will screen out a large percentage of all uninteresting imagery. Performance of such screens is discussed in a general way in terms of false alarm and false dismissal rate. Two
hardware implementable operators are proposed to privide low-level
automatic screening. These operators detect symmetry and linearity/
angularity that are very general features useful in discriminating
interesting man-made objects from noninteresting natural terrain.
Software implementable model-directed recognition algorithms are
proposed for study as higher level screens in a multistage screening system that attempts to minimize the work of the system by performing progressively more detailed analysis on progressively smaller sets of imagery.

I. INTRODUCTION

This paper addresses the problem of designing an inter-active
system for the screening of reconnaissance imagery with the view
that such a system should be realizable within the next 5 years.
Current needs and practices are discussed and functional requirements

---

* This work was sponsored by the 6570th Aerospace Medical Research
Laboratory, Aerospace Medical Division, Air Force Systems Command,
USAF, Wright-Patterson AFB, Ohio, under contract F33605-75-C-5056
to L.N.K. Corporation, Silver Spring, Maryland, 20904.

[1] L.N.K. Corporation and the University of Maryland.

[2] Laboratory for Pattern Analysis, University of Maryland, College
Park, Maryland, and L.N.K. Corporation.

for a screening system are specified. An assessment of state-of-the-art techniques in image analysis is given which concludes that automatic techniques of the required efficiency and reliability will not be available in the predictable future. As a consequence, present computer power can only be brought into use in a system which is interactive. Configuring a man-machine coupled system has severe problems of its own, namely, delegation of tasks and authority and control of communication.

A skeleton system design is proposed which remains inside present day constraints by delegating to the machine those functions which can be automated economically and reliably and by delegating to the man all other functions. A hierarchy of processing is set up and likely candidates for each processing stage are described. A scheme for analyzing and testing the performance and reliability of the total hierarchical screening system is given in terms of the performance and reliability of its stages.

Section II gives functional requirements for a semi-automatic imagery screening system with special attention to change detection given in Section III. Section IV emphasizes the need for an interactive system while Section V describes the special problem of man-computer coupling. The skeleton of a screening system is proposed in Section VI, Section VII shows how the performance and reliability of such a system can be analyzed, and Section VIII proposes implementations for two stages of system.

II. FUNCTIONAL REQUIREMENTS FOR AN IMAGERY SCREENING SYSTEM

Air to ground acquired imagery provides a huge amount of non real-time information. Target information can be broken down into the categories of natural and cultural, with the latter broken down again into millitary and nonmillitary. All types of information have ultimate millitary significance. (See Figure 1) Practical considerations will limit the kinds of objects inventoried and the frequency of update. Information for strategic decision making has urgency perhaps in units of months, while tactical information has urgency in units of hours or days. The load on the inventory system (whether automated or not) is determined by the amount of area surveyed, the resolution of the imagery, the frequency of scanning, and the number of categories being inventoried. (See Harley [1] or Appendix A for hypothetical situations.) Not only is the *presence* of objects important, but also important is a *change* in the presence of objects. Because changes are important, particularly the appearance of cultural activity in areas formerly void of that activity, it is necessary to scan all areas repeatedly, even though a previous inventory shows them void. Automation is quite desireable in the functions of 1) searching imagery for cultural activity and 2) comparing new information with old inventory information for change detection. These two points will receive considerable technical attention later.

421

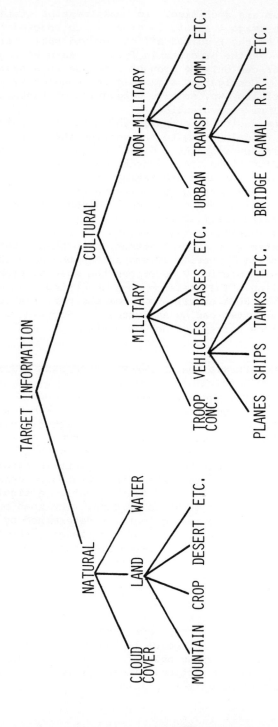

FIG. 1. HIERARCHICAL CLASSIFICATION FOR EARTH INVENTORY INFORMATION.

To screen and inventory imagery of the earth the system must perform three basic functions -- 1) input/output, 2) internal information storage and retrieval, and 3) analysis of data. State of the art equipment and techniques in scanning, plotting, and data base management can presently provide functions 1 and 2 but data analysis techniques necessary for the screening and inventory operations are still not perfected.

Multimode and sophisticated I/O facilities are required to deal with real imagery, symbolic imagery, and logical information. Real imagery such as grey scale, film, or multispectral must be readily handled. Maps, templates, and models must also be input and output and stored. The medium of maps is particularly important for handling the very high information bandwidth which the system must be capable of producing.

The storage and retrieval function is crucial to the data analysis function in that it must make available in a timely manner any real or symbolic data that is required during analysis. The state of the art is well advanced in this area and adequate for screening purposes largely because a) the approximate coordinates of all input and map imagery is known and b) the non-real time aspect of screening allows for sequential accessing and sorting out of information from a huge data base. While it is not necessary to have all real and symbolic imagery on-line for random access to all of the software tools and information that the algorithms or human users may need to do their analysis of an arbitrary image, it will be necessary to have on-line access to general modeling and analytic tools. In particular templates for objects must be on-line at all times.

The data analysis function must provide algorithms for transformation, recognition, abstraction and interpretation. Algorithms will range in sophistication from simple discriminant analysis to complex scene analysis. Many proposed algorithms exist and there is active research producing many more. However, reliability or efficiency has not been proven for any complex automatic image analysis procedures.

III. CHANGE DETECTION

Neither the cultural nor natural features of the earth are static. As in any other inventory system *changes* to an earth inventory must be made via transactions or updates. Types of changes include erection of new buildings, earth work or the movement of a vehicle from one set of coordinates to a new set (2 changes). Such changes must be evaluated for military significance.

Figure 2.a shows how most photointerpretation for change detection is done. New update imagery is compared with archived imagery of the same area by the photo-interpreter and a report of interesting changes is produced. The interpreter usually relies on personal files which contain reference pictures and old reports

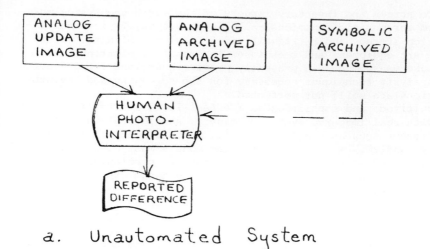

a. Unautomated System

b. Automated Registration & Subtraction

Figure 2. Alternate change detection systems

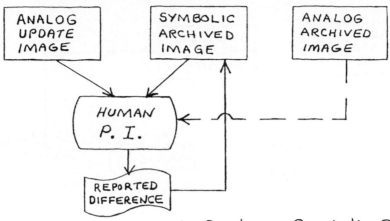

c. Unautomated System, Symbolic Base

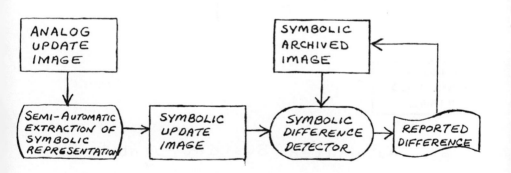

d. Semiautomatic abstraction & automatic difference detection.

Figure 2. Alternate change detection systems (continued)

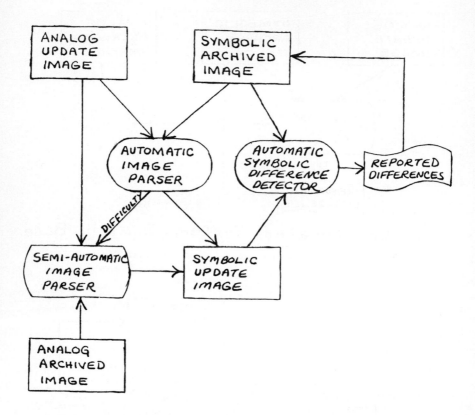

e.   Automated System, Symbolic Base

Figure 2.   Alternate change detection systems (continued)

for the areas for which he is responsible. He may call for con-
sultation on difficult problems and sometimes consensus decisions
are made for the interpretation of ambiguous situations. Archival
storage is usually contained in filing cabinets and common instruments are the light table and magnifying glass [2]. This is an
unautomated system. A simple extension is to automate the delivery
of images to be compared and their registration and to let the
photo-interpreter evaluate the differences revealed. Registration
of images continues to be a sticky problem [3,4] and cannot be
done reliably without human intervention. Automatic delivery of
imagery and automatic image subtraction (after semi-automatic registration) would assist the photo-interpretive process. See Figure 2.b for a diagram of such a system. Note that all interpretation is to be done by the human.

Even if image registration techniques were perfected there
would still be a great problem because a large proportion of the
differences between perfectly registered images would be *trivial
differences*. The determination of the *significance* of differences
is part of the interpretive process [3]. Thus, simple registration and differencing techniques are of little help to reducing
the load on the human photo-interpreter. We conclude that *image
differencing must be done at the symbolic level*.

Figure 2.c shows a system where a human does symbolic change
detection by comparing the contents of new update imagery with a
symbolic representation of that earth area. In the present situation this would involve examination of the new image with respect
to a text report previously compiled on the area.

The system depicted in Figure 2.d produces a symbolic representation of the new image by man-machine interaction. This representation is then automatically compared with the representation
in the inventory. Any differences reported are used to update the
inventory given user approval. This system does not utilize the
knowledge of the area to help analyze the new imagery. A system
which would use stored knowledge in the processing of new imagery
is shown in Figure 2.e. In this system the archived description
of the given earth region is used as an icon and the new data will
be interpreted for change and will be reported to the human operator. Construction of such a system depends on the matching algorithm being insensitive to trivial changes and sensitive to significant changes. In general this is a very difficult research problem, but in several specific cases this approach seems feasible.
Examples are given below.

A) *LAND-WATER BOUNDARIES*

Monitoring of land-water boundaries includes a broad spectrum
of reconnaissance activity such as monitoring rivers for presence
of bridges or boat traffic or checking on harbor or coastline activity. Except for tidal coastline, land-water boundary changes
are usually non-trivial changes. The icon of such a boundary
could be used as a *plan* for isolating the boundary in new imagery.

Use of such a priori information would promote both more accurate and more efficient analysis of the new image. Severe perturbations of the new data with respect to the icon would be an indication of change. For instance, detection of a new gap in a river feature with presence of a near perpendicular linear feature could indicate a new bridge. Presence of ships in docks could be similarly detected.

B) *TRANSPORTATION NETWORKS*

Road and railroad networks are relatively stable and regular image features. An iconic representation of such a network could easily be used as a plan for extraction as in the case of land-water boundaries. Most new road or railroad construction involves a connection to a previous network. Thus, new transportation network features could be detected by examination of image areas adjoining those known to be in the old network. New road development that is unconnected to a previously recorded transportation network would have to be detected by other means, as new cultural activity.

C) *NEW CULTURAL ACTIVITY IN FORMERLY VOID AREAS*

One of the most difficult reconnaissance tasks is the detection of significant activity in areas which were previously devoid of activity. Such areas may represent 98% or more of all imagery to be screened while icons exist for only about 2% of the images. Since new activity can appear at random it is necessary to scan all imagery even though 98% of it will not be of interest. To do this effectively, low-level, hardware implementable filters must be built to detect general cultural activity. A few general features of cultural activity are available. Three of them are symmetry, angularity, and linearity. These features do not usually appear in nature at the scale of reconnaissance photography and should be good features for use in a low level detector for man-made objects. Detection of lines and angles can be done by using the Hough transform [5]. Symmetry detection is discussed in Section VIII.

IV. THE NEED FOR AN INTERACTIVE SYSTEM

Several general principles can be extracted from the last ten years of experience in pattern recognition and artificial intelligence, some of which have produced a generally accepted view that fully automated systems are not currently possible for complex tasks. First of all, the training of machine algorithms always involves the human in a non-trivial way. Unsupervised self-organization is at an impasse which may not yield until human learning itself is better understood. Secondly, it has been found that trade-offs exist between algorithm efficiency and reliability with relia-

bility bounded away from 100%. Semi-automatic procedures are usually necessary to maintain satisfactory efficiency and reliability.
Thirdly, automation is not accepted unless users have confidence
in its product. Perhaps the best way to achieve confidence and
gauge reliability is to have the human intimately involved in the
analysis loop. Fourth, and most important, is the fact that some
recognition tasks which humans do easily are very difficult to
automate. Most human recognition processes are not yet understood
so it is no wonder that recognition tasks are difficult to program.
Even when implementations are achieved the computer is usually
slower than the man. (It is possible for a human to recognize a
familiar object with a tachistoscopec exposure of only 4×10^{-6}
seconds. [6] Also, there is much special logic which perhaps
should never be programmed; for example, the assessment of the importance of buildings by consideration of the snow removal from
their access.

The above discussion gave arguments for keeping the human in
the image analysis loop. There are also arguments for retaining
the computer and automatic procedures. A human might not recognize a familiar object out of a typical orientation [7]. His memory access is unreliable and his judgement often inconsistent.
Also, his performance degrades with fatigue and lack of motivation.
The relative strengths and weaknesses of man and machine are summarized in Table I.

V. PROBLEMS FOR MAN-MACHINE SYNTHESIS

The four principles given in the previous section focus attention on semi-automatic recognition systems that would synthesize the strong properties (or alternatively avoid the weak properties) of man and machine to achieve reliable and efficient performance of complex tasks. Such a synthesis has many problems of
its own due to the facts that the two components do indeed have
different capabilities, and that those of the machine are well
understood while those of the human are not.

The first problem of man machine systhesis is the problem of
language of communication. Clearly, a graphic channel is necessary
from machine to man to provide the necessary bandwidth and to present visual tasks to the human where he can be of most help. Graphic input from man to machine is possible but is insufficient in
bandwidth and freedom of expression.

A second problem involves the representation of a problem and
its analysis steps as it is being solved by man-machine cooperation.
Little is known about the representations used by the human brain.
We are forced by computer characteristics to use fixed and feasible
representations. Given these circumstances and the distortions ef-
fected by the communication medium true man-machine cooperation is
difficult to set up. As far as machine representations are concerned, there has been much progress regarding data structures;

TABLE I. RELATIVE STRENGTHS AND WEAKNESSES OF COMPUTER

	STRENGTHS	WEAKNESSES
C	. VERY FAST AND ACCURATE IN BASIC NUMBER AND CHARACTER OPERATIONS	. INFO. STRUCTURING DIFFICULT, LIMITED AND EXPENSIVE
O	. NEVER BORED, TIRELESS	. PROGRAMMING/DEBUGGING IS DIFFICULT
M		
P	. OBJECTIVE AND CONSISTENT	. COMMUNICATION LIMITED AND INTOLERANT
U		
T	. MODERATELY FAST ACCESS TO A MODERATE AMOUNT OF PRECISELY STORED INFO.	. INFLEXIBLE
E		
R	. CAPABILITY OF INTERFACING/ MANAGING OTHER MACHINES	. DOESN'T LEARN
	. EASY/RAPID PROPAGATION OR REPORTING OF STORED INFORMATION	. NO VISUAL PERCEPTION HARDWARE

TABLE I (CONT.). RELATIVE STRENGTHS AND WEAKNESSES
OF HUMAN.

	STRENGTHS	WEAKNESSES
H	. FLEXIBLE/ADAPTABLE	. BORES EASILY, DISTRACTED EASY, NEEDS MOTIVATION
U	. INTUITION/NATURAL HEURISTICS	. DOESN'T PERCEIVE STATISTICAL OR COMPLEX DETERMINISM WELL
M	. ELABORATE WORLD MODEL	. SUBJECTIVE/INCONSISTENT
	. LEARNS EASILY	. MAKES AND RATIONALIZES MISTAKES
A	. MEMORY SIZE SEVERAL ORDERS MAGNITUDE GREATER THAN COMPUTER	. UNRELIABLE ACCESS TO MEMORY
N	. ACCESS TO A VARIETY OF INSTRUMENTS AND SOURCES OF KNOWLEDGE	. UNAVAILABILITY OF INTERMEDIATE STEPS OF THOUGHT PROCESS FOR RECORDING/CHECKING
	. WELL-DEVELOPED VISUAL SYSTEM	. LACK OF PRECISION IN OUTPUT FORMAT PRODUCES ERRORS IN FURTHER PROCESSING

take for instance, the large number of works reported using trees, graphs, and multi-lists [8,9]. In addition, many very general methods have appeared, such as state space search, problem reduction, theorem proving, and syntactic parsing [10,11,12]. Study must be done in order to evaluate their merits relative to supporting man-machine problem solution.

A third problem involves design of a control mechanism under which man and machine can cooperate to solve a problem. Contribution to the solution from each participant must be facilitated while interference is reduced. Simultaneous manipulation of the problem representation must be carefully controlled. A theory of cooperating sequential processes has arisen out of computer system practices [13]. Techniques are available which offer nice solutions to certain problems but general theory is still in the making. Indeed, effective distribution and synchronization of tasks is now a creative act, out of the realm of theory, and very application dependent. Thus, it seems necessary to induct principles from careful case studies.

The proposal for a screening system given in the next section attempts to circumvent the difficult problems of true man-machine cooperation by preassigning certain low complexity tasks to the machine and certain high complexity tasks to the human. In this manner the problem of control and delegation of responsibility are clear cut, thus permitting a maximum amount of design attention to be paid to the specific problems of imagery screening itself.

VI. A PROPOSED SYSTEM FOR THE INTERACTIVE SCREENING OF RECONNAISSANCE IMAGERY

The ideas discussed in the previous section are incorporated here in outlining a proposed earth inventory system. Module functions are loosely defined and design specifications are not considered. Figure 3 gives a schematic of the processing flow through the system. All discussion below refers to the functional blocks in the flow chart.

The system will have to handle several kinds of data and data structures.
- o Data input and handling
  - o Film imagery
  - o Digitized imagery
  - o Abstracted imagery
    - o Maps
    - o Indexes/Tables
    - o Text
    - o Icons
  - o Models
  - o Templates

The set of all film or digitized imagery that can be accessed

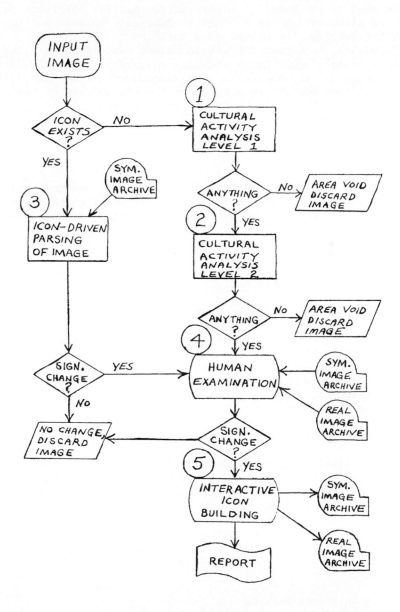

Figure 3.   General algorithm for updating the earth inventory.

by the system is referred to as the Real Image Archive. The set of abstracted imagery will be called the Symbolic Image Archive. Models are used by the human in interpreting imagery; for instance, a model for illumination can be used to duplicate an observed image shadow for gauging the height of a building.

Templates are stored for use in object classification; for instance, templates would exist for each aircraft type so the user or machine could do correlation on real image regions for classification

Data output must be in a form for the consumption of humans who may not understand the mechanism creating it.

o Data output
   o Standard maps
   o Pictures
   o Text

The ease with which computers can be used to document the analysis they perform is well known. Preparation of graphic and text output should be regarded as an important function of any screening system.

SCREENING SYSTEM COMPONENTS

1. Cultural Activity Analysis Level 1

Images of areas which are known from past analysis to contain no interesting activity are passed into this screen. Analysis such as symmetry detection, angle detection, and line detection are performed in hardware since perhaps 98% of all imagery will pass into this screen. If cultural activity is suspected in the image, the image is passed on to block 2 for higher level analysis; otherwise the image is discarded from the system as containing nothing of interest.

2. Cultural Activity Analysis Level 2

Higher level analysis is performed focused on the suspicious regions detected by level 1. This is basically an object detector subsystem which integrates level 1 inputs and searches for complete objects in the image. Block 2 analysis is done in sequential software and need only operate on 10% or so of all imagery if the level 1 screen can be properly set. Confirmation of interesting activity in the image causes it to be passed to block 4 for human examination, otherwise the image is discarded as being uninteresting.

3. Icon Driven Parsing

Images which are known (via their earth coordinates) to contain objects of military significance are initially passed to a subsystem which analyzes the new data with respect to the old data

icon. An image icon is a symbolic map in the ordinary sense augmented by special information and structure that would facilitate
a match of it to real data. Any difficulty in parsing the image
into regions represented by the icon, or detection of any significant perturbation of the image in the areas of interest causes the
operator to be alerted to the image contents.

4. Human Examination

The photo-interpreter is alerted to all suspected changes detected by the lower level automatic screens. At this time he may
use a variety of display aids and comparative material (real imagery, templates, models, etc.) to determine if real change is
present in the image. He may discard the image or record detected
change in the inventory system.

5. Interactive Icon Building

If any significant change has occurred in the area covered by
the image it must be recorded in symbolic form in the inventory.
Through man-machine dialog, the existing icon is modified to reflect the new situation, i.e. the map is altered, and report material is automatically generated.

VII. ESTIMATING THE CHARACTERISTICS OF A SCREEN

Since the system proposed in section VI makes a series of decisions, we need to examine the characteristics expected at each
node of the decision tree. We use the term *screen* to denote an
operator which operates on a set of inputs and creates two or more
sets of outputs. Screens are of use at nodes in decision trees because of their subsetting capabilities. For specificity, only two
output sets are considered here, making any resulting decision tree
a binary tree.

To examine the characteristics of screen, let the universe U
of inputs be divided into two classes w_1 and w_2, where w_1 may be
the class of interesting imagery and w_2 the class of uninteresting
imagery. In the screening application, the number of elements in
w_2 is likely to be much greater than the number of elements in w_1.
Note that $w_1 \cup w_2 = U$ and $w_1 \cap w_2 = \emptyset$. See Figure 4.

When we apply a binary screen, the net result is that the
universe is divided into two sets $w_1{}^*$ and $w_2{}^*$. If the screen were
perfect, $w_1{}^* = w_1$ and $w_2{}^* = w_2$. However, it is very rare to be
able to find a perfect screen.

To test the characteristics of a real screen, we would input
samples of known class, i.e. labeled w_1 or w_2 and examine the output classes into which each is placed. Since we certainly could
not test on all possible inputs (there are, for instance, $64^{64 \times 64}$
images which are 64x64 and have 64 grey levels), our test could

only be regarded as a random experiment.

In order to evaluate the outcome of an experiment with a screen, the usual probability measure is assumed for the universe of inputs. We can characterize the performance of a screen in terms of the conditional probabilities $p(w_1*/w_1)$, $p(w_1*/w_2)$, $p(w_2*/w_1)$ and $p(w_2*/w_2)$. To simplify the notation we write $p(1/2)$ for the probability that the input is from w_2 and the output is to w_1*. The other probabilities are similarly defined. We write $P(1)$ and $p(2)$ for the priori probabilities that an arbitrary input is interesting, and noninteresting, respectively. A screen is now diagrammed in Figure 5.

The matrix of conditional probabilities is called the *characteristic matrix* of the screen, and the vector $[p(1), p(2)]$ is called the *input mix*. The *positive output mix* is the dot product of the input mix and the first column of the characteristic matrix. Similarly, for the *negative output mix*. The two independent elements of the characteristic matrix which are commonly known are $p(2|1)$, known as the false dismissal rate (FDR), and $p(1|2)$, known as the false alarm rate (FAR). Evaluation of the *power* of a screen involves estimation of these two probabilities only since $p(2|2) = 1 - p(1|2)$ and $p(1|1) = 1 - p(2|1)$.

Theoretically, FAR and FDR are not related, and each could lie in the constrained interval $[0,1]$ independently of the other. Practically, however, we know that building a screen with a very low FDR usually results in a high FAR. There is no alternative to setting stringent limits on false dismissals and thus incurring a resultant increase in false alarms. In different terms, the positive output of a practical screen will be increased as the false dismissal rate is decreased. Since decreasing positive output is the goal of screening, it is clear that screens must be built with satisfactory false alarm rates.

Consider the following example illustrated in Figure 6. Imagery with mixed $[10^{-3}, 1-10^{-3}]$ interesting and noninteresting frames respectively enters a screen with FDR 10^{-4} and FAR 0.5. The positive output of the screen is roughly 0.5 meaning that about half of all input images will be screened out. This is helpful, but the ratio of noninteresting to interesting images is 500 to 1; better than 1000 to 1, but still bad. Further improvement can be achieved by concatenating two screens as shown in Figure 7, which also uses more desirable characteristics for the individual screens. The table below the screen diagram summarizes the utility of the 2 stage screen for several possibilities of input mix.

Note that the FDR and FAR of the 2 stage screen are independent of input mix by definition. The output mix, of course, is highly dependent on the input mix. For input mix parameter p=0.5, 0.1,0.01 the output mix is appropriate for human examination. However, for p=0.001 the mix is diluted 40 to 1 with noninteresting output and for p=0.0001 it is 400 to 1. Another stage should be added to the screen for processing imagery with such rare instances of positive data. The additional stage would lower the volume of

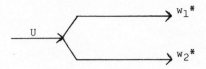

Fig. 4. A binary screen.

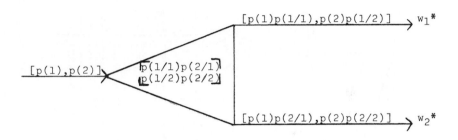

Fig. 5. A screen with probabilistic properties.

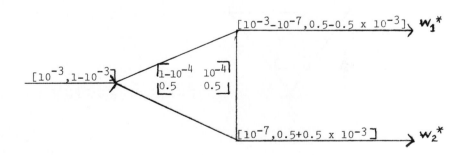

Fig. 6. A screen with FDR = 10^{-4} and FAR = 0.5 .

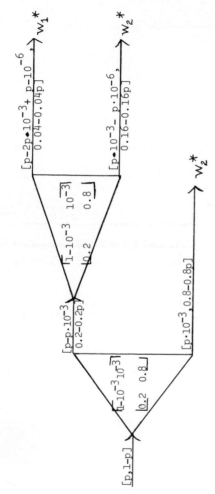

INPUT MIX PAR. p	FALSE DISMISSAL RATE	FALSE ALARM RATE	OUTPUT MIX	POSITIVE OUTPUT
0.5	0.002	0.04	[0.499,0.020]	0.519
0.1	0.002	0.04	[0.100,0.036]	0.136
0.01	0.002	0.04	[0.0100,0.0396]	0.0496
0.001	0.002	0.04	[0.0010,0.0400]	0.0410
0.0001	0.002	0.04	[0.0001,0.0400]	0.0401

Figure 7. A 2-stage screen and table of properties

positive output and balance the output mix more in the favor of interesting imagery so not to bore the human receiver of the output.

It is important to note that the FDR of the 2-stage screen is twice as bad as that of the single screen, and that a 3-stage screen would have FDR 3 times as bad. This phenomena must be taken into account when designing multiple stage screens and can be handled by using more stringent FDR specifications for the individual stages.

The previous discussion considered the analysis of concatenated screening stages in terms of overall false dismissal rate and amount of positive output. Clearly, practical systems can be created with some care provided that individual screens can be built which meet the specifications. The question of testing the characteristics of a given screen is now taken up. Since false dismissal rate and false alarm rate are independent characteristics of a screen, two controlled experiments can be performed to test a given screen. To determine $p(2|1)$ we merely input to the screen a number of images known to be interesting, i.e. in class w_1. Since the behavior of the screen on one input can be assumed to be independent of its behavior on any other input a binomial model for estimating $p(2|1)$ applies. The same reasoning applies for estimating $p(1|2)$ by inputting only images in class w_2.

Given a real screen for testing and a set specification d for false dismissal rate, the statistical hypothesis to be tested is clearly $H_0:p(2|1) \leq d$ against $H_1:p(2|1) > d$. Bartels and Wied [14] have shown how such a hypothesis can be tested by sequentially inputting positive samples to the screen and considering the number of (false) dismissals in a given number of trials. Table II was built by computing the smallest value of N such that at lease 95% of the probability under the binomial distribution $B(p,N,k) =$

$$\sum_{x=0}^{k} \binom{N}{x} p^x(1-p)^{n-x}$$ was massed above $k=k_0$. This gives 95% confidence in the conclusion of the test. For example, 2995 positive images must be input to a screen without a single dismissal to test the hypothesis that its FDR does not exceed 0.001. If a single dismissal occurs in those 2995 trials then the trials must be extended to N=4742 without an additional dismissal. If 2 dismissals appear in the first 2995 trials then the testing must be extended to 6292 trials, etc. Since FDR's of less than 10^{-3} and confidence rates of 95% or more are desirable specifications for a reconnaissance imagery screening system it is clear that thorough but not impossible testing procedures are in order. Such testing has been done in OCR and blood cell classification but to our knowledge has not been done on reconnaissance imagery. Most experiments have been carried out under the goal of complete automation of recognition and the resulting techniques have been too costly and too unreliable to undergo such a rigorous sequence of tests.

Table   II.   Requirea sample sizes N for testing
                      hypotheses about the false dismissal
                      rate of a screen.

Hypothesis   Number of false dismissals k

p ≤ d	0	1	2	3
p ≤ 0.10	29	46	64	76
p ≤ 0.05	59	93	124	153
p ≤ 0.01	299	473	628	773
p ≤ 0.001	2995	4742	6292	–
p ≤ 0.0001	29,956	–	–	–

VIII. HARDWARE SCREEN STAGE

A) *A Transform for Symmetry Detection*

As mentioned in section VI, the large amount of data to be handled at the first level of cultural activity analysis requires that low-level operations such as line, angle, and symmetry detection be implemented in hardware. The capability of detecting symmetry in reconnaissance imagery by a low level detector would be valuable to an image screening operation because most of what is man-made is symmetrical and most of what is natural (at that scale) is assymmetrical. Higher level processing of symmetry is important in other applications of image and scene analysis. A transform is described here, called the "midpoint transform", which can be used in tandem with the well-known Hough transform [5] to define a "symmetry transform" for any set of picture points. Some simple mathematical examples are given as well as some computer runs on sample data.

1. Intuitive Transformation

The symmetry transform is quite simple. The midpoints of all pairs of picture points in the original set are "accumulated" in an intermediate image. This image of accumulated midpoints is then passed through the Hough transform for detection of straight lines. If an *axis* of symmetry exists in the original set of picture points then many midpoints will be colinear and a heavy line will appear in the accumulated image. This line can be detected by the Hough transform. It should be noted that *points* of symmetry are detectable immediately in the accumulated image. Also, linear sets of picture points may be detected as usual by the Hough transform because the midpoint of any two points of the set will lie on the same line. Since linear sets of points are usually of interest it should not be necessary to inhibit such responses.

2. Definitions

Let $P(x,y)$ be a quantized picture function defined on a quantized domain. $P(x,y)$ may represent either a binary or grey scale image and may well be a partial function.

A midpoint transformation M of the image defined by P yields a new image as follows:

$$M(x,y) = \sum_{\substack{x=(x1+x2)/2 \\ y=(y1+y2)/2}} P(x1,y1) \cdot P(x2,y2)$$

where the sum is taken only of products where $P(x_i,y_i)$ are defined.

The Hough transformation H applied to M results in another "image" albeit in a different parameter space.

$$H(r,\theta) = \sum_{\theta \epsilon T, (x,y) \epsilon M} M(x,y)$$
$$r = X\cos\theta + y\sin\theta \ \epsilon \ R$$

T and R are the sets of angle and radius quantizations respectively. The symmetry transform is then just the composite $S=M \cdot H$.

3. Practical Use of S

For an $r \times r$ image with t quantization levels on θ computation of S would require on the order of tr^4 operations. Such a procedure is impractical in sequential software for all reasonable values of r. For sequential software a subset of p representative points such that $p << r^2$ can be selected for computation of the symmetry. Extensive testing is yet to be done to evaluate this transform and the many variations of it which are possible. Good results would imply a search for an efficient hardware solution.

4. Examples

Three examples of the S transform are given below to clarify its operation and to give insight to the selection of thresholds to be used with the accumulator array produced. The first two examples are mathematical analysis and the third gives the results of a computer run on synthetic data.

a) Example 1 (See Figure 8).

A binary picture consists of ℓ points on a line AB and one point C off the line. The $(\ell+1)\ell/2$ midpoints all lie on two lines, $\ell(\ell-1)/2$ lie on the line AB itself and the other ℓ lie on the midline between C and AB. For $\ell>3$ the response of S is much stronger along AB than it is on the midline. Negligible responses occur due to the 1 point and 2 point lines made by other pairs of midpoints.

b) Example 2 (See Figure 9).

The picture consists of a rectangle ABDC of points, ℓ and ω points along each parallel pair of sides. (Assume no point at a corner of the rectangle) From example 2 it follows that the response along the major axis of symmetry is ℓ^2 while it is ω^2 along the minor axis. Thus the response of the major axis will dominate the minor one in proportion to the square of the ratio of the sides. Other weak responses can be gotten by considering the interaction of single points on one side with the entire set of points on a perpendicular side as done in example 1. Symmetrical spacing of the points on the rectangle will strengthen the response on the major and the minor axes, having a greater effect on the minor axis response, and will also produce a point of symmetry at the rectangle's center.

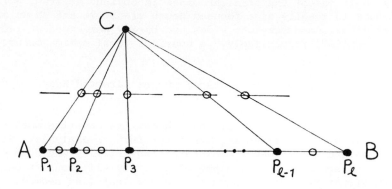

FIGURE 8. Midpoints o of a set of picture points • all but one of which lie on a line.

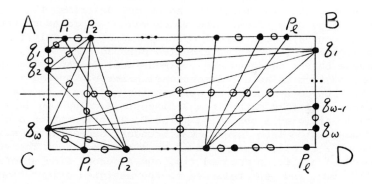

FIGURE 9. Midpoints o of a rectangular set of points • .

c)   Example 3 - Prop.

Figure 10 shows an abstract propeller-shaped object.   Both
axes of symmetry, the point of symmetry, and the two long straight
sides are evident in the midpoint transform of figure 11.   In figure 12 only one of the straight sides is obvious at (r=0, θ=120°).
In figure 13 results of a focused Hough transform are shown and
the major axis and straight sides are barely perceived at 140°,
120°, and 160°, respectively.   A spurious local maxima occurs at
130°.

B)   *Software Screening Stage: Model Directed Edge Following*

Under the hierarchical strategy proposed in Section VI, the
hardware screening stage would pass along its positive output to
a software directed screening stage for further analysis.   Both
the image and the evidence of interesting activity would be passed.
For this discussion the evidence of activity will consist of a detected structural primitive such as a straight line segment, an
angle, an axis of symmetry, etc.   The structural primitive detected in the image is used by the software to *evoke* a set of models,
or plans, which will direct a search for other structures in the
image necessary to detect a complete object.   Note that the search
in model space has the efficiency of applying only those models
relevant to the existing primitive and the search of image data
has the efficiency of focus in the relevant data area.
We suppose that the model for an object describes the object
in terms of edge primitives.   The model may be a procedure for
finding the boundary or a formal description of it.   Only for ease
of discussion is the latter alternative pursued.
Because object contours are 1-dimensional we can write descriptions of them using a 1-dimensional grammar.   Appended to the
grammar must be some concept of orientation and scale so that we
can describe geometric paths in a 2-dimensions.   Any boundary
structure is assigned a beginning point P, an orientation angle θ,
and a decomposition into lower level boundary sub-structures.   Figure 14 shows a formal description of an airplane wing.   The wing
is composed of a side, a rounded tip, and a second side at orien-
tation 15°, 90°, and 165° relative to the assigned orientation of
the entire wing.   The substructures side and cup are primitive
(have no decomposition) and can be viewed as predicates which
search an image at (P,θ) and return a measure of success or quality.
Primitive predicates can be given other parameters such as shape
and scale and can be made sloppy.   Figure 15 shows 3 possible structural descriptions of an airplane.   The first two are equivalent
except for starting point (P$_1$ or P$_2$) and the third description indicates that a partial boundary will also be called that of an airplane provided only the tail is missing.
The process just described can be viewed as a 2 level state
space search.   The top level search proceeds through states which
are elemental edges in a grammar graph while the bottom level

444

```
                PROP  :   BINARY IMAGE
•••••VIRTUAL•    0    59    0    59•SCREEN•   0   59   0   59 •••••
        0123456789012345678901234567890123456789012345678901234567 89
59  000000000000000000000000000000110000000000000000000000000000000000
58  000000000000000000000000000000000000000000000000000000000000000000
57  000000000000000000000000000000000000000000000000000000000000000000
56  0000000000000000000000000000000000000000000000000000000000000000000
55  00000000000000000000000000000000000011000000000000000000000000000
54  00000000000000000000000000000000000101000000000000000000000000000
53  000000000000000000000000000000000010010000000000000000000000000000
52  000000000000000000000000000000000001000110000000000000000000000000
51  000000000000000000000000000000000010000001000000000000000000000
50  000000000000000000000000000000000001000000100000000000000000000
49  000000000000000000000000000000000010000001100000000000000000000
48  000000000000000000000000000000000100000000110000000000000000000
47  000000000000000000000000000000000100000000010000000000000000000
46  000000000000000000000000000000001000000000001000000000000000000
45  000000000000000000000000000000010000000000001000000000000000000
44  000000000000000000000000000001100000000000000110000000000000000
43  000000000000000000000000000001000000000000000011000000000000000
42  000000000000000000000000000001000000000000011000000000000000000
41  000000000000000000000000000001000000000000110000000000000000000
40  000000000000000000000000000010000000000001000000000000000000000
39  000000000000000000000000000100000000000010000000000000000000000
38  000000000000000000000000000100000000001000000000000000000000000
37  000000000000000000000000001000000000010000000000000000000000000
36  000000000000000000000000010000000001100000000000000000000000000
35  000000000000000000000000100000011000000000000000000000000000000
34  000000000000000000000000100000011000000000000000000000000000000
33  000000000000000000000001000011000000000000000000000000000000000
32  000000000000000000000001000110000000000000000000000000000000000
31  000000000000000000000001011000000000000000000000000000000000000
30  000000000000000000000011100000000000000000000000000000000000000
29  000000000000000000000111000000000000000000000000000000000000000
28  000000000000000000011001000000000000000000000000000000000000000
27  000000000000000000011000100000000000000000000000000000000000000
26  000000000000000000110000100000000000000000000000000000000000000
25  000000000000000011000001000000000000000000000000000000000000000
24  000000000000000110000000100000000000000000000000000000000000000
23  000000000000011000000001000000000000000000000000000000000000000
22  000000000001000000000001000000000000000000000000000000000000000
21  000000000001000000000001000000000000000000000000000000000000000
20  000000000001000000000001000000000000000000000000000000000000000
19  000000000001100000000001000000000000000000000000000000000000000
18  0000000000010000000000001000000000000000000000000000000000000000
17  000000011000000000000001000000000000000000000000000000000000000
16  000001110000000000000001000000000000000000000000000000000000000
15  000010000000000000000001000000000000000000000000000000000000000
14  000010001000000000000001000000000000000000000000000000000000000
13  000000110000000000000001000000000000000000000000000000000000000
12  000000010000000000001000000000000000000000000000000000000000000
11  000000010000000001000000000000000000000000000000000000000000000
10  000000000010000000010000000000000000000000000000000000000000000
9   000000000010000000010000000000000000000000000000000000000000000
8   000000000000110000010000000000000000000000000000000000000000000
7   000000000000010001000000000000000000000000000000000000000000000
6   000000000000001001000000000000000000000000000000000000000000000
5   000000000000000100100000000000000000000000000000000000000000000
4   000000000000000011000000000000000000000000000000000000000000000
3   000000000000000000000000000000000000000000000000000000000000000
2   000000000000000000000000000000000000000000000000000000000000000
1   000000000000000000000000000000000000000000000000000000000000000
0   000000000000000000000000000000000000000000000000000000000000000
```

Figure 10.

445

PROP $\mathcal{M}$-TRANSFORM

PROP : HOUGH TRANSFORM

RHO	THETA 0	15	30	45	65	75	90	105	120	135	150	165
10	18	20	21	23	19	19	20	17	5	0	1	3
8	22	20	23	19	22	20	20	20	13	4	3	19
6	28	25	18	13	16	22	24	23	30	15	16	29
4	34	25	19	17	19	19	24	29	32	32	33	20
2	37	27	21	19	17	23	27	36	26	66	62	31
0	36	29	33	39	36	31	29	44	(101)	89	82	93
-2	34	27	24	20	22	24	24	39	45	70	69	45
-4	27	26	20	21	22	22	28	36	22	31	41	22
-6	23	22	20	13	17	23	27	24	29	15	18	35
-8	15	18	19	19	22	19	21	14	14	7	5	17
-10	6	16	15	18	13	16	14	16	4	1	0	7

Figure 12.

PROP : HOUGH TRANSFORM

RHO	THETA 115	120	125	130	135	140	145	150	155	160	165	170
3	12	18	13	24	24	18	25	26	12	10	9	14
2	14	9	16	29	31	31	32	32	19	11	11	22
1	29	18	33	27	44	39	35	32	28	23	34	24
0	31	(58)	49	(57)	39	(52)	46	38	66	(69)	50	34
-1	39	51	56	37	50	52	46	47	36	50	43	30
-2	29	15	26	30	33	33	40	35	28	13	21	25
-3	16	19	12	27	24	23	27	29	17	12	10	18

Figure 13.

447

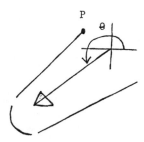

<WING> → (θ+15°) SIDE(θ+90°) CUP (θ+165°)SIDE

Fig 14. The starting point P, orientation θ, and decomposition
assigned to the contour of an airplane wing.

<PLANE> → (θ+90°)<WING>(θ+180°) <TAIL>(θ+270°)<WING>(θ+360°)<NOSE>

<PLANE> → (θ+270°)<WING>(θ+360°)<NOSE>(θ+450°)<WING>(θ+540°)<TAIL>

<PLANE> → (θ+270°)<WING>(θ+360°)<NOSE>(θ+450°)<WING>

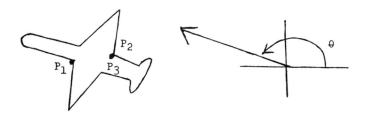

Fig 15. Several possible structural decompositions of an
airplane boundary.

search proceeds through states which are elemental edges in the image itself. Martelli [15] has described methods of carrying on the lower level search but has had difficulty in changing heuristics because of the absence of the higher level space. We have recently developed an algorithm which can be used for the 2 level search described above, and hope to test it soon for tracking object boundaries.

IX. SUMMARY

Information storage and retrieval, preparation of maps and reports, and implementation of recognition logic are all currently available on computers to aid in reconnaissance imagery screening. Problems of data bulk, reliability, and task complexity forbid use of fully automatic methods. Use of computer power in imagery screening is therefore restricted in the near future to interactive systems where the human user is responsible for the complex task and relieved of the trivial. A hierarchical system was proposed to successively apply more power to the screening out of images with no interesting activity. Performance of such a system was analyzed in terms of performance of its individual stages and some insight was gained on specifications for individual screens. Algorithms were proposed for hardware and software levels of the system which are felt to have the characteristics necessary to perform the required functions. Implementation and testing of such algorithms is left for future work.

REFERENCES

1. Harley, T. J., Kanal, L. N., and Randall, N. C., "System Considerations for Automatic Imagery Screening", in *Pictorial Pattern Recognition,* Thompson Book Co., (1968).

2. *Minutes of the 13 May 1975 Meeting of the ARPA Image Understanding Workshop* Science Applications, Inc., 1911 North Fort Myer Drive, #1200 Arlington, Va. 22209.

3. Harley, T. J., Jr., *Electronic Correlation Techniques for Change Detection,* ASTIA document AD-276746, (1962).

4. Kanal, L. N., *Prospects for Pattern Recognition: Workshop and Survey Report,* sponsored by EIA, NSF, and Univ. of Md., (1975).

5. Duda, R. O. and Hart, P. E., "Use of the Hough Transformation to Detect Lines and Curves in Pictures", *CACM,* Vol. 15, No. 7, pp. 11-15, (Jan. 1972).

6. Platt, J. R., "How a Random Array of Cells Can Learn to Tell Whether a Straight Line is Straight", *Principles of Self-Organization,* H. von Foerster and G. W. Zopf, Jr., eds., pp. 315-323, Pergamon Press, New York, (1962).

7. Rock, I., "The Perception of Disoriented Figures", *Scientific American,* pp. 78-85 (1974).

8. Knuth, D. E., *Fundamental Algorithms*, Addison-Wesley, Reading, Mass., (1968).
9. Knuth, D. E., *Sorting and Searching*, Addison-Wesley, Reading, Mass., (1973).
10. Nilsson, N. J., *Problem Solving Methods in Artificial Intelligence*, McGraw-Hill Book Co., (1971).
11. Hopcroft, J. E., and Ullman, J. D., *Formal Languages and Their Relation to Automata*, Addison-Wesley, Reading, Mass., (1969).
12. Vanderburg, G. and Minker, J., "State-Space, Problem Reduction, and Theorem Proving - Some Relationships", *CACM*, Vol. 18, No. 2, Feb. 1975, pp. 107-115.
13. *Interprocess Communications Workshop, ACM SIGCOMM/SIOPS Proceedings*, March 24-25, 1975, Santa Monica, CA.
14. Bartels and Wied, "Performance Testing for Automated Pre-screening Devices in Cervical Cytology", *Journal of Histochemistry and Cytology*, Vol. 22, No. 7, (1974) July, pp. 660-662.
15. Martelli, A., "Edge Detection Using Heuristic Search Methods", *Computer Graphics and Image Processing*, Vol. 1, No. 2, Aug. 1972, pp. 169-182.

APPENDIX A
THE DATA BULK PROBLEM: AN EXAMPLE

We consider a contrived, but hopefully reasonable, tactical system that would monitor a 100 km x 100 km battlefield on a daily basis.

The type of objects being monitored--land vehicles, camps, fortifications, would require a resolution element as fine as 0.1 square meters. Thus, the battlefield presents 10^5m x 10^5m = 10^{10} square meters or 10^{11} resolution elements. Since 1 day$\approx 10^5$ seconds, a daily scan of the entire battlefield requires a data rate of 10^{11} resolution elements / 10^5 seconds = 10^6 elements per second.

10^6 elements would constitute a nice picture or frame of an area about 300 meters x 300 meters. A large scale conventional digital computer could barely process 10^6 resolution elements per second and results would be dubious even if 100 seconds rather than 1 second were spent per frame.

The lesson in this is not that automatic methods cannot provide cost effective performance in this application, but that (1) conventional methods and/or (2) digital methods cannot do the job. Any automatic method must deal with *the bulk of the data* in analog form in order to achieve satisfactory rates.

Pursuing another consideration, we assume that there are 1000 objects of interest in our 100 km x 100 km battlefield imaged on 10^5 frames. Thus, *at most* 1 frame of every 100 is interesting and human performance is known to degrade in such a situation. Assuming human performance is good only when better than 1 frame in 10 is interesting an automatic filter of power 10 or better would be useful in this case. If false negatives could be satisfactorily controlled a false alarm rate of 10 to 1 (ten cries for each wolf) would be tolerable for a combined man-machine screening system.

AN ICONIC/SYMBOLIC DATA
STRUCTURING SCHEME*

Steven L. Tanimoto
University of Connecticut
Storrs, CT.

ABSTRACT

Databases of pictorial information are usually structured
from components that may be considered either strictly iconic
(digitized visual images) or strictly symbolic (picture properties expressed in relational format). The distinction between
these schemes is studied. A new approach to structuring pictorial
data is suggested in which advantages of both schemes may be captured. It is shown that iconic/symbolic data structures permit a
new kind of information retrieval called "iconic indexing" to be
implemented efficiently.

I. MOTIVATION

The object of this study is to examine some fundamental issues of image representation in digital computers. One hypothesis
raised here is that the simple data structure of the intensity matrix and the relational descriptions have been unduly restrictive
and that the time has come for the consideration of more sophisticated pictorial data structures. Indeed many agree that the future
progress of artificial intelligence is resting upon our learning
how to store "semantic knowledge", and in the case of visual intelligence this means learning how to represent pictorial knowledge. Some reasons for studying the organization of pictorial
knowledge come from an information retrieval context [1] and others
from computer vision [2]. We now briefly describe some of these
reasons.

One question arising from the information retrieval context
asks how pictures can be indexed. Can they be indexed according
to content rather than according to external attributes such as
who put them in the database, or artist's name in the case of
paintings? There are many related questions also. Should pictures be grouped into hierarchies, be described by relational
databases, or be treated as nodes of a graph? Should common subpictures be factored out so as to reduce storage requirements?
The development of a new scheme for image representation may get
us closer to answers to these questions.

---

* Research supported by NSF Grant ENG76-09924.

An important area where we especially need new methods to store pictorial semantic knowledge is in image segmentation. One possible approach to the improvement of image segmentation systems is to make them interact with a library of analyzed pictures. This may be justified using a goal-based model of segmentation. The organization and representation of the library of analyzed pictures then becomes a key problem.

A Model for Goal-based Segmentation

We define a *segmentation problem* to be a 4-tuple $(\alpha, \gamma, \tau, \sigma)$ where α is a "prototype segmentation", γ is an input gray level picture, τ is a set of "allowable transformations" and σ is a similarity predicate on pairs of segmentations.

A *solution* $T \epsilon \tau$ is a transformation satisfying $\alpha(T(\gamma), \alpha)$. The prototype segmentation can be expressed in several ways: as a full-resolution matrix, as a graph whose nodes correspond to regions and whose arcs connect nodes corresponding to adjacent regions, as lists encoding the boundaries of regions, or as a combination of these. We generally may assume that γ is always expressed as a full-resolution matrix. The set τ of allowable transformations is more elusive. In a simple case it may simply constrain the merging process to preserve the uniformity of a picture property within regions. In more complicated cases, it might allow elimination of regions interpreted to be mere shadows of objects. Since the study of the transformation sequences is tangential to the scope of this paper we merely mention that standard techniques of edge detection and region analysis are relevant here [3,4]. The similarity predicate may be expressed as a combination of procedures to test similarity and parameter values (e.g. tolerances) to guide the procedure.

A system based on this model may be said to "see" α when the input picture is γ and a $T \epsilon \tau$ has been found such that $\alpha(T(\gamma), \alpha)$.

The system may be given many prototypes and many corresponding similarity predicates so that a wide variety of pictures can be handled. A chief consideration, however, is the space that all these prototype segmentations require. As the number of prototypes stored grows, it is more and more essential that the size of each be minimal. Concurrently, there is the problem of keeping prototype information accessible to the segmentation routines; therefore, storage compaction of prototypes by devious encoding schemes that require slow decoding are to be avoided.

In this context of segmentation our efforts are directed toward problems of efficient prototype storage and access. We make some assumptions about the pictorial information desirable in a segmentation system and proceed from there to discuss means of representing it. Alternatively, one may see the type of information handled as a consequence of, rather than motivation for, the data structuring scheme.

II. ICON VS. SYMBOL

The Distinction

symbol -- 1. something that stands for or represents another thing.

        2. a written or printed mark, letter, abbreviation, etc. standing for an object, quality, process, quantity as in music, mathematics, or chemistry.

icon -- 1. an image, figure, representation.

From the definitions given in *Webster's New World Dictionary of the American Language* [5] the distinction between icon and symbol seems subtle. It will be useful to emphasize that distinction between these two means of representation.

A symbol may be considered an object whose value is associated with it without regard to any physical properties of the symbol itself. Thus a symbol may bear an apparently arbitrary relation to the value it is bound with and need not share any visual or other "likeness" with that which it represents.

An icon is an image or pattern which bears a "natural resemblance" to that which it represents. The ability to "understand" an icon depends primarily on an ability to extract pictorial features and discover shape, discover structure and recognize objects. It does not depend heavily on an ability to recall definitions (retrieve bindings) of symbols.

This distinction is represented in Figure 1.

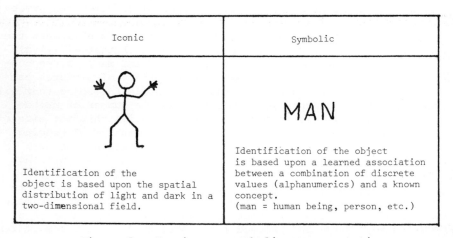

Iconic	Symbolic
Identification of the object is based upon the spatial distribution of light and dark in a two-dimensional field.	**MAN** Identification of the object is based upon a learned association between a combination of discrete values (alphanumerics) and a known concept. (man = human being, person, etc.)

Figure 1. Iconic vs. symbolic representation.

The distinction we have just drawn is *functional*. Whether a
given object is an icon or an abstract symbol depends contextually
on the association mechanism used to determine what the object represents. Since ambiguities may exist with regard to such association mechanisms, there arise situations in which the distinction
seems to break down. In order to better understand the dichotomy,
let us discuss some of its paradoxes.

A) Breakdowns and Paradoxes of the Dichotomy

One apparent breakdown in the distinction between symbolic
and iconic representations is based on the observation that in a
computer both must be represented as finite bit strings:

(1) As soon as an icon (spatial image) is digitized, it can
be represented as a string of discrete values and on that level
can be considered a symbol.

(2) Any symbol, when written out on paper, or stored physically in the computer as a string or array of discrete values, has
spatial characteristics which cannot be denied (be them visible or
invisible but electromagnetic in any case). Of course, these spatial properties will be dependent upon the way the string of symbols is "folded" if it is folded at all. For example, consider
the two foldings of a string shown in Figure 2.

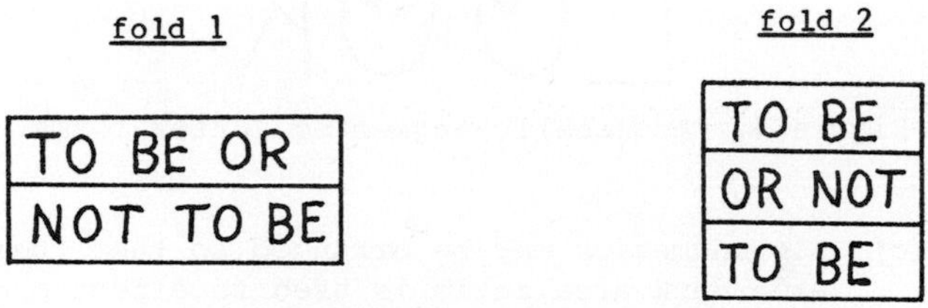

fold 1

TO BE OR
NOT TO BE

fold 2

TO BE
OR NOT
TO BE

Figure 2. Two folds of a character string.
An iconic property of fold 2 is that the top
section of the picture is the same as the
bottom one.

This possible paradox that both symbol and icon must be bit strings
in the computer can be rejected as a look at data structures at
too low a level of abstraction.

Another source of temporary confusion is the use of objects
normally regarded as icons as symbols, and the iconic use of objects normally regarded as symbols.

(3) In Egyptian Hieroglyphics elaborate (but "small") images
have a 1-1 correspondence to phonemes (a finite number of them).
Thus these images may be considered members of a finite alphabet,

and their occurrences in strings makes them symbols functionally.

(4) The forms of symbols may be used for their iconic effect in various ways.

   (a) Images may be composed of segments which are letter shapes (Figure 3).

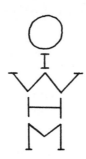

Figure 3. Representation of a man with letter forms.

   (b) Letter forms may be augmented to communicate both symbolically and iconically (Figure 4).

Figure 4. Iconically augmented letter forms.

   (c) Alphanumerics may be arranged so that their light area/dark area ratio is used to effect a global iconic effect. (digital pictures output by a line-printer; typewriter pictures, Knowltons gray scales based on symbol sets [6]).

(5) A source of greater difficulty comes from Art. The intentions of a painter are not always clear to an observer. A canonical question which arises is whether a given object in a painting, say a tree, is to have special symbolic significance (reference through allegory, etc.) or is the iconic designation of a probable object without special significance. A complete knowledge of the context in which the painting was created would be required to resolve the ambiguity [7].

Having discussed the basic difference between iconic and symbolic representation, let us now attempt to compare universes of objects representable by each scheme.

B) The Power of Representation Methods

We have already mentioned that both symbols and icons must be
represented in the computer as bit strings. But are the domains
of objects representable by the two methods the same? We will attempt to answer this question in two different general arguments,
the first dealing with interpretation schemes, and the second with
"simulation".

A simple scheme for organizing symbolically stored data is in
terms of relations [8,9]. An example relational tableau is shown
in Figure 5.

Word	Type of Object	Size	Animate?
MAN	material	3-7'	Yes
HAPPINESS	state of mind	---	No
BASKET	material	$\frac{1}{2}$-3'	No
'	'	'	'
'	'	'	'
'	'	'	'

Figure 5.

The universe of objects that can be represented by single n-
tuples of such a relation is the cartesian product of all the relation's domains except the primary key which gives the *symbols*
associated with the objects. A given symbol is interpreted in
this scheme by first matching it in the list of entries for the
primary key, then reading out the corresponding information in the
other domains.

On the other hand, let us suppose that we have an iconic representation scheme in which we may only interpret icons by applying "segment detectors" to them. These segment detectors may return coordinate and angular position information that can be used
to recognize known forms. These forms may then be associated with
further information as in the relational scheme above. However,
since this association is to be iconic, the object represented
must have a "natural resemblance" to the recognized form. An *a
posteriori* way of defining iconic association is to select a recognition system and then declare that the associations it makes
are iconic. The extent to which such association agrees with
"natural resemblance" may then be an indicator of how well the
recognition system models human form perception.

Because of this restriction that iconic association imposes
on the universe of objects representable, it should be clear that
iconic association is a special case of symbolic association and
cannot be used to represent all objects representable by general
symbolic association.

An alternative line of argument is more daring and may lead to different conclusions. We conjecture now that iconic and symbolic schemes are equally powerful in that each method can simulate the other. We first describe translation of the icon into symbols [1]. Here we assume that an icon (light intensity array) represents a finite number of objects and/or qualities and/or relations. One such quality is "spatial predication" of objects, that is, positioning. Such a predicate can be expressed symbolically as (OBJECT,X,Y,THETA) meaning that the named object has its "keypoint" located at picture coordinates (X,Y) and is inclined by an angle THETA. Eventually, using more or less than a thousand words, all desired objects, qualities, and relations can be spelled out symbolically.

Translating symbolic structures into icons is more difficult. Let us assume a specific fixed realm of objects to be represented, some of which have clear iconic qualities and others of which do not. For example, we take the vocabulary of a child of four. The concept represented by the word "dog" can easily be represented iconically, but the concept for "patience" does not have a simple and obvious iconic encoding. The argument on behalf of "iconic power" asserts that one icon or a sequence of icons can be found that communicate the notion of "patience" to a human observer without using non-iconic symbolism [10]. Note that a movie is a sequence of icons. This argument, of course, will remain highly subjective until a complete visual communication system can be formalized and studied.

III. COMBINING THE ICONIC AND SYMBOLIC

There are two simple ways to combine iconic and symbolic data structuring methods. The first has been used by Tenenbaum et al[2] for interactive scene analysis. In this scheme, the symbolic or relational portion of the data structure is expressed as a graph and the iconic element is introduced by letting some of the nodes be icons. Thus a semantic net [11] of related objects may have object descriptions that are either iconic or symbolic or both. The iconic descriptions, while sometimes requiring more time to access specific facts, are less committed to a small set of specific facts than are the symbolic descriptions. In addition to the simple icon, an iconic node of their net may be a reference to a subpicture of a simple icon; this permits flexibility and storage efficiency.

The second way of combining the iconic and symbolic may be considered a dual to the first in the following sense. Where in the first method icons may replace nodes of the symbolic structure (expressed above as a graph), in the second method, symbols may replace intensity information in the pixels of an icon. Thus we extend the notion of an icon to be an array of pixels which now may represent either light intensities (iconic information) or any object in a given universe (symbolically). The overhead associated with this option is 1 bit per pixel for a flag that indicates whether the pixel is iconic or symbolic. The primary advantage of this method is that the original icon may be efficiently used as a pictorial index to other information, represented either iconically, symbolically or by a mixed scheme. We proceed now to develop this idea of "symbolic pixels".

IV. THE EXTENDED ICON

Definitions

We call an icon or picture matrix in which pixels cannot only represent local light qualities (eg., hue, intensity) but also arbitrary data items an *extended icon*. In a typical implementation a pixel might be represented by 8 bits with 256 potential values. The first 64 of these may correspond with gray values and the remaining 192 may be symbols capable of representing arbitrary data objects. In order to discuss basic definitions in an implementation-independent way, we proceed to define a data type ISDS (for Iconic/Symbolic Data Structure) using an axiomatization scheme like that of the PASCAL programming language [12,13]. The use of such methods to describe picture data structures was suggested by Zahn [14], where it was mentioned that definitions of lower level structures (eg., intensity ranges) could easily be changed without necessitating rethinking of the higher level structures (eg., "picture" in his case). In the first set of definitions, we assume that a mechanism with a symbol table already exists to associate symbols with other entities. Thus, we are concerned only with the relationship of symbols to the extended icons of which they may be parts.

```
constant   black = Ø; white = 127;
           symbol_Ø = Ø; symbol_127 = 127;
           pix_size = 64;
type       indicator = (iconic, symbolic);
           intensity = black .. white;
           symbol = symbol_Ø .. symbol_127;
           pixel = record
                       case  ind : indicator of
                           iconic : (intens : intensity);
                           symbolic : (symb : symbol);
                       end;
           pix_range = 1 .. pix_size;
           extended icon = packed array [pix_range, pix_range]
                               of pixel;
```

The data type extended_icon would in this case be implemented as a 64 x 64 array of 8 bit byte pixels. Each pixel has one of its 8 bits used as an indicator, flagging it as either iconic or symbolic. The remaining 7 bits give either the intensity value or the symbol number. Such a pixel may be called an *iconic/symbolic pixel*.

Let us now ignore implementational considerations and generalize the notion of "symbol" so that it may be considered a pointer
to some structure. We now define this structure and then redefine
the type "symbol". The types "property" and "value" are defined
in a simple way for didactic purposes.

```
type    property  =  (area, surface, shape1, shape2);
        value     =  Ø.Ø .. 1.Ø;
        plist     =  array [property] of value;
        nodetype  =  (pictorial, relational);
        ISDS      =  record
                         case nodeindicator : nodetype of
                             pictorial : (icnc : extended_icon);
                             relational : (rein : plist)

                     end;
        ISDStype  =  class 1ØØ of ISDS;
        symbol    =  ↑ISDStype;
```

At this point we have defined an ISDS as either an extended_icon
or a plist. A plist is an array of property values and with a
slight generalization could be considered a relation in the sense
of Codd [8]. A symbol is now defined to be a pointer to any member of the class of all ISDS's. Thus since a symbol can be a component of an ISDS, the structure of a general ISDS is recursive.

An example of the type ISDS is shown in Figure 6. Symbols,
being pointers, are indicated by arrows emanating from pixels.
Iconic pixels are left blank to simplify the figure, but of course
they normally contain intensity information.

Justification for the Extended Icon

The advantages of ISDS's are their efficiency of space, representational power and the convenience they provide for pictorial information query answering. It is instructive to mention that
the use of symbolic pixels can be avoided, keeping much the same
general structure, but that a corresponding sacrifice of either
accessing efficiency or storage efficiency will result. Figure 7
shows an ISDS and Figure 8 shows a similar data structure in which
the symbolic pixel has been avoided. A general method of pictorial information retrieval that we call "iconic indexing" can work
efficiently using the extended icon, but must make an extra pass
doing unnecessary distance calculations if a "reverse pointer"
method is substituted.

A primary objection to the use of pixels both iconically and
symbolically in the same icon is that where symbols appear, the
continuity of intensity information is interrupted. A simple
method to correct this possible problem is to create separate arrays for the iconic and symbolic components of the extended icon.
But this sacrifices too much storage. Under some fair assumptions,

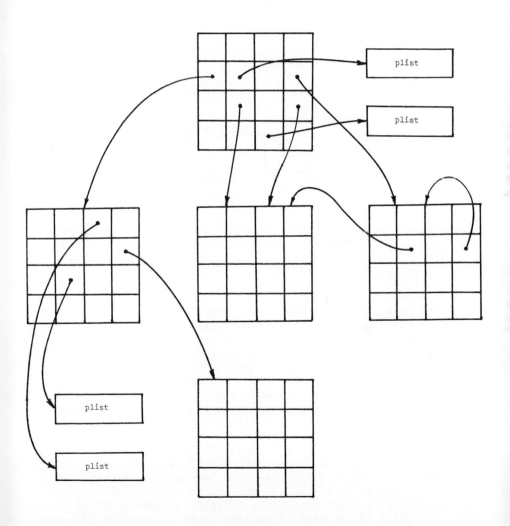

Figure 6. The structure of an example of type ISDS

we maintain that the discontinuity of intensity information is
not a problem.

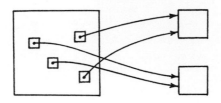

Figure 7.   A simple ISDS employing symbolic pixels.
Iconic indexing can work efficiently to
retrieve an object.

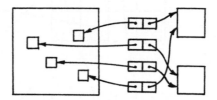

Figure 8.   Another data structure representing identical
information without the use of symbolic pixels.
Iconic indexing requires an extra pass through
a table of links.

The main assumption we make is that the relative numbers of
symbolic pixel occurrences to iconic pixel occurrences is small.
Thus, only a relatively few intensity points are missing. When
necessary, values may be obtained for these locations by interpolation among neighboring intensity values. Such picture patch-
ing takes place in the human visual system; many people are not
even aware that they have a blind spot on their retina where the
receptor array is interrupted by the optic nerve making its exit
from the eyeball to communicate with other parts of the visual
system.
Another assumption we make about the pictorial information
represented in the icon is that it is not sensitive to the loss
of a few intensity points. Note that the loss of an intensity
point is a wholly different phenomenon from the introduction of
noise; in the case of noise there is false intensity information
present; while in the case of an ISDS there is no false information introduced at symbolic pixels. Most picture matrices, even

after a high degree of compaction, are still sufficiently redundant to permit removal of a few intensity samples. Finally we assume that in the process of constructing an extended icon, methods are available with sufficient flexibility to avoid eliminating an intensity point that is somehow crucial to the iconic representation. When cartographers superimpose lettering on maps they place labels near the map feature being described without obscuring any features likely to be important.

In order that processing routines not have to worry about the possibility that a pixel might not be iconic, the following technique may be useful. We assume now that a collection of ISDS's are under the management of a pictorial database management system (PDMS) which supplies requested information to a vision algorithm on demand. As an extended icon is read out from the database and passed to the vision algorithm, the iconic and symbolic parts are separated into two matrices. Since only a small number of ISDS's are actively in use by the algorithm at a time, the extra storage required is not usually a problem. Of course, the PDMS interpolates, filling in the blind spots of the icon during the separation. In case storage is a problem, the PDMS can pack the symbolic matrix using a hash-coding sparse-matrix technique or a double-chained sparse matrix encoding scheme referred to as "grid representation" [13(p154)].

V. ICONIC INDEXING

An information retrieval system must provide a variety of logical access paths to data if the system is to be useful in varied applications. For example, in a relational database system, it should be possible to retrieve an n-tuple by specifying the values of any combination of its domains. In cases where the values do not uniquely identify an n-tuple, those n-tuples that match should be retrieved [15].

With a database of information about a picture or collection of pictures, it is also desirable to permit access to information by a variety of "keys" and types of queries. To this end we describe an indexing method we call "iconic indexing" that accommodates a wide variety of query types, while maintaining fast access to the sought information. The technique makes use of iconic/symbolic data structures as defined previously.

A *one-level iconic index* is an extended icon whose symbolic pixels point to the data items of the pictorial database. The *iconic search mechanism* is a procedure capable of accepting a query, exploring the iconic index, and in case of success, returning one or more symbolic pixels whose locations satisfy the iconic constraints of the query.

The general form of query answerable by the proposed system is "Retrieve the information associated with X" where X falls into a category such as one of the following:

1. Absolute coordinates (X, Y). If the pixel at position (X, Y) is symbolic, the search succeeds, returning the symbol (pointer to desired information). Otherwise the search fails. Note that this operation works independently of intensity information.

2. The locality of (X, Y). This is similar to (1) except that a specified search pattern (e.g. finite diverging spiral) is followed if no symbol is found at (X, Y). This kind of search may be tremendously sped up with the addition of an auxiliary "pyramid of symbol locations" where a small hierarchy of binary pictures is constructed from the projection of the extended icon consisting of the indicator bit of each pixel (see [16,17,18,19]).

3. A point reachable from (X, Y) by moving in direction D = θ. Pixels along a path of some width W starting at (X, Y) and moving in direction D (i.e. angle θ measured clockwise from North) are examined until a symbol is found, a picture border is encountered, or a maximum number of pixels have been examined. This search may also be sped up through use of pyramids. An alternative to searching in a path is searching a sector that radiates out from (X, Y).

4. A feature point of type F. Feature points may be defined in terms of top down search algorithms employing templates in a pyramid [18]. For such a query, all or prespecified parts of the icon can be searched for local or global maxima, minima, corners at particular angles, etc., and then a small neighborhood of the found point(s) can be examined for symbols. Here the intensity information of the iconic index is indispensable.

5. A point a little way along a line or edge emanating from (X, Y). Here the iconic search mechanism must find an edge or line near (X, Y) and follow it in one or more directions until a symbol is found or a prespecified maximum distance has been transversed. A pyramid may be used to speed edge following and also to reduce the likelihood of "just missing" a symbol lying near the edge.

6. Color C. In the case of gray-valued pictures, the iconic search mechanism must locate an area of the icon having the specified intensity (within a tolerance), then search locally for a symbol. In the case of color pictures, this search process can be done efficiently with a pyramid and is analogous to the highly efficient color search by humans [20,21].

Iconic Indexing and Pyramid Search

In order to answer a query of the general form just described, three tasks must be done by the PDMS. First a locality of the icon must be determined. Call this task phase 1. Second, the locality must be searched for a symbol. Call this phase 2. Thirdly the symbol must be extracted and its value retrieved (phase 3).

Now let us compare two PDMS's. System A uses a 1-level iconic index (or extended icon). System B uses an icon without symbol capability and stores a list of (X, Y, SYMBOL) triples instead. Phase 1 is done the same way by A and B. However, phase 2 evokes differences. System A searches the locality of the index quickly, employing "pyramid searching" to cover an area R in $\log_2 R$ steps. PASCAL definitions for the binary pyramid follow:

```
type    sflag      =     (nosymb, symb);

        bpyramid   =     record
                         pic_0:    array[1,1] of sflag;
                         pic_1:    array[2,2] of sflag;
                         pic_2:    array[4,4] of sflag;
                            .
                            .
                         pic 6:    array[64,64] of sflag;

                         end;
```

The binary pyramid is constructed in the following way. pic_6 is just taken to be the projection of all the indicator bits of the extended icon. The bpyramid may be considered a hierarchy in which any sflag in pic_0 to pic_5 has 4 sons in a 2 x 2 block in the successive pic [17]. An sflag is set to 1 (representing value symb) if any of its four sons are 1. Since pic_6 is sparse by assumption, one must go up several levels before any of the pic's get dense. An example of this structure is shown in Figure 9.

One searches for a symbol as follows. We assume that phase 1 is complete and that a cursor is now positioned in the middle of the locality to be searched by phase 2. First find a "lead" by checking successively (until an sflag w/value symb is found): the current sflag, its 4 direct neighbors, its father, the father's 4 direct neighbors, the father's father, etc. If pic_0 is reached and no leads found, then no symbols exist in the iconic index. Assume now that a lead has been found in some pic. As long as the lead has a unique son with value symb, let the son be the lead and keep working back to pic_6. If a lead has two, three or four sons with value symb, choose the one closest to the starting point (using a Manhattan distance function but scaling coordinates for the level change) as the new lead. A lead in pic_6 is a successful solution to phase 2.

Phase 2 by System B

System B must scan through a list of the coordinates of symbols (say N items) calculating distances to the starting point to find that symbol achieving the minimum distance. Binary search *cannot* be used effectively to achieve $O(\log_2 N)$ search time because location of an item "close to" (X_0, Y_0) cannot be done simply by

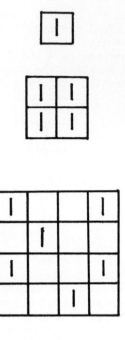

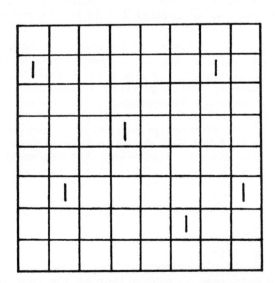

Figure 9. An example of type bpyramid. The largest array (in this case pic_3) consists of the indicator bits of some extended icon. Values of other cells are the inclusive or of their four descendants.

searching on X and then searching on Y. Projected distances along X or Y can be used only as lower bounds on the actual distance between a symbol and the starting point. System B uses $O(N)$ time to execute phase 2.

Since phase 3 is identical for both systems, the comparison is all in phase 2 with $O(\log_2 R)$ vs $O(N)$ search times for systems A and B where again R is the area of the locality to be searched. In a worst case for system A and moderate case for system B, assume R is the whole icon, and $N = \sqrt{R}$. Clearly as R and N grow, the search time for A grows only very slightly compared with that of B.

In practice, symbols will usually be located near distinctive feature points of the icon such as corners, local brightness extrema, etc. Since the phase 1 task is often to find such feature points, the amount R of area needing search in phase 2 is either negligible or very small. Thus system A can determine the symbol associated with a particular image feature extremely rapidly where system B must employ an inefficient search procedure. Difference in performance increases as both the number of symbols in a picture increases and the number of queries to be processed increases.

VI. DISCUSSION

There are many potential uses of iconic/symbolic data structures. One is simply to express a system of two-dimensional relationships among arbitrary entities; this may be referred to as "spatial predication". Another use is to efficiently represent plane maps with labeled regions; such applications may employ "minimal colorings" and symbol concatenation. In a compromise between purely iconic and iconic/symbolic techniques, one may employ "iconic symbols". Finally iconic/symbolic techniques may be used in "image macro" languages that embedding or superposition of images. These uses can be related to data structural needs of computer vision system.

Spatial Predication

The association of an arbitrary symbol with an (X, Y) coordinate pair we call *spatial predication,* and a triple (SYMBOL, X,Y) we call a *spatial predicate.* Whenever such predicates are to be retrieved using the domain SYMBOL as key, relational representation is sufficient, but when they are to be accessed by coordinates, iconic indexing employing an ISDS is likely to be better (as discussed earlier).

Minimal Colorings

Segmentation maps are often represented as icons with regions whose pixels uniformly indicate a unique identification number of the region. A disadvantage of this is that the total storage re-

quired depends not only on the spatial resolution but on the number of regions in the segmentation which can be quite large. Normally there is a feature vector associated with each region giving
attributes such as color and size. A more compact representation
would use 3 bits/pixel with 8 possible values. The first 5 (or
possibly 4) of these correspond to "colors", the last 3 (or possibly 4) correspond to symbols. The ISDS is constructed by first
finding a 5 (or 4) coloring for the map, then carefully superimposing symbolic labels on the interiors of regions. These labels
act as pointers into the table of feature vectors for regions.
Since there are only 3 distinct symbols, the identification of a
particular region may require the concatenation of several symbols
together. Region shapes may sometimes force such symbol strings
to wind around. A somewhat remote but instructive analogy is to
liken these symbol strings to DNA molecules inside genes. String
labeling techniques used in cartography may also be adaptable to
region labeling in ISDS's.

Iconic Symbols

The symbolic capabilities of ISDS's may be had, without the
necessity of symbolic pixels, at the expense of a more complex
symbol identification procedure. Rather than use a pixel as a
pointer into a table of symbol definitions, one may treat a group
of pixels, a subimage, as a symbolic entity. The detection and
matching of these subimages or iconic symbols might be efficient
on a parallel machine but is vastly more time-consuming on a sequential machine than the detection and evaluation of symbolic
pixels.

Image Macros

The display languages of computer graphics systems have employed subroutining for a long time [22,23]. The advantages of
subroutining include conciseness of image representation, convenient updating and ease of describing complex pictures. The systems using subroutining most effectively have been line-oriented
graphics systems. The use of subroutining for representation of
half-tone pictures must deal with one problem that was ignored in
the line-drawing case. The composite image, composed of parts
represented by individual subroutine calls, must combine the pieces.
In the line-drawing case, subimages were superimposed; lists of
line segments to be displayed could simply be concatenated. With
halftones, a number of embedding methods and superposition schemes
are possible. Embedding may allow translation, scaling and shape
or other distortions. Superposition may mean "write-over", "average with", "take maximum with", or "add to". An extended icon
whose symbols represent icons or other extended icons is the data
structure to be used to represent pictures with "subroutining".
Note that where in computer graphics a subroutine is a procedure

to *display* a subimage, in image representation we treat a subroutine as the *representation* of a subimage.

VII. APPLICATIONS IN COMPUTER VISION

The ability to represent both visual and symbolic information in one data structure is perhaps more important to machine perception of scenes than to any other area. Both pictorial knowledge and knowledge of a general nature is useful in segmentation of images into regions. Riseman and Hanson have outlined knowledge representation as a major obstacle in the design of semantically-directed vision machines [24]. Speaking of the form for specific information about the environment they note, "This might vary from a list of the objects that are likely to appear in the image to a complete topographical map of all objects in the environment".

One data-structuring scheme for scene analysis was called a "recognition cone" by Uhr [25] and could be described as a three-dimensional array of processing elements capable of passing along symbolic information in an iconic context. An ISDS may be used to implement such cones. The use of symbolic pixels may also enhance the power of other iconic data structures appearing in the literature [16,17,19,26].

The use of ISDS's in top-down segmentation is straightforward. Harlow and Eisenbeis [27] used a top-down region-growing technique to analyze chest radiographs. Segmentation was guided by a tree, stored as part of the segmentation system. This tree has associated with each node a set of parameters to be used in isolating a particular region represented by the node. The regions so represented were allowed to overlap. In fact, the root node corresponded to the whole chest X-ray picture so that all decendants corresponded to subregions.

An iconic/symbolic data structure may be used to represent their tree. At the top level (zero) of this structure is a matrix, giving a rough segmentation into the regions of level 1. Embedded in each region is a pointer to level 1 matrices. These too may have embedded pointers to structures at levels of greater refinement.

Alternatively the symbolic pixels of a model ISDS may represent procedures that are to be called in the process of examining a corresponding locality on a test picture. In this way, the knowledge about how different kinds of pictures are analyzed is stored procedurally (after Winograd) [28]. This representation form is both procedural and iconic. Not only are the subroutines image processing subroutines, but the calls are spatially predicated as well. Since an extended icon by itself is not a procedure, there is some ambiguity about what the main procedure is; the main procedure is usually regarded as the one in which the subroutine calls are embedded. The philosophical problems that arise in discussions of representation are fascinating [29].

VIII. CONCLUSION

A data structuring method for pictorial information has been presented in which pixels in an array may represent either local light information (iconically) or arbitrary entities (symbolically). Advantages of the technique include compactness of representations, convenient implementation of iconic indexing, and simplified simulation of data structures used in the literature of image analysis.

REFERENCES

1. Firschein, O. and Fischler, M. A., Describing and abstracting pictorial structures, *Pattern Recognition 3*, 4 (Nov. 1971) pp. 421-443.
2. Tenenbaum, J. M., Garvey, T. D., Weyl, S., and Wolf, H. C., An interactive facility for scene analysis research, Stanford Research Institute A. I. Center, Tech. Note 87 (Jan. 1974).
3. Davis, L. S., A survey of edge detection techniques, TR-273, GJ-32258X, Computer Science Center, Univ. of Maryland, (Nov. 1973).
4. Zucker, S. W., Region growing: Childhood and adolescence, TR-370, GJ-32258X, Computer Science Center, Univ. of Maryland, (April 1975).
5. Guralnik, D. B. (ed), *Webster's New World Dictionary of the American Language* (second college edition). N.Y.: The World Publishing Co. (1972).
6. Knowlton, K. and Harmon, L., Computer-produced grey scales, *Computer Graphics and Image Processing 1*, 1 (1972) pp.1-20.
7. Gombrich, E. H., *Art and Illusion: A Study in the Psychology of Pictorial Representation*. Princeton, N. Y. : Princeton Univ. Press (1960).
8. Codd, E. F., A relational model of data for large shared data banks, *Comm. A. C. M. 13*, 6 (June 1970) pp. 377-387.
9. Kunii, T. L., Weyl, S. and Tenenbaum, J. M., A relational database scheme for describing complex pictures with color and texture. Second Int'l Joint Conf. on Pattern Recognition, Copenhagen (Aug. 1974). IEEE #74CHO885-4C, pp. 310-316.
10. Arnheim, R., *Visual Thinking*, Berkeley, Calif: Univ. of California Press (1969).
11. Preparata, F. P. and Ray, S. R., An approach to artificial nonsymbolic cognition. *Information Sciences 4* (1972) pp. 65-86.
12. Wirth, N., The programming language PASCAL, *Acta Informatica 1*, 1 (1971) pp. 35-63.
13. Hoare, C. A. R., Notes on data structuring .In *Structured Programming* by O. J. Dahl, E. W. Dijkstra and C. A. R. Hoare, Academic Press (1972) pp. 83-174.

14. Zahn, C. T., Data structures and pattern recognition algorithms: a case study, *Proc. Conf. on Computer Graphics, Pattern Recognition and Data Structure,* Beverly Hills, CA., (May 1975) pp. 191-195.
15. Date, C. J., *An Introduction to Database Systems,* Reading MA., Addison-Wesley (1975).
16. Hanson, A. R. and Riseman, E. M., Preprocessing cones: a computational structure for scene analysis, COINS Tech. Rept. 74C-7, Univ. of Mass., Amherst (Sept. 1974).
17. Tanimoto, S. L. and Pavlidis, T., A hierarchical data structure for picture processing, *Computer Graphics and Image Processing 4,* 2 (June 1975) pp. 104-119.
18. Tanimoto, S. L., Hierarchical approaches to picture processing. Ph.D. dissertation, Dept. of Electrical Engineering, Princeton Univ. (Sept. 1975).
19. Klinger, A. and Dyer, C. R. Experiments on picture representation using regular decomposition. *Computer Graphics and Image Processing 5,* 1 (March 1976) pp. 68-105.
20. Green, B. F. and Anderson, L. K., Color coding in a visual search task, *J. Exp. Psychol. 51,* (1956) pp. 19-24.
21. Smith, S. L., Color coding and visual search, *J. Exp. Psychol. 64,* 5 (1962) pp. 434-440.
22. Sutherland, I. E., SKETCHPAD: a man-machine graphical communication system, MIT Lincoln Lab. TR296, (May 1965).
23. Newman, W. M. and Sproull, R. F., *Principles of Interactive Computer Graphics,* New York: McGraw Hill (1973).
24. Hanson, A. R. and Riseman, E. M., The design of a semantically directed vision processor (revised and updated). COINS Tech. Rept. 75C-1, Univ. of Mass., Amherst (Feb. 1975).
25. Uhr, L., Layered 'recognition cone' networks that preprocess, classify and describe, IEEE Trans. on Computers 21 (July 1972) pp. 758-768.
26. Tanimoto, S. L., Pictorial feature distortion in a pyramid, *Computer Graphics and Image Processing* (to appear).
27. Harlow, C. A. and Eisenbeis, S. A., The analysis of radiographic images. *IEEE Trans. on Computers C-22,* 7 (July 1973) pp. 678-689.
28. Winograd, T., *Understanding Natural Language,* N. Y.: Academic Press (1972).
29. Goodman, N., *Languages of Art,* N. Y.: Bobbs-Merrill (1968).

IGS: A PARADIGM FOR INTEGRATING
IMAGE SEGMENTATION AND INTERPRETATION*

J. M. Tenenbaum
H. G. Barrow
Artificial Intelligence Center
Stanford Research Institute
Menlo Park, CA.

ABSTRACT

This paper presents a new approach for integrating the segmentation and interpretation phases of scene analysis. Knowledge
from a variety of sources is used to make inferences about the
interpretations of regions, and regions are merged in accordance
with their possible interpretations.

The deduction of region interpretations is performed using a
generalization of Waltz's filtering algorithm. Deduction proceeds
by eliminating possible region interpretations that are not consistent with any possible interpretation of an adjacent region.
Different sources of knowledge are expressed uniformly as constraints on the possible interpretations of regions. Multiple
sources of knowledge can thus be combined in a straightforward way
such that incremental additions of knowledge (or equivalently,
human guidance) will effect incremental improvements in performance.

Experimental results are reported in three scene domains,
landscapes, mechanical equipment, and rooms, using, respectively,
a human collaborator, a geometric model and a set of relational
constraints as sources of knowledge. These experiments demonstrate that segmentation is much improved when integrated with
interpretation. Moreover, the integrated approach incurs only a
small computational overhead over unguided segmentation.

Applications of the approach in cartography, photointerpretation, vehicle guidance, medicine, and motion picture analysis are
suggested.

I. INTRODUCTION

A major goal of scene analysis has been the ability to partition images into regions that could then be interpreted as
semantically important entities such as objects or surfaces. The
conventional approach of performing segmentation followed serially

---

*   The research reported herein was supported by the National
    Aeronautics and Space Administration under Contract NASW-2865.
    Additional Support was furnished by the Advanced Research
    Projects Agency under contract DAHC04-75-C-0005.

by interpretation is frequently ineffective because semantically important pictorial features can be visually indistinct while visually prominent features can be artifacts in the context of the current task. Consider, for example, partitioning an image of a black and white cat on a black and white rug.

This paper presents a new approach, called Interpretation-Guided Segmentation (IGS), for integrating segmentation and interpretation in the analysis of natural scenes. Knowledge from a variety of sources is used to make inferences about the interpretations of regions, and regions are merged in accordance with their possible interpretations. General knowledge, domain specific knowledge, and picture specific knowledge (contributed interactively by a human collaborator) are used uniformly and thus the quality of the analysis can be progressively improved by incremental additions of knowledge.

II. BACKGROUND

The key concept underlying IGS is that picture elements (pixels) can be clustered into regions more reliably if clustering is based on semantic interpretations rather than raw pictorial data. The development of this idea can be traced through almost a decade of region analysis research. The earliest algorithms, such as those of Brice and Fennema[1] and Barrow and Popplestone,[2] clustered raw brightness data and were consequently limited to blocks world scenes where surfaces had uniform brightness and high contrast with adjacent surfaces.

Additional pictorial features were invoked to extend the applicability of region growing. Yachida and Tsuji,[3] for example, used brightness data from three color separations, while Muerle and Allen[4] and Rosenfeld and Thurston[5,6] used a variety of statistically based texture measures. Tomita et al.,[7] and more recently Ohlander,[8] exploited multiple features by using histogram analysis to determine the single feature providing the best discrimination at various stages of analysis. Both Tomita and Ohlander obtained impressive looking results in selected images, but scenes could easily be concocted to expose their fundamental weakness--that pictorial similarity is not always a reliable criterion for segmenting a scene into regions that correspond to objects.

Some of the first explicit attempts at clustering pixels on a semantic basis occurred in the analysis of earth resource satellite imagery. Individual pixels first were classified into crop categories by comparing their multispectral signatures with training sets and then were grouped with contiguous pixels of the same category.[9,10] Unsupervised classifiers were alternatively used to invent categories empirically.[10,11] Tenenbaum[12] and Hanson et al.[13] used supervised and unsupervised classification of pixels respectively to segment landscape scenes viewed from ground level. Pixel attributes, however, are generally insufficient for unique semantic interpretations; the context in which the attributes occur is crucial.

Recent research has emphasized semantic interpretation at the region and interregion levels. Yakimovsky and Feldman,[14] for example, classified regions on the basis of brightness, hue, saturation, size, position in image, and overall shape as well as the length, shape, orientation, and contrast of their boundaries with adjacent regions. Harlow and Eisenbeis[15] used brightness, position in image, and the interpretations of adjacent regions to label areas in chest X rays.

Our work can be viewed as an extension of these efforts in two directions: The use of additional sources of knowledge for constraining region interpretations and the use of more effective deductive mechanisms for integrating knowledge. Our central concern in this paper is to promote the concept of IGS which lies latent or subjugated in the works summarized above..

III.   INTERPRETATION-GUIDED SEGMENTATION: AN OVERVIEW

If interpretations could be assigned to every pixel, then segmentation would be reduced to the trivial process of collecting adjacent pixels with the same labels. There are two difficulties in automating interpretation at the pixel level; namely, the excessive volume of data and the absence of global attributes (e.g., shape, texture, boundary relations). These attributes emerge only after a region structure has been imposed on the pixels, but without them, interpretation is usually ambiguous.

Following Yakimovsky,[14] the integration of segmentation and interpretation is accomplished in our system by proceeding incrementally. A scene is partitioned first into elementary regions consisting of individual pixels or perhaps groups of adjacent pixels with identical attributes. Beginning at this level, the system performs the most complete interpretation possible in the current partition. On the basis of this interpretation and previous knowledge about the domain, the system next merges the pair of adjacent regions that are least likely to represent different objects. The process then iterates by revising the interpretation to fit the current partition and performing another merge (see Figure 1).

The risk associated with a merge is evaluated by assessing the likelihood that the adjacent regions (or pixels) are fragments of the same object. Merges are never allowed between regions whose sets of possible interpretations are known to be disjoint because they must correspond to distinct objects. The safest merge combines regions that already have been assigned the same unique interpretation. It is also safe to merge adjacent regions whose interpretations, while not yet unique, have been narrowed to the point where previous knowledge constrains both regions to take the same interpretation. For example, suppose that Pictures

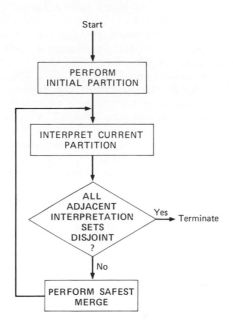

Start

PERFORM
INITIAL PARTITION

INTERPRET CURRENT
PARTITION

ALL
ADJACENT
INTERPRETATION   Yes   Terminate
SETS
DISJOINT
?

No

PERFORM SAFEST
MERGE

FIGURE 1   OVERVIEW OF INTERPRETATION-GUIDED
SEGMENTATION PARADIGM

were constrained to hang only on Walls and thus could never appear
adjacent to Doors in an image. Two adjacent regions with Door and
Picture as possible interpretations, could thus be safely merged
since both regions must be interpreted either as parts of a Door
or as parts of a Picture. If there are no safe merges, as defined
by the above criteria, then the regions separated by the lowest
contrast boundary are merged, provided that their possible interpretations are not disjoint. When the possible interpretations of
all adjacent regions in the current partition are disjoint, the
analysis terminates.

After each merge, the resulting partition is reinterpreted.
This process assigns to each region a set of possible interpretations that are consistent with the region's attributes and also
with at least one possible interpretation of each adjacent region.
The reinterpretation is performed incrementally as follows: When
regions merge, the resultant region initially inherits the possible interpretations shared in common by its parent regions. (These
are obtained by intersecting the interpretation sets of the parent
regions.) Some of these common interpretations may be incompata-
ble with the expanded range of attribute values found in the enlarged region and can therefore be immediately ruled out. A small
region, for example, will admit interpretation as either a small

475

object or part of a large object, but a large region can correspond only to a large object.

Interpretations eliminated in the course of region merging
may, in turn, allow semantically related interpretations to be
dropped as possibilities of other regions. For example, if a newly merged region becomes too large to be a Chairseat, the possibility Chairback can be dropped for the region above it. These
secondary eliminations may themselves propagate additional eliminations extending throughout the image. The deduction of region
interpretations is explained more fully in Section IV.

The interpretation process requires knowledge of how given
region interpretations can appear in legal scenes. In the absence
of such knowledge each region is assumed to have all possible interpretations. Hence any adjacent regions can be merged, but no
merge is guaranteed to be safe. The system will thus function as
a conventional regiongrower, merging regions in order of boundary
contrast. Knowledge acts by constraining the possible interpretations of regions, and thereby prevents merges between semantically incompatible regions. Ideally, with sufficient knowledge,
all permitted merges will be safe and therefore correct.

IV. DEDUCING REGION INTERPRETATIONS WITH RELATIONAL CONSTRAINTS

The process of deducing region interpretations using constraints is a generalization of Waltz's[16] filtering algorithm
similar to that developed independently by Rosenfeld.[17] Every
region initially is assigned a set of possible interpretations
that are consistent with its own attributes. Deduction proceeds
by eliminating those locally possible interpretations that are not
consistent with any possible interpretation of an adjacent region.
After a region interpretation is eliminated, the interpretations
of all adjacent regions must be re-examined to determine whether
they are still compatible with the surviving interpretations. De-
ductions may thus propagate, as in Waltz filtering.

The consistency of an interpretation is determined by relational constraints that specify, for each interpretation, the allowed interpretations for adjacent regions in a specified relationship. A region labeled Lake, for example, cannot appear above
an adjacent region labeled Sky. For each pair of adjacent regions,
a set of applicable relations is determined on the basis of properties of their common boundary. For example, one region may be
spatially *above* and to the *right* of the other, with strong brightness contrast along the boundary. An interpretation is allowed if
at least one interpretation of the other region simultaneously
satisfies all the applicable relational constraints in conjunction
with the interpretation being filtered.

A) An Example

The deduction of region interpretations by filtering is illustrated in Figure 2. The example involves an image of an empty room that has been correctly partitioned into six regions corresponding to the objects Floor, Wall, Door, Baseboard, Picture, and Doorknob. The problem is to determine an assignment of interpretations to regions that satisfies the constraints defined at the bottom left of Figure 2. Initially, every region is assigned all six possible interpretations, but immediately Picture and Knob are dropped from Regions 1, 3, and 6 because their size violates Constraint 4. This stage of labeling is shown in Figure 2(a). Regions are now filtered pairwise in order of region number, beginning with the pair R1, R2. Region 2 is located within region 1 and thus constraint 1 applies. This constraint can be satisfied in two ways: by instantiating Region 2 to Picture and Region 1 to Wall or Region 2 to Knob and Region 1 to Door. Consequently, Wall and Door are retained as possible interpretations for region 1 while Picture and Knob are kept as possibilities for region 2. Next, regions 1 and 3 are filtered by constraint 2. This constraint is satisfied when regions 1 and 3 are instantiated jointly as either Door and Wall, Wall and Door, or Door and Baseboard. The interpretation Floor, cannot appear beside any interpretation and is thus eliminated as a possibility for region 3. Finally, regions 1 and 5 are filtered by constraint 3, which is satisfied only when region 5 is instantiated as Floor or Baseboard.

The state of interpretation after filtering region 1 with all its neighbors appears in Figure 2(b). Region 2 is now due for filtering against its neighbor region 1 but since no interpretations have been eliminated from either region since the last time the pair was filtered, we proceed to region 3 and its neighbors. Applying constraint 1 (within) to regions 3 and 4, constraint 2 (beside) to regions 3 and 5, and constraint 3 (above) to regions 3 and 6, leaves the interpretation possibilities shown in Figure 2(c). The few remaining ambiguities are quickly resolved: Constraint 1 applied to regions 4 and 3 eliminates the interpretation Picture from region 4 and Constraint 3 applied to regions 5 and 1 eliminates the interpretation Door from region 1. At this point all pairs of regions have been filtered once. The process now reconsiders those pairs of regions whose interpretation sets have changed since the last time they were filtered. In particular, Constraint 1 is reapplied to regions 1 and 2, and eliminates the interpretation Knob from region 2. The final (correct) interpretation of the scene is shown in Figure 2(d).

B) Discussion of Filtering

Consistent region interpretations are conventionally found by performing a case analysis or backtrack search.[18-20] Such search

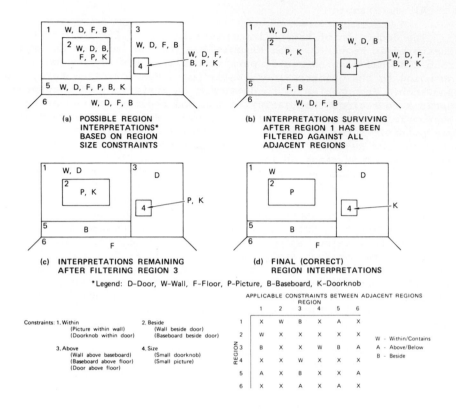

(a) POSSIBLE REGION
INTERPRETATIONS*
BASED ON REGION
SIZE CONSTRAINTS

(b) INTERPRETATIONS SURVIVING
AFTER REGION 1 HAS BEEN
FILTERED AGAINST ALL
ADJACENT REGIONS

(c) INTERPRETATIONS REMAINING
AFTER FILTERING REGION 3

(d) FINAL (CORRECT)
REGION INTERPRETATIONS

*Legend: D-Door, W-Wall, F-Floor, P-Picture, B-Baseboard, K-Doorknob

Constraints: 1. Within
(Picture within wall)
(Doorknob within door)

2. Beside
(Wall beside door)
(Baseboard beside door)

3. Above
(Wall above baseboard)
(Baseboard above floor)
(Door above floor)

4. Size
(Small doorknob)
(Small picture)

APPLICABLE CONSTRAINTS BETWEEN ADJACENT REGIONS

		REGION				
	1	2	3	4	5	6
1	X	W	B	X	A	X
2	W	X	X	X	X	X
3	B	X	X	W	B	A
4	X	X	W	X	X	X
5	A	X	B	X	X	A
6	X	X	A	X	A	X

W - Within/Contains
A - Above/Below
B - Beside

FIGURE 2   DEDUCING REGION INTERPRETATIONS USING RELATIONAL CONSTRAINTS

methods are ordinarily impractical on the scale with which we are dealing (hundreds of regions). Filtering, however, drastically reduces the number of cases that must be considered by eliminating inconsistent interpretations, once and for all, the first time the inconsistency is discovered. This also forestalls the characteristic thrashing of a backtrack search.

Filtering is not guaranteed always to terminate with unique interpretations for every region, first because a given set of constraints may not have a unique solution and second because only interpretations that are locally inconsistent are eliminated. Hence, a case analysis may still be needed. In our experiments, case analysis is implicit in the performance of unsafe merges. The merge represents the case that two regions have the same interpretation. The alternative case, namely, that the regions have different interpretations is not pursued because the pictorial evidence makes it much less likely.

In practice, many diverse sources of knowledge can augment symbolic relations to constrain region interpretations. The following section illustrates how region interpretations can be constrained, for example, by manual interaction, geometric models, maps, or partial descriptions produced by other scene analysis programs. The more knowledge available, the more likely it is that filtering will converge to unique interpretations.

V. EXPERIMENTS

A) Introduction

This section describes various experiments with the IGS paradigm involving different sources of knowledge. The first experiment was performed without knowledge of interpretations to provide a basis for comparison. In subsequent experiments, interpretations were constrained by user interaction, a geometric model, and prior knowledge about the spatial relationships of objects in a limited domain.

B) Implementation

A restricted version of the IGS paradigm was implemented in FORTRAN as an extension of a previously described region and analysis program.[12] The possible interpretations of a region were represented by patterns of bits as were the interpretations required to satisfy particular constraints. This representation was chosen to take advantage of the parallelism inherent in logical machine operations.

The region merging routine maintains a list of boundaries, with each boundary corresponding to a pair of adjacent regions. A flag is associated with each boundary to indicate whether its

constraints should be checked for possible elimination of interpretations from the adjacent regions; when the boundary list is
first created, after the initial partition, all boundaries are
flagged to ensure that each will be checked. When a boundary is
checked, its flag is reset; if any interpretation is eliminated
from a region, all other boundaries involving that region are
flagged. The filtering subroutine makes repeated passes through
the boundary list and checks the flagged boundaries until it makes
a complete pass without encountering any flags. At this point, if
it is possible, a merge is performed, the boundary list is updated,
and all boundaries of the newly created region are flagged for
checking.* If no merge is possible, the program terminates.

The consistency of region interpretations across a flagged
boundary is checked by first determining the applicable relations,
based on characteristics of the boundary. For each interpretation
of one region, there is, for each applicable relation, a bit pattern representing the set of possible interpretations for the
other region. These sets are ANDed together to give the subset of
interpretations that simultaneously satisfies all constraints,
given the interpretation of the first region. This set is then
ANDed with the possible interpretations of the other region and if
this intersection is empty, the interpretation of the first region
is eliminated.

The above filtering routine also is used to determine whether
two regions have the same interpretation and thus can be safely
merged. This condition requires that each interpretation of one
region be supported in the other region only by that same interpretation. It is checked by testing whether the deletion of each
interpretation of one region would result in the elimination of
the same interpretation from the other region.

C) Unguided Segmentation

This first experiment demonstrates problems that can arise
when segmentation is based directly on pictorial attributes. A
color photograph of a (Monterey, California) landscape was digitized to 8 bits/color at 240 x 240 resolution [Figure 3(a)]. For
efficiency, the actual experiment was performed in a 40 x 40 resolution image obtained by using every sixth resolution element of
the original digitization. An initial partition (at 40 x 40 resolution) was formed by grouping adjacent pixels of identical
brightness into regions [Figure 3(b)]. At this stage, each region
still consists of pixels belonging to only one object (e.g., sky,

---

* Note that checking is required even when a newly created region has the same interpretation possibilities as both its
parents. This is because its boundary relations with adjacent
regions may be different from those that previously held for
its parent regions.

(a) DIGITIZED IMAGE (8 BITS AT
256 x 256 PIXEL RESOLUTION)

(b) INITIAL PARTITION
(806 REGIONS)

(c) PARTITIONED SCENE AFTER
206 MERGES (600 REGIONS
REMAINING)

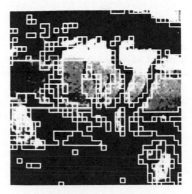

(d) PARTITIONED SCENE AFTER
350 ADDITIONAL MERGES
(250 REGIONS)

FIGURE 3   UNGUIDED SEGMENTATION OF LANDSCAPE SCENE (MONTEREY, CALIFORNIA)

grass, water, and so on). Since the system contained no knowledge about interpretations, it simply proceeded serially to merge adjacent regions with the lowest average absolute color contrast* along their common boundary. The results of merging are illustrated in Figures 3(c) and 3(d) with 600 and 250 regions remaining.

Figure 3(c) shows that elementary regions from the same object (e.g., sky, treetop, ground, and such) initially tend to agglomerate into larger regions representing that object. Without semantics, however, regions from different objects are inevitably merged [Figure 3(d)], and there is no stopping criterion. These failings are fundamental and occur regardless of resolution.

D) Interactively Guided Segmentation

1. Introduction

Initial experiments were performed with region interpretations obtained interactively from a human collaborator. In these experiments, adjacent pairs of regions were again proposed for merging, in an order determined by the average color contrast along their common boundaries. A region resulting from a merge inherited the set of possible interpretations formed by intersecting the interpretation sets of the parent regions. If this intersection set was empty, the proposed merge was not performed.

2. Interpretations Solicited by the System

In this series of experiments, users were requested to manually assign a correct interpretation to all regions in the initial partition larger than six pixels. The majority of regions smaller than 6 pixels were assigned the default set of all possible interpretations. These small regions could therefore merge either with any large region (and inherit that region's interpretation) or with another small region. Two large regions could merge only if they had the same interpretation. When two uninterpreted regions merged, if the size of the resultant region exceeded 6 pixels,

---

*Boundary contrast = $\sum\limits_{i=1}$ $(|r_{ai} - r_{bi}| + |g_{ai} - g_{bi}| + |b_{ai} - b_{bi}|)/N$

where r_{ai}, g_{ai}, and b_{ai} are the brightnesses of the ith boundary element from region a as seen through red, green, and blue filters respectively; r_{bi}, g_{bi}, and b_{bi} are the corresponding brightnesses from region b; and N is the number of boundary elements.

the program would request the user to supply manually a correct
interpretation. Merging terminated when all adjacent regions had
disjoint interpretations.

The above algorithm was applied to the initial partition of
the Monterey landscape scene shown in Figure 3(b). Twenty (out of
806) initial partitition regions exceeded six pixels and were
manually assigned an interpretation from the seven possibilities--
Bark, Crown, Ground, Mountain, Rock, Sea, and Sky. Twenty additional interpretations were assigned during the subsequent analysis when uninterpreted regions attained the required size by merging. The analysis terminated with the regions and interpretations
given in Figure 4. The low spatial resolution at which the analysis was performed is responsible for the jaggedness of some of the
boundaries and for a few minor errors, such as leakage of the Sea
(Region 5) through the Bark (Regions 6 and 7).

Comparable results were obtained with this approach in partitioning an indoor room scene (Figure 5). All major surfaces in
the room have been outlined and labeled correctly except for
chairlegs and tablelegs. These interpretations were not used in
the experiment because the corresponding surfaces were not adequately sampled at the 40 x 40 pixel resolution of the initial
partition. The size threshold of 6, used in both experiments, was
chosen because in previous experiments with unguided segmentation,
fatal merge errors virtually never involved smaller regions.
There are two advantages in deferring interpretation by setting
a high size threshold. First, fewer regions have to be interpreted. Second, the attributes of the region to be interpreted
are better defined. This latter factor becomes significant when
the use of pattern recognition techniques is contemplated for assigning region interpretations automatically.

3.   Interpretations Volunteered by the User

A second series of experiments on interactively guided segmentation were performed based on an alternative means of obtaining region interpretations. Initially, all pixels were assigned
the set of all possible interpretations. Using interactive graphics, a user could then outline an area of the image and assign an
interpretation to all pixels within the area, or delete an interpretation from the possibility sets of all pixels outside the area.
These actions correspond to inscribing or circumscribing an object,
respectively. The user also could point at isolated pixels and
designate an interpretation. Subjects were instructed to crudely
outline and label the major objects in a scene before the initial
partitioning so as to thwart anticipated merge errors. The resulting interaction produced an annotated image array in which
every pixel had an associated set of possible interpretations.

An initial partitioning of the annotated image array was performed in two steps. First, adjacent pixels with unique, identi-

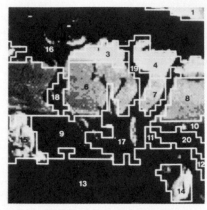

Final Region Interpretations

Interpretations	Regions
Sky	1,2,3,4
Mountain	5,6,7,8
Sea	9,10,11,12
Ground	13
Rock	14,15
Tree (Crown)	16
Tree (Bark)	17,18,19,20

FIGURE 4   FINAL SEMANTIC PARTITIONING OF LANDSCAPE SCENE

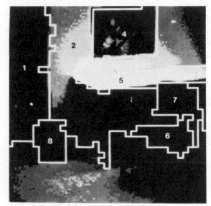

Final Region Interpretations

Interpretations	Regions
Door	1
Wall	2
Floor	3
Picture	4
Tabletop	5
Chairseat	6
Chairback	7
Waste Basket	8

FIGURE 5   FINAL SEMANTIC PARTITIONING OF SRI OFFICE SCENE

cal interpretations were grouped into regions; then all remaining adjacent pixels with both identical brightness and identical interpretation sets were grouped. Grouping uniquely interpreted regions independent of brightness reduces the total number of regions in the initial partition and makes the analysis of higher resolution images computationally feasible. The pictorial attributes of the larger regions that result are also more representative of the underlying object structure, which reduces the risk of proposing an incorrect merge.

After completion of initial partitioning, the merge interpretation cycle commenced. Since the system had no general semantic knowledge, all merges had to be regarded as unsafe. As such, merging proceeded at each stage by deleting the lowest contrast boundary between adjacent regions with nondisjoint interpretation sets.

Some typical results are shown in Figures 6 and 7. Figure 6(b) shows a manual partitioning of the Monterey scene used in the previous experiments. The initial partition (at 60 x 60 resolution) based on both brightness and manual labeling appears in Figure 6(c) and is far superior to that in Figure 3, which was based solely on brightness (at 40 x 40 resolution). The final partition and labeling appears in Figure 6(d). The Point Reyes scene analyzed in Figure 7 contains less occlusion. Consequently, fewer manually inscribed regions were needed adequately to constrain the final partition.

It is difficult to evaluate an experiment whose results are subject to the variability of human input. The results shown are, however, representative of the ten experiments of this type that have been performed. The final partition in Figure 6(d) appears to be subjectively better than the result previously obtained in Figure 4 where interpretations were solicited during the analysis. This improvement is probably attributable principally to the increased (60 x 60) resolution and to an initial partition that more closely resembled the desired final partition.

E)   Model-Guided Segmentation

1.   Introduction

An experiment was performed to demonstrate the feasibility of guiding segmentation with interpretations provided by a three-dimensional structural model. Specifically, the objective was to segment an image into regions that corresponded to the parts of an object articulated in the model. For this experiment, a color TV image of an air compressor was digitized to 6 bits/color at 60 x 60 resolution (Figure 8). This digitized image was then partitioned into elementary regions composed of adjacent pixels with identical brightness, as shown in Figure 9. Because of the uniform coloring of the compressor, which is typical of mechanical equipment, a nonsemantic region-merging program proved to be

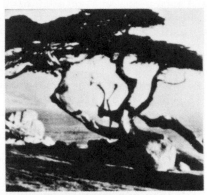

(a) DIGITIZED IMAGE
(8 BITS AT 256 x 256 RESOLUTION)

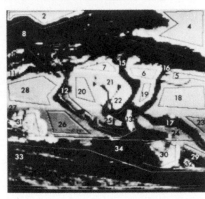

Interpretations	Regions
Sky	2,4,5,6,7,10*,11*
Mountain	18,19,20,21*,22*,28
Sea	23,24,25*,26,27*
Ground	33,34**
Rock	30,31,32*
Tree (Crown)	8
Tree (Bark)	12,13,15*,16*,17

(b) CRUDE MANUAL PARTITION AND LABELING

*Single point region.
**Circumscribed boundary.
All other regions are inscribed boundaries.

FIGURE 6   INTERACTIVELY GUIDED SEGMENTATION OF MONTEREY SCENE

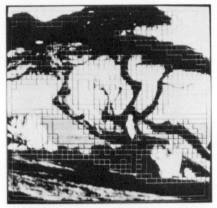

(c) INITIAL PARTITION (AT 60 x 60
RESOLUTION) BASED ON BRIGHTNESS
AND MANUAL LABELING; CONTAINS
481 REGIONS

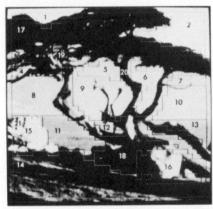

Interpretations	Regions
Sky	1-7
Mountain	8-10
Sea	11-13, 21
Ground	14
Rock	15-16
Tree (Crown)	17
Tree (Bark)	18-20

(d) FINAL PARTITION AND LABELING (21 REGIONS)

FIGURE 6   INTERACTIVELY GUIDED SEGMENTATION OF MONTEREY SCENE   (Concluded)

(a) DIGITIZED IMAGE
(8 BITS AT 256 x 256 RESOLUTION)

Interpretations	Regions
Sky	3,4
Tree	11*,12*,13*
Tree and Sky	2
Shrubs	14,15
Grass	6,7,9*,10*
Path	5

(b) CRUDE MANUAL PARTITION AND LABELING

*Single point region.
All other regions are inscribed boundaries.

FIGURE 7   INTERACTIVELY GUIDED SEGMENTATION OF POINT REYES SCENE

(c) INITIAL PARTITION
(AT 60 x 60 RESOLUTION);
CONTAINS 286 REGIONS

Interpretations	Regions
Sky	1
Tree	6,9
Tree and Sky	2
Shrubs	7,8
Grass	3,5
Path	4

(d) FINAL PARTITION AND LABELS (9 REGIONS)

FIGURE 7   INTERACTIVELY GUIDED SEGMENTATION OF POINT REYES SCENE
(Concluded)

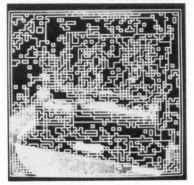

FIGURE 8   DIGITIZED IMAGE OF
COMPRESSOR (5 BITS AT
120 x 120 RESOLUTION)

FIGURE 9   INITIAL PARTITION (AT
60 x 60 RESOLUTION);
CONTAINS 931 REGIONS

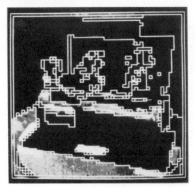

FIGURE 10   UNGUIDED PARTITION
WITH ERRORS (200 REGIONS)

highly unsatisfactory. Figure 10, for example, shows the partition that results from successively merging together pairs of adjacent regions with lowest color contrast, until 200 regions remain. It is evident that several significant errors, such as merging of the tank and base into a single region, already have occurred. Though pointless, the merging process obviously could be continued until the entire scene was included in one big region.

A structural model of this compressor was developed previously by Agin for use in planning assembly and disassembly sequences.[21] The model contains polyhedral representations for the major components of the compressor and associated metrical information. Given this polyhedral model and a simple projective camera model, a graphics program can display how the compressor in known position and orientation will appear from an arbitrary viewpoint shown in Figure 11. With the straightforward addition of a hidden surface algorithm, the display program also can determine which component of the compressor (e.g., tank, pump, motor) will actually be visible at each point in the image. This knowledge can be represented in the form of a visibility matrix, as shown in Figure 12.

2. Methodology

For this experiment, it was assumed that the relative location and orientation of the camera and compressor were known approximately. This undertainty in relative position introduces a corresponding uncertainty in the prediction of which compressor component will be visible at a given point in the image. The uncertainty in prediction can be represented by a set of overlapping regions, each of which expresses the composite for all compressor positions within the assumed range of uncertainty. Figure 13 shows the composite regions for the compressor parts distinguished in this experiment. These regions were transcribed manually from a series of displays showing the compressor at various positions over the allowed range. The transcription process, however, would be straightforward to automate.

The regions shown in Figure 13 were used to make initial interpretations of each pixel in the same way that manually designated region interpretations were used in the previous experiment. Specifically, the bit representing the interpretation of each retion was turned on for all pixels within that region and turned off for all those outside the region. An initial partition was then formed in which all adjacent pixels with identical brightnesses and interpretations were grouped into regions. Regions were then merged, as in the previous experiment, in order of weakest boundary contrast, subject to the existence of at least one common interpretation. Resultant regions again acquired interpretation sets formed by intersecting the possible interpretations of both parent regions.

FIGURE 11   POLYHEDRAL (WIRE FRAME) MODEL
SUPERIMPOSED ON T-V IMAGE
OF COMPRESSOR

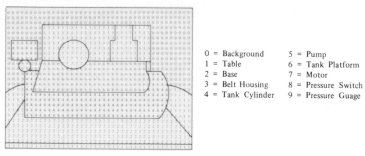

0 = Background   5 = Pump
1 = Table   6 = Tank Platform
2 = Base   7 = Motor
3 = Belt Housing   8 = Pressure Switch
4 = Tank Cylinder   9 = Pressure Guage

FIGURE 12   VISIBILITY MATRIX SHOWING PIXEL INTERPRETATIONS FOR COMPRESSOR
IN KNOWN RELATIVE POSITION TO CAMERA

FIGURE 13   COMPOSITE REGIONS DELINEATING
POSSIBLE AREAS OF IMAGE FOR
EACH INTERPRETATION

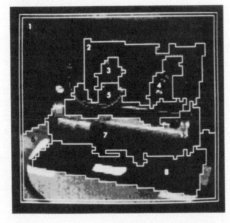

Region	Interpretations
1	Background
2	Belt Housing
3	Motor
4	Pump
5	Tank Platform
6	Table
7	Tank Cylinder
8	Base

FIGURE 14   FINAL PARTITION AND LABELS AFTER MODEL-GUIDED MERGING

3. Results

The merging process terminated with a partition in which all
adjacent regions had disjoint interpretations as shown in Figure 14.
Although the result is by no means perfect, it represents a considerable improvement over the attempt at unguided segmentation.
The result could be further improved by using a more detailed model, by iterating the analysis to refine the position estimate of
the compressor, and by using additional knowledge about compres-
sors such as the visual appearance of parts.

F) Constraint-Guided Segmentation

1. Introduction

In the previous experiments, segmentation was guided by interpretations that were specified for particular regions in a
particular image. In this experiment, region interpretations are
deduced as described in Section III, by using relational constraints that apply to generic interpretations over all images in
a given domain. These constraints specify conditions on the attributes and spatial relationships of regions that must be satisfied for given region interpretation to be valid.
An experimental test of constraint-guided segmentation was
performed in an elementary room scene, Figure 15(a), which resembles the idealized scene used in Figure 2. In this experiment,
the six possible region interpretations--Wall, Door, Picture,
Floor, Baseboard, and Doorknob--were constrained by eight relations
defined by the boxes in Table 1. Each box gives for each interpretation of a region R1, the permissible alternative interpretations for a related Region R2. For example, if Region R1 is *above*
R2, then R1 can be Floor only if R2 can also be Floor. On the
other hand, if R1 is *below* R2, then R1 can be Floor provided R2 is
either Floor, Door, or Baseboard. These constraints were compiled
into the filtering program in the form of bit tables so that bits
representing required interpretations could be rapidly matched
with logical operations against those representing possible region
interpretations. Interpretations were not constrained with respect to region attributes such as size, shape, or brightness.
The applicable relations between a pair of regions were determined in this experiment by factors that could be most easily extracted from an existing region data structure. The conditions
of applicability are summarized in Table 2. Applicability of the
relations *above, below,* and *beside* was based on the relative image
coordinates of the regions' centers of mass and vertices of their
bounding rectangles (derived from X, Y boundary *extrema*). Region
R1, for example, is defined to be *above* Region R2 provided that
its highest boundary point is higher in the image than the highest
point of R2 and that its lowest point is higher than R2's centroid.

494

(a) DIGITIZED IMAGE
(8 BITS AT 256 x 256
RESOLUTION)

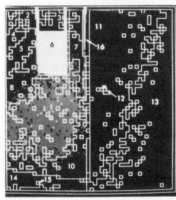

INTERPRETATION POSSIBILITIES
FOR SELECTED REGIONS
FOLLOWING INITIAL FILTERING

Region	Possible Interpretations
1-5	Picture Wall
6	Picture
7-10	Wall
11	Door
12	Knob
13	Door, Baseboard
14-15*	Baseboard
16*	Universal

(b) INITIAL PARTITION OF ROOM SCENE (264 REGIONS BASED ON 4
SIGNIFICANT BITS OF BRIGHTNESS AT 60 x 60 RESOLUTION)
*Manually assigned interpretation.

FIGURE 15   CONSTRAINT-GUIDED SEGMENTATION OF ROOM SCENE

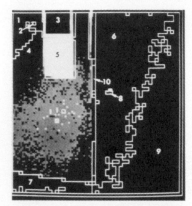

INTERPRETATION POSSIBILITIES
FOR SELECTED REGIONS
FOLLOWING REFILTERING

Regions	Possible Interpretations	Average Brightness
1	Picture, Wall	52
2	Picture	188
3	Picture, Wall	16
4	Wall	89
5	Picture	182
6	Door	13
7	Baseboard	27
8	Knob	64
9	Door, Baseboard	17
10	Wall, Door	48

(c) ROOM SCENE PARTITION AFTER 200 SAFE MERGES

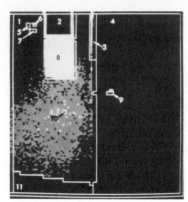

FINAL REGION INTERPRETATIONS

Region	Interpretation
1	Wall
2	Picture
3	Universal
4	Door
5	Picture
6	Picture
7	Picture
8	Picture
9	Knob
10	Picture
11	Baseboard

(d) FINAL PARTITION OF ROOM SCENE

FIGURE 15   CONSTRAINT-GUIDED SEGMENTATION OF ROOM SCENE   (Concluded)

Table 1

RELATIONS GOVERNING INTERPRETATIONS
OF ADJACENT REGIONS IN ROOM SCENE DOMAIN

R1 Above R2*	
R1	R2
Baseboard	Floor, Baseboard
Door	Knob, Floor, Door
Floor	Floor
Wall	Picture, Wall, Baseboard
Picture	Picture, Wall
Knob	Knob, Door

R1 Below R2	
R1	R2
Baseboard	Wall, Baseboard
Door	Knob, Door
Floor	Floor, Door, Baseboard
Wall	Picture, Wall
Picture	Picture, Wall
Knob	Knob, Door

R1 Beside R2	
R1	R2
Baseboard	Door, Baseboard
Door	Knob, Wall, Door, Baseboard
Floor	Floor
Wall	Picture, Wall, Door
Picture	Picture, Wall
Knob	Knob, Door

R1 Adjacent to R2	
R1	R2
Baseboard	Wall, Floor, Door, Baseboard
Door	Knob, Wall, Floor, Door, Baseboard
Floor	Floor, Door, Baseboard
Wall	Picture, Wall, Door, Baseboard
Picture	Picture, Wall
Knob	Knob, Door

R1 Contrasts with R2	
R1	R2
Baseboard	Knob, Picture, Wall, Floor, Door
Door	Knob, Picture, Wall, Floor, Baseboard
Floor	Knob, Picture, Wall, Door, Baseboard
Wall	Knob, Picture, Floor, Door, Baseboard
Picture	Knob, Picture, Wall, Floor, Door, Baseboard
Knob	Picture, Wall, Floor, Door, Baseboard

R1 No Contrast with R2	
R1	R2
Baseboard	Knob, Picture, Door, Baseboard
Door	Picture, Door, Baseboard
Floor	Knob, Picture, Wall, Floor
Wall	Knob, Wall, Floor
Picture	Knob, Picture, Floor, Door, Baseboard
Knob	Knob, Picture, Wall, Floor, Baseboard

R1 Inside R2	
R1	R2
Baseboard	Baseboard
Door	Door
Floor	Floor
Wall	Wall
Picture	Picture, Wall
Knob	Knob, Door

R1 Outside R2	
R1	R2
Baseboard	Baseboard
Door	Knob, Door
Floor	Floor
Wall	Picture, Wall
Picture	Picture
Knob	Knob

*Box lists the interpretations of Region R2 that are compatible with each interpretation of Region R1, given that R1 is above R2. Other relations are analogously defined.

Table 2

CONDITIONS OF APPLICABILITY FOR RELATIONS BETWEEN ADJACENT REGIONS

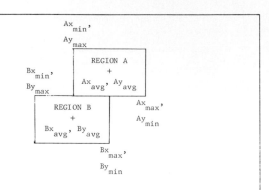

Ax_{min}, Ay_{max}

REGION A
+
Ax_{avg}, Ay_{avg}

Bx_{min}, By_{max}

REGION B
+
Bx_{avg}, By_{avg}

Ax_{max}, Ay_{min}

Bx_{max}, By_{min}

1. Above/below

Region A is above Region B if

$$(Ay_{max} > By_{max}) \wedge (Ay_{min} > By_{avg}) \wedge$$

$$[((Bx_{min} \leq Ax_{min}) \wedge (Ax_{min} < Bx_{max})) \vee$$

$$((Bx_{min} < Ax_{max}) \wedge (Ax_{max} \leq Bx_{max})) \vee$$

$$((Ax_{min} \leq Bx_{min}) \wedge (Ax_{max} \geq Bx_{max}))]^*$$

Region A is below Region B if

$$(Ay_{min} < By_{min}) \wedge (Ay_{max} < By_{avg}) \wedge$$

$$[((Bx_{min} \leq Ax_{min}) \wedge (Ax_{min} < Bx_{max})) \vee$$

$$((Bx_{min} < Ax_{max}) \wedge (Ax_{max} \leq Bx_{max})) \vee$$

$$((Ax_{min} < Bx_{min}) \wedge (Ax_{max} \geq Bx_{max}))]^*$$

2. Region A is beside Region B if

$$[((Ax_{max} > Bx_{max}) \wedge (Ax_{min} > Bx_{avg})) \vee$$

$$((Bx_{max} > Ax_{max}) \wedge (Bx_{min} > Ax_{avg}))] \wedge$$

$$[((By_{min} < Ay_{min}) \wedge (Ay_{min} < By_{max})) \vee$$

$$((By_{min} < Ay_{max}) \wedge (Ay_{max} < By_{max})) \vee$$

$$((Ay_{min} \leq By_{min}) \wedge (Ay_{max} \geq By_{max}))]^*$$

3. Region A contrasts with Region B if

$$|\text{Brightness A} - \text{Brightness B}| > T1$$

4. Region A has no contrast with Region B if

$$|\text{Brightness A} - \text{Brightness B}| < T2$$

*Note: Relations above, below, and beside apply only between regions larger than 5 pixels. Applicability of the relations adjacent, inside, and outside is determined by topological properties of the region data structure.

It was also required that the horizontal extents of R1 and R2 overlap and that the size of both regions exceed 5 pixels. The two last requirements minimize the possibility that a relation will be prematurely applied at an early stage of partitioning (see Section VI-B). *Below* is defined as the converse of *above*. *Beside* is a symmetric relation that applies when regions with vertical overlap are sufficiently displaced in a horizontal direction.

Adjacency is a universal relation that applies between any regions with a common boundary. *Inside* and *outside* refer to regions that are holes within other regions. These three relations are topological properties of the region data structure and not subject to the geometrical artifacts of merging. They are therefore applied regardless of region size.

The relation *contrast* applies whenever the average difference in brightness of two regions across their common boundary exceeds a conservatively large threshold, T1. The relation *no-contrast* applies when the difference is less than a second conservatively small threshold (T2). For the current scene, these thresholds were empirically set at T1 = 42 and T2 = 15 (assuming 256 brightness levels). The *contrast* constraint ensures that two adjacent and strongly contrasting regions will not receive the same interpretation if a surface with that interpretation is known to be approximately uniform in brightness. (It is assumed that all objects in the room domain except Picture have uniform brightness.) The relation *no-contrast* ensures that two regions with similar brightnesses will not receive different interpretations whose brightnesses are known to be significantly different--for example, Wall and Door.

2. Methodology

The image in Figure 15(a) was digitized to 8 bits at 60 x 60 resolution. All pixels were initially assigned the set of all possible interpretations. An arbitrarily chosen pixel within the baseboard area of the image was then manually assigned the unique interpretation Baseboard. This assignment was made to exclude explicitly the case where every region in the image receives the interpretation Picture (i.e., the image portrays a picture of a room scene rather than a room scene). Also, a thin vertically elongated rectangular region was drawn to isolate the bright specular reflection at the top of the image between the Door and Wall. This was done to avoid complicating the initial experimentation by introducing semantics to handle specularity. All pixels within the isolated region were assigned a special universal interpretation that both supports and is supported by any adjacent interpretation. With this interpretation, the anomalous region was effectively removed from the analysis since it could not participate in filtering or safe merges and could merge unsafely only with another region that has the universal interpretation.

The annotated image array was partitioned into elementary regions composed of adjacent pixels with identical brightness (to 4 significant bits) and identical interpretations. The resulting partition, shown in Figure 15(b) contained 264 regions. At this stage, all regions admitted all possible interpretations, except regions 15 (baseboard) and 16 (universal).

The region interpretations were filtered using relational constraints applicable in the initial partition. The results of filtering are shown for selected regions in the caption of Figure 15(b). Note that many parts of the scene already have acquired unique interpretations. These parts include large areas of the Wall (Regions 7-10) and Door (11), as well as the Baseboard (14), the Doorknob (12), and the lower (bright) half of the Picture (6). Many of the smaller regions contained *within* these areas are also labeled with the same interpretation as the containing region.

During filtering, eliminations propagated from the manually assigned Baseboard interpretation. The possibilities for Region 14, *adjacent* to and *noncontrasting* with Region 15 (known to be Baseboard) were immediately reduced to Door or Baseboard. Regions 10 and 14 could then be filtered by the relations *above* and *contrast,* thus leaving those regions with the unique interpretations Wall and Baseboard, respectively. The interpretation of Region 13, beside and noncontrasting with Baseboard Region 14, was then narrowed to the alternatives Door and Baseboard. The interpretation Wall propagated upward from Region 10 to Region 9 through the relations *above* and *no-contrast,* and subsequently to Regions 5, 7, and 8. This, in turn, allowed Region 6 to be interpreted as Picture since it is *above* and *contrasting* with Region 9, now known to be Wall. Meanwhile, Region 11, which is *beside* and *contrasting* with Region 9 (Wall) and *adjacent* and *noncontrasting* with Region 13 (Door or Baseboard), is uniquely constrained to be Door.

The initial stage of filtering leaves two main areas of the image with uncertain interpretations. Region 13 and its interior regions still admit the possibilities Door or Baseboard, while Regions 1-6 in the upper left part of the scene can each be interpreted as either Wall or Picture. The Door/Baseboard ambiguity persists because Regions 11 and 13 do not satisfy the formal conditions defining the relation *above*. The second ambiguity arises because of a brightness gradient across the Wall such that Regions 5 and 8 do not fulfill the conditions for either *contrast* or *no-contrast*. Consequently, the interpretation Picture cannot be eliminated from Region 5 and the resulting Wall/Picture ambiguity then propagates to the other regions in the area. A third and relatively minor area of ambiguity exists among the small regions on the border between Wall and Door. These regions, adjacent to both Door and Wall, are classified as either Door, Wall, or Baseboard.

Based on the interpretations surviving the initial filtering, approximately 200 safe merges are performed. The resulting partition containing about 68 regions, after filtering, yielded the results shown in Figure 15(c). The safe merges primarily involved adjacent regions already having the same unique interpretations. Regions in the upper part of the Wall with possible interpretations Wall and Picture also could be safely merged where the *contrast* constraint did not apply (since a Picture/Wall boundary is required to have *contrast*). Although the resulting partition appears much cleaner, the basic ambiguities described above persist. These ambiguities must now be resolved by postulating unsafe merges, based on the region brightnesses included in the caption of Figure 15(c).

The first unsafe merge significantly affecting interpretation occurred with approximately 43 regions remaining. Regions 6 and 9 [in Figure 15(c)], with a contrast of 4, were merged into a single region with the unique interpretation Door (the intersection of the interpretation possibilities for Regions 6 and 9) and an average brightness of 15. Next, with approximately 25 regions remaining, Regions 1 and 4 (contrast 37) were merged to form one large region of Wall with brightness 87. As a result of this merge, the contrast relation could now be applied to eliminate the interpretation Wall from Region 3. Finally, with about 20 regions left, the small regions, such as Region 10 between Door and Wall, were merged unsafely into Wall. At this point, after a total of 43 unsafe merges and 214 safe merges, the analysis terminated with 11 regions remaining, all having unique and disjoint interpretations.

3. Results

The final partition and associated region interpretations are shown in Figure 15(d). Based on the limited semantics used in the experiment, the analysis is correct. A wall-mounted thermostat was fragmented into three regions (5-7), which were then interpreted as Pictures. A noisy pixel in the center area of the wall area was also assigned the interpretation Picture. These interpretations occurred because Picture was the only legal possibility for a contrasting region contained within a region labeled Wall. The interpretation errors could have been avoided by introducing explicit interpretations for Thermostat and Noise (which would be distinguished from Picture by additional constraints on region size). Finally, the so-called picture, actually a calendar, was split into two regions--a landscape and numeric data--because the spiral binding connecting them was invisible in the digitized image.

A point worthy of note is that no intrinsic classification of regions was made. With two minor exceptions, interpretations were derived entirely from context.

4. Acquisition and Debugging of Knowledge

The constraints used in this experiment were developed empirically. Incorrect or inadequate constraints manifest themselves
ultimately by the elimination of all interpretations from some region. When this situation occurred, the analysis was immediately
halted so that the constraints could be interactively refined.
Unfortunately, because of the way eliminations propagate, the
source of the error was often not the uninterpretable region.
Hence, debugging was difficult.

There are two basic types of error: the elimination of a
correct region interpretation and the unsafe merging of regions
that should represent distinct objects. The first type of error
occurs when a valid supporting interpretation is omitted from the
definition of a relation or when a relation is inappropriately
invoked. An erroneous unsafe merge occurs because an incorrect
region interpretation was not eliminated early enough in the analysis and is therefore an indication that additional constraints
are needed.

VI. DISCUSSION

A) Features

The scene analysis paradigm described in this paper has three
main features. First, segmentation and interpretation are completely and effectively integrated; second, many diverse sources
of knowledge can be used to guide the analysis; and third, the
process of interpretation and its integration with segmentation
can be made tolerably efficient.

Segmenting on the basis of interpretations rather than raw
attributes allows retention of semantically important, but visually indistinct, boundaries [such as the Door/Baseboard boundary
in Figure 15(d)] and at the same time, deletion of high-contrast
edges that are insignificant to the current task (such as interi-
or details of the picture on the wall). A related advantage is
the existence of a well-defined criterion for terminating the
analysis--namely, when all adjacent regions have disjoint interpretations.

The more knowledge sources available, the quicker the filtering process will converge to unique region interpretations. De-
terming region interpretations at an early stage of partitioning
reduces the need to resort to unsafe merges, which are a principal
source of error. To date, we have experimented independently with
three sources of knowledge: Manual interaction, geometric models,
and relational constraints. All these knowledge sources can be
expressed uniformly as constraints on the possible interpretations
of regions. They can thus be combined in a straightforward way.
Many other sources of knowledge are expressible as constraints on

the possible interpretations for given areas of a scene and can therefore also be integrated. In particular, this provides a possible mechanism for integrating partial descriptions of the scene produced by several independent modules, or even other scene analysis programs.

In the current implementation, the overheads associated with region merging completely dominate the computation expended in filtering. The room scene experiment (Figure 15) took 5 minutes on a KA-10 processor, of which only about 1 minute was spent deducing region interpretations. The relative efficiency of the interpretation process stems from the advantages of filtering vis a vis case analysis, as summarized in Section IV and from our use of bit-parallel logical operations in performing constraint checking.

B) Shortcomings

The paradigm has some unresolved problems. The first concerns relations that apparently were applied appropriately, but that may later prove to have been inappropriate--after they have already been used to eliminate "correct" interpretations. (See Figure 16.) Again, because of the way eliminations propagate, this type of error is extremely difficult to trace.

A second fundamental issue concerns whether the IGS approach can be extended to less constrained domains. The existing system has been demonstrated in a variety of domains that each contain fewer than 10 objects and 10 relations. The real world contains millions of objects and millions of relations. Clearly, a more concise initial symbolic description at a general level is required, perhaps in terms of surface characteristics such as curvature (planar, convex, concave), orientation (vertical, horizontal), texture and material (e.g., metal, plastic, wood), and relations such as occlusion, joining, and support. Bajcsy's[22] work on symbolizing texture and that of Marr[23] and Paton[24] on symbolizing shading are relevant. Once the scene has been analyzed in general terms, that analysis can be used to guide a more detailed specific analysis.

In addition to the above conceptual problems, come implementational compromises were adopted for efficiency. First, constraints currently are restricted to be binary-valued (all or nothing) relations between pairs of adjacent regions. Clearly, the filtering process could be extended to handle not only relations among more than two entities that are not necessarily pictorially adjacent, but also relations that involve degrees of uncertainty. We have experimented with a LISP program called MSYS,[25] which performs region interpretations based on real-valued, procedurally represented constraints. However, MSYS has not yet been integrated with a segmentation program to perform a complete scene analysis. Second, there is no provision for backup in the event of an erroneous unsafe merge. Elsewhere, we have conjectured that

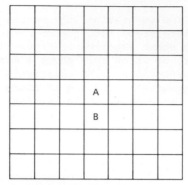

(a) SECTION OF IMAGE AT AN
     EARLY STAGE OF PARTITIONING
     (REGION A ABOVE REGION B)

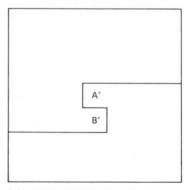

(b) SAME SECTION OF IMAGE:
     REGIONS A AND B HAVE BEEN
     MERGED INTO REGIONS A'
     AND B' RESPECTIVELY, WITH
     (REGION B' ABOVE REGION A')

FIGURE 16   INAPPROPRIATE USE OF THE RELATION "ABOVE"
             AT AN EARLY STAGE OF PARTITIONING

a vision system with *enough* knowledge would not need backup,[26] but this ideal has yet to be realized in practice. Finally, candidate regions for unsafe merges are currently selected on the basis of average color contrast. Comparing the textures and brightness gradients of regions, in addition to their average colors, should significantly improve the basic decision regarding whether two regions belong to the same surface and thereby reduce the risk of an erroneous merge.

C) Applications

Applications of interpretation-guided segmentation come readily to mind. For example, we are currently applying our methodology of interactively guided segmentation to boundary tracing tasks in cartography[27] and photo interpretation. The extraction of object boundaries in aerial imagery is too difficult to do completely automatically and uneconomical to do in quantity completely by hand (e.g., by detailed tracing on a digitizing table). A gradual transition toward more automatic operation can be made by providing relational knowledge that lessens dependence on manual specification of interpretations.

The use of structural models for guiding segmentation is well suited to industrial inspection tasks in which the structure of a manufactured item is fixed and its position is known approximately. The resulting analysis can be used to locate the item's position exactly and also to locate the boundaries of parts of the item as a prelude to inspection. This inspection scenario is representative of a variety of tasks involving knowledge about the approximate image location of objects in a relatively static scene. Maps can be used in a similar fashion as structural models to guide the interpretation of medical imagery such as x-rays and thermograms. A previous analysis of a scene is yet another source of knowledge about object location that can be used in tasks such as change detection, motion tracking (i.e., analyzing a series of scenes taken from slightly different viewpoints), and the analysis of a sequence of movie frames.

In conclusion, the apparent facility with which multiple sources of knowledge may be integrated and the resulting improvements observed in segmentation make Interpretation-Guided Segmentation a promising paradigm for future research and application.

D) Acknowledgments

The authors wish to acknowledge the help of Stephen Weyl, who programmed most of the FORTRAN region finding system, and Helen Wolf, who provided valuable additional programming support.

REFERENCES

1. C. Brice and C. Fennema, "Scene Analysis Using Regions", *Artificial Intelligence 1*, pp. 205-226 (1970).
2. H. Barrow and R. Popplestone, "Relational Descriptions in Picture Processing," in *Machine Intelligence*, Vol. 6 (Edinburgh University Press, Edinburgh, Scotland, 1971).
3. M. Yachida and S. Tsuji, "Application of Color Information to Visual Perception", *Pattern Recognition, 3*, p. 307 (1971).
4. J. L. Muerle and D. C. Allen, "Experimental Evaluation of Techniques for Automatic Segmentation of Objects in a Complex Scene," in *Pictorial Pattern Recognition*, Cheng et al. (Eds.) pp. 3-14 (Thompson Book Co., Washington, D. C., 1968).
5. A. Rosenfeld and M. Thurston, "Edge and Curve Detection for Visual Scene Analysis," *IEEE Trans. Comput.*, C-20, p. 562 (1971)
6. A. Rosenfeld, M. Thurston, and Y. Lee, "Edge and Curve Detection: Further Experiments," *IEEE Trans. Comput.*, C-21, p. 677 (1972).
7. F. Tomita, M. Yachida, and S. Tsuji, "Detection of Homogeneous Regions by Structural Analysis", *Proc 3IJCAI*, pp. 564-571 (August 1973).
8. R. Ohlander, "Analysis of Natural Images", Ph. D. Thesis, Department of Computer Science, Carnegie-Mellon University, Pittsburgh, Pennsylvania (April 1975).
9. J. Gupta and P. Wintz, "Multi-Image Modeling", TR-EE 74-24 School of Electrical Engineering, Purdue University, Lafayette, Indiana (September 1974).
10. T. V. Robertson, K. S. Fu, and P. H. Swain, "Multispectral Image Partitioning", Information Note 071373, Laboratory for Application of Remote Sensing, Purdue University, Lafayette, Indiana (1973).
11. A. G. Wacker and D. A. Landgrebe, "Boundaries in Multispectral Imagery by Clustering", 1970 IEEE Symposium on Adaptive Processes, University of Texas, Austin, Texas (December 1970).
12. J. M. Tenenbaum and S. A. Weyl, "A Region Analysis Subsystem for Interactive Scene Analysis", Proceedings Fourth International Joint Conference on Artificial Intelligence, Tblisi, USSR (September 1975).
13. A. Hanson, E. Riseman, and P. Nagin, "Region Growing in Textured Outdoor Scenes", Technical Report 75C-3, Department of Computer and Information Science, University of Massachusetts, Amherst, Massachusetts (February 1975).
14. Y. Yakimovsky and J. Feldman, "A Semantics-Based Decision Theoretic Region Analyzer", *Proc. 3IJCAI*, pp. 580-588 (1973).
15. C. Harlow and S. Eisenbeis, "The Analysis of Radiographic Images", *IEEE Trans. Computers*, C-22, pp. 678-688 (1973).
16. D. G. Waltz, "Generating Semantic Discriptions from Drawings of Scenes with Shadows", AI TR-271, Artificial Intelligence Laboratory, Massachusetts Institute of Technology, Cambridge, Massachusetts (August 1972).

17. A. Rosenfeld, A. Hummel, and S. Zucker, "Scene Labelling by Relaxation Operations", TR-379, Computer Science Department, University of Maryland, College Park, Maryland (1975).

18. R. O. Duda, "Some Current Techniques for Scene Analysis", Technical Note 46, Artificial Intelligence Center, Stanford Research Institute, Menlo Park, California (October 1970).

19. A. Guzman, "Analysis of Curved Line Drawings Using Context and Global Information", *Machine Intelligence,* Vol. 6, pp. 325-376, B. Meltzer and D. Michie (eds.) (Edinburgh University Press, Edinburgh, Scotland, 1971).

20. Y. Y. Yakimovsky, "On the Recognition of Complex Structures: Computer Software Using AI Applied to Pattern Recognition", *Proceedings International Joint Converence on Pattern Recognition,* pp. 345-353, Copenhagen, Denmark (August 1974).

21. G. J. Agin, "Artificial Intelligence--Research and Applications," N. Nilsson (Ed.), Report on Contract DAHCO4-75-C-0005, pp. 90-100, Artificial Intelligence Center, Menlo Park, California (May 1975).

22. R. Bajcsy, "Computer Description of Textured Surfaces", *Proc 3IJCAI,* pp. 572-579 (August 1973).

23. D. Marr, "Early Processing of Visual Information", AI Memo No. 340, AI Laboratory, Massachusetts Institute of Technology, Cambridge, Massachusetts (December 1975).

24. K. Paton, "Picture Description Using Legendre Polynomials", *Computer Graphics and Image Processing,* Vol. 4, No. 1, pp. 40-54 (March 1975).

25. H. Barrow and J. M. Tenebaum, "MSYS: A System for Reasoning about Scenes", Technical Note 121, Artificial Intelligence Center, Stanford Research Institute, Menlo Park, California (March 1976).

26. H. Barrow and J. M. Tenenbaum, "Representation and Use of Knowledge in Vision", Technical Note 108, Artificial Intelligence Center, Stanford Research Institute, Menlo Park, California (July 1975). (Also published in *SIGART,* June 1975.)

27. T. Garvey and J. M. Tenenbaum, "Application of Interactive Scene Analysis Techniques to Cartography", Technical Note 127, Artificial Intelligence Center, Stanford Research Institute, Menlo Park, California (March 1976).

PATTERN RECOGNITION USING DEGENERATE
REFERENCE DATA

J. R. Ullmann
Department of Applied Mathematics and Computing Science,
The University of Sheffield
Sheffield S10 2TN, England

ABSTRACT

In pattern recognition and scene analysis a well-known technique is to construct a graph which, when labelled with pattern
attributes, abstractly represents a pattern. An unknown pattern
can be recognized by comparing its representative graph with the
reference graphs of specimen patterns. The comparison of representative graphs involves determination of some sort of isomorphism, and there may be many specimen patterns for each recognition class. Recognition involves many computations, each akin to
isomorphism determination, for each recognition class.
To reduce the total amount of computation the present work
aims to achieve recognition by using just one elaborate computation
for each recognition class, instead of a separate computation for
each separate specimen in each recognition class. The basic idea
is to take the union of the representative graphs of all specimens
in a given class, and determine subgraph isomorphism between an
unknown pattern and this union. The idea has been applied in a
watered-down form to hand-printed numeral recognition.

I. INTRODUCTION

Insertion or deletion of spelling errors can be automatically
corrected by matching a word against dictionary words, one by one,
using the dynamic programming method of Lowrance and Wagner [1].
This is computationally extravagant if there are many thousands of
words in the dictionary. Instead of executing a matching algorithm
for each dictionary word in turn, it may be more economical to use
a single complicated computation that does the whole job in one
step, instead of working word by word [2].
To recognize a distorted pattern we could match it in turn
against stored reference patterns, using for instance the short-
cut dynamic programming algorithm of Fischler and Elschlager [9].
An unknown pattern could be assigned to the class of the best-
matching reference pattern. If there were many reference patterns
per class, this nearest neighbor method might be more extravagant
than a method that required just one computation per recognition
class. The problem of achieving elastic matching by one computation per class, instead of by one computation per reference specimen per class, is analogous to the problem of correcting insertion

508

and deletion errors by just one computation instead of one computation per dictionary word. This analogy deserves to be noted because it conforms to the recurrent suggestion [3,4] that a recognition system ought to have many hierarchical levels, the logical structure at all levels being similar. The method introduced in the present paper for dealing with contextual relationships between parts of a single character is similar to a method [2] for dealing with contextual relationships between characters in a word.

To recognize a distorted pattern, most practical speech recognition and character recognition systems do not use a nearest neighbor method like that mentioned in the previous paragraph. Since this paper is concerned with mitigating the computational cost of iterative elastic-matching nearest neighbor methods, we ought to say why such methods may deserve attention.

The part of a practical recognition system that deals with deformation or distortion of patterns is often regarded as adhoc and outside the scope of basic theory. We think that this assessment is incorrect and that the problem of recognizing distorted patterns can usefully be tackled theoretically from first principles. One such investigation [6] suggests that an iteratively computed distance measure will give lower recognition error rates than a structurally comparable non-iterative method.

Informally, the iterative method [6] makes use of contextual relationships ("springs") between parts of a pattern. To achieve given error rates there appear to be two options:

(i)   To use simple features and exploit contextual relationships between them.

(ii) To use larger and more complicated features and ignore their interdependencies.

Here the word *feature* is not very meaningful. Nevertheless it is plausible that the simpler the features, the lower the cost of determining them automatically (e.g. by the method of section 10.3 of [7]). It is this consideration that has roused our interest in option (i), which generally demands iterative computation [9,8,6]. The overall strategy of our research is to devise the logical structure of a recognition system *so that* the complicated details of the design can be determined automatically. Without such automation, progress in pattern recognition may slow down when design complexity overwhelms the intuitive grasp of a human designer.

Because of their conceptual simplicity, it is natural to choose nearest neighbor methods as a practical framework for the investigation of option (i). Against the advantage of logical simplicity we must weigh the disadvantage of the high computational cost of nearest neighbor methods that use iterative distance calculations. The present paper contributes just one basic idea towards avoiding this economic disadvantage: we do not claim to present a fully developed practical technique of recognition.

In this paper we use handprinted character recognition in its old, but no longer fashionable, role as a dropsophylla of pattern recognition. To master the problem of making a machine recognize distorted patterns we do not initially need an application more complicated than the recognition of handprinted characters. Hand-printed character recognition has not finally been "done"; otherwise mail-order companies would use it more widely. It remains a research area that still has potential commercial value.

A handprinted character recognition machine should tolerate some distortions but not others. For instance, if a machine tolerated a distortion that pulled the middle of the character '1' leftwards and upwards to make a '7', then this machine might mis-recognize 7's as 1's. *Admissible* distortions are those that we require a machine to tolerate [6].

Experimentally we have worked with black/white edge detectors. The elementary theory that is outlined in the next section is sure-ly not restricted to character recognition.

II. CORRESPONDENCE OF EDGES

A distortion is a 1:1 continuous function whose inverse is a continuous function. This paper is concerned with distortions that map a two-dimensional space into a two-dimensional space. Prior to spatial quantisation or digitisation, a binary character is an assignment of black or white to every point in a two-dimensional space. When this space is distorted, the distortion takes each black point to exactly one black point in the distorted space, and the same is true for white points. Furthermore the distortion takes each point that lies on a black/white edge to a point that lies on a black/white edge. We shall assume that at any two edge-points that correspond in any given admissible distortion, the tangential directions of the edges differ by not more than $\pm\theta^o$, where θ^o is substantially less than 180°.

If a binary character K_2 is identical to that which is produced by applying distortion D to K_1 then we say that K_1 and K_2 *match* in D. To determine whether any two given characters K_1 and K_2 match in an admissible distortion D, we can in principle determine whether each edge point in K_1 corresponds in D to an edge point in K_2, and vice versa, subject to the condition that tangential directions at corresponding edge points differ by not more than $\pm\theta^o$. (If K_2 matches K_1 in D, then this condition prevents $\overline{K_2}$ from matching K_1, where $\overline{K_2}$ is the complement of K_2, obtained by changing every black point in K_2 to white and every white point in K_2 to black). It may not, however, be practical to consider an infinite number of edge-points. Instead some sort of discretisation is required, and the following approach is perhaps the simplest.

We partition the underlying space into a set U_1 of $|u_1|$ zones, e.g. as in fig. 1(a), and we divide 0°–360° into a set U_2 of $|u_2|$

ranges, e.g. as in fig.1(b).

1	6	11	16	21
2	7	12	17	22
3	8	13	18	23
4	9	14	19	24
5	10	15	20	25

Fig. 1 a

A 5 x 5 grid U_1

Fig. 1 b

A set, U_2, of 16 Angular ranges

It is convenient to represent the elements of the Cartesian product $U_1 \times U_2$ by $y_1, y_2, \ldots, y_{|u_1|x|u_2|}$. Thus

$$U_1 \times U_2 = Y = \{y_1, \ldots y_i, \ldots y_{|u_1|x|u_2|}\}$$

If and only if distortion D would take an edge-point whose position and tangential direction correspond to y_i to an edge-point whose position and tangential direction correspond to y_j we say that y_i *corresponds* to y_j in D.

Let $Y_1 = \{Y_{11}, Y_{12}, \ldots Y_{1i} \ldots Y_{1|u_1|x|u_2|}\}$ be a vector corresponding 1:1 to Y, with elements defined by

$$Y_{1i} = \begin{cases} 1 & \text{if } K_1 \text{ contains an edge-point with position and} \\ & \text{tangential orientation corresponding to } y_i. \\ 0 & \text{otherwise} \end{cases}$$

We define Y_2 similarly corresponding to K_2.

We say that Y_1 matches Y_2 in D if

(a) for all i, $y_{1i}=1$ implies that there is at least one j such that $y_{2j} = 1$,

and   (b) for all j, $y_{2j} = 1$ implies that there is at least one i such that $y_{1i} = 1$ and y_i corresponds to y_j in D.

Our approach to recognition is based on comparing Y_1 with Y_2 instead of comparing K_1 with K_2 because the number of elements of

Y_1 is finite whereas K_1 comprises an infinite number of elements. Ideally we would like the matching of Y_1 with Y_2 to be tantamount to the matching of K_1 with K_2. Thus we would like

(i) K_1 not to match K_2 in D if Y_1 does not match Y_2 in D, and
(ii) K_1 not to match K_2 in D if Y_1 does not match Y_2 in D.

Condition (i) is more nearly satisfied the smaller the zones and angular ranges employed in the construction of Y. It follows from our definitions that (ii) is necessarily satisfied.

To prove this we assume that K_1 matches K_2 when Y_1 does not match Y_2, and show that this leads to a contradiction. If Y_1 does not match Y_2 then for some i such that $y_{1i} = 1$ there is no y_j corresponding in D to y_i such that $y_{2j} = 1$. (Or there is some $y_{2j} = 1$ such that there is no y_i corresponding in D to y_j such that $y_{1i} = 1$, but the same reasoning applies to this as to the other case.) If $y_{1i} = 1$ then there is at least one edge-point in K_1 in the zone and angular range corresponding to y_i, and this point corresponds in D to a point in K_2, since K_1 and K_2 match in D. This point in K_2 lies in the zone and angular range corresponding to y_j, and therefore $y_{2j} = 1$ for some j such that y_j and y_i correspond in D. This contradicts our previous assertion and thus completes the proof.

This elementary proof depends on the stipulation that each edgepoint in K, corresponds to at least one element of Y. This stipulation also means that, in any distortion whatsoever, every element of Y corresponds to at least one element of Y. In this sense Y is closed under distortion. If we change our construction and redefine Y, it appears necessary to arrange that Y is still closed under distortion. For instance in the character recognition system of Patterson [10] the shape of the black-white edge at each point is detected, and the shape detectors are designed so that any distortion takes every edge-shape to at least one other detected edge-shape: the set of edge-shapes is closed under distortion. The requirement for closure appears to be basic, general, and not confined to character recognition, but it has not (so far as we know) been studied in the pattern recognition literature.

As a further illustration of this basic requirement we now outline a further practical scheme that we have used experimentally. The tangential direction at each-edge point is detected, and the directions of neighboring edge-points are compared, as described in detail in [6]. The result is that every edge-point is labelled with at least one of the edge-pair symbols shown in fig. 2. Besides each symbol in fig. 2 is an index number. If, for example, an edge point is labelled with index number 4 this means that neighboring tangents near that point are both in a $22\frac{1}{2}°$ incrementally sloping direction. If an edge-point is labelled with index number 5 this means either that near that point there is a $22\frac{1}{2}°$ tangent above a vertical tangent or that the configuration of the neighboring tangents is any one of those shown in fig. 3.

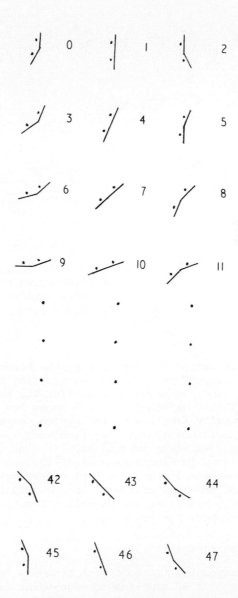

Fig. 2. Tangent-pair symbols with their index numbers. The dots show which side black is on.

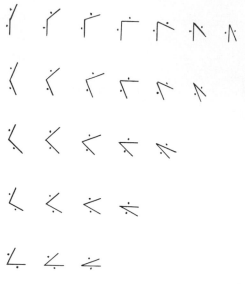

Fig. 3

The logic has been designed so that if
a pair of neighboring tangents has any
of these configurations then the top
left pair (index number 5) will be detected.

This design-specification ensures that at the black corner-point
in fig. 4(a) the tangent pairs shown in fig. 4(b) are detected,
and at the black line-end shown in fig. 4(c) the tangent-pairs
shown in fig. 4(d) are detected. Fig. 5 shows how a portion of a
character was actually labelled by the system described in [6],
and note that any picture element may have many labels.

In recognition we use a grid u_1 such as that shown in fig.1(a).
The symbols in fig. 2 in fact represent 48 classes of edge-shapes,
and the system has been designed so that every edge-point belongs
to at least one of these 48 classes. Let us call this set of 48
classes U_3, so $|U_3| = 48$; and let us define $X = U_1 \times U_3 = \{x_1 \ldots x_i \ldots x_{|u_1|x|u_3|}\}$, where $Y = |u_1|x|u_3|$.

Let $X_1 = \{x_{11}, \ldots x_{ij}, \ldots x_{1|u_1|x|u_3|}\}$

be a vector corresponding 1:1 to X with elements defined by

$$x_{1i} = \begin{cases} 1 & \text{if } K_1 \text{ contains an edge-point labelled with the} \\ & \text{index number and located in the positional zone} \\ & \text{corresponding to } y_i \\ 0 & \text{otherwise} \end{cases}$$

And let us define Y_2 similarly corresponding to K_2.

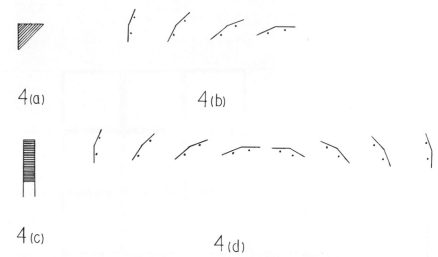

4(a)

4(b)

4(c)

4(d)

Fig. 4 a. A black corner.
   4 b. Tangent-pairs that would be detected at the corner in
         Fig. 4 a.
   4 c. A black end.
   4 d. Tangent-pairs that would be detected at the end in
         Fig. 4 c.

Matching of X_1 and X_2 is defined just the same as matching of Y_1 and Y_2 and as before we would like

(i) K_1 to match K_2 in D if X_1 matches X_2 in D, and
(ii) K_1 not to match K_2 in D if X_1 does not match X_2 in D.

A simple amendment to our previous proof establishes that (ii) is necessarily satisfied. This is true because the construction is such that X has the closure property that any distortion takes each element of X to at least one element of X. If we had not appreciated the need for closure we might not have hit on the idea of, so to speak, *or*ing together the shapes shown in fig. 3, which has allowed us to work with 48 edge-pairs instead of the 200 edge-shapes of Patterson [10].

III. HAMMING DISTANCE NEAREST NEIGHBOR RECOGNITION

An over-simple assumption is that every admissible distortion takes the ith element of X to be i^{th} element of X. According to this (unrealistic) assumption no black/white edge-point is moved from any of the fig. 1(a) zones to any other. We have thought it

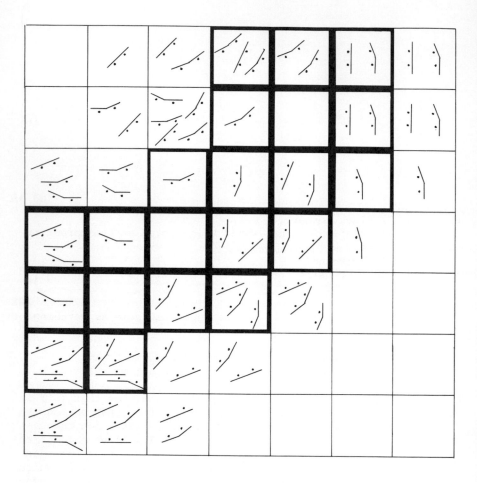

Fig. 5. A portion of the lower curve of a handprinted '3'. In
this figure each grid-cell corresponds to a single bit in
the binarised character. Cells corresponding to black
bits have heavy black edges. Cells corresponding to white
bits have fine edge lines. Within each cell tangent-pair
symbols indicate which tangent-pairs have been detected
within a window [6] centered on that cell.

worthwhile to investigate this simplification experimentally in the case where the grid U_1 is very coarse, actually comprising 5x5 cells.

Fig. 6 is a reject versus substitution error curve for the simple nearest neighbor recognition ruls:- assign $X^?$ to the class of the reference X' to which the Hamming distance is least. The data, experimental method, and the actual stored reference patterns and the test patterns were as described in [6]. Thus the data comprised handprinted numerals 0 - 9 written by eighty writers. There were 1600 test patterns and an average of 195 stored reference patterns automatically selected by a trivial elaboration of Hart's method [11].

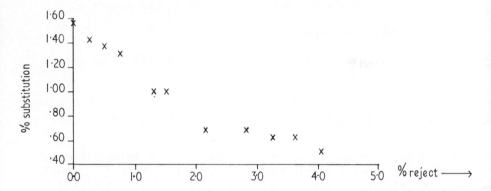

Fig. 6.   Reject versus substitution results for Hamming distance nearest neighbor method.

This simple nearest neighbor method is based on a very naive assumption, and we shall be more realistic in Section 5. Meanwhile let us attend to a further shortcoming of the Hamming distance nearest neighbor method. This is that the method, in its simplest implementation, requires computation of Hamming distance between $X^?$ and every stored X' separately. Thus for each recognition class, the method generally requires many distance computations, not just one. In the following section we revise a classic method that requires just one distance computation per class.

IV.   DEGENERATE NEAREST NEIGHBOR METHOD

To reduce the computational requirements of a simple nearest neighbor method, techniques are available [11] for selecting a good subset of a given set of specimen patterns for use as reference patterns. Another idea is to average various subsets of

specimen patterns, and use a set of averages as reference data
[12,13], but such averages would not serve the purposes of the
present work. A still further idea is that of Bledsoe and Browning [14] which bears a simple relationship to Hamming distance
nearest neighbor methods [p. 119 in 7].

Let $\rho = \{X_1, \ldots X_i, \ldots X_\nu\}$ be a given set of reference patterns
in the rth recognition class, and recall that X_i contains one bit
corresponding to each element of the Cartesian product X that was
defined in Section 2. Let $V_1, \ldots V_h, \ldots V_r$ be artibrarily chosen
n-element subsets of X whose union is X. Let X_{ih} be the projection
of X_i on V_h, that is, the subset of n-elements of X_i that corresponds to the n-elements of V_h; and let us define
$$R_h = \{X_{1h}, \ldots X_{ih}, \ldots X_{\nu h}\} \, .$$
Montanari [15] has shown that in a sense $\{R_1, \ldots R_h, \ldots R_\nu\}$ is an
optimal approximation to the ν-ary relation ρ. Finally let us define
$$b_{rh} = \begin{cases} 1 \text{ if the projection of } X^? \text{ on } V_n \text{ belongs to } R_n \\ 0 \text{ otherwise.} \end{cases}$$

Bledsoe and Browning's method of recognition [14] is to assign $X^?$
to the Xth recognition class such that

$$\sum_{h=1}^{v} b_{rh} > \sum_{h=1}^{v} b_{sh} + \tau$$

for all recognition classes $s \neq r$, where τ is a reject threshold.
An advantage over a simple nearest neighbor is that $\sum b_{rh}$ need
only be calculated once for each recognition class, not once per
specimen per recognition class. The value of b_{rh} can be determined by the table look-up method of Bledsoe and Browning [14]
which does not involve serial searching. As explained in [7],
Bledsoe and Browning's method is a degenerate nearest neighbor
method in that it discards information specifying joint occurrences of, for instance, particular members of R_1 and R_h in members of ρ. The method does not require ρ to be stored for active
use in recognition: $R_1, \ldots R_v$ can be stored instead.

Steck's statistical theory [5] suggests that Bledsoe and
Browning's method should work best when in every pattern each bit
has probability 0.5 of being '1'. In the patterns $X^?$ used in Section 3, we found experimentally that each bit had probability 0.12
of being a '1'. Rough preliminary experiments indicated that
Bledsoe and Browning's method gave poor results with these patterns.

To remedy this we or'ed together bits so as to increase the
percentage of 1's in the patterns to which we finally applied
Bledsoe and Browning's method. Experimentally our set U_1 of zones
(fig. 1(a)) comprised 5x5 zones, as in [6]. We used 48 tangent-
pairs as indicated in fig. 2, so X comprised 48 x 5 x 5 = 1200
bits. To explain our oring, it may be helpful to regard X as

comprising 25 48-bit vectors, one 48-bit vector for each of the 5x5 zones, the jth of these vectors being $\hat{x}_j$. Thus

$$X = (\hat{x}_1, \ldots, \hat{x}_j, \ldots \hat{x}_{25})$$

and

$$x_j = (x_{j0}, \ldots, x_{jk}, \ldots, x_{i47}).$$

The oring process can be regarded as comprising two steps. First for each $j = 1, \ldots 25$ we determine

$$T_j = \{t_{j0}, \ldots, t_{jk}, \ldots t_{j47}\}$$

where

$$t_{jk} = x_{jk} \vee x_{j,k+3}$$

and addition in the subscript is in modulo 48. The symbol $\vee$ denotes inclusive OR. Thus each tangent-pair is or-ed with one in which the relative orientation of the two tangents is the same but the absolute orientation differs by 22.5°. This can be checked by looking at the indexing in fig. 2.

Using the notion that

$$T_i \vee T_j = ((t_{i0} \vee y_{g0}), \ldots, (t_{iK} \vee t_{jK}), \ldots, (t_{i47} \vee t_{j47}))$$

and indexing the 5x5 zones as shown in fig. 1(1), we define

$$Z_1 = T_1 \vee T_2 \vee T_6 \vee T_7$$

$$Z_2 = T_2 \vee T_3 \vee T_7 \vee T_8$$

$$Z_3 = T_3 \vee T_4 \vee T_8 \vee T_9$$

$$Z_4 = T_4 \vee T_5 \vee T_9 \vee T_{10}$$

$$Z_5 = T_6 \vee T_7 \vee T_{11} \vee T_{12}$$

.

.

.

$$Z_{16} = T_{19} \vee T_{20} \vee T_{24} \vee T_{25}.$$

Thus each of $Z_1, \ldots Z_{16}$ is obtained by oring over four adjacent zones, and this can be checked by reference to the indices in fig. 1(a). Finally we concatenate $Z_1 \ldots Z_{16}$ to form a single vector

519

$$Z = (Z_1, \ldots, Z_{16})$$

which comprises a total of 16 x 48 bits.

Using this process we have converted every specimen vector Z' and every pattern $X^?$ to a corresponding Z' or $Z^?$, and have applied Bledsoe and Browning's method using Z's instead of X's. Fig. 7 shows reject versus substitution results of Bledsoe and Browning's method with $\nu = 10$, 60 and 140, using the same test set of 1600 numerals used elsewhere in this paper.

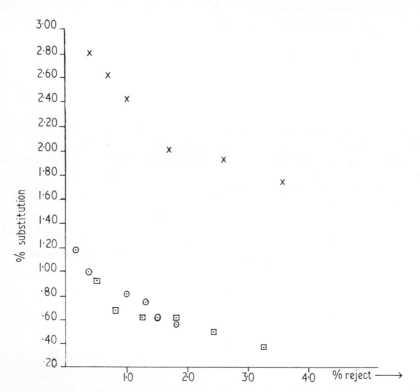

Fig. 7.   Reject versus substitution results for Bledsoe and Browning's method with $\nu = 10$ (crosses), $\nu = 60$ (circles), and $\nu = 140$ (squares).

We used an experimental procedure employing eight constituent experiments, exactly as described in [6]. We used 192 randomly chosen 4-tuples, so that V_h was a 4-element subset of Z. The union of $V_1, \ldots, V_h, \ldots V_{192}$ was Z and no element of Z belonged to more than one of these n-tuples.

Because Bledsoe and Browning's method is a degenerate nearest neighbor method, methods like Hart's [11] can be used to select subsets of a training set for use as reference patterns. In

Method 1 in [11], the number of patterns in the selected subset depends on a parameter ξ. In a preliminary experiment we varied ξ using a test set of 400 Z's, and results are shown in fig. 8.

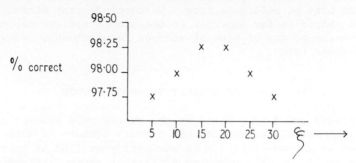

Fig. 8. Results of preliminary experiment: percent correct recognition versus ξ.

Using this method with $\xi = 20$ and a test set of 1600 Z's, with the experimental method of [6] we obtained the results presented in fig. 9.

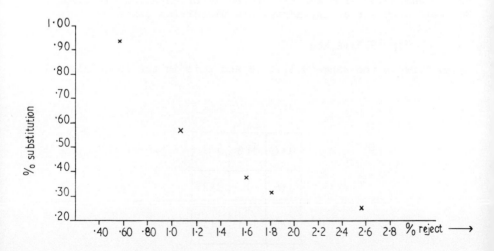

Fig. 9. Reject versus substitution for Bledsoe and Browning's method using reference data automatically selected with $\xi = 20$.

The data and procedure were identical to those used in obtaining fig. 6, and fig. 9 shows a reduction in error rates obtained at no extra cost in storage or in time taken in recognition, when compared with the fig. 6 results. The simple nearest neighbor method of section 3 used 195 stored reference patterns, each of 1200 bits, to yield the fig. 6 results, and 195 x 1200 = 244,000. Bledsoe and Browning's method yielded the fig. 9 results using 192 x 10 x 2^4 = 30,720 bits of reference data. We conclude that Bledsoe and Browning's method is far superior to the simple nearest neighbor method from the points of view of storage requirements, computer time, and error rates.

V. AN ITERATIVE NEAREST NEIGHBOR METHOD

Sections 3 and 4 were based on the over-simple assumption that every admissible distortion takes every element of X to itself. When we abandon this simple assumption we find it appropriate to use an iteratively computed similarity score, instead of Hamming distance, in nearest neighbor recognition. The present section introduces the simplest iterative technique that we have been able to devise: its relationship to a general technique is explained in [6].

An element of X corresponds to a particular grid cell, and to a particular orientation. It is convenient now to refer to the eight neighbors of the jth grid-cell by subscripts j+1,j+2,...,j+8, as shown in Fig. 10. Similarly it is convenient to use k-1 and k+1 as indices for the orientations that respectively differ by -22.5° and 22.5° from the kth of the 16 orientations (Fig.1(b)). We shall assume that any admissible distortion takes

$$x_{jk} \text{ to } x_{j+\delta,k+\epsilon}$$

where δ is in the range 0,1,...,8 and ϵ is in the range -1,0,+1.

$j+7$	$j+8$	$j+1$
$j+6$	j	$j+2$
$j+5$	$j+4$	$j+3$

Fig. 10. Indexing of the eight neighbors of the jth cell of grid U_1.

In a nearest neighbor method, when an unknown pattern $X^?$ is compared with a reference pattern X', the similarity score should be higher or lower according as $X^?$ is or is not related to $X^?$ by an admissible distortion. Roughly speaking, a machine must determine whether $X^?$ is an admissibly distorted (and possibly noisy) version of X' in order to assign an appropriate matching score to the pair $X^?$, X'.

To test whether $X^?$ and X' are related by an admissible distortion, we could test whether each '1' in $X^?$ could correspond, in an admissible distortion, to at least one '1' in X', and vice versa. To reduce the amount of computation, our simple iterative procedure uses a weaker test. This test determines, for each $\delta = 0,1,\ldots,8$, whether any $x^?_{jk}$ could correspond to $x'_{j+\delta,k+\varepsilon}$, where ε is in the range $-1,0,+1$. The computational advantage is that the determination is made separately only for the nine values $\delta = 0,1,\ldots,8$, and not for all combinations of j,k,δ.

We define

$$P_\delta = \begin{cases} 1 \text{ if for any } j,k,x^?_{jk} \text{ could correspond to} \\ \qquad x'_{j+\delta,k+\varepsilon} \\ 0 \text{ otherwise.} \end{cases}$$

We define Q_δ to be the set of all values of γ such that, for some $\alpha,\beta,x^?_{\alpha\beta}$ corresponds to $x'_{\alpha+\gamma,\beta+\phi}$ in at least one admissible distortion in which $x^?_{jk}$ corresponds to $x'_{j+\delta,k+\varepsilon}$. We define Q'_δ to be the inverse of Q_δ, that is, the set of all values of γ such that, for some α,β, $x'_{\alpha\beta}$ corresponds to $x^?_{\alpha+\gamma,\beta+\phi}$ in at least one admissible distortion in which $x^?_{\alpha\beta}$ corresponds to $x'_{\alpha+\gamma,\beta+\phi}$.

From these definitions it follows that if $X^?$ and X' are related by an admissible distortion in which any x_{jk} corresponds to $x_{j+\delta,k+\varepsilon}$ then

(a) for all α,β, if $x^?_{\alpha,\beta} = 1$ then $(\exists\gamma) \atop \gamma\varepsilon Q_\delta$ $(\exists\phi) \atop -1\leqslant\phi\leqslant+1$ $(P_\gamma \cdot x'_{\alpha+\gamma,\beta+\phi})$.

And

(b) for all α,β, if $x'_{\alpha\beta} = 1$ then $(\exists\gamma) \atop \gamma\varepsilon Q'_\delta$ $(\exists\phi) \atop -1\leqslant\phi\leqslant+1$ $(P_\gamma \cdot x^?_{\alpha+\gamma,\beta+\phi})$

Thus $P_\delta = 1$ if conditions (a) and (b) are satisfied, and $P_\delta = 0$ otherwise. We regard binary variables ambiguously as Boolean or as having numerical values 1 or 0. Accordingly we can write

$$P_\delta = \underset{1\leqslant\alpha\leqslant25}{(\forall\delta)} \quad \underset{0\leqslant\beta\leqslant47}{(\forall\beta)} \quad ((\overline{x}^?_{\alpha\beta} \lor q^?_{\alpha\beta}(\delta)).(\overline{x}'_{\alpha\beta} \lor q'_{\alpha\beta}(\delta)))$$

where

$$q^?_{\alpha\beta}(\delta) = \underset{\gamma\varepsilon Q_\delta}{(\exists\gamma)} \quad \underset{-1\leqslant\phi\leqslant+1}{(\exists\phi)} \quad (P_\gamma \cdot x'_{\alpha+\gamma,\beta+\phi})$$

and

$$q'_{\alpha\beta}(\delta) = \underset{\gamma \in Q'_{\delta}}{(\exists \gamma)} \underset{-1 \leq \phi \leq +1}{(\exists \phi)} \quad (P_{\gamma} \cdot x^?_{\alpha+\gamma, \beta+\phi}) .$$

This unrealistically presupposes that no noise will be present in an unknown $X^?$. To remedy this we redefine

$$P_{\delta} = \sum_{\alpha=1}^{25} \sum_{\beta=0}^{47} ((\bar{x}^?_{\alpha\beta} \vee q^?_{\alpha\beta}(\delta)) + (\bar{x}'_{\alpha\beta} \vee q'_{\alpha\beta}(\delta))) > \tau \dots \quad (1)$$

where τ is a threshold.

The binary value of P_4 may depend on P_3 and P_5. To cope with such interdependence we evaluate P_{δ} recursively as follows.

Initially we set $P_{\delta} = 1$ for all $\delta = 0, \dots, 8$. Using a fixed threshold τ, $P_0, \dots, P_8$ are evaluated in turn using (1). $P_0, \dots, P_8$ are then evaluated in turn again using (1), and so on again and again iteratively until there is no further change in $\sum_{\delta=0}^{8} P_{\delta}$.

At that stage the computation is said to have converged. We define the matching score $d(X^?, X')$ to be the largest value of τ such that

$$0 < \sum_{\delta=0}^{8} P_{\delta} \quad \text{at convergence.}$$

In nearest neighbor recognition, $X^?$ can be assigned to the class of X' such that $d(X^?, X')$ is maximal.

This method has yielded 0.75% reject and 0.5625% substitution errors, using exactly the same experimental data, reference patterns, and experimental procedure as in Section 3. Further details (including details of sets Q_{δ}, but in a different notation) are given in [6]. Comparison with fig. 6 shows that the interative technique has yielded far lower error rates than the Hamming distance method of Section 3, but the cost of the iterative computation is too great to be practical.

VI. INTERIM DEVELOPMENTS

By combining the ideas of Sections 4 and 5 we might hope to achieve further reduction both in error rates and in computational cost of recognition, as compared with Section 5. Such a combination of ideas is not easily achieved, and the present Section is devoted purely to introductory steps towards Section 7.

Let us define

$$X''_{\delta} = \{x''_{\alpha\beta}\} = \{q'_{\alpha\beta}(\delta)\}$$

and let us say that

$$X'' \supseteq X'$$

if and only if

$$(\forall \alpha)\,(\forall \beta)\,(\bar{x}'_{\alpha\beta} \lor x''_{\alpha\beta})$$

which is the same as requiring

$$\sum_{\alpha=1}^{25} \sum_{\beta=0}^{47} (\bar{x}'_{\alpha\beta} \lor q'_{\alpha\beta}(\delta)) = 25 \times 48.$$

It is also convenient to redefine

$$q^?_{\alpha\beta}(\delta) = (\exists \gamma)\,(\exists \phi) \quad (P_\gamma \cdot x''_{\alpha+\gamma,\,\beta+\phi})$$
$$\gamma \epsilon Q_\delta \quad -1 < \phi < +1$$

Expression (1) (Section 5) has two parts, and as a crude expedient, not as an improvement, we can apply a noise-tolerating threshold to one part and not to the other. Specifically, it is expedient to redefine:-

$$P_{\delta\delta} = (X''_\delta \supseteq X') \cdot (\sum_{\alpha=1}^{25} \sum_{\beta=0}^{47} ((\bar{x}^?_{\alpha\beta} \lor q^?_{\alpha\beta}(\delta)) > \tau)\,.$$

This admittedly unbalanced definition can be used in the method of Section 5, but its use may cause deterioration of error rates.

Alternatively, we can obtain exactly the same result by evaluating P_δ by

Procedure (A): For each α, β in turn, if $x''_{\alpha\beta} = 1$ then set $x''_{\alpha\beta} = 0$ unless $X''_\delta \supseteq X'$ and $x'_{\alpha\beta} = 1$. Then compute

$$P_\delta = (\sum_{\alpha=1}^{25} \sum_{\beta=0}^{47} (\bar{x}^?_{\alpha\beta} \lor q^?_{\alpha\beta}(\delta)) > \tau)\,\, \ldots\ldots \qquad (2)$$

As a further step in the right direction, we can obtain similar results by a method that uses the *oring* and n-tuples of Section 4. Z' is obtained from X' by the *oring* process. Let $V_h(Z')$ be the projection of Z' on the hth n-tuple.

Each bit of Z belongs to exactly one n-tuple. Because of the *oring*, each bit $x_{\alpha\beta}$ of X corresponds to a number, $\theta_{\alpha\beta}$, of bits of Z, and thus to $\theta_{\alpha\beta}$ different n-tuples. If $X' \subseteq X''_\delta$ and $x''_{\alpha\beta} = 1$ then for each of these $\theta_{\alpha\beta}$ n-tuples, $V_h(Z') \subseteq V_h(Z''_\delta)$ and the bit in $V_h(Z')$ that corresponds to $x''_{\alpha\beta}$ is "1". Instead of procedure (A) we can now use:-

Procedure (B): For each α, β in turn, if $x''_{\alpha\beta} = 1$ then set $x''_{\alpha\beta} = 0$ unless for each of the $\theta_{\alpha\beta}$ n-tuples that correspond to $x_{\alpha\beta}, V_h(Z') \subseteq V_h(Z''_\delta)$ and the bit in $V_h(Z')$ that corresponds to $x''_{\alpha\beta}$ is '1'. Work through all α, β again and again iteratively in this way until there is an iteration in which no $x''_{\alpha\beta} = 1$ is changed to $x''_{\alpha\beta} = 0$. At that time (i.e. Convergence) evaluate P_δ using (2).

The rest of the recognition process is the same as in Section 5.

The iterative process of procedure (B) checks that $X''_\delta \supseteq X'$ (c.f. procedure (A)) by using projections on n-tuples instead of simply using X''_δ and X'. To understand this, suppose that there is an $x'_{\alpha\beta} = 1$ such that $x''_{\alpha\beta} = 0$. The condition $V_h(Z') \subseteq V_h(Z''_\delta)$ may in this case not be satisfied for some of the $\theta_{\alpha\beta}$ n-tuples that correspond to $x_{\alpha\beta}$. This will mean that any other $x''_{\alpha\beta} = 1$ that corresponds to any of these n-tuples will be changed to $x''_{\alpha\beta} = 0$. This may cause the condition $V_h(Z') \subseteq V_h(Z''_\delta)$ to be violated for further n-tuples, and so on iteratively.

VII. ITERATIVE METHOD USING DEGENERATE REFERENCE DATA

The final method of section 6 uses procedure (B) in the computation of $d(X^?, X')$ for each stored reference pattern separately. We now introduce a method that computes just one matching score for each recognition class. It is convenient here to use the term *state* of an n-tuple [14]: for example $V_h(Z')$ and $V_h(Z'')$ are *states* of the hth n-tuple.

We assign $X^?$ to the class that yields the maximum matching score computed as follows. We describe the computation in terms of the rth recognition class. Initially we set $P_\delta = 1$ for all $\delta = 0, \ldots 8$ and evaluate P_δ over and over again iteratively until convergence, using procedure (C). The matching score for the rth class is the largest value of τ such that

$$0 < \sum_{\delta=0}^{\delta=8} P_\delta \quad \text{at convergence.}$$

Procedure (C) is a simple development of procedure (B):-

Procedure (C):- for each α, β in turn, if $x''_{\alpha\beta} = 1$ then set $x''_{\alpha\beta} = 0$ unless for each of the $\theta_{\alpha\beta}$ n-tuples that correspond to $x''_{\alpha\beta}$ there is a state in R_h which $\subseteq V_h(Z'')$ and the bit in this state that corresponds to $x''_{\alpha\beta}$ is '1'. Repeat this procedure again and again iteratively until there is an iteration in which no "$x''_{\alpha\beta} = 1$ is changed to 0. At that time (i.e. convergance) evaluate P_δ using (2).

Fig. 11 shows error/reject curves for this method, with $\nu = 10$ and $\nu = 60$ respectively. For $\nu = 10$ the result is an improvement on Bledsoe and Browning's method (Fig. 7), possibly because of our more realistic assumption about admissible distortions. For $\nu =$ 120 the result is far worse than Bledsoe and Browning's, possibly because of a saturation effect that might perhaps be obviated by making the n-tuples in [6] the same as those used in the present work.

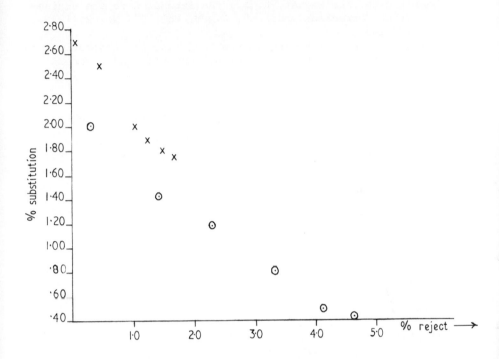

Fig. 11. Reject versus substitution for iterative method
using degenerate reference data with $\nu = 10$
(crosses) and $\nu = 60$ (circles).

Section 5 has led us to require $X_\delta^{\shortmid\shortmid} \supseteq X'$ which cannot straight-forwardly be done by Bledsoe and Browning's method. Bledsoe and Browning's method looks for $X^? = X'$, that is, identity rather than inclusion. To allow for points to move across the zone boundaries of fig. 1(a) we have ored 1's but not 0's. Bledsoe and Browning's method treats 1's and 0's equally, but the method of the present Section does not.

ACKNOWLEDGMENTS

The experimental work reported in this paper was carried out at the National Physical Laboratory and this paper is published with the permission of the Director of the National Physical Laboratory.

REFERENCES

1. Lowrance, R. and Wagner, R. A., "An Extension to the String-to-string Correction problem". *J.ACM*. Vol. 22, No. 2, 1975, pp. 177-183.
2. Ullmann, J. R., "A Binary n-gram Technique for Augomatic Correction of Substitution, Deletion, Insertion and Reversal Errors in Words". To appear in *The Computer Journal* (of the British Computer Society), 1977.
3. Fain, V. S., "Construction of a Machine for Pattern Recognition". *Radio Engineering* (Radiotechnika), Vol. 15, No. 3, 1960, pp. 16-23.
4. Romanov, V. P., "System of Machine Analysis, Recognition and Coding of Images". *Astia Document* AD 739299, December 1971.
5. Stech, G. P. "Stochastic Model for the Bledsoe-Browning Pattern Recognition Scheme", *IRE Transactions on Electronic Computers*, Vol. EC-11, April 1962, pp 274-282.
6. Ullmann, J. R., "Subset Methods for Recognizing Distorted Patterns", Submitted for publication.
7. Ullmann, J. R., "Pattern Recognition Techniques", London, Butterworth's, and New York: Crane Russak, 1973.
8. Davis, L. S. and Rosenfeld, A., "Applications of Relaxation Labelling, 2: spring-loaded Template Matching". Technical Report TR-440, Computer Science Center, University of Maryland, College Park, Maryland 20742, USA, Feb. 1976.
9. Fischler, M. A. and Elschlager, R. A., "The Representation and Matching of Pictorial Structures". *IEEE Transactions on Computers*, Vol C-22, Jan. 1973, pp. 67-92.
10. Patterson, J. V., "Character Reader with Handprint Capability" *UK Patent* No. 1320243, June 1973.
11. Ullmann , J. R., "Automatic Selection of Reference Data for Use in a Nearest-Neighbour Method of Pattern Classification". *IEEE Transactions on Information Theory*, Vol. IT-20, No. 4, July 1974, pp.541-543.
12. Firschein, O, and Fischler, M., "Automatic Subclass Determination for Pattern Recognition Applications". *IEEE Transactions on Electronic Computers*, Vol. EC-12, April 1963, pp. 137-141.
13. Chang, C. L., "Finding Prototypes for Nearest Neighbour Classifier", *IEEE Transactions on Electronic Computers*, Vol-C-23, No. 11, Nov. 1974, pp.1179-1184.
14. Bledsoe, W. W. and Browning, I., "Pattern Recognition and Reading by Machine" Proceedings of the Eastern Joint Computer Conference, 1959, pp. 225-232.
15. Montanari, U. "Networks of Constraints: Fundamental Properties and Applications to Picture Processing". *Information Sciences*, Vol. 7, 1974, pp. 95-132.

SERIAL PATTERN ACQUISITION:
A PRODUCTION SYSTEM APPROACH

D. A. Waterman
The Rand Corporation
Santa Monica, CA.

ABSTRACT

A production system technique for recognizing regularities in
serial patterns is presented in the context of the letter series
extrapolation problem. The learning technique consists of creating an ordered set of production rules to represent the concept or
a pattern, such that each rule is a hypothesis about which pattern
contexts lead to which new pattern elements. The production system learning technique is compared with other series extrapolation
methods and examples of series concepts learned by a computer implementation of the technique are given.

I. INTRODUCTION

A major hurdle to be faced in implementing computer models of
complex learning is the basic task of recognizing regularities in
data. This is particularly critical for so-called "induction"
type learning where a large number of specific data-representations
must be mapped into a single more general data-representation.
Much work has already been done on induction programs, particularly in the area of pattern recognition[1,2,3] and sequence extrapolation.[4-12]   A somewhat different approach to the problem of machine
induction will now be presented.

Ideally, what is needed is a simple uniform technique for
recognizing regularities in data, a technique which can be considered a natural extension of basic associative learning techniques such as rote learning. Such a technique would tend to
bridge the gap between simple learning like memorizing the addition table, and complex learning like inducing the concept of a
series.

In this paper a technique for recognizing regularities will
be presented in the context of the series extrapolation problem.
No attempt will be made here to generalize this technique to other
induction type problems, although some sort of generalization
seems feasible. First the problem of data representation will be
discussed. Then, the learning technique will be described as it
applies to letter series extrapolation problems. Finally, examples
will be presented of series concepts learned by a computer implementation of the learning technique.

II. DATA REPRESENTATION

Basic associative learning can be thought of as associating a stimulus A with a response B. This can be represented very naturally as a set of production rules,[13] since a production rule is just a set of conditions associated with a particular set of actions. Thus a portion of the addition table for integers could be represented as the following ordered set of rules:

$$1,1 \rightarrow 2$$

$$1,2 \rightarrow 3$$

$$1,3 \rightarrow 4$$

$$1,4 \rightarrow 5$$

This is interpreted: if you have 1 + 1 then the sum is 2, else if you have 1 + 2 it is 3, etc. Only ordered production systems will be considered, that is, to obtain a result the conditions in the left-hand sides of the rules are compared to elements in some data base, and the highest priority rule (topmost rule) whose conditions all match data base elements has its actions executed.

More complex information, such as, letter series concepts can also be expressed in production system notation. For example, the concept of the series CDCDCD can be represented as:

$$1.1 \quad C \rightarrow D$$

(1)

$$1.2 \quad D \rightarrow C$$

This can be interpreted: if the last letter in the series is C then the next is D, else if the last is D then the next is C. It is clear that this is all that is needed to extend the series indefinitely.

A) Simple Letter Series Concepts

The concept of a series will be defined to be a set of extrapolation rules, as in (1) above, together with a set of initialization rules. The extrapolation rules contain enough information to extend the series, but both extrapolation and initialization rules are needed to generate the series from scratch. Initialization in (1) can be provided by including * →C as the last rule of the production system, where the asterisk (*) represents a condition defined to match any data base, even an empty one. Thus if no extrapolation rules match the data base then the initialization rule * → C will match by definition. In this paper the extrapolation rules will be referred to as the concept of the series, with the understanding that the actual concept also includes initialization rules.

Consider the more interesting series, GBDGBGBDGBG. This series is composed of repeated occurrences of the string GBDGB.
Furthermore, its description does not require the use of predecessor or successor relations on an alphabet. Series like this
which can be described using nothing more than the *equality* or
same relation will be called *simple repetition* type series. A
production system (PS) representation of the concept of this series is shown below.

$$2.1 \quad D \; G \; B \rightarrow G$$

$$2.2 \quad \quad G \; B \rightarrow D$$

$$(2)$$

$$2.3 \quad \quad \quad D \rightarrow G$$

$$2.4 \quad \quad \quad G \rightarrow B$$

This is interpreted: if the last 3 letters in the series are DGB
the next letter is G, otherwise if the last 2 are GB the next is
D, etc. The rules are always applied to the growing end of the
series and always result in the prediction of a single letter. To
indicate that the series starts with G, the initialization rule
*→G is needed at the bottom of the production system.

In production system (1) the regularities represented are the
facts that D always follows C, and C always follows D. In production system (2) they are that G always follows the string DGB, D
follows all GB's not immediately preceeded by D, G always follows
D, and D always follows G. This shows, at least, that a production system representation is adequate for expressing the concept
of a simple repetition type series in terms of its regularities.

B) Sequence Prediction Tasks

In the literature on induction and learning the work most
closely related to production system representation of regularities is the analysis made by Restle[14] of subjects performing sequence prediction tasks. The subjects were given a series of
binary events equivalent to a sequence of 1's and 0's, and were
asked to predict each event in the sequence, given the partial
sequence prior to that event. Pretraining and test sequences were
analyzed in terms of generative rules*, i.e., grammar-like replacement rules that could be used to generate the sequences. The
test sequence used was 111001000111001..., which has a period size
of nine. Figure 1 compares Restle's replacement rules for the
test sequence with a production system representation of that

---

* These rules were inferred by a manual analysis of the test sequence, rather than by a computer model of the induction task.

sequence. The replacement rules in no sense constitute a production system or even a Markov normal algorithm[15,16] for generating the series. Instead they define a grammar which can generate a number of series, including the test sequence. For example, the top replacement rule generates the seventh item of the sequence and is interpreted "if you have 1 then replace it with 0". Thus the test sequence can be generated by starting with 000 and applying the rules as shown below:

$$000 \overset{1}{\Rightarrow} \underline{1} \overset{2}{\Rightarrow} 1\underline{1} \overset{3}{\Rightarrow} 11\underline{1} \overset{4}{\Rightarrow} \underline{0} \overset{5}{\Rightarrow} 0\underline{0} \overset{6}{\Rightarrow} \underline{1} \overset{7}{\Rightarrow} \underline{0} \overset{8}{\Rightarrow}0\underline{0} \overset{9}{\Rightarrow} 00\underline{0}.$$

Item Predicted	Replacement Rules	Production Rules
(7)	1 → 0	1 0 0 1 → 0
(6)	0 0 → 1	1 1 0 0 → 1
(3)	1 1 → 1 1 1	0 1 1 → 1
(2)	1 → 1 1	0 0 1 → 1
(9)	0 0 → 0 0 0	1 0 0 → 0
(1)	0 0 0 → 1	0 0 → 1
(8,5)	0 → 0 0	0 → 0
(4)	1 1 1 → 0	1 1 → 0

Figure 1. Comparison of Restle's replacement rules and production system rules for the series with period 111001000.

The reason the replacement rules generate series other than the test sequence is that some rules (7 and 2, 6 and 9) contain identical left hand sides. Restle found that subjects make the most errors predicting items that these "optional" rules generate.
  The production rules in Figure 1, unlike the replacement rules, represent the concept of the test sequence since they have associated with them a general control mechanism (interpreter for ordered PS's) which defines their use. Notice, however, that the replacement and production rules are pair-wise isomorphic, i.e., for each replacement rule that predicts a symbol there is a corresponding production rule that predicts the same symbol. The production rules which correspond to the "optional" replacement rules are the most complex, since they have the most symbols in their left hand sides. This occurs because enough context must be

retained in the left hand side of the production rule to discriminate between similar alternatives. Thus within the PS framework
one would expect the most errors during learning to occur on items
generated by the most complex rules, which corresponds to the result obtained by Restle. We will now consider the problem of *generating* a concept from a series and will describe a learning technique capable of creating the production rule representation shown
in Figure 1.

III. BASIC LEARNING TECHNIQUE

A learning technique will now be described that is a simple,
uniform procedure for generating the concept of a series by finding regularities in the series. In general terms, the technique
consists of creating a hypothesis about a particular type of regu-
larity in the data, adding this hypothesis, in the form of a production rule, to the current set of hypotheses (the production
system), and then using the data to test the hypotheses. When the
data prove a hypothesis false, a new hypothesis is added above the
error-causing one.

In terms of series concepts, each hypothesis consists of a
production rule formed from a consecutive sequence of letters from
the series (the condition) and the letter assumed to follow that
sequence (the action). The action always consists of just a single letter.* Sequences of the series are presented to the production system (first letter, first-two letters, first-three letters,
etc.) and it predicts what the next letter should be. The prediction is checked by comparing it to the next letter in the actual
series. When the prediction is in error a new rule is added to
the system above the error-causing rule. The new rule contains
one more letter in its condition than the error-causing rule and
the actual next letter as its action. The principle is one of
minimum local consistency. A new rule is always a correct statement about the sequence, and is only created following an error
at precisely that point in the sequence. When no prediction is
made (the sequence of letters fails to match any of the rules) a
new rule with a condition equal to the rightmost letter of the sequence and an action equal to the actual next letter is added.

A learning *cycle* for a series containing n+1 letters consists
of presenting the system with the first letter, the first-two letters, on up through the first-n letters, and obtaining a prediction

---

* Rules which predict more than one letter can also be used to
form production system concepts of series. Such systems can be
generated using the same learning techniques described in this
paper. One problem with such systems is that they generate unduly complicated rules when the number of letters predicted by
the rules exceeds the period size of the series being represented.

in each case. The learning *phase* consists of repeated learning
cycles and is complete when a learning cycle is encountered which
produces nothing but correct predictions. At this point the production system represents the concept of the series and can be
used to predict the extensions of the series.

An example of this technique applied to the series GBDGBGB
will now be presented. Initially the system contains no rules and
thus fails to predict the first letter of the series. This error
leads to the creation of the default rule $* \rightarrow G$. Now G is given
to the system and matches the default rule. This is considered an
error* so the rule $G \rightarrow B$ is added. Now GB is presented, does not
match $G \rightarrow B$, but does match the default rule. Since this is considered an error $B \rightarrow D$ is added. Next GBD is presented and also
matches only the default rule, leading to the addition of the rule
$D \rightarrow G$. The system now looks like:

$$3.1 \quad D \rightarrow G$$

$$3.2 \quad B \rightarrow D$$

$$3.3 \quad G \rightarrow B$$

$$3.4 \quad * \rightarrow G$$

(3)

Next GBDG is presented, which matches 3.3, predicting that the
next letter is B. From the series we see this is indeed the next
letter so no new rule is necessary. Next, GBDGB is presented
which matches 3.2, predicting that the next letter is D. From the
series we see the next letter is actually G, so the rule $G B \rightarrow G$
is added. Next GBDGBG is presented and matches 3.3, correctly
predicting B. Now the first cycle is complete, but since errors
occurred the process starts over, and G is presented to the system,
which is now:

$$4.1 \quad G B \rightarrow G$$

$$4.2 \quad D \rightarrow G$$

$$4.3 \quad B \rightarrow D$$

$$4.4 \quad G \rightarrow B$$

$$4.5 \quad * \rightarrow G$$

(4)

G matches 4.4 and the correct prediction is made. But now GB is
presented and leads to an incorrect prediction, thus $G B \rightarrow D$ is

---

* Default (or initialization) rules are always considered to make
erroneous predictions in order to accelerate the learning process.

added. GBD and GBDG both elicit correct predictions but GBDGB
matches G B → D which predicts D instead of G. Thus D G B → G is
added. After one more correct prediction the third cycle begins,
but this time all predictions are correct and thus the learning
phase terminates. Figure 2 diagrams the rule acquisition process
for this particular series, showing the first two cycles. The
rules learned are:

$$5.1 \quad D\ G\ B \rightarrow G$$

$$5.2 \quad G\ B \rightarrow D$$

$$5.3 \quad G\ B \rightarrow G$$

$$5.4 \quad D \rightarrow G \tag{5}$$

$$5.5 \quad B \rightarrow D$$

$$5.6 \quad G \rightarrow B$$

$$5.7 \quad * \rightarrow G$$

We will consider the concept of the series to be the set of non-
redundant* rules learned, i.e., the rules that can be accessed

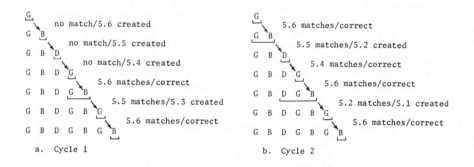

a. Cycle 1   b. Cycle 2

Figure 2. Diagram of Learning Technique on GBDGBGB
           for first two cycles. (Underlined letters
           at tail of arrow indicate letters used as
           rule left hand sides. Letter at head of
           arrow is rule right hand side).

*   See Waterman (1970) for a discussion of redundancy as applied
    to ordered production systems.

using this series as context. We see that G B → D (rule 5.2)
makes G B → G (rule 5.3) unconditionally redundant, and B → D
(rule 5.5) contextually redundant (since, in this particular series, G always occurs before B). The default rule is always contextually redundant. Removing these redundant rules from production system (5) gives the concept of the series as shown in production system (2).**

This learning technique will handle all letter series based
on simple repetition and thus is a theory for recognizing regularities in such series. In fact, it is an instantiation of the
compound stimulus hypothesis[17] in which a response is assumed to
be associated with some sequence of adjacent past events. Restle
and Brown found a positive but weak relationship between number of
errors at a position and number of previous events required to
specify the next event. During production system learning, the
number of errors made at each position in the pattern tends to be
proportional to the number of elements in the condition side of
the rule that predicts an element for that position. This is true
because each error during learning is corrected by effectively
adding one new stimulus element to the condition side of the error-
causing rule. Now we will see how an extension of this technique
can be applied to more complex letter series extrapolation problems.

IV.   REPRESENTATION OF COMPLEX LETTER SERIES

The simplest type of letter series other than those characterized by simple repetition are those requiring the use of predecessor and successor operations on the alphabet or any explicitly
defined ordered list of symbols. Examples of such series are
ABCDEF, AAABBBCCC, and DEFGEFGH. To represent series of this
type, the system must be able to handle the concept of variables
and must be given the capability for executing both predecessor
and successor operations on the alphabet.

A)   Production System Representation

In the production system representation of complex letter
series variables will be indicated by the symbols x1, x2, x3, ...,
and predecessor and successor operations by an apostrophe (')

** The system does not have to remove these rules since their presence cannot affect system output. In the current implementation the rules are left in; however, they could be removed by
having the system keep track of non-firing rules, eventually
eliminating them.

before or after a variable. Thus 'x1 represents the predecessor of x1, and x1' its successor. A variable in the condition side of a rule matches anything and is temporarily bound to the value of what it matches, thus a bound variable can be used in the action side of a rule.

With these refinements, the concept of the series ABCDEF can be represented as x1 → x1'. This rule is interpreted: if the last letter of the series is *any letter* then the next letter in the series is the successor of that letter. Initialization would be accomplished by the rule * → A. Conversely, the series ZYXWVU can be represented as x1 → 'x1, with * → Z for initialization.

Simple repetition can now be represented in a very compact manner, i.e., consider the two simple repetition series discussed earlier. The first CDCDCD, instead of requiring the two rules shown in production system (1) only requires one rule to represent its concept:

$$x1 \ x2 \rightarrow x1. \tag{6}$$

The second series, GBDGBGBDGBG, instead of requiring the four rules shown in production system (2) also requires only one rule to represent its concept:

$$x1 \ x2 \ x3 \ x4 \ x5 \rightarrow x1. \tag{7}$$

It should be clear that any simple repetition series of period *n* can be represented by a single rule of the form:

$$x1 \ x2 \ x3 \ \dots \ xn \rightarrow x1. \tag{8}$$

Now consider the more complicated series AZCXEVGT. Its concept can be represented as:

$$x1 \ x2 \ x1'' \rightarrow ''x2$$
$$\tag{9}$$
$$x1 \ x2 \rightarrow x1''$$

where double apostrophes stand for double predecessor or successor. If we apply these rules to the series the first rule fails to match (since T is not the double successor of V) but the second matches, predicting that the next letter is I. If the rules are now applied to AZCXEVGTI, the first rule matches, predicting the letter R. Thus (9) can be used to extrapolate the series as shown below.

$$AZCXEVGT\mathit{IRKPMNO} \ \dots \tag{10}$$

B) Comparison with other Representations

Other programs have been written which solve letter series extrapolation problems[5, 9-12] The Klahr and Wallace (K&W) model represents series concepts solely on the basis of inter-period relations, i.e., relations between letters occupying the same relative position in adjacent periods. For example, letting s stand for *same*, n for *next*, p for *prior*, n^2 for double next, and p^2 for double prior, the concept of series (10) would be: n^2p^2. The number of relations is the period size (in this case 2), and the representation is called the pattern template. Simple repetition is represented as a sequence of m *same*'s, where m is the period size. Thus the concept of GBDGBGBDGBG is just sssss.

The Hedrick model represents series concepts as a set of unordered, grammar-like productions which can be used to parse a given input sequence to determine if it is an instance of the series in question. For example, the series ABCDEF... would have a representation equivalent to the grammar:*

$$sl \rightarrow A\ B$$

$$sl \rightarrow sl\ next\ (last\ letter\ of\ sl).$$

Thus when given the sequence ABCD the system would recognize it as an instance of sl (the series ABCDEF...), since the above rules lead to the parse shown below.

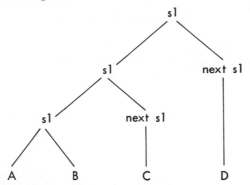

The Hedrick model learns the concept of a series from a set of examples (positive instances) by creating and generalizing productions which classify the components of the series. The model would have to be given AB, ABC, and ABCD before it could acquire the concept of the above series.

The Williams model is part of a more general program for inducing performance strategies from examples taken from aptitude tests. Series concepts are represented in a way very similar to

---

* This is a gross simplification of the actual representation. The rules are condition-action pairs where the conditions are pattern matches on both the series and an intermediate semantic net which can be modified by the actions. Thus the model is effectively a production system implementation of a grammar.

the template representation of Klahr and Wallace. Rules are constructed which define the inter-period relations *same* and *next,* one rule for each element in the period. For example, series (10) would be

Rule	Relation	Iteration	Start	Move	Alphabet
1.	next	2	1	2	Forward English
2.	next	2	2	2	Backward English

Rule 1 states that the double next (next with iteration 2) relation on the forward alphabet holds between letters which are 2 positions apart, starting at position 1. Rule 2 is the same except that the starting point is position 2 and the alphabet is the backward one. This representation is essentially a generalization of the template representation.

The Hunt and Poltrock model represents series concepts on the basis of both inter-period and intra-period relations. This model uses the same three basic relations used by the other models: *same, next,* and *predecessor.* These relations can be applied either to adjacent letters within a period or to letters with corresponding positions in adjacent periods. The series concept is represented as a set of rules, one for each letter in the period, and relates each letter to some other letter in the series. A series of period n is shown below.

$$s_1 \ s_2 \ s_3 \ \cdots \ s_n \ z_1 \ z_2 \ z_3 \ \cdots \ z_n$$

The model represents the series as n rules, the first relating z_1 to either s_n or s_1, the second relating z_2 to either z_1 or s_2, etc. Thus the concept of the series AAABBBCCC would be:

$$z_1 = next(s_3)$$

$$z_2 = same(z_1)$$

$$z_3 = same(z_2) \ .$$

Simple repetition is handled by a set of inter-period rules. To illustrate, the concept of GBDGBGBDGBG is shown below.

$$z_1 = same(s_1)$$

$$z_2 = same(s_2)$$

$$z_3 = same(s_3)$$

$$z_4 = same(s_4)$$

$$z_5 = same(s_5)$$

Initialization information, such as s_1 = G, s_2 = B, s_3 = D, s_4 = G, and s_5 = B, must also be included as part of the concept. The Hunt and Poltrock model does not recognize multiple next or predecessor relations; nor does it permit the description of relations between letters with non-corresponding positions in adjacent periods. Thus the concept of series (10) cannot be described. However, this is more a deficiency of the model than of the representational technique used to describe series concepts.

The Simon and Kotovsky (S&K) model represents series concepts primarily on the basis of intra-period relations. This requires a mechanism for stepping a pointer forward through an arbitrary alphabet (the successor operation), a mechanism for resetting the pointer to any arbitrary location in the alphabet, and a mechanism for constructing arbitrary circular alphabets. The standard forward and backward circular alphabets are initially available. The concept of the series AAABBBCCC would be:

$$m1 = [alphabet];A$$

$$m1,m1,m1,n(m1) \qquad , \tag{11}$$

where m1 is the forward alphabet with pointer initialized to A. The n(m1) represents the act of stepping the pointer to the next position in the alphabet and does not represent the generation of a letter of the series, as do the m1's. The concept of series (10) would be:

$$m1 = [alphabet];A$$

$$m2 = [backward\ alphabet];Z \tag{12}$$

$$m1,n(m1),n(m1),m2,n(m2),n(m2) \quad .$$

Here two separate alphabets, m1 and m2, are required. Simple repetition can be handled by creating an arbitrary alphabet from the letters comprising one period of the series, i.e., the concept of GBDGBGBDGBG would be:

$$m1 = [GBDGB];G$$

$$m1,n(m1) \quad .$$

A comparison of the PS, S&K, and K&W representations is given in Table 1, using series taken from Simon and Kotovsky.[5] Note that in the S&K notation inter-period relations are implicit rather than explicit, while in the K&W notation intra-period relations cannot be described at all. However, in production system notation both can be explicitly described, as illustrated by the first two columns of the Table.

540

Series	PS inter-period	FS intra-period	S&K	K&W
1. ABABAB	x1 x2 → x1 x1 → B * → A	B → A A → B * → A	m1, n(m1) m1 = [AB];A	ss AB
2. AAABBBC	x1 x2 x3 → x1' x1 x2 → A x1 → A * → A	x1 x1 x1 → x1' x1 → x1 * → A	m1, m1, m1, n(m1) m1 = [alphabet];A	nnn AAA
3. ABMCDMEF	x1 M x3 x1'' → M x1 x2 x3 → x1'' x1 x2 → M x1 → B * → A	M x1 x1' M x1'' → x1''' x1 x1' M → x1'' x1 x1' → M C → D A → B * → A	m1, n(m1), m1, n(m1), M m1 = [alphabet];A	$n^2 n^2 s$ ABM
4. DEFGEFGHFG	x1 x2 x3 x4 → x1' x1 x2 x3 → G x1 x2 → F x1 → E * → D	x1 x1' x1'' x1''' → x1' x1 → x1' * → D	m1, n(m1), m1, n(m1), m1 n(m1), m1, n(m2), E(m1,m2) m1 = m2 = [alphabet];D	nnnn DEFG
5. URTUSTUTT	U x2 x3 U → x2' x1 x2 x3 → x1 x1 x2 → T x1 → R * → U	x1 T U → x1' U x1 T → U U x1 → T U → R * → U	U, m1, n(m1), T m1 = [alphabet];R	sns URT
6. NPAOQAPR	x1 A x3 x1' → A x1 x2 x3 → x1' x1 x2 → A x1 → P * → N	x1 x1'' A → x1' x1 A ' x1 → x1' x1 x1'' → A N → P * → N	m1, n(m1), m2, n(m2), A m1 = [alphabet];N m2 = [alphabet];P	nns NPA

Table 1. Comparison of Production System, Simon & Kotovsky, and Klahr & Wallace notations for representing letter series concepts. (Extrapolation rules are shown above the dotted lines, initialization rules below the dotted lines.)

One advantage of using a PS representation is that it permits initialization rules to be represented in a form identical to extrapolation rules. Furthermore, there is a certain degree of independence between initialization and extrapolation which makes it possible to extrapolate a given series without using initialization information. With the K&W representation this is also possible, but the system must effectively regenerate the series from scratch in order to extrapolate it. To extrapolate a series using S&K extrapolation rules the system must obtain the initialization information from the series (a non-trivial task) and then use it to regenerate the series from scratch.

C) Representation of Hierarchical Sequences

Sequential behavior can be analyzed in terms of hierarchical systems,[18],[19] and we will now compare one such analysis with a corresponding production system analysis. Restle[19] developed a notation for describing a hierarchical sequence as a series of nested operators: T_i, R and M, which can transpose (add or subtract by i), repeat, or mirror (reflect) sequences given as arguments. For example, $T_{+1}(3)$ is (3 4) and $T_{+3}(3\ 4)$ is (3 4 6 7). Similarly, R(3) is (3 3) and R(1 2) is (1 2 1 2)*. Thus the pattern 3 1 3 1 6 4 6 4 can be represented as $T_{+3}(R(T_{-2}(3)))$. This is equivalent to representing the pattern as a regular binary tree.

The hierarchical pattern 3 1 3 1 6 4 6 4 can also be represented by the following production system:

13.1   x1 x2 x3 x4 → x1'''

13.2   x1 x2 → x1   (13)

13.3   x1 → ''x1

The pattern is generated from the initial element 3 by one application of rule 13.3 (to produce 3 1), two applications of 13.2 (to produce 3 1 3 1) and four applications of 13.1 (to produce 3 1 3 1 6 4 6 4). Note that each production rule is analogous to one of the Restle operators (or one level in the corresponding binary tree). Hierarchical sequences based on transposition and repetition can be described in terms of this PS notation since these operations map directly into the predecessor, successor, and *same* relations used by the PS's in this paper.

Greeno and Simon[20] have analyzed the problem of converting sequence information stored as a hierarchy of operators into serially ordered performance. The analysis was made on information represented in Restle's notation and considered questions about

---

* For a description of the 'mirror' operation see Restle[19].

the requirements made by the interpretive process on memory storage and computational complexity. Three interpretive processes (push down, recompute, and doubling) were presented for producing the sequence 5 6 2 3 4 5 1 2 from $T_{-1}(T_{-3}(T_1(5)))$, and each was analyzed in terms of storage and computational requirements. One of these processes, called doubling, involves the application of identical operators several times in succession, as illustrated in Figure 3. This particular interpretive process is identical to the one used to interpret a production system representation of this pattern. For example, the above sequence can be represented in PS form as:

14.1   x1 x2 x3 x4 → 'x1

14.2   x1 x2 → '''x1   (14)

14.3   x1 → x1'   .

If we map rule 14.1 into the operator T_{-1}, 14.2 into T_{-3}, and 14.3 into T_1, we see that the sequence of rule applications which generates the series is the same sequence given in Figure 3. Greeno and Simon found that the doubling interpretation process, when compared with the other two, minimized the number of operator applications and operator retrievals from memory, while maximizing the amount of short-term memory required.* Thus we conclude that a production system representation of serial patterns implies a process for which computational complexity has been reduced at the expense of memory requirements.

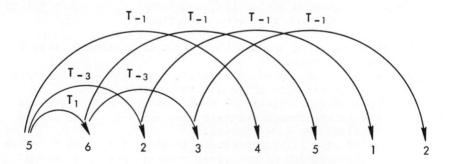

Fig. 3 — Doubling interpretive process for producing
a sequence from $T_{-1}(T_{-3}(T_1(5)))$.

(Taken from Greeno and Simon, 1974).

---

* For m operators the number of operator applications was $2^m - 1$, operator retrievals was m, and maximum memory capacity 2^{m-1}.

V. EXTENSION OF LEARNING TECHNIQUE

The primary interest here is in developing a simple uniform
technique for generating the concept of a complex letter series.
The creation of compact or minimal sets of rules is considered to
be of secondary importance. An extension of the previously discussed learning technique will now be presented. Since series
based on alphabets are used, rules must now be generalized before
being added to the system. For example, the series ABCD cannot be
extrapolated from the rules A → B, B → C, and C → D. A generalized version of these rules, namely xl → xl', provides the needed
predictive power. But the need to generalize rules leads to another problem: that of determining which relations between letters should be made explicit in the generalization. This is a
non-trivial problem because the system will either make errors or
become bogged down in backtracking if spurious relations are made
explicit.[21] This problem is solved by hypothesizing a period size
and then making explicit only relations between letters which occupy the same relative position within adjacent periods. This
method for limiting the search for relevant relations is called
the *template strategy*. Since this technique deals only with inter-
period relations it creates production systems similar to those
shown in column 1 of Table 1.

A) Example of Production System Series Extrapolation

The new production system learning technique is identical to
the earlier one with the following exceptions:

1. Only one cycle through the series is necessary, regardless of errors.
2. New rules are added *immediately* above the error-causing
   rule, rather than above all the current rules.
3. A *generalized* version of each rule is added to the system, rather than a specific one, and only inter-period
   relations are made explicit.
4. Period size is hypothesized, in order from 1 to n, where
   n is the length of the given series. For each period
   size hypothesis one learning cycle is attempted. The cycle is aborted and the period size hypothesis incremented
   whenever (a) no relation can be found between letters occupying the same relative position in adjacent periods,
   or (b) the number of rules added exceeds the period size
   hypothesis.

An example using the series ABMCDMEF will illustrate this
procedure. The initial period size hypothesis is 1, and no rules
are present. The context A is presented to the system; since
there are no rules an error results and the rule A → B is general-

ized and added to the system. Since the period is assumed to be 1 the relation between A and B is made explicit and A → B is added as x1 → x1'. Next the context AB is presented which matches the rule just added and C is predicted, rather than the correct letter M. Thus a new rule must be added. However, this would make the number of rules (2) larger than the period size (1), so the cycle is aborted and starts over with a period size hypothesis of 2 and no rules present.

Now the context A is presented; it leads to an error since no rules are present, and the rule A → B is generalized and added as x1 → B, since A and B are now both in the same period. Next AB is presented which matches the rule just added and B is predicted rather than the correct letter M. Thus the rule A B → M is generalized and added, except that here the generalization fails since no relation can be found between A and M (nothing higher than triple predecessor and successors are considered). As before the cycle is aborted and starts over with no rules present and a period size hypothesis of 3.

Again the context A leads to an error and x1 → B is added to the system. Then AB is presented, leading to the erroneous prediction of B. Thus A B → M is generalized and added as x1 x2 → M, since A, B, and M are all in the same period. The set of rules is now:

$$15.1 \quad x1\ x2 \rightarrow M \text{ (initialization)}$$

$$\text{(15)}$$

$$15.2 \quad \quad x1 \rightarrow B \text{ (initialization)}$$

Here "initialization" indicates that these are intra-period rules needed for initialization of the series but not for extrapolation. To accelerate learning this type of rule is always considered to lead to an erroneous prediction. Next the context ABM is presented, matching 15.1 which predicts M rather than the correct letter, C. So the rule A B M → C is generalized and added above 15.1 to produce:

$$16.1 \quad x1\ x2\ x3 \rightarrow x1'' \quad \text{(1)}$$

$$16.2 \quad \quad x1\ x2 \rightarrow M \quad \text{(initialization)} \quad \text{(16)}$$

$$16.3 \quad \quad \quad x1 \rightarrow B \quad \text{(initialization)}$$

where the (1) indicates that this is the first rule added that counts relative to the abort decision based on the number of rules added (only inter-period rules are counted). Next the context ABMC is presented which matches 16.1 and correctly predicts D as the next letter. Now the context ABMCD is presented, again matching 16.1 but incorrectly predicting O. Thus the rule B M C D → M is generalized and added to produce:

$$17.1 \quad \text{x1 M x3 x1'' } \rightarrow M \quad (2)$$

$$17.2 \quad \quad \text{x1 x2 x3 } \rightarrow \text{x1'' } (1)$$

$$\quad \quad \quad \quad \quad \quad \quad \quad \quad \quad \quad \quad \quad \quad \quad (17)$$

$$17.3 \quad \quad \quad \text{x1 x2 } \rightarrow M \quad (\text{initialization})$$

$$17.4 \quad \quad \quad \quad \text{x1 } \rightarrow B \quad (\text{initialization})$$

Finally, when ABMCDM and ABMCDME are presented they elicit correct predictions and the learning phase is complete. Now the entire series ABMCDMEF is presented and the correct extrapolation, letter M, is made. The concept of the series is considered to be the extrapolation rules (17.1 and 17.2) plus the initialization rules (17.3 and 17.4) shown in (17).*

Rule generalization is straightforward and requires the rule, the series, and the hypothesized period size. For example, if the rule is B B C → B and the series is ABBCBAE with period size 3, then, as shown below, arrows can be drawn between letters whose relations are to be made explicit.

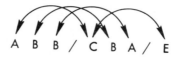

Now the rule B B C → B has only one such arrow, thus only the relation between the first and last B is made explicit. Since it is a *same* relation it can be made explicit by using total generalization to get x1 x2 x3 → x1 or partial generalization to get B x2 x3 → B. Partial generalization can only be used for two letters connected by the *same* relation, and never for letters connected by predecessor or successor relations.

The learning technique just described works when only total generalization on *same* is permitted and also when only partial generalization on *same* is permitted. But in the former case the concept learned for series containing simple repetition is much more compact. Thus in the computer implementation of this learning technique, total generalization on *same* occurs on the first inter-period rule added to the system during each cycle, and

---

* The default rule * → A is also needed to generate the series from scratch. In the current computer implementation of the extended learning technique all initialization rules, except the default one, are learned during the normal execution of the technique. Thus to generate complete series the system must be given either the first letter, the default rule, or a trivial program modification which causes automatic generation of the default rule.

partial generalization occurs on all the subsequent rules added. Since total generalization on *same* always leads to a single rule representation of simple repetition series, this procedure is e- quivalent to the heuristic: "check to see if you have a simple repetition series before proceeding with the more complex series extrapolation methods".

B) Comparison with Other Series Extrapolation Techniques

The production system learning technique just illustrated is a method for learning series concepts based solely on inter-period relations. In this respect it is similar to the K&W template matching technique for series extrapolation. There are some dif- ferences, however. First, for template matching the series must always exhibit two complete periods or the template will not be complete, and no predictions can be made. In the PS technique two periods are not always required since the method automatically hy- pothesizes that the inter-period relations not yet specified are similar to those already learned. For example, the template tech- nique fails on the series AABBACB, even though this can be extra- polated AABBACB*DAEBFA*. It can be thought of as the series ABABABA interleaved with ABCDEF. The PS technique* applied to AABBACB produces the series concept:

$$x1 \; x2 \; x3 \; x4 \; x1 \rightarrow x2''$$

$$x1 \; x2 \; x3 \; x4 \rightarrow x1 \quad ,$$

(18)

from which the correct extrapolation can be made. A second dif- ference between the template technique and the PS technique is that the former always finds a concept based on the shortest pe- riod whereas the latter may find a concept based on some multiple of the shortest period. Even when this occurs the predictions made by the PS technique are identical to those made by the tem- plate technique.

A production system learning technique based on intra-period relations has not yet been developed, but might prove to be a promising area for continued research. One of the major problems with this approach is the difficulty during the learning phase of distinguishing between relevant and spurious intra-period rela- tions. Both the Simon-Kotovsky and Hunt-Poltrock models dealt with this problem with a certain degree of success, thus the heur- istics they used should provide useful guidelines for an adaptive production system implementation.

---

* For this example only, the technique consists of using only total generalization on *same*.

C)   Computer Implementation of Production System Learning
Techniques

Both the basic learning technique (applied to simple repetition series) and the extended learning technique (applied to series using circular alphabets) have been realized as computer programs written in the PAS-II system.[22] Each program is a short
production system which can modify itself by adding new production
rules. The rules added by the system represent the concept of the
series being learned. A complete description of these self-modi-
fying production systems is given elsewhere.[21]
Examples of series concepts learned by SC1, the program employing the basic learning technique, are shown in Figure 4. Both
Figure 5* and Table 1 (first column) contain series concepts
learned by SC2, the program employing the extended learning technique. Here redundant rules have been eliminated from the concept
descriptions. Figure 6 contains more difficult series concepts
learned by SC2. The S&K program, or any program based on intra-
period relations, would tend to have difficulty with these series.
Note that series 4 in Figure 6 is another that the K&W template
matching procedure would be unable to solve.

Series	Concept	Predictions
1. AABAABA	B → A A A → B A → A	AAB
2. ABACABA	C → A B A → C B → A A → B	CAB
3. GBDGBGBDG	D G B → G G B → D D → G G → B	BGB
4. BBABCBBBBA	B B B B → A B B B → B C B B → B C → B A B → C A → B B → B	BCB

Figure 4.   Series Concepts Learned by the
SC1 Series Extrapolation Program.

---

*   The series in Figure 5 were taken from Williams.[10]

Series	Concept	Prediction
1. CDCDCD	x1 x2 → x1	CDC
2. AAABBB	x1 x2 x3 → x1'	CCC
3. ATBATAATB	x1 x2 x3 x4 x5 x6 → x1	ATA
4. RSRTRURV	R x2 R → x2' x1 x2 → x1	RWR
5. ABMCDMEF	x1 M x3 x1'' → M x1 x2 x3 → x1''	MGH
6. DEFGEFGH	x1 x2 x3 x4 → x1'	FGH
7. QXAPXBQXA	x1 x2 x3 x4 x5 x6 → x1	PXB
8. ABCDABCEA	C x2 x3 x4 C → x2' x1 x2 x3 x4 → x1	BCF
9. MABMBCMCDM	M x2 x3 x4 x5 x6 M → x2'' x1 x2 M x4 x5 x6 x1'' x2'' → M x1 x2 x3 x4 x5 x6 x1'' → x2'' x1 x2 x3 x4 x5 x6 → x1	DEM
10. URTUSTU	U x2 x3 U → x2' x1 x2 x3 → x1	TTU
11. MNLNKNJ	x1 N 'x1 → N x1 x2 → 'x1	NLN
12. ABYABXAB	B x2 x3 B → 'x2 x1 x2 x3 → x1	WAB
13. RSCDSTDE	x1 x2 x3 x4 → x1'	TUE
14. NPAOQAPR	x1 A x3 x1' → A x1 x2 x3 → x1'	AQS
15. MNOMOOMPO	M x2 x3 M → x2' x1 x2 x3 → x1	MQO
16. WXAXYBY	x1 x2 x3 → x1'	ZCZ
17. JKQRKLRS	x1 x2 x3 x4 → x1'	LMS
18. PONONMNM	x1 x2 x3 → 'x1	LML
19. CEGEDEHEEE	x1 E x3 x4 x1' → E x1 x2 x3 x4 → x1'	IEF

Figure 5. Series Concepts learned by the SC
Series Extrapolation Program.

549

Series	Concept	Predictions
1. ABCCDEFFG	x1 x2 x3 x4 → x1'''	HII
2. DDCCDDBDEAD	x1 D x3 'x1 → D D x2 x3 D → x2' x1 x2 x3 → 'x1	FZD
3. BADBADCE	x1 x2 x3 x4 'x1 → x2''' x1 x2 x3 x4 → 'x1	ZGB
4. AAABBBCACBD	x1 A x3 x4 x5 x6 x1'' → A x1 B x3 x4 x5 x6 x1'' → B x1 x2 x3 x4 x5 x6 → x1''	BEA
5. ABCBCDCDEF	C x2 x3 x4 C x2'' → x3'' x1 C x3 x4 x1'' → C x1 x2 x3 x4 → x1''	CFG
6. ADUACUAEUABUAF	x1 U A x4 x5 x6 'x1 U A → x4' U A x3 x4 x5 x6 U A → 'x3 A x2 x3 x4 x5 x6 A → x2' x1 U x3 x4 x5 x6 'x1 → U x1 x2 x3 x4 x5 x6 → x1	UAA

Figure 6. Difficult Series Concepts Learned
by the SC2 Series Exatrapolation Program

Even though the SC2 program is an extension of SCl they do
not always make the same predictions, particularly when given ambiguous series. For example, given the series ABBA, SCl makes the
simple extrapolation: BBA..., or simple repetition of period 3.
However, SC2 (and the K&W program) would find a more complex extrapolation of period 2, i.e., CZD... . For unambiguous simple
repetition series, SCl and SC2 always make the same predictions,
but SC2 produces a simpler concept after a much greater computational effort.

VI. CONCLUSION

A learning technique has been presented for finding regularities in sequential patterns. It consists of nothing more complex
than forming an ordered set of hypotheses about which pattern contexts lead to which new pattern elements. The learning system
starts with very general hypotheses, i.e., rules which apply to
particular classes of patterns. As these rules are proven erroneous their generality is reduced by adding new rules above them
which apply to subclasses of these patterns. More specifically,
learning proceeds by first assuming that only one element in a
particular pattern context is relevant and then, as this is proven
false, falling back to the less general assumption that other elements in that pattern context are also relevant. When the learning phase is complete, the system has learned which pattern elements are relevant given any particular pattern context.

The preceeding remarks apply to both the basic learning technique and to the extension of that technique. However, in the extension of the basic learning technique an additional generalization process is present. This is the process of characterizing the relations between elements of the pattern in a very general way before adding the rule containing these pattern elements to the system. Here a specific rule is made more general subject to constraints imposed by the current strategy for recognizing relations. Only one such strategy (the template strategy) was presented in this paper. As mentioned earlier it involved hypothesizing a period size and only recognizing relations between corresponding elements of adjacent periods. However, by making the strategy for recognizing relations a little more sophisticated it should be possible to create a single unified program which can learn series concepts based on both inter-period and intra-period relations.

The production system learning technique was presented primarily as an artificial intelligence implementation of sequence extrapolation, rather than as a model of human problem solving. In fact, comparison with Restle's work indicates that the learning technique may more closely model human sequence prediction than sequence extrapolation, even though the two are very closely related. Since both extrapolation and prediction require pattern acquisition, it might be useful to examine the implications of this learning technique for a general theory of human serial pattern acquisition. First, it implies that some portion of human long term memory is organized in the form of a production system or set of condition-action rules. Second, it implies that these rules have an order imposed on them, i.e., given any rule, one can find the next rule in the list. However, this ordering does not imply that conditions on rules are accessed serially. The matching of production rule conditions against data in short term memory is considered to proceed in parallel*, leading to a set of rules whose conditions match the data. A single rule is chosen from this conflict set on the basis of relative location in long term memory, and its actions are executed. Thus response latency is not necessarily proportional to production system size. Third, the learning technique implies a memory for the locations of rules recently fired. This follows from the necessity of incorporating new rules into the system in front of error-causing rules. Finally, it implies that learning serial patterns involves a liberal use of memory capacity in order to reduce computational complexity.

It is felt that this learning technique can be generalized to other indiction-type tasks. A similar, though much simpler, technique has already been used in a production rule simulation of verbal learning.[21] Another similar, but more complex, technique has been used in a production system program which learns heuristics for draw poker.[23]

---

* This is currently implemented as a simple serial process.

ACKNOWLEDGMENTS

The author wishes to thank David Klahr for his many ideas relevant to this paper. The comments and criticisms of Herbert Simon, Dick Hayes, and Allen Newell are also gratefully acknowledged. This work has been supported in part by the NIH Grant MH-07722, and in part by the Advanced Research Projects Agency of the Secretary of Defense (1-58200-8130).

REFERENCES

1. Selfridge, O. G., and U. Neisser, Pattern recognition by machine. *Computers & Thought*. E. A. Feigenbaum and J. Feldman, (Eds.), McGraw-Hill, 1963, pp. 235-267.
2. Zobrist, A. L., The organization of extracted features for pattern recognition, *Pattern recognition*, Vol. 3, 1971, pp. 23-30.
3. Uhr, L., *Pattern Recognition, Learning and Thought*, Prentice-Hall, 1973.
4. Feldman, J., Simulation of behavior in the binary choice experiment, *Computers & Thought*, Feigenbaum, E. A., and Feldman, J. (Eds.), 1963.
5. Simon, H. A., and K. Kotovsky, Human acquisition of concepts for sequential patterns, *Psychological Review*, Vol. 70, no. 6, 1963, pp. 534-546.
6. Uhr, L., Pattern-string learning programs, *Behavioral Science*, Vol. 9, no. 3, July 1964, pp. 258-270.
7. Solomonoff, R. J., A formal theory of inductive inference, Part II, *Information and Control*, 7, 1964, pp. 224-254.
8. Ernst, G. W., and A. Newell, *GPS: A Case Study in Generality and Problem Solving*, Academic Press, 1969, pp. 232-246.
9. Klahr, D., and J. G. Wallace, The development of serial completion strategies: An information processing analysis, *British Journal of Psychology*, Vol. 61, 1970, pp. 243-257.
10. Williams, D. S., Computer program organization induced from problem examples, *Representation and Meaning*, Simon, H. A., and Siklossy, L. (Eds.), Prentice-Hall, 1972, pp. 143-205.
11. Hedrick, C. L., A computer program to learn production systems using a semantic net, Ph.D. Dissertation, GSIA, Carnegie-Mellon University, 1974.
12. Hunt, E. B. and S. E. Poltrock, The mechanics of thought, In Kantowitz, B. H. (Ed.), *Human Information Processing: Tutorials in Performance and Cognition*, L. Erlbaum Associates, N.J., 1974, pp. 277-350.
13. Newell, A., and H. Simon, *Human Problem Solving*, Prentice-Hall, 1972.
14. Restle, F., Grammatical analysis of the prediction of binary events, *Journal of Verbal Learning and Verbal Behavior*, 6, 1967, pp. 17-25.

15. Markov, A. A., The theory of algorithms (tr. from the Russian by J. J. Shorr-kon), U. S. Dept. of Commerce, Office of Technical Services, OTS 60-51085. (Teoriya Alborifmov, USSR Academy of Sciences, Moscow, 1954).
16. Galler, B., and A. Perlis, *A View of Programming Languages*, Addison-Wesley, 1970.
17. Restle, F., and E. R. Brown, Serial pattern learning, *Journal of Experimental Psychology*, Vol. 83, no. 1, 1970, pp. 120-125.
18. Chomsky, N., Formal properties of grammars, in *Handbook of Mathematical Psychology*, R. P. Luce, R. R. Bush, and E. Galenter, (Eds.), Vol. 2, Wiley, 1963.
19. Restle, R., Theory of serial pattern learning: Structural trees, *Psychological Review*, Vol. 77, no. 6, 1970, pp. 481-495.
20. Greeno, J. G., and H. A. Simon, Processes for sequence production, *Psychological Review*, Vol. 81, n. 3, 1974, pp. 187-198.
21. Waterman, D. A., Adaptive production systems, CIP working paper #285, Psychology Department, Carnegie-Mellon University, December, 1974.
22. Waterman, D. A., and Newell, A. PAS-II: An interactive task-free version of an automatic protocol analysis system. Proceedings of the Third International Joint Conference on Artificial Intelligence, 1973, pp. 431-445.
23. Waterman, D. A. Generalization learning techniques for automating the learning of heuristics. *Artificial Intelligence*, Vol. 1, nos. 1 and 2, 1970, pp. 121-170.

DABI--A DATA BASE FOR IMAGE ANALYSIS WITH
NONDETERMINISTIC INFERENCE CAPABILITY

Y. Yakimovsky
R. Cunningham
Jet Propulsion Laboratory
California Institute of Technology
Pasadena, CA.

ABSTRACT

The following is a description of the data base used in the perception subsystem of the Mars robot vehicle prototype being implemented at the Jet Propulsion Laboratory. This data base contains two types of information. The first is generic information that represents general rules conformed to by structures in the expected environments. The second kind of information is a specific description of a structure, i.e., the properties and relations of objects in the specific case being analyzed. The generic knowledge is represented so that it can be used by the approximate reasoning subsystem to obtain information on the specific structure which is not directly measurable by the sensory instruments. Raw measurements are being input either from the sensory instruments or a human operator using CRT or TTY.

The generic model of the rules is substantially a representation of the statistics of the environment. It contains nondeterministic general rules relating properties of, and relations between, objects. The description of a specific structure is also nondeterministic in the sense that all properties and relations may take a range of values with an associated probability distribution.

I. INTRODUCTION

There were a few attempts to build useful representation models of generic information. The traditional method of modeling in the mathematical physical sciences is the use of a set of deterministic axioms expressed in mathematical logic. This approach was used successfully in generation and analysis of mathematical and physical models and theories. Unfortunately, attempts to use this method of representation by computer programs for automatic reasoning ([1];[2] Chaps. 6,7,8) ran into the problems of computational impracticability as was foreseeable in hindsight from complexity theory [3]. In addition to the inherent computational impracticability of the use of nontrivial axiom systems, most rules in the real world are nondeterministic. That is, for almost all rules, exceptions can be found.

Since logic-based (deterministic) rule systems were found to be impractical, attempts to implement practical nondeterministic inference systems were made [4,5].

This article presents our approach to the representation of nondeterministic generic rules, the representation of nondeterministic facts about the specific cases being analyzed, and the approximate reasoning process which applies the generic information to obtain more information on the specific cases. In some sense, we integrated semantic net approach with sequential decision theory. The semantic net approach contributed flexible hierarchical organization, while the sequential decision theory contributed flexibility by use of probabilities and systematic control structure.

Researchers in scene analysis used or suggested use of the data base approach [6], the semantic base approach [4] or deterministic hierarchical structures [7,8,9] before. However, it appears that our system is a step forward in providing for powerful control and rule-based probabilistic inference under time constraints in a way which was not attempted before and which seems to be potentially and practically useful.

The data base is implemented in SAIL, an algol-based associative data base language for the DEC PDP-10 computer. The machine being used at the present is the Caltech PDP-10, but implementation started on the Stanford Artificial Intelligence Lab. PDP-10. The sensory instrument, e.g., the stereo pair of TV cameras and laser range finder (Fig. 1) are controlled and interfaced to the real time minicomputer GA SPC-16/85 (see Fig. 2). The Caltech PDP-10 can control the SPC-16 via telephone line, and many of the preprogrammed attributes (feature extractors) are implemented as low-level image analysis routine on the SPC-16. The SAIL language is described in Refs. 10 and 11.

The sensory system itself and low-level routines for feature extraction out of images are described in Refs. 12-15. Appendixes A and B contain a self-contained description of a simple application of the data base in the analysis of the traversibility (safety) of area for the vehicle. It may be helpful to refer to these appendixes at this point.

II. ENVIRONMENT DESCRIPTION - SPECIFIC STRUCTURE REPRESENTATION

In the abstract, a specific structure (an analyzed case) can be represented as a set of objects, properties of those objects and relations between objects. Our domain of specializations is the representation and the analysis of pictorial information. Appendix 1 explains a computer printout of a generic model, and Appendix 2 describes a computer printout of a specific model. Both of these models are dedicated for the analysis of traversibity of areas by a robot vehicle. Typically, when modeling the VISUAL WORLD in an attempt to understand pictures there are the following

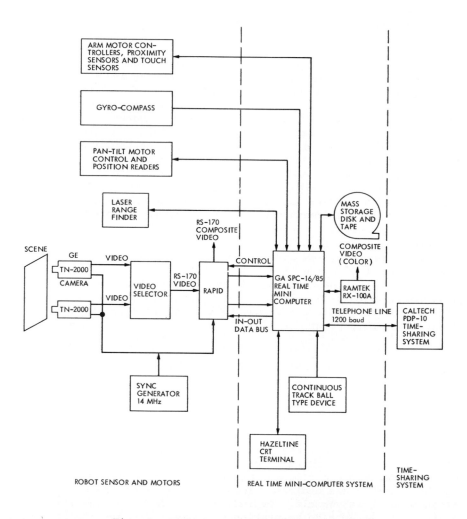

Fig. 1.   Robot system configuration

classes of objects: (1) scenes (picture frames), (2) three-dimensional bodies, (3) two-dimensional regions (pictorial images of
three-dimensional surfaces), (4) one-dimensional lines, (5) one-
dimensional boundaries between regions, (6) vertices, and (7) 3-D
surface sample point, etc.

In each specific instance of the environment (in vision research it will be a specific picture frame), there appear a few
objects of those types. Each one of these objects has properties
and is related to other objects. Figure 3 gives a partial data
structure describing an image.

A) Objects and Classes

The list of possible "classes" of objects is predetermined by
the repertoire of the generic model. When representing an instance
structure, each "class" is a "set" data structure. Such a "set"
is a data structure containing an unsorted list of nonrecurring
pointers to the data structures representing the known objects of
that class in the specific structure. For instance, the set associated with the class "regions" when representing the model in
Fig. 3 will contain pointers to regions R_1, R_2, R_3, and R_4. The
object data structure itself is an item containing the object's
name (for man-machine interaction), the name of its class and some
basic preprogrammed properties. Usually each object in a structure
is in relation "part of" with a global object (the "scene" in the
visual pictures case). The global object allows the definition of
global properties like lens iris setting, camera position, and external lighting conditions which affects the analysis of all sub-
structures.

Fig. 2. Hardware configuration: two cameras and arm

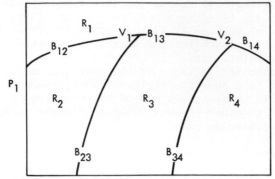

CLASSES OF OBJECTS: SCENES, REGIONS, BOUNDARIES, VERTICES

OBJECTS

    OF CLASS   SCENES: P_1

    OF CLASS   REGIONS: R_1, R_2, R_3, R_4

    OF CLASS   BOUNDARIES: B_{12}, B_{13}, B_{14}, B_{23}, B_{34}

    OF CLASS   VERTICES: V_1, V_2

FEATURES

    OF REGIONS: SIZE, GRAY LEVEL, LABEL

    OF BOUNDARIES: LENGTH, AVERAGE DIFFERENCES

RELATIONS

    REGIONS IN: SCENES ⟶ REGIONS

    BOUNDARY OF: REGION ⟶ BOUNDARY

    ADJACENT: REGION ⟶ REGION

    COMPOSES: VERTEX ⟶ BOUNDARY

PROPERTIES:

$$\text{size} \ \otimes \ R_1 \equiv (10 \ \ 1.0)$$

$$\text{label} \ \otimes \ R_1 \equiv \begin{pmatrix} \text{"SKY"} & .5 \\ \text{"CLOUD"} & .5 \end{pmatrix}$$

RELATION - OBJECT LIST:

$$\text{BOUNDARY OF} \ \otimes \ R_1 \ \equiv \ \begin{pmatrix} B_{12} & 1.0 \\ B_{13} & 1.0 \\ B_{14} & 1.0 \end{pmatrix}$$

$$\text{COMPOSES} \ \otimes \ V_1 \ \equiv \ \begin{pmatrix} B_{13} & 1.0 \\ B_{23} & 1.0 \\ B_{12} & 1.0 \end{pmatrix}$$

$$\text{REGIONS IN} \ \otimes \ P_1 \ \equiv \ \begin{pmatrix} R_1 & 1.0 \\ R_2 & 1.0 \\ R_3 & 1.0 \\ R_4 & 1.0 \end{pmatrix}$$

Fig. 3.   Partial representation of a segmented scene

B)   Representation of Properties

The generic model of the environment defines a set of attributes that are functions that act on elements of a specified class
and map into the integer domain. For example, the following are
some of the attributes which apply to objects of class regions:
"area", "color", "average light intensity", "shape". Attributes
which apply to objects of type boundary include "length", "difference in light intensity across the boundary line", etc.
The value of an attribute when applied to an object is a property of the object. For instance, application of the attribute
"area" to region R_1 may result in the value 7, which is a property
of R_1.
The representation of properties is made a bit more complicated, because measurements may be unreliable and take a range of
possible values. For instance, estimating the "label" (meaning)
of the body imaged on R_1 may be speculative. To represent ambiguity, properties are allowed to take range of values with an associated probability estimate of the validity of that value.
The association of attribute, object, and property is represented by the associative data structure of SAIL, and may look
like this:

$$\text{Area} \; \textcircled{X} \; R_3 = \left\{ \begin{array}{ll} 16 & 0.05 \\ 15 & 0.9 \\ 14 & 0.05 \end{array} \right\}$$

This will mean that the current estimate of the area of R_3 is
16 with probability 0.05, 15 with probability 0.9, and 14 with
probability 0.05. Note, that the probabilities add up to one.
This is so because the property values are assumed to be mutually
exclusive (e.g., one and only one value is actually true even
though we cannot tell which one).
The properties data structure is further complicated by two
factors. First, a property may change in time; hence, some estimate on the period of validity of that property must be given.
Secondly, often the reliability of the estimate of a property depends on the resources spent in measurement and analysis. Hence,
an indication of: (1) the amount of resources (compute time) allocated to obtaining the specific property, (2) the amount of resources actually used to obtain that estimate, and (3) the real
time when the estimate was obtained is associated with the property estimate. As a result, the property data structure (the
item's content, which is a linear array here) contains the following information:

(1)   Start of validity period date.
(2)   End of validity period date.
(3)   Date when the estimate was computed.

(4) Resources allocated to obtain the property's estimate.
(5) Resources used to obtain the estimate.
(6) Last access data - used by the "forget" mechanism to release storage taken by usused information.
(7) Estimated values list.

$$
\begin{bmatrix}
val_1 & P_1 \\
val_2 & P_2 \\
\cdot & \cdot \\
\cdot & \cdot \\
\cdot & \cdot \\
val_n & P_n
\end{bmatrix}
$$

(more compact representation of the probability distribution of values is used when practical.)

All dates are measured in absolute time, and stored in standard PDP-10 format in a 36-bit word specifying the date and time of day down to about a third of a second accuracy. If a property is assumed constant in the effective time, the validity dates may be set to $-\infty$ or to $+\infty$ to indicate permanency in one or two time directions in the scope of the analysis.

Resources are measured in the number of milliseconds of compute time that were used or were allocated to be used to obtain that estimate.

There can be more than one property associated with a pair of an attribute and a specific object. For instance, the color of an object may be blue from $06\underline{00}$ to $17\underline{35}$, red from $17\underline{35}$ to $18\underline{30}$, and black afterwards in the period of interest. The associative storage mechanism of SAIL provides for that type of multiplicity of associations of few properties with a single pair of an attribute and an object.

Attributes values (properties) and relation values (object lists) can be put in manually in the specific model data base as training samples for a learning process where the generic model is being improved or analyzed. Such properties are marked as "special" knowledge for training purposes. The learning process is not described at all within the scope of this article, and no further reference to that point will be made.

C) Representation of Values of Relations (Objects List)

A number of relations are defined for each class of objects in the generic model. The value of a relation applied to an object of the appropriate class will be a list of objects all of one class (possibly different from the class of the object operated on) which satisfy the relation. For instance, "boundary of" will be a relation which operates on object of class "regions" and will come back with a list of objects of class "boundary lines" which are boundaries of that region.

The limitation that relations apply to one object at the time was imposed to simplify implementation.

In general, relations are n-ary, not binary, as in the present implementation; that is, the relation is between more than two objects. The limitation may be bypassed by defining "combination" objects; that is, define an object class whose elements stand for an ordered list of a fixed number of simpler objects.

Typically, application of a relation to an object results in the following association being put in the data base:

$$
\text{Relation } \bigotimes \text{ object}_0 = \begin{bmatrix} \text{object}_1 & W_1 \\ \text{object}_2 & W_2 \\ \text{object}_3 & W_3 \\ \cdot \\ \cdot \\ \cdot \\ \text{object}_N & W_N \end{bmatrix}
$$

The relation is the name as defined in the generic model. Object_0 is an instance of an object of the class of objects upon which the relation works. Each one of object_i ($1 \le i \le N$) is estimated to satisfy the relations with the corresponding probability W_i. In fact, the relations values define fuzzy sets [16]. All of these objects belong to the same class of objects which is the range of the relation. Clearly, N varies with different applications of the relation. We also imposed the constraint that the W_i must be higher than 0.5; otherwise, the corresponding object is not included in the list to save storage. Note that the W_i's do not have to add up to one. There may be cases where more than one object satisfies the relation, e.g., the objects which satisfy a relation are not mutually exclusive. In other cases the list is empty; that is, no object appears to satisfy the relation. The distinction between operators which have mutually exclusive values (attributes) and others (relations) is important. Failure to account for these two types of operators results in mathematical logical distortions when the modeling process is bent to fit reality [5].

As is the case with properties, the "list' of objects which satisfy a certain relation is time and resource dependent. The more the resources are expanded for searching for such objects, the more of them are likely to be found. Similarly, the period of time during which the relation will be valid may be limited. As a result, the data structure of the object list also contains the following information:

(1) Start of validity period date.
(2) End of validity period date.

(3)   Approximated date when list was computed.
(4)   Type of computation.
(5)   Resources (compute time) allocated to obtaining the list.
(6)   Resources used in obtaining the list.
(7)   Last access date (used for storage cleanup).

There are two types of evaluations of relations. The first corresponds to the existential quantifier (∃) in logic. This existential search tries to find an object which satisfies the relation with high enough probability as specified in the call, and it terminates successfully as soon as one is found. The second type of evaluation is an exhaustive search. Its aim is to find as many objects that satisfy the relation with high probability within the bound of the resources allocated. The object list contains also a mark as to which type of search was used to obtain it.

There is an indirect call on relations which return a property-like value. This is a filter call. It operates on a pair of objects (object$_0$, object$_1$) and it takes only two values, 0 or 1. It takes the value 1 if object$_1$ appears to satisfy the corresponding relation to object$_0$ and 0 otherwise,

Example:

$$\text{Filter (Relation}_1,\ \text{object}_0,\ \text{object}_1,\ \text{res)} \quad = \quad \begin{bmatrix} 0 & 0.4 \\ \\ 1 & 0.6 \end{bmatrix}$$

is equivalent to

$$\text{Relation}_1\ \textcircled{X}\ \text{Object}_0 = \begin{bmatrix} \cdot & \cdot \\ \cdot & \cdot \\ \cdot & \cdot \\ \text{Object}_1 & 0.6 \\ \cdot & \cdot \\ \cdot & \cdot \end{bmatrix}$$

III.   THE GENERIC MODEL

The generic model does not describe an instance of the environment (a specific structure) but contains information on general rules that objects and structures in the environment will generally satisfy. The generic model is designed so as to allow direct use of the rules to compute properties and find objects which satisfy certain relations when this kind of information is requested by a user.

The basis of the knowledge representation in the generic model is, of course, the repertoire of: (1) classes of objects, (2) attributes of those objects, and (3) relations. With each attribute and relation, there is an associated algorithm which, when applied to an object of the adequate class, will come back with the value. These algorithms are constructed so that they may use only the resources (compute time) available to get an estimate of the value of the relation or attribute.

At the present the rules are man-made. Using a special interactive editor, experts generate and update the information contained in the rules expressed in the formats described later. The data base system was designed with the intent that it will be expandable to include a statistical learning subsystem. When the learning subsystem will be implemented, the rules will be largely machine generated. The learning subsystem will integrate principles of adaptive learning [17] with statistical structure learning [18,19].

A) Attributes

The data structure of each attribute contains information defining the class of objects it operates on and the range of (integer) values that it can take.

There is an option to associate a name (an alpha-numeric string) with some or all of the integer values that the attribute can take. These names are intended to facilitate man-machine interaction when properties are transmitted to or received from human operators. Similarly, the attribute names are selected so that they will be self-explanatory as to their semantic meaning.

There are three types of attributes as determined by the type of the unique algorithm that is associated with the attribute and which is used to compute the properties of objects. The first type is programmed. Here, a preprogrammed routine is used to compute the value of the attribute when applied to an object. Many of these properties are actually stored in the data structure of the object itself in which case they are not saved in the associative storage. These routines typically control directly the sensory instruments interfaced to the real time computer (SPC-16/85) and perform what we call low level analysis. We distinguish between preprogrammed attributes implemented on the SPC-16 and the PDP-10. The second type of attributes are those whose values are obtained from a human operator or experts. When the value of one of those attributes for an object (the property) is required, the system issues a console (teletype or CRT) message requesting those values from the operator. The text of the message with blanks to be filled with the object names is stored in the data structure of the attribute. The last type of attribute is that which is evaluated by the inference system using the classification tree (the probabilistic semantic net) associated with the attribute. A unique dedicated classification tree is associated with each such attribute. This tree represents a sequential classification process. When a property of an object (the value of an attribute) of that type is requested, the property is estimated by classifying the *object* into one of few small categories of objects of that class, using other (hopefully simpler to obtain) properties. For each of the small categories, the generic model has an estimate of the property distribution for objects in that category. That distribution estimate is then taken as the property of that object. The sequential classification tree can be easily edited to obtain finer categories and to update the estimates of the distribution of the property for objects in the category. This facilitates learning of the generic model. More detail on the classification tree data structure is given below.

B) Relations

The data structure of a relation specifies the class of objects it operates on and the class of objects on which it ranges. As is the case with attributes, there are three classes of relations as defined by the way they are computed. The first is the preprogrammed search where the search is done by a purely programmed algorithm. The second kind of relation requires that the list of objects will be provided by the operator. The third kind of relations, which we call inference relations, is computed from other (simpler) relations by union, intersection, and filtering the output of the simpler relations and attributes. The third type of relations is not yet fully developed in the existing system.

The rest of this article describes the representation of the sequential classification process associated with computation of inferred attributes, followed by a description of the driver system, which computes values of attributes and relations.

IV. INFERRED ATTRIBUTES -- THE CLASSIFICATION TREE

The essence of the inference process which computes the value of an inferred attribute applied to an object is classification of the object. The object is classified into categories such that the range of values of that attribute for objects in the small category is very limited and, hence, the property can be well estimated.

Example: Consider three-dimensional bodies in an environment where three-dimensional bodies may be labeled only oranges, bananas, or table tops. Then, without any test, the *a priori* probability distribution of the attribute "label" applied to an object of class "three-dimensional body" selected at random will be something like orange with probability 0.6, table with probability 0.3, and banana with probability 0.1.

If we break the class of "three-dimensional bodies" into two categories, the first category contains those objects which have some planar surfaces, and the second category contains those objects which are purely curved surface. Then, the first category will include almost exclusively objects whose label takes the value tables, while the second category will be almost exclusively bananas or oranges. Testing the color and shape of objects in the second category will allow further subclassification of objects in that category into finer subcategories, some almost exclusively containing objects labeled bananas and the others almost exclusively containing objects labeled oranges.

The classification tree for an inferred attribute actually represents the classification process. The top node of the tree stands for the category of all objects of the class. With each node, there is an associated category of object and each son node stands for a (finer) subcategory of the category of objects in the parent mode.

Each node contains the following information (to be described in more detail below):

(1) *Calling attribute*. Each node is part of a unique classification tree dedicated to one attribute. A pointer to that attribute is contained in the node.

(2) *Default value*. This is the distribution of the property over all objects which belong to the category associated with the node. This probabilistic information can either be put in manually or can be collected by going over (manually) analyzed examples and counting the distribution. If the inference algorithm reaches the node without sufficient resources to expand the node this estimate is returned as the answer. If there is not a default estimate (insufficient training set or too wide range of values to be stored practically), a marker to that effect is put in.

(3) *Node expansion plan (optional)*. This information designates either how to get a finer classification of the objects in the node's category so as to get a better estimate of the property or how to get a better estimate of the property directly without finer classification. Finer classification is obtained by selecting sons of the node which stand for subcategories of the category of objects. If there is no such plan associated with the node, the default estimate is the only possible answer.

(4) *Integration procedure*. This specifies how to integrate estimates returned from the activated sons to get a unique answer to be returned from the current node. This

integration type is needed where, because of ambiguity, more than one son is activated (that is, the object may have been estimated to belong with positive probability to more than one subcategory).

(5) *Text (optional)*. Describes the rate of the node in the classification tree. This text is put in by the person or procedure who generated the node.

The node expansion procedure (ANODE-EXPAND) is described in detail later in the paper. However, it will be outlined here to justify the data structure of the son selection plan. The node expansion procedure operates on one node at a time. When a node expansion is completed, the expanding procedure returns an estimated property. This estimate will be the default value associated with the node in the case where the node does not have a node *expansion plan* or there are not sufficient resources to activate the node expansion plan. When the node expansion plan is activated the estimate returned from the node will be either the weighted average of the estimates returned from recursive application of the node expansion procedure on sons of the node or the value Q (to be defined shortly) if the node expansion plan does not call for son expansion.

The son nodes where they exist correspond to subcategories of the objects in the category associated with the node. This finer classification is made based on other properties of the specific structure analyzed. Those other properties are requested in the node expansion plan stored in the parent node. Since these other properties may be nondeterministic, this selection of the subcategories may be nondeterministic. In such a case, the object will be assumed to belong to different sons (subcategories) with different positive probabilities. The property estimate of the answer returned from the parent node is the average of the estimates obtained from the activated son weighted by the probability that the object belongs to each of the corresponding subcategories. The integration procedure specifies which kinds of averaging are used for the node.

A node expansion plan contains the following information:

(1) An array of R activation records of relations which are used by the procedure RRECORD-EXPAND (see Sect. VI-E) (R is an integer associated with the node). The ith relation activating record ($1 \leq i \leq R$) specifies: (a) the name of the relation REL [i], (b) the associated index SUBJECT [i] ($0 \leq$ SUBJECT [i] < i) which specifies the objects upon which REL [i] operates (SUBJECT [i] = 0 means the original object and OBJECT [i] = j, $1 \leq j < i$ means that REL [i] should be applied to the objects satisfying the jth relation activation record), (c) the portion of the resources which will be allocated to com-

pute the ith relation activating record out of the total balance of the resources available for the node expansion, (d) the son which should be expanded if no object appears to satisfy the relation with probability greater than a specific threshold, (e) RMODE [i] which specify the mode of operation of RRECORD-EXPAND when it will expand that record.

(2) An array of N attributes activating records (N an integer associated with the node). This record is used by ARECORD-EXPAND (see sect. VI-D). The ith attribute activating record specifies: (a) ATT [i] the attribute it activates, (b) an index IND [i] to the objects operated on (IND [i] = 0) corresponds to the original object, $1 \leq$ IND(i) $\leq$ R means ATT [i] should be applied to the objects computed to satisfy IND [i]-th relation), (c) the portion of the balance of the available resources that should be allocated to that evaluation, and (d) AMODE [i] the mode of application of ARECORD-EXPAND the objects satisfying the IND [i]-th relation.

(3) Two arrays: A, which is a N by N real numbers array and B, which is a N real number array). When the node is expanded, each of the N attribute records is activated and it returns a property value. These N values are stored in N element array of values P. If N > 1 (e.g., more than one call on ARECORD-EXPAND is made) P(i) is the mean of the estimated values which ARECORD-EXPAND returned when N = 1 (only one call on ARECORD-EXPAND in that node), P(i) will be the property itself. The A and B are used to reduce the N properties into a single value Q.

$$Q = \vec{P}^{T} \cdot A \cdot \vec{P} + (\vec{B} \cdot \vec{P})$$

(4,a) Indicator whether Q is the value to be returned by ANODE_EXPAND.

(4,b) The alternative to (4,a) is to have an array of M sons with an associated array of threshold T_i $1 \geq i \geq m$. T_i are such that $T_i < T_{i+1}$ and $T_m = +\infty$. The ith son will be selected to be expanded if Q has positive probability of satisfying

$$T_{i-1} < Q \leq T_i$$

This will mean that there is a positive probability that the object at hand belongs to the ith subcategory which is associated with the ith son. That probability will be the weight given to that son.

Now since Q can take a range of values with different probabilities, it is nondeterministic. As a result, the object may have positive probability of being in more than one subcategory, which will require integrating the estimates returned from each son node so as to get a unique answer from the parent node. Typically, we use the arithmetic average (weighted by the probabilities that the object belongs to the son) of the answers coming back from the different activated sons. This implies real nondeterministic son selection. Alternatively, weighted geometrical averaging is used which implies that we treat each son's answer as an independent estimate.

V. INFERRED RELATION - COMBINATION SEARCHES

Combination searches are not implemented in the current system; we anticipate organizing them in a search tree. The nodes of a search tree will contain a node expansion plan which will be used for resource allocation and expansion of the node. The son selection plan data structure organization will be similar to the son selection plan used in the classification tree. However, clearly there will be no default answer associated with the node (the generic model cannot know the specific objects that will satisfy the relation when applied on a specific object). Also, the dominant form of integration of answers from sons will be probably to take the union of the objects lists returned from the different activated sons.

The default answer of the attribute inference node will most likely be replaced in the nodes of the search tree by calls on other (hopefully simpler) relations and filters.

VI. THE CONTROL STRUCTURE OF THE ACCESS OF THE DATA BASE

Typically an initial access to the data base is a request for the value of a relation or an attribute applied to an object. This request comes from an external user, either a human or another subsystem of the robot system. The external user specifies how much compute time he wishes to allocate to that request. This compute time will be allocated for retrieval of the information. This request is immediately translated into the appropriate calls on ATTR_EXPAND and REL_EXPAND (sections A and B). From that point on control and execution progress in the normal way (see below). The initial access may find an empty specific model (all class sets are empty). In this case the object in the initial request of the access is put into the proper objects class in the data base and other objects are found in the natural way by expanding relations. Description of the 6 recursive procedures which compose the data base access and inference process is given immediately below.

A)   The Attribute Expanding Routine

The first procedure of the data base control is:

ATTR_EXPAND(ATTRIBUTE,OBJECT,RES)

It expands a request for the property which is the value of the
ATTRIBUTE (a pointer to an attribute in the generic model) applied
to OBJECT (a pointer to an object in the specific model).   RES
specifies the total resources (machine time) allocated for that
task.   A pointer to the computed property is returned as the value
of the procedure and also the association ATTRIBUTE (X) OBJECT=
PROPERTY is inserted to the data base.   The three major steps of
the procedure are:

(1)   Checks the validity of the request.   That is, verify
      that the ATTRIBUTE is in the generic model, the OBJECT
      is in the specific model and the OBJECT belongs to the
      class of objects upon which the attribute operates.

(2)   Checks whether the data base already contains the as-
      sociation of that attribute with that object.   If that
      is the case, a decision is made whether to use one of
      the estimates of the property in the data base or to
      compute a new estimate of that property.   The decision
      is made based on the period of validity of the stored
      estimates, the time when the stored estimate was ob-
      tained, and the amount of resources allocated and used
      to obtain the existing estimates.   The idea is that if
      one of the existing estimates is recent and was obtained
      with about the same or more resources as available now
      there is no point in doing redundant work.   In that case,
      the best existing estimate in the data base is returned
      as the value of the procedure immediately.

(3)   The action here depends on the type of the attribute.
      For a pre-programmed attributes, a call is made on the
      library routine which computes the property estimate on
      the PDP-10 or via the communication line on the SPC-16.
      The value returned by the library routine is then stored
      in the data base (in the proper association) and a point-
      er to it is returned as the value of the procedure.   For
      interactive (console) attributes, a request for the val-
      ue is issued to the user's terminal.   For the inferred
      attributes, a call on

      ANODE_EXPAND (ATTRIBUTE,NODE,OBJECT,ATTR,NRES)

      is issued.   (ANODE_EXPAND is the third procedure of the
      driver and is described below.)   NODE is the top node
      of the classification tree of that attribute (which is

specified in the attribute description in the generic
world model). The OBJECT is the same object as the OB-
JECT in the original call and NRES is the balance of resources left after processing steps 1 and 2. The value
returned by ANODE_EXPAND is taken as the property value
and is stored in the data base in the proper association
and a pointer to it is returned as the value of ATTR_
EXPAND in that call.

B)   The Relation Expanding Routine

The second procedure of the inference system driver is

RELAT_EXPAND(RELATION,OBJECT,RES,MODE,THRESHOLD)

This procedure returns as a value a pointer to the object list
(relation value). This object list is the list of the objects
which appear to satisfy the RELATION (which is a pointer to a relation in the generic model) applied to OBJECT (a pointer to an
object in the specific model). RES is the resources allocated for
that search. MODE specifies the type of call, e.g., whether the
procedure should return immediately as soon as an object which
satisfies the relation with probability higher than THRESHOLD is
found or whether it should attempt to find as many objects which
satisfy the relation exhausting the resources allocated. The procedure operates in three steps corresponding to the three steps of
ATTR_EXPAND.

(1)   Checks the validity of the call, e.g., RELATION must be
      defined in the generic model, OBJECT is in the specific
      model, and belongs to the class of objects upon which
      the relation operates as specified in the relation data
      structure.

(2)   Checks whether the information requested is already sub-
      stantially stored in the data base, in which case it re-
      turns the stored information immediately.

(3)   Depends on which kind of relation is being evaluated.
      If the relation is preprogrammed, a call on the comput-
      ing library routine on the SPC-16 or the PDP-16 is made.
      Where the relation is interactive, a console message re-
      questing the list of objects is issued to the operator.
      In the case of inferred relation when it will be imple-
      mented, a call on the top node of the relation, infer-
      ence tree node will be issued RNODE_EXPAND(NODE,OBJ,RE-
      LATION,NRES,MODE,THRESHOLD) corresponding to the ANODE_
      EXPAND in the case of inferred properties. The value
      returned by RNODE_EXPAND will be taken as the value of
      RELAT_EXPAND. In either case the object list (the re-

lation value) is also stored in the data base in the
association RELATION $\otimes$ OBJECT=OBJECT LIST.

C)   The Routine Which Expands a Node in an Attribute Inference Tree

The third recursive procedure of the driver is

ANODE_EXPAND ATTRIBUTE (NODE,OBJECT,PARAM,RES)

This procedure returns with an estimate of the property values
distribution represented in the same form as it is represented in
a property (except that validity time, etc. are not included).
The expansion of the node is made in the following steps:

(1)   Verifies the validity of the call. Check to see that
the NODE actually is a valid one and this node is dedicated to the analysis of the specified ATTRIBUTE. This
check is made only for debugging purposes.

(2)   Checks whether the node should be expanded. If the node
is not going to be expanded, the value returned by the
routine will be the default answer stored in the node
and no further processing will be made. Otherwise, the
node expansion plan will be activated. Decision to expand the node is made if two conditions are satisfied.
First, the node must have a node expansion plan and,
secondly, the resources allocated to this call of the
procedure must exceed a certain threshold which is considered minimum for expansion of that node.

(3)   Computes the R relations in the relation array in the
node (if $R \geq 1$). These relations are evaluated in the
order of 1 to R by recursive calls on the RRECORD_EXPAND
(REL[i],OBJAR[SUBJECT[I]],NRES,RMODE[I],THRESHOLD[I]).
(RRECORD_EXPAND is the 5*th* data base driver of the inference system.) A pointer to the object list returned
by the i*th* call on RRECORD_EXPAND whether empty or not
is stored in OBJAR [i].   OBJAR is an R-ele-
ment array of pointers to object lists associated with
the present expansion of the node. The subject on which
the ith relation operates can be any of the objects already pointed at in OBJAR, e.g., SUBJECT[i] must be less
than i. Clearly, the first relation must be applied to
the original object (e.g., OBJAR[i] = 0) since no other
object is pointed to yet. Where there is call on OBJAR
[i] = 0 a direct call on REL_EXPAND with the appropriate
variables is issued. If no object appears to satisfy
the i*th* relation the node expansion will branch to $RSON_i$
which corresponds to the subcategory where no object
satisfies the i*th* relation. NRES is computed to be the

571

portion of the compute time left for the node expansion that the plan recommends applying for that call.

(4) Computes the N properties associated with the node. The property is computed either by call on ARECORD_EXPAND (the 4th driver routine) with the proper parameter, subject, type of call and resources; or, if the index is 0, by a call on ATTR_EXPAND directly to apply the current attribute to the original object. The values returned by the property are stored into a vector (array) of property values, P [1:n].

(5) Integrates the N values in P into a single property like quantity Q:

$$Q = P^T A P + B P$$

where A is a two-dimensional array N by N and B a one-dimensional array (vector) of N elements. If N=1, Q looks like a typical property estimate, that is

$$Q = \left\{ \begin{array}{cc} val_1 & P_1 \\ val_2 & P_2 \\ . & . \\ . & . \\ . & . \\ val_k & P_k \end{array} \right\}$$

$$P_1 + P_2 + \ldots + P_k = 1$$

and $Val_{i+1} > Val_i$. If N > 1 for computational complexity reasons the P[i]'s are made deterministic values which is the average of the values in the property, and hence Q is also made deterministic.

(6) If Q is marked as the value to be returned by the expansion plan that value is returned as the value of ANODE_ EXPAND.

(7) If the case where the node expansion plan calls for son-nodes expansion the next step is to compare the range of values of Q against a list of threshold and sons

$$\left(\begin{array}{ccc} son_1 & son_2 & son_m \\ T_1 & T_2 & T_m \end{array} \right) .$$

SON_i is expanded if the sum of the probability of Val_j falling into (T_i, T_{i+1}) is positive. The sum of probability is the portion of the available resources for the ith son expansions by recursive call on ANODE_EXPAND out of the remaining resources.

(8) The answer returned from the different expanded sons is integrated by averaging them and returning that value as the value of that call on PNODE_EXPAND. The weight of the answer returned from the node is the same as the weight used to allocate resources to the sons.

D) The Routine Which Expands an Attribute Activating Record in Nodes

The 4th procedure of the driver system is:

ARECORD_EXPAND(ATTR,POBJL,MODE,RES)

POBJL is a pointer of an object list which will be referred to as OBJL. ARECORD_EXPAND starts as the other routine by checking the validity of the call for debugging purposes. The next action depends on the MODE in the call. When the system was implemented originally, there was only one mode of operation [20], but unfortunately the complexity of the simplest application forced us to implement plurality of modes. In all cases, it returns a property-like value which is computed in the following ways:

Mode 1: The attribute ATTR is applied by a call on ATT_EXPAND to each object in OBJL with a portion of the resources RES proportional to the probability that the object belongs to OBJL. The values returned by those calls are added together with proper weights to generate a single property-like value returned by ARECORE_EXPAND.

Mode 2: ATTR is applied to all objects in OBJL but the value returned is the property of the object whose mean is the maximum among all other objects.

Mode 3: Same as mode 2 except that the minimum is returned.

Mode 4: The mean of all values computed by application as in Mode 1 is returned, e.g., a single deterministic value which is the mean (average) of the property value which would have been returned by similar call with Mode 1.

Mode 5: The variance of the values computed by application as in Mode 1 is returned.

Mode 6: ATTR is applied only to the one object which maximizes the probability that it belongs to OBJL among all other objects in the list.

E) The Routine Which Expands Relation Record in Nodes

The 5*th* procedure of the driver

RRECORD_EXPAND(RELATION,POBJL,RES,MODE,THRESH)

POBJL is a pointer to an object list referred to as OBJL. RRECORD_EXPAND will return a pointer to an object list that it generated.

MODE = 0 means REL_EXPAND is going to be called only once to apply the RELATION to the object which maximizes the belong feature among all objects in the list pointed to by POBJL.

MODE = 1 means REL_EXPAND is going to be applied on all objects in the list. The new object list is generated by taking the object which satisfies each call of REL_EXPAND with highest probability.

MODE = 2 means REL_EXPAND is going to be applied on all objects in the list. All the object's lists generated are going to be united into a single long list.

F) The Routine Which Expands Nodes in Relation Inference Tree

The sixth routine of the driver is RNODE_EXPAND. This routine when implemented will be similar to PNODE_EXPAND with two differences:

(1) If the search operates in the existential mode, then as soon as one object which appears to satisfy the relation with high enough probability is found, the procedure returns immediately.

(2) There are no default answers. Instead of the default answer, a node may have a call on other relations and a filter property. If there is such a relation in the node, it is always evaluated with a portion of the resources. Then the filter is applied to those objects which satisfy that relation. The filter can have only two values, 0 and 1. The weighted average of the two values is taken as the probability that the object satisfies the original relation. If that probability is high enough, the object is added to the object list.

VII. PERMANENT STORAGE

The associative data base representing a specific structure
is meaningless without the associated generic model which defines
the classes of objects, the attributes, and the relations. Hence,
there are two types of permanent storage options on a magnetic
disk or tape file. One is the generic model by itself, and the
other is a generic model coupled with a description of a specific
structure using the terms defined by the generic model. The system can store files containing either kind of data and accept them
so as to continue analysis or editing from the status as saved.

VIII. MEMORY REFRESH

We plan on implementing a memory garbage collection mechanism.
This mechanism will be called when the data base runs out of storage. It will erase properties values and object lists giving priority according to the following factors:

(1) The amount of resources used to obtain the estimate.

(2) The length of time left for that information to be valid.

(3) The time lapsed after the last access for that information.

IX. CONCLUDING REMARKS

The foregoing material describes our approach to the representation of perceptual information. This system is an evolving
effort, and is expanded as experience is gained in using the inference capabilities of the data base. Control options are added
when necessary or when they appear to help convenience of use. We
believe this work is an improvement on our previous efforts described in Refs. 4, 17, 20. We consider our major contribution
to be the integration of the concepts of (1) inference and search
bound by time constraints, (2) nondeterministic hierarchical inferences, and (3) nondeterministic data representation.

Our present goal is to apply the system to image recognition
using the low-level segmentation routines described in Refs. 13
and 14 so as to create a more effective system than the one described in Ref. 17. We are also looking for practical ways to
save the status of inference processes which exhausted their resources so that if additional resources become later available,
the inference process may be resumed from the status it was in
when it was terminated. Currently, it has to be started from the
beginning again, but it can make use of any properties and values
of relations that are already in the data base.

We also consider the theoretical merit of integrating the resources (compute time) available more elaborately into the node

expansion plan. Adding such an option may allow more effective and sophisticated use of limited resources in special cases. That is, branching to special options where there are very limited resources.

APPENDIX A

EXAMPLE OF A GENERIC MODEL

I. INTRODUCTION

This section describes a generic model which DABI uses to solve a traversability problem for the JPL Robot Vehicle. The model is used to obtain an estimate of whether or not the vehicle can safely occupy a specified location in the environment. A complete listing of the model is included at the end of this appendix (Table A-1).

For a location to be classified "safe", several criteria must be satisfied. The weight of the vehicle should be nearly equally distributed on all four wheels. This implies that the four points which support the wheels should be "nearly" planar. The vehicle should be supported at a slope which is acceptable within limits imposed by wheel traction, driving and braking power, and the center of gravity. Once it has been determined that the vehicle will be adequately supported, the area that would be covered by the vehicle in that location must be examined for obstacles. The area around each wheel support point is checked first to see that the wheels are free of obstacles, then the entire region is checked to see if there are any obstacles which would interfere with any other part of the vehicle.

As the classification tree is expanded, each of the above criteria is tested as the value of an attribute defined in the model, in the order presented above. If each test is satisfied with probability 1, the location is classified "safe". If any test fails with probability 1, the location is classified "unsafe". Otherwise a value (safe, p_1), (unsafe, p_2) is assigned to the location where $p_1 + p_2 = 1$.

II. DESCRIPTION OF THE MODEL

The generic model consists of four data structure type CLASSES, RELATIONS, ATTRIBUTES, and NODES. A CLASS stands for a set of objects of the same type. RELATIONS and ATTRIBUTES are mappings f: A → B. In either case the domain A is a class defined in the generic model. In the case of RELATIONS, B is also a class defined in the model. For ATTRIBUTES, B is a specified set of integers. Each NODE of the classification tree is described in terms of the relations and attributes to be expanded by that node, and

the manner in which the expansion proceeds from that node.
A 3-dimensional cartesian coordinate system fixed in the environment is defined such that the x- and y-axes determine a horizontal plane and the positive z-axis points up. All references to
the coordinates of a point are with this coordinate system in mind.
The unit of measurement is inches.

III. CLASSES

A) VEHICLE!LOCATION

An object in this class specifies a vehicle location and is
represented by an ordered triple (x_0, y_0, θ_0). The vehicle is at
location (x_0, y_0, θ_0) if:

(1) The coordinates of a fixed point P rigidly attached to
the vehicle are (x_0, y_0, z);

(2) θ_0 is the angle formed by the positive x-axis and a vector $\vec{V}$ pointing toward the front of the vehicle (see
Fig. A-1).

Implicit in this definition is a rectangular region which contains
the projection of each point of the vehicle onto the xy-plane.
This region will be referred to as the *vehicle region*.

B) TILE

The vehicle region corresponding to a vehicle location $(x_0,
y_0, \theta_0)$ is subdivided into 8 by 8 in. squares or tiles. Each of
these subregions is an object of class TILE and is specified by
the (x,y) coordinates of its center point. The four tiles which
contain the support points of the wheels will be referred to as
the *wheel tiles*.

C) SAMPLE!POINT

A real world surface point (x, y, z) is an object of SAMPLE!
POINT. The coordinates of a SAMPLE!POINT are obtained by the robot sensory instruments, using either the LRF (laser range finder)
or stereo correlation [15].

IV. RELATIONS

SUPPORT: VEHICLE!LOCATION → TILE. This relation is preprogrammed to return a list of the four wheel tiles corresponding to
a vehicle location (x_0, y_0, θ_0). The list is generated in the following order: right front (wheel), right rear, left rear, and
left front.

A) WHEEL!AREA: TILE → TILE

This relation is preprogrammed. This relation is applied to each wheel tile and returns a list of nine tiles forming a square with the wheel tile in the center (see Fig. A-2).

B) GET!REGION: VEHICLE!LOCATION → TILE

This relation is preprogrammed to return a list of all the tiles covering the vehicle region defined by (x_0, y_0, θ_0).

C) SAMPLE: TILE → SAMPLE!POINT

This relation is preprogrammed to drive the sensory instrument to find a real world surface point (x, y, z) whose (x, y) coordinates are in the map tile.

V. ATTRIBUTES

A) SAFETY: VEHICLE!LOCATION → $\{1,2\}$

The value of this inferred attribute is taken as the estimate of whether the location (x_0, y_0, θ_0) is safe or unsafe for the vehicle. The values that this attribute can take are 1 and 2, corresponding to safe and unsafe, respectively. Nodes 1, 3, 4, 6, 7, 9, 10, 11, and 12 are controlled by SAFETY. The values computed at each of these nodes are integrated into a single value which node 1 returns as the value of SAFETY.

B) ZCOORD: SAMPLE!POINT → $\{integers\}$

This attribute is preprogrammed to return the z-coordinate of a sample point.

C) PLANE!FIT: VEHICLE!LOCATION → $\{non-negative\ integers\}$

This attribute is computed in node 2 using ARECORD_EXPAND. The attribute ZCOORD is applied to the sample point of each wheel tile in the order that they are generated by the relation SUPPORT. If the wheel tiles are labeled in order T_1, T_2, T_3, T_4 with Z_i $(1 \leq i \leq 4)$ the corresponding z-coordinate of T_i then the value of PLANE!FIT can be expressed as

$$d = \left| (z_1 + z_3) - (z_2 + z_4) \right| .$$

If the four points are planar, the value of d is 0. Otherwise d represents the distance in the z direction from any one point to a plane passing through the other three points. Thus d can be thresholded to determine if all four wheels of the vehicle will be adequately supported at the location (x_0, y_0, θ_0).

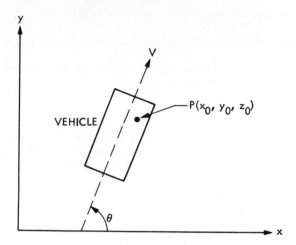

Fig. A-1. A vehicle location

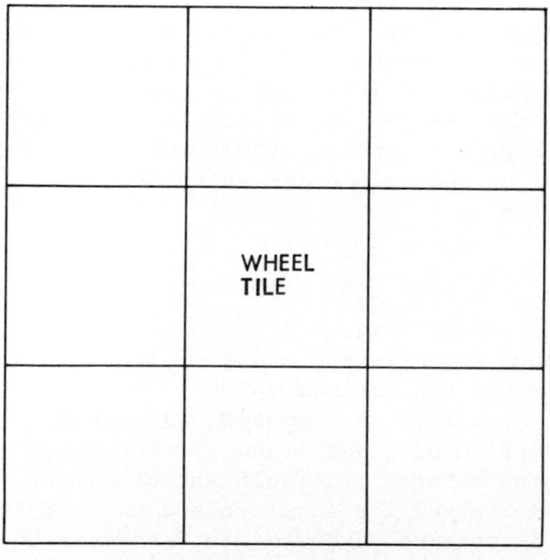

Fig. A-2. Configuration of tiles
computed by WHEEL!AREA

D) SUPPORT!VAR: VEHICLE!LOCATION → {non-negative integers}

The value of this attribute is computed in node 5 in a manner similar to PLANE!FIT. The value of SUPPORT!VAR is (max $\{z_i\}$ - min $\{z_i\}$), where z_i, $1 \leq i \leq 4$, represents the z-coordinates of the sample points of the four wheel tiles as above. This value is a measure of the slope of the vehicle region.

E) SUPPORT!HGT: VEHICLE!LOCATION → {integers}

This attribute is computed in node 14 as the average of the z_i, $1 \leq i \leq 4$ (z_i as above).

F) WHEEL!OBST: TILE → {non-negative integers}

This attribute is computed in node 8. For each wheel tile (obtained by SUPPORT), the relation WHEEL!AREA is expanded. ZCOORD is called for the sample point of each tile ARECORD_EXPAND. The value w_i = max $\{z\}$ - min $\{z\}$, $i = 1 \leq i \leq 4$ is computed for each wheel area. The value of WHEEL!OBST is taken as the worst case of w_i over the four wheel areas i.e.,

$$\max_{1<i<4} \left\{ w_i \right\}$$

A large value of WHEEL!OBST indicates the presence of an obstacle near one of the wheels.

G) HIGH!POINT: VEHICLE!LOCATION → {non-negative integers}

Using the list of all tiles obtained by the relation GET!REGION (in node 13), this attribute finds the maximum z-coordinate taken over the sample points of all tiles in the vehicle region. The z-coordinates are obtained by successive calls to ZCOORD in ARECORD_EXPAND. The difference between HIGH!POINT and SUPPORT!HGT is taken as an indication of whether or not there are obstacles present in the vehicle region.

H) NODES

The tree structure (Fig. A-3) is designed to compute the attributes described above in the order of increasing amounts of data necessary to compute the desired value.

In node 1, PLANE!FIT is computed. This value is used to determine the selection of nodes 3 and 4. For large values, node 4 is expanded, which returns a default answer UNSAFE.

In node 3 (expanded for small values of PLANE!FIT) the value of SUPPORT!VAR is obtained and used to determine the selection of nodes 6 and 7. For large values, node 7 is expanded which returns a default answer UNSAFE.

In node 6 (expanded for small values of SUPPORT!VAR) the value of WHEEL!OBST is computed, and used to determine the selection of nodes 9 and 10. For large values, node 10 is expanded which returns a default answer UNSAFE.

In node 9 (expanded for small values of WHEEL!OBST) the value of HIGH!POINT and SUPPORT!HGT are computed. The difference between these two values is used to determine the selection of nodes 11 and 12. If difference is large (indicates a vehicle obstacle is present), node 12 is expanded which returns a default answer UNSAFE. If the difference is small, node 11 is expanded and returns a default answer SAFE.

This completes the expansion of the nodes controlled by SAFETY. The values at each node are integrated and returned by node 1 in the form (SAFE, p_1), (UNSAFE, p_2) as the value of SAFETY ($p_1 + p_2 = 1$).

Nodes 2, 5, 8, 13, and 14 are controlled by the attributes PLANE!FIT, SUPPORT!VAR, WHEEL!OBST, HIGH!POINT, and SUPPORT!HGT respectively. Each of these nodes returns the value

$$Q = P \times A \times P^T + P \times B$$

as described in section VI-C (6).

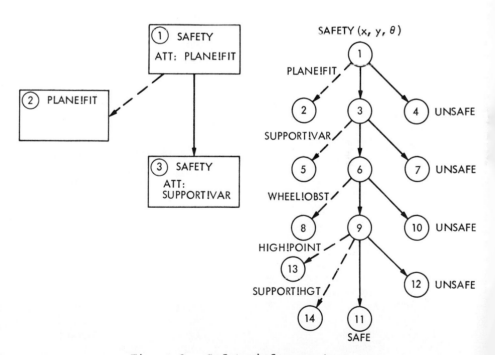

Fig. A-3. Safety inference tree

Table A-1. A generic model for vehicle obstacle detection

CLASSES:
    SAMPLE!POINT
    TILE
    VEHICLE!LOCATION

RELATIONS:
    NAME: SUPPORT
    TYPE: PDP10
    DOMAIN: VEHICLE!LOCATION
    RANGE: TILE

    NAME: WHEEL!AREA
    TYPE: PDP10
    DOMAIN: TILE
    RANGE: TILE

    NAME: SAMPLE
    TYPE: SPC16
    DOMAIN: TILE
    RANGE: SAMPLE!POINT

    NAME: GET!REGION
    TYPE: PDP10
    DOMAIN: VEHICLE!LOCATION
    RANGE: TILE

ATTRIBUTES:
    NAME: HIGH!POINT
    TYPE: TREE
    DOMAIN: VEHICLE!LOCATION
    RANGE: UNBOUNDED
    DEFAULT VALUE: NONE

    NAME: SUPPORT!HGT
    TYPE: TREE
    DOMAIN: VEHICLE!LOCATION
    RANGE: UNBOUNDED
    DEFAULT VALUE: NONE

    NAME: PLANE!FIT
    TYPE: TREE
    DOMAIN: VEHICLE!LOCATION
    RANGE: UNBOUNDED
    DEFAULT VALUE: NONE

    NAME: ZCOORD
    TYPE: PDP10
    DOMAIN: SAMPLE!POINT
    RANGE: UNBOUNDED
    DEFAULT VALUE: NONE

    NAME: SAFETY
    TYPE: TREE
    DOMAIN: VEHICLE!LOCATION
    RANGE: 2
    DEFAULT VALUE:
        SAFE,1
        UNSAFE,1

    NAME: WHEEL!OBST
    TYPE: TREE
    DOMAIN: TILE
    RANGE: UNBOUNDED
    DEFAULT VALUE: NONE

    NAME: SUPPORT!VAR
    TYPE: TREE
    DOMAIN: VEHICLE!LOCATION
    RANGE: UNBOUNDED
    DEFAULT VALUE: NONE

NODES:

1   TEXT: SAFETY TOP NO
    TYPE: EXPAND SONS
    ATTRIBUTE: SAFETY
    DEFAULT VALUE:
        SAFE,1
        UNSAFE,1
    RELATION BLOCK: EMPTY
    SELECTION BLOCK:

        VECTOR B: 1
        SELECTION ATTRIBUTES:
            ATTRIBUTE: PLANE!FI
            OBJECT INDEX: 0
            WEIGHT: 1
            MODE: 0

    SON BLOCK:
        SON: 3   4
        THRESHOLD: 6   INF
    INTEGRATION TYPE: 2

2   TEXT: COMPUTE PLANE!FI
    TYPE: TERMINAL--RETURN
    ATTRIBUTE: PLANE!FIT
    DEFAULT VALUE:
        1,1

RELATION BLOCK:

    RELATION: SUPPORT
    OBJECT INDEX: 0
    WEIGHT: 1
    THRESHOLD: 0.5
    SON: 2
    MODE: 0

    RELATION: SAMPLE
    OBJECT INDEX: 1
    WEIGHT: 1
    THRESHOLD: 0.5
    SON: 2
    MODE: 2

SELECTION BLOCK:

    VECTOR B: 1

    SELECTION ATTRIBUTES:
        ATTRIBUTE: ZCOORD
        OBJECT INDEX: 2
        WEIGHT: 1
        MODE: 2

SON BLOCK: EMPTY
INTEGRATION TYPE: 2
3   TEXT: ALL 4 WHEELS ON THE GROUND
   TYPE: EXPAND SONS
   ATTRIBUTE: SAFETY
   DEFAULT VALUE:
     SAFE,1
     UNSAFE,1
   RELATION BLOCK: EMPTY
   SELECTION BLOCK:

    VECTOR B: 1

    SELECTION ATTRIBUTES:
        ATTRIBUTE: SUPPORT!VAR
        OBJECT INDEX: 0
        WEIGHT: 1
        MODE: 0

    SON BLOCK:
        SON: 6   7
        THRESHOLD: 6 INF
    INTEGRATION TYPE: 2

```
4    TEXT:              ONE WHEEL OFF THE GROUND
     TYPE:              TERMINAL--RETURN DEFAULT ANSWER
     ATTRIBUTE:         SAFETY
     DEFAULT VALUE:
         UNSAFE,1
     RELATION BLOCK:  EMPTY
     SELECTION BLOCK: EMPTY
     SON BLOCK:       EMPTY
     INTEGRATION TYPE: 2

5    TEXT:              COMPUTE SUPPORT!VAR
     TYPE:              TERMINAL--RETURN Q
     ATTRIBUTE:         SUPPORT!VAR
     DEFAULT VALUE:
         1,1
     RELATION BLOCK:

         RELATION:        SUPPORT
         OBJECT INDEX:    0
         WEIGHT:          1
         THRESHOLD:       0.5
         SON:             5
         MODE:            0

         RELATION:        SAMPLE
         OBJECT INDEX:    1
         WEIGHT:          1
         THRESHOLD:       0.5
         SON:             5
         MODE:            2
     SELECTION BLOCK:

         VECTOR B:     1    -1

         SELECTION ATTRIBUTES:
             ATTRIBUTE:    ZOOORD
             OBJECT INDEX: 2
             WEIGHT:       1
             MODE:         3

             ATTRIBUTE:    ZOOORD
             OBJECT INDEX: 2
             WEIGHT:       1
             MODE:         4

     SON BLOCK:          EMPTY
     INTEGRATION TYPE:  2

6    TEXT:              LOOK FOR WHEEL!OBSTACLE
     TYPE:              EXPAND SONS
     ATTRIBUTE:         SAFETY
```

```
DEFAULT VALUE:
    SAFE,1
    UNSAFE,1
RELATION BLOCK:

    RELATION:       SUPPORT
    OBJECT INDEX:   0
    WEIGHT:         1
    THRESHOLD:      0.5
    SON:            6
    MODE:           0


SELECTION BLOCK:

    VECTOR B:       1


    SELECTION ATTRIBUTES:
        ATTRIBUTE:      WHEEL!OBST
        OBJECT INDEX:   1
        WEIGHT:         1
        MODE:           3

SON BLOCK:
    SON:            9    10
    THRESHOLD:      6    INF
INTEGRATION TYPE:   2
```

```
7   TEXT:               DANGEROUS SLOPE
    TYPE:               TERMINAL--RETURN DEFAULT ANSWER
    ATTRIBUTE:          SAFETY
    DEFAULT VALUE:
        UNSAFE,1
    RELATION BLOCK:     EMPTY
    SELECTION BLOCK:    EMPTY
    SON BLOCK:          EMPTY
    INTEGRATION TYPE: 2
```

```
8   TEXT:               WHEEL!OBST COMPUTE NODE
    TYPE:               TERMINAL--RETURN 0
    ATTRIBUTE:          WHEEL!OBST
    DEFAULT VALUE:
        1,1
    RELATION BLOCK:

        RELATION:       WHEEL!AREA
        OBJECT INDEX:   0
        WEIGHT:         1
        THRESHOLD:      0.5
        SON:            8
        MODE:           0
```

```
ELECTION BLOCK:

    VECTOR B:          1  -1

    SELECTION ATTRIBUTES:
        ATTRIBUTE:        ZOOORD
        OBJECT INDEX:     2
        WEIGHT:           1
        MODE:             3

        ATTRIBUTE:        ZOOORD
        OBJECT INDEX:     2
        WEIGHT:           1
        MODE:             4

SON BLOCK:          EMPTY
INTEGRATION TYPE:   2
```

```
9   TEXT:               SAFE SO FAR...LOOK FOR VEHICLE OBSTACLE
    TYPE:               EXPAND SONS
    ATTRIBUTE:          SAFETY
    DEFAULT VALUE:
        SAFE,1
        UNSAFE,1
    RELATION BLOCK:     EMPTY
    SELECTION BLOCK:

        VECTOR B:          1  -1

        SELECTION ATTRIBUTES:
            ATTRIBUTE:        HIGH!POINT
            OBJECT INDEX:     0
            WEIGHT:           2
            MODE:             0

            ATTRIBUTE:        SUPPORT!HGT
            OBJECT INDEX:     0
            WEIGHT:           1
            MODE:             0

    SON BLOCK:
        SON:            11      12
        THRESHOLD:       6     INF
    INTEGRATION TYPE:    2
```

```
10  TEXT:               FOUND A WHEEL OBSTACLE
    TYPE:               TERMINAL--RETURN DEFAULT ANSWER
    ATTRIBUTE:          SAFETY
    DEFAULT VALUE:
        UNSAFE,1
```

```
        RELATION BLOCK:    EMPTY
        SELECTION BLOCK:   EMPTY
        SON BLOCK:         EMPTY
        INTEGRATION TYPE: 2

11   TEXT:               NO OBSTACLES
     TYPE:               TERMINAL--RETURN DEFAULT ANSWER
     ATTRIBUTE:          SAFETY
     DEFAULT VALUE:
         SAFE,1
     RELATION BLOCK:    EMPTY
     SELECTION BLOCK:   EMPTY
     SON BLOCK:         EMPTY
     INTEGRATION TYPE: 2

12   TEXT:               THERE IS A VEHICLE OBSTACLE
     TYPE:               TERMINAL--RETURN DEFAULT ANSWER
     ATTRIBUTE:          SAFETY
     DEFAULT VALUE:
         UNSAFE,1
     RELATION BLOCK:    EMPTY
     SELECTION BLOCK:   EMPTY
     SON BLOCK:         EMPTY
     INTEGRATION TYPE: 2

13   TEXT:               COMPUTE HIGHEST POINT IN REGION
     TYPE:               TERMINAL--RETURN 0
     ATTRIBUTE:          HIGH!POINT
     DEFAULT VALUE:
         1,1
     RELATION BLOCK:

             RELATION:       GET!REGION
             OBJECT INDEX:   0
             WEIGHT:         1
             THRESHOLD:      0.5
             SON:            13
             MODE:           0

             RELATION:       SAMPLE
             OBJECT INDEX:   1
             WEIGHT:         1
             THRESHOLD:      0.5
             SON:            13
             MODE:           2

     SELECTION BLOCK:

             VECTOR B:       1
```

```
        SELECTION ATTRIBUTES:
             ATTRIBUTE:       ZOOORD
             OBJECT INDEX:    2
             WEIGHT:          1
             MODE:            3

        SON BLOCK:           EMPTY
        INTEGRATION TYPE:    2

14  TEXT:                COMPUTE SUPPORT!HGT
    TYPE:                TERMINAL--RETURN 0
    ATTRIBUTE:           SUPPORT!HGT
    DEFAULT VALUE:
       1,1
    RELATION BLOCK:

        RELATION:        SUPPORT
        OBJECT INDEX:    0
        WEIGHT:          1
        THRESHOLD:       0.5
        SON:             14
        MODE:            0

        RELATION:        SAMPLE
        OBJECT INDEX:    1
        WEIGHT:          1
        THRESHOLD:       0.5
        SON:             14
        MODE:            2

    SELECTION BLOCK:

        VECTOR B:        1

        SELECTION ATTRIBUTES:
             ATTRIBUTE:       ZOOORD
             OBJECT INDEX:    2
             WEIGHT:          1
             MODE:            1

        SON BLOCK:           EMPTY
        INTEGRATION TYPE:    2
```

APPENDIX B

AN EXAMPLE OF A SPECIFIC MODEL

This section presents an application of the generic model described in Appendix 1. Table B-1 lists the contents of the associative data base after the expansion of SAFETY for the location
$(x,y,\theta) = (0,0,0)$ is complete. The listing in Table B-1 consists
of three parts: OBJECTS, RELATION VALUES, and ATTRIBUTE VALUES.
Objects are listed under the class they belong to. The number in
parentheses after each class name indicates the number of objects
present in that class. Objects names consists of a letter to help
identify the class of the object, and the numbers that specify
that object to the system. For example, S-5!49!30 (line 300) is
the SAMPLE!POINT with (x,y,z) coordinates $(-5,49,30)$; T-5!49 (line
800) is the TILE centered at $(x,y) = (-5,49)$; VO!0!0 (line 1300)
is the VEHICLE!LOCATION $(x,y,\theta) = (0,0,0)$. VO!0!0 is defined in
the initial request to expand SAFETY of VO!0!0. The objects in
classes TILE and SAMPLE!POINT are defined as the result of relation values (SUPPORT and SAMPLE) obtained during the expansion.
Relation values are listed starting at line 1500. Each relation defined in the generic model is listed with a number in parentheses indicating how many objects (subjects) the relation was
applied to in this expansion. Each subject of the relation is
followed by three quantities in parentheses indicating the resources allocated and the resources used for the expansion on that
subject, and the time the value was obtained. For example (line
1700) 672 milliseconds were allocated to obtain the value of SUP-
PORT (VO!0!0). The expansion required 50 milliseconds and the
value was obtained at 90:9:28:46 (day:hour:minute:second, with the
days counted from Jan. 1, 1976). Under each subject, the objects
satisfying the relation are listed with the corresponding probabilities. Thus the value of SUPPORT (VO!0!0) is a list of four
(wheel) TILES - T-5!49, T-101!49, T-101!-7, T-5!-7, each satisfying the relation with probability 1. The relation SAMPLE (line
2300) was applied to four TILES and one SAMPLE!POINT was obtained
for each TILE.
The listing of attribute values follows the same format as
the relation values with a list of (value, count) pairs under each
object instead of (object, probability pairs). In the case of
SAFETY, names have been defined for the range values (1=SAFE,
2=UNSAFE) and the value name appears (line 5100).
The expansion in this example involves nodes 1,3, and 7
(SAFETY); 2 (PLANE!FIT); and 5 (SUPPORT!VAR). The relation values
for SUPPORT and SAMPLE are originally obtained in node 2, along
with the value of ZCOORD for each SAMPLE!POINT. Node 2 returns
$|(30\pm10) - (30+10)| = 0$ as the value of PLANE!FIT (see Appendix A).
This value is thresholded in Node 1 and the expansion proceeds to
Node 3 which is expanded for small values of PLANE!FIT.
The values of SUPPORT, SAMPLE and ZCOORD are required again

in Node 5 to compute SUPPORT!VAR. The existing values are retrieved from the associative data base and the value 30-10 = 20
is returned to node 3 as the value of SUPPORT!VAR (see Appendix A).
This value is thresholded and the expansion proceeds to node 7
where it is assumed that the support slope of the vehicle is greater than the allowable slope. Node 7 returns the value (UNSAFE, 1),
which is ultimately returned by node 1 as the value of SAFETY
(VO!0!0).

Table B-1. A specific model based on
the generic model of A-1

```
00100    OBJECTS
00200      SAMPLE!POINT(4)
00300        S-5!49!30
00400        S-101!49!10
00500        S-101!-7!10
00600        S-5!-7!30
00700      TILE(4)
00800        T-5!49
00900        T-101!49
01000        T-101!-7
01100        T-5!-7
01200      VEHICLE!LOCATION(1)
01300        VO!0!0
01400
01500    RELATION VALUES
01600      SUPPORT(1)
01700        VO!0!0(672,50,90:9:28:46)
01800          T-5!49,1.0,
01900          T-101!49,1.0,
02000          T-101!-7,1.0,
02100          T-5!-7,1.0;
02200      WHEEL!AREA(0)
02300      SAMPLE(4)
02400        T-5!49(151,33,90:9:28:48)
02500          S-5!49!30,1.0;
02600        T-101!49(151,33,90:28:50)
02700          S-101!49!10,1.0;
02800        T-101!-7(151,50,90:9:28:51)
02900          S-101!-7!10,1.0;
03000        T-5!-7(151,33,90:9:28:53)
03100          S-5!-7!30,1.0;
03200      GET!REGION(0)
03300
```

```
03400   ATTRIBUTE VALUES
03500       HIGH!POINT(0)
03600       SUPPORT!HGT(0)
03700       PLANE!FIT(1)
03800           VO!0!0(4500,317,90:9:28:53)
03900           0,1;
04000       ZOOORD(4)
04100           S-5!49!30(380,16,90:9:28:53)
04200           30,1;
04300           S-101!49!10(380,0,90:9:28:53)
04400           10,1;
04500           S-101!-7!10(380,0,90:9:28:53)
04600           10,1;
04700           S-5!-7!30(380,17,90:9:28:53)
04800           30,1;
04900       SAFETY(1)
05000           VO!0!0(10000,500,90:9:28:53)
05100               UNSAFE,1;
05200       WHEEL!OBST(0)
05300       SUPPORT!VAR(1)
05400           VO!0!0(3915,83,90:9:28:53)
05500           20,1;
```

REFERENCES

1. McCarty, J., and Hayes, P. S., "Some Philosophical Problems From the Standpoint of Artificial Intelligence," Stanford University, Artificial Intelligence Lab., A.I.B.-73, Nov. 1968.
2. Nilsson, N., *Problem Solving Methods in Artificial Intelligence,* McGraw-Hill Book Co., Inc., New York, 1971.
3. Rabin, M.O., "Theoretical Impediments to Artificial Intelligence," *Proceedings of I.F.I.P.,* 1974, pp. 615-619.
4. Feldman, J., and Yakimovsky, Y., "Decision Theory and Artificial Intelligence: A Semantics Based Region Analyzer," *A. I. Journal,* 5 (1974), 349-371.
5. Shortliffe, E.H., *Mycin: A Rule-Based Program for Advising Physicians Regarding Antimicrobal Therapy Selections,* Stanford University Technical Report STAN-CS-74-465, 1974.
6. Kunii, T., Weyl, S., Tenenbaum, J., "A Relational Data Base Schema for Describing Complex Pictures With Color and Texture," in *Proceedings of the Second Joint International Pattern Recognition Conference,* Aug. 1974, p. 310.

7. Barrow, H., Popplestone, R., "Relations Description in Picture Processing," *Machine Intelligence,* 6, pp. 377-296, B. Metzer (ed.), American Elsevier Pub. Co., N.Y., 1971.

8. Winston, P., "Learning Structural Description From Examples," Mac-TR-76, Massachusetts Institute of Technology, Artificial Intelligence Lab., Sept. 1970.

9. Minsky, M., *A Framework for Representation of Knowledge,* TR-306, Massachusetts Institute of Technology, Artificial Intelligence Lab., 1974.

10. Van-Lehn, K., et al., "SAIL Manual," Stanford University Technical Report CS-STAN-73-373, July 1973.

11. Feldman, J., and Rovner, P.D., "An Algol-Based Associate Language," C.A.C.M. Vol. 12, No. 8, pp. 439-449, 1969.

12. Yakimovsky, Y., Eskanazi, R., and Rayfield, M., *RAPID - A RANDOM ACCESS PICTURE DIGITIZER DISPLAY AND MEMORY SYSTEM,* Technical Memorandum 33-772, Jet Propulsion Laboratory, Pasadena, Calif., April 1976.

13. Yakimovsky, Y., "Boundary and Object Detection in Real World Images," to appear in *JACM.* Also appears in *Proceedings of the Fourth International Joint Conference on Artificial Intelligence,* Tbilisi, Russia, Advance Papers. Cambridge, Mass., International Joint Council on Artificial Intelligence, 1975.

14. Yakimovsky, Y., and Cunningham, R., *On the Problem of Embedding an Image Point in a Region,* Technical Memorandum 33-774, Jet Propulsion Laboratory, Calif., April, 1976.

15. Y. Yakimovsky and Cunningham, R., *A System for Extracting 3-Dimensional Measurements from a Stereo Pair of TV Cameras,* Technical Memorandum 33-769, Jet Propulsion Laboratory, Pasadena, Calif., April 1976.

16. Zadeh, L.A., "Fuzzy Sets," *Information and Control,* Vol. 8, pp. 334-353, 1965.

17. Yakimovsky, Y., *Scene Analysis Using Sematic Base for Region Growing,* Stanford University Artificial Intelligence Lab., A.I.M.-209, June 1973 (Ph.D. Thesis).

18. Michalski, R., "Variable Valued Logic and Its Application to Pattern Recognition and Machine Learning," in Monograph *Multiple Valued Logic and Computer Science,* American Elsevier Pub. Co., New York, 1975.

19. Fu, K. S., *Sequential Methods in Pattern Recognition and Machine Learning,* Academic Press, New York, 1967.

20. Yakimovsky, Y., *Nondeterminant Data Base for Computerized Visual Perception,* Technical Memorandum 33-761, Jet Propulsion Laboratory, Pasadena, Calif., January 1976.

RELAXATION LABELLING, LOCAL AMBIGUITY,
AND LOW-LEVEL VISION

Steven W. Zucker*
Computer Science Center
University of Maryland
College Park, MD 20742

ABSTRACT

The use of knowledge in the form of constraint expressions
arises very naturally in many problem solving systems and in many
machine perception systems. Knowledge in such a form is useful
at various levels in vision systems, particularly in the resolution of local ambiguities or uncertainties. For example, ambiguities may arise when an original intensity image is interpreted
into a low-level, symbolic description. To reduce this uncertainty,
it is often sufficient to use processes which are restricted to a
purely local perspective. Relaxation labelling is one such class
of processes. The knowledge that it employs is in the form of compatibility relationships between neighboring objects. Abstractly,
relaxation labelling is a class of computational processes which
manipulate labels on graphs. This paper describes relaxation labelling processes and several of their applications in vision systems. It is shown that they can provide consistent sets of local
symbols to serve as enhanced input for more active, global processes.

I. INTRODUCTION

Computing correct interpretations for local symbolic variables
is an integral part of many problem-solving and understanding systems. Ambiguities in these variables arise when each may assume
one of a large set of possible values. In order to restrict this
set of possibilities, that is, to reduce local ambiguities, additional sources of knowledge must be used (e.g., [33]). One very
natural source arises when considering interactions between the
variables. Such knowledge can be represented in the form of constraint or compatibility expressions. This paper describes the
use of knowledge in this form by a class of computational processes, called relaxation labelling processes, to reduce or remove
ambiguities in local descriptions. Before defining these notions
more precisely, it is instructive to introduce them qualitatively
in the context of some familiar problems.

---

* Current address: Dept. of Electrical Engineering, McGill Univ.,
  Montreal, Quebec H3C 3G1, Canada.

First, consider the scheduling of daily activities within a university environment. To solve this problem it is convenient to partition the day into blocks of time and to attempt to assign appropriate activities to these time blocks. For instance, given a list of local activities, e.g., teaching, meetings, lunch, preparation time, etc., and a list of constraints between these activities, e.g., the lecture preparation time block should precede the lecture, meetings with students should occur after lunch, etc., then the problem is to determine the global pattern of the activities for the day. In other words, we wish to determine a daily plan in which each time block contains an activity and in which no constraints between activities are violated. (For a more detailed discussion of this problem, see [13].)

Because time is strictly ordered, this scheduling example is, to a first approximation, one dimensional. An analogous problem in two dimensions is that of determining spatial layouts. More specifically, given a set of physical objects (such as tables and chairs) and a set of binary relations between these objects (e.g., the chair is NEAR and LEFT-OF the table), the problem is to construct a global layout of the objects such that all of the local constraint relations are satisfied. The task of representing such conceptual notions as NEAR and LEFT-OF in the form of local constraint relationships and of using them to determine spatial configurations is currently being investigated by R. Haar (personal communication); see also [7].

Many other problems fit nicely into this general format, such as the cryptarithmetic task [26, 12] and theorem proving [19]. For still other examples, see [10].

The main thrust of this paper is that there are many situations which arise within vision systems, particularly at the lower levels, which also fit into this general paradigm. It must be noted at the outset, however, that there is an important difference between the relaxation labelling algorithms to be developed here and the traditional approaches to constraint satisfaction. Most of the computational mechanisms developed previously (such as generate and test, backtrack programming, and sequential filtering) were sequential in nature*. However, in vision systems there are many places in which sequential algorithms create difficulties. For one, there is the problem of selecting a starting point for the algorithm and of determining whether the final result is independent of it [40]. There is also the problem of handling the very large amounts of data which must be processed, particularly in the lower levels of vision, and of maintaining the resultant large numbers of potential hypotheses and their alternatives. These difficulties, together with the prevalence of parallelism in human low-level vision [5], provide sufficient incentive to develop parallel relaxation labelling processes.

---

* Mackworth [21] gives an excellent review of these techniques, with important insights into their inherent computational efficiency.

II. RELAXATION LABELLING PROCESSES

Many different kinds of symbolic objects, at various levels
of abstraction, arise in the course of understanding an intensity
array. For our present purposes it is convenient to think of
these objects as being assigned to positions in the visual array.
This induces a neighbor relation over the set of objects and suggests a graph representation. In such a graph the nodes correspond to the objects and the edges indicate neighboring pairs of
objects. Attached to each object-node is a set of labels indicating possible semantic interpretations for that object. The relaxation labelling process attempts to decide, on the basis of local evidence, which of these possible interpretations is the correct one. Note that this formulation is, in a very strict sense,
dual to that in the previous section, in which the object interpretations were fixed and the positional labels were variable.
That is, in the spatial layout example we were given what the objects were (i.e., their interpretations) and had to determine their
positions; in the time scheduling example we were given the activities and had to determine their locations on the time axis. In the
present case, conversely, we are given the positions and we have to
determine the interpretations.

Selection of the label set for an object determines the space
of possible interpretations for (or relevant assertions about)
that object. For example, we will consider the interpretation of
picture points into a space of oriented line segments, and the interpretation of lines into a space of physical edge configurations.
Both of these interpretive spaces consist of symbols which provide
a basis for describing (or computing) compound objects within a
larger interpretive universe (see also Marr's remarks about the
principle of explicit naming [22]). Namely, long curves can be
constructed from oriented unit line segments and solid objects can
be described by their edges. More generally, relaxation labelling
processes should be useful whenever labels are being assigned to
data (i.e., assertions made about the data) and whenever knowledge
is available about how these labels can interact. These labels
need not fit as neatly into a descriptive hierarchy as the above
examples indicate, even in low-level vision. Another, more abstract possibility is suggested by stereo imaging problems, in
which it may be useful to define second order labels such as positional difference or relative error symbols.

Once the label set and semantic universe are determined, it
is necessary to evaluate a *priori* the ways in which the labels can
interact. This knowledge is represented in the constraint or compatibility functions.

Given an input in this form, i.e., a graph with a label set
attached to each node, relaxation labelling processes use the constraint expressions to eliminate node labels which are inconsistent with the labels still residing on neighboring nodes. This is
done in parallel on every node in the graph and then re-iterated
until there is no change in the label set. The final labelling

ordinarily contains a smaller number of interpretations for each
object than was originally possible. With fewer local interpretations, the combinatorial number of possible global interpretations
which can be synthesized from them is reduced. The reduction of
local ambiguities in this manner simplifies the design of the algorithms which subsequently build the global interpretations. It
also improves their operational efficiency, because some of the
(incorrect) data which they would have had to process have already
been eliminated. These general remarks will become more clear in
the next section, in which we begin to discuss relaxation labelling processes in some detail.

2.1 *Discrete Relaxation Labelling*

Semantic labels can be assigned to objects in an all-or-none
fashion in which the label is either appropriate or not, or they
can be assigned with some level of certainty (or appropriateness)
attached to them. We will first consider the all-or-none case.
This will lead to the discrete relaxation labelling process, a
parallel, iterative version of the Waltz algorithm [38].

Discrete relaxation labelling will be developed in the context of simplified line drawing interpretation, in which the problem is to build the interpretation of the entire drawing from the
interpretations of its component lines. This simplified domain
is used because it offers a very clear picture of what is going
on in the abstract symbol-manipulating processes. The particular
universe of interpretation is illustrated in Figure 1a (after [17,
4]). In this universe a line can denote (i) a convex edge, (ii)
a concave edge, (iii-iv) an occluding edge with the forward object
below or above*. It is now straightforward to determine all pairs
of labels which can actually occur on neighboring line segments
(i.e., line segments which meet at a vertex); see Figure 2.

Suppose that, as an example, the particular input to the discrete relaxation process is the one shown in Figure 1b. It involves the set of objects a_i (i = 1, 2, 3), the neighbor relationships, and the initial labelling. In principle, these initial label sets were determined *a posteriori*. That is, measurements were
made on the original image to determine which labels were appropriate.

The measurements for sides a_2 and a_3 were ambiguous, resulting in the labels shown. Side a_1 was impossible to observe, leaving only the default alternative of assigning it the complete label set Λ.

---

* Note that while (iii) and (iv) are rotationally equivalent,
  for clarity in this example it is convenient to label them
  distinctly.

$$
\text{LABEL SET } \Lambda = \left\{
\begin{array}{ll}
+ \; ; & \text{CONVEX EDGE} \\
- \; ; & \text{CONCAVE EDGE} \\
\longrightarrow ; & \text{OCCLUDING EDGE: FORWARD OBJECT BELOW} \\
\longleftarrow \; ; & \text{OCCLUDING EDGE: FORWARD OBJECT ABOVE}
\end{array}
\right.
$$

(a)

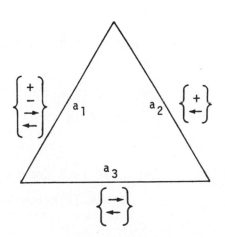

(b)

Figure 1. Labelling simple line drawings:
a) the label set
b) input picture and initial
   labelling.

With this as input, the relaxation process discards labels according to the following rule: Keep the label λ at a_i if and only if for every neighbor a_j there is a label λ' ϵ Λ_j which is compatible with λ (i.e., Λ_{ij} $(\lambda, \lambda') \neq \Phi$). Beginning with the initial label set at each node, this rule is applied to every node in parallel until no additional labels are discarded. (For a proof that this procedure always terminates, see [30].) If this sequence of operations is performed on the input picture in Figure 1b using the constraints in Figure 2, then the final labelling in Figure 3a is obtained. Note that while sides a_1 and a_2 still remain uncertain of their interpretation (but less so), side a_3 is now completely certain. It has been entirely determined by information contained in the distribution of labels in its neighborhood.

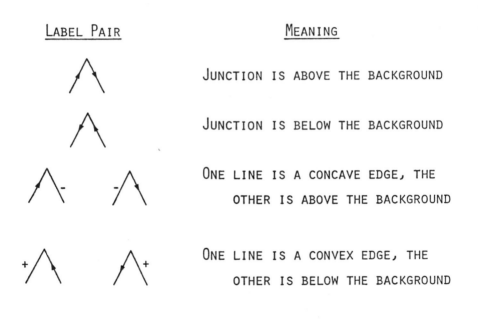

LABEL PAIR	MEANING
	JUNCTION IS ABOVE THE BACKGROUND
	JUNCTION IS BELOW THE BACKGROUND
	ONE LINE IS A CONCAVE EDGE, THE OTHER IS ABOVE THE BACKGROUND
	ONE LINE IS A CONVEX EDGE, THE OTHER IS BELOW THE BACKGROUND

Figure 2. The constraint set of allowable label pairs $\Lambda_{ij}(\lambda, \lambda')$.

598

(a) **F**INAL **L**ABELLING

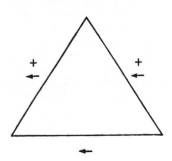

(b) **L**ABELLING **N**ETWORK

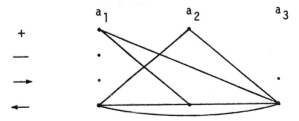

(c) **C**LIQUES ◄──► **C**ONSISTENT GLOBAL INTERPRETATIONS

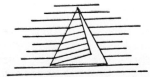

Figure 3. The line drawing final labelling and its
          interpretations.

The size of the neighborhood is a function of the iteration number. It grows radially outward as the iterations proceed. This implies that the number of iterations required for termination is determined by the maximum distance that information must travel in order to disambiguate the worst (i.e., least locally determined) node.

Finding the legitimate global interpretations for Figure 3a should now be easier because there are fewer possible interpretations for each side. One approach is to use the labelling network (Figure 3b), a graph in which the nodes correspond to object-label pairs and in which two nodes, (a_i, λ) and (a_j, λ'), are joined by an edge if and only if $(\lambda, \lambda') \varepsilon \Lambda_{ij}$. Cliques in this graph then correspond to consistent global interpretations -- these are drawn in Figure 3c.

There is, however, a limitation inherent in the relaxation labelling process which arises because of its restricted local perspective. This can be domonstrated by attempting to label a Penrose impossible figure [28] (Figure 4a). Note that while this figure is well-formed locally, in that each corner could actually occur in a real triangle, it is ill-formed globally. There is no single point of view from which a real triangle would give this projection.

Since the irregular aspect of this figure concerns the depth orientations of its sides, the label set describes these orientations as either into (λ_I) or out of (λ_O) the plane of the paper. To obtain the constraint set, it is necessary to examine the ways in which these labels can be combined at a vertex. It is easy to see (by examining a real triangle) that all pairwise combinations are possible. Thus the constraint set is

$$\Lambda_{ij}(\lambda,\lambda') = \{ (\lambda_O, \lambda_O), (\lambda_I, \lambda_I), (\lambda_O, \lambda_I), (\lambda_I, \lambda_O) \}$$

The process begins with both labels on every side; each label is then consistent with one of the labels on each of its neighbors, so no labels are discarded. The labelling network, however, immediately reveals the unusual side configuration for the Penrose figure (Figure 4c) -- namely, that the object-spanning cycles over this network are of length six. This is clearly impossible for a figure with only three sides.

2.2 Probabilistic Relaxation Labelling

Often, during the understanding process, interpretations are not just possible or impossible, but are possible with some degree of certainty. Such is the case in low-level vision, where the problem is to interpret the intensity array into a vocabulary of low-level symbols. The typical approach to the problem has been to evaluate a local feature detector on the intensity array, and then, on the basis of this measurement, to assert the existence of

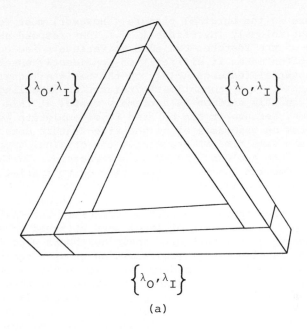

(a)

$$\Lambda = \left\{ \begin{array}{l} \lambda_O; \text{ SIDE ORIENTED OUT OF THE PLANE OF THE PAPER} \\ \\ \lambda_I; \text{ SIDE ORIENTED INTO THE PLANE OF THE PAPER} \end{array} \right.$$

(b)

λ_O

λ_I

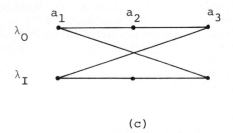

(c)

Figure 4.   a) Penrose impossible triangle and initial
                labelling
            b) label set
            c) labelling network
            Note that the object spanning cycles are
            of length six.

an actual feature in the original picture. However, most feature detectors are not uniquely invertible [22]. They respond not only to the presence of the feature, but also to various noise configurations. This often makes it difficult to confidently assert the existence of pictorial features solely on the basis of single detector measurements. The probabilistic relaxation labelling process introduced in this section is extremely useful at this level in vision systems, because it can be used to disambiguate feature detector responses on the basis of neighboring feature detector responses. At the same time it translates the original array of intensity values into another kind of data structure. In this new data structure, symbolic assertions are attached to spatial locations derived from the original array.

The probabilistic relaxation process can be thought of as a generalization of the discrete relaxation process. The discrete model was developed on the basis of label sets attached to nodes in a graph. Labels inconsistent with their neighbors were discarded from these label sets. This discarding process can be modeled by attaching an additional binary variable to each label. When the label is present, the variable is set to one; when the label is discarded it is changed to zero. The probabilistic relaxation process can now be described as an extension of the discrete relaxation process in which the range of this variable is extended to the interval $[0,1]$. This variable, denoted $p_i(\lambda)$, can now be interpreted as an estimate of the probability that label λ is correct for object a_i. In other words, it serves as a measure of our confidence in assigning label λ to object a_i.

Now, instead of discarding the labels, the probabilities on the labels are updated. This is done using heuristic knowledge embedded in what are termed compatibility functions. Compatibility functions are the probabilistic counterparts to the discrete constraint relations. More specifically, the compatibility function $r_{ij}(\lambda,\lambda')$ controls the contribution that the probability attached to label λ' on object a_j makes to the probability attached to label λ on object a_i during the updating process. In a loose sense, the compatibility function resembles a correlation function, because it assumes values according to the following bench-marks:

$$
r_{ij}(\lambda,\lambda') = \begin{cases} -1 & \text{if } \lambda \text{ at } a_i \text{ is incompatible with } \lambda' \\ & \text{at } a_j \\ 0 & \text{if } \lambda \text{ at } a_i \text{ is independent of } \lambda' \text{ at} \\ & a_j \\ +1 & \text{if } \lambda \text{ at } a_i \text{ is perfectly compatible} \\ & \text{with } \lambda' \text{ at } a_j \end{cases}
$$

Since the compatibility can assume both positive and negative values, both positive and negative influences can propagate around the graph. This often has the effect of organizing the different interpretations into sets of cooperating and competing [24] subprocesses.

With the compatibility functions specified (often in a procedural form), the probabilities are updated according to an appropriate rule, e.g.,

$$p_i^{k+1}(\lambda) = \frac{p_i^k(\lambda) \ [1+q_i^k(\lambda')]}{\sum_\lambda p_i^k(\lambda) \ [1+q_i^k(\lambda')]} \tag{1}$$

$$\text{where } q_i^k = \sum_j c_{ij} \sum_{\lambda'} r_{ij}(\lambda,\lambda') \ p_j^k(\lambda') \tag{2}$$

This rule states that the probability for label λ on object a_i at the (k+1)st iteration is a function of both the previous estimate for that probability, $p_i^k(\lambda)$, and the contribution from the probability distributions on the neighboring label sets, $q_i^k(\cdot)$.

The most straightforward way in which the neighboring probabilities can contribute to the updating process is shown in Eq. 2. For each neighbor j, the probability on each label λ' is weighted by the compatibility function, and the result is then summed. The total neighborhood contribution is then a weighted (c_{ij}) sum of all these neighbor contributions. Thus the more certain a label is, the more influence it has. More complex schemes could consider pairwise (or higher order) combinations of the probabilities by incorporating conditional expressions into above rule [41].

Once the neighborhood contribution has been determined, it enters the updating rule in a nonlinear fashion (i.e., the term $[1+q_i^k]$). A nonlinearity is essential to the process because it can be proven that linear schemes iterate to terminal values which are independent of the initial probabilities [30]. Thus linear processes are independent of any a posteriori information. The denominator in Eq. 1 guarantees that the updating rule maps probabilities into probabilities.

In this probabilistic model, as in the discrete model, the process is limited to a local perspective on the neighborhood of each node. The sphere of influence for each node does, however, grow with the iteration number.

III. APPLICATIONS OF PROBABILISTIC RELAXATION LABELLING

3.1 Line and Curve Enhancement

The first application of the probabilistic model will be the enhancement of lines and curves. Consider interpreting an intensity array into the extremely simple symbolic universe of oriented line segments. A picture point can either correspond to a unit line segment in any of eight orientations, or it can correspond to a background point (the no-line label) [41]. See Figure 5.

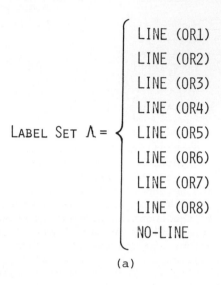

LABEL SET Λ =
$\begin{cases} \text{LINE (OR1)} \\ \text{LINE (OR2)} \\ \text{LINE (OR3)} \\ \text{LINE (OR4)} \\ \text{LINE (OR5)} \\ \text{LINE (OR6)} \\ \text{LINE (OR7)} \\ \text{LINE (OR8)} \\ \text{NO-LINE} \end{cases}$

(a)

COMPATIBILITY FUNCTIONS (LINE - LINE)

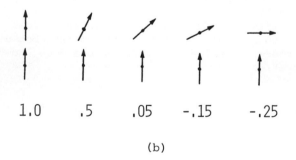

1.0　　.5　　.05　　-.15　　-.25

(b)

Figure 5. a) Label set for line and curve enhancement.
b) Line-to-line compatibilities.

The underlying object graph for this application is composed of the individual picture points, with each point joined to its eight nearest neighbors. The label probabilities are initialized by evaluating a local line detector [32] in eight orientations at every picture point. The results are scaled so that a single strong response gives a large value to the appropriate line-label probability; otherwise, the weight is distributed proportionally over all the line labels. The no-line probability is one minus the sum of the line probabilities.

The line-line compatibilities are shown in Figure 5b. Line segments oriented in the same direction support one another, while perpendicular line segments detract support. Since it is possible for curves to make right angle turns, however, the negative coefficient is smaller than the maximum permitted. The no-line label is supported by neighboring no-line labels and line segments not directed toward (or away from) it, and it is weakened by line segments directed toward it.

The result of applying this process to a satellite photograph of a winding river is shown in Figure 6. While the local line detector responds to some extent everywhere in the noisy background (Figure 6b), the relaxation process enhances the river quite dramatically (Figure 6f). It is now a simple matter to design a tracking routine to actually follow the river.

The curve enhancement application makes apparent two additional and more general aspects of probabilistic relaxation processes. The first of these concerns the robustness of the process. The more detailed paper [41] demonstrated the insensitivity of the process to proportional changes in the compatibility coefficients. In other words, the final result is not particularly sensitive to specific numerical values, but rather is sensitive to their proportional relationships. If this were not the case, the usefulness of these processes would be severely limited. For then, it would be insufficient to determine proportional working values from an understanding of the problem domain. Instead, specific numbers would have to be determined, and, because these numbers would be picture dependent, the process would have no generality.

The second additional aspect of the probabilistic model is the empirical observation that the line enhancement process can be conceptualized as two competing subprocesses. One subprocess attempts to establish a line label at each point, and the other subprocess attempts to establish a no-line label. More generally it has been found that while relaxation labelling processes are designed with only one label set in mind, they often act as if there were several label subsets, each defining its own subprocess. It seems as if competition takes place between the subprocesses and cooperation takes place within each subprocess. This conceptualization of the internal organization of these processes is often a useful aid in their design. Similar labels can be lumped together and treated as a single module in relation to the others.

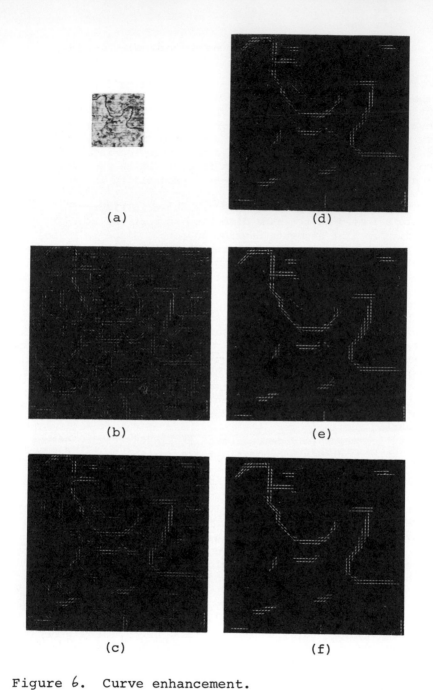

(a)

(d)

(b)

(e)

(c)

(f)

Figure 6. Curve enhancement.
a) LANDSAT subimage containing river.
b) The initial probability assignments
   for (a). The intensity for each line
   segment is proportional to the maximum
   probability at that position.
c-f) Iterations 1, 3, 5, and 7 for the
   relaxation process applied to (a).

3.2 *Labelling Dot Clusters*

The second application of probabilistic relaxation labelling extends the low-level symbolic universe to include shapes with interiors, not just thin lines and curves. More specifically, the problem is to label all of the dots in a planar distribution with one of the following interpretations (i) interior point, (ii) edge point (with some orientation), and (iii) noise point. This dot labelling problem is relevant to two different areas, clustering algorithms and scene segmentation. Most clustering algorithms are based on a metric notion of proximity [2,15]. Under some conditions this produces final clusters which are rather different from those which humans would perceive [39]. The above labels can provide some indication of the role each point plays in determining the overall shape of the dot cluster. This, in turn, should lead to more visually satisfying results. The labelling of dot clusters can also be considered as a first step toward the general scene segmentation problem, i.e., the problem of segmenting a gray-level picture into regions of homogeneous intensity separated by well-marked lines and edges [31].

The underlying graph for this dot labelling application is constructed by considering each dot as an object and joining it with its k nearest neighbors. For the examples to be presented in this paper, $k = 4$ and $k = 8$ produced effectively the same results. The initial probabilities are estimated loosely in terms of the disparity between a point and the center of gravity of its k nearest neighbors. If a point is surrounded uniformly, the interior label is given strong probability. If most of a point's neighbors are skewed to one side, the appropriate edge-value is given a strong initial probability. If a point is very far away from its neighbors (with respect to most interpoint distances), the noise label is given a strong initial weight. In general, the initial probabilities are a weighted combination of these three possibilities.

The compatibility functions are shown in Figure 7b. Basically the edge-to-edge compatibilities behave like the line-to-line compatibilities in the line enhancement example, except that the mutual influence decreases as the distance separating them increases. Interior points are strengthened by nearby edge points that are on the proper side of the edge, by other nearby interior point and by noise points which are far away. They are weakened by distant interior points, by improperly oriented edge points, and by nearby noise points. The analogous compatibilities for edge and noise points are straightforward.

The results of applying this labelling process to a figure eight shaped dot cluster are shown in Figure 8 (after [39]). Note that all points are labelled unambiguously except for the two points in the neck of the figure. The process was unable to decide whether this figure consisted of two clusters just touching or whether it consisted of just one connected cluster. Rather than forcing a decision one way or another on the basis of purely

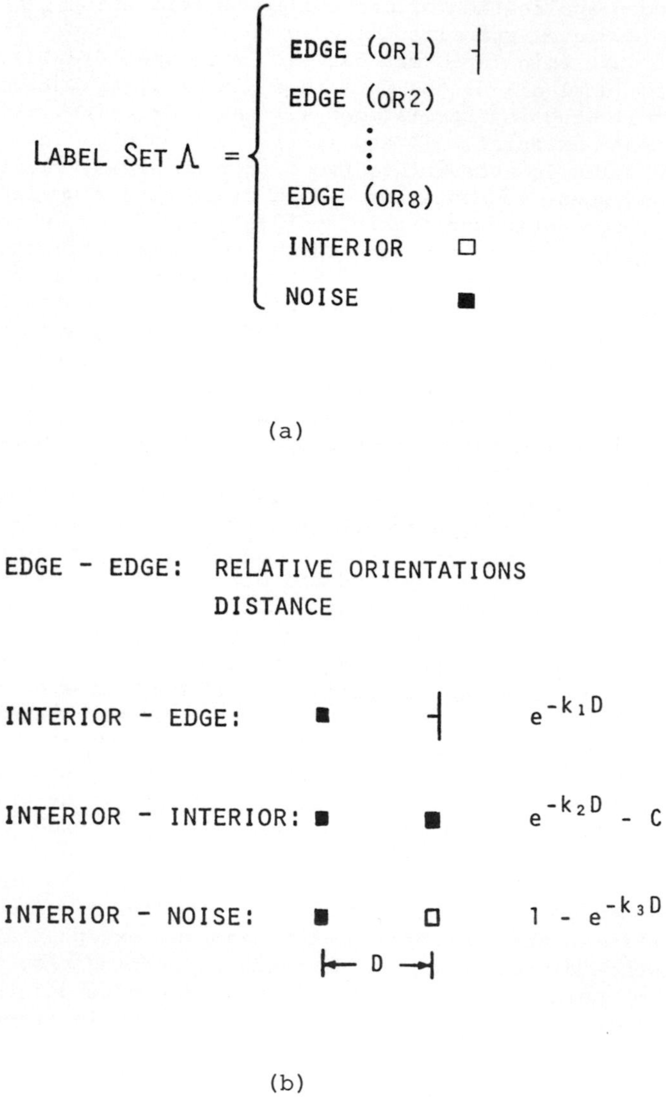

$$\text{LABEL SET } \Lambda = \begin{cases} \text{EDGE (OR1)} \quad \dashv \\ \text{EDGE (OR2)} \\ \quad \vdots \\ \text{EDGE (OR8)} \\ \text{INTERIOR} \quad \square \\ \text{NOISE} \quad \blacksquare \end{cases}$$

(a)

EDGE - EDGE: RELATIVE ORIENTATIONS
              DISTANCE

INTERIOR - EDGE: ■   ┤ $e^{-k_1 D}$

INTERIOR - INTERIOR: ■   ■ $e^{-k_2 D} - c$

INTERIOR - NOISE: ■   □ $1 - e^{-k_3 D}$

$\longmapsto D \longrightarrow$

(b)

Figure 7.   Labelling dot clusters:
            a) label set and symbols
            b) compatibility functions.

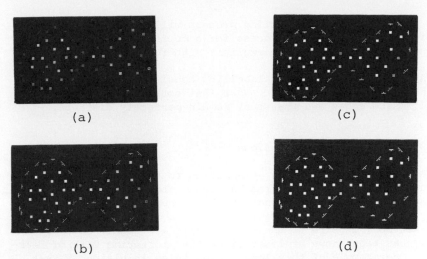

(a) (c)

(b) (d)

Figure 8. Labelling dot clusters
a) Initial probability assignments
b-d) Iterations 5, 10, and 20 of
the relaxation process applied to (a).

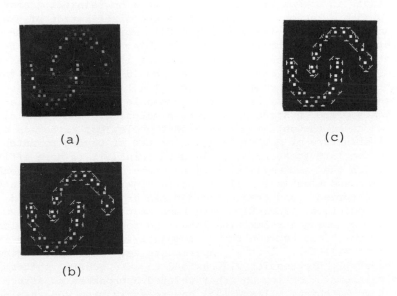

(a) (c)

(b)

Figure 9. Intertwined clusters
a) Initial probability assignments
b-c) Iterations 10 and 20 of the
relaxation process.

local information, the labelling process will pass the two possibilities to a more global process for a decision. Thus the different interpretations are made explicit with respect to the shape of
the dot cluster.

A second example of dot labelling consists of the two intersecting C-shapes in Figure 9. Note that both C's are properly enclosed inside edges and that they remain perfectly distinct.

3.3 *Additional Applications*

Relaxation labelling is an approach to the reduction of local
ambiguities which only requires knowledge about how local symbols
can interact. These techniques should be applicable to problems
in any domain which are specifiable in this fashion.

That many aspects of the visual world are highly determined
locally has been known at least since the pioneering work of Helm-
holtz. One example of this local determinism in vision, rather
different from those already presented is that of perceptual transparency. Matelli [23] has recently shown that degrees of transparency can be computed on the basis of certain lightness ratios
that are evaluated at the borders between adjacent regions. Another example is the scene analysis problem of region growing, in
which other kinds of regional interaction have been found to be
useful. The system of Feldman and Yakimovsky [9], in particular,
has many ideas in common with the present work on relaxation processes. Within a region, knowledge about the distribution of gray
levels can be used for noise cleaning [20]. More generally, because arbitrary scene segmentation is a problem involving both regional interactions and the kinds of edge and line interactions
discussed in Section 3.1 and 3.2, it too should be appropriate for
a relaxation labelling formulation (e.g., [34]).

Another kind of local interaction amenable to relaxation labelling takes place in structured pattern matching. For example,
a template can be thought of not as a unit whole, but rather as a
relational structure of subtemplates. Instead of trying to match
the entire template to every possible data point, it is more efficient to match the subtemplates [37] and then combine them together. Fischler and Elschlager [11] proposed linking the subtemplates
with elastic springs, and then using dynamic programming to find
the optimal solution. Recently there have been attempts to solve
this problem by using a relaxation labelling formulation, in which
the elastic relations between the subtemplates are incorporated into the compatibilities. Initial experiments have been encouraging
[6] and hopefully the results will extend to more general pattern
matching problems. Working on other related approaches to structural pattern matching, Ullmann [35] has recently proposed an algorithm for subgraph isomorphism which is very close to the discrete relaxation process, and Hinton [16] has been using relaxation techniques to find globally best figures in ambiguous drawings.

610

IV. PERSPECTIVES AND EXTENSIONS ON PROBABILISTIC RELAXATION
     LABELLING

Probabilistic relaxation labelling introduced an explicit notation for the likelihood that a label is correct. This took the
form of a continuous variable (in the interval [0,1]) attached to
each label. We called this variable the probability that the label is correct because it serves, in the sense of Carnap [3], as
a measure of the evidence supporting such a hypothesis. As the
process iterates, and more evidence is examined, this probability
value is updated. The process terminates either when all of the
evidence has been examined or when sufficient evidence has been
examined for each probability to become sufficiently stable. Thus
the number of iterations required depends on the distance that information must travel in order to disambiguate the most uncertain
assignments. The more that a label is determined by its immediate
neighbors, the smaller the number of iterations needed.
     The probability estimates are updated by the rule which de-
fines how neighborhood information is used. One of the simplest
ways to do this was to form a weighted sum of neighboring label
probabilities which act through the compatibility functions. Sometimes, as in the line enhancement application [41], more complex
schemes are required. In that example, in order to prevent lines
from thickening during updating, it was necessary to incorporate
some information about the distribution of probabilities over the
neighborhood rather than just information about their algebraic
sum. This new information was obtained from a difference relation
across two labels. More generally, it might be necessary to include arbitrary conditionals in the updating rule so that structural characteristics of the neighborhood can enter the updating
computation. Along the same lines, rather than just considering
binary constraints between variables, n-ary constraints could be
used [25].
     For applications in which many labels have to be updated at
each node, it may be advisable to parameterize some of the variable label dimensions. In the line enhancement application, for
example, instead of having a separate label for each possible line
orientation, a single label could be used to denote a unit line
segment. The orientation of this line segment would then be indicated by a parameter. With this formulation, only two labels woul
have to be updated -- the no-line label and the line label. However, the line orientation parameter would then have to be updated on the basis of the line orientations around it [36]. This
last point reveals the price that has to be paid for increased
computational efficiency: less accuracy in the orientation variable. That is, instead of updating orientation on the basis of a
distribution of probabilities over all possible orientations, only a single value is available from each distribution. However,
the more accurately this value represents the distribution, the
closer it comes to the non-parameterized formulation.

The foundations for this remark about parameterization were already laid in the section on line and curve enhancement. There it was described how the process behaved as if there were two subprocesses -- one for lines and one for no-lines. Each of these subprocesses had to remain distinct, hence at least two labels were needed. However, the internal conflicts within each subprocess could have been lumped into a single parameterized variable just as orientation was in the above reformulation.

In addition to parameterization, knowing the type of an object, or certain of its characteristic features, can often be used to partially restrict the label set which may legitimately apply to it. To take advantage of such partial evidence, a program could be attached to each node. This program could then either generate the label set (cf. [38]) or refine the node label set on the basis of partial evidence accumulated by the relaxation process. This, in turn, would improve the operational efficiency of the process, because only subsets of the labels would have to be updated on each iteration. A more extreme possibility is to allow these node programs to treat a portion of the object graph (or perhaps the entire graph) as data, thereby giving the local nodes more of a global perspective. In this way, many diverse sources of knowledge could be used simultaneously (cf. [8]).

Another possibility for generalization is the actual construction of the object graph. For example, in the line enhancement application, the graph was completely determined by the matrix underlying the intensity array. In the clustering application, on the other hand, the graph was built by a program which searched for the k nearest neighbors of a given point. In other situations, the design of this graph can have important effects on the final results. For instance, in the sub-template matching application, a basic criterion had to be met (i.e., a significant match) before a node was established. Varying this criterion affected the number and the distribution of the nodes that were established [6].

In addition to these remarks about how relaxation labelling processes can be extended, it is interesting to note that entirely different approaches to them are possible. For example, one can conceive of the label probabilities as inequalities over a set of variables which take values in the range [0,1]. More traditional, mathematical relaxation techniques can then be applied [1]. Or, from another point of view, these processes can be conceived of as networks of automata. The discrete model would then correspond to a network of finite automata [29], and the probabilistic model to a network of probabilistic automata [27]. Perhaps these alternate points of view will reveal more general results about the convergence of relaxation labelling processes.

V. CONCLUSIONS

Relaxation labelling processes, as described in this paper, are techniques for deciding among alternative symbolic interpretations for local variables. They use a specific kind of knowledge about the ways in which these variables can interact. When the variables are domain-specific, e.g., when their interpretations are only meaningful within a domain such as the blocks world, then the knowledge about how they can interact will also be specific to the domain. However, when the variables are general purpose [42], i.e., when they are common to many different semantic domains, then the knowledge of how they can interact is also general purpose.

General purpose knowledge, at least in terms* of low-level vision, is knowledge about the structure of the intensity array and how it relates to symbolic constructs such as edge and line segments. It is useful in a variety of semantically-specific domains, including bubble chamber physics, satellite imagery, and the blocks world. Furthermore, it is useful even before domain-specific questions or expectations are formulated. For example, in Figure 8 it was possible to use very general knowledge about how line segments can interact to enhance lines. It was not necessary to know that the lines specifically represented roads. Moreover, once these long lines were labelled, they might be able to serve as highly salient features important for associating the image with more specific and appropriate semantic domains.

Thus, relaxation labelling processes begin to provide us with a mechanism through which general-purpose and domain-specific processes can communicate. One possibility is to let the compatibility functions be sensitive to the requirements of domain specific experts. In terms of the line enhancement application, for example, bubble chamber experts might bias the compatibilities in favor of very straight lines. In the absence of this specialization, values derived from more general-purpose considerations could be used, and the processing would proceed to accumulate evidence useful in the search for more relevant and specific domains. While this does not suggest a mechanism for directly inferring the correct semantic domain, it does offer a means for obtaining reliable low-level data to be used by the mechanism.

ACKNOWLEDGMENT

This paper stems from earlier, more mathematical work done with A. Rosenfeld and R. Hummel. I would especially like to thank A. Rosenfeld for his continued interest and for our many fruitful discussions. The support of the National Science Foundation under Grant MCS-72-03610 is gratefully acknowledged, as is the help of Shelly Rowe in preparing this paper.

---

* For a discussion of a more complete vocabulary for low-level vision, see Marr [22].

REFERENCES

1. Agmon, S., The relaxation method for linear inequalities, *Can. J. Math.*, Vol. 6, No. 3, 1954, pp. 382-392.
2. Anderberg, M. R., *Cluster Analysis for Applications,* Academic Press, New York, 1973.
3. Carnap, R., *Logical Foundations of Probability,* (2nd Ed.), The University of Chicago Press, 1962.
4. Clowes, M. B., On seeing things, *Artificial Intelligence,* Vol. 2, 1971, pp. 79-116.
5. Cornsweet, T., *Visual Perception,* Academic Press, New York, 1970.
6. Davis, L. S., and A. Rosenfeld. Applications of relaxation labelling, 2: Spring-loaded template matching, *Technical Report TR-440,* Computer Science Center, University of Maryland, February 1976.
7. Eastman, C. M., Automated space planning, *Artificial Intelligence,* Vol. 4, 1973, pp. 41-64.
8. Erman, L. D., and V. R. Lesser., A multi-level organization for problem solving using many, diverse, cooperating sources of knowledge, *Adv. Papers Fourth International Joint Conf. Artificial Intelligence,* Tbilisi, Sept. 1975, pp. 483-490.
9. Feldman, J. A., and Y. Yakimovsky, Decision theory and artificial intelligence: I. A semantics-based region analyzer, *Artificial Intelligence,* Vol. 5, 1974, pp. 349-371.
10. Fikes, R. E., REF-ART: A system for solving problems stated as procedures, *Artificial Intelligence,* Vol. 1, 1970, pp. 27-120.
11. Fischler, M. A. and R. A. Elschlager. The representation and matching of pictorial structures, *IEEE Trans. Computers,* Vol. C-22, 1973, pp. 67-92.
12. Gaschnig, J., A constraint satisfaction method for inference making, *Proc. 12th Annual Allerton Conf. on Circuits and System Theory,* Univ. of Illinois, Urbana-Champaign, 1974.
13. Goldstein, I. P., Bargaining between goals, *Adv. Papers Fourth International Joint Conf. Artificial Intelligence,* Tbilisi, Sept. 1975, pp. 175-180.
14. Gregory, R. L., *The Intelligent Eye,* McGraw-Hill, New York, 1970.
15. Hartigan, J. A., *Clustering Algorithms,* Academic Press, New York, 1973.
16. Hinton, G., Using relaxation to find a puppet, Draft, Cognitive Studies Programme, University of Sussex, 1976.
17. Huffman, D. A., Impossible objects as nonsense sentences, in B. Meltzer and D. Michie (eds.), *Machine Intelligence 6,* Edinburgh U. Press, Edinburgh, 1971, pp. 295-323.
18. Koffka, K., *Principles of Gestalt Psychology,* Harcourt, Brace, and World, Inc., New York, 1935.
19. Kowalski, R., A proof procedure using connection graphs, *Journal of the ACM,* Vol. 22, No. 4, 1975, pp. 572-595.

20. Lev. A., Zucker, S. W., and A. Rosenfeld. Iterative enhancement of noisy images, *Technical Report TR-445*, Computer Science Center, Univ. of Maryland, March 1976.
21. Mackworth, A. K., Consistency in networks of relations, *Technical Report 75-3*, Department of Computer Science, University of British Columbia, Vancouver, July 1975.
22. Marr, D., Early processing of visual information, *A. I. Memo 340*, Artificial Intelligence Lab., M.I.T., Dec. 1975.
23. Matelli, F., The perception of transparency, *Scientific American*, Vol. 230, No. 4, 1974, pp. 90-98.
24. Montalvo, F. S., Consensus versus competition in neural networks: A comparative analysis of three models, *Int. J. Man-Machine Studies*, Vol. 7, 1975, pp. 333-346.
25. Montanari, V., Networks of constraints: Fundamental properties and applications to picture processing, *Information Sciences*, Vol. 7, 1974, pp. 95-132.
26. Newell, A., and H. A. Simon. *Human Problem Solving*, Prentice Hall, Englewood Cliffs, N. J., 1972.
27. Paz, A., *Introduction to Probabilistic Automata*, Academic Press, New York, 1971.
28. Penrose, L. S., and R. Penrose, Impossible objects: A special type of illusion, *Brit. J. Psychol.*, Vol. 49, 1958.
29. Rosenfeld, A., Networks of automata: Some applications, *IEEE Trans. Systems, Man, and Cybernetics*, Vol. SMC-5, 1975, pp. 380-383.
30. Rosenfeld, A., Hummel, R., and S. W. Zucker. Scene labelling by relaxation operations, *IEEE Trans. Systems, Man, and Cybernetics*, vol. SMC-6, no. 6, 1976, pp. 420-433.
31. Rosenfeld, A., and A. C. Kak. *Digital Picture Processing*, Academic Press, New York, 1976.
32. Rosenfeld, A., and M. Thurston. Edge and curve detection for visual scene analysis, *IEEE Trans. Computers*, Vol. C-20, 1971, pp. 562-569.
33. Sussman, G. J., A computational model of skill acquisition, *A. I. TR-297*, Artificial Intelligence Lab., M.I.T., August, 1973.
34. Tenenbaum, J. M., et. al. An interactive vacility for scene analysis research, *Technical Note 87*, Stanford Research Institute, Menlo Park, 1974.
35. Ullmann, J. R., An algorithm for subgraph isomorphism, *Journal of the ACM*, Vol. 23, No. 1, 1976, pp. 31-42.
36. VanderBrug, G. J., Experiments in iterative enhancement of linear features, *Technical Report TR-425*, Computer Science Center, Univ. of Maryland, 1975.
37. VanderBrug, G. J. and A. Rosenfeld. Two-stage template matching, *Technical Report TR-364*, Computer Science Center, Univ. of Maryland, March 1975.
38. Waltz, D., Understanding line drawings of scenes with shadows, in P. H. Winston (ed.), *The Psychology of Computer Vision*, McGraw Hill, New York, 1975.

39. Zahn, C. T., Graph-theoretical methods for detecting and describing Gestalt clusters, *IEEE Trans. Computers*, Vol. C-20, 1971, pp. 68-86.

40. Zucker, S. W., Region growing: Childhood and adolescence, *Computer Graphics and Image Processing*, in press, 1976.

41. Zucker, S. W., Hummel, R., and A. Rosenfeld. An application of relaxation labelling to line and curve enhancement, *IEEE Trans. Computers*, to be published.

42. Zucker, S. W., Rosenfeld, A., and L. S. Davis. General purpose models: Expectations about the unexpected, *Adv. Papers Fourth International Joint Conf. Artificial Intelligence*, Tbilisi, Sept. 1975, pp. 716-721.

SUBJECT INDEX

A 6
B 7
C 8
D 9
E 0
F 1
G 2
H 3
I 4
J 5